KB161187

DOKDO
DO
1947

Dokdo 1947

**The Postwar Dokdo Issue and Tripartite Relations
between Korea, the US, and Japan**

First published   August 9, 2010
English edition   November 11, 2022

Written by Jung Byung-joon

Publisher   Han Chul-hee
Published in Korea by Dolbegae Publishers

Dolbegae Publishers
Registered August 25, 1979 No. 406-2003-000018
Address   77-20 Hoedong-gil, Paju-si, Gyeonggi-do, Republic of Korea (10881)
Tel   (+82) 31-955-5020
Fax   (+82) 31-955-5050
Website   www.dolbegae.co.kr
E-mail   book@dolbegae.co.kr

Editorial Director   Yoo, Yeilim
Book Design   Lee, Eun-jeong
Cover Design   Kim, Minhae
Printing & Bookbinding   Sangjisa P&B

ISBN 979-11-91438-89-5 (93910)

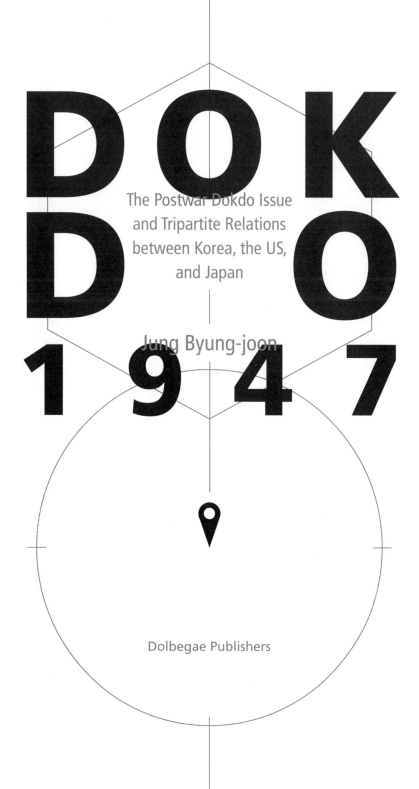

DOKDO

DO

The Postwar Dokdo Issue
and Tripartite Relations
between Korea, the US,
and Japan

Jung Byung-joon

1947

Dolbegae Publishers

Preface

The idea for this book came about in 2001 when I was studying the U.S. State Department's diplomatic documents from the 1950s in the National Archives and Records Administration. The records were telling a different story from what average Koreans know about Korea-Japan relations and the Dokdo issue. Although much of the documents about Korea-Japan relations and the Dokdo issue were still classified, I was able to see that the 1951 Treaty of San Francisco was the starting point of, as well as a turning point for, the U.S. policies and diplomatic decisions on Dokdo. So I started delving into the archives of the U.S., Japan, Korea, and the UK. I looked into how the San Francisco Treaty—which officially settled the war between Japan and the U.S.-led Allies—relates to Korea and how it became a turning point for Korea-Japan relations, Korea-U.S. relations, and U.S.-Japan relations. I found myself on a journey of exploring how the San Francisco system shaped the new post-war order in Northeast Asia; how Korea, the U.S., Japan, and the UK viewed and responded to Japan's territorial issues including that of Dokdo; and how Korea-U.S. relations, U.S.-Japan relations, and Korea-Japan relations had changed over the years.

This book is a summary of what I learned during my journey, and it delineates how and when Korea, the U.S., and Japan began introducing policies, as they became more aware of Dokdo after the Second World War, and how these policies evolved before and after the San Francisco Treaty.

I retraced the steps that Korea, the U.S., and Japan took after the Second World War and found out that 1947 was a watershed year for the Dokdo issue. That is why I chose to name this book "Dokdo 1947". It was a year in which Korea started conducting comprehensive surveys on Dokdo and made Korean people see the island in a fresh new light. Japan, on the other hand, distributed a pamphlet that contained false information about Dokdo and Ulleungdo being Japanese territories. Meanwhile, the U.S. completed the draft of the San Francisco Treaty, which stipulated that Liancourt Rocks (Dokdo) belonged to Korea. The interplay between the views and policies of these three countries on Dokdo led to the San Francisco Treaty in 1951, but later, they each went on their separate paths.

Japan's disagreement with its neighbours, such as Korea, Russia (the former Soviet Union), and China, over the sovereignty of certain islands escalated into full-blown territorial disputes in the early 1950s. These territorial disputes centering around Japan may appear to be purely bilateral on the surface, but the underlying cause is regional. The seeds of contention have been sown when a new order was established in Northeast Asia after the Second World War. In fact, it was the peace conference between Japan and the Allies, otherwise known as the San Francisco Peace Conference, that enabled Japan to assert Dokdo is an disputed island even though it has been returned to Korea after the war.

Many think that the differences between Korea and Japan over the historical title to the island are what caused the Dokdo issue. From my studies, however, I came to learn that the Dokdo issue is a ramification, or one of the shadows, of the sway and decision power the U.S. exerted on the post-war policies for Northeast Asia. Therefore, it would be more accurate to say that the dispute over the sovereignty of Dokdo after the Second World War involves the U.S. as well and that it is a matter of regional and international politics rather than that of history. Thus, I devoted much of this book to explaining the post-war structure of Korea-Japan, Korea-U.S., and U.S.-Japan relations and how they have manifested as the issue of Dokdo as we know it.

Indeed, the Second World War put an end to the hostility between the Allied and Axis powers, but the power struggle between the U.S. and the Soviet Union, and between the Western Bloc and the Eastern Bloc, set off the so-called Cold War. Diplomatic relations remained intact between the key players and no military hostilities occurred at the center of the Cold War rivalry, but local clashes were abound along the boundaries. The

Chinese Civil War, the Korean War, the Vietnam War, and the Indonesian War of Independence broke out in Asia one after the other. These were all civil wars, but international wars at the same time. They were also variants of a typical anti-colonial independence war. The Chinese Civil War and the Korean War highlighted the geostrategic value and importance of Japan in Northeast Asia, which prompted the hurried signing of the peace treaty between Japan and the Allies.

The peace treaties of the First World War were inherently a peace dictated by the victors and imposed harsh terms on war responsibility, territorial cessions, and reparations payments upon those who had started the war. Peace treaties signed with Italy and Romania after the Second World War were similar in nature in that they were punitive. However, Japan's case was different. There was a delay in the process and the Allies signed a peace treaty with Japan in 1951, six years after the war ended. The primary purpose of the San Francisco Treaty was to strengthen the Allies' position against their Cold War rivals, as opposed to fixing the damage caused by the war. This is what sets the San Francisco Treaty apart from other peace treaties. The text of the treaty was simpler, the emphasis was on peace rather than on war responsibility, and territorial cessions and reparations payments were left out of the picture for the most part. By signing the San Francisco Treaty, Japan restored peace with 48 countries. However, China and Korea, who suffered the most from Japan's aggressions, were not invited to the conference and Russia refused to sign the treaty. In short, the treaty paved the path for a Northeast Asian peace order led by the U.S. without Japan having to correct the wrongdoings it had committed against its neighbouring countries. The fact of the matter was that the U.S. was in a crisis situation when the treaty was in the works. China had already been communized and South Korea was about to fall into the hands of the communists, so the voice of Japan, which was its only brigdehead into Northeast Asia, carried weight.

The San Francisco Treaty, another wall in the anti-communism fortress that the U.S. built in the Cold War era, left enduring legacies in Northeast Asia. Japan was able to restore peace with Korea, China, and Russia through bilateral agreements, but issues of war responsibility, historical misdeeds, colonization, and territorial rights remained unsettled, which later became a breeding ground for conflicts. The treaty also handed down legacies to Japan including issues pertaining to Okinawa, the U.S. military bases, the constitution, and the U.S.-Japan Security Treaty. The conflict between Korea and Japan over Dokdo is just one of the many legacies left by the San Francisco Treaty.

In writing this book, I received tremendous help from the National Institute of Korean History, National Assembly Library, National Archives, Dokdo Museum, Seoul National University Library, and Corean Alpine Club in Korea; the National Archives and Records Administration, Air Force Historical Research Agency in the Maxwell Air Force Base, and MacArthur Archives in the U.S.; the Diplomatic Archives of the Ministry of Foreign Affairs of Japan; and the National Archives of the UK. I am also grateful to Pang Sunjoo, Son Kyungseok, Kim Hanyong, Park Jongpyeong, Lee Hanwoo, and Lee Myunghwan for their comments and testimonies and for providing me with valuable materials.

This book was first published in 2010 by Dolbegae. Since then, many researchers and institutions have asked for an English version, and I felt it was about time that I obliged to their request and put the English version out into the world. I have reorganized the book and reduced the number of pages in half for the English readers. My sincere thanks go to all those who have helped to publish and translate this book.

Jung Byung-joon
September 30, 2022

CONTENTS

[005]   Preface

          Introduction

[017]   1 The San Francisco Peace Conference and the Dokdo Issue

[017]   1) The San Francisco Peace Conference as the source of the postwar Dokdo
                issue
[021]   2) Disclosure of US diplomatic documents and new approaches to the study
                of the Dokdo issue

[027]   2 Perspective, Composition, and References Related to the Study

[027]   1) The Dokdo issue as part of the tripartite relations between Korea, the US,
                and Japan
[030]   2) The events of 1947 and their significance

Chapter 1 Korea's Perception of Dokdo: Exploration of Dokdo (1947)
           and Bombing of Dokdo (1948)

[037]   1 From Dokdo to Seoul: Reenactment of the 1905 "Invasion"

[037]   1) Dokdo crisis: Unlawful encroachment and shooting incident by Japanese
                fishermen
[039]   2) Seoul's response: Combination of the Dokdo incident and relaxation of
                the MacArthur Line

[043]   2 Exploration of Ulleungdo and Dokdo by the Interim Government
             and Corean Alpine Club (1947)

[043]   1) Organization of the Survey Committee by the Interim Government
[046]   2) Joining forces with the Corean Alpine Club
[048]   3) First Dokdo survey

[054]   3 Legacies of the 1947 Dokdo Survey

[054]   1) Debriefing session, exhibition, and survey reports
[057]   2) Coverage by newspapers and magazines
[058]   3) Emergence of major concepts, discussion points and perceptions about
           Dokdo

[064]   4 Parangdo and Tsushima Regarded as One Issue

[064]   1) Parangdo: Worries of another Japanese invasion attempt
[065]   2) Interim Legislative Assembly: Participation in the peace conference with
           Japan and the reversion of Tsushima

[069]   5 1948 Bombing of Dokdo

[069]   1) Bombing incident over Dokdo
[070]   2) Investigation by USAFIK and CINCFE
[075]   3) Claims review and compensation
[077]   4) Facts of the bombing incident and points of dispute

[090]   6 Recognition of Dokdo among the Koreans in 1948

[090]   1) Public consensus: Dokdo as Korean territory
[096]   2) Petition by the Patriotic Old Men's Association: Regarding Dokdo,
           Parangdo, and Tsushima as one issue

Chapter 2   Japan's Preparations for the Peace Treaty and Perception of Dokdo
            (1945~50): Dokdo and Ulleungdo as Japanese Territory

[103]   1 Preparations by the Japanese Government for the Peace Treaty
           (1945~1950)

[104]   1) The Executive Committee for Research on a Peace Treaty (November 1945
           to May 1947): Launch of peace treaty preparations
[108]   2) Establishment of an Executive Committee for Coordination between
           Ministries for a Peace Treaty (May 1947) and discussion on general
           principles by the Japanese government
[113]   3) Start of negotiations with the Allied Powers (July 1947) and establishment
           of the Policy Review Committee
[124]   4) Review of the peace treaty formula: Reverse course and de facto peace
           policy (1948)
[126]   5) Choice of a "separate peace" and "majority peace" (1949~1950)

[132] 2 Japan's Preparation and Lobbying on Territorial Issues

[132]   1) The Japanese Foreign Ministry's preparations on territorial issues
[139]   2) Were there lobbying activities for territorial interests?

[148] 3 Maneuvering by the Japanese Foreign Ministry in 1947: Drafting of a
          Pamphlet to Publicize Dokdo and Ulleungdo as Japanese Territory

[148]   1) Publication of the "Minor Islands Adjacent to Japan Proper" series by the
              Japanese Foreign Ministry
[155]   2) The Japanese Foreign Ministry's announcement of Dokdo and Ulleungdo
              as Japan's annexed islands
[162]   3) Origin of the Japanese Foreign Ministry's perception of Dokdo in 1947

Chapter 3   The US Draft Treaty of Peace with Japan and Its Relation to Dokdo
               (1947-1951)

[175] 1 The Peace Conference and Peace Treaty with Japan
[175]   1) Formulation and finalization of the Peace Treaty with Japan
[180]   2) Evolution of the draft treaty of peace with Japan

[188] 2 Dokdo in the Draft Treaties of the US Department of State, Part I
          (1946-1947): The Liancourt Rocks (Dokdo) under Korean sovereignty

[188]   1) Establishment of Working Group on Japan Treaty in 1946
[192]   2) Draft treaty of the Working Group on Japan Treaty during the period
              1947-1948
[212]   3) Dokdo in the draft treaties of 1949

[226] 3 Dokdo in the Draft Treaties of the US Department of State, Part II
          (1949-1950): Sebald's Posturing

[226]   1) Sebald's review of the draft treaty and his insistence that the Liancourt
              Rocks (Dokdo) be placed under Japanese jurisdiction
[235]   2) Request by the US Ambassador to Korea for Korea to be a party to the treaty
[240]   3) Change of ownership of Dokdo (Late 1949-1950)

[248] 4 Dokdo in the Draft Treaties of the US Department of State, Phase III
          (1950-1951): Dokdo-related Provisions Deleted

[248]   1) John Foster Dulles and the crafting of a new draft treaty

[250]   2) Draft treaty of August 7, 1950: Japanese territorial clauses under the
        Potsdam Declaration discarded
~[253] 3) Draft treaty of September 11, 1950: Revised draft treaty
[254]   4) The "Seven Points" Proposal on the Japanese Peace Treaty of September
        11, 1950: Territorial clauses deleted
[257]   5) Provisional memorandum of February 9, 1951 (initialed by the US and Japan)
[259]   6) Provisional draft treaty of March 1951 (official draft treaty sent to the
        Allied Powers)

[264]   5 The Formulation of Joint Anglo-American Draft Treaties and the
          Final Treaty (1951)

[264]   1) The first joint Anglo-American draft treaty of May 3, 1951: Sent to the
        British Commonwealth countries
[275]   2) The second Anglo-American draft treaty of June 14, 1951: Exclusion
        of Korea from Allied Power status and the abandonment of the Allied
        Powers' war-time provisions on Japanese territory
[277]   3) The third joint Anglo-American draft treaty of July 3 and July 20, 1951:
        Sent to all countries involved
[278]   4) Final draft treaty of August 13, 1951

Chapter 4   British Draft Treaties of Peace with Japan and Anglo-American
            Consultations (1951)

[283]   1 Confirmation of Korea's Sovereignty over Dokdo in the British Draft
          Treaties (March 1951)

[283]   1) The UK's formulation of a draft treaty of peace with Japan
[289]   2) Korea-related provisions in the British draft treaty
[296]   3) Characteristics of the British map / Korean sovereignty over Dokdo
        reaffirmed

[303]   2 Anglo-American Consultations of 1951 and Discussions on Terri-
          torial Issues

[304]   1) Consultations of March 1951
[307]   2) The first Anglo-American talks (April 25-May 4, 1951) including
        discussions on Korea's participation in the peace treaty settlement and
        territorial issues
[325]   3) The second series of Anglo-American meetings (June 2-14, 1951) and the
        decision to exclude Korea altogether from participation in the treaty

Chapter 5   US-Japan Negotiations (1951)

[337]   1 The First Visit to Japan by Dulles in 1951 and Major US-Japan Treaty-Related Agreements

[337]   1) Japan's preparations for the Seven Principles of the Treaty with Japan (November 1950 to January 1951)
[339]   2) Dulles' first visit (January to February 1951) and the de facto initialing of principal treaties
[352]   3) The Japanese government's reply to the US Provisional Draft of March 1951 on April 4, 1951

[354]   2 Dulles' Second Visit to Japan in 1951 and Japan's Opposition to Korea's Participation

[355]   1) Dulles' intentions vs. Japan's intentions
[358]   2) US-Japan discussion on the UK draft treaty and the Dokdo issue
[365]   3) Japan's opposition to Korea's participation and false accusations

Chapter 6   The Korean Government's Response to the Treaty of Peace with Japan and Korea-US Negotiations (1951)

[381]   1 The Korean Government's Preparations for the Peace Treaty from 1948 to 1950

[381]   1) Four items on the agenda: reparations, participation in the treaty, territorial issues, and the MacArthur Line
[384]   2) The MacArthur Line at issue

[391]   2 Provisional Draft Made Available to Korea (March 1951) and the Korean Government's First Reply (April 27, 1951)

[391]   1) Diplomatic efforts in Washington and Tokyo
[394]   2) Seoul's response: Establishment of the Foreign Affairs Committee
[398]   3) The Korean Government's first reply (April 27, 1951) and request for the return of Tsushima
[405]   4) The US Department of State comments (May 9, 1951)

[409]   3 The US-UK Draft of July 1951 and the Korean Government's Response

[409]   1) Denial of Korea's status as a signatory by the US (July 9, 1951)
[411]   2) The Korean government's second reply (July 19, 1951)
[416]   3) Korea-US dialogue (July 19, 1951) and the issue of Dokdo and Parangdo

[419]   4 US Department of State Research on Dokdo and Parangdo and Its
           Conclusion
[419]   1) Review by Samuel Boggs of Dokdo as Korean territory
[425]   2) The Korean Government's third reply (August 2, 1951)
[429]   3) The Rusk Letter (August 10, 1951) and conclusion of Korea-US negotiations
[434]   4) Significance and limits of the Rusk Letter

[438]   5 Korea's Participation in the San Francisco Peace Treaty in an Informal
           Capacity

Chapter 7   Invisible Battle: Prelude to the Dispute over Dokdo and Actions
             taken by Korea, the United States, and Japan

[445]   1 Korea: The Peace Line and Expedition to Parangdo and Dokdo
[445]   1) Dokdo inside the Peace Line
[453]   2) 1952 Dokdo expedition by the Corea Alpine Club and the Dokdo
              bombing incidents
[458]   3) 1953 Dokdo expedition by the Corea Alpine Club and erection of a territorial
              signpost

[464]   2 Japan: Propaganda and Stratagem
[464]   1) Propaganda of 1951: Japanese claims of sovereignty over Dokdo
[474]   2) Japan's stratagem in the period 1952-1953: Designation and release of
              Dokdo as a bombing rang
[491]   3) Mid-1953: Japanese encroachment on Dokdo and installation of Japanese
              signposts

[509]   3 The United States: From Active Intervention to a Position of Neutrality
[509]   1) Disparate views in Busan, Tokyo, and Washington in 1952
[522]   2) The responses of Korea and Japan to the release of Dokdo as a bombing
              range in 1953
[531]   3) Request for intervention by the US Embassy in Tokyo and Dulles'
              declaration of neutrality

[545]   Bibliography   [573]   Index
[581]   Index of Names   [585]   Index of Place Names
[589]   List of Figures & Tables

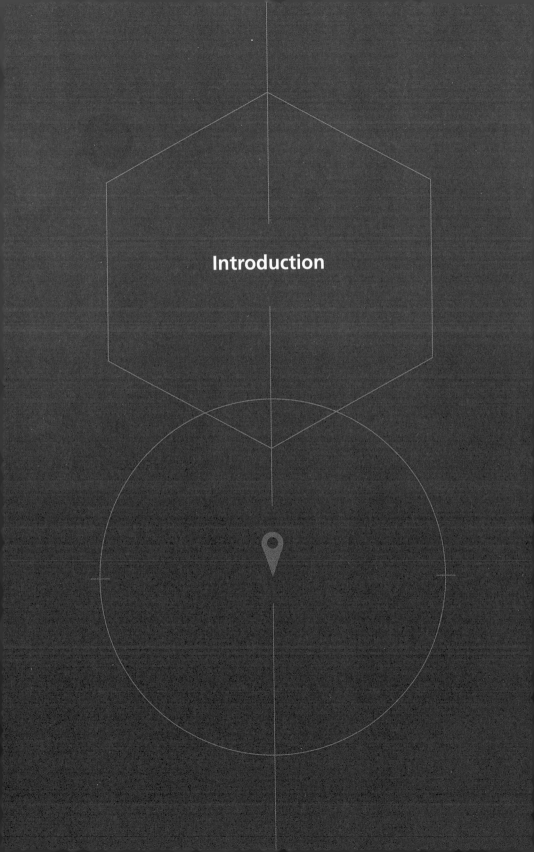

Introduction

1

The San Francisco Peace Conference and the Dokdo Issue

1) The San Francisco Peace Conference as the source of the postwar Dokdo issue

Japan's 1952 claim of sovereignty over Dokdo vis-à-vis Korea was based more on the argument that the island remained part of Japan's territory as a result of the 1951 San Francisco Peace Conference, rather than on the argument that Dokdo was Japan's inherent territory or its illegal annexation of 1905. The illegal annexation was part of the one-sided and imperialistic invasion by Japan of Korea, the latter which had by then practically lost its sovereignty and could not resist any unjust measure forced upon it due to the Japan-Korea Protectorate Treaty of 1905. Therefore, the annexation was uniquely ill-founded and lacked legitimacy. On the other hand, the Treaty of Peace with Japan Signed at San Francisco in 1951 signed by Japan and 48 other nations was judged to be acceptable by the international community and served as a basis for universal agreement.

The 1951 Treaty of Peace with Japan led by the US was a framework treaty, which defined the order of postwar Northeast Asia but its basic nature was limited as it was concluded during the Korean War. The 1949 communization of mainland China, the 1950 outbreak of the Korean War, and the intervention of Chinese communist forces in the war served as the main driving forces in the establishment of this regional political system.

Firstly, the Treaty of Peace with Japan was a one-sided peace treaty whose negotiation was led by the United States and was anticommunist and anti-Soviet in nature. Among the Allies of World War II (WWII), the Soviet Union and China were excluded, and Great Britain did not play much of a role. The Allies agreed on the principle of non-exclusive pacification to avoid unilateral engagement in peace negotiations with enemy nations, but as the Cold War aggravated, separate peace settlements, rather than an overall peace, and a peace formula that included many individual parties, instead of an overall peace formula, were adopted. It all boiled down to anticommunist and anti-Soviet maneuvering as the Cold War aggravated with the communization of China and the outbreak of the Korean War.[1]

Secondly, though Japan restored peaceful relations with the signatories of the Treaty of Peace with Japan, China and Korea, the two Asian nations which suffered greatest and for the longest period, were not included in the treaty. The reason for China's exclusion was its debatable representativeness due to the separation of Taiwan and the mainland while in Korea's case, because it had been a Japanese colony. Exclusion of the Northeast Asian nations injured the most showed that the treaty placed priority on prevention of the spread of communism rather than on peace, and was centered on US needs and not those of Northeast Asia.

Thirdly, the Treaty of Peace with Japan also bequeathed a harmful legacy to postwar Japanese history. More than twenty million people were sacrificed during the Asia-Pacific War, but the treaty specified neither Japan's war responsibilities nor its responsibility for compensation, indemnification or apology. In addition, the Emperor system was not revoked nor was the then Emperor not replaced. Though Japan restored peace, it was not a new Japan but a different version of the same aggressor which had victimized other Asian nations, and Japanese people were deprived of an opportunity to put an end to their miserable past. It was therefore only natural that Japan and its Asian neighbors had a variety of disputes in the postwar era over previous sources of conflict. On the other hand, though Japan managed to restore its sovereignty and gain peace, it ended up with limited sovereignty along with unequal and subordinate

---

1   *Mainichi Shimbun* published *The Treaty of Peace with Japan* in 1952 and characterized it with three traits: the first was 'pacification with the anti-communist movement bloc'; the second was 'pacification as a result of defeat'; and the third was 'pacification that left the resolution of important matters to future negotiations between involved nations due to the pressing international situation.' (Mainichi Shimbun, 1952, *The Treaty of Peace with Japan*, Preface).

relations with the US.[2]

Fourthly, after the Treaty of Peace with Japan, Northeast Asia witnessed the establishment of security and regional order through bilateral alliances with the US. When the U.S. was concluding peace and security treaties with Japan, the Philippines, Australia, and New Zealand, who were both former WWII Allies and allies of the US, were enraged at the US for granting security to Japan, their former enemy. To soothe them, around the time of the conclusion of the US-Japan Security Treaty in 1951, the US concluded security treaties with the Philippines, and with Australia and New Zealand (ANZUS) the same year. After the Korean War ended in a ceasefire in 1953, Korea demanded a security treaty with the US, and the ROK-US Mutual Defense Treaty came into being. The establishment across Asia of these security alliances with the US resulted in a chain of security linking Japan, Korea, and the Philippines, and Japan, Australia, and New Zealand. These became major pillars to Asia's new regional order, and all were chain-linked to the US.

The Treaty of Peace with Japan became the basic principle behind the regional order of postwar Northeast Asia and the starting point of Korea-Japan relations. Korea, which neither participated in nor signed the treaty, could do little to negate the treaty in its relations with its former occupier. The treaty also became the source of three main issues in bilateral relations, all of which have been the topic of major research.

The first of the three is Korea's status under international law. From 1947, Korea demanded Allied Power status and qualification to participate in and be a signatory state to the peace negotiations with Japan. However, none of these demands were granted at the San Francisco Peace Conference, and Korea was regarded as a "nation liberated after WWII." The legal status of ethnic Korean residents in Japan was linked to this decision: the interpretation was that they were neither Japanese during occupation by US forces under the Supreme Commander of the Allied Powers (SCAP)

---

2   Narahiko Toyoshita, 2009, *Hirohito and MacArthur (Showa Tenno, Makkasa Kaiken)*, translated by Gwon Hyeok-tae, Gaemagowon.

nor Allied nationals, but instead occupied a third position and were thus classified as "foreigners" after the treaty.[3]

The second is the territorial conflict over Dokdo. The Treaty of Peace with Japan did not mention Dokdo, but it was subsequently interpreted differently by Korea and Japan, with the conflict regarding sovereignty over Dokdo becoming serious by 1952.[4] Japan's position that Dokdo was acknowledged as Japanese territory at the 1951 San Francisco Peace Conference as seen in the 1952 memoranda of the Japanese Ministry of Foreign Affairs to Korea became official in Japan, and since then, Kenzo Kawakami and other Japanese researchers have supported this claim.

The third is the right to demand compensation and indemnification. This later became one of the main issues in the conclusion of the Korea-Japan Basic Relations Treaty, which involves both Korea's claims against Japan and Japan's claims against Korea. The property in Korea owned by the Japanese government and its nationals was confiscated and listed as enemy property during the US military government and was legally transferred to the Korean government. This was also specified in the Treaty of Peace with Japan. However, Japan demanded its right to those properties while trying to undermine or ignore Korea's right to compensation.[5]

---

3   Jeong In-seop, 1995, *Legal Status of Ethnic Korean Residents in Japan*, Seoul National University Press; Lee Jong-won, 1995, "International Political Background of the Korea-Japan Talks," *Reinterpretation of the Korea-Japan Talks*, Asea Culture Publishing; Kim Tae-gi, 1996, "The Japanese Government's Policy regarding Korean Residents: Focusing on the Period of the Japanese Occupation over Korea," an annual academic conference of the Korean Political Science Association; Kim Tae-gi, 1999, "The GHQ/SCAP Policy toward Korean Residents in Japan," *The Korean Journal of International Relations*, Vol. 38, No. 3

4   Sin Yong-ha, 2001, "Criticism of Japan's Claim that the Exclusion of Dokdo from the Korean Territory in the 1951 Treaty of Peace with Japan Acknowledged Dokdo as Japanese Territory," *Criticism on Japanese Claims of Sovereignty over Dokdo*, Seoul National University Press; Sin Yong-ha, comp., 2000, "Part 7: SCAP's Materials on Sovereignty over Dokdo and Explanation," *Study of Materials on Sovereignty over Dokdo*, Vol. 3, Dokdo Research and Preservation Association; Lee Seok-woo, 2002, "Some Observations on the Territorial Disputes over Dokdo (Liancourt Rocks) and Interpretation of the Territorial Clauses of the San Francisco Peace Treaty," *Seoul International Law Journal*, Vol. 9, No. 2.

5   Lee Won-deok, 1996, *The Starting Point of Dealing with the Past Affairs between Korea and*

The intent of the treaty was for the Allies of WWII and Japan to discuss conditions regarding the cessation of hostile relations and occupation status and to restore peaceful relations. One of these conditions was defining Japan's postwar territorial boundaries. Dokdo was dealt with as part of the territorial aspect of the treaty.

2) Disclosure of US diplomatic documents and new approaches to the study of the Dokdo issue

The memoranda of the foreign ministries of Korea and Japan during the 1950s were the expression of their official positions, but due to the non-disclosure of the relevant documents at the time, it was not clearly known how the Dokdo issue was specifically dealt with in the process leading up to conclusion of the Treaty of Peace with Japan. The different arguments by the two governments ran parallel, and though there were different positions and arguments, it was difficult to ascertain the truth. Serious research into the issue began only in the latter part of the 1970s when the US began to disclose diplomatic documents related to the treaty. Once diplomatic documents of the US Department of State (DoS) began to be released, including the Japanese Peace Treaty Files of John Foster Dulles, the US special envoy to the treaty; those of John Moore Allison, an aide to Dulles and the US Ambassador to Japan (Records Relating to the Treaty of Peace with Japan–Subject File, DoS Office of Northeast Asia Affairs); those of the US Embassy in Tokyo; and those of the US Embassy in Seoul, study began in earnest. This was before the disclosure of Korean and Japanese diplomatic documents.

It was Takashi Tsukamoto who first took note of how Dokdo was indicated in the treaty-related diplomatic documents disclosed by the US, and in the drafts of the treaty in particular. He tracked how Dokdo-related

---

Japan: Japan's Postwar Diplomacy and the Korea-Japan Talks, Seoul National University Press; Park Jin-hui, 2008, *Korea-Japan Talks: the First Republic's Policy toward Japan and the Process of the Korean-Japan Talks*, Sunin Book; Osamu Ota, 2008, *Korea-Japan Talks: Study on the Right of Claim*, translated by Song Byeong-gwon, Park Sang-hyeon, and O Mi-jeong, Sunin Book.

clauses were written and changed through the various drafts of the treaty included in the *Foreign Relations of the United States (FRUS)*, officially published in 1983, and published an article, based on this research, claiming that Dokdo was confirmed as Japanese territory in the Treaty of Peace with Japan.[6]

He continued to discover and introduce various treaty drafts and documents related to the bilateral negotiations from the US National Archives and Records Administration (NARA) and the UK Public Record Office (PRO, predecessor to the current National Archives, TNA).[7] His conclusion confirmed the official position of the Japanese Foreign Ministry that Dokdo was defined as Japanese territory in the treaty. Tsukamoto built his career as a specialist on Japan's territorial issues such as the Northern Territories dispute and the Dokdo issue.

His findings had a direct impact on Korea as well, where they were introduced through a domestic journal in the mid-1990s[8], and documents from the US and UK government that he identified and selectively used to back up the Japanese Foreign Ministry's position were also introduced in Korea.[9]

Though Tsukamoto suggested a new approach to the study of the Dokdo issue as dealt with at the San Francisco Peace Conference, the purpose of his research and criteria for choosing references were neither impartial nor rational. Firstly, he chose, sorted, and analyzed references with the purpose of championing Japan's claims of sovereignty over Dokdo and carried out

---

6   Takashi Tsukamoto, 1983, "The Treaty of Peace with Japan and Takeshima - FRUS," Research and Legislative Reference Department, National Diet Library, *The Reference*, No. 389 (Jun. 1983).

7   Takashi Tsukamoto, 1994, "The Treaty of Peace with Japan and Takeshima (Review)," Research and Legislative Reference Department, National Diet Library, *The Reference*, No. 518 (Mar. 1994).

8   Takashi Tsukamoto, 1996, "A Full Account of the Omission of Takeshima in the Treaty of Peace with Japan," Korea Institute of Military Affairs, *Korean Military Affairs Journal 3* (Aug. 1996).

9   Kim Byeong-ryeol, 1997, *Dokdo: Comprehensive Survey of Dokdo Materials*, Dada Media, pp. 418-525.

his research with the same focus. As such, he emphasized references that were advantageous to the Japanese claim and deleted or minimized those that were disadvantageous, to a large extent, in his selection, introduction, and interpretation of materials. For instance, he placed a great emphasis on a letter dated August 10, 1951 and written by Dean Rusk, the then US Assistant Secretary of State, but did not even mention the memoranda of Secretary of State Dulles dated November 19 and December 4, 1953, which became the official position of the US DoS regarding the Dokdo issue. He also failed to disclose that Dokdo had been indicated as Korean territory in the territory clauses of the drafts written by the US DoS since January 1947, the existence of a map attached to the treaty drafts by the US DoS dating back to 1947 and Dokdo's inclusion as Korean territory thereon, and the map attached to the official draft treaty (the third draft) of the UK Foreign and Commonwealth Office (FCO) drawn up in April 1951. As such, he intentionally highlighted references that favored Japan's position and excluded or omitted unfavorable ones. It was difficult for him to overcome the limits of his official position as a territorial issues specialist for the National Diet Library.

Secondly, he did not examine at all the structural context of the treaty including the process of drafting it, changes to its nature through the process, and background to the writing of drafts and their characteristics. The process that dragged on over four and a half years (from 1947 to 1951) reflected geopolitical changes in the world as a whole and Northeast Asia in particular. The parties involved and the reason for the writing of the treaty changed while the purpose for and method of its conclusion also varied greatly between 1947 and 1951. It is a daunting task to analyze how the enormous structure of the San Francisco Peace Conference was conceived, coordinated, formed, and changed. It is clearly different from simply reviewing the Dokdo-related clauses of the treaty drafts.

Thirdly, the lack of specific clauses relating to Japanese territory in the treaty and the fact that there was no open discussion or agreement among the Allies on Japanese territory in the lead up to or during the peace conference were overlooked. To be specific, the principle that Japanese territory was limited to its main four islands and the surrounding islands to be determined by the Allies was rescinded (a clause on Japanese territory agreed upon by the Allies in the Cairo Declaration and Potsdam Declaration at the end of WWII), but no clause on Japanese territory was agreed on during the peace conference. According to the clause on Japanese territory agreed upon by the Allies and by Japan, the Allies had the right to determine which of the surrounding islands should be designated as Japanese territory. Specifically, this right covered the ① specific designation of the islands to be included in or excluded from Japanese territory; ② indication of Japanese territory with longitude and latitude lines to delineate its exact boundaries; ③ and attachment of a map for a clear visual representation. The treaty drafts by the US DoS beginning in 1947 and the 1951 draft of the UK FCO were drawn up according to this clause. However, in 1950 when Dulles appeared at the negotiation table, priority was given to a peace treaty that would be lenient, non-punitive and simpler. As a result, the clause defining Japanese territory was virtually removed and nothing placed in the void afterwards.

Regardless of what the US determined regarding Japanese territory in the course of the San Francisco Peace Conference, there was no general consensus among the Allies. The Japanese Foreign Ministry argues that the failure to mention Dokdo as territory to be excluded from Japan confirmed it as Japanese territory, but this was never discussed or decided at the peace conference. The Japanese territory clause agreed to by the Allies during WWII was basically scrapped without ever being officially discussed, and the treaty was concluded with no agreement on a new territory clause. What remains valid is Korea's explanation that Dokdo was validated as Korean territory by being considered an outlying island around Ulleungdo and its interpretation that the territorial clause agreed to by the Allies remains in effect is accurate.

On December 4, 1953, when the Dokdo conflict between Korea and Japan had reached a crescendo, US Secretary of State Dulles sent a memorandum to the US Embassies in Seoul and Tokyo to clarify these issues for all parties concerned. This later became America's official position on the Dokdo issue.

Studies on Dokdo from the mid-1990s attempted to reveal that Dokdo was recognized as Korean territory at the San Francisco Peace Conference based on the materials found and publicized by Japan.[10] Starting in the 2000s, researchers conducted research based on relevant materials that they found by visiting foreign archives such as US NARA and UK TNA directly.

Lee Seok-woo is believed to be the first Korean researcher who searched such archives and made use of materials found there.[11] In 2005, Jung Byung-joon found a map attached to the official draft treaty written by the UK FCO in April 1951. He used the map to declare that Dokdo was excluded from Japanese territory and defined as Korean territory and that Dokdo was given precedence as Korean territory during the peace conference.[12] Also, he shed light on the role of postwar diplomats who were sympathetic towards Japan by highlighting the career and activities of William J. Sebald, who served as a US political adviser in Japan and head of the Diplomatic Section of SCAP and was cited as a key figure in Japan's lobby in the US.[13] He pointed out that the Dokdo issue is not just a Korea-Japan issue or an issue of historical sovereignty or geographical references but a regional issue derived from both Korea-US relations and US-Japan relations as a byproduct of the US strategy in Northeast Asia, its policy regarding Japan in particular, after WWII starting with the San Francisco Peace Conference.[14]

---

10   Sin Yong-ha, 2001, *Study of Materials on Sovereignty over Dokdo* 4, Dokdo Research and Preservation Association, pp. 284-301 and 313-329.

11   Lee Seok-woo, 2002, "Some Observations on the Territorial Disputes over Tokdo (Liancourt Rocks) and Interpretation of the Territorial Clauses of the San Francisco Peace Treaty," *Seoul International Law Journal*, Vol. 9, No. 1.

12   Jung Byung-joon, 2005, "The UK FCO's Draft of the Treaty of Peace with Japan and Its Attached Map (Mar. 1951) and Reconfirmation of Korea's Sovereignty over Dokdo," *Journal of Korean Independence Movement Studies*, Vol. 24.

13   Jung Byung-joon, 2005, "William J. Sebald and the Dokdo Territorial Dispute," *Historical Criticism*, Vol. 71.

14   Jung Byung-joon, 2006, "Essay: Korea-Japan Dispute on Sovereignty over Dokdo and the Role of the US," *Quarterly Review of Korean History*, No. 60; Jung Byung-joon, 2006, "Viewpoints of Korea, the US, and Japan regarding the Territorial Dispute over Dokdo Island," *Sarim*, No. 26; Jung Byung-joon, "Korea's Post-Liberation View of Dokdo and Dokdo Policies (1945-1951),"

In the 2000s, Dokdo sourcebooks about the peace conference were published.[15] Volumes 1 to 3 of *Dokdo Data Collection*, compiled and annotated by Park Jin-hui, contain the most systematic and detailed Dokdo-related US materials produced before and after the peace conference with a focus on the files of the US DoS. They elucidate the policies and position of the US DoS related to Dokdo after conclusion of the treaty in 1951 along with the treaty drafts.[16]

As seen above, the studies based on the US diplomatic documents took note of how Dokdo was assessed and dealt with in the process of the peace conference. The focus of the analysis was on how the reversion and sovereignty of Dokdo was worded in the treaty drafts.

Journal of Northeast Asian History, Vol. V-2 (Winter 2008).

15   Lee Seok-woo, 2006, *Data Collection on the Treaty of Peace with Japan*, Northeast Asian History Foundation.

16   Park Jin-hui, 2008, "Sovereignty over Dokdo and Korea, Japan, and the US," *Dokdo Data Collection*, Vol. 1 to 3 (with regard to the US), National Institute of Korean History.

2

Perspective, Composition, and References Related to the Study

1) The Dokdo issue as part of the tripartite relations between Korea, the US, and Japan

The basic perspective taken by this study is as follows: firstly, the Korea-Japan conflict on sovereignty over Dokdo originated from Japan's imperialist invasion and its greed for territory even after its defeat in the war. In this regard, Japan has produced documents and employed diverse strategies at the government level. When Japan incorporated Dokdo into its territory in 1905, a Japanese fisherman Yozaburo Nakai, who petitioned the Japanese government for fishing rights around Dokdo, and high-ranking officials of the Japanese government, went ahead with the unlawful act in full knowledge of the fact that Dokdo belonged to Korea. They argued prior occupation according to *terra nullius* (land belonging to no one), and promulgated the incorporation through a Shimane Prefecture Public Notice, which they hid from Korea. In 1947, the Japanese Foreign Ministry distributed a pamphlet to the US and Allied Powers that falsely argued that Dokdo and Ulleungdo were part of Japanese territory, and propagated another argument, through Sebald and others between 1949 and 1951, that Korea had never objected to Japan's claim that Dokdo was Japanese territory. Taking advantage of Washington's friendly attitude during the lead up to the San Francisco Peace Conference, Japan first proposed the designation and, afterwards, the removal of Dokdo as a bombing range for the occupation forces in Japan between 1952 and 1953, involving the US as a co-conspirator to confirm its sovereignty over Dokdo and securing evidence for its claim of sovereignty.[17] The stratagem successfully employed by the Japanese Foreign Ministry in 1905 was readopted from 1952 to 1953.

Secondly, the Korea-Japan conflict over Dokdo came to the surface with the Korean government's Declaration of Sovereignty over Adjacent Seas (the Peace Line) in January 1952 and Japan's claim of sovereignty over Dokdo in response. However, this originated from the preparation process for the peace conference and the conclusion of the peace treaty in 1951 and its aftermath. This was evident in 1952 when the Japanese Foreign Ministry contended through a series of diplomatic memoranda that Dokdo was Japan's inherent territory and was incorporated according to the principles of modern law in 1905, and suggested the peace treaty as the most significant basis for its claim. Since then, both the Japanese Foreign Ministry and Japan's international law jurists have continually pushed the treaty as the most important basis for Japan's argument in terms of international law.

Thirdly, the postwar Dokdo issue seemed to be a conflict over the historical sovereignty of Dokdo between the two nations, but in essence, it was an international political issue deriving from the process of building postwar regional order in Northeast Asia based on the San Francisco Peace Conference, namely "the San Francisco System". As such, it is more of a regional issue. The San Francisco System was the postwar peace regime that replaced wartime hostilities and the hostile postwar occupation between Japan and the Allied Powers. Though Korea was neither a participant in the peace conference nor a signatory state to the treaty, it could not escape the regulations and influence of the San Francisco System, which provided the basis for regional order. Korea was bound by them not only with regard to the Korea-Japan Basic Relations Treaty of 1965 but also with regard to Korea-Japan relations and other regional issues throughout the 1950s and 1960s.

Fourthly, though on the surface, the postwar Dokdo issue was a bilateral conflict between Korea and Japan and the cause of hostile relations

---

17 Jung Byung-joon, "Japan's Fabrication for 100 Years," *Hankyoreh* (Mar. 16, 2005); Jung Byung-joon, 2005, "William J. Sebald and his role in the beginning of so-called Dokto Dispute," *Historical Criticism*, Vol. 71.

between them, in reality, the decisive role and status that the US had in Northeast Asia was ever-present, always lurking in the background. In fact, the Dokdo issue was part of the tripartite relations of Korea, the US, and Japan and derived from US construction of the new postwar regional order in Northeast Asia. A study by Lee Jong-won on the role and importance of the US in Korea-Japan relations opened a new horizon for the study of the history of the 1950s and that of Korea-Japan and Korea-US relations.[18] From the perspective of Korea-Japan-US relations, the Dokdo issue of the 1950s was a byproduct of the regional order construction process rather than a bilateral issue between Korea and Japan or the verification of historical sovereignty. It was a shadow in the shade cast by single-minded US hegemony.

Fifthly, the political relations and positions of the three nations differed on the Dokdo issue. Japan deliberately devised and carried out strategic diplomatic maneuvers against Korea, mired as the latter was in the ravages of colonization, national division, military rule, and war, to induce intervention and consent by the US and secure its sovereignty over Dokdo. The US, in possession of hegemonic power over Northeast Asia in the 1950s, provided the cause for the Dokdo dispute by allowing the replacement of high-level policy with administrative opportunism by working-level members in the process of preparing the treaty. The Dokdo issue unintentionally resulted from the US' decisive diplomatic power, and when it recognized what had happened, the US adjusted itself so as to take up a neutral position on the issue. Korea, whose very survival as a nation had been threatened during the Korean War, was swept up in the unexpected controversy and was able to defend Dokdo only through desperation in making its case. In a nutshell, Japan positioned itself as a

---

18   Lee Jong-won, 1996, *East Asia Cold War and Korea-US-Japan Relations*, University of Tokyo Press; Lee Jong-won, 1995, "International Political Background of the Korea-Japan Talks," *A Second Look at the Korea-Japan Basic Relations Treaty*, compiled by the Institute for Research in Collaborationist Activities, Asea Culture Publishing; Lee Jong-won, 1994, "Normalization of Korea-Japan Relations and the US - 1960 to 1965," *Journal of Modern Japanese Studies 16*, compiled by the Research Group on Modern Japan, Yamakawa Publishing.

planner, a schemer, and an aggressor when it came to Dokdo. On the other hand, Korea had no choice but to play the role of a newly-independent nation, a diplomatic novice, and to adopt a defensive posture. The US remained in its role as a decision-maker and arbitrator.[19]

Based on the judgment that it gained recognition from the US of its sovereignty over Dokdo in the process of concluding the 1951 treaty, the Japanese government initiated the Dokdo dispute. This argument was iterated in a January 1952 statement by the Japanese Foreign Ministry regarding the Peace Line. The designation and subsequent removal of Dokdo as a bombing range for the occupation forces in Japan between 1952 and 1953 was openly pursued by the Japanese Foreign Ministry and Diet, intending to give prominence to the US as a third party that could decide on and was responsible for sovereignty over Dokdo. At the core of the postwar Dokdo issue was the US role and decisive power in the formation of regional order. This newly-created regional system based on the peace treaty had a lasting impact.

2) The events of 1947 and their significance

This book deals with the time period from 1945 after the end of WWII to 1953. The focus is on the period from 1947 when the Treaty of Peace with Japan was first conceived and began to be drafted in earnest to 1951 when it was signed in San Francisco. The periods before 1947 and after 1951 are also partially dealt with as needed. The reason for the importance of the year 1947 is that it was when Korea, Japan, and the US, the three main players in the Dokdo issue, started to create many of the most important perceptions, policies, and judgments.

Firstly, Korea began to take interest in and explore Dokdo in earnest from 1947. It was only two years after national liberation and before the

---

19   Jung Byung-joon, 2006, "Essay: Korea-Japan Dispute on Sovereignty over Dokdo and the Role of the US," *Quarterly Review of Korean History*, No. 60; Jung Byung-joon, 2006, "Viewpoints of Korea, the US, and Japan regarding the Territorial Dispute over Dokdo Island," *Sarim*, Vol. 26.

establishment of the Republic of Korea (ROK) government, but under the instruction of An Jae-hong, the Minister of Civil Affairs of the South Korean Interim Government, a government survey team and members of the Corean Alpine Club jointly formed the Dokdo Scientific Expedition. They were dispatched to the island because of the news of the impending peace treaty, the landing of Japanese fishermen on Dokdo, and Japan's claim of sovereignty over it. The Koreans, who had failed to properly respond to Japan's unlawful incorporation of Dokdo during the colonization process of the nation after the Japan-Korea Protectorate Treaty of 1905, began preparations in earnest to protect its sovereignty over the island in 1947 even before the nation was standing on its own feet. That year, Korea and its people began recognizing the importance of the postwar Dokdo issue and taking action and exploring the island in earnest. The determination of the Koreans to defend it led to interest in Parangdo Island which was known to be under the threat of reinvasion by Japan and extended to the demand for the return of Tsushima, which was an offensive response to Japan's aggression. Dokdo, Parangdo, and Tsushima came to represent to the Koreans the territorial sovereignty boundary to be protected against Japan from 1947 onwards. As evidenced in the 1948 petition by the Patriotic Old Men's Association, which asked General Douglas MacArthur to define the three islands as Korean territory and return them, they were regarded as one set. In the same context, the Korean government demanded sovereignty over them in negotiations with the US with regard to the 1951 peace conference.

Secondly, in the eyes of Japan, the conclusion of a peace treaty emerged as a matter of grave national concern immediately after WWII. The Japanese Foreign Ministry set out to prepare for a treaty from late 1945 and completed all that was required from it by 1947. For instance, a pamphlet produced by the Japanese Foreign Ministry and distributed to the US and Allied Powers in June 1947 was used as decisive evidence with regard to Dokdo. The pamphlet indicated Dokdo and Ulleungdo as "islands annexed to Japan" and further propagated false information that there was no Korean name for Dokdo and that Dokdo was not shown on Korean-made maps. This misinformation became documentary evidence that caused confusion in the Dokdo-related judgments made by General MacArthur's headquarters, the US Department of State (DoS), and other such parties beginning in 1948. In this light, 1947 is when false claims and intrigues by Japan to gain sovereignty over Dokdo gained traction.

Thirdly, the US began preparing for the peace treaty from the latter half of 1946 and began creating draft treaties from early 1947. The various drafts written by the US DoS in early 1947 clearly indicated the Liancourt Rocks (Dokdo) as Korean territory. In 1947, the Policy Planning Staff (PPS) of the US DoS was in charge of promoting the position of the US DoS and representing it with drafts and maps: this policy position was maintained until Sebald, a US political adviser in Japan and Head of the Diplomatic Section of SCAP, argued that Dokdo was Japanese territory in November 1949. After that, the US policy position on Dokdo went through innumerable changes, and Dokdo was not mentioned in the final treaty.

As seen above, the year 1947 witnessed a clear manifestation of the respective positions and policy choices of the three nations with regard to Dokdo and was the invisible starting point of the postwar Dokdo issue. That same year, the three nations began formulating their own perceptions, judgments, and policies on Dokdo for the first time since WWII according to their separate needs and judgments. The antagonism between the three nations that remained just beneath the surface was settled for the time being with the conclusion of the 1951 peace treaty. After that, as a strategic choice to secure sovereignty over Dokdo, Korea included Dokdo within the Peace Line and carried out a full-scale exploration of the island. Japan induced the US to designate and later remove Dokdo as a bombing range. The conflict regarding Dokdo came to the fore through the heated exchanges of diplomatic memoranda from January 1952 and gradually escalated into the unlawful encroachment onto the island and armed conflicts. Recognition of and policy on Dokdo by the three nations began to gain momentum in 1947, which represents the starting point of the postwar Dokdo issue.

This book has two focal points: the first looks at each nation's policy, and more specifically, how Korea, Japan, and the US recognized Dokdo and established policy relating to it in preparation for the peace treaty. The second is about tripartite relations: how the three nations negotiated with and influenced one another. As the subtitle of this book reveals, it is about the postwar Dokdo issue and the tripartite relations between Korea, the US, and Japan.

Chapter 1

Korea's Perception of Dokdo

: Exploration of Dokdo (1947) and
Bombing of Dokdo (1948)

1

From Dokdo to Seoul

: Reenactment of the 1905 "Invasion"

1) Dokdo crisis: Unlawful encroachment and shooting incident by Japanese fishermen

When Korea was liberated in 1945 with Japans' defeat in WWII, sovereignty over the Korean peninsula and its annexed islands naturally reverted back to Korea. The initial recognition of Dokdo by the Koreans after liberation followed the same course of action as in 1905 when Dokdo was illegally incorporated into Japanese territory. In 1947, a Korean fishing boat engaged in fishing in the waters around Dokdo was shot by Japanese who came ashore at Dokdo. The residents of Ulleungdo were enraged and their rage was reported to the central government by the provincial government of Gyeongsangbuk-do, which had jurisdiction over the island. As in 1905, the residents of Ulleungdo, who relied on the waters around Dokdo to make a living, stressed the importance of sovereignty over Dokdo and news of the situation spread to the central government through the local government.

It was in 1947 when the name "Dokdo" and the issue of its sovereignty received attention in the Korean press, after the nation had been liberated. An article carried by the *Daegu Shibo*, a newspaper published in the city of Daegu, helped improve awareness of Dokdo among Koreans and had an impact on deciding how to respond to Japan's provocations.[1] This article was noteworthy in three aspects:

---

1   "Stupidity of the Enemy Japanese: Ownership Claimed over a Small Island near Ulleungdo as a Fishing Area," *Daegu Shibo* (Jun. 20, 1947).

Firstly, it clearly defined Dokdo as Korean territory and provided information on its geographical location. The article stated, "Dokdo lies about 49 miles to the east of Ulleungdo, Gyeongsangbuk-do(province), and consists of two islands, Jwado (Seodo) and Udo (Dongdo), which are uninhibited, running 1.5 miles and 0.5 miles in circumference, respectively."

Secondly, it reaffirmed awareness of Korea's historical sovereignty over Dokdo and Korea's sovereignty over the island. The article described Dokdo as "part of the nation" and "an island of Korea's" and accurately accounted for the visit to Ulleungdo by Shimane Prefecture officials and the notification regarding the illegal incorporation of Dokdo into Japan in 1906. It went on to point out the existence of a document in which Sim Heung-taek, then Magistrate of Ulleungdo, who received verbal notification, provided a full account of the incident to the Gangwon-do government and requested response to the matter.[2] It stated that Gyeongsangbuk-do, the governing authority over Dokdo, demanded action on the issue by the central government based on the history of invasion by Japan and the current situation in Dokdo.

Thirdly, it recorded the intrusion of Dokdo by the Japanese after national liberation. The article went on to say, "It seemed that a Japanese resident in Sakai Minato Port of Shimane Prefecture believes he owns Dokdo as his personal fishing ground, and when a fishing boat from Ulleungdo went out fishing near Dokdo this past April, it was fired on by machine guns." This means that after having claimed ownership of the island, the Japanese man used the region as his personal fishing grounds and attacked the Ulleungdo fishing boat near Dokdo in April 1947.

Sakai Minato Port is an advance base of the present Tottori Prefecture from where ships depart to Oki Islands or Ulleungdo and Dokdo.

On the other hand, SCAP Instruction No. 677 of January 29, 1946 had already excluded Dokdo from the governmental and administrative authority of Japanese. Paragraph 3 of SCAPIN No. 1033 of June 22, 1946

---

2   A copy of the Sim Heung-taek report was found at the Ulleungdo government office by the Ulleungdo·Dokdo scientific expedition in August 1947.

(subject: Area Authorized for Japanese Fishing and Whaling) stipulated, "Japanese vessels or personnel thereof will not approach closer than twelve (12) miles to Takeshima (37°15′ North Latitude, 131°53′ East Longitude) nor have any contact with said island." This MacArthur Line clearly removed Dokdo from Japanese territory. Accordingly, Shimane Prefecture deleted clauses related to Dokdo and sea lion hunting from the "Shimane Prefecture Fisheries Control Regulation" through Prefecture Ordinance No. 49 (July 26, 1946).[3]

As such, the Japanese attempt to invade and occupy Dokdo, claiming fishing rights and banning fishing by Koreans in 1947 was an illegal act that violated not only the SCAP instructions but also Japanese law. Furthermore, the firing upon the Korean fishing boat was an act of brutality and illegality.

2) Seoul's response: Combination of the Dokdo incident and relaxation of the MacArthur Line

On June 19, 1947, Gyeongsangbuk-do reported to the central government Japan's attempt to plunder Dokdo and the *Daegu Shibo* covered the incident. One month later, Dokdo was no longer a regional issue but emerged as an issue that concerned the central government in Seoul and furthermore, a matter of national interest.

By late July, media outlets in Seoul started to follow up on the *Daegu Shibo* report with a tone similar to the original article. An article from one of these media outlets, *Dong-A Ilbo*, was built on the previous *Daegu Shibo* article and increased recognition of Dokdo by the Korean population and impacted the policy response at the central-government level.[4] The *Dong-A Ilbo* article speculated on the prospect of Dokdo becoming the subject of a sovereignty dispute with Japan, urging action by the South Korean

---

3   Seizaburo Tamura, 1965, *Shimaneken Takeshima No Shin Kenkyu (A New Study of Takeshima, Shimane Prefecture)*, General Affairs Department, General Affairs Section, Shimane Prefecture, p. 73.
4   "Invasion Tendency of Japanese Who Can't Abandon Territorial Greed, Resuscitation of the Issue of Dokdo off the Coast of Ulleungdo," *Dong-A Ilbo* (Jul. 23, 1947).

Interim Government. As such, the response to the incident that occurred during the fishing operation off Dokdo in 1947 was passed up to Seoul through the local governments in Ulleungdo and Gyeongsangbuk-do. The seemingly insignificant incident involving a small island in the East Sea resonated with the press in Seoul and started to receive national attention. This is when the Dokdo incident expanded into an issue of sovereignty over Dokdo.

Another reason for the heightened awareness of Dokdo by the Koreans from June to July 1947 was the threat from the sea due to the easing of the MacArthur Line. On July 2, 1947, General MacArthur's headquarters dispatched two Americans from the National Resources Survey Agency to Korea to survey its fishery status to address the food shortage in Japan.[5] The MacArthur Line had delimited the fishing boundaries for the Japanese and a strong concern that this line might be further expanded into Korea's territorial waters was raised in Korea. Korea's fishing industry was worried that, as Korea's fishing techniques were less advanced and its fishermen only able to fish inshore and unable to go offshore, the sea fishing industry along the southern coast would be ruined and fall into decline if Japan's fishing boundaries were to be widened. They demanded that the MacArthur Line, which was curved to the south of Jeju Island, be straightened to reduce Japan's fishing zone.[6]

The concern surrounding the illegal landing at Dokdo and shooting on a Korean vessel by the Japanese, which began in Ulleungdo in June 1947, was combined with concerns over the widening of the MacArthur Line and the reduction of Korea's fishing zones. These concerns eventually gained a stronger voice.

Looking back, it was more likely that Korea then started to pay full attention to the Dokdo issue and take action to defend its sovereignty over the island by mere chance and circumstance. The interest in Dokdo, which

---

5   *Fisheries Economic Newspaper* (Jul. 4, 1947).

6   "Japanese Fishermen Illegally Fished in the South Sea Violating the Fishing Boundaries; the So-Called MacArthur Line Should Be Corrected and Curtailed," *Fisheries Economic Newspaper* (Jul. 30, 1947).

started in Ulleungdo in 1947 and carried over to Daegu and eventually to Seoul, was the starting point that made an important contribution to firmly securing Korea's sovereignty over Dokdo after WWII.

A report by the *Hanseong Ilbo* on August 13, 1947 showed that the Korean press and intellectuals of the time were interested in both the Dokdo issue and the easing of the MacArthur Line.[7]

The increased recognition of the Dokdo issue by the Koreans after national liberation reflected multifaceted judgments of the situation such as worries over a possible reinvasion by Japan as evidenced by the unlawful encroachment onto Dokdo; the Korean determination to firmly establish the territorial sovereignty of Korea which had been liberated but was not yet fully independent; and the need to secure the survival of Korean fisheries in view of the expansion of the MacArthur Line. The general understanding was that sovereignty over Dokdo was directly related to the MacArthur Line.

To sum up, the illegal encroachment of Dokdo, the attempt to prevent Koreans from fishing in their own waters, and the discharge of firearms on a Korean vessel by the Japanese all happened in April 1947. The Gyeongsangbuk-do government received a petition from Ulleungdo residents who fished off Dokdo and reported the situation to the South Korean Interim Government on June 19, 1947. In response, the Fisheries Bureau of the Interim Government's Ministry of Agriculture demanded that the MacArthur Line be redrawn by MacArthur's headquarters in mid-July of the same year. In other words, the reasons for the increased public interest in Dokdo after WWII were the overfishing, crossing of the fishing boundaries, illegal encroachment onto Dokdo, and the shooting incident by the Japanese. The Dokdo issue became a national issue, moving from Ulleungdo to the Gyeongsangbuk-do provincial authorities and finally to the Interim Government in Seoul, following the very same route used to report Japan's illegal incorporation of Dokdo in 1906. First, the Magistrate

---

7   "Invasion and Plunder by Japanese Fishing Vessels in the Adjacent Seas; Correction of the MacArthur Line Was Also Proposed," *Hanseong Ilbo* (Aug. 13, 1947).

of Ulleungdo back then, Sim Heung-taek, reported it to the Gangwondo provincial government, when then reported it to the central government of the Korean Empire. Japan's invasion of Dokdo was reenacted in much the same way 41 years later.

Korea had just been liberated from years of colonization, and was experiencing great conflict in the process of establishing itself as a new nation state, and the fate of the nation itself was still undecided. Under these circumstances, Dokdo, the first Korean territory to fall victim to Japanese imperialist forces in the early 20th century, was again at the forefront of a new crisis and this warranted a proactive response from Koreans who vividly remembered it.

2

Exploration of Ulleungdo and Dokdo by the Interim Government and Corean Alpine Club (1947)

1) Organization of the Survey Committee by the Interim Government

At the time, the Japanese Ministry of Foreign Affairs was carrying out a large-scale propaganda campaign targeting MacArthur's headquarters, former Allied Powers, and the like with a pamphlet that falsely alleged that Dokdo was Japanese territory. The Ministry promoted the idea that, practically, Ulleungdo was also, closer to Japanese territory.

The fishermen from Shimane Prefecture resorted to physical violence at Dokdo while the Japanese Foreign Ministry employed diplomatic means concurrently. With Korea having been recently liberated from occupation and yet divided and caught up in chaotic political, economic, and social upheaval amid a flood of conflicts between the US and the Soviet Union, the two opposing Koreas, and the right and left sides of the political spectrum, the Koreans were ultimately left clueless. Their foremost goal was to build a unified and independent nation engaged in reconstruction for survival.

Despite being unaware of the tricks employed by the Japanese Foreign Ministry, they began to respond intelligently and on the spot to Japan's attempts to take Dokdo. With no sovereign government of their own, their responses were limited as they were still under the control of the US Army Military Government in Korea (USAMGIK). After the illegal encroachment onto Dokdo and the shooting incident came to light, there were basically two responses taken by the Koreans.

First, the South Korean Interim Government conducted an exploration of Dokdo and relevant literature studies. Second, the Corean Alpine Club, a private organization, surveyed Ulleungdo and Dokdo in close cooperation with the Interim Government as a complementary measure. That is, as officials of the Interim Government who were not capable of exerting any authority over territorial issues under USAMGIK, they were able to actively engage in research activities through the Corean Alpine Club.

A task force was immediately organized that centered on An Jae-hong, a well-known intransigent nationalist and center-right politician, who was also the Minister of Civil Affairs in the Interim Government. As seen in the remarks made by Sin Seok-ho, the Director of Guksagwan (the present National Institute of Korean History) that "MacArthur's headquarters should confirm Dokdo as Korean territory" as it had been Korea's geographical and historical territory,"[8] Koreans had no choice but to pursue the confirmation of Korea's sovereignty over Dokdo indirectly, such as by reporting to and pleading with MacArthur's headquarters.

When newspapers covered the Basic Post-Surrender Policy for Japan adopted by the Far Eastern Commission on July 11, 1947, ownership of Dokdo drew attention in Korea.[9] In early August, the Interim Government established the Dokdo Survey Committee headed by the Minister of Civil Affairs and held a meeting with relevant specialists at the Minister's Office at Capitol Hall on August 4, 1947.[10] The most important agenda item was to dispatch an expedition to determine the actual situation on Dokdo and secure needed evidence. The meeting naturally came up with two main tasks: finding historical references and conducting a field survey.[11]

The Interim Government decided to dispatch a Dokdo survey team. On instructions from Civil Affairs Minister An Jae-hong, a four-member onsite survey team consisting of Sin Seok-ho (Guksagwan Director), Chu In-bong (Manager for Japanese Affairs, Office of Foreign Affairs), Lee Bong-su (textbook editor, Ministry of Culture and Education), and Han Gi-jun (technician, Fisheries Bureau) was formed and dispatched to

---

8 "Naturally Ours: Interview with Guksagwan Director Sin," *Dong-A Ilbo* (Jul. 23, 1947).
9 Bureau of State Affairs, Ministry of Foreign Affairs, 1955, *Introduction to the Dokdo Issue*, p. 34.
10 "Grave Dokdo Issue: Discussion on Organization of the Dokdo Survey Committee," *Dong-A Ilbo* (Aug. 3, 1947).
11 "Our Territory: Interview with Manager Chu In-bong," *Dong-A Ilbo* (Aug. 3, 1947).

Dokdo.[12]

The Dokdo survey team, under the direct supervision of the Minister of Civil Affairs, arrived in Daegu on August 16, 1947[13] and was joined by two officials of the Gyeongsangbuk-do government (regional manager Gwon Dae-il and one other official). Now a six-member team (four specialists in the areas of history, foreign relations, education, and fisheries from the central government plus two local officials) began their on-site survey. They were accompanied by the Ulleungdo and Dokdo expedition team of the Corean Alpine Club.

In the meantime, though not part of the Dokdo survey team, a significant number of government personnel were part of the Ulleungdo and Dokdo expedition of the Corean Alpine Club. According to several records, there were 18 officials belonging to the Interim Government: four from the central government, two from Gyeongsangbuk-do and 12 who joined the Corean Alpine Club.

However, their dispatch was kept quiet and the survey carried out secretly. USAMGIK made no public mention of and did not officially recognize their dispatch. The team appeared only once in USAMGIK's records, in one of the South Korean Interim Government Activities reports. In this report, the military government wrote, "Dokdo is an excellent advance base for fishing and consists of two small islets located southwest (as written in the original text) of Ulleungdo. Sovereignty over the island is currently being disputed." In other words, it relayed the idea that Dokdo was formerly occupied by Japan but was currently demarcated as part of Korea's fishing zone by the MacArthur Line, and its ultimate ownership would be determined at the forthcoming San Francisco Peace Conference.[14]

As the purpose of dispatching the Interim Government's Dokdo survey

---

12 Sin Seok-ho, 1948, "Who Dokdo Belongs To", *Sahae*, December Issue (Vol. 1, No. 1), p. 90.

13 "Departure of the Dokdo Survey Team on the 16th," *Daegu Shibo* (Aug. 17, 1947).

14 USAFIK, United States Army Military Government in Korea, South Korea Interim Government Activities, No. 23 (Aug. 1947), prepared by the National Economic Board and Statistical Research Division, Office of Administration, p. 7.

team was to serve the Dokdo Survey Committee as initially proposed, they focused on learning about the historical and geographical traits, actual on-site conditions, and other aspects of Dokdo.

2) Joining forces with the Corean Alpine Club

The team that joined the Interim Government's Dokdo survey team in their exploration of the island was from a private organization known as the Corean Alpine Club. It was the predecessor of the present Corea Alpine Club and not a typical social or recreational club but rather a territory-surveying exploratory group. It was a large, elite group of the brightest minds in their young adult and middle-aged years. Having explored the nation, visited remote areas, and opened up hiking paths, the club also had the experience, skills, and personnel necessary for a survey and exploration of Dokdo. It was natural for a club equipped with such people and experience to join the government's survey team and, in the end, to lead the survey. What they had in common was their affiliation with An Jae-hong and the Chindan Society. The Corean Alpine Club was closely related to and worked together with the Chindan Society and had made numerous independent efforts to learn more about the nation's territory.

Formation and dispatch of the Dokdo expedition in 1947 was led by Minister of Civil Affairs An Jae-hong, Guksagwan Director Sin Seok-ho, Song Seok-ha and Do Bong-seop of the Corean Alpine Club, and others. They had previously participated in the Chindan Society, an academic society for Joseon studies (Sin Seok-ho, Song Seok-ha, Yu Hong-ryeol) and led the Joseon studies movement (An Jae-hong and Song Seok-ha) during the Japanese colonial period. Those who had led studies in Korean culture, history and geography with a great affection for and determination to find the essence of Korea during colonial rule played a leading role in forming the Dokdo survey team after national liberation. In particular, An Jae-hong, in his government role as the Minister of Civil Affairs, pulled strings to seek the help the Corean Alpine Club needed for the Dokdo survey.

Song Seok-ha led the formation of the scientific expedition within the Corean Alpine Club, but the idea to survey Dokdo under the pretext of a survey of Ulleungdo was conceived by the Interim Government. After having decided to survey Dokdo, the government, which had to be cautious about its relationship with USAMGIK, invited the Corean Alpine Club, with their relevant experience and skilled personnel to carry out the actual survey activities.

With the support of the Interim Government, the Corean Alpine Club invited the foremost domestic specialists in a variety of areas and formed the "Ulleungdo Scientific Expedition" (hereinafter referred to as "the expedition"). The expedition consisted of a head team and a survey division, the former with 15 members responsible for directing and supervising the expedition, taking care of general affairs, and securing and shipping equipment and food. Some of these personnel also joined the survey division.[15] The latter consisted of eight teams: ten members in social science team A (history, geography, economics, sociology, archeology, folk studies, and linguistics); 11 in social science team B (living status survey carried out by the head team members); six in the zoology team; nine in the botany team; four in the agriculture and forestry team; two in the geology and mineralogy team; eight in the medical team; and eight in the media coverage team (photography and radio), bringing the total number to 63.[16] This was the largest number of people ever mobilized for a survey after national liberation, and was also the best qualified, with the participants considered the top experts in their fields at the time. Two belonged to Seoul National University (SNU)'s College of Arts and Sciences, one to SNU's College of Commerce, two to Suwon College of Agriculture (Predecessor of SNU's College of Agriculture and Life Sciences), one to Daegu University's College of Education, two to a college of pharmacy, six to SNU's College of Medicine, one to a women's college of medicine, one to the Suwon Agricultural Research Station, three to the National Science Museum, one to the National Museum, one to the National Folk Museum,

15 "Ulleungdo Scientific Expedition Report (1) by Hong Jong-in," *Hanseong Ilbo* (Sept. 21, 1947).

16 "Expedition to Be Dispatched to Ulleungdo by the Corean Alpine Club," *Hanseong Ilbo* (Aug. 3, 1947); "Ulleungdo Scientific Expedition Arrived and Started Survey Activities," *Seoul Shinmun* (Aug. 22, 1947).

two to the Korea Institute of Geoscience & Mineral Resources, one to the National Quarantine Laboratory (predecessor of the National Institute of Health) and one to the Gyeonggi-do Bacteriological Laboratory. There were also 11 middle school teachers, one radio technician from the Ministry of Communications, and one electrician from the Ministry of Commerce. Being scholars and technicians from universities and national agencies put them among the highest-qualified people in their respective fields nationwide.

The mobilization of personnel from universities, public offices, and other relevant organizations demonstrated that this survey was organized by the Interim Government and was the result of thorough preparations that made possible the concurrent participation of experts from different fields. With four from the government survey team, two from Gyeongsangbuk-do, and the police officers from the Fifth Precinct included, the total number of people involved in the expedition of 1947 was 80.[17]

3) First Dokdo survey

The government survey team and the Corean Alpine Club's scientific expedition left Pohang for Ulleungdo on August 18, 1947 on a Coast Guard vessel with an escort of Fifth Precinct police. Their final destination was to be Dokdo. On the surface, it was advertised as a scientific investigation of Ulleungdo by a private organization, the Corean Alpine Club, but in essence, it was meant to be an official survey of Dokdo, the island at the center of the controversy regarding the illegal encroachment attempts by the Japanese.

The Department of Internal Security (presently the Ministry of National Defense) provided the patrol craft *Daejeonhwan* to allow for the convenient transportation of the large-scale expedition of some 80 people

---

17   Personnel from the Gyeongsangbuk-do provincial government, the Coast Guard, and Kyungpook National University who were initially not part of the expedition, demanded to be part on account of Ulleungdo being under their jurisdiction. They joined the team in Daegu.

and equipment. The craft transported them from Pohang to Ulleungdo and then on to Dokdo. It was more than a simple job of assisting with transportation: it was only possible because the Interim Government was behind the expedition. Patrol craft could be used only for official business and one was assigned to the Ulleungdo and Dokdo expedition under the government's auspices. Also, the provincial government of Gyeongsangbuk-do, the Fifth Precinct police headquarters, which had jurisdiction over the province, and Ulleungdo rendered their full support. The itinerary of the expedition was as follows:[18]

August 16   The lecture team departed as an advance party in the morning and the main unit, in the afternoon. Sixty-three members of the Corean Alpine Club arrived in Daegu: four from the government survey team, two from Gyeongsangbuk-do, police officers from the Fifth Precinct, and several more joined the expedition.

August 17   Travelled via Daegu. A lecture held at Daegu University's College of Education by the Gyeongbuk Education Association (Sin Seok-ho, Do Bong-seop, and Hong Jong-in lectured to an audience of some 400 people). All gathered in Pohang in the afternoon.

August 18   Left Pohang on the Coast Guard's patrol craft *Daejeonhwan* at 7 am and arrived at Ulleungdo's Dodong Port at 6 pm.

August 19   Rested, delivered care packages to Ulleungdo residents, held a lecture, and participated in a nighttime meeting.

August 20   Departed from Ulleungdo's Dodong Port at 5:10 am, arrived at Dokdo at 9:40 am, surveyed Dokdo, and returned to Dodong Port at 8:30 pm.

August 21   The survey division, with the exception of the medical team,

---

18   "Expedition to Be Dispatched to Ulleungdo by the Corean Alpine Club," *Hanseong Ilbo* (Aug. 3, 1947); "Departure of the Dokdo Survey Team on the 16th," *Daegu Shibo* (Aug. 17, 1947); "Dokdo Explored," *Daegu Shibo* (1947. 8. 22); "The Ulleungdo Scientific Expedition Unexpectedly Found Seals at Dokdo," *Chosun Ilbo* (Aug. 23, 1947); "Seonginbong Tramped All Over: Korea on the Science Front," *Gongeop Shinmun* (Aug. 28, 1947); "Ulleungdo Scientific Expedition Report (2) by Hong Jong-in," *Hanseong Ilbo* (Sept. 24, 1947); Hong Gu-pyo, 1947, "Wrapping up the Expedition of the Unmanned Island Dokdo (travel essay)," *Geongukgongron*, November Issue (Vol. 3, No. 5)

was divided into two to climb Seonginbong Peak on Ulleungdo. They got up at 7 am and reached the top at noon. Team A descended southeast to lodge in Namyang-dong while Team B went down northeast to be put up in Nari-dong.

August 22 Team A left Namyang-dong and lodged in Daeha. Team B left Nari-dong, went by way of Cheonbu-dong and stayed in Hyeonpo.

August 23 Team A left Daeha, went by way of Hyeonpo, and stayed in Cheonbu-dong while Team B left Hyeonpo, went by way of Daeha, and stayed in Namyang-dong.

August 24 All gathered in Dodong in the afternoon. For their part, the medical team spent two days in Dodong, two days in Cheonbu-dong, and one day in Nari-dong. They offered medical treatment to residents free of charge and performed research. They also climbed Seonginbong and returned to Dodong.

August 25 Rested and organized collected materials. A special lecture was held in the morning at Usan Middle School.

August 26 Left Dodong at 9:30 am, arrived in Pohang at 10:30 pm, and stayed overnight.

August 27 Left Pohang in two teams in the morning and afternoon and travelled via Daegu.

August 28 The main unit arrived in Seoul in the morning.

The first thing the team did was to visit Dokdo (initiating the survey on August 20) because the Interim Government placed the highest priority on the Dokdo survey, which was also its key objective. Everything was done to keep it secret as the head team informed the rest of the expedition that a survey of Dokdo was the first item on their official schedule only on the day after their arrival in Ulleungdo.

Though they brought specialists in the areas of social science, zoology, botany, agriculture and forestry, geology and mineralogy, medicine, media coverage, and telecommunications, there was not much for them to investigate on Dokdo. Being an uninhabited island, it did not offer anything for the social science, medical, and agriculture and forestry teams to look into. The geology and mineralogy survey must have been simple on these

[Figure 1-1] Territorial signposts installed at Dokdo by the Corean Alpine Club (Aug. 20, 1947) © Hong Jong-in/Corea Alpine Club

islands of volcanic rocks. The most important aspects of the 1947 survey were collecting zoological and botanical specimens, measuring distances with the naked eye, learning about the islands' geographical features, and creating photographic records.

According to geographer Ok Seung-sik, the expedition could not perform any actual measurements as there was no surveyor or geodesist present and instead the geology and mineralogy team had to make measurements with the naked eye. The diameter of the island was estimated to be about 200 to 205m.[19] Actual measurement was carried out in 1953.[20] The zoology and botany teams did a surface-level investigation to learn about the island's vegetation and ecology. With their rifles, they shot three young animals that looked like seals in the northeastern lowland of Dokdo's western island (Seodo or often called Namdo, or "Man Island").[21] They collected some 50 botanical and insect specimens which belonged to the same plant and animal kingdoms as those present on Ulleungdo.[22]

The survey on Dokdo ended at around 3:30 in the afternoon, which was about five hours and 30 or 40 minutes after the initial landing. As such, it was considered a rough survey of the land.

The most noteworthy of their activities was their installation of signposts on Dongdo, Dokdo's eastern island, bearing the names of the Interim Government and the Corean Alpine Club (refer to Figure 1-1).[23] During the first-ever Dokdo survey, the expedition installed signposts that declared Dokdo to be Korean territory and by doing so, completed its main task of confirming sovereignty over it. They installed two signposts on Dongdo: the right post was inscribed "Joseon, Ulleungdo, Nam-myeon, Dokdo"; and the left "Commemorative Signpost of the Ulleungdo & Dokdo Scientific Expedition". The date of installation was August 20, 1947. A photo of these posts remains as part of Hong Jong-in's contribution to *Korean Mountains* in 1977.[24] They were the first outward physical signs

---

19 "Brief Report on the Geological Survey of Ulleungdo and Dokdo" (geology and mineralogy team, Ok Seung-sik), Dokdo Museum, p. 3.
20 "Brief Report on the Geological Survey of Ulleungdo and Dokdo" (geology and mineralogy team, Ok Seung-sik), Dokdo Museum, p. 10 and 14.
21 "Nature of Ulleungdo by Seok Ju-myeong," *Seoul Shinmun* (Sept. 9, 1947); Hong Gu-pyo, 1947, "Wrapping up the Expedition of the Unmanned Island Dokdo (travel essay)," *Geongukgongron.*, November Issue, p. 20.
22 "Alpine Club Expedition Fascinated by the Ecology of Dokdo: A Mysterious Land in the East Sea," *Jayu Shinmun* (Aug. 24, 1947).
23 "Our Land in the East Sea, the Deplorable Record of a Bloody Scene: Reminiscences of the Expedition by Hong Jong-in," *Chosun Ilbo* (Jun. 17, 1948).
24 Hong Jong-in, 1977, *Korean Mountains*, p. 102.

that marked Dokdo as Korean territory. The name *Joseon* was used because it was before the establishment of the ROK government and therefore the nation was still under the control of USAMGIK and the Interim Government. That signposts were installed has been known about for a while, but the photo has been made public only recently.

The signposts of 1947 are believed to have been removed by the Japanese who illegally landed on Dokdo in 1953. They installed their own signpost, which was removed by the Corea Alpine Club expedition upon its revisit to Dokdo in October 1953. During this second expedition, they erected a granite landmark.[25] However, this one was also removed by the Japanese Coast Guard some time later. The stone marker that currently stands on Dokdo is a replica of the 1953 landmark restored by Gyeongsangbuk-do in 2009.

As explained above, the most significant achievements of the Dokdo expedition were the basic survey of the island and the confirmation of Dokdo as Korean territory. Having completed their mission, the expedition left Dokdo around 3:30 pm, sailed around the island once, and returned to Dodong Port on Ulleungdo around 8:30 pm.

After their return to Ulleungdo, they conducted research on that island during the remainder of the trip. They visited and surveyed Seonginbong Peak, the first time a Korean research team had done so, as well as other major areas of the island. The survey of Ulleungdo took four days. They left Ulleungdo on August 26 and arrived in Pohang after an 11-hour trip, the return journey taking the same amount of time as the trip to Ulleungdo. They travelled via Daegu to arrive in Seoul on August 28 to wrap up the expedition.

The expedition itself took nine days including one day for the Dokdo survey (August 20) and four days spent surveying Ulleungdo (August 21 to 24), coming to a total of 13 days including travel time.

---

25 The photos of the stone landmark and activities by the expedition have been recently made public. Lee Jeong-hun, 2005, "Root out the Trace of 'Takeshima' in Dokdo in 1953," *Weekly Dong-A*, Mar. 15, Serial No. 476.

3
Legacies of the 1947 Dokdo Survey

After the return of the survey team, the results of the Ulleungdo and Dokdo expedition were made public through various channels. The first was through a debriefing session and an exhibition; the second was through survey reports and extended media coverage; and the third was through newspapers and magazines while distributing materials written by individual members of the expedition. Through these efforts, Dokdo was rediscovered and entered the public's consciousness, resulting in heightened social and cultural awareness and interest in the island. In addition, the scholars who participated in the expedition continued to produce theories, logic, evidence, and other relevant references that helped increase Koreans' recognition of Dokdo and develop subsequent policies.

1) Debriefing session, exhibition, and survey reports

The official debriefing session by the Corean Alpine Club was held at 2 pm on September 2, 1947 at Seoul's National Science Museum.[26] At a meeting with a reporter on August 31, the head of the expedition, Song Seok-ha, mentioned Dokdo, saying, "What's more interesting is the unmanned island Dokdo and we found *haero* (animals similar to *otdosei* [seal in Japanese]) inhabiting the island."[27] He did not place much emphasis on the sovereignty issue.

---

26 "A Debriefing Session by the Ulleungdo Expedition," *Seoul Shinmun* (Sept. 9, 1947); "A Lecture to be Held on the 10th to Report on Ulleungdo," *Gongeop Shinmun* (Sept. 9, 1947); "Ulleungdo Scientific Expedition Report (3) by Hong Jong-in," *Hanseong Ilbo* (Sept. 25, 1947).
27 *Jayu Shinmun* (Sept. 1, 1947).

The Corean Alpine Club also held an exhibition to report on the Ulleungdo scientific expedition in the fourth-floor gallery of Seoul's Donghwa Department Store (on the site of the current Shinsegae Department Store) from November 10 to 18, 1947. Featured was a comprehensive display of the research findings from the survey of the two islands, including news photos; zoological, botanical, mineral, agricultural, and forestry specimens; archeological and folklore materials that dated back to the Stone Age; research findings from the medical team, and more.[28]

The display included 16 large photos (2.4m~4.0m), 281 photos in full-sheet and quarto sizes, some 50 graphs of various types, and some 600 scientific specimens. They were viewed by 7,000 to 10,000 people on a daily basis, bringing the total number of visitors to about 85,000.[29] At the exhibition, "the photos of Ulleungdo were worth seeing but those of Dokdo drew a surprisingly large amount of attention from the public." It is believed that this was the first time Dokdo photos were displayed in downtown Seoul. Hong Jong-in said that one of the goals of the exhibition was to "give a complete picture of Dokdo, the uninhibited and isolated island about which reversion may be disputed, to the public".[30] Though it was not fully recognized then, the survey of Dokdo, the exhibition, and other such efforts in 1947 provided an important turning point in the recognition of Dokdo among Koreans and served as a firm step towards the establishment of sovereignty.

After Seoul, the exhibition toured two cities, Daegu and Busan, and finally ended on Ulleungdo,[31] where it all started. This signified that the joint efforts by the Interim Government and the Corean Alpine Club to conduct research on Dokdo had been concluded, at least for the time being.

---

28   "Ulleungdo Exhibition," *Dokrip Shinbo* and *Seoul Shinmun* (Nov. 5, 1947).

29   Kim Jeong-tae, 1977, "30 Years' History of the Corea Alpine Club," *Korean Mountains* XI (1975-1976), Corea Alpine Club, p. 25.

30   "Opening the Ulleungdo Exhibition: Hong Jong-in," *Seoul Shinmun* (Nov. 15, 1947).

31   "Ulleungdo Scientific Expedition Report (3) by Hong Jong-in," *Hanseong Ilbo* (Sept. 25, 1947).

After completion of the survey, the four people dispatched by the Interim Government, namely, Sin Seok-ho (Guksagwan Director), Chu In-bong (Manager for Japanese Affairs, Office of Foreign Affairs), Lee Bong-su (textbook editor, Ministry of Culture and Education), and Han Gi-jun (technician, Fisheries Bureau) must have all written official reports. It is not clear whether the government survey team itself produced a comprehensive official report, but the members are believed to have produced individual reports in their respective realms.

First, Guksagwan Director and historian Sin Seok-ho contributed an essay on sovereignty over Dokdo to the history magazine *Sahae* in 1948. He wrote, in the first part, on the background to the dispatch of the Dokdo expedition and gave a full account, which made the essay a *de facto* official report.[32]

Lee Yeong-ro (an Ewha Women's University professor), who participated in the 1947 Dokdo expedition, documented 35 species of Dokdo's flora in the second issue of *Susan* (July 1952), while Jeong Yeong-ho (a professor of Seoul National University's College of Natural Sciences) wrote about 36 species in the first issue of *Korean Journal of Pharmacognosy*.[33] Fisheries Bureau technician Han Gi-jun is also believed to have written a report.[34] "Ulleungdo Scientific Expedition Reports," a series of four reports by Hong Jong-in, then the vice president of the Corean Alpine Club and deputy head of the Ulleungdo expedition, can be seen as the expedition's final official report.[35] In the reports carried by the *Hanseong Ilbo*, Hong made a very brief reference to Dokdo: "Our trip to Dokdo, an unmanned island located in the sea 48 li (18.9 km) southeast of Ulleungdo and reversion over which is said to be disputed, was not announced before it was conducted but had

---

32　Sin Seok-ho, 1948, "Who Dokdo Belongs To", *Sahae*, December Issue (Vol. 1, No. 1).

33　Park Bong-gyu, 1985, "Section 2 Nature of Ulleungdo and Dokdo of Chapter I Outline," *Dokdo Research*, Korea Modern Historical Research Society, p. 22.

34　Heo Yeong-ran, 2008, "Main Discussion Points of the Dokdo Sovereignty Issue and Dilemma of Inherent Territory Theory," *Ewha Sahak Yeongu (Bulletin of the Ewha Historical Research Center)*, Vol. 36, p. 110.

35　Hong Jong-in, "Ulleungdo Scientific Expedition Reports (1) to (4)," *Hanseong Ilbo* (Sept. 21, 24, 25, and 26, 1947)

been planned all along as a surprise move."[36]

Thanks to the 1947 Dokdo survey and the subsequent debriefing, exhibition, press coverage, and reports, Dokdo came to receive ever more attention not only from the Interim Government but also from academia and the press as well as the general public.

2) Coverage by newspapers and magazines

In the meantime, the expedition members wrote for newspapers and magazines to introduce Ulleungdo and Dokdo to the public and the press took the lead in carrying articles on Dokdo. On August 30 and 31, immediately after the return of the expedition, photos of Dokdo were shown in Seoul and Daegu for the first time. Photos first shown in Seoul were those carried by the *Jayu Shinmun* on August 30. They were taken and provided by Kim Hong-rae, a Corean Alpine Club member who participated in the expedition. In Daegu on August 31, the *Daegu Shibo* printed three Dokdo photos taken by reporter Choi Gye-bok.[37] They were the first Dokdo photos taken by Koreans and carried by newspapers after national liberation and later displayed in Daegu. Ulleungdo photos taken by Choi were also carried by the *Daegu Shibo*.[38] There were also several articles introducing Dokdo itself.[39]

---

36 "Ulleungdo Scientific Expedition Report (1) by Hong Jong-in," *Hanseong Ilbo* (Sept. 21, 1947).
37 "Dokdo Photography," *Daegu Shibo* (Aug. 31, 1947).
38 "Ulleungdo Photography," *Daegu Shibo* (Sept. 3, 4, and 5, 1947).
39 "Alpine Club Expedition Fascinated by the Ecology of Dokdo: A Mysterious Land in the East Sea," *Jayu Shinmun* (Aug. 24, 1947); "This is Dokdo," *South Korean Economic Daily* (Aug. 27 and 28, 1947); "The Nationality of Dokdo is Joseon: Clear Evidence Exists," *Gongeop Shinmun* (Oct. 15, 1947); *Fisheries Economic Newspaper* (Oct. 16, 1947); Hong Gu-pyo, 1947, "Wrapping up the Expedition of the Unmanned Island Dokdo (travel essay)," *Geongukgongron*, November 1947 Issue (Vol. 3, No. 5).

3) Emergence of major concepts, discussion points and perceptions about Dokdo

The most important outcome of the 1947 survey by the Interim Government and the Corean Alpine Club of Dokdo was that the opinion leaders of Korean society who would lead the formation of perceptions, policies, and public opinion on Dokdo after the establishment of the ROK government in 1948 clearly realized the importance of the Dokdo issue and the possibility of conflict. They came to know the history of Korea's sovereignty over the island, evidence in the relevant literature, details of the Japanese invasion, and the like. As such, they formed a social consensus about the need to actively respond to the Dokdo issue. This is a clear achievement of the 1947 Ulleungdo and Dokdo expedition. When a dispute broke out regarding the sovereignty over Dokdo with the 1948 bombing and the 1952 declaration of the Syngman Rhee Line (Peace Line), Korea was able to proactively cope with the situation thanks to the reverberations created by the 1947 survey.

The 1947 survey served as an important milestone with regard to the recognition of Dokdo by the Korean public, Korean scholars, and the Korean government as well as in regard to policies relating to the island. The documents produced between 1947 and 1948 by three scholars who participated in the expedition laid the foundation for research and the recognition of Dokdo as Korean territory. These scholars were: Song Seok-ha, President of the Corean Alpine Club and head of the Ulleungdo and Dokdo expedition; Bang Jong-hyeon, a professor of Korean literature at Seoul National University, Korean linguist, and dialectologist; and Sin Seok-ho, the Guksagwan Director and a historian.

Song Seok-ha: Dokseom and Sambongdo

Few writings on Dokdo by Song Seok-ha, president of the Corean Alpine Club and head of the Ulleungdo expedition have been found up to date, which is strange since he played the most significant role as head of the expedition. However, research has revealed that Song wrote a one-page piece for a magazine called *Pictorial Korea* in January 1948 about the Ulleungdo survey.[40] In the piece, he mentioned Dokdo's other names, Dokseom and Sambongdo which appeared in *Joseon Wangjo Sillok* (the Annals of the Joseon Dynasty).

Bang Jong-hyeon: Dokdo = Dokseom = Dolseom = Seokdo

Bang Jong-hyeon, a professor of Korean literature at Seoul National University's College of Arts and Sciences, participated in the 1947 Dokdo expedition. He wrote a diary-style travel essay titled "A Day at Dokdo" for the *Gyeongseong University Premed Newspaper* in 1947.[41] The most noteworthy aspect of this article is a trace of the origin of the name *Dokdo*. Bang presumed that the origin of Dokdo was Dokseom and this comes from Dolseom or Seokdo ("Stone Island"). His presumption was actually an outstanding idea as it was later learned that the Seokdo described as being under the jurisdiction of Uldo-gun County (Ulleungdo) in Imperial Decree No. 41 of 1900, actually refers to Dokdo.

Bang first argued that the name Dokdo did not come from it being solitary (the Chinese characters that constitute Dokdo mean "Lone Island") nor from Yangdo or Daedo, names derived from it having two islands.

Next, he raised the possibility that the "Dok" in Dokdo might have come from Dokdo having a hollowed-out interior like a water pot ("dok" in Korean). Then he withdrew this possibility: he argued islands were often named based on their shapes and the shape of Dokdo did not necessarily resemble that of a water pot. He also concluded that Dokdo consisting of two islands (Dongdo and Seodo) made it difficult to be likened to a water pot.

The last possibility left was that the name came from Seokdo, meaning "Stone Island." There are two reasons for this presumption: there is no

---

40 Ulleungdo Expedition Head Song Seok-ha, 1948, "A Visit to Ulleungdo, Historical Remains!" (Dec 1, 1947), *Pictorial Korea*, International Publicity League, p. 10.

41 Bang Jong-hyeon, 1947, "A Day at Dokdo," *Gyeongseong University Premed Newspaper*, pp. 568-572.

evidence of soil on Dokdo as the island is composed of many rocks; in addition, "dol (stone)" is called "dok" in the dialect used along the west coast of Jeollanam-do. This was how he came to the conclusion that Dolseom, Dokseom, and Seokdo all referred to Dokdo.[42]

Sin Seok-ho: Historical and literature research

Sin Seok-ho, a member of the government survey team, published an essay that confirmed Korea's historical sovereignty over Dokdo in the history magazine *Sahae* in December 1948. The article was meaningful in four aspects: firstly, it was more of an official report of the Dokdo survey team than a personal record.[43] Secondly, this suggested the historical basis for Korea's sovereignty over Dokdo in a logical manner, the first attempt at such a feat after national liberation. Thirdly, the materials Sin identified and referred to in his article are among the most important evidence backing up Korea's claim to sovereignty over Dokdo. Fourthly, Sin's historical research and arguments served as a milestone in the research on Dokdo. In short, his article summarized materials and evidence for Korea's sovereignty over Dokdo that were discovered in 1947 and 1948, and opened up a new angle in the field of research related to Dokdo. Sin's findings can be summarized as follows:

(1) Dokdo is the current name for Sambongdo, of which records date back to the reign of King Seongjong of the Joseon dynasty. This means it has been Korean territory since the 15th century.

(2) During the reign of Sukjong of Joseon, Japan acknowledged Takeshima

---

42　The presumption that Seokdo was actually Dolseom or Dokseom as called by some 120 people from Jeollanam-do who worked on Ulleungdo before 1883 was suggested by Song Byeong-gi at a 1981 discussion (Baek Chung-hyeon, Song Byeong-gi, Sin Yong-ha, 1981, "Shedding New Light on the Dokdo Issue (academic discussion)," *Hankuk Hakbo (Journal of Korean Studies)*, No. 24, p. 201).

43　In his essay, Sin Seok-ho wrote that it was intended to report on the background, members, results and the like of the 1947 Dokdo expedition to the Minister of Civil Affairs An Jae-hong (Sin Seok-ho, 1948, the above essay, p. 99).

(Ulleungdo) as Joseon territory. Thereby Takeshima (Dokdo), which belonged to Ulleungdo, was recognized as such (as indicated in the original text).

(3) According to the Japan Navy Ministry publication *Chosen Engan Suiroshi (Korean Sea Directory)* and witness accounts given by Hong Jae-hyeon, an elder in Ulleungdo and others, it is clear that Dokdo was used by Ulleungdo settlers from when the island was first settled until the ninth year of Gwangmu (1904, the 39th year of Meiji) and thereby clearly belongs to Joseon.

(4) Based on a report by the Ulleungdo magistrate dated March 5 of the year of Byeongo, the tenth year of Gwangmu (based on the lunar calendar); *Gazetteer of Japan*; and documents by Japanese geographers, it is clear that Japan robbed Korea of Dokdo during the Russo-Japanese War.

(5) Dokdo originally belonged to Joseon and this is clearly rational in terms of geographical location. That is why Japan's official and semi-official documents such as *Korean Sea Directory* and *Korean Marine Directory* as well as civilian Japanese scholar Hibata Fukiko all recognized Dokdo as belonging to Joseon even after the unlawful incorporation.

(6) Even the MacArthur Line, which currently demarcates the Japanese fishing zone, passes 12 nautical miles (22.224 km) east of Dokdo, leaving the island in Joseon's fishing zone.[44]

Sin's essay served as the most important reference and basis for Korea's recognition of and policy towards Dokdo. Additional references were gradually identified throughout the 1950s when Korea continued clashing with Japan over Dokdo but the basic framework continued to be his logic and materials.

---

44 Sin Seok-ho, 1948, "Who Dokdo Belongs To," *Sahae*, December Issue (Vol. 1, No. 1) pp. 98-99.

References and testimonies: Sim Heung-taek's report and Hong Jae-hyeon's testimony

The 1947 Dokdo survey discovered two significant references: the first is a copy of the Sim Heung-taek report found at the Ulleungdo government office, and the second is a witness account given by Hong Jae-hyeon, who had lived on Ulleungdo for 60 years. The former was written in 1906 by the Magistrate of Ulleungdo (Sim Heung-taek) who, upon learning of the incorporation of Dokdo from a Japanese survey team from Shimane Prefecture, immediately reported it to the Gangwon-do Governor. In this famous report, Sim stated that "Dokdo, belonging to Ullengdo" had been unlawfully incorporated into Japanese territory. The report was mentioned in the essay Sin Seok-ho published in *Sahae*.[45]

The latter is a witness account given by Hong Jae-hyeon, who was then 85 years old and had settled in Ulleungdo 60 years previous. His testimony was also mentioned in Sin's essay and his entire statement can be found in a 1955 publication by the Bureau of State Affairs of the Ministry of Foreign Affairs.[46]

Hong's testimony was important in several aspects and was later used as a key piece of evidence to reinforce Korea's claim of sovereignty over Dokdo. Firstly, his testimony verified the recognition of Dokdo as an island belonging to Ulleungdo. All residents on Ulleungdo have known this since the first immigrants moved to the island in 1883.

The second important aspect to this testimony is that Dokdo can be seen clearly from Ulleungdo on fine days and some of the ships sailing from Ulleungdo out into the East Sea had been found on the shore of the island, resulting in great interest in it. In addition, Dokdo was being used mainly as an anchorage or a shelter during sailing or fishing trips, further strengthening the recognition that it belonged to Ulleungdo. Namely, it

---

45 Sin Seok-ho, 1948, "Who Dokdo Belongs To," *Sahae*, December Issue (Vol. 1, No. 1); Sin Seok-ho, 1960, "Origin of Dokdo," *Sasangge*, August Issue.

46 Bureau of State Affairs, Ministry of Foreign Affairs, 1955, *Introduction to the Dokdo Issue*, pp. 35-38.

was Korean ships that sailed around Ulleungdo and on the East Sea that could use Dokdo.

Thirdly, Hong said that he had been to Dokdo about four or five times since the year of the hare 45 years previous, which was 1903, to collect sea mustard or catch sea lions. Hong's testimony confirmed that Dokdo was an annex to Ulleungdo, whose residents used Dokdo as an anchorage or a shelter and went there to collect sea mustard or catch sea lions.

Fourthly, he recounted that a group led by the Oki Island Magistrate from Shimane Prefecture visited Ulleungdo in the tenth year of Gwangmu or 1906 and made an absurd claim that Dokdo was Japanese territory. In response, several people reported this fallacy to the higher authorities, including Magistrate Sim Heung-taek and village head Jeon Jae-hang.

Those who participated in the 1947 Dokdo expedition laid an important foundation for Korea's recognition, policy, and research on Dokdo. After the ROK government was established in 1948, the Corean Alpine Club changed its name to the Corea Alpine Club, and many key figures of this Korean society were lost during the Korean War. As a result, when the Corea Alpine Club went on another expedition of Dokdo in 1952, An Jae-hong, Song Seok-ha, Do Bong-seop, Seok Ju-myeong, and others who had led the 1947 expedition were no longer around to participate. It was left to those who survived, including Hong Jong-in, the only surviving executive member, to lead the second expedition, which this time included Parangdo.

4

Parangdo and Tsushima Regarded as One Issue

1) Parangdo: Worries of another Japanese invasion attempt

In the summer of 1947, the Koreans saw provocations by the Japanese and did all they could under the circumstances including performance of an on-site survey, reconfirmation of their sovereignty over Dokdo, and building and popularizing social consensus. It was only natural for the Koreans to bear enmity toward Japan, as it was this eastern neighbor which had put them under military rule and national division, a situation from which they were now attempting to recover. The news of Japan's invasion of fishing grounds far offshore and its attempt at territorial expansion and encroachment stirred up emotional resistance among Koreans.

Korean interest, incited by the Dokdo incident in 1947, extended to the Parangdo issue, which was interpreted as yet another Japanese attempt to encroach on Korea's fishing grounds to expand its territory and therefore received media attention.

An October 22, 1947 article by the *Dong-A Ilbo* raised the need to respond to Japan's actions at Parangseo (Parangdo) (attempting to plunder Korea's fishing grounds and incorporate the rock into Japanese territory) as in the case of Dokdo.[47] The source of this article and relevant facts cannot be confirmed now but it can be easily surmised that Parangseo in the article refers to present-day Ieodo based on the map attached to the article. This article is believed to be the first case of Korea arguing its sovereignty

---

47 "Japan's Aggressive Ambition: This Time, It Claimed the West Sea's Parangseo as Its Territory to MacArthur's Headquarters," *Dong-A Ilbo* (Oct. 22, 1947).

over Parangdo.

2) Interim Legislative Assembly: Participation in the peace conference with Japan and the reversion of Tsushima

While Dokdo was making news in Seoul in July and August of 1947, the easing of the MacArthur Line and the peace negotiations between the former Allied Powers and Japan were also emerging as key issues.

The South Korean Interim Legislative Assembly (SKILA) delivered an official request for the attendance of a Korean representative at the peace negotiations with Japan to USAMGIK on July 17, 1947, and received a reply on August 10 from Brigadier General and Acting Military Governor Charles G. Helmick, which stated, "As the US Department of State (DoS) has a clear intention to have Joseon nationals present in the international meeting as soon as circumstances allow, it is possible to have them at the meeting as specialists and advisers. As such, your participation in the planned peace conference with Japan is currently under consideration."[48]

At the 131st meeting of the SKILA on August 18, 1947, Yang Je-bak and five other assemblymen submitted a "Resolution to Notify and Gain Approval for Korea's Intention to Participate in the Allied Powers' Peace Conference with Japan." The reasons for participation they enumerated in the resolution are as follows: Korea consistently fought for its own independence against Japan before and after the 1910 Korea-Japan annexation and Korean youth fought against Japanese forces during WWII alongside the US and Chinese troops, which makes the representation of Korea at the conference justifiable. Korea was entitled to demand compensation for enormous losses and damage caused by Japan during its rule of about 40 years such as shedding the blood of so many Koreans, robbing the nation of above-ground and underground resources to produce

---

48 Interim Legislative Assembly Secretariat, *South Korean Interim Legislative Assembly Stenographic Records*, Vol. 8, No. 135, pp. 1-2; Kim Hyeok-dong, 1970, *Interim Legislative Assembly under the US Army Military Government*, Pyeongbeom Publishing, p. 120.

war supplies and thereby impeding the development of its industries and economy, and forcing Koreans to change their names to Japanese names.[49] These reasons for Korea's participation in the peace negotiations with Japan provided the basis of logic for the official Korean government to use in its negotiations with the US.

This resolution was passed at the meeting attended by 56 assemblymen, with 50 in favor, 0 against, and 6 abstaining. As such, an official request was sent on August 18 to US President Harry Truman, British Prime Minister Clement Attlee, USSR Premier Josef Stalin, and Chinese Government Chairman Chiang Kai-shek.[50] Then US Secretary of State George C. Marshall delivered the letter from SKILA Chairman Kim Gyu-sik to President Truman and reported that a reply had been made to the effect that the US DoS would devise a way so that Korea's interests could be well represented in relation to the peace negotiations.[51] On August 27, SKILA Chairman Kim requested again in Telegram No. 306 from Seoul to the US DoS, the actual entity that was pursuing the peace treaty with Japan, Korea's participation in the peace conference. The Working Group on the Treaty with Japan at the US DoS which received the telegram sent a reply indicating that they would do their best in the name of the US DoS.[52]

In response to the SKILA's expression of its will to participate in the peace conference, Joseph E. Jacobs, the US political adviser to the occupation commander in Korea, replied on September 15, 1947, "The message about the Joseon nationals' interests with regard to the peace negotiations with Japan has been delivered to President Truman and the US DoS is considering granting them the right to speak in the interests of

---

49 Kim Hyeok-dong, 1970, *Ibid.*, pp. 120-121.
50 Kim Hyeok-dong, 1970, *Ibid.*, pp. 97 and 119.
51 Memorandum for the President. Subject: Message from the Interim Legislative Assembly of South Korea (Sept. 11, 1949), RG 59, Department of State, Decimal File, 740.0011 PW(Peace)/9-1147.
52 Working Group on the Treaty with Japan (Sept. 3, 1947), RG 59, Office of Northeast Asia Affairs, Records Relating to the Treaty of Peace with Japan-Subject File, 1945-51, Lot 56D527, Box 5.

the Joseon people at the peace conference."[53]

The SKILA also put to a vote a proposal to suggest to the peace conference that Tsushima revert to Korea at its session on February 17, 1948.[54] This resolution, however, was never deliberated on.[55]

Though it was unlikely that Tsushima would revert to Korean territory, as the USSR had once considered the move after WWII, it was not a totally groundless claim. The USSR made reference to Korea in a document prepared for the London Conference of Foreign Ministers (September 11 to October 2, 1945):

> In defining Japan's and Korea's future national boundaries, a suggestion of reverting Tsushima to Korea should be made. The reason is that Tsushima has been the advance basis in Japan's aggression toward the continent, and toward Korea in particular, since the dawn of history.[56]

The USSR's suggestion that Tsushima revert to Korea can be interpreted not as a matter related to historical sovereignty but a punitive measure against Japanese imperialism. In other words, its reversion to Korea would depend on where the Allied Powers would be willing to draw the lines delimiting Japan's territory.

As seen so far, the Japanese invasion of the fishing grounds of Dokdo and Parangdo and its attempt to incorporate them, which started in 1947, led to Korea's resistance and subsequent research activities, and as a responding offensive towards Japan, the reversion of Tsushima began to be widely discussed. This historical experience from 1947 had an impact on

---

53 The 142nd meeting of the Interim Legislative Assembly (Sept. 18, 1947).

54 *Dong-A Ilbo* (Feb. 17, 1948).

55 Kim, *Interim Legislative Assembly*, p. 97.

56 *Запискаквопросуо бывшихяпонскихколонияхи подмандатны хterritoriях (Note on the Issues of Japan's Colonies and Mandated Territories)*, АВПРФ, Фонде0431, Описы 1, Папка6в 8, Пор52, c.42-43 (re-quoted in: Kim Seong-bo, 1995, "The USSR's Policy toward Korea and the Process of National Division Shaped in North Korea, 1945-1946," compiled by the Institute of Korean Historical Studies, *Fifty Years of National Division and Tasks for Unification*, Critical Review of History, p. 65).

preparations for the 1951 San Francisco Peace Conference by the Korean government where it highlighted Dokdo, Parangdo and Tsushima.

5
1948 Bombing of Dokdo

1) Bombing incident over Dokdo

Korean interest in Dokdo triggered by the 1947 Dokdo expedition was heightened by the bombing of the island on June 8, 1948. While the expedition had been led by opinion leaders belonging to the Interim Government and the Corean Alpine Club, the tragic bombing of Dokdo made the general public keenly aware of the situation and assured them that Dokdo was Korean territory.[57]

The news of bombing was delivered by a fishing boat which went fishing around Dokdo the day after, leading the Ulleungdo police to dispatch two rescue boats at 7 pm on June 9. However, with boats weighing less than four tons, the search and rescue operation could not be completed properly.[58] The bodies and boat fragments which had been scattered in and around Dokdo had been swept away by the waves overnight and only the bodies of two people, Kim Jun-seon and Choi Tae-sik, were recovered from what remained of the boat *Gyeongyanghwan* that was found wrecked on the rocks.[59] The boats returned to Ulleungdo at 6 pm on June 10. It was then believed that the bombing killed at least 9 people instantly and

---

57   Hong Seong-geun, 2003, "Analysis of the Bombing Incident from an International Law Perspective," *Research History of Korea's Sovereignty over Dokdo*, Association for the Study and Preservation of Dokdo; Mark Lovmo, "In-depth Study of the Dokdo Bombing on June 8, 1948" (May 2003), http://www.geocities.com/mlovmo.

58   *Kyunghyang Shinmun* (Jun. 16, 1948).

59   "Names of the Innocent Victims," *Fisheries Economic Newspaper* (Jun. 15, 1948); "Fourth Newsflash on the Dokdo Bombing: No Human Shadows Can Be Seen on Dokdo, the Missing Confirmed Killed Instantly, Ulleungdo Grief-Stricken," *Chosun Ilbo* (Jun. 15, 1948).

perhaps also the five others who were missing. Twelve of the 14 dead were never found.

2) Investigation by USAFIK and CINCFE

The US Army Forces in Korea (USAFIK) first learned about the incident on June 10, 1948. According to "History of Claims Service: USAFIK," the Chief of the Ulleungdo police reported to the Deputy Commander of the Joseon Coast Guard's Pohang base of the bombing, the sinking of boats, and the occurrence of casualties and requested a rescue team at 1 pm on June 10, 1948. Accordingly, the Military Governor of Gyeongsangbuk-do immediately dispatched a USAMGIK investigation team and medical staff to Dokdo. The survivors said that they were not only bombed by the aircraft but also strafed.[60]

The bombers were first described as of unknown origin but the only possibilities were that they belonged to the US occupation forces in Korea and Japan, or the Soviet forces stationed in North Korea. US aircraft were soon suspected as the witnesses gave similar accounts of seeing "four-engined aircraft bearing the star and circle insignia on the wings," which is the star-insignia of the US Air Force.[61]

However, the Gimpo Air Base denied that any USAFIK planes were in the area of the bombing on June 8.[62] The only possibility left was the US forces in Japan, or more specifically, the US Far East Air Force (FEAF). USFEAF revealed the launch of an investigation and its progress in three statements made after the incident.

First, on June 12, USFEAF Headquarters revealed that US aircraft practiced a live-fire exercise in the waters where the Korean fishing

---

60 Investigation of Military Government, June 1948. AG files, 333.5; "History of Claims Service, USAFIK," RG 554 Records of General HQ, Far East Command, Supreme Commander Allied Powers, and United Nations Command, XXIV Corps, G-2, Historical Section, Box 41.
61 "FEAF Headquarters Announcement: It Might Have Been US Aircraft," *Chosun Ilbo* (Jun. 15, 1948).
62 *Ibid.*

boats were bombed on June 8 and it was studying the photos of the site to determine the possible involvement of the US planes.[63] A USFEAF Headquarters spokesperson stressed that Dokdo was a live bombing range, a reconnaissance overflight was made to visually check the area before dropping the bombs from a high altitude, and flatly denied there had been any intentional strafing.[64]

The interim findings of the FEAF Headquarters investigation were announced on June 15. The summary was that the "involvement of US aircraft in the bombing has not been confirmed. If that is the case, the bombing would have been an unforeseen accident. The area in question is a designated bombing range, and the target was a series of small rocks near large rocks in the middle of the Sea of Japan, which has been used as a bombing range from some time ago. The unit that flew on June 8 flew at a high altitude so that it would have been difficult for them to spot small boats among the rocks or within the bombing range, though it might have been possible." In addition, it was confirmed that no machine gun was fired by the FEAF unit.[65]

On the same day, a USAMGIK agent in Pohang stated the following in a report about the bombing and strafing of Dokdo: "Survivors who are residents of Pohang-dong have returned to their homes. Eight people were severely wounded, twenty-one slightly wounded, and seventeen people unharmed. Sixteen people were killed or missing, of which two bodies have been recovered. Twenty-three fishing vessels were involved in the incident."[66]

Finally, on June 17, USFEAF Headquarters announced that it had been

---

63   *Ibid.*

64   "USFEAF Announcement: Currently Investigating the Possible Involvement of US Aircraft in the Bombing of Fishing Boats in the Sea near Dokdo," *Fisheries Economic Newspaper* (Jun. 15, 1948).

65   "USFEAF Headquarters Releases the Findings of the Investigation into the Dokdo Bombing Incident," *Kyunghyang Shinmun* and *Chosun Ilbo* (Jun. 16, 1948).

66   CG XXIV Corps to CINCFE (Jun. 15, 1948), "AG 684 Target and Bombing Ranges, 1948," RG 554, Entry A1 1378, United States Army Forces in Korea (USAFIK), Adjutant General, General Correspondence (Decimal Files) 1945-1949, Box 141.

US planes that bombed Dokdo and described it as a "most unfortunate and regrettable accident."[67]

According to the statement, a weather plane had flown six circuits around the bombing range, carrying out reconnaissance of the area up to 30 minutes prior to the bombing and had given the "all clear" sign. However, they enlarged and studied photographs that were taken 30 minutes after the bombing and found three small boats just 30 feet (9.144 meters) from the rocks in the danger zone. The statement went on to say that the "area has been publicized as a practice bombing area and was not usually sailed by vessels either large or small because of the danger from rocks. Vessels have been repeatedly warned to stay out of the area since it became an American practice bombing run. As the area features many small rocks, they may have failed to see the small boats among the rocks through visual reconnaissance using the naked eye and the fishing vessels may have been mistaken for the grey rocks that protrude from the sea by the bombardiers at the altitudes flown during the practice mission."[68]

In a nutshell, although FEAF Headquarters admitted that B-29s flying from Okinawa dropped the bombs on Dokdo, it reported that entry into the bombed area was banned for vessels due to its designation and notification as a bombing range; the unit did not identify the fishing boats through visual reconnaissance and mistook them for rocks; they dropped practice bombs from a high altitude of 23,000 feet (7,010 meters) and no machine guns were fired.

The US Commanding General in Korea, John R. Hodge, drafted a press release to be distributed to the Korean press, reported the incident to the US Department of State on June 15 and sent it on to Chang Myun of the Foreign Affairs Committee on June 16.[69] The press release was carried by

---

67 "USFEAF Headquarters Issues a Statement on the Dokdo Bombing Incident," *Seoul Shinmun* and *Chosun Ilbo* (Jun. 18, 1948); "Formal Announcement by FEAF Headquarters: The Dokdo Bombers were B-29s," *Saehan Minbo*, 2-13, first & second ten-day issues of July 1948, p.11.
68 "USFEAF Headquarters Announcement: "Most Unfortunate and Regrettable Accident" Boats Mistaken as Rocks?" *Fisheries Economic Newspaper* (Jun. 18, 1948).
69 Seoul POLAD no. 460 (Jun. 15, 1948) ZPOL 882 (150815/Z), Hodge to Department of

the Korean press the same day.[70]

Having admitted that the bombing was undertaken by the US Air Force stationed in Japan, Hodge had no choice but to promise a thorough investigation and compensation while urging Koreans to suspend judgment until a full report could be made. While Hodge was struggling to overcome the political mess created by the incident, the US forces in Japan were not fully aware of the magnitude of the situation due to their geographical distance. On June 14, the Fifth Air Force sent a radio message strongly urging the USAFIK Commander to allow Dokdo to be used as a bombing range once more:

Request earliest date Liancourt Rocks bombing and gunnery range (37 deg 15 min north-131 deg 37 min east) can be cleared for bombing practice.[71]

On the same day, the Fifth Air Force Commander notified the USAFIK Commander that the Liancourt Rocks (Dokdo) were one of the nine bombing and gunnery ranges used by the Fifth Air Force.[72]

Hodge was enraged by the unreasonable request of the Fifth Air Force amid the political turmoil of the Dokdo bombing incident. He sent a third-class classified radio message, ZGCG 883 (150817/Z) to the Commander-in-Chief Far East (CINCFE) (General MacArthur) on June 15, 1948 to state that the Fifth Air Force "requested a permit at the earliest date for the

---

State, RG 554, Entry A1 1380 USAFIK, Adjutant General, Radio Messages 1945-49, Box 193.

70   *Chosun Ilbo, Dong-A Ilbo, Seoul Shinmun*, and *Fisheries Economic Newspaper* (Jun. 17, 1948). Refer to the following for the original text: Press Release (Jun. 16, 1948), RG 554, Entry A1 1404 USAFIK, US Army Office of Military Government, Box 311; RG 554, USAFIK, XXIV Corps, G-2, Historical Section, Box 77, "Political 3rd Year: Miscellaneous," "Fishing Boats Bombed off Korean Coast".

71   5th Air Force to CG USAFIK (Jun. 14, 1948), "AG 684 Target and Bombing Ranges, 1948," RG 554, Entry A1 1378, USAFIK, Adjutant General, General Correspondence (Decimal Files) 1945-1949, Box 141.

72   CG 5th Air Force to CG 8th Army, CG USAFIK (June 14, 1948), "AG 684 Target and Bombing Ranges, 1948," RG 554, Entry A1 1378, USAFIK, Adjutant General, General Correspondence (Decimal Files) 1945-1949, Box 141. According to this, the Fifth Air Force used nine practice ranges and the USAFIK used one.

use of the Liancourt Rocks bombing and gunnery range for their bombing practice" and "USAFIK shall withhold approval for any bombing practice in the subject area until further notice."[73]

This message reveals several important facts. Firstly, of the bombing and gunnery ranges used by the Fifth Air Force, Dokdo was used as a daily practice range. Secondly, according to CINCFE policy, the USAFIK Headquarters would have needed to be notified of any bombing practice two weeks in advance. Thirdly, there was no such advance notice given before the June 8, 1948 bombing. Fourthly, the Fifth Air Force strongly requested permission from USAFIK for the use of Dokdo as a bombing range on June 14, soon after the June 8 bombing.

On June 15, Hodge sent radio message CGT 6525 (150828/Z) to the Fifth Air Force Commander to deliver a strong message that USAFIK would withhold approval for any bombing practice in the subject area until further notice.[74] In other words, immediately after the bombing incident, the USAFIK Command discovered the Liancourt Rocks in the list of bombing ranges from FEAF and the Fifth Air Force and recognized them as Dokdo. Furthermore, the Fifth Air Force requested permission by USAFIK to use the Liancourt Rocks as a bombing range.

The Fifth Air Force Headquarters notified USAFIK only on June 28 that the Liancourt Rocks Air to Ground Range would be closed until further notice.[75] Hodge sent a second-class classified radio message to CINCFE on June 17 to report that the "(Dokdo bombing) issue is of significant importance here in the field" and asked General MacArthur to issue an order not to use Dokdo as a bombing or gunnery range for US aircraft.[76]

---

73 CG USAFIK (Hodge) to CINCFE (Jun. 15, 1948), RG 554, Entry A1 1380 USAFIK, Adjutant General, Radio Messages 1945-49, Box 193.

74 CG USAFIK (Hodge) to CG Fifth Air Force (Jun. 15, 1948), "AG 684 Target and Bombing Ranges, 1948," RG 554, Entry A1 1378, USAFIK, Adjutant General, General Correspondence (Decimal Files) 1945-1949, Box 141.

75 HQ, Fifth Air Force, Subject: Warning Notice-Bombing and Gunnery Ranges (Jun. 28, 1948), RG 554, Entry A1 1378, USAFIK, Adjutant General, General Correspondence (Decimal Files) 1945-1949, Box 141.

76 Secret, ZGCG 893 (170645/Z) (Jun. 17, 1948), Hodge to CINCFE. RG 554, Entry A1 1380

USAMGIK also sent an official request to CINCFE via the USAFIK Command on June 24 for a halt to all bombing on Dokdo. This letter, under the name of the USAMGIK Governor, Major General William F. Dean, went on to say, "The waters in the vicinity of Liancourt Rocks are among the best fishing areas available to Korean fishermen...These waters are the principal source of livelihood for 16,000 fishermen and their families living on Ullung Do and nearby islands."[77]

Along with the above letter, Hodge asked CINCFE again for favorable action to make the area available to Korean fishermen (June 28, 1948). Hodge concurred with the request by USAMGIK and said favorable action on this issue would do much to counteract the unfavorable conditions created by the recent bombing.[78]

3) Claims review and compensation

Regarding the bombing of Dokdo, no official apology was made for the deaths and injuries of innocent victims and property losses by any of the parties involved: USAMGIK, CINCFE, FEAF or Fifth Air Force. The Korean press offered their own optimistic and ungrounded prospects including the referral of the bomber pilots to a court-martial,[79] but there was no follow-up.

USAMGIK took the position that the bombing was an accident that had occurred in the course of a legitimate military operation and the case

---

USAFIK, Adjutant General, Radio Messages 1945-49, Box 193.

77 CG, USAMGIK (Dean) to Commander in Chief, Far East (Jun. 24, 1948), Subject: Bombing off Liancourt Rocks, "AG 684 Target and Bombing Ranges, 1948," RG 554, Entry A1 1378, USAFIK, Adjutant General, General Correspondence (Decimal Files) 1945-1949, Box 141.

78 John R. Hodge to CINCFE (Jun. 28, 1948), "AG 684 Target and Bombing Ranges, 1948," RG 554, Entry A1 1378, USAFIK, Adjutant General, General Correspondence (Decimal Files) 1945-1949, Box 141.

79 "Soon to Be Announced: Pilots Who Dropped Bombs to Stand before a Court-Martial?" *Fisheries Economic Newspaper* (Jul. 8, 1948); "The Democratic Independence Party Demands a Full Investigation of the Dokdo Bombing Incident," *Chosun Ilbo* (Jul. 8, 1948).

[Table 1-1] Claims by Koreans during US Military Rule

Amount / Classification	(A) Amount requested	(B) Amount paid	(C) Ratio of requests vs. compensation (B/A100)
Aug. 10, 1946 to Jun. 30, 1947	35,560,529.80	9,543,425.30	26.83%
Jul. 1, 1947 to Jun. 30, 1948	138,899,828.34	13,203,784.04	9.50%
Contract claims (entire period)	16,868,133	4,873,213	6.72%
Claims for the Dokdo bombing	72,478,000	9,108,680	12.56%
Total	263,806,491.14	36,729,102.34	13.92%

[Source] "History of Claims Service: USAFIK", (undated), RG 554 Records of General HQ, Far East Command, Supreme Commander Allied Powers, and United Nations Command, XXIV Corps, G-2, Historical Section, Box. 41.

would be closed by making monetary compensation to the victims. *The New York Times* covered the incident and remarked that all claims resulting from the accident should be promptly and generously paid while arguing that the US crews who dropped the bombs from a high altitude should not be held accountable as it was difficult to distinguish rocks and small vessels in the sea.[80]

USAMGIK immediately went ahead with the compensation process. Hodge announced on June 19 through the Department of Public Information that a special claims commission had been established and its members sent to the East Sea and Ulleungdo to discern the magnitude of the losses and damage and to determine the subsequent compensation.[81]

---

80 "Even *The New York Times* Criticizes in its Editorial: Delayed Compensation for the Tragic Dokdo Incident Is Unforgivable," *Daegu Shibo* and *Chosun Ilbo*, Jun. 19, 1948.

81 Headquarters, South Korea Interim Government, Department of Public Information, Daily Activity Report of Departments and Offices (Jun. 21, 1948), RG 554, USAFIK, XXIV Corps, G-2, Historical Section, Box 31; A Special Claims Commission Established for Compensation Payments: Announced through the Department of Public Information, *Chosun Ilbo* (Jun. 20,

USAMGIK expected the investigation to be completed by the end of June. The Foreign Claims Commission No. 63 consisted of Captain Andrew W. Winiarczyk (USAFIK Claims Service member), Thomas McClure (Fisheries Bureau, Ministry of Agriculture), Captain Millopda Mann (JAG officer, Daegu Military Government), and a few interpreters.[82] The Commission finished reviewing 33 out of a total of 36 compensation claims by June 27 and after reporting to Seoul, headed back to the site on June 29 to finalize them. The reason for the three unreviewed claims was that the addresses of the claimants were not known.[83]

The Commission visited Pohang, Ulleungdo, Dokdo, Mukho, Jukbyeon, and Hupo-ri and tallied up the casualties as 14 dead or missing, three bodies collected (including one unidentified body), three fishermen severely wounded and several slightly wounded; and property damage totaling seven motorboats and ten sailboats. The total amount paid by the Commission was 9.1 million won, only 12.56% of the 72.47 million won claimed by the victims of the bombing. The final findings of the investigation into the Dokdo bombing incident were never announced. None of the parties involved, including USAMGIK, CINCFE, FEAF and Fifth Air Force ever released a report of final findings. The truth of the incident was never revealed and there was no heartfelt apology. USAMGIK closed the case with Dean, not Hodge, declaring the completion of compensation at a press conference on July 8.

4) Facts of the bombing incident and points of dispute

Resolution of the incident left several questions unanswered. Still

---

1948).

82 "Investigation of the Losses and Damage from the Dokdo Incident to Be Completed by Month-End?" *Fisheries Economic Newspaper* (Jun. 26, 1948); "Compensation for the Dokdo Incident Proposed, Great Interest in the Findings by the Claims Commission," *Chosun Ilbo* (Jun. 26, 1948).

83 "The Department of Public Information Announces the Findings of the Claims Commission," *Seoul Shinmun* (Jun. 30, 1948); *Chosun Ilbo* (Jun. 30, 1948).

unknown were the military units involved and the number of bombers, the time and altitude of the bombing, whether machineguns were fired, the complete number of dead and missing, the number of damaged fishing boats, and more. What remains most troubling about the background of the incident was how, when, and why Dokdo had been designated as a bombing range for FEAF.

First, according to "History of Claims Service: USAFIK," the waters around Dokdo had been a fishing ground for Korean fishermen for a long time. Fishermen from the mainland and Ulleungdo had not visited Dokdo because of the high seas for some time before the incident, and as the weather improved, some 60 went to Dokdo on June 7 to 8 on seven motor boats and 12 sailboats. Around 11:30 am on June 8, 11 planes dropped bombs from an altitude of 23,000 feet.[84]

Survivors' accounts

The reports carried by the press immediately after the bombing suggested the bombing occurred at approximately 11 am, for about 20 minutes from 11 am, around 11:30 am, and around noon, and that nine to 11 bombers were involved. They all agreed that three to six bombers initiated the bombing and the area was bombed a total of four times. Also confirmed were that the bombers dropped stone-like bombs and fired machineguns. Regarding the bombing altitude, Lee Wan-sik, the surviving captain of the boat *Gungjanghwan*, testified to the fact that they bombed and strafed the fishing boats from a low altitude. The survivors declared that they had waved *Taegeukgi*, the Korean national flag, and made hand signals but the bombing continued.[85]

---

84   USAFIK Key File No. K-3231. In JAGO files; "History of Claims Service, USAFIK," (undated), RG 554 Records of General HQ, Far East Command, Supreme Commander Allied Powers, and United Nations Command, XXIV Corps, G-2, Historical Section, Box 41.

85   *Chosun Ilbo* (Jun. 12, 1948); *Kyunghyang Shinmun* (Jun. 16, 1948); *Fisheries Economic Newspaper* (Jun. 13, 1948); Hankuk University of Foreign Studies, 1995, *Dokdo Research Society's Source Book: Dokdo's Yesterday and Today (Aug. 24 to 30, 1995)*, pp. 16-18 (re-quoted on pp.

Descriptions in US Air Force records

US Air Force records also provide clues to the incident. At around noon on June 8, 1948, 20 B-29s belonging to the FEAF Headquarters bombed the area four times. The B-29s involved belonged to the 93d Bombardment Group (BG) (VH-Very Heavy) of the 93d Bombardment Wing (Very Heavy) of the Fifteenth Air Force. The 93d BG was deployed at Kadena Air Base in Okinawa, Japan at the time of the bombing.[86]

"History of the 93d Bombardment Group (VH), Kadena Air Force Base, Okinawa, for the Month of June 1948" describes the circumstances of the 93d BG at the time of the bombing.[87] It was the first unit assigned to the Strategic Air Command (SAC) and its mission was outlined in SAC Field Order No. 16 of April 15, 1948. SAC chose the 93d BG for a 90-day deployment to FEAF,[88] replacing the B-29s of FEAF's 22nd Bombardment Group belonging to the Fifth Air Force, which bombed Dokdo on March 25, 1947 and returned to the continental US in May 1948.[89]

During the month of June 1948, the 93d BG carried out eight long-range, maximum-effort missions consisting of four actual bombing

---

377-378 of "Analysis of the Bombing Incident from an International Law Perspective" by Hong Seong-geun)

86   The fact that the 93d BG was the unit that bombed Dokdo was made known by Lovmo, from references he found at the Air Force Historical Research Agency (AFHRA) at Alabama's Maxwell Air Force Base. His articles can be found on the Internet and have been translated into Korean (http://www.geocities.com/mlovmo).

87   "History of the 93d Bombardment Group (VH), Kadena Air Force Base, Okinawa, for the Month of June 1948," Air Force Historical Research Agency, Maxwell Air Force Base, Alabama - During my visit to US NARA from January to February 2008, I was able to get in touch with AFHRA with the help of senior military archivist Richard Boylan. Marcie T. Green, an AFHRA archivist, found and mailed this document. I wish to take this opportunity to express gratitude to Boylan and Green for their help.

88   "History of the 93d Bombardment Group (VH), Kadena Air Force Base, Okinawa, for the Month of June 1948," p. 7.

89   United States Air Force, "Strategic Air Command Rotation Program," FEAF 1948 History, 68, History Office, Pacific Air Forces, Hickam AFB, Hawaii. pp. 70-71 (Quoted in *In-depth Study of the Dokdo Bombing on June 8, 1948* by Lovmo).

missions and four camera bombing missions (photographing the targeted drop points instead of dropping bombs). All missions were carried out according to the field orders disseminated through the First Air Division and 316th Bombardment Wing to the 93d BG.[90] These missions shed light on the context of the bombing of Dokdo.

In its missions, the 93d BG set Tokyo Imperial Palace, downtown Manila, Busan, and other large cities as well as US air bases and islands as bombing targets and carried out both camera bombing and actual bombing missions. Comprised of three bombardment squadrons, the 93d BG included all of its more than 20 bombers and reconnaissance planes in each mission. Actual bombs were used at uninhabited small islands like Dokdo (Liancourt Rocks), Maug in the Philippines, and Farallon de Medinilla in the Northern Marianas. General-purpose (GP) bombs that weighed 500 lb were mainly used, with 63 or 64 bombs dropped per run. GP bombs that weighed 1,000 lb or 454 kg were used in the bombing of Dokdo.

Dokdo was bombed by the 93d BG on its third mission. The sequence of events that took place on that critical day is as follows:[91] The 93d BG was ordered on June 7, 1948 to fly a maximum effort mission to bomb the Liancourt Rocks with 1,000-lb GP bombs per aircraft. A total of 23 planes plus a weather aircraft were scheduled to participate in the mission but two aircraft were unable to take off due to mechanical failures. The 93d BG departed in the morning.

The 22 planes of the 93d BG, after departing from Kadena Air Force Base in Okinawa, assembled over the northern tip of Kamino-shima of Kagoshima Prefecture in southern Kyushu and departed on course at 11:05 for the initial point (Ulleungdo), arriving there at 11:47. The weather aircraft flew 30 minutes ahead of the group relaying weather information en route. Leaving Ulleungdo, the 93d BG changed to a squadron formation, with the 330th Bombardment Squadron (seven planes) in front, the 328th

---

90   "History of the 93d Bombardment Group (VH), Kadena Air Force Base, Okinawa, for the Month of June 1948," p. 11.

91   *Ibid.*, pp.14-16.

(six planes) next and flying at a lower altitude, and the 329th (six planes) bringing up the rear and flying at a higher altitude. The island was bombed four times: three squadrons released their bombs at 11:58:30 am, 12:00 pm, and 12:01 pm, respectively, and two of the B-29s, which failed to drop on the initial bombing run, flew back to the target to do so.

The 21 B-29 bombers dropped a total of 76 1,000-lb bombs on the island, with an average CEP (circular error probability) of 300 feet.[92] This was an excellent rate of accuracy, meaning that no less than 38 out of the 76 bombs hit within 300 feet (91.44m) of the target. Most of the small boats which had come alongside the island or in the surrounding waters must have been destroyed without a trace due to the detonation blasts, flares, shards, and shock immediately after the bombing.

Yonhap News discovered and photographed, on July 24, 2008, unexploded 1,000-lb, AN-M-65 GP bombs about 15m below the surface of the water under Buchae ("fan") Rock near the Dongdo wharf and about 10m below near Chotdae ("candlestick") Rock between Dongdo and Seodo.[93] They are enormous in size.

As pointed out by Mark Lovmo, based on "History of the 93d Bombardment Group," it is apparent that the survivors' statements and the Air Force records match, particularly in regard to the fact that the island was bombed at noon, the planes came from the direction of Ulleungdo, and the island was bombed four times.[94]

"History of the 93d Bombardment Group" offers two clues believed to be related to the Dokdo bombing. The first is the replacement of the 93d BG Commander. Colonel Lee B. Coats was the Bombardment Wing

---

92   Circular error probability (CEP) is a measure of a weapon system's precision. It is mostly used for ballistic missiles or guided bombs, not for typical missiles. It is defined as the radius of a circle, centered about the mean, whose boundary is expected to include the landing points of 50% of the rounds. For instance, when ten rounds are fired, a circle is drawn around five of them, and if the radius of the circle is 5m, the CEP is 5m (definition found on the Wikipedia site (http://ko.wikipedia.org.) on Feb. 11, 2009).

93   "Bombs in the Sea off Dokdo, Evidence of the Tragedy of 60 Years ago," *Yonhap News* (Aug. 10, 2008).

94   Lovmo, *In-depth Study of the Dokdo Bombing on June 8, 1948* (May 2003).

Commander who came to Okinawa with the 93d BG. He left Okinawa on June 19 and Colonel Robert H. Terrill took over his position. The reason for the replacement of the commander in the middle of a 90-day deployment was never fully explained.[95]

The second is careful concern paid to the signs of human habitation in the target areas by the 93d BG immediately after the Dokdo incident. According to "History of the 93d Bombardment Group," the 93d BG captured some 10,000 feet of film during the month of June with the help of the First Motion Picture Unit during its deployment to Okinawa.[96]

The biggest unresolved issues are the altitude of the bombing and whether strafing took place at Dokdo that day. In general, it is known that B-29s should fly at an altitude of no lower than 10,000 feet when engaged in a high-altitude bombing mission to be safe from fragments, shock waves, heat, and back blast released by the detonation of bombs. "History of the 93d Bombardment Group" did not indicate the altitude of the bombers at the time of the bombing, but after considering the altitudes of its other missions conducted in June 1948, the statement by FEAF that the 93d BG flew at an altitude of around 20,000 feet during the bombing of Dokdo is likely true.

The reason that the crews of the 93d BG failed to see the fishing boats at Dokdo is probably related to the altitude at which they were flying. Fishing boats at anchor do not leave any traces behind them and it would be difficult to spot them from high up in the sky. More fundamentally, there had been several bombing practices in the area since the designation of Dokdo as a daily practice range in September 1947, and therefore, it was a case of inertia at work based on the experience of having incurred

---

95 According to "History of the 93d Bombardment Group," Coats was temporarily dispatched on May 10 from Castle Air Force Base in California to command the unit until Colonel Terrill arrived and his departure was postponed until the 93d BG could properly perform its missions. ("History of the 93d Bombardment Group (VH), Kadena Air Force Base, Okinawa, for the Month of June 1948," p. 2).

96 "History of the 93d Bombardment Group (VH), Kadena Air Force Base, Okinawa, for the Month of June 1948," pp. 5-6.

no problems before and after previous bombing missions. The experience-based confidence gained through several previous bombings that Dokdo was a small uninhabited island not accessed by fishing boats and fishermen must have created a sense of complacency towards advance reconnaissance and careful observation by the weather plane. Also, the pilots and crews of the bombers must have not paid the appropriate amount of attention, simply assuming this mission would go as smoothly as all the previous ones.

The bombing survivors consistently testified to strafing taking place after the bombing. In general, a bombing by B-29s at a specific target usually lasted between 30 seconds to one minute and was characterized by the planes flying at a high speed. It is absurd for them to drop bombs while flying low and remain to circle 180 degrees to fire machineguns. It is especially unlikely in light of how bombing missions were carried out at that time.

In general, machine-gunning is a kind of low-altitude attack, performed at heights of no more than 1,000 feet (about 305m). According to Clause 14 of "Air Reconnaissance and Observation" (1942 edition), US Army Field Manual 1-20, the height from which a person aboard an aircraft can recognize a person on the ground is about 2,500 feet (762m) and the airplane would need to descend down to about 500 feet (152m) to be able to tell whether the person in question is a soldier or civilian based on his/her clothes and equipment.[97]

Therefore, the B-29s would have had to fly at an altitude of about 2,500 feet for the argument to be valid that they flew at a low altitude, recognized the fishing boats and their crews who were waving Korean flags at the planes in vain, and fired machineguns specifically at them, as stated by the survivors and in reports by the Korean press. However, it is highly unlikely that heavy bombers, which are not fighters, to fly at a lower altitude in consideration of safety concerns and the general bombing procedure for

---

97   Truth and Reconciliation Commission, 2008, "Bombing of Wolmido by the US Forces," *Investigation Report for the First Half of 2008*, Vol. 2, p. 56.

B-29s. As such, the strafing testified to by the bombing survivors was likely bomb fragments hitting the water surface and rocks and flying in all directions, along with the flare, noise, and shock. As indicated in "History of Claims Service: USAFIK," every survivor was certain they had been strafed but they must have confused the noise and chaos from the detonation of the bombs as machinegun fire.

Questions about SCAPIN No. 1778 (September 16, 1947)

In the end, all of this was caused by the designation of Dokdo as a bombing range. FEAF Headquarters stated on June 15 that Dokdo was the US Air Force's designated bombing range, a "series of small rocks near large rocks in the middle of the Sea of Japan," and had been used as a bombing target from some time ago.[98] This statement referred to SCAPIN No. 1778 dated September 16, 1947. In the instruction, SCAP designated Dokdo (indicated as the Liancourt Rocks or Take-Shima in the original text) as a bombing range and ordered that the inhabitants of the Oki Islands and of all ports on the west coast of the island of Honshu north of the 38th parallel should be warned prior to bombing exercises:

GENERAL HEADQUARTERS
SUPREME COMMANDER FOR THE ALLIED POWERS

AG 684 (16 Sept 47) GC-TNG (SCAPIN 1778)   16 September 1947 APO500

MEMORANDUM FOR: JAPANESE GOVERNMENT
THROUGH: Central Liaison Office, Tokyo
SUBJECT: Liancourt Rocks Bombing Range

1. The islands of Liancourt Rocks (or Take-Shima), located 37° 15' north, 131° 52' east, are designated as a bombing range.

---

98   *Kyunghyang Shinmun, Chosun Ilbo* (Jun. 16, 1948)

2. The inhabitants of Oki-Retto (Oki-Gunto) and the inhabitants of all the ports on the west coast of Honshu north to the 38th parallel, north latitude, will be notified prior to each actual use of this range. This information will be disseminated through Military Government units to local Japanese civil authorities.

FOR THE SUPREME COMMANDER:

R. M. LEVY,

for Colonel, AGD,

Adjutant General[99]

The following questions regarding SCAPIN No. 1778 warrant being addressed: firstly, why was Dokdo designated as a bombing range in September 1947? Secondly, it was SCAP that did the designation but it was air units under the Command of FEAF that actually used Dokdo as a bombing range. This begs the question as to what places they had used previously for bombing exercises. Thirdly, where did SCAP and FEAF get the idea of using Dokdo as a bombing range?

On June 14, 1948 after the bombing of Dokdo, the Fifth Air Force notified USAFIK of a list of nine bombing and gunnery ranges used by its subordinate units and that the Liancourt Rocks were one of the locations on the list.[100]

H. Liancourt Rocks Air to Ground Range: 07:00 to 17:00 daily at 37 deg 15′ N-131 deg 37′ E with danger area extending for 5 miles in all directions.

2. The Korea Aerial Gunnery Range is located at coordinates 38 deg 07′ N-125 deg 30′ E, 37 deg 07′ N-125 deg 53′ E, 37 deg 35′ N-125 deg 30′ E,

---

99   GHQ, SCAP, "SCAPIN no.1778: Memorandum for Japanese Government: Liancourt Rocks Bombing Range," (Sept. 16, 1947).

100 NG 1505 (140625/Z) CG 5th Air Force to CG 8th Army, CG USAFIK (Jun. 14, 1948), "AG 684 Target and Bombing Ranges, 1948," RG 554, Entry A1 1378, USAFIK, Adjutant General, General Correspondence (Decimal Files) 1945-1949, Box 141.

37 deg 35′ N-125 deg 53′ E.[101]

Lovmo pointed out in his research that the two bombing and gunnery ranges (Geocheomdo Island and maritime gunnery range) located on Korea's west coast were under the control of USAFIK while the other nine ranges including the Liancourt Rocks were under the Fifth Air Force. After the Dokdo incident, USAFIK closed the ranges on the west coast for safety reasons and did not want the decision to be made public.

As seen above, the Fifth Air Force notified USAFIK of its use of Dokdo as a bombing range only on June 14, long after the June 8 bombing of Dokdo had occurred. USAFIK had been left in the dark of this fact before that time. The list above indicates the Liancourt Rocks (Dokdo) as one of the bombing and gunnery ranges near Japan.

No clear answer has been given as to why and through which channel Dokdo was designated as a US forces' bombing range in SCAPIN No. 1778. More detailed research is necessary into the background that SCAP used as a basis to write the instruction that affected the designation.

First, let us look at why the Far East Command and FEAF Headquarters did not relay the bombing of Dokdo to USAFIK Headquarters. In a radio message from Hodge to MacArthur on June 15, 1948, according to standards, the use of a bombing range was to be made known to the US forces in the corresponding region two weeks prior to the actual bombing but there was no such advance notice for the June 1948 bombing of Dokdo.[102] In addition, Hodge received the list of bombing ranges, which included the Liancourt Rocks, from the Fifth Air Force only on June 14.

As stipulated in SCAPIN No. 1778 (September 16, 1947), the local Japanese civilian authorities should have been notified by the US military government units of every bombing exercise held at Dokdo two weeks prior to warn the "inhabitants of the Oki Islands and of all the ports on the west coast of Honshu north to the 38th parallel." However, the records that

---

101 *Ibid.*

102 RG 554, Entry A1 1380 USAFIK, Adjutant General, Radio Messages 1945-49, Box 193.

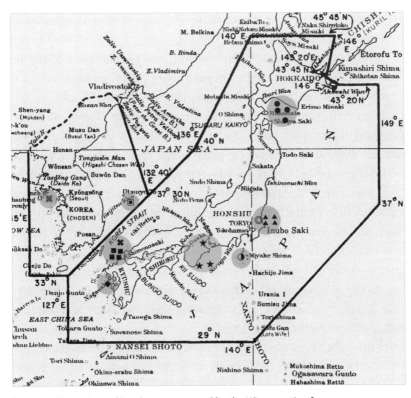

[Figure 1-2] Locations of bombing ranges used by the US occupation forces

Remark: Indicated on a map (H.O. 1500) attached to a draft of the Treaty of Peace with Japan by the US DoS (Nov. 2, 1949).

■ Kyushu
  34° 10' north latitude, 130° 20' east longitude
  34° 10' north latitude, 130° 40' east longitude
  34° 40' north latitude, 130° 20' east longitude
  34° 40' north latitude, 130° 40' east longitude

▲ North Honshu
  36° north latitude, 140° 55' east longitude
  36° north latitude, 141° 20' east longitude
  36° 30' north latitude, 140° 55' east longitude
  36° 30' north latitude, 141° 20' east longitude

★ South Honshu
  33° 50' north latitude, 136° 23' east longitude
  33° 46' north latitude, 136° 14' east longitude
  33° 50' north latitude, 137° east longitude

◆ Omura
  32° 53' north latitude, 129° 52' east longitude

◑ Onohara Island
  34° 2' 30'' north latitude, 139° 23' east longitude

● Hokkaido
  42° 5' north latitude, 141° 40' east longitude
  42° 20' north latitude, 141° 50' east longitude
  42° 1' north latitude, 142° 20' east longitude
  41° 55' north latitude, 142° 10' east longitude

✖ Ashiya
  33° 52' north latitude, 130° 37' east longitude

▣ Liancourt Rocks
  37° 15' north latitude, 131° 37' east longitude

◎ Mito
  36° 23' 15'' north latitude, 140° 36' east longitude

▨ Aerial bombing ranges in Korea
  38° 7' north latitude, 125° 30' east longitude
  37° 7' north latitude, 125° 53' east longitude
  37° 35' north latitude, 125° 30' east longitude
  37° 35' north latitude, 125° 53' east longitude

87

are currently kept in Japan do not clearly indicate when bombing exercises were conducted at Dokdo.

Work Reports and *Monthly Work Reports* (June 1947 to June 1951) by the Chugoku Liaison Office and the Chugoku Liaison and Coordination Office, which were responsible for communication between the US military and civilian government authorities in the Chugoku region (Tottori, Shimane, Okayama, Hiroshima, and Yamaguchi Prefectures), do not record any advance warning about bombing practice over Dokdo. However, advance notice of bombings in areas other than Dokdo can be found sporadically.

In February 1950, 2,000 fishermen from Shimane Prefecture submitted a petition to move the bombing range out of their prefecture. The petition wrote that the coast of Shimane Prefecture was the location of the second best fishing grounds after those near Hokkaido, but one-third of these grounds were lost to them because of the range.[103] All things taken together, it is apparent that there were a number of bombing practices near Shimane Prefecture and it is likely that there must have been advance notice of bombing practice at Dokdo.

In this light, there must have been several bombing runs by the US Air Force at Dokdo starting in September 1947,[104] and in fact, testimony was made after the Dokdo bombing incident that a bombing run had been made in April.[105] This was confirmed as taking place on April 16, 1947, with no casualties.[106] Ulleungdo Governor Heo Pil said in an interview with

---

103 Chugoku Liaison and Coordination Office, *Half-monthly Work Report*, Vol.4, No.4, Mar. 1 of the 25th year of Showa, compiled and annotated by Takashi Ara, 1994, the above publication, p.258.

104 Witnesses of the 1948 Dokdo bombing incident revealed that Dokdo was bombed at different times during both 1947 and 1948. (Hong Seong-geun, 2003, "Analysis of the Bombing Incident from an International Law Perspective," *Research History of Korea's Sovereignty over Dokdo*, pp. 377-378).

105 "Breaking News from the Site of the Dokdo Bombing: A Great Shock to Public Sentiment, 23 Fishing Boats Sunk, 24 Dead and Injured," *Chosun Ilbo* (Jun. 12, 1948); "Fishing Boats Bombed during Operation, 11 Fishing Boats Sunk and Some 20 Dead and Injured at Dokdo," *Fisheries Economic Newspaper* (Jun. 12, 1948).

106 "Bombing of Dokdo by US Aircraft," *Kyunghyang Shinmun, Seoul Shinmun,* and *Dong-A Ilbo* (Jun. 12, 1948).

Seoul Shinmun correspondent Han Gyu-ho that he himself experienced the bombing on April 16, 1947.[107] This incident also warrants further investigation.

Also, as Lovmo discovered in his research, the 22nd Bombardment Group, which was stationed at Kadena Air Base in Okinawa in 1948, bombed Dokdo on April 25, 1948. This is additional evidence that FEAF bombed Dokdo over several occasions since its designation in September 1947. The June 8, 1948 incident was tragic, but from the perspective of FEAF, it was a single accident in a long series of bombing exercises that had remained uneventful since 1947.

The US Commanding General in Korea, John R. Hodge, issued a press release on June 17, 1948, where he stated that no US planes based on or assigned to units in Korea were involved in the bombing and a careful investigation was still underway.[108] USAFIK issued an order to stop all bombing practices at Dokdo and FEAF followed suit by officially and permanently closing the bombing range at Dokdo.[109] As such, Dokdo, which was included in the list of bombing and gunnery ranges issued by the Fifth Air Force on June 17, was indicated as closed on the list dated June 28.[110]

---

107 Han Gyu-ho, 1948, "Tragic Dokdo (on-site report)," *Shincheonji*, July Issue (Serial No. 27), p. 99.

108 *Chosun Ilbo, Dong-A Ilbo*, and *Seoul Shinmun* (Jun. 17, 1948).

109 *Dong-A Ilbo* & *Chosun Ilbo* (Jun. 23, 1948).

110 CG 5th AF to CG 8th Army, FASA-Com Navel Forces Far East (Jun. 17, 1948); HQ, Fifth Air Force, Subject: Warning Notice-Bombing and Gunnery Ranges (Jun. 28, 1948), RG 554, Entry A1 1378, USAFIK, Adjutant General, General Correspondence (Decimal Files) 1945-1949, Box 141.

6

Recognition of Dokdo among the Koreans in 1948

1) Public consensus: Dokdo as Korean territory

The Dokdo bombing incident occurred while administrative control was being transferred from the US occupation authorities to the Korean government, newly established after the May 10 general elections. This had considerable implications on many aspects of how the Koreans recognized Dokdo and responded to any issues related to the island going forward.

First, the overall public sentiment immediately after the bombing was that the dignity and lives of Koreans were brutally trampled upon before they could reassert sovereignty over their land and while under the control of the US military government. The *Seoul Shinmun* reported that the "murderous" bombers flew in from the East Sea and hit fishing boats, sinking 11 and killing 9, and quoted Jang Hak-sang, one of the survivors, who testified to the fact that they had been strafed.[111]

The *Chosun Ilbo* stated, "It is illegal by public law to open fire at non-combatants and, if it was a prank by individuals, it is even more savage" and "Dokdo is clearly Korean territory both in terms of literature and geography, and the Japanese government has created an issue by making unreasonable claims for the island after national liberation."[112] Hong Jong-in published memoirs on the 1947 expedition to Dokdo by the Corean Alpine Club where he wrote that Dokdo, which used to be called Sambongdo, was

---

111 *Seoul Shinmun* (Jun. 12, 1948).
112 "A Formation of Nine Aircraft Heavily Bombed Fishing Boats, Those Responsible Should Be Held for Innocent Victims," *Chosun Ilbo* (Jun. 12, 1948).

a strategic point in aviation and called it "Our Land in the East Sea."[113] The newspapers were critical in unison, calling the bombing "brutality using fishermen as test subjects" and demanding an "investigation of real facts and public punishment of those responsible."[114]

The then Constitutional Assembly in Seoul also discussed the Dokdo incident during its 11th session on June 15, 1948, when 11 assemblymen including Kim Jang-ryeol submitted an urgent motion to investigate the "attack on Ulleungdo fishing boats." Yun Chi-yeong of the Foreign Affairs and National Defense Committee made a report on July 6 entitled the "Dokdo bombing incident near Ulleungdo." Yun reported that he was unofficially informed by USAMGIK that it intended to see this matter properly resolved by court-martialing those responsible after an investigation.[115]

What Hodge was particularly concerned about was propaganda and instigation by the Communists. In his radio message dated June 15 to MacArthur, he expressed his concern that "no matter how (the Dokdo bombing incident) is dealt with, the reputation of the US in Korea will be injured under heavy attack by the communists." In another message, he wrote that the Dokdo bombing issue was "of significant importance here in the field and adding to the flare of the communists who are doing everything to heighten anti-American sentiment using every incident and excuse no matter how small. I believe considerable effort is required to overcome and respond to its negative effects."[116]

Immediately after the incident, all media outlets, political parties, and social organizations demanded, in unison, a thorough investigation,

---

113 "Our Land in the East Sea, the Deplorable Record of a Bloody Scene: Reminiscences of the Expedition by Hong Jong-in," *Chosun Ilbo* (Jun. 17, 1948)

114 The Gyeongbuk Branch of the Federation of Korean Cultural Organizations issued a statement on June 22, 1948 demanding a "public execution of American soldiers who bombed our compatriots at Dokdo" [*South Korean Economic Daily* (Jun. 23, 1948)].

115 National Assembly Secretariat, "The First National Assembly Stenographic Records No. 26" (Jul. 6, 1948), *Constitutional Assembly Stenographic Records* (May 31 and Sept. 8, 1948), Vol. 1, p. 455.

116 RG 554, Entry A1 1380 USAFIK, Adjutant General, Radio Messages 1945-49, Box 193.

compensation, and punishment. In connection with the political situation at the time, many showed a tendency to bind the Dokdo bombing incident to anti-American as well as anti-Japanese sentiment, leaving the US occupation authorities baffled. According to USAMGIK records, all Korean political parties and social organizations were condemning the incident as brutality and suspecting that it was related to the US intention to rearm Japan.[117]

Rumors spread that the US occupation authorities in Korea were employing former high-ranking Japanese officials, which led to strong anti-Japanese, anti-American, and anti-USAMGIK sentiment.[118] The Publicity Department of the Democratic Independence Party issued a statement that the US was training Japanese Special Forces to rearm Japan while suspicion and indignation was very high that the Dokdo bombing might have been "conducted by those Japanese invaders."[119] In other words, the Dokdo bombing incident combined the shock from the death of innocent people with the fear of reinvasion by Japan and the dispute regarding sovereignty over Dokdo, and exerted political pressure on the US occupation authorities in Korea. With anti-Japanese sentiment at work, the political parties overcame their differences and there were virtually no parties or organizations that did not offer their opinions or issue a statement on the incident.

At the staff conference of the US XXIV Corps in charge of governing Korea, the Chief of Staff for Intelligence, G2 remarked as follows:

The 'Dokdo bombing incident' united the Koreans like never before. They killed each other for a long time without blinking an eye, but at the news of the recent bombing of fishing boats, they now howl like Indians.[120]

---

117 USAFIK, South Korean Interim Government Activities, No. 33 (Jun. 1948), USAMIG, prepared by the National Economic Board, p. 152.

118 *Chosun Ilbo* (Jun. 10, 1948); *Seoul Shinmun* and *Dong-A Ilbo* (Jun. 11, 1948).

119 "The Publicity Department of the Democratic Independence Party: An Outrageous Incident," *Fisheries Economic Newspaper* (Jun. 20, 1948).

120 Corps Staff Conference 18 June 1948, RG 554 USAFIK, XXIV Corps, G-2, Historical

After the press release issued by Hodge on June 17, 1948 in response to the bombing, the rumors that the Japanese were behind the incident died away. It is clear that the Dokdo bombing incident coalesced with anti-Japanese sentiment and served as a central force that united the newly independent Korea. A military attaché to the US Embassy in Seoul said that any hint of a resurgent Japan or infringement from any other source upon the rights of the Korean people would rapidly weld the heterogeneous and bickering factions in Korea and this susceptibility was and would continue to be exploited by the Soviets and their communist propaganda machine.[121] The American authorities emphasized that the incident was not intentional but an accident and blamed the resulting uproar on anti-American sentiment and on the hatred Koreans held towards Americans.

In a 1992 interview with the national broadcaster, Korean Broadcasting System (KBS), Donald McDonald, who had been Second Secretary in charge of political affairs at the US Embassy in Seoul at the time of the bombing, claimed that it was not an intentional attack, but a mistake and the result of a practice run by an air unit. The interviewer said he himself had visited Dokdo and disputed McDonald's statements, arguing the bombing amounted to an attack. Nevertheless, McDonald stressed that the bombing did indeed happen and that it was an accident also admitted to by the US authorities.[122]

The 1948 bombing of Dokdo provided Koreans with an important lesson and served as an opportunity to build a national consensus on Dokdo being Korean territory and jumpstarted efforts both at home and abroad to confirm Korean sovereignty there. Press coverage was generally based on the premise that those injured or killed during the bombing were all Korean fishermen from Gangjin and Mukho (Gangwon-do), and Ulleungdo who were fishing at Dokdo, which was Korean territory. After the incident, USAMGIK dispatched an investigation team that included

---

Section, Box 25, "Historical Journal of Korea, June-August 1948".

121 Military Attaché in the Embassy at Seoul, Joint Weeka, No. 25 (Jun. 19, 1948), p. 9.

122 KBS Discovery of Modern History team, "Interview with Donald McDonald" (Nov. 12, 1992), *Interviews with Americans as Part of Modern Korean History Research*, pp. 272 -273.

army surgeons and relief workers to Dokdo, demonstrating that it was indeed under the jurisdiction of USAMGIK. *The New York Times* reported, "Coastal residents were involved in the accident while fishing in the area for their livelihood, as they have done for many generations," recording Dokdo as Korean fishing grounds.[123]

Messages of consolation and contributions for the bereaved families came from all over the country. The Fisheries Association, middle school students, and others delivered contributions and care packages.[124] This was an expression of national interest and consolation related to the misfortunes of fellow countrymen, similar to relief funds for flood or fire victims.

All these perceptions and actions were clear proof that Dokdo, where the incident occurred, was Korean territory. Neither the Japanese authorities nor SCAP was involved in the investigation and handling of the incident. The Japanese press did not cover it. The Dokdo bombing helped establish a national consensus that Dokdo was Korean territory without doubt and that a close eye should be kept on the island annexed to Ulleungdo where the tragedy occurred.

To Koreans, who had fallen for games played by more powerful nations amid the chaos of national liberation and division, military rule, and the lack of national sovereignty, Dokdo became a spiritual center that could unite them. Dokdo, the first victim of the Japanese invasion, was the frontline for a country whose sovereignty continued to be threatened by Japan even after that nation's defeat, and ended up being a bombing range for US air units. To Koreans, it became a symbol of the ordeals suffered by a small, weak nation and its territorial inviolability as a sovereign nation.

The bombing of Dokdo also had an impact on the art scene. Lee Kwae-dae, one of the masters of modern Korean art, produced a large painting *Crowd IV* (oil painting on canvas, 177×216cm) that described the incident.

Tragic though the bombing of Dokdo was, in the end, it was an opportunity to recognize Dokdo as Korean territory. The effort to confirm

---

123   *Chosun Ilbo* (Jun. 19, 1948).
124   *Chosun Ilbo* (Jun. 26, 1948); *Dong-A Ilbo* (Jul. 25, 1948).

Korea's sovereignty there was started by the Interim Government and the Corean Alpine Club in 1947, and the bombing in 1948 allowed the public to vividly realize its importance and even provided clear evidence of that sovereignty. The tragedy paradoxically became the driving force that instilled in Koreans a sense of confidence about their sovereignty over Dokdo and allowed them to take the measures necessary to safeguard Dokdo and actively respond to Japan's claims over it, which began in 1952.

The Dokdo bombing incident was settled for the time being with the unveiling of a memorial stone that was erected for the victims at Dokdo. It was held at 10 am on June 8, 1950, right before the outbreak of the Korean War, and attended by some 100 people including Gyeongsangbuk-do Governor Jo Jae-cheon.[125] Korean fishing boats and fishermen had been attacked on Korean territory, compensation by the US occupation authorities had been completed, and representatives from the agencies of the newly-established government such as the Ministry of Finance and the Bureau of Public Information were present at the unveiling ceremony, proving that the island was Korean territory.[126] Governor Jo read a funeral oration to the effect that the incident was the result of a bombing mistake by the US Air Force.[127] The Japanese government neither claimed sovereignty over Dokdo nor protested with USAMGIK or the Korean government between 1947 and 1951.

In a written demand for reparations from Japan, the Interim Government included "Demands Regarding Dokdo Island" as an official clause, demonstrating the importance placed on its sovereignty over Dokdo.[128] The

---

125 *Chosun Ilbo* (Jun. 8, 1950); *Hanseong Ilbo* (Jun. 9, 1950).

126 *Chosun Ilbo* (Jun. 8, 1950); *Hanseong Ilbo* (Jun. 9, 1950).

127 "Funeral Oration (Gyeongsangbuk-do Governor Jo)," *Hanseong Ilbo* (Jun. 9, 1950). Jo Jae-cheon made a record of his visit to Ulleungdo and Dokdo from June 7 and 8, 1950, in his "Photo Album to Record the Erection of the Dokdo Memorial Stone to Comfort Ulleungdo Residents," and dedicated it to President Rhee Syngman. The album included 50 photos taken by Choi Gye-bok, who accompanied the Corean Alpine Club in its 1947 Dokdo expedition, and is kept at Ihwajang, a historic building in Seoul. *Dong-A Ilbo*, YTN, and other media outlets covered it on March 21, 2005.

128 "Claims of the Korean Government, Government Departments, Bureaus and Agencies,

Constitutional Assembly mentioned sovereignty over Dokdo in the process of writing the Constitution of the Republic of Korea and composing Article 84 about nationalizing fishery resources.[129] The Koreans' awareness of Dokdo, triggered in 1947 when the Interim Government was in place and which had since heightened, the public consensus on the need to reaffirm sovereignty, and the threat of reinvasion of Dokdo by Japan were reflected in the Constitution, opening a new era for Korea's recognition of and policy on Dokdo. Guarding Dokdo was a way to block aggression and defend the country and the Constitution and the ideas they uphold.

2) Petition by the Patriotic Old Men's Association: Regarding Dokdo, Parangdo, and Tsushima as one issue

The amplified interest in Dokdo and Parangdo in 1947 was related to a peace treaty to be concluded with Japan. In 1947, the former Allied Powers led by the US planned to conclude a peace treaty with Japan early and opinions were being actively exchanged between them in this regard. Koreans' awareness of Dokdo became clear right before the establishment of the ROK government after the 1947 Dokdo expedition and the 1948 Dokdo bombing. Korea's territorial policy toward Japan, characterized by concerns that the latter would take Dokdo and the active response to it, a new emphasis placed on Parangdo, and an offensive attitude toward Tsushima, became serious and the tendency to regard Dokdo, Parangdo, and Tsushima as one set of issues became evident. A good example of this tendency is the petition sent by the Patriotic Old Men's Association to MacArthur on August 5, 1948.

Korean Individuals and Juridical Persons against the Japanese Government, Japanese Individuals and Juridical Persons," (May 15, 1948). RG 554, Entry A1 1404, United States Army Forces in Korea (USAFIK), US Army Office of Military Government, Public Relations File 1947-1948, Box 311.

129 National Assembly Secretariat, "The First National Assembly Stenographic Records No. 26" (Jul. 6, 1948), *Constitutional Assembly Stenographic Records* (May 31 & Sept. 8, 1948), Vol. 1, p. 475.

The association was established on January 10, 1946 by senior citizens (60 years of age or more) with the purpose of opposing foreign trusteeship over Korea, which was decided at the Moscow Conference of 1945.

Its relationship with MacArthur started when it visited USAMGIK Commanding General Hodge on February 20, 1946 and asked him to deliver to MacArthur a demand for the return of the Japan–Korea Annexation Treaty document signed in 1910.[130] On the occasion of National Liberation Day on August 15, 1946, General MacArthur returned Korea's eight Seals of State that had been stolen by Japan and kept at its Imperial Household Agency in addition to the requested treaty document. In return, the Association sent a letter of appreciation to MacArthur.[131] On August 5, 1948, the Association sent another petition to MacArthur for the return of Docksum (Dokdo), Ulleungdo, Tsushima, and Parangdo to Korea as they were Korean territory.[132]

They seem to have been encouraged by the fact that their 1946 petition achieved the desired results. Cho Sung-whan, one of the key figures of the Provisional Government of Korea, served as the head of the association. The petition epitomized the Korean view of Dokdo, Parangdo and Tsushima that began to take shape in 1947, and was significant in that, of all the documents that had been produced before the establishment of the ROK government in 1948, it most accurately described the historical basis of Korea's sovereignty over Dokdo.

The letter contained the universal sentiment felt by Koreans and the belief that they should defend the islands (Dokdo and Parangdo) against Japan's attempt to take them, which had intensified since 1947, and

---

130 *Dong-A Ilbo* (Feb. 20, 1946).

131 *Chosun Ilbo* (Aug. 15, 1946); *Dong-A Ilbo* (Aug. 20, 1945). The Seals of State, the Japan–Korea Annexation Treaty document, and other returned items were displayed at the National Museum in February 1949 [*Dong-A Ilbo* (Jan. 25, 1949)].

132 US Political Adviser for Japan No. 612 (Sept. 16, 1948), Subject: Korean Petition Concerning Sovereignty of "Docksum", Ullungo Do, Tsushima, and "Parang" Islands, RG 84, Entry 2828, Japan: Office of US Political Adviser for Japan (Tokyo), Classified General Correspondence (1945-49, 1950-), Box 34.

demarcate Tsushima as Korean territory in response to Japan's actions.[133]

First, let us look at "Part I. Return of 'Docksum.'" The petition was as accurate about the Dokdo issue as could be expected in 1948. It stated that Japan was first after Ulleungdo but failed and had turned its eyes to Dokdo in recent times.[134]

Except for the erroneous indication of Shimane Prefecture as Tottori Prefecture, the petition stated the relevant facts accurately and offered a complete picture of Koreans' awareness of Dokdo and what they had learned about the island by 1948. In conclusion, it wrote that Japan should "return" Dokdo, upon which it was illegally encroaching, to Korea. This part of the petition concerning sovereignty over Dokdo and Japan's aggression was accurately written in detail.

However, "Part II. Transfer of 'Tsushima' to Korea," was more of a political argument. The petition asked for the transfer of Tsushima to Korea for the following reasons:

1. To permanently remove one threat to the survival of Korea
2. To prevent Japanese aggression toward the Continent
3. To prevent the possible invasion of the Asian Continent by the robbers[135]

This reveals that the request for the transfer of Tsushima to Korea was not about the issue of sovereignty. The letter argued that the transfer of the island to Korea stood to reason since the Potsdam Declaration left out Okinawa and Tsushima.[136] Thwarting any Japanese attempt to invade the Asian continent, one of the reasons it cited, coincided with the note from the USSR about transferring Tsushima to Korea.

Lastly, in "Part III. Clarifying Where Parangdo Belongs," the petition

---

133 Cho Sung-whan, Chairman, Patriotic Old Men's Association to Gen. Douglas MacArthur, Supreme Commander, SCAP, Subject: Request for Arrangement of Lands between Korea and Japan (Aug. 5, 1948) (hereafter referred to as "petition").

134 "Petition," p. 2.

135 "Petition," p. 3.

136 "Petition," pp. 4-5.

stated that the name "Parangdo" meant "Green Island" in Korean and reprinted the aforementioned *Dong-A Ilbo* article of October 22, 1947. It alleged that Japan intended to reoccupy Dokdo, the Paracel Islands in the South China Sea, Parangdo, and more, one after another. Ultimately, the petition asked the US to redefine the boundaries between Korea and Japan.

However, arguing that Tsushima and Parangdo were Korean territory even in consideration of the lack of geographical information in 1948 had more than a little potential to make the US and other former Allied Powers doubt Korea's genuine intentions, as Tsushima clearly belonged to Japan and the very existence of Parangdo was yet to be confirmed. Nevertheless, this petition by the Patriotic Old Men's Association is important in that it shows the heights Korea's territorial awareness had reached as of August 1948. The arguments by the ROK government over sovereignty relating to Tsushima, Parangdo, and Dokdo, one after another, made after its establishment were neither incidental mistakes nor unexpected acts.

In the end, the letter had both positive and negative effects. Although it rationally contended for Korea's historical sovereignty over Dokdo and Ulleungdo, the letter also contended for sovereignty over Parangdo, whose location was unknown, and sovereignty over Tsushima, which the international community could not accept. These requests greatly marred the credibility and authenticity of the petition.

An officer who reviewed the petition at US Far East Command G-3 severely criticized the petition, noting that the name "Docksum" was unidentifiable, the name and location of Parangdo remained unexplained, the letter was written in poor English and contained many historically inaccurate facts, including what it said about Tsushima.[137] He also said that SCAP did not need to answer letters from an unidentifiable association and suggested that a copy be submitted to SCAP's Diplomatic Section for reference. On August 27, R.B. Finn at SCAP's Diplomatic Section and Lt. Col. Anderson at G-3 discussed the petition over the phone and decided

---

137 GHQ, FEC, G-3 Section, Memorandum for the Chief of Staff, Subject: Petition of Patriotic Old Men's Association of Seoul, Korea (Aug. 25, 1948).

not to take any action but to submit a copy to the Diplomatic Section for reference.[138]

---

138 GHQ, FEC, Check Sheet, G-2 to Diplomatic Section, Subject: Petition of Patriotic Old Men's Association of Seoul, Korea (Sept. 27, 1948).

Chapter 2

Japan's Preparations for the Peace Treaty and Perception of Dokdo (1945~50)

: Dokdo and Ulleungdo as Japanese Territory

1

Preparations by the Japanese Government for the Peace Treaty (1945~1950)

After its defeat in the Pacific War, Japan was deprived of the two most important elements of national sovereignty: military and diplomatic independence. The Army Ministry and Navy Ministry, which had carried out the war, were dismantled while the Ministry of Foreign Affairs remained. With no right to engage in diplomacy, the Foreign Ministry's primary task was to prepare for an eventual peace treaty. These preparations were made in three steps: first, an Executive Committee for Research on a Peace Treaty was established within the Foreign Ministry to discuss relevant matters internally and undertake preparatory research (November 1945 to April 1947); second, an Executive Committee for Coordination between Ministries for a Peace Treaty was launched on May 8, 1947 to promote discussion between the Foreign Ministry and other relevant ministries; and third, after discussion between the relevant ministers, a Review Department was set up in September 1947 within the Foreign Ministry where working-level officials from different ministries had regular meetings to prepare for the peace treaty. Having arrived at the last step, the Foreign Ministry came to an approximate end of its preparations for the peace treaty.

By July 1947, it was evident that the US wanted to see a peace treaty concluded at the earliest possible date, and accordingly, Japan was fully engaged in official and unofficial contact with the former Allied Powers. Although the holding of a peace conference with Japan was delayed due to disagreement and opposition between the US and the Soviet Union over procedures and goals, negotiations with the US became full-fledged with John Foster Dulles' designation as US special envoy to the Treaty of Peace with Japan in May 1950. By the middle of 1950 when it became clear that a separate peace settlement would be made early under the leadership of the US, the Japanese government had already been preparing for it for more than five years and the Foreign Ministry and relevant ministries had already discussed and made decisions on key issues and strategies at the national level.

1) The Executive Committee for Research on a Peace Treaty (November 1945 to May 1947): Launch of peace treaty preparations

The Japanese government began to lay the groundwork for a peace treaty right after its defeat in the war. Shigeru Yoshida, who served as Foreign Minister of the Shidehara cabinet, became Foreign Minister in September 1945 and described Japan as a "carp on the chopping board" at his inauguration ceremony, with its fate in the hands of the former WWII Allies and asked for all involved to do their utmost to get the nation out of this predicament.[1] In the fall of 1945, Yoshida and former Foreign Affairs Ministry diplomats Mamoru Shigemitsu and Hitoshi Ashida summoned and urged the Directors of the Treaties and Political Bureaus, the key departments of the Foreign Ministry, to help Japan escape the harsh fate that Germany faced with the 1919 Treaty of Versailles after World War I.[2] Based on their experience of having participated in the Paris Peace Conference as diplomats, the three veterans advised the Foreign Ministry officials to avoid a "forced peace." Takeso Shimoda, Director of Treaties Section I of the Foreign Ministry's Treaties Bureau and who was present at the meeting, was advised that the US occupation would not be prolonged and Japan would definitely be made free, so preparations should be made to defend the completely disarmed Japan.[3] Accordingly, an Executive Committee for Research on a Peace Treaty was established on November 21, 1945, with

---

1   Takeso Shimoda, 1984, *Sengo Nihon Gaiko No Shogen (Testimony to Japan's Postwar Diplomacy: How Japan Revived) Vol. 1*, edited by Nobutoshi Nagano, Tokyo, Research Institute for Public Administration, pp. 50-51.

2   Makoto Iokibe et al., 2002, *The Diplomatic History of Postwar Japan*, translated by Jo Yang-uk, Darakwon, p. 73.

3   Shimoda, *Sengo Nihon Gaiko No Shogen*, p. 51.

the Foreign Ministry's Treaties Bureau at its center. While Arata Sugihara, Director General of the Treaties Bureau, was the Committee head, the Committee itself consisted of ten managers from the Foreign Ministry's Political, Economic, Treaties, Investigation, and Management Bureaus and one manager from the Central Liaison Office, with Shimoda serving as Executive Secretary.[4]

From that time onward, the Foreign Ministry predicted that discussion would start in earnest with the former Allies in early 1947 and promptly proceeded with the necessary preparations. According to "Basic Guidelines for the Conclusion of a Peace Treaty," written as part of research on a peace treaty on January 31, 1946, the Foreign Ministry set up a three-step plan of ① completing its own research on a peace treaty by the first half of the year; ② establishing an organization within the Ministry that would coordinate the relevant ministries and review research findings to suggest improvements (civilians would be introduced at an appropriate time) by the latter part of the year, and ③ proposing its own ideas depending on the willingness of the Allies to accept Japanese suggestions by early 1947.[5] The Foreign Ministry made preparations for a peace treaty according to this timeline.

Makoto Iokibe, a historian, has suggested that the research and writing of a proposal by the Foreign Ministry were carried out in four steps. The first was to analyze the Allied plan for Japan contained in the Potsdam Declaration and afterwards to discover ways to restore Japan's independence. The second was to explore ways to restore the minimum conditions to be a sovereign State by disclosing the outline of a draft of Japan's postwar constitution in March 1946. The third step corresponded to the time after the commencement of the Cold War and the fourth step occurred when the peace treaty was concluded under the direction of

---

4   "Establishment of the Executive Committee for Research on a Peace Treaty" (Nov. 21, 1945), Ministry of Foreign Affairs of Japan, 2006, *Japanese Diplomatic Documents: Preparations for the San Francisco Peace Treaty*, p. 12.
5   "Basic Guidelines for the Conclusion of a Peace Treaty" (Jan. 31, 1946), Ministry of Foreign Affairs of Japan, 2006, *Ibid.*, pp. 41-42.

Foreign Minister Yoshida during the Korean War.[6]

The Executive Committee meeting on January 19, 1946 divided the peace treaty into three different categories of general affairs (four clauses), political matters (six clauses), and economic matters (seven clauses). They divided the research subjects among themselves to write papers on each by January 31. The political subjects included constitutional, territorial, and military issues.[7] Another meeting on January 26, 1946 compared a proposal expected from the Allies and Japan's own desired outcomes. The basis for the comparison was the Treaty of Versailles from WWI. They characterized the treaty as a ① forced peace complete with ② conditions that distorted the original principles. Firstly, it was a forced peace as the rights of Germany were only mentioned once in the document and the Allied Powers presented their revision of the peace treaty along with an ultimatum demanding it be signed within five days. There were no negotiations and compromises between the victorious and defeated countries. Secondly, although the surrender of Germany was based on the Fourteen Points suggested by US President Woodrow Wilson, those principles were distorted in the actual treaty. As such, a forced peace failed to have binding force over Germany and the Treaty of Versailles ended up with the notorious reputation of being a "tainted document" due to its distortion of the principles on which it had been based.[8]

The Executive Committee's first report was completed in May 1946 and distributed to the relevant ministries. This report contained the results of research conducted from January to May 1946 in five areas. "Expected Political Clauses in a Peace Treaty and Countermeasures against Possible Discrepancies (draft) (Peace Treaty Research for Political Clauses-1)" defined the Foreign Ministry's principles at that time regarding political

---

6   Iokibe, *The Diplomatic History of Postwar Japan*, pp. 73-74.

7   "Dividing Research Subjects on a Peace Treaty" (Jan. 19, 1946), Ministry of Foreign Affairs of Japan, 2006, *Japanese Diplomatic Documents: Preparations for the San Francisco Peace Treaty*, pp. 13-14.

8   "Comparison and Analysis of the Allied Powers' Presumable Proposal and Japan's Own Desired Outcomes" (Jan. 26, 1946), Ministry of Foreign Affairs of Japan, 2006, *Ibid.*, p. 17.

clauses that would be included in a peace treaty. The key points were the independent and unrestricted selection of the Japanese government by its own people; pledges to renounce war and become a permanently neutral nation, international measures for the guarantee of security for Korea, and the like to firmly establish a national policy of permanent peace.[9] The Foreign Ministry wrote that if the conditions were harsh or unfair, Japan should refuse to sign the treaty, and if that option was unavoidable, it should refuse its ratification.[10] It is hard to believe these words were written by a defeated and occupied country as a plan for a peace treaty. Japan intended to firstly keep its Emperor as head of government and secondly eliminate the influence of powers such as the US and the Soviet Union from its affairs.

The Executive Committee for Research on a Peace Treaty came up with a second work plan on May 22, 1946. It aimed to complete a second round of research by the end of June 1946 based on the directions defined in the first report and to prepare a package of information by the end of July 1946 that the Japanese delegation to a peace conference could carry around and use as reference material.[11]

The second round of research was meant to be finished by the end of June 1946 but most of the documents appear to have been completed in the latter part of the year. "Relations between Existing Treaties Which Involve Japan as a Concerned Party and a Peace Treaty" (Peace Treaty Research for Economic Clauses-6)[12] was completed on July 20, 1946 and "Japan's

---

9   "Expected Political Clauses in a Peace Treaty and Countermeasures against Possible Discrepancies (draft) (Peace Treaty Research for Political Clauses-1)" (May 1946), Ministry of Foreign Affairs of Japan, 2006, *Ibid.*, pp. 91-92.

10   *Ibid.*, p. 99.

11   "Second Work Plan of the Executive Committee for Research on a Peace Treaty" (May 22, 1946), Ministry of Foreign Affairs of Japan, 2006, *Japanese Diplomatic Documents: Preparations for the San Francisco Peace Treaty*, pp. 114-115.

12   "Relations between Existing Treaties Which Involve Japan as a Concerned Party and a Peace Treaty" (Peace Treaty Research for Economic Clauses-6) (Jul. 20, 1946, Treaties Section, Treaties Bureau), Ministry of Foreign Affairs of Japan, 2006, *Ibid.*, pp. 122-129.

Participation in the United Nations" later in September.[13]

2) Establishment of an Executive Committee for Coordination between Ministries for a Peace Treaty (May 1947) and discussion on general principles by the Japanese government

The first step of preparations envisioned by the Japanese Foreign Ministry, namely, internal preparations by the Ministry, appears to have been completed around May 1947. With MacArthur's statement that advocated an early peace with Japan in March 1947 and the US government's proposal in July that year for a preliminary peace conference, there was a clear possibility of an early peace. Accordingly, the Foreign Ministry suggested the establishment of an unofficial organization within the Ministry for close cooperation between different ministries. The official name of the new organization was the Executive Committee for Coordination between Ministries for a Peace Treaty. Each ministry dispatched one secretary to the committee, which was chaired by Toru Hagiwara, Director General of the Treaties Bureau. Ten government entities participated including the Economic Stabilization Board, the Foreign Ministry, the Central Liaison Office, and the Ministries of Internal Affairs, Finance, Justice, Agriculture and Forestry, Commerce and Industry, Trade, and Transport.[14]

With preparatory research already completed on specific issues, this Executive Committee focused on working out the Japanese government's overall stance on a peace treaty. As discussion on individual subjects had been completed, they moved from particulars to generalities. Director general Hagiwara submitted a report based on the discussion and each ministry made suggestions for improvement.

"General Observations on a Peace Treaty by the Japanese Government,"

---

13 "Japan's Participation in the United Nations" (Sept. 1946, Treaties Section, Treaties Bureau) Ministry of Foreign Affairs of Japan, 2006, *Ibid.*, pp. 129-146.

14 "Establishment of the Executive Committee for Coordination between Ministries for a Peace Treaty" (May 17, 1947), Ministry of Foreign Affairs of Japan, 2006, *Ibid.*, p. 180.

first draft (May 1947)

1. Japan's wishes should be fully heard in the process of laying the foundation for a peace treaty.

2. A peace treaty should be in agreement with the Atlantic Charter, Joint Declaration by the United Nations, Cairo Declaration, and Potsdam Declaration.

3. Japan should be given an opportunity to be responsible for implementing the terms of a peace treaty on its own, including such conditions as democratization and demilitarization.

4. An international organization should be immediately established that can fully guarantee Japan's political independence, preservation of its territory, and its security in tandem with Japan's complete demilitarization.

5. Aid should be made and necessary measures (e.g. the freedom to pursue peaceful industrial development and acquire raw materials) taken until Japan can stand on its own economically.[15]

The basic position of the Japanese Foreign Ministry in this report was that Japan should be left alone to do what was required of it and the Allies should suggest a treaty document based on the promises they made in the existing declarations and charters. Its argument was that Japan, the defeated country, would take care of the aftermath of the war on its own and the Allies should guarantee its political and economic freedom and security while providing economic aid. The report did not touch on the most important issue: Japan's remorse. No mention was made of taking responsibility for the war, making apologies for and promises to compensate for the losses and damage caused by wars, invasions, and colonial rule, punishing war criminals, and establishing an international watchdog to guarantee Japan's democratization and demilitarization. There

---

15 "General Observations on a Peace Treaty by the Japanese Government (first draft)" (May 1947); "General Observations on a Peace Treaty by the Japanese Government" (Hagiwara's first draft), Ministry of Foreign Affairs of Japan, 2006, *Ibid.*, p. 181.

was no trace of remorse anywhere in the report.

Toshikazu Kase, a General Affairs Bureau councilor[16] who reviewed the draft by Hagiwara, pointed out that the Cairo Declaration should be removed from the second paragraph. This was because the Cairo Declaration included territorial clauses that were difficult for the Japanese government to accept and therefore no promise should be made for the acceptance of such by the Japanese government. The clauses stipulated that ① Japan should be stripped of all the islands in the Pacific which she had seized or occupied since the beginning of the First World War in 1914; ② all the territories Japan had stolen from the Chinese, such as Manchuria, Formosa, and the Pescadores, should be restored to the Republic of China; and ③ Japan would also be expelled from all other territories which she had taken by violence and greed.

This comment vividly shows that the basic stance taken by Foreign Ministry officials was to disregard and neutralize the terms of surrender Japan had accepted. The framework of the occupation of Japan was drafted in the Cairo Declaration, Potsdam Declaration, and Japanese Instrument of Surrender, which, in fact, constituted one integrated scheme. As the Potsdam Declaration was based on the Cairo Declaration, Japan was not free to choose one and disregard the other. Nevertheless, Kase suggested referring to the Potsdam Declaration but omitting all references to the Cairo Declaration. Basically, Japan's strategy was that they should reject even the previously-accepted terms of surrender, if at all possible.

Kase offered that, instead of directly approaching MacArthur with a proposal drawn up by the Japanese Foreign Ministry, they should unofficially contact those close to George Atcheson, Jr., a political adviser to SCAP, to provide indirect assistance, and there should be a separate organization in the Ministry for the preparation of a peace treaty. He went

---

16   Toshikazu Kase as a veteran diplomat helped draft the declaration of war on the US and held important posts such as Secretary to the Foreign Minister and head of the North American Section. He participated in the signing of Japan's surrender in 1945 as a close aide to then-Foreign Minister Mamoru Shigemitsu (Lee Chang-wi, 2008, *The Rise and Fall of the Empire of Japan*, Kungree, p. 106).

further to suggest tasks for this committee such as gathering data and writing preparatory documents; unofficially contacting GHQ (General Headquarters) and foreign delegations; and producing propaganda materials to distribute to the media, the foreign press in particular. He pointed out that it was essential to win over two to three trustworthy foreign correspondents stationed in Japan who could inform the Japanese government of the events at both GHQ and in the United States.[17]

The efforts to build personal connections paid off whenever the leaders of the Japanese Foreign Ministry and the government as a whole were required to promptly make decisions and take action in the process leading up to the San Francisco Peace Conference in 1951. The sources of information that was treated with the utmost importance in the files of Japanese diplomatic documents regarding the San Francisco peace treaty must have been American officials, newspapers, and reporters who were seen as favorable to Japan, though not specifically mentioned.

The second draft by Hagiwara was submitted on June 2, 1947 and reviewed at the Vice Minister's office on June 4. The second draft deleted the reference to the Cairo Declaration and emphasized only the Atlantic Charter and Potsdam Declaration. The tone was much softened[18] but its intention was essentially the same as that of the first draft.

Hagiwara produced the third draft, a partial revision of the second, on June 5, 1947 as seen below:

"General Observations on a Peace Treaty by the Japanese Government,"
third draft (June 5, 1947)

1. The Japanese government wishes to be given an opportunity to fully present its case so that the Japanese people's rational hopes can be granted to the full extent possible.

---

17 "Regarding a Peace Treaty" (Jun. 5, 1947, Kase), Ministry of Foreign Affairs of Japan, 2006, *Japanese Diplomatic Documents: Preparations for the San Francisco Peace Treaty*, pp. 186-187.
18 "General Observations on a Peace Treaty by the Japanese Government (second draft)" (Jun. 1, 1947), Ministry of Foreign Affairs of Japan, 2006, *Ibid.*, pp. 194-196.

2. A peace treaty should be based on the spirit of the Atlantic Charter that abides by the principles of international law and also be concluded according to the intention of the Potsdam Declaration.

3. The Japanese government and people have the confidence and ability to faithfully implement a peace treaty that we agree to and accept. As such, we hope to be granted an opportunity by the Allied Powers to responsibly implement a peace treaty on our own and regain the trust of the international community.

4. We hope for Japan's inclusion in the United Nations and a security guarantee to be considered as part of a peace treaty.

5. We ask that the principle that provides for a certain standard of living for the Japanese people and Japan's economic independence be the basis of a peace treaty.[19]

The third draft was a representation of a completely Japan-centered stance. The first paragraph talked about Japan's rights, and the second paragraph can be construed as expressing distrust of the Cairo Declaration by arguing that the Atlantic Charter meets the principles of international law. The third paragraph demanded that the Allied Powers present conditions that Japan would find acceptable and that Japan be left alone to implement a peace treaty on its own. The fourth paragraph stipulated Japan should be allowed to join the United Nations and its security be guaranteed. The fifth paragraph did not even mention war reparations and instead merely demanded a guarantee for a certain standard of living and economic independence. This was an expression of the strong determination to make only the bare minimum of reparations. Japan stated only its rights and demands but made no mention of responsibility, apology, remorse, or reparations.

The Foreign Ministry sought advice from its elders in diplomatic circles on the third draft. On June 24, four veteran diplomats, Hachiro Arita,

---

19   "General Observations on a Peace Treaty by the Japanese Government (third draft)" (Jun. 5, 1947), Ministry of Foreign Affairs of Japan, 2006, *Ibid.*, pp. 201-204.

Masaaki Hotta, Shigeru Kuriyama, and Tsuneo Matsudaira, were invited to the official residence of the Vice Foreign Minister and their opinions on the draft were heeded.[20] All four had previously worked for the Foreign Ministry.

Hagiwara wrote a final version on July 17 based on the results of the review thus far: even the manner in which thoughts would be expressed in sentences was thoroughly thought through. As such, the Foreign Ministry worked out the Japanese government's basic principles and a position paper on a peace treaty by July 1947. The paper defined principles and procedures for achieving the most advantageous treaty possible for Japan and avoiding potential pitfalls such as the previously-mentioned clauses in the Cairo Declaration.

3) Start of negotiations with the Allied Powers (July 1947) and establishment of the Policy Review Committee

As the US Department of State (DoS) and MacArthur came to support an early peace treaty in early 1947, the Japanese government approached the Allies through various channels starting that summer. With the Truman Doctrine announced and the Cold War becoming ever more serious, the need to start a discussion for the conclusion of a peace treaty was gathering momentum. The Japanese government intended to find ways to enter into negotiations with the Allies in order to avoid a "forced peace", and additionally, to feel out the Allies about the possibility of changing the established Allied policy of a total demilitarization of Japan from the early stages of the Allied occupation of Japan through to the subsequent onset of the Cold War.[21]

Japan had already started to contact the Allies in 1946 through various channels. Koichiro Asakai, Chief of the General Affairs Department of the

---

20 "Opinions Heard on General Observations on a Peace Treaty by the Japanese Government" (Jun 25, 947, recorded by Nishimura), Ministry of Foreign Affairs of Japan, 2006, *Ibid.*, pp. 209-214.

21 Iokibe, *The Diplomatic History of Postwar Japan*, p. 75.

Central Liaison Office, met with George Atcheson (the US delegate to the Allied Council for Japan (ACJ), political adviser to SCAP, and head of the Diplomatic Section of SCAP) and W. McMahon Ball (the Commonwealth delegate to the ACJ) on several occasions. The Central Liaison Office was established immediately after the end of the war (August 26, 1945) at the request of SCAP to serve as a liaison office to wrap up war-related issues. It served as an official channel of communication between SCAP and Japan. Asakai met McMahon Ball three times (January 20, April 15, and June 24, 1947) and Atcheson seven times (May 1, July 17, October 7, and December 17, 1946 & January 23, March 12, and July 3, 1947) and delivered Japan's opinions on the Allies' policy toward Japan and the forthcoming peace treaty.

Macmahon Ball was an Australian academic and diplomat who studied at the London School of Economics from 1929 to 1932 and also in Germany and the United States. He later became a professor of political science at Melbourne University. Asakai criticized him for being friendly toward the Soviet Union, which differed from the US stance, and delivered the Foreign Ministry's proposal on a peace treaty with Japan during their second talk behind closed doors (April 15, 1947).[22]

Asakai's approach to George Atcheson, who strongly believed Japan should be punished for its war actions and was a China specialist, required more caution. Atcheson visited Washington at the end of January 1947 and stayed for one month to explain the occupation policy in Japan to George C. Marshall, the newly-appointed Secretary of State. In time for this visit, Asakai delivered "A Compilation of Japan's Honest Opinions Vol. 1" to Atcheson, with permission by the Treaties Bureau of the Foreign Ministry.[23] What is interesting is how this file landed in Atcheson's hands.

---

[22] "Asakai and McMahon Ball Talks (second talk)" (Apr. 15, 1947, Koichiro Asakai, Chief of the General Affairs Department, the Central Liaison Office), Ministry of Foreign Affairs of Japan, 2006, *Japanese Diplomatic Documents: Preparations for the San Francisco Peace Treaty*, p. 178.

[23] "Asakai and Atcheson Talks (seventh talk)" (Jul. 3, 1947, Koichiro Asakai, Chief of the General Affairs Department, the Central Liaison Office), Ministry of Foreign Affairs of Japan,

It was delivered to him on January 28, one day before his departure, not directly, but by way of Sebald,[24] whom the Japanese government used to deliver information and materials to the US. Even during the days when Atcheson, a hardliner on Japan, served as US political adviser to SCAP, the Japanese government's documents were delivered through a route put in place that went through the Japanese Foreign Ministry represented by Asakai, Sebald, Atcheson, and finally to the US DoS. At the sixth talk they had on March 12, 1947, after Atcheson's return to Japan, Asakai asked about the US DoS's response to the compilation and Atcheson replied that, "there was not much reaction to talk about" and "those materials were informative."[25] Atcheson informed him that the US was arguing at the UN for trusteeship of Japan's former mandated territories as its strategic possessions and that there was no specific change in position regarding other areas.

At the seventh talk on July 3, 1947, Asakai delivered the second volume of the compilation to Atcheson. Volumes 2 & 3 were sent to the Diplomatic Section of SCAP on July 5.[26] That is, the Japanese Foreign Ministry handed over materials it prepared for a peace treaty to Atcheson on three separate occasions: Volume 1 on January 28, 1947, Volume 2 on July 3, 1947, and Volumes 2 and 3 on July 5, 1947.

After having provided materials prepared by the Foreign Ministry to the United States and Australia through Asakai between January and early July 1947, the Japanese government decided to establish full contact with the Allied Powers. Towards this end, the Foreign Ministry summarized

---

2006, *Ibid.*, p. 228.

24 "Asakai and Atcheson Talks (fifth talk)" (Jan. 23, 1947, Koichiro Asakai, Chief of the General Affairs Department, the Central Liaison Office), Ministry of Foreign Affairs of Japan, 2006, *Ibid.*, pp. 167-168.

25 "Asakai and Atcheson Talks (sixth talk)" (Mar. 12, 1947, Koichiro Asakai, Chief of the General Affairs Department, the Central Liaison Office), Ministry of Foreign Affairs of Japan, 2006, *Ibid.*, p. 168.

26 "Asakai and Atcheson Talks (seventh talk)" (Jul. 3, 1947, Koichiro Asakai, Chief of the General Affairs Department, the Central Liaison Office), Ministry of Foreign Affairs of Japan, 2006, *Ibid.*, p. 228.

the Japanese government's desires into a draft request of nine items to be submitted to Atcheson:

Japan's draft request to be submitted to Atcheson

1. Procedures related to the writing of a peace treaty (The Japanese government should be given a full opportunity to express its position; fairness should be ensured in the procedures and methods)
2. Basis of a peace treaty (Treaty in accordance with the Atlantic Charter and Potsdam Declaration)
3. Independent implementation of a treaty
4. Japan's inclusion in the UN (Prompt inclusion of Japan in the UN should be prescribed in the treaty)
5. Domestic peace and order (The occupation forces should withdraw and domestic public order be maintained by a proper police force)
6. Trial jurisdiction
7. Territorial issues
8. Reparations
9. Economic restrictions[27]

With the above nine-point document finalized, Foreign Minister Hitoshi Ashida met Atcheson and delivered an English version on July 26, 1947.[28] A visit to Courtney Whitney, head of the Government Section of SCAP, was made on July 28 and the same document was delivered.[29] This is the so-called Ashida Initiative, where the defeated Japan took the initiative to bring up the conclusion of a peace treaty before the Allied Powers had even started to seriously discuss it. This move naturally created strong

---

27 "Plan for Talks with Ambassador Atcheson" (Jul. 24, 1947), Ministry of Foreign Affairs of Japan, 2006, *Ibid.*, pp. 245-247.
28 "Ashida and Atcheson Talks" (Jul. 26, 1947), Ministry of Foreign Affairs of Japan, 2006, *Ibid.*, pp. 249-253.
29 "Ashida and Whitney Talks" (Jul. 28, 1947), Ministry of Foreign Affairs of Japan, 2006, *Ibid.*, pp. 261-262.

resistance from SCAP and the Allies.

In the afternoon of July 28, Atcheson and Whitney both summoned Ashida separately and refused to accept the document.[30] Atcheson notified him that it would be disadvantageous to the Japanese government if the US DoS were to find out that it had written this document. The perception that Japan wanted a "peace conference through discussion" was a troublesome development. Whitney pointed out that acceptance by the US of this kind of unofficial document from the Japanese government or Japanese Foreign Minister might rub other Allies, who were opposed to Japan, the wrong way and advised that it would be wise for Japan to remain patient and wait for a peace conference to be held.[31]

On July 31, Prime Minister Tetsu Katayama and Ashida met Australian Foreign Minister Herbert Vere Evatt and discussed a peace conference.[32] On August 11, Ashida met McMahon Ball and delivered an eight-point request.[33] However, with the rejection by Atcheson and Whitney already complete on July 28, Japan's preemptive proposal for a peace conference through the so-called Ashida Initiative ended in failure.

At this point, Japan's attempts to secure a peace treaty were temporarily thwarted as up to that time, the Allies that remembered Japan's war atrocities were inclined to push for a punitive treaty. However, the US policy on Japan changed from 1948 onwards. This reverse course policy signaled a shift away from anti-militarism and pro-democratization towards anti-communism had to wait for the Cold War to kick into high gear in Europe prior to its spread to Asia. The Cold War in Europe reflected in the Truman Doctrine of March 1947 would have an impact on Asia one year later.

---

30 "Return of the Ashida Initiative Delivered to Atcheson and Whitney" (Jul. 28, 1947), Ministry of Foreign Affairs of Japan, 2006, *Ibid.*, pp. 262-265.

31 *Ibid.*; Shimoda, *Sengo Nihon Gaiko No Shogen*, p. 57.

32 "Katayama, Ashida and Evatt Talks" (Jul. 31, 1947), Ministry of Foreign Affairs of Japan, 2006, *Japanese Diplomatic Documents: Preparations for the San Francisco Peace Treaty*, pp. 265-270.

33 The first of the nine items about the procedures of writing a peace treaty was deleted. "Ashida and McMahon Ball Talks" (Aug. 11, 1947), Ministry of Foreign Affairs of Japan, 2006, *Ibid.*, pp. 276-280.

From August to September 1947, the Japanese Foreign Ministry took a step back from its preparations for a peace treaty. On September 3, 1947, Toru Hagiwara, director general of the Ministry's Treaties Bureau invited the former Prime Minister Kijuro Shidehara, Tsuneo Matsudaira, the former Ambassador to the USSR Naotake Sato, and the former Foreign Minister Shigeru Yoshida and heard their opinions on the preparations.[34]

At the same time, a Review Department was established to supervise the preparations across the entire government on September 15, 1947. Its establishment was finalized on August 6, 1947 at a cabinet meeting.[35]

This means that the Japanese government had completed peace-treaty preparations within the Foreign Ministry and by then had come to set up a permanent organization enabling the Ministry to closely cooperate with other relevant ministries to review the preparations together. From August to September 1947, after the failure of the Ashida Initiative, two important incidents occurred within the Diplomatic Section of SCAP which had a great impact on the peace treaty process.

The first was that George Atcheson, who strongly believed Japan should be punished for its war actions, died in an airplane crash in August 1947. Atcheson held the most important civilian position in Tokyo between 1945 and 1947. He served concurrently as a ① political adviser (POLAD) dispatched by the US DoS to MacArthur; ② head of the Diplomatic Section of SCAP; and ③ US delegate and chairman of the Allied Council for Japan (ACJ). The post of political adviser was created by the Secretary of State to advise MacArthur on political and diplomatic matters and the US DoS's policy toward Japan, and was the most important non-military position in postwar Japan. The Diplomatic Section of SCAP was designed to handle all diplomatic matters for Japan, which had lost its diplomatic independence with its surrender. For its part, the ACJ was established as a result of the

---

34 "Opinions Heard on the Status of Preparations for a Peace Treaty" (Sept. 3, 1947, recorded by Toru Hagiwara), Ministry of Foreign Affairs of Japan, 2006, *Ibid.*, pp. 281-284.
35 "High Court Draft on the Establishment of a Review Department and Its Operational Regulations" (Sept. 15, 1947, authorized), Ministry of Foreign Affairs of Japan, 2006, *Ibid.*, pp. 296-299.

Moscow Conference of 1945 to give guidance and advice to SCAP. The four delegations to the ACJ represented the US, the UK, the Soviet Union, and China. MacArthur saw the ACJ as meddling with SCAP and handed over his position as ACJ chairman to Atcheson. As the holder of these three positions, Atcheson was the most influential American official in Tokyo and MacArthur's civilian adviser.

Atcheson was also a China specialist who started as a student interpreter in Beijing in 1920. His diplomatic career began as Deputy Council in China in February 1924, later serving as Council in Tianjin, Fuzhou, Nanjing, and Chongqing. He was dispatched to SCAP as a minister-level political adviser as of September 7, 1945, and then promoted to an ambassador-level diplomat on May 30, 1946.[36]

As political adviser representing the US DoS's position, Atcheson often came into conflict with MacArthur. The general, who came to be known as the "new Japanese emperor" for his strong support of an Asia-first policy, argued for the reconstruction of Japan based on a policy of anti-communism. MacArthur saw that the postwar Japanese reforms would allow for the "so-called liberals" who were actually "Soviet agents" to incite a "communist revolution." He believed that measures such as purges of officials from the former regime, payment of compensation and reparations, and anti-trust policy would only make things worse. As such, he was inclined to only pretend to engage in reforms while in fact maintaining the old power structure so that Japan could reestablish itself as the "natural leader of Asia."[37] Asakai recalled that Atcheson was no match for MacArthur in terms of power, but nevertheless, he kept a close watch on the occupation from the perspective of the US DoS to a degree that he sometimes criticized MacArthur in front of Asakai.[38]

---

36 "Background of Atcheson, George, Jr." MacArthur Archives (MA), RG 5, Box 107, Folder 1.

37 Michael Schaller, 2004, *Douglas MacArthur: The Far Eastern General*, translated by Yu Gang-eun, Imagine, p. 254.

38 Ministry of Foreign Affairs, ed., 1978, *Early Occupation Policy of Japan (Vol. 1) - Report by Koichiro Asakai*, Mainichi Shimbunsha, p. 33.

Debate over policy toward Japan had started during the Pacific War. During the course of devising plans for the occupation of Japan from 1944 to 1945, US Undersecretary of State and former US Ambassador to Japan Joseph C. Grew, US diplomat Eugene Dooman, and other officials maintained that, though Japan had strayed from the right path, it could easily rejoin the civilized world by implementing the necessary reforms. On the other hand, New Dealers and economists asserted that only structural political and economic reforms would allow for the development of a democratic and peaceful Japan. The debate ended in 1945 with the defeat of Grew and his followers.[39] After the war, there was a conflict in the Office of the US Political Adviser for Japan, more specifically between China specialists such as Atcheson and Service and Japan specialists like Max W. Bishop and Sebald. The basic difference between the two groups was over the "degree of harshness with which the Japanese should be dealt."[40]

With the death of Atcheson, the Japan specialists gained power over the China specialists within SCAP. Focus shifted from a punitive and democratizing policy on Japan to a moderate, status quo or reverse course policy. In general, those who were friendly toward and well-acquainted with Japan started to gain stronger voices.

The second was the coming to the fore of William Sebald, a representative Japan specialist. Sebald started his career as a navy officer, then became

---

39   Makoto Iokibe divided the different opinions that existed in the US Department of State about the after-war reform of Japanese politics. The first was to be careful about intervening in post-war Japanese politics as the frantic military was responsible for the war and that the Japanese moderate party should be allowed to pursue voluntary reform. This opinion was represented by Joseph Ballantine. The second blamed Japan's institutional defects for the war and maintained that proactive institutional reform by the moderate party should be induced. Hugh Borton was a representative advocate of this opinion. The third saw the Emperor system and militarism as inseparable and that democracy should be firmly rooted as a universal doctrine through direct intervention in Japanese politics. The fourth was thoroughly pessimistic about the Japanese and asserted that they were incorrigible in every way and therefore should be left isolated and neglected. Hornbeck was a representative pessimist (Makoto Iokibe, 1993, *Beikoku No Nihon Senryo Seisaku (US Occupation Policy of Japan)*, Vol. 1, Chuokoronsha, pp. 256-282).

40   William J. Sebald with Russell Brines, *With MacArthur in Japan: A Personal History of the Occupation*, W.W. Norton & Company, Inc., New York, 1965, p. 43.

a lawyer, and finally a diplomat.[41] Upon graduating from the US Naval Academy, he was assigned to the US Embassy in Tokyo, and became a lawyer to take over his father-in-law's law firm after his marriage to a British-Japanese woman. After the war, he served as a diplomat stationed in Tokyo, Japan from December 1945 to April 1952 and played an important role throughout the reconstruction of Japan, the Korean War, and the San Francisco Peace Conference. From 1947 to 1952, he served simultaneously as an acting US political adviser to SCAP, head of the Diplomatic Section of SCAP, and chairman and US delegate of the ACJ. Later, he served as US Ambassador to Burma (1952-1954), Deputy Assistant Secretary of State for Far Eastern Affairs (1954-1957), and US Ambassador to Australia (1957-1961). Well-versed in the Japanese language, culture, society, and law and enchanted with Japanese culture, he was openly pro-Japanese.[42]

After the death of Atcheson, MacArthur used his authority to appoint Sebald to the two important posts of head of the Diplomatic Section of SCAP and chairman and US delegate of the ACJ.[43] The US DoS opposed Sebald's appointment as US political adviser to SCAP citing his lack of experience and intended to appoint Maxwell M. Hamilton, the former head of the Division of Far Eastern Affairs of the US DoS, to the post. However, MacArthur rejected Hamilton on the grounds that he was one of the "old China hands." Sebald gained the reputation of being an "excellent student of the 'School of General MacArthur'" and "MacArthur's faithful subordinate" who had changed his naval uniform to a diplomat's morning coat.[44]

Sebald's perceptions of Japan are characterized by his devotion to it and strong anti-communist sentiments. He was captivated by the Japanese

41 Department of State, Office of Public Affairs, *Register of the Department of State, April 1, 1950*, p. 454; Department of State, *The Biographic Register 1956* (Revised as of May 1, 1956), pp. 568-569.

42 Regarding Sebald, refer to: Jung Byung-joon, 2005, "William J. Sebald and the Dokdo Territorial Dispute," *Historical Review*, Vol. 71.

43 Sebald, *With MacArthur in Japan*, p. 60.

44 Sebald, *With MacArthur in Japan*, p. 61; Ministry of Foreign Affairs, ed., *Early Occupation Policy of Japan (Vol. 1)*, p. 33.

people and their culture, marrying a British-Japanese woman and keeping company with many leading figures in Japan. As a US political reporter immediately after the war, Sebald met openly with right-wing political leaders. He believed that a handful of Japanese militarists were responsible for the Pacific War and not any defects in the country's political, economic, and ideological structures. Sebald justified his pro-Japanese stance with the alleged communist infiltration of Japan. He was opposed to any purges of Japanese war criminals and economic reforms such as the dismantling of the *zaibatsu* system (industrial and financial business conglomerates), arguing that they were orchestrated by communists. He even sympathized with the claims of Japanese rightists that SCAP and the US were encouraging the spread of radical leftism and communism in Japan.

On the other hand, his perceptions of Korea, which he visited six times, could not have been worse. Sebald described the Koreans he met as "sad, downtrodden, miserable, impoverished, quiet, and gloomy." He wrote that the postwar situation and President Rhee's harsh character made Korea an even more unbearable place and Koreans more intransigent for many American political advisers assigned to the US Commanding General in Korea.[45] He clung to this view during his active participation in the preparations leading up to the peace treaty with Japan and in the early stages of the Korea-Japan Talks.

When the Japanese Foreign Ministry's efforts to contact the Allies through SCAP had failed, Sebald took up an important role. Around September 20, 1947, a message from the Japanese Emperor himself was forwarded to him by a Foreign Ministry official assigned to the royal family and Sebald relayed it to Washington. The Emperor's message indicated that Japan would allow the US to continue its military occupation of Okinawa for a 25- to 50-year period in the form of a long-term lease.[46] As pointed out by Narahiko Toyoshita, this was a representative case where the symbolic Emperor intervened in actual politics under the "Peace Constitution"

---

45   Sebald, *With MacArthur in Japan*, p. 181.

46   Iokibe, *Beikoku No Nihon Senryo Seisaku*, p. 76.

system.[47] In the end, Japan was able to restore its peace and sovereignty at the expense of Okinawa. The US-championed policy of concluding a separate peace treaty with Japan after the war started with the Emperor, who had no authority under the constitution to put Okinawa up for lease.

During their fourth meeting on May 6, 1947, the Japanese Emperor had already told MacArthur that it should be the US, not the UN nor the Far Eastern Commission, that should be directly responsible for the safety of Japan. Having replaced Atcheson after his accidental death, Sebald actively pursued the conclusion of a peace treaty from a perspective that was advantageous to Japan.

The Japanese Foreign Ministry contacted Lieutenant General Robert L. Eichelberger, Commanding Officer of the US 8th Army, regarding Japan's defense after the establishment of a peace treaty and discussed different forms of security guarantees through other channels.[48]

By the end of 1947, responses by the 11 member nations of the Far Eastern Commission (FEC) were known regarding the US proposal for the convening of a preliminary conference on Japanese peace made on July 11, 1947. The US proposed that the conference be composed of the 11 nations of the FEC and that it decide by a two-thirds majority vote. The USSR threatened to use its veto and argued that the Japanese peace settlement should be examined by the Council of Foreign Ministers composed of the representatives of the governments of the Soviet Union, China, the UK and the US. The UK concurred to the US proposal at the Canberra Conference (August 25 to September 2, 1947), but China announced its intention not to attend a peace conference without the USSR (Sept 9, 1947). China

---

47   Narahiko Toyoshita, 2009, *Hirohito and MacArthur (Showa Tenno, Makkasa Kaiken)*, translated by Gwon Hyeok-tae, Gaemagowon, p. 8.

48   "Kuma Suzuki and Eichelberger Talks" (Sept. 13, 1947); "Ashida and Gascoigne Talks on the Prospects on a Peace Treaty, Security Assurance for Japan, Etc." (Sept. 24, 1947); "Guarantee of Japan's Security after the Conclusion of a Peace Treaty" (Oct. 6, 1947, Hitoshi Ashida); "Technical Observations on the Guarantee of Japan's Security after the Conclusion of a Peace Treaty" (Oct. 18, 1947, recorded by Hagiwara), Ministry of Foreign Affairs of Japan, 2006, *Japanese Diplomatic Documents: Preparations for the San Francisco Peace Treaty*, pp. 284-296, 301, 314-315, 316-324.

proposed a compromise that included a vote by the four Big Powers as well as a majority vote by the FEC members (November 17, 1947). As such, by the end of 1947, the Allies were split among the three proposals on peace treaty negotiations with Japan by the US (a two-thirds majority vote by the 11 FEC member nations and no veto granted), by the USSR (deliberation by the Council of Foreign Ministers and vetoes accorded), and China (a simple majority vote by the 11 nations and vetoes granted to the four Big Powers). The Japanese Foreign Ministry determined that the prospect of the US proposal eventually being accepted was gradually growing excluding the Soviet proposal except for the issue of whether China would agree to it.[49] With the delay in reaching an agreement among the Allies on the procedures, a peace conference had to wait several years until new momentum surfaced.

4) Review of the peace treaty formula: Reverse course and *de facto* peace policy (1948)

By mid-1948, with the US gradually removing or progressively relaxing many restrictions and controls on Japan, the Japanese government judged that it was possible to put the country on a *de facto* peace footing even before a peace treaty was signed. They noticed the great importance that the US placed upon Japan. Based on this judgment, the Japanese government studied the cases of other nations which had restored relations to their pre-war state before signing peace treaties. From studying the cases of Italy (peace treaty effective on September 15, 1947), three Balkan countries (Romania, Bulgaria, and Hungary: peace treaty effective on September 15, 1947), and Austria (peace treaty effective on July 18, 1946), they deemed that they could establish diplomatic relations, exchange ambassadors, resume trade, and join international organizations even before signing a

---

49   "Current Status of the Proposal for the Convening of a Preliminary Conference on Japanese Peace" (Dec. 1947, Treaties Section, Treaties Bureau), Ministry of Foreign Affairs of Japan, 2006, *Ibid.*, pp. 328-344.

peace treaty.[50] Especially with regard to their relations with the US, they predicted that a *"de facto* peace" and a "partial peace" would be possible before a peace treaty was in place. Japan foresaw a possibility to patch things up by declaring that it was no longer in a state of war even without a formal peace treaty.

More specifically, the Japanese Foreign Ministry saw that partial restoration of sovereignty and restoration of diplomatic rights would be achievable. Once diplomatic rights were restored, they expected that the rights to conclude treaties, participate in international meetings, negotiate trade terms, dispatch and receive diplomatic delegations and consuls, and do other such things would be granted. Japan determined that the longer the convening of a peace conference was delayed, the wider the scope would become of *de facto* peace. Similarly, the sooner the conference was held, the narrower the scope would be.[51]

The Foreign Ministry organized research data on *de facto* peace into the areas of diplomacy, trade and navigation, and domestic affairs in December 1948.[52] This *de facto* peace was realized when the US allowed in February 1950 the establishment of Japanese government offices in four American cities: New York, San Francisco, Los Angeles, and Honolulu. By May 1951, the Japanese government was allowed to open government offices in Washington, DC, Sweden, France, the Netherlands, Belgium, Uruguay, Pakistan, Thailand, Burma, Peru, Mexico, Canada, the UK, Brazil, Indonesia, India, and other places.[53]

Into 1948, the relationship between the Japanese government and SCAP became closer and more amicable. According to the 1948 activity report by the Review Department, it held a total of 82 meetings about 22 research subjects in which the Foreign Ministry and relevant ministries participated

---

50   *Ibid.*, pp. 363-368.

51   *Ibid.*, pp. 370-375.

52   "About Inquiries into the Details of 'de Facto Peace'" (Dec. 25, 1948), Ministry of Foreign Affairs of Japan, 2006, *Japanese Diplomatic Documents: Preparations for the San Francisco Peace Treaty*, pp. 376-384.

53   Shimoda, *Sengo Nihon Gaiko No Shogen*, p. 45.

throughout the year. The papers produced from those meetings were delivered to the Diplomatic Section of SCAP.[54]

In 1949, the Foreign Ministry established a Policy Review Committee within the Ministry to review and coordinate the highest-level policies (January 27, 1949).[55]

The greatest interest of the Foreign Ministry beginning in late 1948 was how Japan could assure its security after a peace treaty with no army and no right of belligerency under Article 9 of the Peace Constitution. In 1949, the Ministry considered different ways to assure this security including a ① declaration of permanent neutrality; ② conclusion of a treaty of alliance with a specific country, and ③ establishment of an organization to mutually guarantee security.[56] A Foreign Ministry manager looked into the possibility of Japan's neutrality and concluded that it would be difficult to maintain wartime neutrality, and if US troops withdrew from Japan and Japan desired neutrality, the Soviet Union would not let it remain neutral.[57] There was a notion that, even if Japan became neutral on the surface, it would need to make domestic preparations to eventually choose a specific side or country.

5) Choice of a "separate peace" and "majority peace" (1949~1950)

Into the latter half of 1949, new prospects for a peace conference were raised. As agreement between the US and the USSR was delayed on the procedures for a peace treaty with Japan, the possibility of a separate peace opened up. Under this separate peace, Japan would restore relations with

---

54　"Review Department Activity Report for the 23rd Year of Showa," Ministry of Foreign Affairs of Japan, 2006, *Japanese Diplomatic Documents: Preparations for the San Francisco Peace Treaty*, pp. 384-386.

55　"Composition of the Policy Review Committee (draft)" (Feb. 2, 1949), Ministry of Foreign Affairs of Japan, 2006, *Ibid.*, p. 394.

56　"Observations on Ways to Assure Japan's Security" (May 1949, Legal Studies Section, Treaties Bureau), Ministry of Foreign Affairs of Japan, 2006, *Ibid.*, p. 396.

57　"Observations on Japan's Neutrality" (Jun. 2, 1949, manager Usiroku), Ministry of Foreign Affairs of Japan, 2006, *Ibid.*, pp. 399-403.

some countries, which would include the US and the UK, but technically remain at war with others, including the USSR and Communist China.[58] The Allied Powers had agreed to separately negotiate neither ceasefires nor peace treaties with enemies through the UN Declaration of January 1, 1942. In addition, by signing the Declaration of the Four Nations on General Security on October 30, 1943, the US, the UK, the USSR, and China promised to act in unison regarding the surrender and disarmament of common enemies. However, with escalation of the Cold War, the possibility of a separate peace that excluded the USSR was raised and Japan examined various possibilities where such a thing might be realized, indeed highly likely, especially in consideration of the internal condition of the US attitude toward Japan rapidly taking an amicable turn and the external condition of continually worsening US-USSR relations. Its conclusion was that, when a separate peace was in place, the US forces would inevitably be stationed in Japan for the long term, and therefore the issue of security assurance for Japan would come into question. Furthermore, the USSR would exercise its veto to object to Japan joining the UN and Japan would therefore not be able to declare itself a neutral nation. As such, US forces should remain on Japanese soil to protect the country, and though there existed concerns over the negative consequences, such as erosion of the Japanese sense of independence due to the prolonged presence of US forces, this was better than an everlasting occupation.[59]

The Japanese government believed that if a separate peace excluded the USSR and other such parties, it would not be an overall peace but a majority peace led by the US and the UK, both of whom advocated peace with Japan, and began examining the pros and cons, including security assurances (the most important to Japan), economic issues, and other relevant matters. Emphasis was placed on the US commitment to Japan's security and much more was involved than just a peace treaty: it was more

---

58 "The Possibility of a Separate Peace and Its Gains and Losses" (Sept. 24, 1949), Ministry of Foreign Affairs of Japan, 2006, *Ibid.*, p. 406.
59 *Ibid.*, pp. 412-414.

about building a bilateral military relationship with the US and having it provide such a guarantee.

A Foreign Ministry document written in December 1949 stated that if a majority peace was forthcoming, the stationing of foreign forces and military installations within Japanese territory should be avoided if possible, and if that was inevitable, they should be located on outlying islands, not the Japanese mainland. If that was also implausible, then the period of them being stationed on the mainland should be limited. Any foreign force deployment should be limited to US forces and allowed only for a short period.[60] Another document pointed out that Japan should make known to the outside world that it was completely disarmed and had no choice but to rely on the US for defense. It also agreed with the former document in that the stationing of US troops on the Japanese mainland should be avoided as far as possible and their presence limited to the outlying islands. If stationing on the mainland was inevitable, it should be limited to a minimum of different locations, and the details of any US military presence strictly defined in a treaty.[61]

The Foreign Ministry completed research on a peace treaty as it related to different subjects on December 10, 1949. Discussion once again put the highest priority on Japan's security and pointed out that whether foreign troops were stationed on the mainland or outlying islands did not make much difference in the eyes of the law but it actually exerted considerable influence on domestic politics.

The disputes between an overall peace and separate peace continued in Japan. Prime Minister Yoshida accused Shigeru Nanbara, President of Tokyo University who advocated an overall peace, of sophistry and published a statement on June 1, 1950 arguing that a separate peace would be signed first and peace would gradually be restored at a later date with

---

60 "Basic Policy on Security Assurance in Case of a Majority Peace" (Dec. 3, 1949), Ministry of Foreign Affairs of Japan, 2006, *Japanese Diplomatic Documents: Preparations for the San Francisco Peace Treaty*, pp. 441-442.

61 "Statement on Security Assurance" (Dec. 8, 1949), Ministry of Foreign Affairs of Japan, 2006, *Ibid.*, pp. 445-446.

countries which did not participate in the separate peace now. A separate peace was closely related to Japan's intention to overlook its invasion of China and colonial rule of Korea and other nations.[62]

In May 1950, John Foster Dulles was appointed US special envoy to the Treaty of Peace with Japan. Shortly thereafter, the Korean War broke out, putting things in motion for the convening of a peace conference. In August 1950, the Japanese Foreign Ministry predicted the possibility of a bilateral separate peace, which meant Japan concluding a separate peace with individual countries. This could be either with each former Allied Power concluding a prearranged treaty of the same content with Japan and ending the formal state of war (a formal bilateral separate peace) or each Ally individually working out a practical treaty with Japan with no prearrangement on conditions (a practical bilateral separate peace). The Japanese government predicted that a series of formal bilateral separate peace treaties would actually have the same results as a majority peace in reality while the former could result in harsher conditions being placed on Japan than the latter, keeping the nation in an extremely unstable state until the final treaty was concluded with the last remaining Ally. As such, formal bilateral separate peace treaties had to be avoided at all costs.[63]

The final position of the Japanese government was defined in the final version of "Outline of a Hypothesis on a Peace Treaty with Japan" in September 1950. This systematically brought together the government's official position on a peace treaty and would be used as the basis for negotiations with the Dulles delegation in 1951. This classified document was first drafted in March 1950 and completed after reference to Italy's peace treaty. It consisted of one preamble and six chapters of territorial, political, military, and economic clauses, guarantee of treaty implementation, and assurance of security. The document deserves special mention for several

---

62   Akira Fujiwara, Shoji Arakawa, Hirofumi Hayashi, 1993, *Modern Japanese History (1945-1992)*, translated by No Gil-ho, Guwol, p. 90.

63   "Observations on Bilateral Separate Peace Treaties" (Aug. 29, 1950), Ministry of Foreign Affairs of Japan, 2006, *Japanese Diplomatic Documents: Preparations for the San Francisco Peace Treaty*, pp. 515-519.

reasons.

Based on Italy's peace treaty, the Japanese government reckoned that in the preamble a Japanese peace treaty would state the fact that Japan had concluded a Tripartite Pact with Germany and Italy, started the wars of aggression, and thereby shared war responsibility and that it surrendered unconditionally and signed an instrument of surrender. However, the eventual Treaty of Peace with Japan mentioned neither remorse for wartime aggression nor responsibility for Japan's part of that aggression.

Regarding territorial clauses, the document stipulated that Japan would ① return Formosa and the Pescadores to China; ② return the southern part of Sakhalin and transfer the Kurils to the USSR; ③ relinquish its claim to Joseon; and ④ return the Kwantung Leased Territory to China.[64] The ethnic Korean residents in Japan would become Joseon nationals with the independence of their home country.

Regarding compensation, it mentioned ① domestic facilities, ② current production, and ③ overseas properties. The first was about dismantling domestic facilities to come up with resources for compensation and was part of the so-called interim reparations program. The second was also mentioned in Italy's peace treaty and the Basic Post-Surrender Policy for Japan and the Japanese thought that they might be able to avoid this kind of compensation depending on where the US stood. The third was Japan's abandonment of claims, which included ① abandonment of all claims to the Allied Powers arising from the war; ② the Japanese government being charged with fairly compensating specific claims made for individuals' losses due to the waiver of claims; ③ waiver of claims to the Allies which severed diplomatic relations with Japan; and ④ waiver of claims to Germany and Italy.[65]

As seen above, the Japanese government completed preparations for a peace treaty in the latter half of 1950, a process which it had embarked

---

64 "Outline of a Hypothesis on a Peace Treaty with Japan" (Sept. 1950), Ministry of Foreign Affairs of Japan, 2006, *Ibid.*, pp. 519-521.
65 *Ibid.*, pp. 526-527.

on in late 1945. With thorough preparations completed, what remained were negotiations with the Allies, and with the US in particular. When Japan began the preparation process in 1945, it expected a severe punitive treaty, but as the US-Soviet confrontation intensified from 1947, a change in policy on Japan became obvious, and with the reverse course policy in 1948, Japan came to consider a *de facto* peace and a separate peace. Finally, with the outbreak of the Korean War in 1950, the conclusion of a bilateral separate peace became imminent and the Japanese government came up with the "Outline" document.

2

Japan's Preparation and Lobbying on Territorial Issues

1) The Japanese Foreign Ministry's preparations on territorial issues

Once in place, the Executive Committee for Research on a Peace Treaty conducted its research in the three areas of general, political, and economic issues, with the focus of political issues placed on territorial issues. By January 26, 1946, the Executive Committee figured out the Allies' general principles on territorial issues: the Allies declared that they had no intention of seeking expansion of their own territory in the Atlantic Charter, Potsdam Declaration, and Cairo Declaration on which their actions were based. The committee encouraged Japan to use this principle to its advantage. Japan had accepted that there was nothing they could do about the decisions made in the Potsdam Declaration and Cairo Declaration to limit Japanese territory to the islands of Honshu, Hokkaido, Kyushu, Shikoku and minor islands; strip Japan of all its former islands in the Pacific; and oblige it to return Manchuria, Formosa, and the Pescadores to China, withdraw from occupied territories, and free Joseon. What mattered was how to secure minor islands so that the Allies would determine they belong to Japan. What concerned the Japanese Foreign Ministry in early January 1946 were the cession of the Kurils (Chishima) and Southern Sakhalin (Minami-Karafuto) to the USSR and the recognition of China's sovereignty over the Ryukyu Islands. The Ministry argued that there was no absolute need to cede the Kuril Islands and Southern Sakhalin to the USSR, and even if China's sovereignty over the Ryukyu Islands was to be recognized, it should be done so through a popular vote or other such measures. And the US should be allowed to use a military base on the main island of Okinawa only when it was recognized by the US as Japanese territory.[66]

"Territorial Clauses" (draft proposal, Political Bureau) submitted by the Executive Committee on January 31, 1946 was the first report resulting from Japan's peace treaty preparations and offered a comprehensive view of territorial issues. According to this document, the Allies' thoughts on Japanese territory could be seen in the Cairo Declaration (December 1943), Potsdam Declaration (July 1945), and General of the Army Douglas MacArthur's Instruction to his Commands Concerning the Basic Purpose of the Allied Occupation of Japan and the Manners in which They Are Carried Out by the Allied Forces (December 19, 1945) as follows:

- **Cairo Declaration:** ① Japan shall be stripped of all the islands in the Pacific which she has seized or occupied since the beginning of the First World War in 1914; ② all the territories Japan has stolen from the Chinese, such as Manchuria, Formosa, and the Pescadores, shall be restored to the Republic of China, and ③ Japan will also be expelled from all other territories which she has taken by violence and greed.
- **Potsdam Declaration (Paragraph 8):** The terms of the Cairo Declaration shall be carried out and Japanese sovereignty shall be limited to the islands of Honshu, Hokkaido, Kyushu, Shikoku and such minor islands as we shall determine.
- **General of the Army Douglas MacArthur's Instruction:** Japanese sover-eignty shall be limited to the islands of Honshu, Hokkaido, Kyushu, Shikoku and some 1,000 nearby, minor islands including Tsushima.[67]

Accordingly, the Foreign Ministry expected three main territorial issues. The first was that US military bases would be set up on the Ryukyu Islands, Bonin Islands (Ogasawara Islands), and Volcano Islands (Kazan Retto),

---

66 "Comparison and Analysis of the Allied Powers' Presumable Proposals and Japan's Own Desired Outcomes" (Jan. 26, 1946), Ministry of Foreign Affairs of Japan, 2006, *Japanese Diplomatic Documents: Preparations for the San Francisco Peace Treaty*, p. 19.
67 "Territorial Clauses" (Jan. 31, 1946), Ministry of Foreign Affairs of Japan, 2006, *Ibid.*, pp. 46-47.

while it argued that the issue of where the Ryukyu Islands belonged should be decided by referendum. The second was that the reversion of Southern Sakhalin and the Kuril Islands was not dealt with in the Cairo Declaration and Potsdam Declaration. However, according to the announcement by US Secretary of State James F. Byrnes (January 29, 1946) about the Yalta secret agreement that decided the fate of these islands, the US, the UK, and the USSR agreed that they would be part of Soviet territory, and this would be confirmed in a peace treaty with Japan. The third issue was that it would lose such territories as Joseon (which would become independent), Formosa, the Pescadores, and Manchuria (which would be returned to China), Southern Sakhalin and the Kuril Islands (which would revert to the USSR), mandated territories (which would be placed under UN trusteeship and the Mariana Islands under US trusteeship), and occupied territories (already reverted to their previous status).[68]

The Ministry wrote that, in accordance with international treaties, if the title to even those areas acquired by Japan by lawful means was questioned from a historical and geographical view, such issues should be decided through a popular vote, and once Japan's territory was defined in a peace treaty, the Japanese residents in the areas to be ceded should be given rights to sell real estate and take out their movable assets.[69] In a nutshell, regarding territorial issues, the Ministry focused on "securing important minor islands (especially from geographic, historical, and ethnic perspectives)" as Japanese territory was defined as the four major islands and nearby minor islands in the Cairo Declaration and Potsdam Declaration as of late January 1946.[70]

The Executive Committee's first report was distributed to the relevant ministries in May 1946. Part of the report, "Expected Political Clauses in

---

68   *Ibid.*, pp. 47-48.

69   *Ibid.*, pp. 48-49.

70   "Study to Produce a Basic Policy on a Peace Treaty and Comparison of the Allied Powers' Proposals and Japan's Own Desired Outcomes" (Feb. 1, 1946), Ministry of Foreign Affairs of Japan, 2006, *Japanese Diplomatic Documents: Preparations for the San Francisco Peace Treaty*, pp. 74-75.

a Peace Treaty and Countermeasures for Possible Discrepancies (draft) (Peace Treaty Research for Political Clauses-1)" contained principles regarding the favorable resolution of territorial issues as follows:

① **Fair reversion of territories:** The Allied Powers repeatedly declared that they had no intention of seeking the expansion of their own territory (Paragraph 1 of the Atlantic Charter, Cairo Declaration, and Navy Day address by the US President in 1945), and the Potsdam Declaration stated they did not intend that the Japanese should be enslaved as a race or destroyed as a nation. As such, efforts should be made for fair resolution.

② **Nearby minor islands:** Maximum efforts should be made to expand the scope of nearby minor islands to be determined by the Allies to be Japanese territory based on geographic, historical, economic, and ethnic grounds. Regarding the January 29, 1946 memorandum, "Governmental and Administrative Separation of Certain Outlying Areas from Japan," authoritative scientific materials should be used to offer valid reasons why Amami Oshima and Izu Oshima belong to Japan historically, geographically, and ethnically.

③ **Ryukyu Islands:** The odds are high that the Ryukyu Islands will be placed under joint trusteeship by the Allies or exclusive US trusteeship and quite low that it will fall in the hands of the Republic of China. We cannot oppose the former, and in the case of the latter, we should strongly argue against it, and if necessary, refer the issue to a popular vote. Okinawa Island is expected to be designated by the US as a strategic area of a trust territory under Article 82 of the UN Charter and Japan will not be able to oppose it.

④ **Southern Sakhalin and Kuril Islands:** The Yalta Conference included a secret agreement that handed over the Kurils to the Soviet Union but Japan is not bound by the agreement. Japan is to relinquish its sovereignty over Southern Sakhalin by having accepted the Potsdam Declaration, but according to the principle not to recognize territories seized through war, further research should be made to determine the ownership of these areas through a popular vote and certain other just conditions.

⑤ **Iwo Jima:** It is expected to be designated by the US as a strategic area of a trust territory as in the case of Okinawa and, similarly, Japan will not be able to oppose it.

⑥ **Joseon and Formosa:** The independence of Joseon and return of Formosa to China is approved and there should be regulations in place on security assurance for Joseon.[71]

According to the above, Japan's most significant interest was its ownership of nearby minor islands to be determined by the Allies – namely Amami Oshima, Izu Oshima, the Ryukyu Islands (and Okinawa), Southern Sakhalin, the Kurils, Iwo Jima, Joseon, and Formosa. After the Executive Committee's first report (May 1946) was released, the Japanese Foreign Ministry produced pamphlets on the small islands in the seas adjacent to Japan and widely distributed them to the Allies.

According to the Executive Committee's second work plan, it was to complete a second round of research by the end of June, 1946, which included "Study on Territorial Clauses" (Peace Treaty Research for Political Clauses-3)[72]. The content of this document is unknown.

The Japanese government provided peace treaty research papers drawn up by the Foreign Ministry to the US and Australia by the beginning of July 1947 and summarized its desires into a draft request consisting of nine items on July 24 to be submitted to Atcheson. Its seventh paragraph was about territorial issues.[73] It reads, "The Potsdam Declaration stipulated that the Allies will determine which minor islands in the vicinity of Japan belong to Japan. Regarding this decision, Japan wishes that sufficient consideration should be placed on the close historical, ethnic, economic and cultural relations between these small islands and mainland Japan."

---

71 "Expected Political Clauses in a Peace Treaty and Countermeasures for Possible Discrepancies (draft) (Peace Treaty Research for Political Clauses-1)" (May 1946), Ministry of Foreign Affairs of Japan, 2006, *Ibid.*, pp. 95-96.

72 "Second Work Plan of the Executive Committee for Research on a Peace Treaty" (May 22, 1946), Ministry of Foreign Affairs of Japan, 2006, *Ibid.*, pp. 114-115.

73 "Plan for Talks with Ambassador Atcheson" (Jul. 24, 1947), Ministry of Foreign Affairs of Japan, 2006, *Ibid.*, pp. 245-247.

The Foreign Ministry's attempt to contact the Diplomatic Section and Government Section of SCAP and other such parties between June and July of 1947, which was then known as the Ashida Initiative, failed and the document was returned. Nevertheless, according to Takeso Shimoda, it was clear that the Ashida document had a considerable impact on the drafting of a peace treaty by the US.[74] Both Shigeru Yoshida and Takeso Shimoda agreed that if a peace treaty had been signed shortly after the end of the war, the Allies would have placed harsh conditions on Japan amid strong antipathy and hostility towards it, and therefore, the delayed convening of a peace conference turned out to be "beneficial to Japan."[75] Yoshida further remarked that the duration of the occupation period where Japanese officials were in daily contact with their Allied counterparts was, in fact, a *de facto* peace treaty negotiation process. The Japanese government always placed a priority on contacts with Allied officials and frequently met the leading members of SCAP in a non-official capacity so that they could gain a better understanding of Japan. They also met the leaders of the public and private sectors from the US and other nations whenever they visited to inform them about Japan's situation. These efforts had a profound impact.[76]

The Foreign Ministry delegated work related to a peace treaty on November 12, 1949, with Shimoda the point of contact for "Opinions on Territorial Issues" and the team including director Miyake, Usiroku, Haga, and Matsui, and deputy director Heda.[77] In late December 1949, the publications "Tsushima" and "Treatment of Japanese Nationals Overseas" were submitted to the US Department of State (DoS). "Tsushima" must have been related to Korea's strong claim of sovereignty over Tsushima

---

74   Shimoda, *Sengo Nihon Gaiko No Shogen*, p. 57.

75   Shimoda, *Sengo Nihon Gaiko No Shogen*, p. 57; Shigeru Yoshida, 1958, *Kaiso Junen*, Vol. 3, Tokyo, Shinchosha, p. 23.

76   Yoshida, *Kaiso Junen*, Vol. 3, pp. 23-24.

77   "Assignment of Work on a Peace Treaty" (Nov. 12, 1949), Ministry of Foreign Affairs of Japan, 2006, *Japanese Diplomatic Documents: Preparations for the San Francisco Peace Treaty*, pp. 453-454.

made at that time. It is said that a Foreign Ministry meeting reviewed "Special Statement on Territorial Issues" but its content is not known.[78] The Japanese government's final position on a peace treaty is defined in the aforementioned "Outline of a Hypothesis on a Peace Treaty" written in September 1950.[79]

In October 1950, the Japanese government wrote "Statement to the US (draft)" regarding its negotiations with the US to clarify its position on territorial issues: it first declared that Japan had conformed to the principles of the Atlantic Charter and was therefore fully willing to surrender its title to Formosa and the Pescadores, free Joseon, and give up its mandate over the South Sea Islands. On the other hand, it contended that it should be allowed to retain islands which had always been historically and ethnically Japanese territory because they were not seized through war by Japan but had been part of Japanese territory continuously for a long time. The islands listed by the Foreign Ministry were as follows:

- **Kuril Islands:** We do not understand why we are required to hand over the Kurils in addition to Southern Sakhalin.
- **Habomai Islands, Shikotan:** We naturally expect the restoration of the Habomai Islands and Shikotan currently unduly occupied by the Soviet Union.
- **Nansei Islands, Bonin Islands, and Iwo Jima:** We wish to hold onto possession of the Nansei Islands, Bonin Islands and Iwo Jima that are currently outside Japan's administrative jurisdiction and under US occupation. We also would like to add that, if the US needs to use these islands, we are willing to accept their request.[80]

---

78 "Peace Treaty Work" (Dec. 28, 1949), Ministry of Foreign Affairs of Japan, 2006, *Ibid.*, pp. 441-453.

79 "Outline of a Hypothesis on a Peace Treaty" (Sept. 1950), Ministry of Foreign Affairs of Japan, 2006, *Ibid.*, pp. 519-521.

80 "Statement to the US (draft)" (Oct. 4, 1950), Ministry of Foreign Affairs of Japan, 2007, *Japanese Diplomatic Documents: Negotiations with the US for the San Francisco Peace Treaty*, pp. 25-26.

From the above, it is apparent that Japan took a very hard-line stance on the Kuril Islands, Habomai Islands, and Shikotan. The Japanese Foreign Ministry put Japan's position as follows: "These islands are very small in terms of area. So small that the Allies might think it is absurd for us to seek so strongly to retain them. However, it is difficult for the Japanese to be deprived of even a small part of the homeland when we are losing all our overseas territories. These islands also now are of economic importance that is disproportionate to their area."[81]

The draft "Statement to the US" was written to negotiate with the US regarding a peace treaty and dealt with territorial, political, military, and economic issues in this order, with the greatest focus placed on territorial issues. This document summarized territorial issues and minutely described Japanese sovereignty over the above-mentioned islands. The order the islands appeared in within the document can be thought of as the degree of importance the Japanese government placed on them being included in Japanese territory.

2) Were there lobbying activities for territorial interests?

There was suspicion over Japan's lobbying of the US regarding territorial issues through the Japanese Foreign Ministry's long preparatory process for a peace treaty. This suspicion only intensified as SCAP, POLAD, and other on-site Allied officials became very friendly toward Japan. Against the backdrop of the aggravation of the Cold War in Europe and the communization of China in Asia, Japan's strategic importance heightened and peace negotiations were moving in a direction to grant the defeated Japan the right to negotiate, which was unprecedented in the world's history of diplomacy. For their part, the Japanese did everything in their power to produce an outcome that favored Japan's interests as much as possible. In this regard, let us look at the recollections of the Japanese government's key figures at the time.

---

81   *Ibid.*, p. 26.

The first recollections of note are those of Shigeru Yoshida, who served as Prime Minister of Japan from 1946 to 1947 and from 1948 to 1954. Yoshida recalled: "I believed that something had to be done during the process of drafting a treaty to ensure favorable consideration for Japan. I gave considerable thought to ensuring that the Allies did not wrongly and overly interpret the scope of "territories which Japan had taken by violence and greed" indicated in the Potsdam Declaration. We produced an enormous amount of data on territorial issues alone, which constituted seven volumes."[82]

According to Yoshida, the preparation of general papers in English to help the Allies to better understand Japan's situation at the time started as early as 1947, and "Japan's Status Quo (Economy)" and "Japan's Status Quo (Politics)" were produced. They were written based on the expectation that the US would represent Japan's interests, and over time, were revised and updated. In this regard, the Japanese needed to provide the US with sufficient references. The work targeted the US government, which was less informed about Japan's situation than SCAP. Yoshida remarked that, unlike other Allies which continued to distrust Japan, the US well understood Japan's situation through the occupation and was most sympathetic to its demands and wishes. When they returned back home, American soldiers gave favorable reports about Japan and its people, and as the Americans were inherently generous and well-intentioned, Japan chose the US as the champion of its interests, according to Yoshida.[83]

Yoshida pointed out that the greatest focus in the peace treaty preparations was on territorial issues. The references for the US government gave a detailed account of how indivisible Japan was from such territories as Okinawa, the Bonin Islands, Hokkaido, and the Kuril Islands from the

---

82 Yoshida, 1958, *Kaiso Junen*, Vol. 3. Re-quoted by Lee Jong-hak. According to the website of the Japanese Foreign Ministry (http://gaikokiroku.mofa.go.jp/mon/mon_b.html), *Research on a Peace Treaty*, written by the Executive Committee for Research on a Peace Treaty, had a total of seven volumes. Additionally, a number of other documents are publicly available.
83 Yoshida, *Kaiso Junen*, Vol. 3, pp. 24-25.

perspectives of history, geography, ethnicity, and economy.[84] Yoshida wrote that, from 1948, "(We) produced references that equaled tens of volumes and hundreds of thousands of words covering almost everything related to a peace treaty and submitted them over two years by 1950. By the time the US government started writing draft peace treaties the same year, Japanese-prepared documents had already been delivered to them in sufficient quantity."[85]

Next, let us look at the recollections of Takeso Shimoda, who served as the director of the Treaties Section I of the Foreign Ministry's Treaties Bureau, Executive Secretary of the Executive Committee for Research on a Peace Treaty, and the Executive Secretary of the Review Department.[86] According to Shimoda, SCAP, wary of what the Soviet Union and other Allies might think, was reluctant until 1946 to receive any Japanese-prepared documents relating to a peace treaty. However, with the exacerbating US-Soviet confrontation, "Washington came to see the value of these documents and willingly accepted them in the end."[87]

> I took the role of secretly visiting the office of Ambassador Sebald at the Mitsui head office in the Nihonbashi district in the dead of night and delivered reports several times. In total, dozens of volumes of reports containing hundreds of thousands of words were delivered, covering all aspects of a peace treaty. Accordingly, when the US government later drafted the peace treaty, they were in possession of these materials and used them as references.[88] (underlined by the quoter)

Shimoda's recollection of visiting Sebald's office "in the dead of night" and delivering reports over several occasions reveals the abnormal and secretive relations between Sebald and the Japanese Foreign Ministry. As

---

84   Yoshida, *Kaiso Junen*, Vol. 3, pp. 25-26, 60-70.

85   Yoshida, *Kaiso Junen*, Vol. 3, p. 26.

86   Yoshida, *Kaiso Junen*, Vol. 3, p. 26.

87   Shimoda, *Sengo Nihon Gaiko No Shogen*, p. 54.

88   *Ibid.*

[Table 2-1] 36 Volumes of References in English Forwarded to the US Department of State by the Japanese Ministry of Foreign Affairs

Classification		Title	Publication date
1. General issues		1. Japan's status quo (politics)	Feb. 1950
		2. Japan's status quo (economy)	Dec. 1949
2. Territorial issues		1. Kuril Islands, Habomai Islands, and Shikotan	Nov. 1946
		2. Southern Kurils, Habomai Islands, and Shikotan	Apr. 1949
		3. Sakhalin	Jan. 1949
		4. Ryukyu Islands and Nansei Islands	Mar. 1947
		5. Bonin Islands and Volcano Islands	Jun. 1947
		6. Minor islands in the Pacific and in the Sea of Japan	Jun. 1947
		7. Tsushima	Jun. 1949
3. Political issues		1. Law and jurisdiction	Feb. 1948
		2. Japanese nationals in the territories to be separated from Japan and foreigners who originated from those territories and reside in Japan	Feb. 1948
		3. Japan's police system	Jun. 1948
		4. Status of ethnic Koreans in Japan	Jun. 1950
		5. Japan and international treaties	Mar. 1949
		6. Treatment of Japanese nationals overseas	Oct. 1949
4. Economic issues	A. Related to the future	1. Minimum quality of life for the Japanese people	Aug. 1948
		2. Actual quality of life in Japan	Dec. 1947
		3. Attachment to the above No. 2	Dec. 1947
		4. Fisheries	Jan. 1948
		5. Japan's shipping industry	Mar. 1948
		6. Japan's civil aviation	Jan. 1948

		7. Japan's population	Jun. 1948
		8. Japan's whale hunting	Jan. 1949
		9. Damage Japan suffered in the Pacific War (Attachment: damage by atomic bombs)	Apr. 1949
	B. Related to the existing claims	1. Japan's overseas debts and Japan's claims and obligations in the territories to be separated from Japan	Jun. 1948
		2. Status of rooted property	Sept. 1948
		3. Occupation costs	Jul. 1948
		4. Industrial property	Oct. 1948
		5. Foreigners' copyright	Apr. 1948
		6. Capture and inspection	Feb. 1949
		7. Allied property in Japan	Sept. 1950
		8. Reparations	May 1950
5. Special issues		1. Submarine cable	May 1948
		2. Weather and oceanographic observation in Japan	May 1948
		3. Narcotics	Feb. 1950

[Source] Kumao Nishimura, 1971, *Japan's Diplomatic History 27: The Treaty of Peace with Japan*, Kajima Research Institute Press, pp. 45~47.

such, the Ministry continued to deliver its reference materials related to a peace treaty to the head of the Diplomatic Section of SCAP in a clandestine fashion.

Backed by Sebald's favorable responses, Japanese-prepared documents were forwarded to the SCAP Diplomatic Section secretly "in the dead of night" from 1947 or 1948. They were "willingly" received by the US DoS through the SCAP Diplomatic Section in a "sufficient" amount and Washington thought highly of them as references. Though neither Yoshida nor Shimoda mentioned Dokdo in their recollections, the Dokdo issue must have been dealt with in the same manner.

According to Kumao Nishimura, director general of the Treaties Bureau, the Japanese Foreign Ministry forwarded 36 volumes of English references to the US DoS, with seven of them about territorial issues. According to the Ministry's records, there were four different types of territorial references passed to the SCAP Diplomatic Section up until December 1948.[89] They were pamphlets all published by the Ministry and are explained in detail below.

It is understood that these documents were handed over to the SCAP Diplomatic Section by the director general of the Ministry's General Affairs Bureau and then to the US DoS and other relevant departments of SCAP. The officials of the Diplomatic Section gave comments on the documents such as "valuable references" or "the Japanese government's opinions are not clearly indicated."[90]

Richard B. Finn who worked in the SCAP Diplomatic Section and the POLAD office (POLAD—Japan) left a memoir in the same vein. According to Finn, the Japanese Foreign Ministry launched peace treaty preparations right after the occupation began and conducted in-depth research on territorial, compensation, and other issues. The resulting papers were passed on to the US DoS. Finn claimed some of the papers were sent to Washington but there is almost no evidence that policy makers in Washington used them.[91] Still, he clearly admitted that research papers on a peace treaty drawn up by the Japanese Foreign Ministry were delivered to the US DoS.

William Sebald, head of the Diplomatic Section and a political adviser to SCAP, not only served as an intermediary by faithfully passing the Japanese Foreign Ministry's reports on to the US DoS but also voluntarily and

---

89 "Review Department Activity Report for the 23rd Year of Showa", Ministry of Foreign Affairs of Japan, 2006, *Japanese Diplomatic Documents: Preparations for the San Francisco Peace Treaty*, pp. 384-386.

90 "Review Department Activity Report for the 23rd Year of Showa", Ministry of Foreign Affairs of Japan, 2006, *Ibid.*, p. 386.

91 Richard B. Finn, *Winners in Peace: MacArthur, Yoshida and Postwar Japan*, University of California Press, Berkeley and Los Angeles, California, 1992, p. 246.

actively represented Japan's voice on the side of the Japanese government. He "earnestly persuaded" his subordinates to meet as many Japanese as possible, particularly high-ranking government officials, professors, businessmen, and even those who had been purged by SCAP. Sebald explained the purpose of these contacts to "secure constant communication with Japanese leaders in all areas to a very practical degree" and wrote about the relaxation of restrictions on holding diplomatic parties and contacting the Japanese Prime Minister and cabinet officials on a frequent basis by mid-December 1948.[92]

Koichiro Asakai, chief of the General Affairs Department of the Central Liaison Office, was the point of contact between SCAP and the Japanese government. In his book, published in 1950, he wrote that he "feels reassured that Japan is being continuously introduced" by public figures across the US despite the lack of diplomatic relations between the two countries and confidently stated that this was an "invisible yet great asset." Asakai asserted that the US would side with Japan if Japan were to stand before the UN due to an international dispute with another country after its independence. He cited as an example a hypothetical lecture held in the US with representatives from Japan and another nation where the other nation's representative mentions Japan's past atrocities and criticizes its present errant behavior. He predicted that in such a case someone in the audience would stand up and talk about time spent in Japan as part of the occupation forces for three years and how the Japanese were not like that, criticizing the accuser and strongly defending Japan. Asakai argued that, "through tactful cooperation with the occupation forces by both the high and low-ranking officials of the Japanese government, Japan acquired many valuable friends within the US." Factoring in that this book was published even before the conclusion of a peace treaty, the level of confidence Japan felt about its friendship with the US is readily apparent.[93]

---

92   *Sebald, With MacArthur in Japan*, pp. 66-69.

93   Koichiro Asakai, 1950, *Gaiko No Reimei (Dawn of Diplomacy)*, Yomiuri Shimbun, pp. 185-186.

The documents currently available to researchers show no evidence of the Japanese government, the Foreign Ministry in particular, lobbying the SCAP Diplomatic Section and the US DoS on the Dokdo issue alone. The Foreign Ministry produced a pamphlet that contained false information on Dokdo in June 1947 as part of a series of propaganda efforts, which the SCAP Diplomatic Section and POLAD-Japan accepted as true. Along with trust in the Japanese Foreign Ministry, pro-Japanese sentiment demonstrated by the US diplomats and officials in Japan, close and everyday contact and relations between the Ministry and the SCAP Diplomatic Section, this false document was believed to be true, and it was used in decisions made afterwards by the SCAP Diplomatic Section on the Dokdo issue. As such, the Dokdo issue, though not specifically targeted, was understood and determined in the broader context of the cozy relations between the Japanese Foreign Ministry and the SCAP Diplomatic Section and POLAD-Japan.

With the US taking a reverse course policy with Japan in 1948 and outbreak of the Korean War in 1950, an early peace and rearmament of Japan became inevitable. With the appointment of Dulles as a special envoy to the Treaty of Peace with Japan in 1950, movements for an early peace such as the announcement of the Seven Principles of the Treaty with Japan gained full momentum. The pro-Japanese stance became fully exposed.

The written testimonies by Shigeru Yoshida, Takeso Shimoda, Richard Finn, William Sebald, and more are sufficient evidence of Japan's strong lobbying efforts with the Allies and the US with regard to territorial issues. The Japanese Foreign Ministry produced massive amounts of materials on these issues according to their selective priorities and was able to provide them to the US DoS through the SCAP Diplomatic Section. As confirmed by Shigeru Yoshida, Japan turned the US into Japan's mouthpiece through everyday contact, and furthermore, into a practical channel that reflected Japan's interests. The officials of the SCAP Diplomatic Section, including its head, Sebald, and the US DoS officials of POLAD-Japan, were sympathetic to Japan's concerns and demands and made active efforts to reflect its interests in policy. The opinions of the Japanese government were regarded as reasonable, there was a stable channel to deliver them to the US DoS, and

American diplomats and officials who relayed them were friendly toward Japan. This is the truth about the diplomatic and lobbying efforts by the Japanese Foreign Ministry from 1947 to 1951 regarding territorial issues.

3
Maneuvering by the Japanese Foreign Ministry in 1947
: Drafting of a Pamphlet to Publicize Dokdo and Ulleungdo as Japanese Territory

1) Publication of the "Minor Islands Adjacent to Japan Proper" series by the Japanese Foreign Ministry

The two most important documents related to Japanese territory were the Cairo Declaration and Potsdam Declaration. The Cairo Declaration (December 1943) talked about three groups of territories which were placed under Japanese rule on different dates and through different ways. The first were the islands in the Pacific which Japan had seized or occupied since the beginning of the First World War in 1914, otherwise known as mandated territory in the South Pacific which used to belong to Germany (the South Sea Islands). The second was all the territories Japan had stolen from the Chinese, such as Manchuria, Formosa, and the Pescadores. The third was all other territories which Japan had taken by violence and greed. As the mandated territory in the South Pacific came under the administration of Japan after the defeat of the German Empire in WWI, it was predicted to be placed under UN or US trusteeship. Among the territories to be returned to China, Manchuria was occupied by the Japanese Kwantung Army after the 1931 Manchurian Incident and Formosa and the Pescadores were occupied right after the First Sino-Japanese War. The third group could be interpreted in different ways and included Korea. To Korea, it was most advantageous to apply the year of 1894 when the First Sino-Japanese War broke out as the starting point of Japanese aggression, which is also the starting point for the resolution of territorial issues between Japan and China, but Japan had a different opinion.

The Potsdam Declaration (July 1945) specifically delimited Japanese sovereignty to the four major islands of Honshu, Hokkaido, Kyushu, and Shikoku and such minor islands as the Allies would determine, and excluded all the colonies and occupied and mandated territories. Also, General of the Army Douglas MacArthur's Instruction of December 19, 1945 specified Japan's minor islands to some 1,000 nearby islands including Tsushima. Accordingly, the Japanese government saw that, at stake in the negotiations with the Allies on territorial issues was which islands would be determined as Japan's minor islands according to the Cairo Declaration and Potsdam Declaration.

The basic stance of the Japanese Foreign Ministry was that Japan was responsible for the Pacific War, but not for what had happened before.[94] Its stance on territorial issues was that it would give up territories acquired in ways that had been recognized as conventional under international law and practices at the time of acquisition and long regarded as Japanese territory by the international community. But it would not accept the international community regarding the mere retention of them by Japan as criminal and separating them from Japan as a punitive measure.[95]

The Japanese Foreign Ministry was obsessed with the fate of the islands to be reverted to Japan. In 1946, it started to produce and distribute to the Allies reference material on the islands, islets, and rocks that it believed should be given to Japan. As far as we know at this time, the Ministry produced a total of four pamphlets about the islands, in a series entitled "Minor Islands Adjacent to Japan Proper" with Part 1 published in November 1946, Parts II and III in March 1947, and Part IV in June 1947.[96] The title was the same throughout the series and the subtitles were the

---

94 Ministry of Foreign Affairs, ed., 2006, *Preparations for the San Francisco Peace Treaty*, p. 183 (Jo Seong-hun, 2008, "The US Strategy toward Japan after World War II and the Dokdo Issue," *Journal of International Area Studies*, Vol. 17, No. 2, p. 46).

95 "Representation of the Economic and Financial Treatment of Ceded Territories" (Dec. 3, 1949), microfilm made public in the seventh round of releases by the Diplomatic Archives of the Ministry of Foreign Affairs of Japan, 1982, *Research on a Peace Treaty*, Vol. 5, pp. 740-742 (Soji Takasaki, 1988, *Kensho Nikkan Kaidan (Verification: Japan-Korean Talks)*, translated by Kim Yeong-jin Cheongsuseowon, pp. 7-8).

96 The Korean translation of the title resembles the Japanese title, Japan's Annexed Islands, instead of the English title, Minor Islands Adjacent to Japan Proper.

[Table 2-2] Minor Islands Adjacent to Japan Proper

	Publication date	Subtitle	Subject islands
Part I	Nov. 1946	The Kurile Islands, the Habomais, and Shikotan	Kurile Islands, Iturup, Kunashiri, Shikotan, Habomai Islands
Part II	Mar. 1947	Ryukyu and Other Nansei Islands	Ryukyu Islands and Nansei Islands
Part III	Mar. 1947	The Bonin Island Group, the Volcano Island Group	Bonin Islands and Volcano Islands
Part IV	Jun. 1947	Minor Islands in the Pacific, Minor Islands in the Japan Sea	Daito Islands, Marcus (Minami-Tori-shima), Parece Vela (Okinotorishima), Dokdo (Liancourt Rocks), Ulleungdo (Dagelet Island)

names of the islands each pamphlet dealt with.

The English names of these pamphlets are as follows:

- Minor Islands Adjacent to Japan Proper, Part I: The Kurile Islands, the Habomais, and Shikotan
- Minor Islands Adjacent to Japan Proper, Part II: Ryukyu and Other Nansei Islands
- Minor Islands Adjacent to Japan Proper, Part III: The Bonin Island Group, the Volcano Island Group
- Minor Islands Adjacent to Japan Proper, Part IV: Minor Islands in the Pacific, Minor Islands in the Japan Sea [97]

However, documents released by the Japanese Foreign Ministry have different Japanese titles for parts I, II, III of the pamphlets:

---

97   Minor Islands Adjacent to Japan Proper, Part I. "The Kurile Islands, the Habomais, and Shikotan," November 1946; Part II. "Ryukyu and Other Nansei Islands," March 1947; Part III. "The Bonin Island Group, the Volcano Island Group," March 1947; Part IV. "Minor Islands in the Pacific, Minor Islands in the Japan Sea," June 1947, RG 84, Foreign Service Posts of the Department of State, Office of the US Political Adviser for Japan-Tokyo, Classified General Correspondence, 1945-49, Box 22.

- **Japan's Annexed Islands, Part I:** The Kurile Islands, the Habomais, and Shikotan; Southern Kurils, Habomai Islands, and Shikotan; and Sakhalin
- **Japan's Annexed Islands, Part II:** Ryukyu and Other Nansei Islands
- **Japan's Annexed Islands, Part III:** The Bonin Island Group, the Volcano Island Group[98]

These pamphlets were published based on the order of priority given by the Japanese Foreign Ministry: the Kuril Islands, the Ryukyu Islands (including Okinawa), the Bonin Islands (Ogasawara Islands) and Iwo Jima (Volcano Islands), and Dokdo and Ulleungdo.

The diplomatic documents released by the Japanese Foreign Ministry do not include these pamphlets. The references used here are found at US NARA. The Japanese government has failed to release not only these pamphlets but also documents about their writers and drafting process. Only the Japanese titles of these English pamphlets can be seen in the diplomatic documents made public so far.

There are two important points to note. First, the Japanese and English titles are different. The English title, "Minor Islands Adjacent to Japan Proper" refers to the small islands close to the four main islands of Japan (of Honshu, Hokkaido, Kyushu, and Shikoku) determined as Japanese territory by the Allies in the Potsdam Declaration. However, the Japanese title appearing in the Foreign Ministry documents is "Japan's Annexed Islands."[99] Namely, the Japanese government specified that all the islands mentioned in the pamphlets were small islands annexed to Japan. While the English title for the Allies seemed to refer to the small islands close to mainland Japan as indicated in the Potsdam Declaration, the Japanese title and the Foreign Ministry's official records declared that the islands of the

---

98   "Statement to the US (draft)" (Oct. 4, 1950), Ministry of Foreign Affairs of Japan, 2007, *Japanese Diplomatic Documents: Negotiations with the US for the San Francisco Peace Treaty*, pp. 24-30. The Japanese titles are as follows: *"日本の附屬小島 I, 千島齒舞及び色丹島," "南千島齒舞及び色丹島," "樺太"; "日本の附屬小島 II, 琉球及び他の南西諸島"; and "日本の附屬小島III, 小笠原及び火山列島."*

99   *Ibid.*, pp. 24-30.

pamphlets were annexed to Japan.

Second, and even more importantly, the Japanese Foreign Ministry included Ulleungdo and Dokdo in this series of pamphlets. The Japanese government wrote a document that clearly stated its policy defining Ulleungdo and Dokdo as Japan's annexed islands and launched a major campaign to convince the Allies of this fallacy. The fact that this pamphlet claims not only Dokdo but also even Ulleungdo as islands annexed to Japan is shocking.

According to POLAD—Japan, these pamphlets were sent to the US Department of State (DoS) through the office on three occasions. They were attached to Despatch No. 844 (February 26, 1947), Despatch No. 1166 (July 14, 1947), and Despatch No. 1296 (September 23, 1947).[100] They were forwarded over three occasions as the first part was published in November 1946, the second and third parts in March 1947, and the fourth part in June 1947. Twenty copies of each pamphlet were sent to the US DoS and the different sections of SCAP also received them: four copies for the Economic and Scientific Section (ESS), four for the Legal Section (LS), one for the Government Section (GS), one for the Natural Resources Section (NR), one for the Commander in Chief (CINC), one for the Civil Intelligence Section (CIS), and more.[101] In consideration of these facts, it is apparent that these pamphlets were distributed not only to SCAP but also to the US DoS in large quantities. The US DoS did not have records on which of its offices received them, but it was confirmed that the Bureau of Far Eastern Affairs, geographers, and others did.

Part I dealt with the Kurils and four islands (Etorofu-to, Kunashiri Shima, Shikotan Shima, and Habomais) north of Sakhalin in which Japan is currently involved in a territorial dispute with Russia. The Japanese Foreign

---

100 United States Political Adviser for Japan, Despatch no. 1296, Subject: Minor Islands Adjacent to Japan (Sept. 23, 1947), RG 84, Office of the US Political Adviser for Japan-Tokyo, Classified General Correspondence, 1945-49, Box 22.

101 Minor Islands Adjacent to Japan Proper, Part I. The Kurile Islands, The Habomais, and Shikotan, Foreign Office, Japanese Government, November 1946, Cover, RG 84, Office of the US Political Adviser for Japan-Tokyo, Classified General Correspondence, 1945-49, Box 22.

Ministry argued that the Northern Kurils north of Urup were peacefully acquired through the 1875 Treaty of Saint Petersburg, while the Southern Kurils had always been Japanese territory, with Japan's sovereignty over them confirmed in the 1855 Treaty of Commerce and Navigation between Japan and Russia (Treaty of Shimoda).

It claimed that although the Yalta Conference stipulated that Southern Sakhalin be returned and the Kurils be handed over to the Soviet Union, if the intent was to restore the state to before the Russo-Japanese War, the return of Southern Sakhalin would suffice and the return of the Kurils, including the Southern Kurils, could not be accepted.

Regarding Shikotan and the Habomai Islands, the Ministry contended that they were not part of the Kurils but an extension of the Nemuro Peninsula which extends from the east coast of Hokkaido, and which were occupied by the Soviets after the war. It went on to claim that they had been part of Nemuro Province since the Tokugawa Shogunate and inhabited by the Japanese and were mentioned neither in the Treaty of Saint Petersburg nor in the Treaty of Shimoda. Under SCAP General Order No. 1 (September 2, 1945), the Japanese forces within Manchuria, Korea north of the 38th parallel, Sakhalin, and the Kurils surrendered to the Commander in Chief of the Soviet Forces in the Far East. According to the Japanese, the Soviet forces in the Kurils seized the opportunity to occupy Shikotan and the Habomai Islands and displaced the Japanese. The Ministry wrote, "We naturally hope that the wrongful '*de facto*' occupation of these islands by the Soviets will not be sanctioned as '*de jure* incorporation.'"[102]

In 1956, the USSR and Japan signed the Soviet-Japanese Joint Declaration and agreed to enter into negotiations after the conclusion of a peace treaty on the return of Shikotan and the Habomai Islands, which are relatively small in size and adjacent to Japanese Sakhalin, and on the reversion of Etorofu and Kunashiri, which are large and contested. These

---

102 "Statement to the US (draft)" (Oct. 4, 1950), Ministry of Foreign Affairs of Japan, 2007, *Japanese Diplomatic Documents: Negotiations with the US for the San Francisco Peace Treaty*, p. 27.

territorial issues remain unresolved to this day.

The Ryukyu Islands of Part II are called Nansei Shoto or Ryukyu Retto in Japanese. They went under US trusteeship after the San Francisco peace treaty. Japan argued that the mission of UN trusteeship was meant to "aid development in areas that are far less civilized like those in Africa" and there was not much need to separate the Ryukyu Islands and place them under trusteeship as they were similar to mainland Japan in terms of politics, economy, social structure, and education. It went on to say that Japan understood that the US placed important military value on these islands and was willing to meet US needs and render full cooperation but there should be a way other than trusteeship.[103] Japan emphasized its sovereignty over Amami Oshima of the Nansei Islands and presented large numbers of Amami Oshima-related petitions during the process leading up to the peace treaty. Amami Oshima was excluded from Japanese administration, but not occupied by the US and returned to Japan in December 1953.[104]

Dealt with in Part III are the Bonin Islands and the Volcano Islands, or Ogasawara and Kazan Retto or Iwo Jima, respectively, in Japanese. Japan argued that the former was incorporated into Japanese territory in 1875 and the latter in 1891. They were placed under US trusteeship and returned to Japan in 1968.

Part IV talked about ① the Daito Islands, ② Marcus Island (Minami-Tori-shima), and ③ Parece Vela Island (Okinotorishima) in (1) Minor Islands in the Pacific; and ① Dokdo (Liancourt Rocks, Takeshima), and ② Ulleungdo (Dagelet Island, Matsushima, Utsuryo, Ullung Island) in (2) Minor Islands in the East Sea (Japan Sea).[105] To the dismay of Koreans, the Japanese Foreign Ministry claimed Dokdo and Ulleungdo as its territory in

---

103 *Ibid.*, pp. 28-30.
104 Yoshida, *Kaiso Junen*, Vol. 3, pp. 66-67.
105 Minor Islands Adjacent to Japan Proper, Part IV, "Minor Islands in the Pacific, Minor Islands in the Japan Sea," June, 1947, RG 84, Foreign Service Posts of the Department of State, Office of the US Political Adviser for Japan-Tokyo, Classified General Correspondence, 1945-49, Box 22.

the official booklet published for the Allies in June 1947.[106]

2) The Japanese Foreign Ministry's announcement of Dokdo and Ulleungdo as Japan's annexed islands

"Minor Islands Adjacent to Japan Proper, Part IV: Minor Islands in the Pacific, Minor Islands in the Japan Sea" has a total of 16 pages (two cover pages, 12 pages of body text, and two pages of maps). Dokdo and Ulleungdo are covered in five pages of body text (pp. 8~12) and two pages of maps. [Figure 2-1] is one of the maps where the Japanese Foreign Ministry marked Ulleungdo and Dokdo as Japanese territory. The East Sea is also marked as the Japan Sea.

Let us look at the Ulleungdo text first. As it is important, it is quoted here at length.

II. Dagelet Island (Matsu–shima, Utsuryo or Ul-lung Island)

1. Geography (omitted)

2. History
It was only in 1878 that the island was first mentioned, by the name of Dagelet, in the world history of discoveries by Captain Jean François de La Pérouse of the French navy. In Japanese documents, however, reference was made as early as 1004 to Uruma Island, an old Japanese equivalent for Ul-lung Island.
The Island was known to Koreans also from ancient times. Several attempts at colonization were made by Koreans after the middle of the 12th century. The island became later a convenient hiding-place by criminals and brigands. The Korean Government from 1400 and onward adhered for a long time to a policy of keeping it uninhabited.
As the island was thus virtually abandoned by the Korean government, the

---

106 Written on the inside cover of this pamphlet is "Information for the Allied Authorities"

Japanese continued to frequent it in increasing numbers. The expedition of TOYOTOMI Hideyoshi to Korea in 1592 served to accelerate activities of the Japanese in this area, and for about a century thereafter the island remained in all appearances a Japanese fishing base.[Note 4: In 1618, the feudal lord of Inaba, under the sanction of the Shogunate, authorized two citizens by the name of Otani (Jinkichi Otani) and Murakawa (Ichibe Murakawa) of Yonago, Hoki Province, to visit Take-shima (viz. Dagelet). They made yearly visits to the island for fishing and some of the abalones thus caught were sent from the Inaba Clan to the Shogunate as an annual present.]

From the beginning of the 17th century repeated negotiations were carried on between Japan and Korea on the question of ownership of the island.

In 1692 the arrival of a large number of Koreans in the island gave rise to a dispute, on which negotiations were conducted between the Korean Government and the feudal lord of Tsushima representing the Shogunate. As a result, in 1697 the Tokugawa Shogunate prohibited the Japanese from going to the island for fishing and informed the Korean Government to that effect. The question was thus apparently settled for the time being.

The Korean authorities, however, made no change in their policy to keep the island uninhabited even after the above mentioned incident. They dispatched officials once in three years to have them cut down trees and bamboos and collect native products to be presented to the government. The Japanese, therefore, never stopped fishing near the island [Note 5: in 1837, a shipping agent by the name of Hachiyemon (Aizuya Hachiemon) of the Hamata Clan, Iwami Province, was executed for engaging in contraband trade with Korea under the pretext of visiting Dagelet. The incident let the Shogunate to issue a proclamation prohibiting all journeys to foreign lands. In the proclamation it was stated that whereas Japanese had made frequent trips to Dagelet for fishing in other times, such trips were no longer permitted because the island had been turned over to Korea since 1697.]

Toward the end of the Tokugawa Shogunate and in the early years of Meiji (around 1868), a movement gathered force in Japan urging the development of "Matsu-shima" and petitions were made to the Government. As it was ascertained that "Matsu-shima" was none other than the island which was once the subject of negotiations with the Korean Government and which the

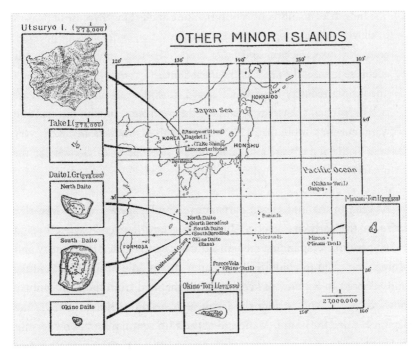

[Figure 2-1] Attached map, Minor Islands Adjacent to Japan Proper, Part IV (June, 1947)

Japanese had been prohibited from entering, the petitions were not taken up by the Japanese Government, although Japanese still continued to go to the island. On the other hand the Korean Government made repeated demands to Japan to keep her subjects out of the island and at the same time tried to develop the island themselves but with negligible results.

The Annexation of Korea in 1910 brought the island under the rule of the Government-General of Chosen.

3. Industry

The development of the island is still in an incipient stage, most of the settlers having come no earlier than several dozens of years ago. The total population, mostly Koreans, as of 1935, was 11,760, the Japanese numbering a little over 500 among them.

The Industries mainly consist of agriculture and fishing. Because of the lack of alluvial soil, farming is limited to the cultivation of dry land for potatoes, corn, soy beans, wheat, and other crops. The total production is barely adequate to meet the needs of the inhabitants.

The fishing industry is actively engaged in as the surrounding waters are rich in fish and sea-weeds because of the confluence of both the cold and warm currents. More than 120,000 yen worth of products are taken every year. Cattle and silk are also raised on the side-line.[107] (underlined by the quoter)

As seen in the underlined parts above, the Japanese Foreign Ministry intended to clearly characterize Ulleungdo as Japanese territory. According to the pamphlet, Japan first recognized Ulleungdo in the 11th century and Korea attempted to colonize it only after the middle of the 13th century and adhered to a policy of keeping it uninhabited from the 15th century onward. For a century after the Japanese invasion of Korea in 1592, the Japanese ruled the island. At the end of the 17th century, Korea's ownership of Ulleungdo was recognized after a long dispute but the Korean authorities continued to keep the island uninhabited and the Japanese never stopped fishing near it. Also, in the latter part of the 19th century, there was a movement and petitions urging the development of Ulleungdo, and despite the government's disapproval, Japanese still continued to go to the island. That is to say, the pamphlet claimed that Japan first recognized Ulleungdo and had it under its rule for a century, there had been disputes over sovereignty, and while Korea practically left it unattended, Japan developed the island.

Why did the Japanese Ministry include Ulleungdo in the "Minor Islands Adjacent to Japan Proper" series? The intention is clear. As these pamphlets were designed to influence the Allies in their determination of which minor islands belonged to Japan, it was meant to claim sovereignty over

---

107 Minor Islands Adjacent to Japan Proper, Part IV: Minor Islands in the Pacific, Minor Islands in the Japan Sea, June, 1947, pp. 10-12.

Ulleungdo. These pamphlets were not aimed just to provide information as a simple gazetteer or coast pilot but to claim sovereignty, and therefore, Ulleungdo, which was undoubtedly Korean territory then as it is now, should not have been mentioned. Most of the islands included in the pamphlets were those the Allies excluded from Japanese administration or over which sovereignty was disputed. As the Japanese title, "Japan's Annexed Islands," indicated, it is unquestioned that Japan regarded Ulleungdo as one such island. Japan did not mask its intentions by including Ulleungdo and not Tsushima in the pamphlet.

If the circumstances had allowed, Japan would have continued to claim sovereignty over Ulleungdo, not over Dokdo. As is well known, when the Japanese discussed the development of Dokdo in the 1870s, it was only as part of the development of Ulleungdo. Dokdo never appeared alone in pre-modern Japanese documents. Dokdo was regarded as an island that could function only in conjunction with Ulleungdo and as an island attached to Ulleungdo. The real reason the Korean Empire issued an Imperial Decree to elevate the island to the status of county was to defend its sovereignty over Ulleungdo in the context of the Japanese invasion. But it failed to dispatch an official at the time of the declaration of Uldo County and the Japanese took advantage of this to illegally enter the island and engage in all manner of illegal behavior such as logging, sales of island produce, pillaging, the use of weapons, and violence. To protect these Japanese thugs, Japanese police were illegally stationed on Ulleungdo despite it being Korean territory.[108]

Following is the Dokdo section of the pamphlet. It is also quoted here at length due to its critical importance.

I. Liancourt Rocks (Take-shima)

1. Geography (omitted)

---

[108] Song Byeong-gi, 1999, "Ulleungdo's Incorporation in the Government System and Seokdo," *Ulleungdo and Dokdo*, Dankook University Press, pp. 93-132.

2. History

As stated in the Introduction, the Japanese knew the existence of the Liancourt Rocks from the ancient times. But the earliest documentary evidence of this knowledge is to be found in the *Inshu Shicho Goki* (Oki Province; Things Seen and Heard), a book published in 1667, which contains the following description:

To the northwest of the Province of Oki there is Matsu-shima at a two days' distance, and at another day's distance further out there is Take-shima. The latter, also called Iso-take-shim, is rich in bamboo, fish, etc.

It is clear that Matsu-shima here refers to the Liancourts (Illustration).

As for European acquaintance with the Rocks, it was in 1849 that the *Liancourt*, a French whaling ship, first sighted them and gave them their present name. The *Palláda*, a Russian frigate under the command of Admiral Putiatin, is said to have taken soundings of the adjacent sea in 1854. In the following year came the *Hornet*, a corvette of the British China Fleet, which also sounded the vicinity of the Rocks.

It should be noted that while there is a Korean name for Dagelet, none exists for the Liancourts Rocks and they are not shown in the maps made in Korea. On February 22, 1905, the Governor of Shimane Prefecture, by a prefectural proclamation, placed the Liancourts under the jurisdiction of the Oki Islands Branch Office of the Shimane Prefectural government. [Note 3: *The United States Hydrographical Survey* at present deals with the Liancourt Rocks under the head of Oki group of islands.]

3. Industry

It is presumed that no one has ever settled on the islets owing to such natural conditions as stated above. In 1904, however, the inhabitants of Oki Islands began to hunt sea-lions on these islets and thereafter each summer the islanders, using Dagelet as their base, went regularly to the Rocks and built sheds as temporary quarters for the season.[109] (underlined by the quoter)

---

[109] Minor Islands Adjacent to Japan Proper, Part IV: Minor Islands in the Pacific, Minor Islands in the Japan Sea, June, 1947, pp. 9-10.

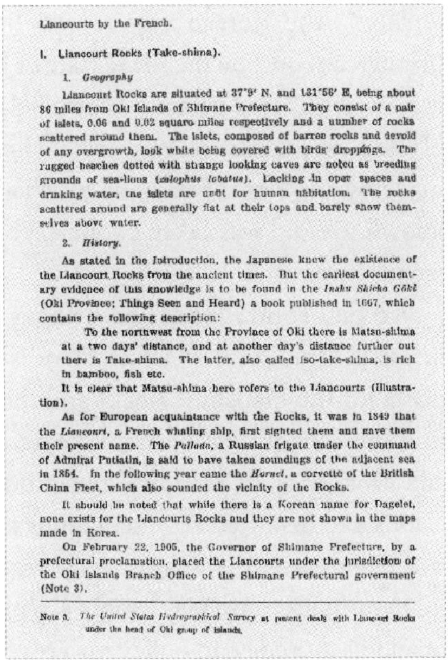

[Figure 2-2] Dokdo section, Minor Islands Adjacent to Japan Proper, Part IV (June, 1947)

According to the Japanese Foreign Ministry, the Japanese had known of the existence of Dokdo, naming it Matsu-shima in 1667, while the Europeans named it the Liancourt Rocks only in 1849. The Ministry also emphasized that, unlike Ulleungdo, there was no Korean name for the Liancourt Rocks and they were not shown on Korean-made maps. This is an entirely fraudulent claim and an undisputed fabrication. The assertion that the Japanese began fishing on the Liancourt Rocks in 1904 and Shimane Prefecture incorporated the Liancourt Rocks on February 22, 1905 was meant to justify the Japanese invasion.

As is well known, in September 1904, Yozaburo Nakai, a fisherman in Shimane Prefecture, requested that the Japanese government incorporate Dokdo as Japanese territory and lease it to him. On January 28, 1905, the Japanese government did so by naming Dokdo Take-shima and promulgated such through the Shimane Prefecture Public Notice. Nakai and the Japanese government were aware of Dokdo being part of Korean territory. The Korean empire was belatedly informed of the situation through a report by the Magistrate of Ulleungdo Sim Heung-taek in 1906. However, the royal palace was invaded by Japanese troops in the turbulence of the Russo-Japanese War and diplomatic rights were lost. The outcries made by the Korean press as to what was happening to Dokdo are well known. Dokdo was taken by violence and greed during the first phase of Japan's invasion of Korea.

As seen above, Japan lied without hesitation to advance its territorial interests. The lie that "while there is a Korean name for Dagelet, none exists for the Liancourt Rocks and they are not shown in the maps made in Korea" vividly demonstrates its stance. When Japan claimed Ulleungdo and Dokdo as its territory and produced a document filled with false claims and distorted representations in June 1947, this was not just about sovereignty over the islands.

In the background lay a more essential issue: Japan's postwar perception of and its attitude and policy towards Korea.

3) Origin of the Japanese Foreign Ministry's perception of Dokdo in 1947

The author of this pamphlet or sources of information used in it are unknown. As testified to by Takeso Shimoda, the leading author was likely Kenzo Kawakami, who was in charge of territorial issues in the Japanese Foreign Ministry's Treaties Bureau.[110] Kawakami was the author of *Takeshima No Ryoyu* (Sovereignty over Takeshima) in 1953, the first ever publication on Dokdo published by the Foreign Ministry's Treaties Bureau, as well as *Takeshima No Rekishi Chirigakuteki Kenkyu* (A Historical and Geographical Study of Takeshima), which summed up Japan's claims to sovereignty over Dokdo in 1966.[111] Kawakami together with Seizaburo

---

110 Shimoda, *Sengo Nihon Gaiko No Shogen*, p. 50.
111 Kenzo Kawakami (1909-1995) graduated from Kyoto Imperial University (today's Kyoto University), worked at the General Staff Office and Ministry of Greater East Asia, and after the war served as Councilor of the Foreign Ministry's Treaties Bureau, Japanese Minister to the

Tamura of Shimane Prefecture provided the key grounds for Japan's claim to sovereignty over Dokdo in the 1950s to 1970s. They exchanged materials and influenced each other in coming up with arguments to support the Japanese position.[112]

This pamphlet distributed by the Foreign Ministry did not indicate references or other sources of information at all. The above pamphlet dealt with Ulleungdo and Dokdo together, argued that there was a Korean name for Dagelet but not for the Liancourt Rocks and that they were not shown in any map made in Korea, and mentioned the February 22, 1905 prefectural proclamation by the Governor of Shimane Prefecture that placed the Liancourts under the jurisdiction of the Oki Islands Branch Office of the Shimane Prefectural Government. Its treatment of Ulleungdo and Dokdo as one entity and reference to the prefectural proclamation by the Governor of Shimane Prefecture regarding the illegal incorporation of Dokdo by Japan is very peculiar and quite at odds with the Japanese government's current position. This shows that the aggressive and imperialistic perspective of regarding Ulleungdo as Japanese territory was in the background and it was the Shimane Prefecture proclamation that

---

Soviet Union, and in other roles. He led the work of writing reports on territorial issues at the Treaties Section I of the Treaties Bureau. He is known as the key drafter of statements from the Foreign Ministry with regard to sovereignty over Dokdo in the 1950s. His *Takeshima No Rekishi Chirigakuteki Kenkyu (A Historical and Geographical Study of Takeshima)* represents Japan's sovereignty claims and has been used as a critical reference by the Japanese government and academics. Regarding this publication, refer to *Critical Review on Takeshima No Rekishi Chirigakuteki Kenkyu* (Park Bae-geun, 2001, Institute of Law Studies, Pusan University, *Journal of Law Studies*, Vol. 42, No. 1). It was translated into Korean in 1990 by Korea's Ministry of Oceans and Fisheries.

112 Seizaburo Tamura worked at the Publicity Documentation Section (Koho Bunshoka) of the General Affairs Department of Shimane Prefecture. He is the author of *Shimaneken Takeshima No Kenkyu (A Study of Takeshima, Shimane Prefecture)* (1954, Shimane Prefecture) which claimed Shimane Prefecture's sovereignty over Dokdo, and *Shimaneken Takeshima No Shin Kenkyu (A New Study of Takeshima, Shimane Prefecture)* (1965, General Affairs Section, General Affairs Department, Shimane Prefecture) which compiled materials from the Japanese side and verbal testimonies on Dokdo. He collected an enormous amount of material on Dokdo which is currently retained at the Prefectural Library of Shimane. This is the source of many materials used by Korean scholars.

served as the basis for the illegal incorporation of Dokdo.

Considering this, the authors of this pamphlet are believed to have referred to *Takeshima Oyobi Utsuryoto* (Dokdo and Ulleungdo) compiled by Fukuichi Okuhara in 1906 and published in 1907. This book was written after a visit to Ulleungdo by dozens of Shimane Prefecture officials under the pretext of inspecting Takeshima one year after the illegal incorporation. They illegally entered Ulleungdo and informed its Magistrate of the incorporation of Dokdo that had occurred one year earlier.

After its illegal incorporation in 1905, Japan made a total of three surveys of Dokdo.[113] In August 1905, Bukichi Matsunaga, Governor of Shimane Prefecture, inspected Dokdo. In March 1906, an inspection team of more than 40 people came with Yutaro Gaminish, a high-ranking Shimane Prefecture government official as its head. The inspection is said to have produced a report on Dokdo written by the Oki Islands Magistrate. *Takeshima Oyobi Utsuryoto* was produced as a result of this second on-site inspection.

The second team was engaged in this "inspection of Takeshima" from March 22 to 30, 1906. They arrived at Dokdo on March 27, "took shelter" at Ulleungdo from March 27 to 28, and returned to Japan on the 30th. Consisting of two parts on Dokdo and Ulleungdo, the book first listed several arguments supporting the idea of Dokdo being Korean territory and refuted each of them. It was the only official publication produced by Shimane Prefecture after the illegal incorporation, and dealt with Dokdo and Ulleungdo as one entity, claiming the prefectural proclamation by the Governor of Shimane Prefecture as the basis for Japan's incorporation of Dokdo. It looked at Dokdo and Ulleungdo from different perspectives, placing stress on sovereignty over Dokdo and on commerce with and Japanese inhabitants on Ulleungdo. That is, *Takeshima Oyobi Utsuryoto*

---

113 "3. Feb. 10, A2, No. 15, Ministry of Foreign Affairs of Japan Memorandum" (Feb. 10, 1954), "The Japanese Government's Opinions Refuting the Korean Government's Shown in the Korean Diplomatic Mission to Japan Memorandum Dated Sept. 9, 1953 Regarding Sovereignty over Dokdo," Bureau of State Affairs, Ministry of Foreign Affairs, 1955, *Introduction to the Dokdo Issue*, p. 148.

was written with intent to defend the illegal incorporation of Dokdo and the advancement of Japanese economic interests in Ulleungdo against the background of the Japanese imperialistic invasion of Korea. This book was almost the only comprehensive reference of Dokdo written after the 1905 illegal incorporation. Also, on issues of historical sovereignty, there was no better reference than this one, researched and written in 1906.

It is believed, while writing "Minor Islands Adjacent to Japan Proper, Part IV: Minor Islands in the Pacific, Minor Islands in the Japan Sea," the Japanese Foreign Ministry borrowed the following points from *Takeshima Oyobi Utsuryoto*: treating Dokdo and Ulleungdo as one entity; characterizing that the Japanese have practically developed Ulleungdo; and that the Japanese knew of the existence of the Liancourt Rocks from ancient times and therefore Shimane Prefecture had incorporated the island into its territory. As such, the recognition of and approach to the Dokdo issue by the Foreign Ministry shown in this pamphlet, written in June 1947, was an extension of the ideas from imperial Japan.

The significance of this pamphlet, produced by the Japanese Foreign Ministry in June 1947 and used in propaganda targeting the Allies, was not widely known. The pamphlet helps better understand the stance and responses taken by Korea, Japan, and the US regarding the Dokdo issue in different spheres, and is significant in the following four aspects:

First, as of 1947, the Japanese government was clearly aware that Dokdo was Korean territory and its claim to the island was seriously ill-founded. The very act of creating this pamphlet is an admission that the Japanese Foreign Ministry itself questioned the claim. In consideration of the fact that SCAPIN No. 677, which excluded Dokdo from Japanese territory, was not mentioned in the pamphlet, it is difficult to see that it was designed to respond to the Allied policy. If it had in fact targeted the Allied policy, it would have used completely different logic and arguments. As such, it is believed to have been intended for use against a possible sovereignty claim by Korea. As of June 1947, when the pamphlet was published, discussion on sovereignty over Dokdo had not started in earnest in Korea, itself still under US and Soviet occupation, and thus the Japanese Foreign Ministry took preemptive action. They provided false information to the

Allies about the events that transpired from 1905 to 1906 to deny Korea's sovereignty while Korea had not yet achieved complete independence or established its own government. The Japanese government did not hide its imperialistic, expansionistic, and aggressive nature even after its surrender as far as Dokdo was concerned. This is the most important factor to be observed about this pamphlet.

Second, the fact that the Japanese Foreign Ministry produced a fraudulent document reflects the Japanese government's perception of and attitude toward Korea and Koreans after its defeat in the war. As Japan understood it, it was defeated by the US-led Allies, not by Korea: liberation alone was a sufficient reward for Korea, and therefore, it did not need to provide any compensation or make apology. The pamphlet, which offers a glimpse into how postwar Korea-Japan relations dawned, was based on Japan's scornful and insulting view of Korea.

According to Yuko Nagasawa, the Japanese government determined that Japan's abandonment of sovereignty over Korea was not decided by acceptance of the terms of the Potsdam Declaration at its surrender, but would be determined through a peace treaty with the Allies. Immediately after the war, this thinking developed into the argument that Japan retained sovereignty over Joseon even after its surrender. This point was consistently argued by the Japanese government, high-ranking officials from the Governor-General of Joseon including Mikio Yamana, retired soldiers, the then Ministry of Health, Labor, and Welfare, and others. This was the basic postwar stance held by the Japanese government toward Korea. Based on such ideas, until a peace treaty with Japan was in place, Japan became independent, and Korea-Japan relations were reestablished, the Japanese government pursued its economic interests dating back from its colonial rule in South Korea through SCAP and other channels despite its defeat in the war.[114] Specifically, the Japanese government's meeting on

---

114 Yuko Nagasawa, 2007, "Japan's Argument for Sovereignty over Joseon and US Policy on Korea with a Focus on Their Effect on the Division of the Korean Peninsula (1942-1951)," doctoral dissertation, Department of Political Science and International Relations, Korea University Graduate School.

the cessation of hostilities, which was held on August 24, 1945, notified the Governor-General of Joseon that sovereignty over the Korean peninsula lay with Japan until a peace treaty was signed. However, the Governor-General predicted Japan's hold on sovereignty would be taken away by the US occupation authorities.[115] In the same light, the Japanese government after its defeat viewed its colonial rule of Korea as an accomplishment and expected that the people of its now-liberated colony and the Japanese nationals living there would be able to peacefully coexist.[116]

Japan reckoned it was fine to trample on the interests of a country like Korea and remained an aggressor that did not hesitate to carry out government-level document manipulation and engage in political maneuvering. The June 1947 pamphlet was no different from the 1905 illegal incorporation of Dokdo despite Japan's knowledge of Korea's sovereignty. At the time, Japan fabricated the fiction that the island was a no man's land and recorded its incorporation in the Shimane Prefecture Public Notice without informing Korea. This is also parallel to Japan's inducing Dokdo's designation and subsequent cancellation as a US Air Force bombing range from 1951 to 1952 to help in its claim of sovereignty. They were all carried out through government-level political maneuvering and fabrication of documents. These repetitive acts throughout recent history reveal Japan's contempt for Korea and inherent aggressive nature.

Third, Korea's situation at the time the Japanese Foreign Ministry created this false document and used it to lobby the Allies and the US warrants looking into. Despite having been liberated, Korea was divided at the 39th parallel and under complete military administration which had been designed with Japan in mind. It was denied exercise of sovereign authority

---

115 "Yamana Memoirs," p. 47; "Outline of the Status of the Japanese Korean Army before and after the End of the War", Nobuyuki Abe-related documents (microfilm) R7, Constitutional Government Documents Collection, National Diet Library (Yuko Nagasawa, 2007, *Ibid.*, p. 86).
116 Choi Yeong-ho, 2008, "Recognition of Colonial Rule as Seen in the Process of Japanese Residents Returning Home from the Korean Peninsula," *Journal of Northeast Asian History*, No. 21, p. 268; Choi Yeong-ho, 1998, "Recognition of Korea and Koreans by Contemporary Japanese," The Korea-Japan Historical Society, *Mutual Recognition of Korea and Japan*, Kookhak, pp. 242-244.

in any aspect of legislation, jurisdiction, government administration, national defense, and diplomacy. In June 1947, the Joint Soviet-American Commission was being held in Seoul according to the Moscow Conference of 1945 which had been the only international agreement on Korea's independence. All the involved parties, South and North Korea, the right and left, the US and the USSR were fiercely pitted against each other over establishment of a provisional government.

On the other hand, Japan, a defeated nation responsible for war crimes, was under US occupation and yet not denied its sovereignty. Its cabinet, chosen through an election, was exercising sovereignty under the indirect control of SCAP. The Japanese Foreign Ministry, while prohibited from engaging in diplomatic activities, was encroaching on Korea's interests through the SCAP Diplomatic Section, POLAD-Japan and other channels by dishonest means. In the meantime, the newly-liberated Korea was struggling to establish its own government despite being divided and under military rule. While Japan enjoyed the support of a large number of Americans who actively defended its interests, Korea had almost no legal channel to represent its side of the story. The only possibilities they had were petitions by the South Korean Interim Legislative Assembly, an advisory body to the US Army Military Government, and investigations by the South Korean Interim Government, all of which had no effect. While Korea continued to suffer from a war that had been waged by Japan, Japan did not hesitate to infringe on its interests anew by confusing the Allies with lies and false claims.

Fourth, this false pamphlet was used as an important reference in the course of the San Francisco Peace Conference to decisively violate Korean interests. The American diplomats and officials in both Tokyo and Washington, in particular, were influenced in no small measure by the false information and misconstrued representations in the pamphlet regarding the Dokdo issue.

According to research, it was used as the basis for the US to deny Korea's claim to Dokdo and instead confirm Japan's claim on four separate occasions. It was first used in this context in August 1948 when the Patriotic Old Men's Association appealed to SCAP over Korea's sovereignty over

Dokdo, Parangdo, and Tsushima. The petition landed in the POLAD office headed by Sebald and it was none other than Richard Finn who reviewed it and rejected their claims, citing the information in the Japanese pamphlet. Both he, at SCAP's Diplomatic Section, and Lt. Col. Colin E. Anderson at the G-3 section of the Far East Command decided not to take any action other than to submit a copy to the Diplomatic Section for reference.[117] For this reason, the Patriotic Old Men's Association's petition was simply dismissed in Tokyo, never making it to Washington.

The second time the pamphlet was used was in the review process by the overseas diplomatic missions of a draft peace treaty sent around by the US DoS in 1949. The draft, written on November 2, 1949, stipulated that Jejudo, Geomundo, Ulleungdo, and the Liancourt Rocks (Dokdo) were excluded from Japanese territory and defined as part of Korean territory. However, Sebald, the acting political adviser in Japan, argued that Dokdo was Japanese territory in his review. In a telegram sent to W. Walton Butterworth, the US Assistant Secretary of State for Far Eastern Affairs, on November 14, 1949 and in a document sent to the US Secretary of State on November 19, 1949, he argued that Japan's claim to the Liancourt Rocks was time-honored and appeared valid, and it was difficult to regard them as islands in the coastal waters of Korea.[118] He suggested that the Liancourt Rocks (Takeshima) be specified as Japanese territory and installation of radar stations on them be considered. Though he did not mention it, there is no doubt that Sebald consulted "Minor Islands Adjacent to Japan Proper, Part IV." As a result, the US draft treaty presented on December 29, 1949 and the "Commentary on the Draft Treaty of Peace with Japan" prepared in July 1950 recorded that ① Takeshima was formally claimed by Japan in 1905, apparently without protest by Korea, and placed under the

---

117 GHQ, FEC, Check Sheet, G-2 to Diplomatic Section, Subject: Petition of Patriotic Old Men's Association of Seoul, Korea (Sept. 27, 1948).

118 William J. Sebald, POLAD Japan to W. Walton Butterworth (Nov. 14, 1949), 740.0011 PW(Peace)/11-1449, *FRUS* 1949, Vol. VII, pp. 899-900; Sebald to the Secretary of State, Subject: Comment on Draft Treaty of Peace with Japan (Nov. 19, 1949), RG 59, Department of State, Decimal File, 740.0011PW(Peace)/11-1949.

jurisdiction of the Oki Islands Branch Office of Shimane Prefecture and ②
unlike Dagelet Island, Takeshima has no Korean name and does not appear
ever to have been claimed by Korea.[119] These views also mirrored the
claims of the pamphlet. Sebald's arguments made in November 1949 had
a decisive influence on the US DoS's decision on sovereignty over Dokdo.

The pamphlet was used a third time during the period from July to
August 1951 when the Korean government was engaged in negotiations
with the US DoS for a peace treaty with Japan and claimed Dokdo and
Parangdo as Korean territory in its second reply dated July 19, 1951 on
the US draft treaty. When looking to resolve sovereignty over Dokdo,
Samuel W. Boggs, a US DoS geographer at the Office of Intelligence and
Research (OIR) referred only to the pamphlet.[120] He wrote reports on
the Liancourt Rocks over three occasions: first he thought the rocks were
Korean territory, but with no supporting materials from Korea, he came to
increasingly depend on the only available reference: the Japanese Foreign
Ministry pamphlet. In the end, he came to the conclusion that Dokdo was
called Takeshima, it had been officially claimed by Japan in 1905, clearly
with no protest from Korea, and it seemed that Korea had never claimed
sovereignty over it before.[121]

The pamphlet was used the last time as follows: Assistant Secretary
of State Dean Rusk sent a memorandum to ROK Ambassador to the US
Yang You-chan on August 10, 1951, which stated that Dokdo was Japanese
territory. It wrote, "...this normally uninhabited rock formation was
according to our information never treated as part of Korea and, since
about 1905, has been under the jurisdiction of the Oki Islands Branch
Office of Shimane Prefecture of Japan. The island does not appear ever

---

119 "Commentary on Draft Treaty of Peace with Japan," RG 59, Department of State, Decimal File, 694.001/7-1850.

120 Memorandum by Boggs, OIR/GE to Fearey, NA, Subject: Spratly Island and the Paracels, in Draft Japanese Peace Treaty (Jul. 13, 1951), RG 59, Department of State, Decimal File, 694.001/7-1351.

121 Memorandum by Fearey to Allison, Subject: Proposed Changes for August 13 Draft (Jul. 30, 1951), p. 3.

before to have been claimed by Korea."[122] The Japanese Foreign Ministry's 1947 pamphlet was used as the most important reference in August 1951 right before the signing of a peace treaty with Japan.

As seen above, the Japanese Foreign Ministry's 1947 pamphlet of falsified information played a decisive role in rendering Korea's claim to Dokdo invalid at critical moments from 1948 to 1951. It is interesting to note that American diplomats and officials in Tokyo not only trusted the document fabricated by the Japanese Foreign Ministry but also forwarded it to Washington where it was also regarded as a valuable reference. That is, the exchange, communication, and mutual influence between the Japanese Foreign Ministry and US diplomats and US DoS officials had a negative impact on Korea's legitimate interests and claims. With no government of its own, Korea was not even aware of Japan's maneuvers and lobbying efforts, and by the time the peace negotiations were in full swing, it was struggling to survive in a civil war that would decide its fate. Japan illegally incorporated Dokdo in 1905 in the midst of dire circumstances for Korea, distributed false information about Dokdo in 1947, and convinced the US DoS with its false information when Korea was otherwise occupied with the Korean War from 1950 to1951.

---

122 Letter by Dean Acheson to You Chan Yang, Ambassador of Korea (Aug. 10, 1951), RG 59, Japanese Peace Treaty Files of John Foster Dulles, 1946-52, Lot 54D423, Box 7; RG 59, Department of State, Decimal File 694.001/8-1051.

The US Draft Treaty of Peace with Japan and Its Relation to Dokdo (1947-1951)

1

The Peace Conference and Peace Treaty with Japan

1) Formulation and finalization of the Peace Treaty with Japan

In the wake of World War II, the US and other Allied Powers ended their hostile relations with the Axis powers and reestablished relations with them. They signed a peace treaty with Italy in 1947 and ended their occupation of Germany in 1949. Following a meeting of the Foreign Ministers of the Big Five and the peace conference of July 1946, the Allied Powers concluded a peace treaty with Italy in February 1947. Their approach to dealing with postwar Italy, which had been an Axis power but later became a member of the Allied Powers after the deposition of Mussolini in 1943, significantly influenced the Allies' policy with regard to the occupation of the other Axis powers and the way peace treaties were formulated and signed.[1]

As a result of the Potsdam Agreement of July 1945, Germany lost nearly a quarter of its prewar territory and later was divided into East and West Germany in 1949, with establishment of the Federal Republic of Germany in the west and the German Democratic Republic in the east. The Allied Powers ended their hostile occupation of Germany without a peace conference. Discussions about a proposed peace treaty with Japan began in 1946 and a treaty was finalized in 1951. Development of the Japanese peace treaty progressed through three distinct stages.

The first stage began in 1947 with the US proposing to conclude an early peace treaty with Japan. After beginning work on a treaty in the second

---

1   Written by Narahiko Toyoshita, translated by Gwon Hyeok-tae, 2009, *Hirohito and MacArthur*, Gaemagowon, pp. 171-177.

half of 1946, the US made such a proposal to the members of the Far Eastern Commission in July 1947 based on the views expressed by General MacArthur on March 17, 1947. The Soviets, however, argued that the major Allied Powers should be given veto rights over any proposed peace treaty with Japan and that such a treaty should only be concluded by a final decision during a meeting of the foreign ministers from the major Allied Powers rather than a majority decision. China also came out in opposition to the US proposal, expressing dissatisfaction over the manner in which the treaty was to be concluded. Thus, by the end of 1947, the initial push by the US to conclude a peace treaty early with Japan had lost its momentum.

The second stage took place from 1948 to 1950 when Cold War tensions between the US and the Soviet Union were at their height and the US sought to sign a peace treaty with Japan that excluded the Soviet Union while at the same time drawing down the spectrum of opinions that existed within the US. As conflict between the US and the Soviet Union intensified from 1947 onwards, the US fully committed itself to a policy of Cold War with the Soviets. This policy was articulated by the Truman Doctrine and enacted by means of the Berlin Airlift. The Cold War in Europe expanded eastward to East Asia in 1948. This caused the US to reverse course on its policies toward Japan, from a focus prior to that time on weakening Japanese militarism and promoting democracy to one on reindustrializing the nation as a fledgling Cold War partner. This new policy focus, which aimed at rebuilding Japan to become a factory powerhouse for Asia, was the brainchild of George F. Kennan, the leading policy planner of the US Department of State (DoS) and the primary architect of the policy of containment as formalized by NSC 13/2 (October 7, 1948).

The unexpected communization of China in 1949 increased the strategic importance of Japan in East Asia even further. This expansion of the communist camp in East Asia—namely the Soviet Union, China, and North Korea—and escalation of Cold War confrontations between this camp and the US made an early conclusion of a peace treaty with Japan a critical and urgent matter. At this point, the US had three key prerequisites that it needed to resolve prior to concluding a peace treaty with Japan, the first of which was the decision of whether or not to reach a compromise with the Soviet Union. The US was at a crossroads, needing to decide whether to go with an overall peace arrangement that included the Soviet Union or pursue a separate peace arrangement with Japan that excluded the Soviets. In the final analysis, the US opted to exclude the Soviets. The second prerequisite was to narrow the spectrum of views that existed among the policy-making authorities within the US Administration. While the US DoS tended to prefer an early conclusion of a peace treaty with Japan, the Department of Defense was adamantly opposed to it on the grounds that the withdrawal or reduction of US forces it would require would put the security of the entire Far East at risk. The Department of Defense emphasized the need to secure Japan's consent to the stationing of US forces on Okinawa and the main island of Japan, and ensure the unrestricted freedom of these forces. The conflict between the Department of State and the Department of Defense on this issue was finally resolved with the decision to reach a US-Japan security agreement along with a peace treaty. At the heart of the security agreement was the guarantee that the US could station its forces in Japan and secure a military base on Okinawa. The third component of the peace accord was the signing of a compromise agreement with Japan with regard to the security needs of the country that, due to Article 9 of its Peace Constitution, lacked the right of belligerency. Thus, in the end, a compromise was reached to conclude a security treaty along with a peace treaty.

The third stage was the period from 1950 to 1951 when John Foster Dulles became the special representative in charge of the peace treaty negotiations with Japan and rendered the peace treaty actually signed.[2]

---

2   The Working Group on Japan Treaty divided the entire process of formulating the peace treaty with Japan into sixteen stages: 1. New York conversations (Dec. 1950; Fifth General Assembly of the United Nations); 2. Further consideration of treaty timing within the United States Government (Dec. 1950–Jan. 1951); 3. Initial formal response to New York conversations (Soviet and Indian governments); 4. Consultation with Congress: Meeting with Mr. Malik (Jan. 11-13, 1951); 5. Mission to Japan, the Philippines, Australia and New Zealand (Jan. 22-Feb. 25, 1951); 6. Circulation of United States Provisional Draft Treaty of March 1951; 7. Second Mission to Japan (Apr. 13-23, 1951); 8. US-UK Washington Conversations (Apr. 25, 1951); 9. Comments of other governments on US March draft; 10. London visit (Jun. 2-14, 1951); 11. Consultations

Dulles was appointed as adviser to the Secretary of State on April 19, 1950 and was later appointed by the President on May 18 of that year as special envoy to Japan for the purpose of concluding a Japanese peace treaty. On June 17, Dulles stopped briefly in Tokyo to feel out the situation on the ground. Secretary of Defense Louis Johnson and Joint Chiefs of Staff Omar Bradley, both of whom harbored differing views from Dulles', made a separate visit to Tokyo at the time. All outstanding issues and discord began to quickly dissipate after the outbreak of the Korean War in June 1950, and especially so with the dramatic turn of the war's tide following intervention by the Chinese in November 1950 and the humiliating retreat of United Nations Forces: the importance of Japan and the need for an early peace treaty quickly emerged as a top priority for US policy makers. From December 1950 to early January 1951, the decision was reached that, as Japan was the only bridgehead in Asia, it was imperative to conclude an early peace treaty with her, and this helped resolve any remaining outstanding differences between the relevant departments. For example, the US DoS and the Department of Defense were able to reach agreement to place the former mandated territories of Japan and Okinawa under the trusteeship of the US, while signing a separate security agreement with Japan to establish a legal basis for stationing US forces in the country. In what later became known as "shuttle diplomacy," Dulles made frequent visits to the nations with major interests in the negotiations with Japan, taking along with him a copy of the draft treaty to mediate differences between the Allies. In short, the Japanese peace treaty was for the most part not the outcome of formal talks between the relevant nations but rather one that resulted from personal contacts between the principal negotiator and

---

at Paris, Karachi, New Delhi, Manila and Tokyo; 12. Circulation of July 3 and July 20 drafts and issuance of invitations to Peace Conference; 13. Comments by other Allied Powers received between June 1 and July 19 (1951); 14. Comments received between July 20 and August 13 (1951); 15. Responses to invitation to San Francisco Conference; and 16. The Peace Conference. "Summary of Negotiations Leading Up To the Conclusion of the Treaty of Peace With Japan," by Robert A. Fearey (Sept. 18, 1951), RG 59, Office of Northeast Asia Affairs, Records Relating to the Treaty of Peace with Japan-Subject File, 1945-51, Lot 56D527, Box 1.

official representatives of the key countries involved. This fundamentally new approach to entering into a peace treaty was unprecedented, the essence of which was a US-led shuttle diplomacy process followed by a majority decision on a peace settlement. Such a process smacked of separate non-inclusive peace settlement, which deviated from the agreement that had been made by the Allied Powers that no country was to reach a peace settlement on its own with enemy nations but rather, would have to do so collectively with the others. A peace treaty based on a majority decision involved the US and the UK camp pursuing a peace settlement with Japan together with the majority of the other Allied Powers while excluding the Soviet Union, China, and other pro-communist nations.

During his two separate visits to Tokyo in 1951, Dulles negotiated with Japan and agreed on a package deal that included a peace treaty and several related security agreements. At the same time, he visited key allied countries like the UK, the Philippines, Australia, and New Zealand, and also met with representatives of key allies in Washington and New York. During consultations with the UK, the two sides voiced conflicting views on the nature of the treaty and the participation of China but soon were able to reach agreement based for the most part on the US draft. After the US and the UK fine-tuned their joint draft treaty during two final rounds of meetings and obtained the consent of the other Allied Powers on it, the peace treaty was signed by the Allied Powers and Japan at the San Francisco Conference in September 1951. The conclusion of the treaty officially ended the state of war between the Allies and Japan and transformed their postwar relationship from one of hostility to one of peace. Since Japan was banned from having a military and the right to engage in belligerency under the Peace Constitution of 1947, the conclusion of a bilateral security agreement with the US that allowed US forces to be stationed in Japan enabled Japan to secure its defense. Conclusion of the US-Japan security agreement and the Japanese peace treaty concomitantly allowed Japan to finalize a peace treaty based on its security agreement with the US.

As a result, the Philippines, Australia, and New Zealand—members of the Allied Powers and allies of the US during World War II—were enraged by the US agreeing to provide for the security of Japan, an enemy country.

To assuage their anger, the US agreed in 1951 to conclude a mutual defense treaty with the Philippines as well as an ANZUS (Australia-New Zealand-United States) Pact with Australia and New Zealand. Following the ceasefire between the two Koreas in 1953, South Korea also demanded a defense treaty with the US, the outcome of which was the Mutual Defense Treaty between the US and Korea. Thus, as of 1953, the US had established a defensive alliance in Asia consisting of Japan, Korea, Australia, and New Zealand. The result was the creation of a chain of defense linking Japan-Korea-the Philippines and Japan-Australia-New Zealand. Such alliances would later form an important pillar for security and order in the region.

2) Evolution of the draft treaty of peace with Japan

The background research and draft treaties leading up to the San Francisco Peace Conference with Japan were carried out in five different stages. In each stage, the draft underwent several rounds of modifications.

The first stage involved the initial formulation of a draft treaty within the US DoS itself, done in early 1947 by the Bureau of Far Eastern Affairs. Ongoing modification of the draft continued until 1948. The entity placed in charge of this task was the Working Group on Japan Treaty of the Bureau. Hugh Borton, the head of the Division of Japanese Affairs of the Bureau of Far Eastern Affairs, oversaw this task at the working level, while another member of the division, Robert A. Fearey, was placed in charge of crafting the treaty's territorial clause. During this process, the most important document of reference was the *PPS/10 Results of Planning Staff Study of Questions Involved in the Japanese Peace Settlement*, a top secret document dated October 14, 1947 that had been put together by the Policy Planning Staff (PPS).[3]

Constructed by Cold War planner George F. Kennan, this document

---

3   "PPS/10 Results of Planning Staff Study of Questions Involved in the Japanese Peace Settlement" Memorandum by George F. Kennan to the Secretary of State (Marshall) and the Under Secretary (Lovett) (Oct. 14, 1947), FW 740.0011PW (Peace)/10-2447, RG 59, Department of State, Decimal File, 740.0011PW (Peace) file, Box 3501.

contained a map in Appendix A. This was the first official map made by the US in its efforts to prepare a draft of a peace treaty with Japan. On the map, Dokdo (Liancourt Rocks) was clearly designated as being under Korean sovereignty. This lends support to the fact that, beginning as early as 1947, the US DoS had already determined that the Liancourt Rocks were a part of Korea.

The second stage involved the US DoS's ongoing revisions of the draft treaty and its circulation to Tokyo and the Department of Defense for further modification prior to sending it to the UK government. The effort to form a draft, which had been suspended in early 1948 due to opposition from the Soviet Union and China, resumed in September 1949 when US Secretary of State Dean Acheson held talks with UK Foreign Secretary Ernest Bevin in Washington. At these meetings, Bevin proposed to circulate the US draft treaty at the British Commonwealth Foreign Ministers Conference scheduled for January of the next year. His intention was that, if the draft treaty was deemed satisfactory, he would support an early conclusion of a treaty with Japan based on the consensus reached at that Conference. The draft formulation process picked up steam in the months of October through December 1949. The US DoS's draft was completed somewhere between November and December of 1949, but the Department of Defense opposed the early signing of a treaty with Japan unless US security interests were addressed and a security agreement secured first. The Defense Department demanded US trusteeship over mandated territories that had formerly been held by Japan in the South Pacific and over the Ryukyu Islands, and the securing of the Port of Yokosuka and army and naval bases on mainland Japan. Due to the failure to reconcile these differences of opinion between the US DoS and the Department of Defense, the goal of submitting the US draft treaty to the British Commonwealth Foreign Ministers Conference of January 9, 1950 proved to be elusive. Meanwhile, the US DoS proceeded on its own to collect opinions from within its own ranks and finalized its own version of a draft treaty on November 2, 1949. This draft had a map attached to it identifying Dokdo (Liancourt Rocks) as being a part of Korean territory. The US DoS sent this draft to three persons only—General MacArthur, his political adviser in Tokyo William

J. Sebald, and the Secretary of Defense. The Department of Defense, which was still opposed to an early conclusion of a treaty with Japan, responded by using the stalling tactic of not providing any feedback on the draft. General MacArthur replied with a brief comment. On the other hand, Sebald submitted a reply mirroring Japanese interests.

A significant event took place at this point with regard to Dokdo. In the *Commentary on the Draft Treaty of Peace with Japan*, Sebald, a diplomat of the US DoS and US political adviser in Japan, argued in favor of Dokdo being a part of Japanese territory on the grounds that it had been formally claimed by Japan in 1905 without any protest voiced by Korea.[4] At the same time, without having received a copy of the draft, US Ambassador to Korea, John J. Muccio, submitted his views that Korea should be granted the status of a participant in the peace conference with Japan and a signatory to the treaty. His stated rationale was that the US and the United Nations were by policy supportive of Korea and that the prestige of the Korean government should be preserved.[5] The US DoS accepted the views expressed by the local diplomatic offices and modified the draft treaty accordingly in December 1949. Although the revised draft reflected the opinions of both ambassadors, i.e. that Korea should be allowed to attend the peace conference and that Dokdo should now be placed under Japanese sovereignty, the draft generously reflected Sebald's pro-Japanese views. The existence of this draft treaty of the US DoS, which mistakenly described Dokdo as being under Japanese sovereignty, subsequently became the strongest factual support for Japan's claim that Dokdo had been confirmed as a part of its territory under the provisions of the Japanese Peace Treaty. Neither the Korean government nor the American Embassy in Korea was cognizant of this development at this point.

---

4   The Acting Political Adviser in Japan (Sebald) to the Secretary of State (Nov. 14, 1949), RG 59, Department of State, Decimal File, 740.0011PW (Peace)/11-1449, *FRUS*, 1949, Vol. VII, pp. 898-900; Sebald to the Secretary of State, Subject: Comment on Draft Treaty of Peace with Japan (Nov. 19, 1949), Department of State, Decimal File, 740.0011PW (Peace)/11-1949.

5   John J. Muccio, Ambassador to Korea to the Secretary of State (Dec. 3, 1949), RG 59, Department of State, Decimal File, 740.0011PW (Peace)/12-349; *FRUS*, 1949, Vol. VII, p. 904.

The third stage involved a revision of the Department of State's draft following the emergence of Dulles on the scene. After being appointed special envoy to Japan in May 1950, John Foster Dulles led out in the negotiations between the Allied countries and Japan for the remainder of the time leading up to the signing of the Japanese peace treaty. He believed that the key to the early signing of this peace treaty lay in it having a "non-punitive" nature. Having attended the Paris Peace Conference as a junior diplomat at the end of World War I, Dulles came to believe that the Treaty of Versailles, which had stipulated the war responsibilities of the defeated enemies in great detail and imposed harsh territorial divisions and punitive reparations on them, had set the stage for Germany to cause the Second World War.[6] Up until that point, the draft of the US DoS was much like the Treaty of Versailles, highly punitive in nature in terms of its reparations clause. The peace treaty with Italy after World War II had also significantly addressed the issues of war responsibilities and reparations. Dulles felt that the US DoS's draft was "too detailed" and was convinced that it should be discussed early on with Japan even if the opinions of the Japanese were not decisively incorporated into the draft.[7] Following the outbreak of the Korean War, he determined to design a peace treaty that was less harsh and as non-punitive as possible, and that would almost completely exclude the idea of requiring war reparations on the part of Japan. The result was the friendliest draft treaty in the history of world diplomacy. Basically, Dulles demanded a whole new draft treaty that was essentially different from the ones that the US DoS had been working on since 1947. The "seven principles" that Dulles set forth as the basis for the Japanese peace treaty in September 1950 were a well-thought-out expression of that position. He would work to develop a draft that would be peaceful and non-punitive and did not make demands for an acknowledgment of war responsibility or specify the need to make reparations. Dulles also wanted a draft treaty that would be distinctly simple, so that the US could reach *ex ante* agreements

---

6   John M. Allison, *Ambassador from the Prairie*, Boston, Houghton Mifflin, 1973, p. 146.

7   *Ibid.*, pp. 146-147.

with the parties involved through shuttle diplomacy rather than through a long drawn-out roundtable conference involving all relevant nations. Thus, all "unnecessary" details were deleted from the draft, leaving only the most important key matters to be addressed in the treaty. More specifically, Dulles' seven principles and the drafts of the Japanese peace treaty made through October 1950 only incorporated simple and general content. With regard to Korea, the draft now only stated that Japan was to acknowledge Korea's independence and renounce all rights, titles, and claims to Korea; it failed to make any mention of the Liancourt Rocks (Dokdo).

The fourth stage of the development of the peace treaty was when the official draft was made in consultation with the other Allied nations. This draft treaty, completed in March 1951, was the first draft worked on in earnest after Dulles' first visit to Tokyo (January-February 1951) in order to send to the other Allied nations. Titled the *Provisional Draft of a Japanese Peace Treaty (Suggestive Only)*,[8] the document was the first official draft treaty used as the basis for negotiations with the other Allies and was unlike any other previous draft treaties that the US had made for its internal use and for limited circulation among its overseas missions. The US sent this draft to the Korean government, thereby suggesting that it regarded Korea as a party to the negotiations and a signatory to the treaty. The other provisions related to Korea were the same as those of the third stage, likewise leaving out any mention of the Liancourt Rocks (Dokdo).

The fifth stage was when the US formalized the joint Anglo-American draft treaty in consultation with the UK, a key Allied partner. After the first joint Anglo-American talks (March 1951) and the joint working group meetings (April-May 1951), the US and the UK completed their first joint draft (May 3, 1951). However, this draft was not forwarded to the Korean government. At this stage, based on a proposal made by the UK government, the draft included the provision that Japan, recognizing the independence of Korea, renounced all rights, titles, and claims to

---

8   RG 59, Office of Northeast Asia Affairs, Records Relating to the Treaty of Peace with Japan-Subject File, 1945-51, Lot 56D527, Box 1.

Korea including the islands of Quelpart, Port Hamilton, and Dagelet. The Korea-related provisions in the first joint draft treaty were incorporated into the final draft. Following a few final minor revisions, the US and the UK completed their second joint draft treaty (July 3, 1951) and sent it to Japan as well as to thirteen countries involved in the peace treaty talks (July 9, 1951). The second joint draft treaty was also sent to the Korean government, but Korea at this point was denied status as a party to the negotiations, a signatory of the treaty, and a participant at the peace conference. Subsequently, the final draft treaty went through a few more minor modifications before it was again sent to the relevant nations on August 13, and then finalized at the San Francisco Peace Conference on September 4, 1951.

Furthermore, based on their nature and key characteristics, as well as how they were received, the various treaty drafts might be further divided into three different groups or clusters. The first cluster of drafts was punitive and strict, much like the Treaty of Versailles after World War I and the Peace Treaty with Italy after World War II. Time-wise, these draft treaties correspond to those drafts made during the first and second stages of the treaty formulation process, and were all made from 1947 to 1949 by the US DoS. Their primary focus and purpose was to clearly establish Japan as bearing the guilt of war and demanding of Japan a series of strict, punitive provisions and reparations. In the history of world diplomacy, such a draft was in keeping with the common, traditional way of concluding a peace treaty. The drafts contained elaborate, complex structures and provisions, and were very lengthy in order to reflect the varying interests of the numerous Allied nations. To a large extent, they were based on the Treaty of Versailles developed after World War I and the Peace Treaty with Italy after World War II. The US assumption at the time these drafts were developed was that the Soviet Union and China would be participating in the peace treaty negotiations with Japan.

The second cluster of treaty drafts emerged after the appointment of Dulles in 1950 as the special Presidential envoy for the negotiations of a Japanese peace treaty. Time-wise, these drafts correspond to the third and fourth stages of the treaty development process in the period between 1950 and early 1951. They were exceptionally generous towards Japan and did not impose any war reparations or assign any war responsibility. They were also based on earnest and sincere negotiations with Japan itself. In this sense, they were "peace treaty" drafts in the true sense of the word, based on the desire for forgiveness and reconciliation. Such treaties had been unheard of in the history of world diplomacy up until that time. In the words of Shigeru Yoshida, they were an "unbelievable proposal." Yoshida's views were well reflected in his dialogue with George Clutton, the Minister at the British Mission to Japan, on April 30, 1951. After the US draft treaty was leaked to the media (March 1951), Clutton queried Yoshida about the lukewarm reaction from Japan. Yoshida's reply was simple. He said that the draft treaty was so generous that the Japanese people and the National Diet doubted America's sincerity. Yoshida said that when he told the Japanese lawmakers that this was a true draft, they did not believe it. Only after Dulles arrived in Tokyo and confirmed that this was a genuine draft, did lawmakers and the general public believe it to be so.[9] At this point, the US was working on a peace treaty that excluded the Soviet Union as well as the two Chinas (i.e., the Communist Government and the Nationalist Government). Rather than revising and fine-tuning the draft treaty text through extensive dialogue between all the relevant parties, as was the case for the Treaty of Versailles and the Italian Peace Treaty, the US opted for a peace treaty process in which it would seek to reach agreements with the relevant nations on an individual basis, then once an overall agreement had been reached, to conclude the treaty at a conference attended by representatives of all the parties to the negotiations. For this reason, the format and content of the draft treaty had to be kept as simple as possible. Dozens of nations were highly involved in the treaty negotiation process, and it was expected that about fifty countries would actually be signing the Japanese peace treaty itself, so it was essential to present the most important

---

9   FO 371/92547, 213351, FJ 1022/383, Mr. Clutton to Mr. Morrison, no. 148 (119/244/51) (May 1, 1951), Subject: Record of Meeting with the Japanese Prime Minister on the 30th April at which the main theme of conversation was the Japanese Peace Treaty.

principles as briefly as possible in a way that reflected the common interests of all those involved.

The third cluster of draft treaties included those modified by the US in consultation with the UK, its most important Allied partner at that time. After a series of talks beginning in March 1951, the US and the UK developed two joint draft treaties, drawn up using the US draft as the primary draft to work from and incorporated key portions of the British draft treaty as well as a number of key views and concerns of the UK. As a result, the US draft treaty underwent a few changes, but no significant ones content-wise. The second joint Anglo-American draft treaty became the final draft treaty.

In summary, the drafts of the Japanese peace treaty evolved significantly based on changing historical circumstances, under which the alliance between the US, the Soviet Union, the UK and China under the Yalta Agreement collapsed. This occurred owing to changes in the international environment, especially with respect to exacerbation of the Cold War confrontation between the Soviet Union and the US and the communization of mainland China. In the end, the US and the UK took part in the conference and signed the peace treaty with Japan; the Soviet Union participated in the conference but refused to sign the treaty; and China was not even invited. The initial harsh and punitive draft treaties developed by the US from the perspective of Japan as an enemy country changed over the course of time owing to the dramatic intensification of the Cold War in 1948 and the outbreak of the Korean War in 1950. In an effort to reestablish its former enemy as a key ally in East Asia, the US decided instead to propose a generous peace treaty. By obtaining trusteeship over the mandated territories formerly held by Japan in the South Pacific, trusteeship over Okinawa, and the right to station its military forces and maintain military facilities on mainland Japan, the US became the greatest beneficiary of the dramatically-revised Japanese peace treaty. Unlike the US, the UK expressed wariness and counseled restraint towards Japan. In the end, however, it consented to the US version of the proposed peace treaty with only a few minor changes.

2

Dokdo in the Draft Treaties of the US Department of State, Part I (1946-1947)

: The Liancourt Rocks (Dokdo) under Korean sovereignty

1) Establishment of Working Group on Japan Treaty in 1946

The US began work on a peace treaty with Japan in the latter half of 1946. At this time, there were conflicting views about whether the US occupation of Japan should end in the short term or whether it should last 25 years or longer. The first view emphasized peace while the latter underscored disarmament and demilitarization. Most Japanese experts within the US Department of State (DoS) were of the view that the occupation of Japan should end in the near future. Hugh Borton, Chief of the Office of Japanese Affairs, was in favor of an early conclusion of a peace treaty with Japan and General MacArthur in Tokyo also agreed with this perspective. Noting that no military occupation longer than five years had ever succeeded in history, MacArthur was convinced that the US occupation of Japan should last for three years at most. He asserted that anything longer than that would weaken the military's morale and corrupt its discipline, ultimately earning the long-term resentment of the local population. This information appears to be credible as it is based on a personal interview that Shigeru Yoshida had with General MacArthur.[10]

Sometime around August 1946, the need for an early signing of a Japanese peace treaty was proposed in Washington and Tokyo. On August 26, a joint meeting was held between the US DoS and the Department of War, attended by General Echols and Dean Rusk from the Department of War, Assistant Secretary of State Acheson, legal adviser Gross, Director

---

10   Shigeru Yoshida, 1958, *Kaiso Junen*, Vol. 3, Tokyo, Shinchosha, pp. 19-20.

Vincent of the Bureau of Far Eastern Affairs, Borton of the Office of Japanese Affairs from the Department of State, special adviser Reischauer, and several Harvard professors.[11] This meeting was organized because General MacArthur had expressed his intention to bring the issue of the Japanese peace treaty before the Far Eastern Commission, which was in charge of Japanese affairs. Discussions were in progress at the time on a German peace treaty, and there was considerable support for linking the Japanese peace treaty with it. However, Borton, Chief of the Office of Japanese Affairs and others at the US DoS opposed this idea, suggesting instead that the US craft a separate peace treaty with Japan.[12]

At the meeting, based on a proposal made by Acheson, it was agreed to establish a Special Committee to work on a Japanese peace treaty. In addition, it was also agreed 1) to craft a Japanese peace treaty befitting the Japanese circumstances and to pattern it along the lines of the German peace treaty, 2) to establish an informal steering committee to deal with Japanese issues and to consult with the State-War-Navy Coordinating Committee, and 3) not to bring the issue of the Japanese peace treaty before the Far Eastern Committee until the US came up with a more unified position on the issue.[13]

The task of crafting a peace treaty with Japan was assigned to the Division of Research for the Far East. However, soon it was assessed that the staff of the division was not up to the task.[14] Borton proposed to the Division's

---

11   Memorandum of Conversation, Subject: Peace Treaty with Japan (Aug. 23, 1946), RG 59, Department of State, Decimal File, 740.0011PW (Peace)/8-2346.

12   Memorandum by Borton (JA) to General Hildring (A-H) and Vincent (FE), Subject: Peace Treaty with Japan (Aug. 14, 1946), RG 59, Department of State, Decimal File, 740.0011PW (Peace)/8-1446; Memorandum by Vincent (FE) to General Hildring (A-H), Subject: Peace Treaty with Japan (Aug. 15, 1946), RG 59, Department of State, Decimal File, 740.0011PW (Peace)/8-1546.

13   Memorandum of Conversation, Subject: Peace Treaty with Japan (Aug. 23, 1946), RG 59, Department of State, Decimal File, 740.0011PW(Peace)/8-2346, p. 2.

14   Memorandum by Warren S. Hunsberger (DRF) to Hugh Borton (JA), Subject: Research Preparation for the Peace Settlement with Japan (Aug. 23, 1946), RG 59, Department of State, Decimal File, 740.0011PW (Peace)/8-2346.

Director Vincent that General John H. Hildring instead be allowed to designate the members of the committee that would conduct research on the treaty.[15] Hildring was Assistant Secretary of State for Occupied Areas and a representative of the Department of State to the State-War-Navy Coordinating Committee. Through guidance from Director Vincent, who accepted Borton's proposal, and upon order of Assistant Secretary of State Hildring, a committee for the preparation of a Japanese peace treaty was organized.

The project was named the Japanese Peace Treaty Project and the task force that oversaw the project was the Working Group on Japan Treaty. Initial members included Edwin M. Martin of the Division of Japanese and Korean Economic Affairs (JK), Warren S. Hunsberger of the Division of Far Eastern Survey, John. K. Emmerson of the Division of Japanese Affairs (JA), and Ruth Bacon of the Bureau of Far Eastern Affairs (FE). The group was chaired by James K. Penfield, the Deputy Director of the Bureau of Far Eastern Affairs.[16] However, actual discussions were led by Hugh Borton, a specialist on Japan and Chief of the Division of Japanese Affairs (later head of the Division of Northeast Asian Affairs). The group held its first meeting on September 6, 1946 and decided to meet every two weeks thereafter.

Initially, the Working Group on Japan Treaty was a task force of experts under the oversight of the Bureau of Far Eastern Affairs of the Department of State. As discussions progressed, the group sought out assistance from other departments and kept close contact with the Department of War and the Department of the Navy.

The group began to get into full swing in October 1946. On October 4, the group reached an agreement on the general outline of a treaty, worked on the list-up of countries that would take part in the treaty, and divided up

---

15   Memorandum by Borton (JA) to Vincent (FE), Subject: Research Preparation for Peace Treaty (Aug. 27, 1946), RG 59, Department of State, Decimal File, 740.0011PW (Peace)/8-2346.
16   Memorandum by Penfield to Vincent, Subject: Japanese Peace Treaty Project (Oct. 18, 1946), RG 59, Office of Northeast Asia Affairs, Records Relating to the Treaty of Peace with Japan-Subject File, 1945-51, Lot 56D527, Box 5.

the tasks.[17] In the beginning, the group expected the peace treaty with Japan to take effect sometime in the autumn of 1947. In early 1948, however, the target completion date was postponed to sometime in the autumn of that year.[18] The working group's main concerns related to the term of the treaty (25 years), how to ensure the long-term disarmament of Japan, whether to establish a new Control Committee (to oversee Japan), and whether an early conclusion of a treaty was in line with US interests.[19] On October 25, 1946, the group finalized a document entitled *Peace Treaty with Japan*. The document contained the key components of a proposed peace treaty, organized by chapters.[20] It had a preamble, 11 chapters, and annexes. More specifically, the Preamble was followed by Chapter I on Territorial Clauses, Chapter II on Clauses Relating to Ceded Territories, Chapter III on Political Clauses, Chapter IV on War Criminals, Chapter V on Disarmament and Demilitarization, Chapter VI on Interim Arrangements, Chapter VII on Claims Arising Out of the War, Chapter VIII on Property Rights and Interests, Chapter VIII on Other Economic Clauses, Chapter X on Final Provisions, Chapter XI on Protocol, and Annexes.

According to a report in December 1946 by Penfield, the head of the Working Group on Japan Treaty and Deputy Director of the Bureau of Far Eastern Affairs, the group conducted research for three months and finalized the outline of the treaty together with draft preamble, Chapter V (Interim Arrangements) and Chapter VI (Disarmament and Demilitarization).[21] This

---

17 Working Group on Japan Treaty, Suggested Agenda for Meeting on Friday, October 4, 3:00 p.m. Room 358, Main Building, RG 59, Office of Northeast Asia Affairs, Records Relating to the Treaty of Peace with Japan-Subject File, 1945-51, Lot 56D527, Box 5.

18 Working Group on Japan Treaty, Minutes of Meeting on Friday, January 31, 1947 (Feb. 10, 1947), RG 59,Office of Northeast Asia Affairs, Records Relating to the Treaty of Peace with Japan-Subject File, 1945-51, Lot 56D527, Box 5.

19 Working Group on Japan Treaty, Notes on Meeting of Friday, October 25, 1946, RG 59, Office of Northeast Asia Affairs, Records Relating to the Treaty of Peace with Japan-Subject File, 1945-51, Lot56D527, Box 5.

20 "Peace Treaty with Japan" (Oct. 25, 1946), RG 59, Office of Northeast Asia Affairs, Records Relating to the Treaty of Peace with Japan-Subject File, 1945-51, Lot 56D527, Box 1. Folder "Drafts (Ruth Bacon)"

21 Memorandum by Penfield (FE) to Vincent (FE) and Hildring (A-H), Subject: Peace

indicates that the initial draft treaty was characterized by a Disarmament and Demilitarization Treaty (D and D Treaty), strongly demanding war reparations and the acknowledgment of war responsibility by Japan while envisioning a long-term occupation of Japan for 25 years or more.

2) Draft treaty of the Working Group on Japan Treaty during the period 1947-1948 and Dokdo

Territorial clauses of the January 1947 draft treaty: the first draft placing the Liancourt Rocks (Dokdo) under Korean sovereignty

Of the various drafts produced, the first draft of the US DoS's Working Group on Japan Treaty that contained territorial clauses was completed in January of 1947.[22] The territorial clauses in Chapter I, which addressed the issue of the postwar boundaries of Japan, were submitted to the Working Group on Japan Treaty on January 30, 1947.[23]

Written by Robert A. Fearey of the Office of Japanese Affairs, Bureau of Far Eastern Affairs of the US DoS, the territorial provisions comprised a simple, two-page document that became the key resource used by the US DoS to develop the relevant provisions in its various drafts of a peace treaty with Japan for the period of 1947-1949. The document was simply named *Draft*, with an opening statement that it dealt with the territorial provisions of the proposed treaty and was the working group's draft of Chapter I of the treaty draft. It was comprised of a number of territorial clauses, i.e., clauses addressing the extent of Japanese territory in the postwar era. The crucial concern of this provision was how to stipulate those islands to be included

---

Treaty with Japan (Dec. 18, 1946), RG 59, Department of State, Decimal File, 740.0011PW (Peace)/12-1846.

22   "Draft," by Robert A. Fearey (JA) (Jan. 1947), RG 59, Office of Northeast Asia Affairs, Records Relating to the Treaty of Peace with Japan-Subject File, 1945-1, Lot 56D527, Box 1. Folder "Drafts (Ruth Bacon)".

23   Working Group on Japan Treaty, Suggested Agenda for Meeting on Friday, January 31, 1947. RG 59, Office of Northeast Asia Affairs, Records Relating to the Treaty of Peace with Japan-Subject File, 1945-51, Lot 56D527, Box 5.

under Japanese sovereignty.

The draft had the following characteristics: first, it specified that Japanese territory would be limited to the territory that Japan had possessed prior to January 1, 1894. This meant that, according to the Cairo Declaration, Japan was to return all land it had seized since the Sino-Japanese War of 1894, including those stolen from the Chinese such as Manchuria, Formosa, and the Pescadores. Second, it provided that the territory of Japan would be comprised of the islands of Honshu, Kyushu, Shikoku, Hokkaido, and a number of minor islands offshore of Japan. It also included the Ryukyu Islands and all the remaining islands in the Inland Sea, Rebun, Riishiri, Okujiri, Sado, Oki, Tsushima, Iki, and the Goto Archipelago, but excluded the Kuril Islands. This provision on Japanese territory was first added in January 1947 and remained a part of the draft treaty until 1949. Third, Article 1-2 stated that a map clarifying Japan's territorial limits would be attached to the draft treaty. Fourth, Article 2 concerned the territories to be ceded to China and Article 3 those to be ceded to the Soviet Union. Fifth, the following was stated in Article 4 regarding Korea:

> Japan hereby renounces all rights and titles to Korea and all minor offshore Korean islands, including Quelpart Island, Port Hamilton, Dagelet (Utsuryo) Island and Liancourt Rock(Takeshima).[24]

The provision stating that Japan hereby renounced all rights to Korea, including Quelpart Island, Port Hamilton, Dagelet Island, the Liancourt Rocks (Dokdo), and all other minor offshore islands belonging to Korea appeared for the first time in the January 1947 draft treaty. It is significant to note that this was the first draft of a peace treaty with Japan and also the first US DoS document to indicate that Dokdo belonged to Korea. This provision was preserved in all subsequent drafts until Dokdo was briefly

---

24　The original text is "Japan hereby renounces all rights and titles to Korea and all minor offshore Korean islands, including Quelpart Island, Port Hamilton, Dagelet(Utsuryo) Island and Liancourt Rock(Takeshima)."

switched to being a part of Japan as a result of William J. Sebald's request in November of 1949.

The author of this document, Robert A. Fearey, had previously been the personal assistant to Joseph C. Grew, the US Ambassador to Japan, before the war and was later appointed by special envoy John Foster Dulles to serve as his assistant during the peace treaty negotiations with Japan.[25] Fearey was a specialist on Japan and became a key figure involved in decisions concerning Korea during development of the Japanese peace treaty.

Partial draft treaty of March 19, 1947: The Liancourt Rocks (Dokdo) under Korean sovereignty

No title was given to this draft. However, it was referred to as the *Peace Treaty with Japan,* a title used by the Working Group on Japan Treaty since the latter half of 1946.

This draft was attached to a document sent on March 19, 1947 by the US DoS to George Atcheson, Jr., head of the Diplomatic Section of SCAP and political adviser to SCAP, requesting feedback on it from MacArthur's Headquarters. It was comprised of three chapters, including a preamble, a chapter on the territory of Japan, and a chapter on the territories to be ceded by Japan and the economy.[26] Although this was clearly the first draft treaty sent to Tokyo, it was not yet a complete draft but only contained a preamble and territorial clauses.

The document was delivered in person rather than by telegram or diplomatic pouch. Hugh Borton, the person in charge of the treaty at the US DoS, along with Bacon of the Working Group, visited Tokyo in March 1947 to seek the views of General MacArthur on the proposed draft. They flew with political adviser Atcheson on his way back to Tokyo after

---

25 Richard B. Finn, *Winners in Peace: MacArthur, Yoshida, and Postwar Japan,* University of California Press, Berkeley and Los Angeles, California, 1992, p. 252.

26 Memorandum by unknown to Ambassador Atcheson (Mar. 19, 1947), RG 59, Office of Northeast Asia Affairs, Records Relating to the Treaty of Peace with Japan-Subject File, 1945-1, Lot 56D527, Box 1.

attending to some business in Washington. Borton visited Tokyo and Seoul from March 8 to April 11, 1947. Upon his arrival in Tokyo, he delivered a copy of the draft to Atcheson who then passed it on to MacArthur.[27] This means that MacArthur's call for a rapid conclusion of a peace treaty with Japan at a March 17 press conference was made after he received the US DoS's draft treaty from the Borton delegation in Tokyo.

The draft treaty had the following chief characteristics. First, as stated above, it was comprised of three chapters including a preamble and a chapter on the territory of Japan, and a chapter on the territories to be ceded by Japan. It was very simple and short, comprising a total of 11 pages. Second, it identified 45 countries as being among the Allied and Associated Powers of World War II and indicated that they would be signatories to the treaty. Korea was not included on the list. Furthermore, this draft clearly identified Japan as the aggressor in the war. It was noted that Japan had been the one to invade China, had taken the initiative to establish an alliance with Nazi Germany and Fascist Italy, and had proceeded to invade much of the rest of the Pacific region. Third, the draft was still in many ways incomplete, so it was not likely that it would receive the unqualified support of the authorities of the military occupation in Tokyo. It did not address how the islands that the US had an interest in would be dealt with (Ryukyu and Iwo Jima), the security concerns of Japan, or the future status of US forces stationed in Japan, all of which were key concerns of MacArthur and the other military authorities there.

According to Makoto Iokibe, the March 1947 draft treaty that the Working Group on Japan Treaty crafted under the direction of Hugh Borton mirrored the mainstream view that, due to its catastrophic impact on the Asian region, Japan should remain under the rule of the Allied Powers in order to forestall the rebirth of Japanese militarism in the future.[28] Subsequent drafts of August 1947 and of January 1948 continued to retain

---

27   Hugh Borton, *Spanning Japan's Modern Century: The Memoirs of Hugh Borton*, Lexington Books, 2002, pp. 189-198, 202-206.
28   Written by Makoto Iokibe et al., translated by Jo Yang-uk, 2002, *The Diplomatic History of Postwar Japan*, Darakwon, pp. 71-72.

this perspective. In his meeting with Borton, MacArthur refrained from making specific comments regarding the content and structure of the draft. This may have been due to reluctance on his part to discuss policy matters with a lower-ranked official like Borton. Instead, he noted that he would reply in writing if a special request was made by Secretary of State George C. Marshall for him to do so.[29]

With respect to territorial issues, the Working Group's second draft was highly reflective of the territorial provisions of the first draft. First, it provided that the territory of Japan should be limited to those it had possessed prior to January 1, 1894. Second, the provisions addressing Japanese territory remained exactly the same as in the previous draft of January 1947. Third, just as the previous draft, this one stipulated that Japan was to agree to cede sovereignty over all of Sakhalin and Kaiba south of 50° North to the Soviet Union as well as sovereignty to the Kuril Islands lying between the Kamchatka Peninsula and Hokkaido, which had been designated for such by the Yalta Agreement. Third, it stated that Japan was to agree to renounce all rights and titles to the Ryukyu Islands, Daito, and Rasa, which had previously been assumed to be part of Okinawa. This was a departure from the January draft, which, under Article 7, had included the parenthetical question: "Should the Ryukyu Islands be included in Daito?"

Finally, the draft's territorial provision addressing Korean territory remained the same as in the January draft, reading as follows:

Japan hereby renounces all rights and titles to Korea and all minor offshore Korean islands, including Quelpart Island, Port Hamilton, Dagelet (Utsuryo) Island and Liancourt Rock(Takeshima).[30]

---

29 Memorandum by George Atcheson, Jr., United States Political Adviser for Japan to Hugh Borton, Chief, Division of Northeast Asia Affairs, Department of State (Apr. 29, 1947), RG 59, Office of Northeast Asia Affairs, Records Relating to the Treaty of Peace with Japan-Subject File, 1945-1, Lot 56D527, Box 1.
30 Memorandum by unknown to Ambassador Atcheson (Mar. 19, 1947)

In March 1947, the US DoS was clearly working under the belief that the Liancourt Rocks were part of Korean territory. However, it only perceived the island by its international name, the Liancourt Rocks, and its Japanese name, Takeshima, but not by its Korean name, Dokdo. This may have been one of the reasons why the US DoS changed its mind about who had territorial sovereignty over Dokdo after November 1949.

A few things are worthy of note. First, at this point in time, the political adviser to SCAP was George Atcheson, a seasoned expert on China. The first US DoS draft treaty placing Dokdo under Korean jurisdiction had been communicated to SCAP while Atcheson was still there, and no opposition or response to the apportionment of Dokdo to Korea had been forthcoming then. It appears that Dokdo was widely recognized at that stage as being under Korean sovereignty. Second, in June 1947, three months after this draft was communicated to SCAP, the Japanese Foreign Office published a pamphlet, arguing that Dokdo and Ulleungdo should actually be considered Japanese territory. Dozens of copies of this pamphlet that contained false information were sent to SCAP and the US Department of State. Third, William J. Sebald, who became the political adviser to SCAP following the death of Atcheson, dismissed outright the September 1948 petition of the Korean Patriotic Old Men's Association on Korea's sovereignty over Dokdo. Meanwhile, on two different occasions in November 1949, Sebald vigorously argued that Dokdo was Japanese territory.

Memorandum dated July 24, 1947: Confirmation by Boggs that the Liancourt Rocks (Dokdo) were Korean territory

This document was submitted as a revised draft containing modifications made by Samuel W. Boggs, a geographer at the US DoS, to the territorial provisions of the February 3 treaty draft.[31] The modifications were made

---

31   "Draft of Treaty with Japan," by Samuel W. Boggs (SA-/GE)(Jul. 24, 1947), RG 59, Office of Northeast Asia Affairs, Records Relating to the Treaty of Peace with Japan-Subject File, 1945-

based on a request by Fearey of the Bureau of Far Eastern Affairs to make several changes to the territorial clauses of the draft treaty.

Boggs' draft was qualitatively different from any previous drafts since it described in a very detailed and precise manner Japanese territory, those areas to be excluded from Japan, Korean territory, and the territory of Formosa. While Fearey's "territorial clauses" and Borton's partial draft only presented area names (island names) with respect to Japan's postwar territorial boundaries, those areas to be excluded from Japan, Korean territory, and the territory of Formosa, Boggs' draft included both area names and the specific degrees of longitude and latitude as well as a line connecting these points to visually delineate territorial boundaries. He also included an attached map. This was the outcome of a geography specialist's efforts to provide visual clarity to the territorial clauses of the Cairo and Potsdam declarations as well as to remove any ambiguities that may lead to territorial disputes in the future. His memorandum of July 24, 1947 noted that the series of lines drawn on the attached map was intended to remove any uncertainties regarding which islands were to be placed under the sovereignty of Japan, Formosa, and Korea.

Boggs' method of 1) specifying in detail the islands to be included or excluded from Japanese sovereignty, 2) drawing a straight line using degrees of longitude and latitude, and 3) displaying this line visually on an attached map was preserved in the territorial provisions of the US peace treaty drafts with Japan until late 1949.

Boggs drew red, bold lines on Chart 1500 of the Hydrographic Office to clearly delineate the territorial boundaries of Japan, Formosa, and Korea. Providing an introduction to the map and the delineation of territorial boundaries using red, bold lines were Boggs' idea. His map became the prototype for drafts that followed until 1949. Following the presentation of Boggs' draft on July 24, 1947, all subsequent US DoS's drafts of a proposed peace treaty with Japan used a bold line to delineate the territorial

---

1, Lot 56D527, Box 5; Memorandum by Boggs (SA-/GE) to Fearey (FE)(Jul. 24, 1947), RG 59, Department of State, Decimal File, 740.0011PW (Peace)/7-447.

boundaries of Japan, Korea, and Formosa.

Boggs' draft carefully specified the territorial boundaries of Japan (Article 1), Formosa (Article 2), and Korea (Article 4). Since it was practically impossible to name all the islands and archipelagos in a text, Boggs drew "lines through the sea encircling" those islands that belonged to Japan, Formosa, and Korea, respectively.[32]

Two things are worth noting regarding the territorial boundaries of Japan in Boggs' draft. First, the four disputed islands of Habomai, Shikotan, Kunashiri, and Etorofu to the north of Japan were marked as being Japanese territory. Second, the Ryukyu Islands were included as being under Japanese sovereignty. Prior to this draft, the four islands in the North and the Ryukyu Islands had all been excluded. For this reason, of all the drafts created in the period 1947-1949, Boggs' was the friendliest and most favorable toward Japan.

Boggs included the following territorial provision regarding the territory of Korea in Article 4 of the draft.

Article 4

Japan hereby renounces all rights and title to Korea (Chosen) and all minor offshore Korean islands, including Quelpart (Saishu To), and Nan How group (San To, or Komun Do) which forms Port Hamilton (Tonaikai), Dagelet Island (Utsuryo To, or Matsu Shima), Liancourt Rocks (Takeshima), and all other islands and islets to which Japan had acquired title lying outside the line described in article 1 and to the east of the meridian 124° 15′ E, longitude, north of the parallel 33° N. latitude, and west of a line from the seaward terminus of the boundary at the mouth of the Tumen River to a point in 37° 30′ N. latitude, 132° 40′ E. longitude. This line is indicated on Map No. 1 attached to the present treaty.[33] (Underlined by the quoter)

---

32 Memorandum by Boggs (SA-/GE) to Fearey (FE)(Jul. 24, 1947), RG 59, Department of State, Decimal File, 740.0011PW (Peace)/7-447, p. 2.

33 *Ibid.*, pp. 3-4.

The territorial boundaries of Korea were also delineated using longitude and latitude lines. More importantly, the Liancourt Rocks, or Dokdo, were also included as being under Korean sovereignty. In fact, it is difficult to accurately delineate the borders of Japan and Korea by use of text alone. But by drawing the coordinates on a map, it became clear that Dokdo was included as a part of Korea, and not Japan. Having reviewed the territorial matters in July 1947, the top geography specialist at the US DoS reaffirmed Korea's sovereignty over Dokdo. And what is more, Boggs had done so in an otherwise pro-Japanese territorial draft that included the four islands in the North as well as the Ryukyu Islands as being Japanese territory. Boggs' text regarding Korean territory was included without further modification in all subsequent draft treaties until the end of 1949.

First official draft treaty of August 1947: The Liancourt Rocks (Dokdo) under Korean sovereignty

Titled the *Draft Treaty of Peace for Japan*, this document is found in a number of government files.[34] The August draft treaty was one of the most important drafts produced in 1947. Not only was it finalized with the expectation that a peace conference would be held in September that year, but it was also the first draft treaty to be officially sent to and circulated among the personnel within the Department of the Navy and the Department of War.[35] The August draft treaty had the following chief characteristics:

First, it was voluminous and complex. The preamble was followed by a total of ten chapters (I- X), nine annexes (A-I), and two maps. The portions

---

34 "Draft Treaty of Peace with Japan," (Aug. 1, 1947), RG 59, Office of Northeast Asia Affairs, Records Relating to the Treaty of Peace with Japan-Subject File, 1945-1, Lot 56D527, Box 5; Memorandum by Borton (FE) to Fahy (Le), Subject: Draft Treaty of Peace for Japan (Aug. 6, 1947), RG 59,

35 Memorandum by the Chief of the Division of Northeast Asian Affairs (Borton) to the Counselor of the Department (Bohlen) (Aug. 6, 1947), RG 59, Department of State, Decimal File, 740.0011PW(Peace)/8-647, *FRUS*, 1947, the Far East, Vol. VI, p. 478.

of the document disclosed to date only include the preamble, the main body, and Annexes D and E. However, the table of contents indicates that originally, in addition to the title page and table of contents, there were 83 pages in the main body, 15 pages of annexes, and two pages of maps, for a total of 102 pages. This made it, with all likelihood, the longest of all the drafts produced from 1947 through 1951.[36]

Next, while fifty countries were specified in the preamble as being members of the Allied and Associated Powers and hence signatories to the treaty, Korea was not included. Again, as in the previous draft treaties, Japan was defined as the aggressor.

Unlike the draft treaty of March 1947, this document offered clear provisions on the postwar boundaries of Japan. In order to remove any doubt, it marked out the territories included in and those excluded from Japan on a map using a bold line. This key characteristic carried over into all succeeding US draft treaties until 1949. Such a method of specifying territorial boundaries was similar to that of the British draft treaty of 1951.

Essentially, the territorial clauses of this draft treaty emulated Boggs' territorial draft of July 24, 1947. For this reason, it appears that Boggs' draft was officially recognized by the US DoS as consistent with its underlying policy at this time.

Such an approach basically arose from a proactive effort to fulfill the Japanese territorial clauses of the Cairo and Potsdam declarations. Both declarations specified that postwar Japanese territory would be limited to the four major islands of Japan and minor islands as the Allies should so determine. Thus, the main issue for the section of the draft related to Japanese territory was how to specify the minor islands that would still belong to Japan. Practically speaking, it would have been extremely difficult to specify which country had sovereignty over which of the thousands of

---

36 The August 5, 1947 draft treaty, which was the longest of any of the drafts, was eventually edited down to a total of 60 pages or so (28 pages in the main text and between 30 and 32 pages in the annexes) between October and November 1949. The draft treaties of 1950 were reduced even further.

islands in the region, and so it was only natural to use a boundary line with degrees of longitude and latitude to distinguish those minor islands included in and those excluded from Japanese sovereignty. Such a boundary line using degrees of longitude and latitude was inserted in the text of the draft treaty and in an annex of the draft as well in order to concisely and visually establish the specified boundaries. As a result, the provision on Japanese territory was comprised of three primary components: 1) detailed specification of islands included in and those excluded from Japanese sovereignty, 2) delineation of Japanese territorial boundaries using degrees of longitude and latitude, and 3) inclusion of a map in an annex to the treaty. Such was the first Japanese territorial provisions agreed upon by the wartime Allies. In summary, they were based on the conditions that Japan had accepted at the time of its surrender. Thus, curiously, both the US draft treaty and the British draft treaty, which appear to have been developed independently and without prior consultation, initially used the same method for their territorial provisions on Japanese sovereignty.

To sum up again briefly, this draft had the following key characteristics with respect to territorial issues. First, its territorial provisions were remarkably amicable and favorable toward Japan. Not only did it specify the four disputed islands in the North—Habomai, Shikotan, Kunashiri, and Etorofu—as being Japanese territory, but it also provided that the Rykyu Islands, including the Sofu Gan (Lot's Wife) and Izu, as a part of Japan as well.

Second, the territorial waters and islands of Japan were marked off by a boundary line.[37] The territory to be included as part of Japanese sovereignty in this draft was the same as that found in Boggs' draft.

Third, the draft also included a section addressing Formosa and its adjacent minor islands in more detail than in the March draft.[38]

Fourth, it recognized Japanese sovereignty over the four islands to the North, over which there were disputes between Japan and Russia.[39]

---

37 Map no. 1 is entitled "Territorial Limits of Japan".
38 Map no. 2 is entitled "Formosa and Adjacent islands Ceded to China".

Though this had already been included as a provision in Boggs' draft (July 24, 1947), this is particularly noteworthy in that it was now officially recognized as being the policy of the US Department of State.

Fifth, the draft included the following in Article 4 with regard to Korea.

Japan hereby renounces all rights and titles to Korea (Chosen) and all offshore Korean islands, including Quelpart (Saishu To)' the Nan How group (San To, or Komun Do) which forms Port Hamilton (Tonaikai); Dagelet Island (Itsiryo To, or Matsu Shima); Liancourt Rocks (Takeshima); and all other islands and islets to which Japan had acquired title lying outside the line described in Article 1 and to the east of the meridian 124°, 15′ E, longitude, north of the parallel 33° N. latitude, and west of a line from the seaward terminus of the boundary at the mouth of the Tumen River to a point in 37° 30′ N. latitude, 132° 40′ E. longitude.

This provision left no room for doubt as to whether the Korean peninsula, Quelpart Island, Port Hamilton, Dagelet, and the Liancourt Rocks (Dokdo) were under Korean sovereignty. Though the islands described as being part of Korea were specified using coordinates that are somewhat difficult to decipher without a map, this provision nonetheless clearly established that the Liancourt Rocks (Dokdo) were Korean territory. Due to the complexity of the wording, which may be difficult for many to understand, the draft treaty also included a map in an accompanying annex.

The extent of Korean territory in the August 5 draft treaty was the same as that found in Boggs' draft of July 24, 1947. It would remain the same in the map attached to PPS/10 (October 14, 1947), a memorandum of the Policy Planning Staff of the US DoS. In each of these documents, Dokdo was clearly and unmistakably identified as Korean territory.

Following dissemination of the draft, the Department of the Navy was

---

39   Takashi Tsukamoto, 1991, "Draft Treaty of Peace with Japan of the US Department of State and Northern Territorial Issue," *The Reference* no. 482 (Mar. 1991) and "Japan and Territorial Issues," Vol. 1 and 2, *The Reference* no. 504-505 (Jan. 1993)

the most proactive in providing feedback on it. It conveyed the opinion that, based on the Joint Chiefs of Staff decision 1619/19(JCS 1619/19), the US should retain Nansei Islands, Nanpo Islands, and Marcus Island (Minami-Tori-Shima), and that the department needed to secure the right to station its forces in a garrison at the Port of Yokosuka and to have an airfield for the garrison's protection (August 18, 1947).[40] A week later, the department sent more detailed comments, requesting that two modifications be made with respect to Korea. The first was to insert the Korean notation "Tomen Kan" after "Tumen River," and second, to add "and thence to a point in 33° N latitude, 127° E longitude" after "to a point in 37° 30' N latitude, 132° 40' E longitude."[41]

Meanwhile, the US DoS also received feedback from MacArthur on the draft (September 1, 1947).[42] According to Richard B. Finn, MacArthur was "the first American leader to publicly advocate a nonpunitive peace settlement" and he stuck to his guns on this point throughout 1947.[43]

PPS/10 of October 14, 1947: The Liancourt Rocks (Dokdo) under Korean sovereignty (indicated on a map)

Of the US DoS's drafts of 1947, the one with the greatest policy implication was the *PPS/10, Results of Planning Staff Study of Questions Involved in the Japanese Peace Settlement* produced by the Policy Planning

---

40 Memorandum by E.T. Wooldridge, Assistant Chief of Naval Operations for Politico-military Affairs, Navy Department to Hugh Borton, Chief of the Division of Northeast Asian Affairs, Department of State, Subject: Draft Treaty of Peace with Japan (Aug. 18, 1947), RG 59, Department of State, Decimal File, 740.0011PW(Peace)/8-847.

41 Memorandum by E.T. Wooldridge, Assistant Chief of Naval Operations for Politico-military Affairs, Navy Department to Hugh Borton, Chief of the Division of Northeast Asian Affairs, Department of State, Subject: Draft Treaty of Peace with Japan (Aug. 25, 1947), RG 59, Department of State, Decimal File, 740.0011PW(Peace)/8-547.

42 Working Group on Japan Treaty, Notes of Meeting on Wednesday, September 3, 1947, RG 59, Office of Northeast Asia Affairs, Records Relating to the Treaty of Peace with Japan-Subject File, 1945-1, Lot56D527, Box 5.

43 Richard B. Finn, *Winners in Peace: MacArthur, Yoshida, and Postwar Japan*, University of California Press, Berkeley and Los Angeles, California, 1992, p. 241.

Staff (PPS) on October 14, 1947. Written by George F. Kennan, who had become well-known as the architect of the policy of containment, this document was the only official policy document pertaining to Japan at the time. The PPS was based on an in-depth, eight-week study of the various issues involving the peace treaty with Japan as well as extensive discussions with officials of the Bureau of Far Eastern Affairs such as W. Walton Butterworth and James K. Penfield, as well as representatives of the Army and Navy, and outside experts like Joseph C. Grew.[44] Kennan proposed the need for high-ranking officials of the US DoS to discuss the Japanese peace treaty with General MacArthur and his staff in Japan prior to submitting a final report on the treaty.

Attached to this memorandum was the 10-page *PPS/10, Results of Planning Staff Study of Questions Involved in the Japanese Peace Settlement* and a one-page map (see Figure 3-1). PPS/10 was groundbreaking in many aspects, the first reason being that it viewed the early ending of the occupation of Japan risky given that Japan was not yet politically and economically stable. Kennan weighed in against an early peace settlement. Second, the report argued that the Soviet Union should be invited to participate in the Japanese peace treaty negotiations and that the US should consent to a request by members of the Far Eastern Commission to be granted veto rights over the proceedings even though the US was reluctant to accede to this request. Third, with regard to territorial issues, it discussed in some detail the issue of to whom the four islands in the North belonged and the proper disposition of the Ryukyu Islands.[45] The map in Appendix A reflected these policy recommendations regarding territorial issues.

The map had the following characteristics with respect to Japanese territory and Korean territory. First, the Ryukyu Islands south of 29°

---

44 George F. Kennan to the Secretary of State (Marshall) and the Under Secretary of State (Lovett) (Oct. 14, 1947), RG 59, Department of State, Decimal File, FW 740.0011PW (Peace)/10-2947.

45 "PPS/10, Results of Planning Staff Study of Questions Involved in the Japanese Peace Settlement," p. 3.

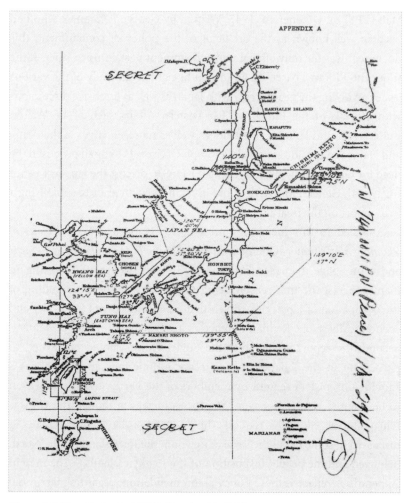

[Figure 3-1] Map attached to PPS/10 (October 14, 1947)

North were excluded from Japanese territory. No changes were made to Korean territory. Thus, from the crafting of Boggs' draft (July 24, 1947) onward up until the completion of the first official draft treaty of the US DoS (August 5, 1947) and PPS/10 (October 14, 1947), the extent of Korean territory remained the same. The only difference was in the description of the mouth of the Dumangang (Tumen River), which was to be the starting point of the boundary line delineating the northern border of Korea.

As noted above, Korean sovereignty over the Liancourt Rocks (Dokdo) was officially confirmed by PPS/10 in October 1947. Since specifying the Liancourt Rocks (Dokdo) as Korean territory in the territorial provisions of the January 1947 draft, the US DoS subsequently adopted the PPS/10 and its attached map as its official policy document, publicly confirming that the Liancourt Rocks (Dokdo) were part of Korea.[46]

The attached map was noteworthy in the following ways:

First, it was an official map produced and disseminated by the US DoS leading up to the conclusion of the Japanese peace treaty. All Japanese peace treaty drafts of the US DoS until August 1947 had been produced at the working-level by the chiefs of bureaus and offices. Though there had been some discussions about producing a map during this timespan, no map had been officially produced and attached to a draft treaty document at this stage. The map attached to PPS/10 was therefore adopted as an official document of the Policy Planning Staff and was the first policy document reported to the Secretary and Undersecretary of State.

Second, the map clearly delineated Japanese territorial boundaries using a bold, straight line. The primary reason why Japan became embroiled in territorial disputes with neighboring countries since the signing of the San Francisco Peace treaty has been because no map was attached to the text of the final treaty.

Third, the map clearly showed the Liancourt Rocks (Dokdo) as being Korean territory. On the map, the eastern edge of Korean territory in the East Sea was at 37 degrees 30 minutes north latitude and 132 degrees 40 minutes east longitude, just beyond Dagelet or Ulleungdo. Near this

---

46   This map was an adaptation of the Hydrographic Office Chart 1500 for use in Boggs' report of July 24, 1947. On September 4, 1947, Fearey of the Office of Northeast Asian Affairs reported to Borton that Military Intelligence (MI) could obtain about 50 charts and general maps of former Japan. Obtaining a variety of accurate maps was a key priority of the US Department of State as it began work to form a draft treaty of peace with Japan. Memorandum by Fearey (NA) to Borton (FE), Subject: Japanese Treaty Maps (Sept. 4, 1947), RG 59, Department of State, Decimal File, 740.0011PW(Peace)/9-47.

[Figure 3-2] Dokdo in the map attached to PPS/10 (October 14, 1947)

boundary line and just below Dagelet, Dokdo can be seen encircled by a dotted line (See Figure 3-2), clearly on the Korean side of the line.

Fourth, the map carries significance in that it clearly shows the territories of Japan, Korea, and Formosa in relation to one another. While the map attached to the April 1951 draft of the British Foreign Office clearly marked out Japanese territory, it did not do so for the territories of other nations. On the other hand, this map had the effect of removing all room for controversy by clearly delineating not only the territory of Japan but also that of Korea and of Formosa.

Fifth, this map was used by the US DoS as the most basic and important map whenever it reviewed the territorial issues involved in the Japanese peace treaty. It was the official map used when discussing the ownership of disputed regions like the Ryukyu Islands and the islands in the North. For this reason, it was the most frequently referenced map in the Japanese peace treaty files of the US DoS.

Draft treaty of November 7, 1947: The Liancourt Rocks (Dokdo) under Korean sovereignty

The draft treaty dated November 7, 1947 was entitled *Draft Treaty of Peace for Japan*.[47] Comprised of a preamble, a total of ten chapters and five annexes, it was a voluminous document totaling about a hundred pages in length.

The general characteristics of this draft treaty are similar in many respects to the previous draft treaties. The number of Allied countries and signatories to the treaty was increased by one to 51, and the part discussing Japan's war responsibilities remained unchanged.

The November 7, 1947 draft treaty succeeded the PPS/10 of October 1947 as the official policy on territorial issues. While providing that the four islands in the North were all still to be considered Japanese territory, it established the southern limit of Japan to 29 degrees north latitude, practically excluding the Ryukyu Islands scattered in between 23 degrees north latitude and 29 degrees north latitude from Japanese territory. Other than that, the draft was pretty much the same as the previous drafts in that it clearly delineated Japanese territory with a straight line and further specified these borders by using degrees of longitude and latitude on an attached map.[48]

In summary, the draft treaties of 1947 incorporated two differing boundary lines when delineating Japanese and Korean territory. The Boggs' draft of July as well as the August draft both included the Ryukyu Islands in Japanese territory, but both the map attached to PPS/10 and the November draft treaty excluded them. Figure 3-3 shows these two boundary lines juxtapositioned to one another for comparison. Meanwhile, come November 1949, the four islands in the North were all excluded from Japanese territory. And in the draft treaty of November 2, 1949, the Japanese territorial boundaries had shrunk to the smallest since 1947.

The November 7 draft treaty delineated the extent of Korean territory in the same way as did the August 1947 draft treaty.[49]

---

47 "Draft Treaty of Peace for Japan," (Nov. 7, 1947), RG 59, Records of the Office of Northeast Asian Affairs Relating to the Treaty of Peace with Japan, Lot 56D527, Box 1. Folder "Drafts (Ruth Bacon)".

48 *Ibid.*, pp. 4-5.

49 "Draft Treaty of Peace for Japan," (Nov. 7, 1947), RG 59, Office of Northeast Asia Affairs, Records Relating to the Treaty of Peace with Japan-Subject File, 1945-51, Lot 56D527, Box 1. Folder "Drafts (Ruth Bacon)," pp. 7-8.

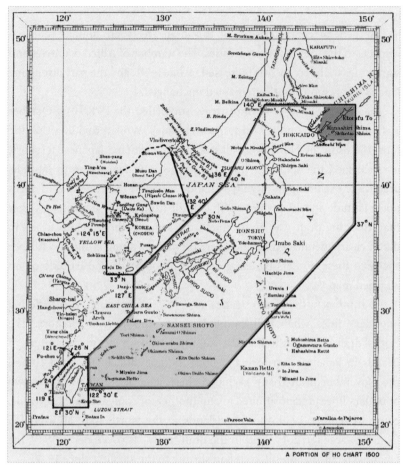

[Figure 3-3] Territorial boundaries in the US Department of State's draft treaties of 1947

——— Boggs' draft (July 24, 1947), August draft (August 5, 1947)
······ PPS/10 (October 14, 1947), November draft (November 7, 1947)
– – – Draft of November 2, 1949
▨ The Ryukyu Islands south of 29° North, excluded from Japanese territory
▮ The four islands in the North, excluded from Japanese territory

I. Japan's latitude and longitude
① 45° 45' North, 140° East ② 45° 45' North, 149° 10' East ③ 37° North, 149° 10' East ③-1 29° North, 139° 55' East ③-2 29° North, 127° East ④ 23° 30' North, 134° East ⑤ 23° 30' North, 122° 30' East ⑥ 26° North, 122° 30' East ⑦ 30° North, 127° East ⑧ 33° North, 127° East ⑨ 40° North, 136° East

II. Korea's latitude and longitude
ⓐ 124° 15' East ⓑ 33° North, 124° 15' East ⓒ 37° 30' North, 132° 40' East ⓓ Headwaters of Duman River

210

Draft treaty of November 19, 1947: The Liancourt Rocks (Dokdo) under Korean sovereignty

This draft treaty was produced on November 19, 1947 and did not include a title. *Redraft* was simply written by hand in a blank on the top page. It was a handwritten revision of the November 7 draft treaty,[50] and included two footnotes regarding the disputed four islands in the North and the Ryukyu Islands south of 29° North.[51]

No major changes were made to the other territorial provisions. Regarding Korea-related provisions, only "all minor offshore Korean islands" was changed to "minor offshore Korean islands." Again, Dokdo was placed as part of Korean territory.

Draft treaty of January 2, 1948

According to Tsukamoto, the January 2, 1948 draft treaty was formulated from December 1947 to January of the next year. In the document, the words *Re-draft 2 January* were transcribed in the Territorial Clauses of Chapter I.[52] This document is found in the Japanese peace treaty files of the Office of Northeast Asian Affairs.[53]

The key characteristic of this draft is that it had notes under each chapter. Chapter I comprised of nine articles, including Article 1 on Japanese territory, Article 2 on Formosa, Article 3 on the island of Sakhalin and the Kurils, and Article 4 on Korea. In Article 4 pertaining to Korea, the only change was the addition of the words "for the Korean people." The rest remained the same as the draft treaty of August 5, 1947.[54]

---

50 "Redraft" (Nov. 19, 1947), RG 59, Office of Northeast Asia Affairs, Records Relating to the Treaty of Peace with Japan-Subject File, 1945-51, Lot 56D527, Box 5.

51 *Ibid.*, p. 4.

52 Tsukamoto, "The Treaty of Peace with Japan and Takeshima (Review)," p. 40.

53 RG 59, Office of Northeast Asia Affairs, Records Relating to the Treaty of Peace with Japan.-Subject File, 1945.51, Lot 56D527, Box 4. Folder "Peace Treaty."

54 "Re-draft 2 January," pp. 7-8, and 59, Bureau of Far Eastern Affairs, Lot 56D527, Records of the Office of Northeast Asian Affairs Relating to the Treaty of Peace with Japan, Box 4. Folder

Draft treaty of January 8, 1948

The original copy of this draft treaty could not be confirmed. However, it can perhaps be reconstructed based on the document titled *Analysis of the Japanese Peace Treaty Draft of January 8, 1948*.[55] The most important sources for the territorial clauses of this draft were the Cairo Declaration (December 1, 1943), the Yalta Agreement (February 11, 1945), and the Potsdam Declaration (July 26, 1945). The section dealing with Korean territory can be found under Article 4 of Chapter I. Given that no special mention was made of changes in the territorial provisions, it can perhaps be safely assumed that the provisions remained the same as in the previous draft treaty. The document presents the Cairo Declaration and the Potsdam Declaration as the primary sources used for the territorial provisions on Korea.[56] The only issues that remained undecided in the territorial provisions were the disposition of the Southern Kurils and the Ryukyu Islands.[57]

3) Dokdo in the draft treaties of 1949

Time interval from January 1948 to September 1949: Efforts for a peace settlement with Japan that excluded the Soviet Union and Korea's status as a signatory to the treaty

The January 1948 draft treaty is believed to be the last draft made by the Working Group on Japan Treaty. From that point onwards, the activities of the working group were practically non-existent. This was due to the

---

"Peace Treaty"

55 "Analysis of the Japanese Peace Treaty Draft of January 8, 1948," (undated), RG 59, Department of State, Decimal File, 740.0011PW(Peace)/1-048.

56 "Source for Articles in Draft Treaty of January 8, 1948," (undated), RG 59, Department of State, Decimal File, 740.0011PW(Peace)/1-048.

57 "Analysis of the Japanese Peace Treaty Draft of January 8, 1948," (undated), 740.0011PW (Peace)/1-3048, p. 5.

fact that, on account of opposition from the Soviet Union and China and the uncooperativeness of other Allied Powers, the hopes of the US to get the peace treaty with Japan signed in the latter half of 1947 were shattered. Meanwhile, the American Council on Japan, otherwise known as the spearhead of lobbying efforts for Japan in the US, was launched on July 19, 1948. The organization included some prominent figures such as Joseph W. Ballantine, special assistant to the Secretary of State (1945-1947), William R. Castle, Ambassador to Japan (1930) and Undersecretary of State (1931-1933), Eugene Dooman, counsel to the US Embassy in Tokyo (1937-1941), Joseph C. Grew, Ambassador to Japan (1932-1941), Admiral Thomas C. Hart, a former Senator (1945), and Harry F. Kern, foreign affairs editor for Newsweek.[58] Against the backdrop of an intensified Cold War, anti-Soviet/pro-Japanese sentiments began to grow in the US.

Work on the Japanese peace treaty picked up speed again in the latter half of 1949. With the acceleration of Cold War conflict between the US and the Soviet Union, new prospects for soon completing the Japanese peace treaty began to emerge. At the heart of these new prospects was the idea of a separate peace settlement with Japan that excluded the Soviets: an idea that began to take on a life of its own as chances of reaching an agreement with the USSR on procedures for a peace conference were becoming increasingly unlikely.

A report by Marshall Green of the Office of Northeast Asian Affairs in July of 1949 entitled *Views of Other Countries toward a Japanese Peace Settlement* reviewed in some detail the views of Australia, Canada, Free China, France, India, the Netherlands, New Zealand, the Philippines, the Soviet Union, and the UK,[59] with the most emphasis being placed on the rising influence of the Soviet Union on Japan and its opposition to the anticipated peace treaty. The report concluded that while the Soviet

---

58   Letter by Harry F. Kern, Chairman, Organizing Committee, The American Council on Japan to Robert A. Lovett, Under Secretary of State (Jul. 25, 1948), RG 59, Records of the Office of Northeast Asian Affairs Relating to the Treaty of Peace with Japan, Lot 56D527, Box 3.

59   "*Views of Other Countries toward a Japanese Peace Settlement* by Marshall Green (Jul. 29, 1949), RG 59, Department of State, Decimal File, 740.0018PW(Peace)/7-949.

Union was more concerned about the rearmament of Japan and the establishment of anti-Soviet military bases in the Far East, the US was, due to the increasing reach of Communism in the Far East and Japan, more concerned about threats posed to its ability to secure military bases in the region and preserve its other interests in Japan and the Ryukyu Islands. The US concluded that given the Soviet proclivity to engage in opposition merely for opposition's sake, as well as the fact that the objectives of the US and the USSR were by this point in time completely at odds with each other, it would be difficult for the two to reach an agreement on such a peace settlement. Consequently, Marshall Green took initial steps toward planning for a peace settlement without the Soviet Union or one where the Soviet Union and Communist China would take part only at the opening of the peace conference. Notable in the July 1949 report is the statement that, at that time, Australia favored a strategic US trusteeship over Ogasawara (Bonin) Islands and the Ryukyu Islands but also over Quelpart, which was indisputably considered a part of Korean territory.[60]

Meanwhile, US Secretary of State Dean Acheson met with British Foreign Secretary Ernest Bevin in September 1949 in Washington. Bevin proposed that if the US could complete their draft treaty by early December, the British Government would try to get it accepted at the British Commonwealth Foreign Ministers Conference scheduled for early 1950. As a result, the Bureau of Far Eastern Affairs of the US Department of State resumed work in earnest on the Japanese peace treaty draft in September and October of 1949. Work progressed quickly, the goal being to submit a draft to the UK and the British Commonwealth countries.

Also in 1949, the executive staff of the Bureau of Far Eastern Affairs of the US DoS was reshuffled. Hugh Borton, who had led the work on the Japanese peace treaty at the working level, had by this time returned to Colombia University, so his position as Director of the Division of Northeast Asian Affairs had been filled first by John Moore Allison in 1947 and then by Max W. Bishop in 1948. H. Merrell Benninghoff, who had

---

60   *Ibid.*, p. 3.

been the political adviser to Korea in mid-1948, was appointed as Deputy Director of the Bureau of Far Eastern Affairs, followed by Allison in late 1948.

In late August 1949, Allison asked Fearey of the Office of Northeast Asian Affairs for an outline of the draft treaty that was being worked on.[61] Fearey submitted a report titled *Substantive Problems in Preparation of Japan Treaty Draft*, in which he suggested that three issues remained unresolved with respect to the territorial provisions of the January 1948 draft.[62] The first was the issue of whether to separate the Ryukyu Islands south of N 29° from Japan, the second the disposition of the Southern Kurils and Habomai, and the third the transfer of Formosa to China. Fearey felt that a change would be necessary in the wording of the text with regard to the Ryukyu Islands should the Soviet Union and China participate in the peace conference. He also believed that the draft treaty should apportion the Southern Kurils and Habomais to Japan and that Formosa should be handed over to China. No additional comments were made at this time regarding the provisions related to Korea.

Meanwhile, in June 1949, the issue of whether or not to have Korea participate in the Japanese peace treaty was reviewed. Ruth Bacon of the Bureau of Far Eastern Affairs reviewed the list of countries that had been at war with Japan and their eligibility to participate in the peace treaty. Bacon organized the countries as: 1) states that declared war against Japan (43 countries), 2) states not recognized by the US that declared war against Japan (2 countries), 3) states that declared themselves in a state of belligerency with Japan (3 countries), or 4) states that were integral parts of other states during the war but have subsequently attained independence or become members of the United Nations (8 countries), with the date of war declaration indicated where applicable.[63] Korea fell into categories 2

---

61   Memorandum by R. Fearey (NA) to Allison (FE), Subject: Japanese Peace Treaty (Aug. 31, 1949), RG 59, Department of State, Decimal File, 740.0011PW(peace)/8-149.

62   "Substantive Problems in Preparation of Japan Treaty Draft," by Robert Fearey (Aug. 31, 1949), RG 59, Department of State, Decimal File, 740.0011PW(Peace)/8-3149.

63   Memorandum by Bacon to Butterworth, Subject: The Japanese Peace Settlement and States

and 4. The countries classified in category 2 were the Mongolian People's Republic and the Provisional Government of the Republic of Korea, with regard to which Bacon had recorded that "according to a letter sent by Rhee Syngman to the US Secretary of State dated May 1, 1945, the 'Provisional Government of the Republic of Korea' duly declared war on Japan on December 10, 1941." Korea was also classified under category 4 along with Burma, Belarus, Ceylon, India, Pakistan, the Philippines, and Ukraine.[64] Countries included under category 3 were Chile, Peru, and Venezuela, which according to the review had been at war with Japan without officially making such a declaration owing to a provision in their Constitution preventing them from doing so.

However, the US DoS's Office of the Legal Adviser was of the opinion that there was no absolute obligation for the US to have all the countries that had been at war with Japan take part in the peace treaty with Japan. The rationale was that at the December 1945 Moscow Conference of Foreign Ministers, it was decided to limit the countries that would take part in the preparation and conclusion of peace treaties with Italy, Romania, Bulgaria, Hungary, and Finland to those European countries that had actually been at war with the Axis powers. In fact, while 29 countries had signed the declaration of war against Italy (January 1, 1942), only 16 countries were invited to the postwar peace treaty with Italy. The remaining 13 countries were not invited.[65] The reason why Korea was brought up at this point was reflective of the US DoS's positive assessment of Korea's participation in the peace conference with Japan. This support for Korean participation perhaps arose in part from the fact that the US DoS wanted to get the Republic of Korea recognized as the sole legal government of Korea at the 3rd General Assembly of the United Nations in December 1948, and

---

at War with Japan (Jun. 20, 1949), RG 59, Office of Northeast Asia Affairs, Records Relating to the Treaty of Peace with Japan-Subject File, 1945-51, Lot 56D527, Box 3.

64   *Ibid.*, p. 2.

65   Burma, India, Pakistan, and the Philippines (countries that became independent after the war) became signatories to the Treaty of Peace with Japan at the 1951 San Francisco Conference. Korea, Belarus, Ceylon, and Ukraine were not invited to the conference.

as such, had developed a particular interest and affection for this new nation that it had helped to establish. Another reason was the persistent requests from the Korean government to be a party to the treaty process. The Korean Government had continued to persistently raise this issue ever since Kim Kyu-sik, Chairman of the Interim Legislative Assembly, first made the request in 1947 that Korea be allowed to participate. These persistent efforts on the part of the newly established Korean Government may have also had an influence on the US DoS.

Draft treaty of September 7, 1949: The Liancourt Rocks (Dokdo) under Korean sovereignty

The first draft treaty produced in 1949 was dated September 7, 1949.[66] Though it came without a title, it read September 7, 1949 at the top of the table of contents page in handwriting.

This draft differed from the January 1948 draft treaty in the following ways: First, it differed in composition. Provisions regarding measures to monitor Japan following the conclusion of a peace treaty including the transfer of authority, disarmament and demilitarization as well as a Council of Ambassadors were deleted, while other provisions were added regarding the security of Japan, economic issues, and settlement of disputes.

Second, two new chapters were added regarding the security of Japan (Chapter IV on the Navy, Army, and Air Forces, and Chapter V on the Allied Security Forces), providing that while Japan would be restrained from rebuilding its army, navy, and air force to pre-war levels, the country would be given access to Allied Security Forces to maintain its borders and the security of its people. These provisions reflected the intent of the crafters of the treaty to prevent the rebirth of Japanese militarism in the future.

Third, with regard to economic issues and the settlement of disputes, the

---

66   [Treaty of Peace with Japan] (Sept. 7, 1949) p. 3. RG 59, Office of Northeast Asia Affairs, Records Relating to the Treaty of Peace with Japan-Subject File, 1945-1, Lot 56D527, Box 6.

draft provided some new provisions: Chapter VIII on General Economic Relations; Chapter IX on the Settlement of Disputes, and Chapter X on Final Provisions. These new provisions were preserved in subsequent draft treaties.

Fourth, in the provisions related to Korea and its territory, some modifications were made to the wording used such as replacing "Koreans" with "the Korean Government and Korea" and replacing "Korea" with "the Korean Peninsula." Overall, however, this draft was not substantially different from the draft treaties of 1947 and 1948. Thus in this draft, the Liancourt Rocks (Dokdo) were upheld as being part of Korean territory.

Draft treaty of October 13, 1949: The Liancourt Rocks (Dokdo) under Korean sovereignty

According to Fearey, from the Office of Northeast Asian Affairs, who led out in its development, this draft treaty was based to a large degree on the January 1948 draft.[67] For the description of Japanese territory, however, a different approach from the one used in the draft treaties of 1947 and 1948 was adopted. Instead of delineating the borders of Japan using degrees of longitude and latitude, the October 1949 draft treaty used the method of spelling out those islands to be included as Japanese territory. This was the method employed in the draft treaties prior to July 1947.

1. The territorial limits of Japan shall comprise the four principal Japanese islands of Honshu, Kyushu, Shikoku and Hokkaido and all adjacent minor islands, including the islands of the Inland Sea (Seto Naikai), Sado, Oki Retto, Etorofu, Kunashiri, the Habomai Islands, Shikotan, Tsushima, the Goto Archipelago, the Ryukyu Islands north of 29° N. latitude, and the Izu Islands southward to and including Sofu Gan (Lot's Wife).

2. These territorial limits are indicated on the map attached to the present

---

67   Memorandum by Fearey (NA) to Allison (NA), Subject: Attached Treaty Draft (Oct. 14, 1949), RG 59, Department of State, Decimal File, 740.0011PW(Peace)/10-1449.

Treaty.[68]

As shown above, the four islands in the North were again identified as belonging to Japan, probably as a sort of compensation in exchange for the designation of Ryukyu and Ogasawara as being under US trusteeship.

Article 4 of Chapter I dealt with Korea and its territory. The provision was modified slightly, but content-wise, it was essentially the same as the draft treaties of 1948.[69] Thus, this draft continued to maintain that the Liancourt Rocks (Dokdo) were Korean territory.

The draft treaties of October 27 and October 31, 1949: "Basic Principles" added

The draft treaty of October 13 was modified on October 27 and again on October 31, 1949. The changes involved the addition of a new first chapter entitled Basic Principles. This new chapter was based on the views of Edwin O. Reischauer, assistant professor at Harvard University and an expert on Japan who served as a special adviser for the US DoS. After reviewing the October 13 draft treaty, Reischauer had submitted some feedback to the Department of State regarding the psychological questions involved in the draft treaty.[70] He pointed out that the draft did not hide its cynicism and doubt about the war-renouncing Japanese Constitution and that a definite declaration of the ideals that the US stood for was missing. As an alternative, Reischauer suggested that the territorial clauses not be placed at the very beginning of the draft and that the provisions of Article 11 and Article 12 in the original draft articulating that Japan confirm to universal principles of mankind and international ethics be organized as

---

68   *Ibid.* p. 3.

69   "Treaty of Peace with Japan," (Oct. 13, 1949), pp. 4-, RG 59, Department of State, Decimal File, 740.0011PW(Peace)/10-449.

70   Memorandum by Reischauer to Hamilton, Subject: Comments on Psychological Questions Involved in the Draft Japanese Peace Treaty (Oct. 19, 1949), RG 59, Department of State, Decimal File, 740.0011PW(Peace)/10-949.

a separate chapter. He also proposed to title this chapter Basic Principles.[71]

The fact that the US DoS chose to accommodate Reischauer's concerns about the anticipated "psychological problems" that may be felt by the Japanese is indicative of the direction that the department had at this point. From this point in time onwards, officials with a deep understanding of or familiarity with Japan at the US DoS became more deeply involved in the drafting of the Japanese peace treaty. Experts on Japan in the US spared no efforts to take Japan and its people into consideration, while experts on Japan in the Office of the US Political Adviser for Japan sought to speak for the interests and concerns of the Japanese government more fervently than anyone else.

The next draft of the Japanese peace treaty was expanded to a total of ten chapters. In addition to the inclusion of a new first chapter, it became clear that the purpose of the treaty now lay not so much in establishing an enduring postwar settlement in a legal sense using such terms as "punishment" and "reparations," but rather in "peacemaking," i.e., the making of a lasting peace with Japan. Just like Reischauer, the officers of the Bureau of Far Eastern Affairs along with the Policy Planning Staff were opposed to including non-executable constraints upon Japan.[72] It became increasingly clear that the overall ambience of the process involved in developing the draft treaty had turned in favor of Japan.

Following a review of the October 27 draft treaty, some further modifications were made on October 31. These changes in the draft continued on into the official draft treaty of November 2.

Draft treaty of November 2, 1949: The Liancourt Rocks (Dokdo) under Korean sovereignty

The official draft treaty finalized on November 2, 1949 was forwarded to

---

71 Subject: Comments on Psychological Questions Involved in the Draft Japanese Peace Treaty (Oct. 19, 1949), p. 2, RG 59, Department of State, Decimal File, 740.0011PW(Peace)/10-949.

72 Memorandum by Hamilton (FE) to Fisher (L) (Oct. 31, 1949), RG 59, Department of State, Decimal File, 740.0011PW(Peace)10-149.

Tokyo under cover of a letter sent to Sebald, the political adviser to SCAP (November 4, 1949).[73] This is a clear indication why efforts to formulate a draft treaty, which had been discontinued in January 1948, were resumed in the second half of 1949. Taking this into consideration, the main characteristics of the November 2, 1949 draft treaty were as follows:

First, the draft treaty formulated in September and October of 1949 was made specifically for the purpose of consulting with the UK and the British Commonwealth countries. In other words, with the prospects of an early conclusion of a peace treaty with Japan becoming bleak due to opposition by the Soviet Union and China and on account of the non-cooperation of other major Allied Powers, the new driving force for the treaty came from the UK. This is indication that the UK government would exert some influence over subsequent work on the draft.

Second, while in 1947 and 1948 the crafting of the draft treaty had been assigned to the Working Group on Japan Treaty led by head of Bureau of Far Eastern Affairs, no new committee was separately established in 1949. It seems, however, that Fearey, from the Bureau of Far Eastern Affairs, took a central role in this latter phase of the development of a draft treaty. After Borton, the officer who had previously played the key role, left the Department of State, his position was filled first by Max Bishop and then by John Allison. Despite these changes in personnel, the overall policy direction appears to have remained unchanged.

Third, the November 2 draft treaty of 1949 was only sent to Tokyo (i.e., to Sebald and MacArthur) and to the Secretary of Defense. The US Department of State instructed Tokyo to send initial feedback promptly by telegram and then a more detailed and technical review of the draft proposal later. Sebald sent to Washington his initial feedback on the draft treaty in the form of a summary comment, and then a more detailed commentary some time later. What is to be noted is that while Korea was kept in the dark, Sebald in Japan sent two reports to the US DoS in which

---

73 Letter by W. Walton Butterworth to William J. Sebald, Acting United States Political Adviser for Japan (Nov. 4, 1949), RG 59, Department of State, Decimal File, 740.0011PW(Peace)/11-49.

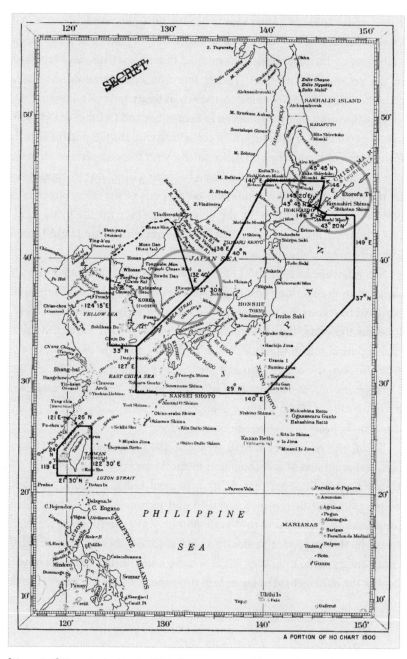

[Figure 3-4] Map attached to the US draft peace treaty with Japan (November 2, 1949)

[Figure 3-5] Four islands in the North in the draft treaty of November 2, 1949

he objected the Liancourt Rocks being placed under the jurisdiction of Korea in the treaty and claimed instead that Japan should have sovereignty.

Following are the key characteristics of the November 1949 draft. First, in terms of organization, the draft now had more chapters than the previous one, with a total of ten chapters including the new Chapter I on Basic Principles and the new Chapter III on Special Political Clauses.[74]

Second, the preamble now listed 49 countries as "The Allied and Associated Powers" but excluded Korea.[75]

Third, Japanese territory was now specified in a different way under Article 3 of Chapter II. Other than that, the most notable changes were the exclusion from Japan of the four islands in the North and the reinstitution of a clear boundary line visualizing its precise, postwar borders.[76]

The four islands to the North that were excluded were Etorofu, Kunashir, Habomai, Shikotan.[77] It was also stated that the US should consider

---

74   Memorandum by Howard to Butterworth, Subject: Security Clauses of the Japanese Peace Treaty (Oct. 20, 1949), RG 59, Department of State, Decimal File, 740.0018PW(Peace)/10.2049; *Security Clauses of Japanese Peace Treaty*, First Draft (Oct. 17, 1949).

75   "Treaty of Peace with Japan," (Nov. 2, 1949), p. 1, RG 59, Department of State, Decimal File, 740.0011PW(Peace)/11.1449. The original text reads as follows: "It is thought that Korea should not participate in a peace treaty with Japan."

76   *Ibid.* pp. 4-5.

77   *Ibid.* pp. 5-6.

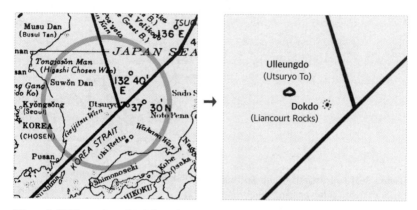

[Figure 3-6] Ulleungdo and Dokdo in the draft treaty of November 2, 1949

proposing to the Soviet Union to put the Kuril Islands under trusteeship.[78]

A clear boundary line was reintroduced to delineate the extent of Japanese territory. The main difference from the August 1947 draft treaty was the exclusion from Japanese sovereignty of the four islands in the North and some additional territory in the Southwest. Figure 3-4 shows the map attached to the November 2 draft treaty of 1949.[79]

Figure 3-5 provides a magnification of a portion of the map in Figure 3-4, showing in greater detail the boundary line in relation to the four islands in the North (marked as A). With the exclusion of these four islands, one can see that the territory in the upper right part of the map is clearly marked as being outside Japan's territorial boundaries. The coordinates showing the extent of Japanese territory in this draft were changed accordingly as well.

Fourth, the provision related to Korea and its territory was included in Article 6 of Chapter II. Overall, it remained the same as that of the October

---

78 *Ibid.* pp. p. 6.

79 This map was found in large numbers in the US Department of State files. This particular map was the one conveyed to General MacArthur together with the November 2, 1949 draft treaty. It is from the MacArthur Archives. MacArthur Archives (MA), RG 5, Box 3, Official Correspondence 1948-1951.

13 draft treaty.[80]

The territorial boundaries of Korea remained unchanged. Figure 3-6 is a scaled-up version of the line delineating the border of Korea in relation to Ulleungdo and Dokdo (marked as B) on the map in Figure 3-4. Ulleungdo (Utsuryo To on the map) is shown clearly on the Korean side (i.e., to the left) of the boundary line dividing Korea and Japan, as is Dokdo (the smaller dot-encircled island to the right of Ulleungdo). The coordinates showing the extent of Korean territory remained unchanged in this draft. However, the dispute over the rightful ownership of Dokdo was triggered after the November 1949 draft treaty was sent to Sebald in Tokyo.

---

80 "Treaty of Peace with Japan," (Nov. 2, 1949), p. 6, RG 59, Department of State, Decimal File, 740.0011PW(Peace)/11-449.

3

Dokdo in the Draft Treaties of the
US Department of State, Part II (1949-1950)
: Sebald's Posturing

1) Sebald's review of the draft treaty and his insistence that the Liancourt Rocks (Dokdo) be placed under Japanese jurisdiction

The US DoS's draft treaty of November 2, 1949 was sent to Sebald in the Office of the US Political Adviser for Japan in Tokyo. Upon request of the Department of State, Sebald quickly sent MacArthur's initial feedback on the draft by telegram and later sent some more detailed commentary. Thus, two different documents were sent by Sebald to the US DoS with regard to the November 1949 draft treaty. The first was a telegram message dated November 14, 1949, two pages in length, containing the initial observations of MacArthur and Sebald.[81] The second was a despatch dated November 19, 1949, 11 pages long, containing more detailed commentary.[82]

Sebald's telegram (November 14, 1949): The Liancourt Rocks (Dokdo) under Japanese sovereignty

According to Sebald, MacArthur emphasized that the treaty with Japan was a "peace" treaty and pointed out the need for careful consideration to be given to the psychological fallout and adverse economic implications

---

81 Telegram by Sebald to the Secretary of State, no. 495 (Nov. 14, 1949), RG 59, Department of State, Decimal File, 740.0011PW(Peace)/11-449.

82 William J. Sebald to the Secretary of State, Subject: Comment on Draft Treaty of Peace with Japan, no. 806 (Nov. 19, 1949), RG 59, Department of State, Decimal File, 740.0011PW (Peace)/11-949.

that the treaty would impose on the Japanese.[83] Viewing things from a broader perspective, MacArthur was more concerned that the nature of the peace treaty be such that it would bring about a definitive peace. While the US DoS had urgently asked Sebald for MacArthur's "first impression" of the draft treaty, Sebald was more focused on expressing his own views and position in the telegram. Stating that he and MacArthur had independently given careful study to the draft treaty, Sebald referred himself to MacArthur's authority by fully concurring with his observations. Following a description of MacArthur's feedback, Sebald added his own comments at length.

Sebald raised some pro-Japanese observations in more detail. He emphasized that they were not his views but those of the Office of the US Political Adviser for Japan. As a tentative reaction, he stated that the mission agreed that it would prefer a shorter treaty with less emphasis upon technical matters and that it was somewhat concerned that the treaty seemingly represented the maximum conditions which the US sought to place upon Japan, and that it left little room for bargaining purposes should a "harder" treaty be desired by the Allies.

Sebald then specifically criticized some of the provisions, raising concerns about 11 articles. He expressed utmost support for Japan with respect to three articles in the territorial clauses and recommended that seven articles unfavorable to Japan be reworded or deleted. There was only one article with which he was in full agreement.

Essentially, Sebald's claim was that the views and interests of the Soviet Union, China, and other Allied Powers could be ignored, while those of Japan should be diligently protected. With regard to territorial issues, Sebald did not approach them with the neutrality and fairness of a diplomat, nor did he take into account the established territorial policy that the Allies had agreed upon during wartime. Instead, his main concern was to keep Japan firmly on the side of the US in its fight against communism and to

---

83 Telegram by Sebald to the Secretary of State, no. 495 (Nov. 14, 1949), pp. 1-2, RG 59, Department of State, Decimal File, 740.0011PW(Peace)/11.1449.

uphold Japan's territorial interests.

Sebald may have decided to take the extremely pro-Japanese position that he did based on prior knowledge that the US was planning on pursuing a separate peace settlement with Japan excluding not only the Soviet Union but also Communist China in Beijing and Free China in Taipei. He was also likely aware that the draft treaty that he had received had not been sent to the other major Allied Powers like the Soviet Union and China.

Sebald's proposal to place Formosa under trusteeship consequent upon plebiscite under Article 4 was in absolute disregard of the Allies' wartime agreement under the Cairo and Potsdam Declarations. Even the Japanese Ministry of Foreign Affairs, after having duly reviewed territorial issues, had accepted as established policy the necessity of returning Formosa to China in accordance with the provisions of the Cairo Declaration, which stated that all the territories that Japan had stolen from the Chinese, such as Manchuria and the Pescadores, be restored. However, there is a curious sense of *déjà vu* upon reading Sebald's proposal for a trusteeship consequent upon plebiscite, as the exact same proposal had been made on Rhyukyu islands, South Sakhalin, and the Kurils by the Japanese Ministry of Foreign Affairs in the first research paper completed by its Executive Committee for Research on a Peace Treaty in May 1946. The document was titled, *The Expected Political Clauses in a Peace Treaty and Countermeasures for Possible Discrepancies (Draft).*[84] In the paper, the Japanese Ministry of Foreign Affairs had taken the position that, while deciding that it would not oppose an incorporation of territory or trusteeship by the US and despite the fact that Japan had accepted the territorial clauses in its wartime agreements with the Allied Powers, it would either radically oppose the transfer of territory to the Soviet Union or China or demand that a "plebiscite" be conducted in each of the territories in question. Thus, it appears probable that Sebald was doing little more than repeating earlier proposals made

---

84 "Expected Political Clauses in a Peace Treaty and Countermeasures against Possible Discrepancies (draft) (Peace Treaty Research for Political Clauses-1)" (May 1946), Ministry of Foreign Affairs of Japan, 2006, pp. 95-96.

by the Japanese Ministry of Foreign Affairs for a trusteeship consequent upon plebiscite. Sebald's stated rationale was to prevent the possibility of Formosa being handed over to communist China. Essentially, it is more likely, however, that he believed that the pro-Japanese natives of Formosa would decide to come under the sovereignty of Japan should a plebiscite be conducted. If the Chiang Kai-shek Government had ever become aware of Sebald's missive in response to the November 14, 1949 treaty draft, it would have triggered an intense backlash and a pronounced increase of discord between the US and China.

Sebald's comment regarding the four islands in the North under Article 5 also strongly advocated the position of the Japanese Ministry of Foreign Affairs.

Sebald's comment on Dokdo under Article 6 is already well known. It says "Recommend reconsideration Liancourt Rocks (Takeshima). Japan's claim to these islands is old and appears valid. Security considerations might conceivably envisage weather and radar stations thereon."[85] Such a claim was, with all likelihood, taken directly from a June 1947 publication of the Japanese Ministry of Foreign Affairs entitled *Minor Islands Adjacent to Japan Proper, Part IV: Minor Islands in the Pacific, and Minor Islands in the Japan Sea.*

It appears, in retrospect, that Sebald either contacted the Japanese Ministry of Foreign Affairs directly in preparing his response to the draft treaty or else depended mainly on the Ministry's publications regarding territorial issues, including the report of the Executive Committee for Research on a Peace Treaty (May 1946) regarding Formosa, the publicity paper of the Ministry entitled *Minor Islands Adjacent to Japan Proper, Part I, The Kurile Islands, the Habomais, and Shikotan* (November 1946) concerning the four islands in the North, and the Ministry's publicity paper entitled *Minor Islands Adjacent to Japan Proper, Part IV, Minor Islands in the*

---

85   The original text reads as follows: "Article 6: Recommend reconsideration Liancourt Rocks (Takeshima). Japan's claim to these islands is old and appears valid. Security considerations might conceivably envisage weather and radar stations thereon."

Pacific, Minor Islands in the Japan Sea (June 1947) with regard to Dokdo.

While the Soviet Union and China were kept in the dark, Sebald proposed radically pro-Japanese alternatives that disregarded the wartime agreements of the Allied Powers. His reactions were so blatantly biased in favor of Japan that, had they been known to other nations, they would have with all likelihood triggered a tremendous uproar not only among America's closest Allies—the UK, Australia, and New Zealand—but also among other allies in Asia such as the Philippines and Burma. Neither the Korean government nor the American Embassy in Korea was made aware of the November 2 draft treaty or of Sebald's recommendation to place Dokdo under the sovereignty of Japan. Owing to Sebald's partial and biased statements in his calculated response to the US DoS's November 2 draft treaty, Korean territory would now suddenly become a subject of dispute.

Sebald's report (November 19, 1949): The Liancourt Rocks (Dokdo) under Japanese sovereignty

Upon request from the US DoS, Sebald sent a prompt reply by telegram on November 14, 1947 with MacArthur's initial reactions to the November 2 draft treaty. He followed this up with more detailed comments by air mail on November 19, 1947.[86] In his memoirs, Sebald said that "To my mind, the document was too long and too complex and its general tone was one of dictation by the victor to the vanquished."[87]

Sebald pointed out that the draft treaty did not fully recognize conditions in the Far East as they existed at that time and failed determinedly to discard the psychology and concepts which prevailed before and at the time of Japan's surrender.[88]

---

86 W. J. Sebald, United States Political Adviser for Japan to the Secretary of State, Subject: Comment on Draft Treaty of Peace with Japan, no. 806 (Nov. 19, 1949), RG 59, Department of State, Decimal File, 740.0011PW(Peace)/11-1949.

87 Sebald with Brines, *With MacArthur in Japan: A Personal History of the Occupation*, p. 249.

88 Subject: Comment on Draft Treaty of Peace with Japan, no.806 (Nov. 19, 1949), p. 3, RG 59,

The Far Eastern situation has undergone a vast change during the past four years, largely to American disadvantage (with the single exception of our relations with Japan); the coming treaty must face this situation and take into account the obvious fact that the United States now has a vital stake, which did not exist four years ago, in a politically stable and friendly Japan. It may accordingly be questioned whether many of the terms of the November 2 draft may not be too severe for a Japan which suffered total defeat, without offering us any conceivable advantage. The draft could possibly be improved by making greater allowances for the fact that the difficult task of rebuilding Japan into a peaceful democratic country, and of meeting deficiencies to enable Japan to achieve a stable economy capable of sustaining its large population, has been primarily the responsibility and burden of the United States.[89]

The 6-page *Detailed Comment on November 2 Draft Treaty* made the following points related to the territorial clauses and the provisions on Korea.[90]

First, Sebald strongly criticized the provisions demarcating Japanese territory in Article 3 of the draft treaty, stating that the method of delineation employed had serious psychological disadvantages for the Japanese people. His primary criticism was of the method of using a boundary line to delineate Japanese territory, a method that had been used since the first drafts were put together in 1947. Sebald argued that "another method of description be employed which avoids circumscribing Japan with a line even if it is necessary to enumerate a large number of territories in an annex." In short, Sebald openly opposed the method of clearly spelling out the borders of Japanese territory on the grounds that it

---

Department of State, Decimal File, 740.0011PW (Peace)/11-1949.

89   *Ibid.*, p. 4.

90   "Detailed Comment on November 2 Draft Treaty," Enclosure to Despatch No. 806 dated November 19, 1949, from Office of United States Political Adviser for Japan, Tokyo, Subject: Comment on Draft Treaty of Peace with Japan, RG 59, Department of State, Decimal File, 740.0011PW(Peace)/11-1949.

may have a detrimental psychological impact on Japan. He concluded by recommending that the map just be deleted from the draft altogether.

After receiving Sebald's recommendations, the US DoS's draft treaty underwent two major revisions relating to territorial issues: first, the method of using a boundary line to clearly demarcate the boundaries of Japanese territory was deleted, and second, the attached map clearly spelling out the extent of Japanese territory was removed. These two features were what the Japanese Ministry of Foreign Affairs most wanted to change. As numerous researchers have pointed out since, the biggest reason why many East Asian countries have become embroiled in postwar territorial disputes with Japan was because no provisions were established clearly demarcating the territory of Japan and no map was used that visually illustrated its borders at the San Francisco Peace Conference. The failure to include such provisions created unnecessary confusion and ambiguity and allowed for conflicting interpretations of the treaty's territorial provisions to emerge.

Basically, there were three ways of stipulating the territory of Japan in the treaty: the first was to merely specify the territory to be included under Japanese sovereignty; the second was to specify the territory to be included under Japanese sovereignty as well as the territories that would be ceded by Japan; and the third was to merely specify the territories that Japan would agree to give up. Japan most favored the approach of merely specifying the territories that it would agree to give up, since it would allow it to assert its sovereignty claims over those areas that remained unspecified in the treaty.[91]

The second point Sebald suggested was that articles 4 through 12 of the draft, which related to the territories that Japan would give up, be omitted, and the disposition of the territories formerly under Japanese jurisdiction be agreed upon by the signatories other than Japan in a document subsidiary to the treaty. He was suggesting that the disposition of Formosa,

---

91   Jung, "The UK FCO's Draft of the Treaty of Peace with Japan and its Attached Map and Reconfirmation of Korea's Sovereignty over Dokdo."

the four islands in the North, and Dokdo be addressed in a subsidiary agreement. It is difficult to ascertain why Sebald would have made such a proposal other than that he was trying to soften the blow to Japan by having deleted from the draft the fact that Japan would be expelled from all territories which it had taken by violence and greed. This initiative on Sebald's part is indication that he was more actively advocating Japan's interests with respect to the draft treaty than was the Japanese Ministry of Foreign Affairs.

Third, as in his telegram of November 14, 1949, Sebald proposed with regard to Formosa that consideration be given to the question of a plebiscite to decide on a United Nations trusteeship, on the grounds that disturbed conditions in China intervening since the Cairo Conference invalidated any automatic disposition of the Island.[92] He was basically saying that the wartime international agreements between the Allied Powers should henceforth be considered null and void.

Fourth, regarding the disposition of the four islands in the North, he argued that the islands listed in his proposed Article 3 as belonging to Japan specifically include Etorofu, Kunashiri, Shikotan, and Habomai Islands. This was again little more than a reechoing of arguments that had been put forward by the Japanese Ministry of Foreign Affairs.

Fifth, he made the following claims regarding the disposition of Dokdo.

With regard to the disposition of islands formerly possessed by Japan in the direction of Korea it is suggested that Liancourt Rocks (Takeshima) be specified in our proposed Article 3 as belonging to Japan. Japan's claim to these islands is old and appears valid, and it is difficult to regard them as islands off the shore of Korea. Security considerations might also conceivably render the provision of weather and radar stations on these islands a matter of interest to the United States.[93]

---

92 "Detailed Comment on November 2 Draft Treaty," p. 2.
93 *Ibid.*

In his missive to the US DoS, Sebald made four claims regarding Dokdo. The first was that Dokdo should be specified in Article 3 as belonging to Japan. The second was that Japan's claim to this island was "old" and "appeared valid." Third, he argued that it was difficult to regard Dokdo as an island off the shore of Korea. And fourth, he conjectured that it would also be in US interests to build weather and radar stations there.

Sebald did not present any documentation supporting his arguments, however. Nowhere in Sebald's reports to the US DoS can one find the documentary basis of support on which his claims were made. Before advancing his claims, Sebald could have at least inquired into why the US DoS had marked Dokdo as Korean territory and then state his reasons for opposing that decision. If that were the case, he would have consulted with the Korean government and the American Embassy in Korea to understand what the position of Korea (government) was with regard to Dokdo. Then, he could have made a more balanced and logical case for his position through a comparison of the claims of Japan with those of the US DoS and Korea.

Sebald's insistence that Dokdo should belong to Japan, not Korea contained what appear to be clear allusions to the June 1947 publication *Minor Islands Adjacent to Japan Proper, Part IV. Minor Islands in the Pacific, Minor Islands in the Japan Sea* published by the Japanese Ministry of Foreign Affairs. For example, he quoted from the material that "attention should be focused on Japan's claims that there was no Korean name for Liancourt Rocks, when Dagelet (Ulleungdo) did in fact have a Korean name, and that these islands did not appear on any Korean maps. On February 22, 1905, the governor of Shimane Prefecture enacted Ordinance No. 87, which declared that Liancourt Rocks belonged to the Oki Islands District of Shimane Prefecture."[94] Thus, it seems likely that he depended heavily on political propaganda put out by the Japanese Ministry of Foreign Affairs as the basis for his arguments.

94　Minor Islands Adjacent to Japan Proper, Part IV, "Minor Islands in the Pacific, Minor Islands in the Japan Sea," June, 1947, pp. 9-10.

Also, Sebald's proposal to install weather and radar stations in Dokdo smacks of a logic that combines US military interests with the aggressive brutality and inhumanity to which Japanese Imperialism had subjected the Korean people. In support of his claims, Sebald used the historical precedent that radio stations and a Japanese Navy observation facility had been installed on Dokdo during the Russo-Japanese War.

As shown above, Sebald made the outrageous claim that Dokdo belonged to Japan in two successive reports to the US DoS. Also, the overall tenor of his comments was openly pro-Japanese and a blatant negation of not only previous international agreements but also the official US policy up until that time.

It was on November 4, 1947 that Assistant Secretary of State for Far Eastern Affairs Butterworth sent the November 2 draft treaty to Sebald.[95] Given that Sebald's first report to the US DoS was dated November 14, one can assume that extensive closed-door discussions took place over that ten-day period at the Office of the US Political Adviser for Japan. The pro-Japanese claims embedded in Sebald's response make it difficult to believe that the comments came solely from that Office without any outside consultation. In other words, it could well be that Sebald received consultative assistance from Japan as he prepared his report.

2) Request by the US Ambassador to Korea for Korea to be a party to the treaty

Report of the US Ambassador to Korea (December 3, 1949)

The November 1949 draft treaty, formulated by the US DoS with the intention of sending to the UK government in December 1949, was in the end communicated only to MacArthur and Sebald in Tokyo and the US Secretary of Defense. No other Allied Powers were informed of it. While

---

95 Letter by W. Walton Butterworth to William J. Sebald, Acting United States Political Adviser for Japan, (Nov. 14, 1949), RG 59, Department of State, Decimal File, 740.0011PW (Peace)/11-449.

Sebald was strongly making his claims in favor of Japanese ownership of Dokdo, neither the Korean government nor the US Embassy in Korea was aware of what was happening.

The only information that the US DoS gave to the American Embassy in Korea related to whether Korea would be allowed to be a party to the treaty. Undersecretary of Defense Webb sent a telegram to US Ambassador to Korea John J. Muccio in this regard on November 23, 1949.[96] Webb announced that the US DoS's plan was to have the countries that had declared war on Japan or that had been at war with Japan during World War II be the signatories to the treaty. The 13 countries of the Far Eastern Committee would be the actual negotiating powers, and the remaining 38 countries would take part in the treaty in a consultative capacity. Stating that Korea was neither a negotiating country nor a consultative party, Webb urgently asked the American Embassy about whether and in what capacity Korea should be allowed to participate in the treaty.

Muccio had little choice but to answer the question in the prescribed manner. Unaware of the substance of the draft treaty, the process by which it was formulated, or the specific inside story involving the ongoing deliberations over it, all he could do was to communicate the sentiments of the local population regarding the draft treaty itself. Thus, Muccio requested that Korea be included in some capacity among nations participating in the Japanese peace treaty. Though Koreans would request to be an actual negotiating party, Muccio believed that if they could be given good reason why that was impossible or impracticable, they could be persuaded to participate in a consultative capacity.[97] Thus, he requested that Korea take part in the treaty process in a consultative role rather than a negotiating capacity.

Muccio also suggested that Korea-Japan problems would be better resolved through an international forum rather than through bilateral

---

96   Telegram by Webb to Muccio, no. 984 (Nov. 23, 1949), RG 59, Department of State, Decimal File, 740.0011PW(Peace)/11-349.

97   Telegram by Muccio to the Secretary of State, no. 1455 (Dec. 3, 1949), RG 59, Department of State, Decimal File, 740.0011PW(Peace)/12-349.

talks, and that such an eventuality should be taken into consideration by the US.[98] Following the San Francisco Peace Conference, a key issue that arose during the preliminary talks held between Korea and Japan was whether the normalization of relations between the two countries should be dealt with through bilateral talks or through some kind of round-table conference involving the US and other key Allied Powers. It seemed to Muccio that the normalization of relations between Japan, the aggressor, and Korea, the victim, may require the presence of an impartial arbitrator or a party that could exercise some pressure as needed to bring about a fair and just outcome to the negotiations. Claims that "perfect bilateral talks" were possible were unfair and, in practice, lent advocacy to Japan's position, as they failed to consider the long history of oppression that the Korean people had experienced at the hands of the Japanese.

From Muccio's perspective, it was important that Korea be included as a party to the treaty in a consultative capacity while preventing it from making additional demands for reparations, and that the normalization of Korea-Japan relations be resolved through an international forum rather than through bilateral negotiations. Such a reply was within the realm of what was considered reasonable and appropriate for a US diplomat to make. From the perspective of the Korean government, Muccio's request was neutral and mildly supportive of Korea. However, it was not in any way as supportive of Korea's political agenda as was Sebald's missive supportive of Japan's.

In contrast to Muccio's reply, Sebald's response in retrospect comes across as being excessive in its advocacy of Japan's position and interests. From this point in time onwards, Sebald made little effort to hide his role as an advocate for the Japanese lobby, conveying to the US DoS various documents supporting the position of Japan.

Meanwhile, following Muccio's report, the Division of Research for the Far East under the Office of Intelligence and Research of the US DoS addressed the participation of Korea in its report No. 163 (December

---

98   *Ibid.*

12, 1949).[99] The report took a negative stance on Korea's request to be acknowledged as a country that had been at war with Japan, pointing out the fact that the Provisional Government of the Republic of Korea had not yet obtained international recognition. It anticipated that Korea's participation in the peace conference may entail: 1) an excessive demand by Korea for repayment and reparations from Japan, 2) a demand by North Korea for a place in the peace settlement process, and 3) more pressure being exerted by North Korea and the Soviet Union on South Korea should North Korea be excluded from the settlement process. It also predicted that Korea's antagonistic attitude towards Japan and the US could be further exacerbated if it were excluded. After receiving reports from Muccio and the Division of Research for the Far East, the US DoS put Korea on the list of the negotiators and signatories to the peace treaty with Japan in its sixth draft (December 29, 1949). This was a strategic US decision to preserve "Korea's prestige" given that the US intervention to aid Korea had already begun. Following the outbreak of the Korean War, even Dulles viewed that Korean participation in the peace settlement with Japan was necessary in light of the heightened psychological and symbolic position that Korea had now attained in the eyes of the Free World.

Agreement Respecting the Disposition of Former Japanese Territories of December 19, 1949 (draft): The Liancourt Rocks (Dokdo) under Korean sovereignty

On December 19, 1949, a document titled *Agreement Respecting the Disposition of Former Japanese Territories* was produced in preparation for a possible agreement between the Allied Powers and Japan on an as-yet undetermined date in 1950.[100] It seems that the document pertained to the new proposals that Sebald had made (November 19, 1949) regarding

---

99   DRF no. 163, "Participation of the ROK in the Japanese Peace Settlement," (Dec. 12, 1949), RG 59, Records of the Division of Research for Far East, Lot 58D245.

100   Lee Seok-woo, 2002, "Dokdo-related materials held by the US National Archives and Records Administration," *Seoul International Law Journal*, Vol. 9, No. 1, pp. 155-156.

the territorial clauses of the draft treaty. Sebald had proposed that the provisions regarding "territories to be ceded by Japan" be entirely deleted from the November 2, 1949 draft and that instead an annex document be included containing the details of the disposition of the territories formerly under the control of Japan along with the documented consent of the Allied Powers to these arrangements. In short, this next document was a sort of experimental revision of the draft treaty to accommodate some of Sebald's recommendations. It was also designed to draw an agreement among the Allied and Associated Powers regarding the disposition of territories formerly held by Japan. Though the format of the document was changed based on Sebald's recommendation, the substance did not entirely conform to his suggestions. His proposal to determine the trusteeship of Formosa consequent upon plebiscite was rejected, while his recommendation that the four islands in the North be placed under the jurisdiction of Japan was accepted. Sebald's insistence that the Liancourt Rocks (Dokdo) belonged to Japan was not accommodated. In other words, despite Sebald's insistence (November 14 and 19, 1949) that the Liancourt Rocks (Dokdo) should be viewed as Japanese territory rather than Korean, the next draft document maintained that Dokdo (the Liancourt Rocks or Takeshima in the document) was Korean territory.[101]

In this sense, it seems like the December 1949 document was primarily made to accommodate Sebald's proposals to delete the Japanese territorial provisions and place a new agreement regarding the disposition of Japanese territory in an annex to the treaty proper. In other words, the Bureau of Far

---

101   The original text reads as follows: "Article 3. The Allied and Associated Powers agree that there shall be transferred in full sovereignty to the Republic of Korea all rights and titles to the Korean mainland territory and all offshore Korean islands, including Quelpart (Saishu To), the Nan How group (San to, or Komun Do) which forms Port Hamilton (Tonaikai), Dagelet Island (Utsuryo To, or Matsu Shima), Liancourt Rocks (Takeshima), and all other islands and islets to which Japan had acquired title lying outside …and to the east of the meridian 124 15 E. longitude, north of the parallel 33 N. latitude, and west of a line from the seaward terminus of the boundary approximately three nautical miles from the mouth of the Tumen River to a point in 37 30 N. latitude, 132 40 E. longitude. This line is indicated on the map attached to the present Agreement."

Eastern Affairs (Office of Northeast Asian Affairs) was making a separate annex to the peace treaty with Japan as it was preparing for a new draft treaty. In that process and in the next completed draft (December 29, 1949), the Liancourt Rocks (Dokdo) were placed under Japanese territory. Thus, the December 1949 document was a transitional one leading up to the next draft treaty.[102]

3) Change of ownership of Dokdo (December 1949-1950)

Draft treaty of December 29, 1949 and memorandum thereon: Korean participation in the treaty upheld and sovereignty over the Liancourt Rocks (Dokdo) switched to Japan

The next draft of a peace treaty was completed on December 29, 1949 and was entitled *Draft Treaty of Peace with Japan*.

The modifications in this version of the draft were made by Robert Fearey of the Office of Northeast Asian Affairs, Bureau of Far Eastern Affairs of the Department of State. A memorandum attached to this draft treaty provided an overview of the principal changes from the November 2 draft.[103]

Overall, the new draft of December 1949 reflected a shift in favor of Sebald's views. Changes were made to the territorial clauses as well as those articles on the economy, the term of the Arbitral Tribunal, and the conference to review the treaty five years after it came into effect. Fearey even noted that "On the whole we have gone quite far in adopting Sebald's suggestions, and have adopted two of the three advanced by General Mac-

102 Memorandum by Fearey to Allison, Subject: Japanese Treaty (Dec. 29, 1949), RG 59, Office of Northeast Asia Affairs, Records Relating to the Treaty of Peace with Japan-Subject File, 1945-1, Lot 56D527, Box 2.
103 Memorandum by Fearey to Allison, Subject: Japanese Treaty (Dec. 29, 1949), RG 59, Office of Northeast Asia Affairs, Records Relating to the Treaty of Peace with Japan-Subject File, 1945-1, Lot 56D527, Box 2.

Arthur."[104]

The form and substance of the December 1949 draft was notable in the following respects:

First, it was shorter overall than the November draft. The number of articles was reduced from 53 to 44, a deduction of nine articles. Of those deductions, four were from Chapter II on territorial clauses.

Second, it was decided that Korea would be a party to the peace treaty with Japan. Korea was placed on the list of "The Allied and Associated Powers" in the preamble of the draft treaty. A total of 53 countries were listed in the preamble, and this was the first draft treaty that listed Korea as a party to the peace treaty. It appears that key to this decision were the report by Ambassador Muccio (December 3, 1949) requesting that Korea participate in the treaty in a consultative capacity as well as the report from the Division of Research for Far East of the US DoS(December 12, 1949).

Along with this draft, the US DoS also produced the *Commentary on Draft Treaty of Peace with Japan*, which explained the reason why Korea was included as a party to the treaty.[105] According to the commentary, the Preamble of the draft provided a list of the "Allied and Associated Powers," which were the countries that had declared war against Japan or had been at war with it. Added to this list were India, Pakistan, Burma (all three of which were members of the Far Eastern Commission), Indonesia, Korea, and Ceylon.

Korea—The Republic of Korea is not an FEC member and is not recognized by the USSR. Nevertheless, as a liberated territory with a decades old resistance movement, a record of active fighting (with the Chinese Nationalist forces) in the war against Japan, and with an important interest in the treaty, it will doubtless feel entitled to participate, and would be resentful if the US did not favor its participation. The US Ambassador at Seoul has reported that

---

104 Memorandum by Fearey to Allison, Subject: Japanese Treaty (Dec. 29, 1949), p. 2.
105 "Commentary on Draft Treaty of Peace with Japan," (Dec. 29, 1949), RG 59, Office of Northeast Asia Affairs, Records Relating to the Treaty of Peace with Japan-Subject File, 1945-1, Lot 56D527, Box 6.

Korean officials expect that Korea will be invited to participate in the peace settlement, but that the Government could probably be persuaded to attend at a later stage in a consultative capacity along with the non-FEC nations at war or in a state of belligerency with Japan, rather than as a member of the negotiating conference.[106]

Given its long history of resistance and struggle against Japan and of being a country that had suffered for the longest period of time under Japanese aggression as the US DoS acknowledged, Korea would be recognized as a party to the treaty until the completion of the March 1951 draft treaty. However, in the face of strong and sustained opposition from the UK and Japan, the US DoS ultimately gave in and withdrew its support for Korea to be a party to the treaty.

Third, the provisions on Japanese territory were significantly modified.[107] For the most part, Sebald's recommendations were adopted. The boundary line delineating Japanese territory was removed based on Sebald's concerns that such a line may have a negative psychological impact on Japan. This decision also implied that the Allied Powers' previously established principles to handle Japanese territories in wartime, which later became part of the Cairo and the Potsdam Declarations, had practically become null and void.

Next, not only were all boundary lines delineating Japanese territory removed, but now in addition to including Dokdo as part of Japanese territory, a new boundary line was drawn connecting Tsushima, Dokdo, and Rebun. This was going a step further from Sebald's recommendations. Furthermore, of the four islands in the North, Habomai Islands and Shikotan were now specified as being a part of Japan. This was also in line with Sebald's proposals. Finally, Sebald's request to add a three-mile belt of territorial waters around the islands was also accommodated. As such, the territorial clauses of the December 1949 draft considerably mirrored

---

106 *Ibid.*
107 *Ibid.*, pp. 4-5.

Sebald's recommendations. Overall, the draft treaty was significantly shorter than the previous one and the use of boundary lines to delineate Japan's territorial boundaries was all but abandoned. Strangely, however, with respect to Dokdo alone, a new territorial boundary line was added, showing Dokdo as part of Japan instead of Korea, making this the sole exception to the new emphasis placed on the elimination of all boundary lines to delineate Japanese territory.

Fourth, Dokdo was deleted from Article 6 of Chapter II, where it was previously specified as being Korean territory.[108]

Fifth, the draft treaty indicated that Japan would cede all territorial rights to Formosa and the Pescadores to China, and all sovereignty over the Southern Sakhalin and the Kurils south of latitude 50° North to the Soviet Union. No mention was made regarding Kunashiri and Etorofu. Based on Sebald's communications regarding the Kurils, the US DoS determined that Habomai Islands and Shikotan would remain under Japan while territorial sovereignty over Kunashiri and Etorofu would be transferred to the Soviet Union.[109] However, no discussion, references, or reasonable explanations were given as far as the change of ownership of Dokdo was concerned. A search of almost all of the US DoS's files on the Japanese peace settlement has availed no such documentation or any basis of any sort explaining how this decision came about or why it was made.

It can be reasonably inferred that the US DoS, and more specifically Robert Fearey of the Office of Northeast Asian Affairs of the Bureau of Far Eastern Affairs, modified the draft treaty in line with Sebald's claims with regard to Dokdo without undertaking any serious or sustained discussions, research, or consultations with others within or outside of the US DoS. Furthermore, it appears that no one raised the issue or requested that further research be done or explanations be provided outlining the reasons for the change. While there appears to be circumstantial evidence of

---

108 *Ibid.*, p. 6.
109 Memorandum by Conrad E. Snow (L/P) to Hamilton (FE), Subject: Southern Kurile Islands and the Shikotan Archipelago (Nov. 25, 1949), RG 59, Department of State, Decimal File, 740.0011PW(Peace)/11-2549.

collaboration between the Japanese Ministry of Foreign Affairs and Sebald in Tokyo and a feeling of trust and good will between Sebald and Fearey in Washington, it appears that no one at the US DoS took the time to consult with anyone that could have spoken out in favor of Korea's interests. These were the circumstances under which Dokdo was turned over to Japan in the draft treaty of December 29, 1949.

Boggs' territorial clauses of January 3, 1950: The Liancourt Rocks (Dokdo) under Japanese sovereignty

From the time that the draft treaty of December 29, 1949 first marked Dokdo as Japanese territory, subsequent documents of the US DoS continued to indicate Dokdo as part of Japan until the early months of 1950. On January 3, 1950, Boggs sent a memorandum entitled *Draft Treaty of Peace with Japan, Territorial Clauses* to Hamilton and Fearey at the Office of Northeast Asian Affairs of the Bureau of Far Eastern Affairs.[110] As a special adviser on geography, Boggs was submitting a modified version of the territorial clauses.

In making his proposed modifications, Boggs used as his primary references the draft of November 2, 1949 and his memorandum dated December 8, 1949. His memorandum proposed changes to Article 3 (Territory of Japan), Article 4 (Formosa and the Pescadores), and Article 6 (Territory of Korea).

The first proposed change was to eliminate the annexed map showing the territorial boundaries of Japan. This proposal was in line with Sebald's proposal that the map be removed on the grounds that it would cause psychological disadvantage to Japan.

Sebald's recommendation that a trusteeship for Formosa be decided by plebiscite was not reflected in Article 4, which dealt with the disposition of Formosa. Article 6 dealing with the territories to be ceded to Korea was the

---

110 Memorandum by Boggs to Hamilton and Fearey, Subject: Draft Treaty of Peace with Japan, Territorial Clauses (Jan. 3, 1950), RG 59, 694.001/1-350.

same as in the draft treaty of December 29, 1949.

Commentary on Draft Treaty of Peace with Japan of July 1950

Work on the draft treaty of peace with Japan, which had resumed in earnest in the second half of 1949 in preparation for the British Commonwealth Foreign Ministers Conference scheduled to be held in January 1950, practically ground to a halt in January 1950. Looking at the history of the draft treaty development process, this was the second time that the work on the treaty had been suspended, the first being in the early part of 1948. The next opportunity to resume work on the draft treaty came following the appointment of John Foster Dulles as special envoy to the Treaty of Peace with Japan in mid-1950.

Other than the *Commentary on Draft Treaty of Peace with Japan* document, which again marked Dokdo as Japanese territory when it was revised between July and August of 1950, the draft treaty of December 29, 1949 was the first and last draft to indicate Dokdo as part of Japanese territory.[111]

The commentary of 1950 was similar in many respects to the initial commentary on the draft treaty of December 29, 1949, only with more detail. With respect to Korea, it first explained the reason why Korea was included as a signatory to the treaty in the preamble. Second, it included Dokdo in Japanese territory, and third it provided an explanation why it was considered as such. This explanation was basically little more than a re-statement of what was said in the draft treaty of December 29, 1949. The reason why Korea was included among the 53 countries listed as the Allied Powers and signatories to the treaty was because, although it was not a member of the Far Eastern Commission, it had a long history of fighting alongside the Chinese Nationalist Army against Japan and was, as such,

---

111 "Commentary on Draft Treaty of Peace with Japan," (Dec. 29, 1949), RG 59, Office of Northeast Asia Affairs, Records Relating to the Treaty of Peace with Japan-Subject File, 1945-51, Lot 56D527, Box 6.

recommended to be a party to the treaty in a consultative capacity.

Next, Dokdo (Takeshima or the Liancourt Rocks) was included in Japanese territory.[112] The revised commentary document gave the following explanation regarding Dokdo:

> Takeshima (Liancourt Rocks): The two uninhabited islets of Takeshima, almost equidistant from Japan and Korea in the Japan Sea, were formally claimed by Japan in 1905, apparently without protest by Korea, and placed under the Jurisdiction of the Oki Islands Branch Office of Shimane Prefecture. They are a breeding ground for sea lions, and records show that for a long time Japanese fishermen migrated there during certain seasons. Unlike Dagelet Island a short distance to the west, Takeshima has no Korean name and does not appear ever to have been claimed by Korea. The islands have been used by US forces during the occupation as a bombing range and have possible value as a weather or radar station site.[113]

The portion of the *Commentary* quoted above is, ironically, practically identical to what was stated in the propaganda leaflet titled the *Minor Islands Adjacent to Japan Proper, Part IV. Minor Islands in the Pacific, Minor Islands in the Japan Sea* published by the Japanese Ministry of Foreign Affairs in June 1947 and distributed widely to the SCAP and the US DoS. The corresponding part from the leaflet read as follows:

> Here, attention should be focused on Japan's claims that there was no Korean name for Liancourt Rocks, when Dagelet (Ulleungdo) did in fact have a Korean name, and that these islands did not appear on any Korean maps. On February 22, 1905, the governor of Shimane Prefecture enacted Ordinance No. 87, which declared that Liancourt Rocks belonged to the Oki Islands District of Shimane Prefecture. (Omitted)
> Because of the natural environment mentioned above, no one has ever

---

112 "Commentary on Draft Treaty of Peace with Japan," (undated), pp. 2-3.
113 *Ibid.*, p. 3.

settled on the islets. In 1904, the inhabitants of Oki islands began to hunt sea-lions on these islets. Each summer, the islanders, using Dagelet as their base, went regularly to the Rocks and built sheds as temporary quarters for the season.[114]

This was the first draft treaty to include a reference to the possible use of Dokdo as a bombing range by US forces. In addition to the rationale that the US DoS appropriated from the Japanese propaganda leaflet, the possible use of Dokdo as a bombing range was given as another reason why ownership of the island should be given over to Japan. The Japanese propaganda leaflet was also quoted in other US DoS documents, providing further indication that the leaflet was a trusted source not only for Sebald in Tokyo but also for Fearey in Washington. The leaflet seems to have been the only reference material that the US DoS used in support of its revised policy on the sovereignty over Dokdo.

---

114 Minor Islands Adjacent to Japan Proper, Part IV, *Minor Islands in the Pacific, Minor Islands in the Japan Sea*, June 1947, pp. 9-10, RG 84, Foreign Service Posts of the Department of State, Office of the US Political Adviser for Japan-Tokyo, Classified General Correspondence, 1945-49, Box 22.

4

Dokdo in the Draft Treaties of the US Department of State, Phase III (1950-1951)
: Dokdo-related Provisions Deleted

1) John Foster Dulles and the crafting of a new draft treaty

With work on the Japanese peace treaty again running into difficulties, US Secretary of State Dean Acheson appointed John Foster Dulles as a special adviser to the US Department of State (DoS) on April 19, 1950. Dulles was a Republican Senator from New York and a seasoned lawyer. An advocate of bipartisan diplomacy, Dulles was appointed the President's special envoy for negotiating a Japanese peace treaty on May 18, 1950. His brief visit to Tokyo on June 17, 1950 presented a new opportunity for moving forward with the Japanese peace treaty.

Dulles thought that the key to a successful peace treaty with Japan lay in it being a "non-punitive treaty," and this was his starting point. Shigeru Yoshida stated that the treaty Dulles envisioned was most characteristic in that it was not to be "a treaty of vengeance but an instrument of reconciliation," pointing to Dulles' speech on the second day of the San Francisco Peace Conference where he talked about a "peace of reconciliation" and "a peace of justice, not a peace of vengeance." According to Yoshida, the peace treaty with Japan contained no provision on Japan's war responsibility. Dulles viewed that unlike the peace treaties with Italy and Romania after World War II, the peace treaty with Japan should impose no restrictions on Japan's future rearmament and should provide for war reparations in a way that was different from the conventional treaties of the past.[115]

According to Allison, the head of the Office of Northeast Asian Affairs

---

115   Yoshida, *Kaiso Junen*, pp. 29-31, 38-39.

and Dulles' aide for the negotiations on the Japanese peace treaty, Dulles' convictions about the shape that the Japanese peace treaty should take were intimately connected with his personal experience. Having attended the Paris Peace Conference as a junior diplomat in the US delegation, Dulles had become convinced that the punitive nature of the Treaty of Versailles and the enormous reparations imposed on Germany had been the root cause of the Second World War.[116] Up to this point, peace settlements generally involved the stipulation of war responsibilities, territorial concessions, and reparations to be imposed upon the defeated nation. But Dulles held the view that such principles, which were also rigorously applied in the making of the peace treaty with Italy after World War II, were not sensible. From this perspective came the principle that the peace treaty with Japan would involve the Japanese from the onset. While the treaty was not meant to accommodate the views of Japan in every respect, such a principle signaled a peace settlement that would be entirely different in nature from any peace settlement of the past.[117]

Meanwhile, aside from Dulles' personal convictions, the outbreak of the Korean War further elevated Japan's geopolitical and strategic position. The US assessed that, since Japan was the last bridgehead against communism in Asia and a key foothold for the defense of the Pacific islands, it was urgent to restore peaceful relations with Japan and make it a friend and ally. As a result, the peace settlement with Japan advanced at a very quick pace following the outbreak of the Korean War, and particularly so after the intervention of the Communist Chinese Army in the war. The outcome was a friendly peace treaty unprecedented in the history of world diplomacy, one without a detailed reference to Japan's war responsibilities, reparations, or territorial cessions and recognizing defeated Japan as a true negotiating partner. In reality, the peace treaty with Japan was more of a bilateral

---

116 John M. Allison, *Ambassador from the Prairie*, Boston, Houghton Mifflin, 1973, p. 146.

117 *Ibid.*, p. 147. According to Allison, the formulation of a peace treaty with Japan was characterized by 1) continuous consultations with Congress, 2) the choice of bilateral negotiations rather than a roundtable conference of the victor nations, and 3) close consultations with Japan. *Ibid.*, p. 140.

agreement exchanging security for peace between the US and Japan.

Dulles' personal convictions combined with the changing situation in East Asia demanded a new approach to the making of a draft treaty of peace with Japan, one that would be entirely different from the punitive draft treaties that the US DoS had been working on since 1947. He requested that the draft treaty be simple and focused on peace. Thus, the previous treaty drafts of the US DoS, which were detailed and complex and underlined Japan's war responsibilities, reparations, and a surveillance system after the treaty went into effect, were all swept from the table.

2) Draft treaty of August 7, 1950: Japanese territorial clauses under the Potsdam Declaration discarded

Shortly before the outbreak of the Korean War in June 1950, Dulles made a short visit to Tokyo and Seoul. This visit was intended to be a preliminary inspection tour and an opportunity to meet with MacArthur to resolve differences regarding the peace treaty with Japan. MacArthur proposed that the US conclude a US-Japan security agreement at the same time the Japanese peace treaty was signed. This idea of seeking security for peace, which would give the US the right to station forces in Japan while at the same time enable the latter to regain its sovereignty, began to appear increasingly attractive after the outbreak of the Korean War. Such a formula garnered the support of the US Secretary of Defense and the Chairman of the Joint Chiefs of Staff, who were also both visiting Tokyo at the time. By September 1950, the US Secretary of State and the US Secretary of Defense were able to agree on resuming negotiations for a peace treaty with Japan on the condition of concomitantly working out a bilateral US-Japan security agreement and trusteeship of the Ryukyu Islands. The outbreak of the Korean War, which presented a crisis for US security interests in East Asia, helped to resolve differences of opinions within the US Administration in short order. The first draft treaty formulated by Dulles and his staff following his preliminary visit to Tokyo came out on August 7, 1950. Enclosed along with a document that Dulles sent to the Assistant Secretary of State for Economic Affairs, this draft treaty was marked *Draft #2* and was later called *Draft Treaty of Peace with Japan: Revised on August 7, 1950.*[118]

In his memorandum, Dulles stated that due to the change in circumstances, it was very desirable to move forward with a "simple draft." As a result, he and Allison worked on a simpler and more concise draft to replace the previous long format. The new draft treaty mirrored Dulles' desire for a "non-punitive and simple draft treaty." According to a footnote in FRUS (Foreign Relations of the United States), it was made based in part on the longer draft treaties of July 18 and August 3, 1950.[119] This first draft treaty by Dulles and Allison, which was unlike any other previous drafts, had the following chief characteristics:

First, peace was proposed as the first and foremost purpose of the draft treaty. The previous chapters and articles on basic principles or punitive provisions against Japan were deleted entirely. Instead, chapters on peace, sovereignty, United Nations, and security were added. In both form and substance, the new draft was reorganized in such a way that it emphasized peace rather than punitive arrangements, war responsibility, and reparations.

Second, the draft treaty became very simple and abbreviated. It was reduced to include less than half of the previous provisions, and the total number of articles was reduced from 44 to 21. Many of the articles dealing with legal issues, which had been taken very seriously in previous drafts, were eliminated. This draft treaty reflected the transitional circumstances leading up to the *Seven Principles of the Treaty with Japan*, which Dulles finalized in September 1950. Thus, it stands out as perhaps the most unique of all the draft treaties in that, in line with Dulles' preference for a simple, "non-punitive peace treaty," it resulted in a significant reduction or omission of much of the content included in previous versions.

---

118 Memorandum by the Consultant to the Secretary (Dulles) to the Assistant Secretary for Economic Affairs (Thorp) (Aug. 9, 1950), RG 59, Department of State, Decimal File, 694.001/8-950; *FRUS*, 1950, Vol. VI, pp. 1267-1270.

119 RG 59, Department of State, Decimal File, 694.001/7-1850. These draft treaties featured a total of 44 articles and 8 annexed documents. The security provision was not included (*FRUS*, 1950, Vol. VI, p. 1267, footnote 2).

Third, the territorial clauses on Japan completely disappeared. Regarding Japan, only Chapter II on Sovereignty provided that "2. Subject to the provisions hereof and of any other relevant treaties, the Allied and Associated Powers accept the full sovereignty of the Japanese people, and their freely chosen representatives, over Japan and its territorial waters." This was a clear break from the territorial clauses of the Potsdam Declaration, i.e. the wartime principles agreed upon by the Allied Powers regarding the disposition of Japanese territories to which the previous draft treaties had attached the utmost importance. All the subsequent draft treaties no longer employed the method of specifying the islands that would constitute Japanese territory or those that would be excluded from it. Only Korea, Formosa, the Pescadores, Southern Sakhalin, Kurils, and Ryukyu were briefly mentioned in this regard.

Fourth, Korea's territorial interests were still addressed briefly in Chapter IV, where it was stated that "Japan recognizes the independence of Korea and will base its relations with Korea on the resolutions adopted by the United Nations Assembly on December _, 1948."[120]

Also, the listing of the islands to be included in and excluded from Japanese territory disappeared, as well as the use of degrees of latitude and longitude to delineate Japanese territory. Not only was this the outcome of a desire for simplicity, but it essentially meant that the territorial clauses of the Potsdam Declaration were discarded. The draft treaty, which Dulles finalized on August 7, 1950, became the most important documentary basis for the final draft of the Japanese peace treaty.

The most notable change in the treaty was the decision to specify neither Japanese territory nor those areas to be ceded by Japan. This was essentially an abandonment of the Japanese territorial clauses under the Potsdam Declaration. The primary motivations prompting this decision were the disintegration of the system of cooperation that the Allied Powers had enjoyed during the World War II era and the pragmatic need to pursue a new order in Northeast Asia, marked by an urgent need for a peace treaty

---

120 *FRUS*, 1950, Vol. VI, p. 1268.

with Japan, the security crisis presented by the Korean War, and a desire to have a separate peace settlement excluding the Soviet Union.

In terms of format, the new territorial provisions had the advantage of keeping the peace treaty simple; however, substance-wise, they gave Japan more leeway to stir up controversy in the future and assert its claims to territories. The lax territorial provisions provided it a green light to engage in territorial disputes with Korea, China, and the Soviet Union, all of which were either not invited to sign the treaty or refused to sign it.

3) Draft treaty of September 11, 1950: Revised draft treaty

The draft treaty of August 7, 1950 was revised on September 11, 1950.[121] The overall organization remained the same as in the August 1950 draft treaty, but the number of articles increased from 21 to 26.

The provisions related to Korea also remained almost the same as in the previous draft treaty, reading "Japan recognizes the independence of Korea and will base its relations with Korea on the resolutions adopted by the United Nations Assembly and Security Council."[122]

In short, the draft treaty of September 11, 1950 reflected only minor revisions to the draft treaty of August 7, 1950. The only provisions that became clearer and more detailed were those related to the territories formerly under Japanese mandate and the Ryukyu Islands, which were to be placed under US trusteeship. In other words, the US made sure to include a clearly worded and detailed provision on those islands for which it had an interest, while completely deleting the other provisions on those islands to be included in and those to be excluded from Japan based on the Potsdam Declaration. This was basically the upshot of the key territorial clause of the draft treaty that Dulles completed on September 11, 1950.

In sum, there were two distinct, significant differences between the draft treaties of December 1949 and August 1950. The first was the overall

---

121　*Ibid.*
122　*Ibid.*, p. 1298.

emphasis on peace and deletion of the punitive and restrictive elements of previous drafts, while the second was the shift from a long, complex draft to a brief, simple one.

4) The Seven Principles of the Treaty with Japan of September 11, 1950: Territorial clauses deleted

While constructing a simpler, revised version of a draft on September 11, 1950, Dulles came up with seven principles to serve as the basis for the US position regarding the peace treaty with Japan. These principles were called the *Seven Principles of the Treaty with Japan*. At this point, Dulles' goal was for the US to come up with some common principles regarding the Japanese peace treaty and to use them as the basis for individual consultations with the other Allied Powers and Japan in order to first finalize a peace treaty and then have it signed at the peace conference, rather than have the major Allied Powers of the Second World War meet conjointly through a Foreign Ministers' meeting or a roundtable conference to work out a peace treaty with Japan. At the source of this plan were the two major changes faced by the Allied Powers, i.e. the possibility of the Soviet Union not taking part in the peace settlement and the exclusion of China. If the US were to pursue a separate peace settlement with Japan and exclude China and the Soviet Union, then the most important remaining Allied partner to work with was the UK. Accordingly, it appeared that the quickest way to a successful early conclusion of a peace treaty with Japan was to first obtain the support of the UK and the British Commonwealth countries and the unqualified support of Japan.

The *Seven Principles of the Treaty with Japan* was made public through UP(United Press) on October 6, 1950. At this point, the Japanese Ministry of Foreign Affairs was already reviewing the document.[123] The date that the

---

123 "Regarding the Seven Points Proposal on Japanese Peace Treaty Made by US" (Oct. 25, 1950), Japanese Ministry of Foreign Affairs, pp. 73-78. The Japanese Ministry of Foreign Affairs identified the seven principles as procedure, membership to the United Nations, geographical area of sovereignty, security, accession to international treaties, and settlement of claims, all of

US Department of State officially announced the principles to the media was November 24, 1950.[124]

(1) *Parties.* Any or all nations at war with Japan which are willing to make peace on the basis proposed and as may be agreed

(2) *United Nations.* Membership by Japan would be contemplated.

(3) *Territory.* Japan would (a) recognize the independence of Korea; (b) agree to United Nations trusteeship, with the United States as administering authority, of the Ryukyu and Bonin Islands, and (c) accept the future decision of the United Kingdom, the USSR, China and the United States with reference to the status of Formosa, the Pescadores, South Sakhalin and the Kurils. In the event of no decision within a year after the treaty comes into effect, the United Nations General Assembly would decide. Special rights and interests in China would be renounced.

(4) *Security.* The treaty would contemplate that, pending satisfactory alternative security arrangements such as United Nations assumption of effective responsibility, there would be continuing cooperative responsibility between Japanese facilities and United States and perhaps other forces for the maintenance of international peace and security in the Japan area.

(5) *Political and Commercial Arrangements.* Japan would agree to join multilateral treaties dealing with narcotics and fishing. Pre-war bilateral treaties could be revived by mutual agreement. Pending the conclusion of new commercial treaties, Japan would extend most-favored-nation treatment, subject to usual exceptions.

(6) *Claims.* All parties would waive claims arising out of war acts prior to Sept. 2, 1945, except that (a) the Allied powers would, in general, hold Japanese property within their territory and (b) Japan would restore Allied property or, if not restorable intact, provide yen to compensate for an agreed percentage of lost value.

---

which conformed with the actual seven principles officially announced subsequently.
124 *Ibid.*, pp. 94-98.

(7) *Disputes.* Claims disputes would be settled by a special neutral tribunal to be set up by the president of the International Court of Justice. Other disputes would be referred either to diplomatic settlement, or to the International Court of Justice.[125]

The provisions on Japanese territory were nowhere to be found in the very simple *Seven Principles of the Treaty with Japan,* and the Korea-related provision was abbreviated into a short sentence reading that Japan recognizes the independence of Korea. Such would henceforth be the key principles of the official draft of March 1951, and they would remain largely unchanged throughout all subsequent drafts of the treaty.

The Dulles Delegation used this *Seven Principles of the Treaty with Japan* extensively in their consultations with other Allied Powers. However, discussing the specifics of a proposed draft treaty solely based on such simple principles was practically impossible. This was perhaps the primary reason why Dulles sought to make the crafting of a simple draft treaty a key objective of negotiations. Dulles wanted a rough framework in order to avoid specific or detailed discussions or issues that may delay the achievement of a quick agreement and the conclusion of an early peace treaty with Japan. A simple draft treaty seemed to him to be a neat and efficient way to block or nimbly sidestep specific demands from various countries involved. It would limit the discussion of varying interests to a general and schematic level. Allowing for all the specific demands of the countries involved to be reflected in and agreed upon in the treaty would have inevitably resulted in a long treaty text, an even longer drawn-out negotiations period, and an inevitable delay in the conclusion of a Japanese peace treaty. Against this backdrop, Dulles presented the *Seven Principles of the Treaty with Japan* to the Allied Powers in the fall of 1950 and also communicated it to the Japanese government.

---

125 "Unsigned Memorandum Prepared in the Department of State," (Sept. 11, 1950), *FRUS,* 1950, Vol. VI, pp. 1296-1297. The Seven Points Proposal announced on November 24, 1951 and the Japanese title "對日講和7原則"; *Ibid.,* pp. 94-98.

In the *Seven Principles of the Treaty with Japan*, the new US position regarding the disposition of Japanese territories was not to specify any islands by name.

5) Provisional memorandum of February 9, 1951 (initialed by the US and Japan)

Dulles' visit to Japan in January and February 1951 culminated in the initialing on February 9, 1951 of five documents with the Japanese Ministry of Foreign Affairs.[126] At the heart of the US-Japan conclave was the exchange of security for peace through the joint conclusion of the Japanese peace treaty and US-Japan security agreement. Such an arrangement allowed the US to station its forces in Japan in exchange for ending the occupation and bringing peace. The security agreement also provided for the security of Japan given that the latter had no right of belligerency under its new constitution.[127]

Following Dulles' visit, the US and Japan were able to conclude a provisional memorandum concerning three important agreements: 1) the Japanese peace treaty, 2) the security agreement, and 3) the administrative agreement. The three agreements involved the exchange of a peace treaty for a US-Japan security agreement and a status of forces agreement, all of which constituted an interconnected package. The provisional memorandum is a key document showing the process by which the US and Japan established a mutually agreed-upon framework for the signing of a peace agreement. With the initialing of this memorandum on February 9, 1951, the content of the proposed Japanese peace treaty was all but finalized.

The provisional memorandum had the following key characteristics:

---

126 RG 59, Department of State, Decimal File, 694.001/2-1051. The agreements were initialed by John Allison and Sadao Iguchi in place of John Foster Dulles on the US side and by Shigeru Yoshida on the Japanese side to highlight the fact that the conclusions were provisionary and temporary, rather than official.

127 "Memorandum," (Feb. 9, 1951), signed by John M. Allison and S. Iguchi, RG 59, Department of State, Decimal File, 694.001/2-1051.

First, it did not contain any provisions on Japan's war responsibilities, such as those on basic principles, special political clauses, and war criminals. As shown by the prominent usage of the word "peace" in the first chapter, the omission of such provisions reflected Dulles' conviction that the Japanese peace treaty should be non-punitive. Japan had been worried about the type of forced peace that would be imposed on it under a treaty modeled after the Peace Treaty of Versailles. Fortuitously, the US attitude turned out to be friendly and cooperative beyond Japan's imagination. No punitive provisions were included. Though the provisional memorandum only presented a basic framework for the peace treaty and the wording or text of the treaty had yet to be fixed, the proposed structure and content of the treaty embraced an overall spirit of amity, peace and good will.

Second, the provisional memorandum was incorporated as a whole into the next official draft treaty of the US that was finalized and distributed in March 1951. Using what had been agreed upon with Japan on February 9, 1951 as a working prototype, the US DoS finalized the first official draft treaty at the end of March 1951 and sent it to the relevant parties for review. The elapse of time is indicative of the fact that the provisional memorandum formed the basis for the official draft treaty of March 1951.

Third, the provisions on Japanese territory, which were emphasized in previous draft treaties, were eliminated from the provisional memorandum. The territories to be excluded from Japan were presented in a much simpler and more concise manner as follows:

Territory: Japan renounces all rights and titles to Korea, Formosa and the Pescadores, and accepts a United Nations trusteeship with the United States as administering authority over the Ryukyu Islands south of 29° north latitude, the Bonin Islands, including Rosario Island, the Volcano Islands, Parcoe Vela [Quoter's note: Parcoe Vela in the original document; an error that should be Parece Vela] and Marcus Island.[128]

While the postwar territory of Japan and the territories to be excluded from it were simplified, the provisions regarding the minor islands as specified under the Potsdam Declaration were removed completely. The

258

only islands mentioned were the Ryukyu Islands and those islands associated with it south of 29° North over which the US would have trusteeship. In other words, at this point, the US was not significantly concerned about what islands were to be included in or excluded from postwar Japan, but only about those islands over which it would have trusteeship. Such an approach was clearly against the policy framework that the Allied Powers had agreed upon at Potsdam. Thus, the policies that the Allied Powers' had agreed to with regard to the territory of Japan in the Cairo and Potsdam declarations was for all practical purposes unilaterally discarded. The US negotiated the Japanese territorial provisions of the peace treaty privately with Japan, even though the provisions should have been discussed, agreed to and decided upon jointly among the Allied Powers. After reaching an agreement with its former enemy and not with the other Allied Powers that had fought alongside it during the war, the US only then consulted the Allied Powers *ex post facto* about the already initialed agreement with Japan. This captures the essence of the process by which the Japanese peace treaty was crafted. The resultant agreement between the US and Japan opened the way for the latter to engage anew in territorial disputes with its neighbors in East Asia.

6) Provisional draft treaty of March 1951 (official draft treaty sent to the Allied Powers)

Upon returning from his visit to Japan, Australia, and New Zealand, Dulles announced on March 1, 1951 that a new draft treaty would be prepared, on which work soon began in full swing.[129] In the third week of

---

128 "Provisional Memorandum," (Feb. 8, 1951), RG 59, Department of State, Decimal File, 694.001/2-1051.

129 Of the documents dated March 1, 1951 and March 9, 1951, the draft treaty is entitled "Provisional Draft of a Japanese Peace Treaty" (RG 59, Japanese Peace Treaty Files of John Foster Dulles, 1946-52, Lot 54D423, Box 12). Of the documents dated March 12 and 20, 1951, the draft of the same title remains in RG 59, Department of State, Decimal File, 694.001/3-1251, 694.001/3-2151.

March, Dulles finished the draft and submitted it on March 19 for review by the Far Eastern Sub-Committee of the Foreign Affairs Committee of the Senate. As a result, the *Provisional Draft of a Japanese Peace Treaty (Suggestive Only)* was finalized in March of 1951.[130]

Unlike previous draft treaties intended only for circulation within the Administration itself, this draft was declared the first official draft to be used for negotiations with other countries. During the last week of March, the draft was sent to 14 key Allied Powers and the Korean Embassy in the US along with a request for review by the respective governments. The draft treaty was also sent to the Korean embassy because the US intended that Korea be a party or a signatory to the peace treaty.

According to a US DoS memorandum, this draft treaty, which was based on Dulles' *Seven Principles of the Treaty with Japan*, was finalized after at least one round of information exchange from September 1950 to January 1951 with the government representatives of 14 countries to which the draft was sent.[131]

The draft treaty of March 1951 had the following characteristics:

First, it was the first official US draft treaty sent to the Allied Powers involved in the Japanese peace settlement process, and its official nature made it stand out as unique from all previous drafts.

Second, the format of this draft was unlike those produced before 1950. The biggest change was that the preamble and those articles on basic principles were eliminated. The basic principles were incorporated into the preamble. The US headed Chapter I with the title "Peace," highlighting the

130 "Provisional Draft of a Japanese Peace Treaty (Suggestive Only)," (March 1951), RG 59, Office of Northeast Asia Affairs, Records Relating to the Treaty of Peace with Japan-Subject File, 1945-51, Lot 56D527, Box 1.

131 Meetings with the countries represented at the Far East Committee were held on the following dates: the Philippines (Sept. 27, 1950), the Netherlands (Oct. 13, 1950), Burma (Oct. 19, 1950), New Zealand (Oct. 19, 1950, Jan. 4, 1951), Great Britain (before and after Jan. 12, 1951), China (Oct. 23, 1950, Dec. 19, 1950), India (Dec. 21, 1950), the Soviet Union (Sept. 28, Oct. 27, Nov. 20, Nov. 24, Dec. 28, 1950, Jan. 13, 1951). "Major Papers Regarding Japanese Peace Treaty and Pacific Pact," (undated), RG 59, Office of Northeast Asia Affairs, Records Relating to the Treaty of Peace with Japan-Subject File, 1945-51, Lot 56D527, Box 3, Folder, "Miscellaneous".

fact that the most important purpose and principle of the treaty was the making of peace. No provisions specifying war responsibility or Japanese obligations to make reparations were included. Also, the list of the Allied and Associated Powers prominently displayed at the beginning of the previous draft treaties were deleted from this draft. This was in accordance with the provisional memorandum agreed upon with Japan on February 9, 1951.

Third, the length and format of the draft became simpler. The draft was now only eight pages long, containing eight chapters and 22 articles as opposed to ten chapters and 44 articles in the December 1949 draft treaty. The US had finally succeeded in coming up with a draft treaty of peace with Japan that was simple and non-punitive.

Fourth, all previous provisions on Japanese territory disappeared from the new draft. The only remaining provision of this sort was the one reading "2. The Allied Powers recognize the full sovereignty of the Japanese people over Japan and its territorial waters" in Chapter II on Sovereignty. All the detailed and elaborate descriptions specifying the postwar limits of Japanese territory, in particular those concerning the minor islands to be included as a part of Japan, disappeared. The clearly-articulated provisions on where Japanese territory began and ended and where its boundary line was to be with respect to other countries in the region were deleted entirely from the text. As explained in the section on the provisional memorandum of February 9, 1951, a draft treaty was formalized that opened the way for Japan to engage in territorial disputes with its neighbors in East Asia.

Fifth, the previous provisions concerning the areas that Japan would give up or cede were also dramatically simplified.[132] This was in line with the provisional memorandum agreed upon with Japan on February 9, 1951. The new draft now only provided a very brief description of the areas that Japanese would give up. On the other hand, it included a very detailed description of those areas over which the US would have trusteeship. It also contained new provisions on the Southern Sakhalin and Kuril Islands.

---

132 "Provisional Draft of a Japanese Peace Treaty (Suggestive Only)," (March 1951).

The key characteristics and significance of this draft treaty with regard to Korea and its territory are as follows: First, the draft treaty was sent to Korea, which was one of the 15 countries to receive it, along with Australia, Burma, Canada, Ceylon, China, France, India, Indonesia, the Netherlands, New Zealand, Pakistan, the Philippines, the UK, and the Soviet Union. By doing this, the US officially acknowledged it as a party and signatory to the treaty. Thus, in addition to the thirteen countries of the Far Eastern Commission that had previously taken part in policy-making with regard to the occupation of Japan, the US now sent the peace treaty draft to Korea and Indonesia as well, recognizing their right as of March 1951 to take part in the peace conference and sign the treaty.

Second, the provisions relating to Dokdo were deleted. Dokdo was now specified neither as Korean territory nor as Japanese. It seems like the deletion came in the process of formulating a briefer provision on Japanese territory, Formosa, Korea and the Kurils. Now, the only provision relating to Korea was the short description in Chapter III reading, "3. Japan renounces all right, title and claim to Korea, Formosa and the Pescadores."

A fallout of the provisional memorandum of February 9, 1951, the deletion of the Dokdo-related provision came as a result of attempts to make the treaty text briefer. It was a reflection of the dramatic change that was taking place in the way the US DoS was proposing to specify Japanese territory. As a defeated foe in the war, Japan made every effort possible to have as many islands as possible included under its sovereignty. Given the circumstances surrounding 1951, a new phase emerged in US policymaking in which a detailed specification of the islands to be included in and those to be excluded from Japan was no longer considered essential. Such was the incredibly favorable situation that emerged for Japan in 1951, and it signified that the provisions established under the Potsdam Declaration with regard to postwar Japanese territory were now effectively null and void.

On the other hand, the US chose to specify in the greatest of detail the provisions regarding the Ryukyu Islands as well as the other islands over which it would have trusteeship in order to avoid the possibility of any future controversies or disputes over them. Thus, the territorial provisions of the March 1951 draft treaty could be summarized as the renunciation of the Japanese territorial clauses under the Potsdam Declaration, the non-specification of those islands to be included in and those to be excluded from Japanese territory, and the specification of all those islands to be included under US trusteeship. The draft also only briefly stated that those areas to be renounced by Japan were Korea, Formosa, the Pescadores, Southern Sakhalin, and the Kurils. All other mention of the names of specific minor islands was completely removed.

5

The Formulation of Joint Anglo-American Draft Treaties and the Final Treaty (1951)

1) The first joint Anglo-American draft treaty of May 3, 1951: Sent to the British Commonwealth countries

At the end of March 1951, the US finalized the *Provisional Draft of a Japanese Peace Treaty (Suggestive Only)* and sent it to the relevant Allied Powers. Then on April 7, 1951, the British government finalized its official draft treaty entitled *A Provisional Draft of a Treaty of Peace with Japan*. Both the US and the UK draft treaties were delivered to the other party respectively, and from April 25 to May 4 of 1951, officials of the British Foreign Office visited the US Department of State (DoS) in Washington for meetings. At the Anglo-American meetings chaired by John Allison, the two sides compared their respective draft treaties, article by article, and finalized the joint Anglo-American draft treaty on May 3, 1951.[133]

The official title of the first joint Anglo-American draft treaty was *Joint United States-United Kingdom Draft Prepared during the Discussions in Washington, April-May 1951*. This first "provisionally agreed-upon joint draft treaty" was the result of incorporating the US draft of March 1951 with the UK draft of April 1951. According to the British Foreign Office, the US draft treaty was used as the basic document, but due to the US delegation's willingness to accommodate many of the points presented in the British draft treaty, the end product was substantially different from the original US draft. As a result, the text of the treaty lengthened slightly,

---

133 "Joint United States-United Kingdom Draft Peace Treaty," (May 3, 1951), Tokyo Post Files: 320.1 Peace Treaty, *FRUS*, 1951, Vol. VI, part 1, pp. 1024-1037.

but it was still assessed as being the shortest peace treaty that came out of the Second World War.[134] According to Fearey, the joint Anglo-American draft of May 3, 1951 "successfully reconciled the United Kingdom concern for a technically precise and comprehensive treaty with the United States desire for a document sufficiently simple and brief to be widely read and understood."[135]

Form-wise, the British draft treaty was much longer and more detailed than the US draft treaty because the UK had used the peace treaty with Italy after World War II as a prototype. Content-wise, the British draft was more punitive in nature in that it underlined Japan's war responsibility and its obligations for war reparations, unlike the non-punitive US draft treaty emphasizing the need for a lasting peace. In other words, the British draft treaty was closer in form and content to the US draft treaties prior to December 1949. Regarding the provisions on territorial issues in particular, reflecting the spirit of the Potsdam Declaration, the British draft treaty specified the islands to be included in Japanese territory using degrees of longitude and latitude and attaching a map in an annex. The UK government had little to gain politically or economically out of the peace treaty with Japan, while most of the British Commonwealth countries such as Australia and New Zealand held strong opinions with regard to Japanese war crimes, the need for reparations for damages, and the future rearmament of Japan.

Meanwhile, having secured trusteeship over the territories formerly under Japanese mandate in the South Pacific as well as the Ryukyu and Bonin islands and having the most to gain from a peace treaty with Japan, the US could not but respect the views of the other relevant Allied Powers.

---

134 FO 371/92547, 213351, FJ 1022/368, Sir O. Franks, Washington to Foreign Office, no. 1382 (May 4, 1951), Subject: Japanese Peace Treaty: given text of line taken by State Department in answer to any press enquiries; FJ 1022/373, C. P. Scott to A. E. Percial, Esq., B/T., no.1(1951. 5. 8), Subject: Japanese Peace Treaty: transmit copy of Joint Draft of the J.P.T. after talks which have taken place in Washington.
135 "Summary of Negotiations Leading Up To the Conclusion of the Treaty of Peace With Japan," by Robert A. Fearey (Sept. 18, 1951), p. 8, RG 59, Office of Northeast Asia Affairs, Records Relating to the Treaty of Peace with Japan-Subject File, 1945-51, Lot 56D527, Box 1.

[Table 3-1] Organization of Draft Treaties of Peace with Japan
(Drafts of February, March, & May 1951)

Draft / Chapter	Draft agreed upon by the US and Japan on February 1951	Provisional draft treaty (Suggestive only) of March 1951	First joint Anglo-American draft treaty of May 1951
	Preamble	[Preamble]	Preamble
Chapter I	Peace	Peace (1)	Peace (1)
Chapter II	Sovereignty	Sovereignty (2)	Territory (2-5)
Chapter III	Territory	Territory (3-5)	Security (6-7)
Chapter IV	Security	Security (6-7)	Political and Economic Clauses (8~14)
Chapter V	Political and Economic Clauses	Political and Economic Clauses (8-13)	Claims and Property (15-20)
Chapter VI	Claims Arising out of the War	Claims and Property (14-16)	Settlement of Disputes (21)
Chapter VII	Settlement of Disputes	Settlement of Disputes (17)	Final Clauses (22-26)
Chapter VIII	Final Clauses	Final Clauses (18-22)	
Chapter IX	General Observation		
Chapter X			
Annexed documents			Protocol

[Source] "Provisional Memorandum" initialed by the US and Japan on February 9, 1951 (February 8, 1951), RG 59, Department of State, Decimal File, 694.001/2-1051; "Provisional Draft of a Japanese Peace Treaty (Suggestive only)" (March 1951)], RG 59, Office of Northeast Asia Affairs, Records Relating to the Treaty of Peace with Japan-Subject File, 1945-51, Lot 56D527, Box 6 and Decimal File, 694.001series, Box 3007; "Draft Japanese Peace Treaty: Revised on May 3, 1951," RG 59, Department of State, Decimal File, 694.001/5-351.

With the Soviet Union excluded, the US saw it as indispensable to gain support and backing of the UK in particular, as the latter and the other British Commonwealth countries were now the most important Allied Powers and partners of the US in the treaty negotiation process. Dulles intuitively knew that the US would have to make some major concessions to the UK in order to move the treaty development process forward.

Perhaps in light of this fact, not only did he present the British draft treaty to the Japanese government for review, he also arranged for an expert of the Japanese Ministry of Foreign Affairs to visit Washington for more in-depth discussions on the British draft before the British Foreign Office officials arrived in Washington.

In summary, the joint Anglo-American draft treaty of peace with Japan of May 3, 1951 was finalized by means of the following process: first, the US completed its draft treaty (March 1951); the UK finalized its draft treaty (April 1951); the US and the UK reviewed each other's draft treaty and Dulles made a second visit to Japan (April 7-23, 1951); the US received feedback from the Japanese government on the British draft and the UK Foreign Office officials came to visit Washington (April 25-May 4, 1951).

The territorial provisions contained in Article 2 of Chapter II of the joint Anglo-American draft treaty are as follows:

Chapter II, Article 2:
Japan renounces all rights, titles and claims to Korea (including Quelpart, Port Hamilton and Dagelet), [Formosa and the Pescadores]; and also all rights, titles and claims in connection with the mandate system, [or based on any past activity of Japanese nationals in the Antarctic area]. Japan accepts the action of the United Nations Security Council of April 2, 1947, in relation to extending the trusteeship system to Pacific Islands formerly under mandate to Japan. (U.K. reserves position on passages between square brackets.)[136]

The provisions on Japanese territory were left out together with Article 2 of the US draft on the sovereignty of Japan.

In the process of finalizing the first joint draft treaty (May 3, 1951), both Japan and the UK had voiced their strong opposition to Korea being a party to the treaty. Faced with such strong opposition, the US sought a

---

[136] "Joint United States-United Kingdom Draft Peace Treaty," (May 3, 1951), *FRUS*, 1951, Vol. VI, p. 1025.

compromise, which consisted of not granting Korea the status of an Allied Power but including special provisions in the treaty that granted Korea the same rights and benefits as the Allied Powers in certain respects at least. This alternative arrangement was first given form and shape in the *Japanese Peace Treaty Working Draft and Commentary* (June 1, 1951).

Revised US draft treaty of May 3, 1951

At the same time as the US and the UK were finalizing their joint draft treaty on May 3, 1951, the US DoS revised its existing draft treaty and entitled it *Draft Japanese Peace Treaty: Revised on May 3, 1951*.[137] The revised US draft treaty of May 3, 1951 was almost identical to the joint Anglo-American draft treaty of the same date. Two changes were made with respect to Korea, however. The first was the inclusion of Quelpart, Port Hamilton, and Dagelet in Korean territory. This was done to partially accept the UK government's request to specify the islands lying between Korea and Japan in the treaty. The second change was the insertion of the statement, "and agree to recognize and respect all arrangements which may be made by or under the auspices of the United Nations regarding the sovereignty and independence of Korea," which was taken verbatim from the draft treaty of the UK government. Thus, the joint draft generally tended to reflect the views of the UK government with regard to the provisions on Korea. However, the statement added to the Korea-related provision that reads "and agree to recognize and respect all arrangements which may be made by or under the auspices of the United Nations regarding the sovereignty and independence of Korea" ended up being removed sometime after May 3, 1951. This provision only made it into the revised draft treaty of the US DoS of May 3, 1951.

The joint Anglo-American draft treaty of May 3, 1951 was circulated by the UK to the British Commonwealth countries. Also, in April and May of

---

137 "Draft Japanese Peace Treaty: Revised on May 3, 1951," RG 59, Department of State, Decimal File, 694.001/5-351.

1951, feedback was received from the relevant governments on the official US draft treaty of March 1951.[138]

The biggest controversy to arise was between the Soviet Union and the US. The Soviet Union's response to the draft, which was received on May 7, 1951, contained what appeared to be the most reasonable and favorable arrangement for Japan.[139] The Soviet's key request was that the peace settlement be concluded at a foreign ministers' conference of the four major Allied Powers including Communist China. In addition, it expressed its opposition to the Ryukyu and Bonin Islands being placed under US trusteeship and turned into US military bases. In a subsequent reply (May 19, 1951), the US rejected the Soviet Union's demand for a foreign ministers' conference.

Japanese Peace Treaty Working Draft and Commentary (June 1, 1951)

This document puts together the feedback received from each state to which the US DoS sent the *Provisional Draft of a Japanese Peace Treaty (Suggestive Only)*, as well as their views on the joint Anglo-American draft treaty of May 3, 1951.

At this point, the US wanted to get the feedback of the various Allied Powers regarding the US official draft treaty (March 1951) and the joint Anglo-American draft treaty (May 3, 1951) and decide whether or not to reflect their views in the new draft treaty. This endeavor resulted in the voluminous *Japanese Peace Treaty Working Draft and Commentary* (June 1, 1951), in which the feedback of every country that had submitted its response were arranged by chapter and article, after which the US position was explained.[140]

---

138 "Summary of Negotiations Leading Up To the Conclusion of the Treaty of Peace With Japan," by Robert A. Fearey (Sept. 18, 1951), pp. 8-9, RG 59, Office of Northeast Asia Affairs, Records Relating to the Treaty of Peace with Japan-Subject File, 1945-51, Lot 56D527, Box 1.
139 *Ibid.*, p. 9.
140 "Japanese Peace Treaty Working Draft and Commentary," (Jun. 1, 1951), RG 59, Office of Northeast Asia Affairs, Records Relating to the Treaty of Peace with Japan-Subject file, 1945-51,

[Table 3-2] Changes in Korea-related Provisions in Draft Treaties of Peace with Japan
(May–June 1951)

Draft treaty \ Classification	Article	Provision
First joint Anglo-American draft treaty (May 3, 1951)	Chapter II. Territory Article 2	Japan renounces all rights, titles and claims to Korea (including Quelpart, Port Hamilton and Dagelet), [Formosa and the Pescadores];
US revised draft treaty (May 3, 1951)	Chapter II. Territory Article 2	(a) Japan renounces all rights, titles and claims to Korea, including Quelpart, Port Hamilton and Dagelet, and agrees to recognize and respect all arrangements which may be made by or under the auspices of the United Nations regarding the sovereignty and independence of Korea.
Japanese Peace Treaty Working Draft and Commentary (June 1, 1951)	Chapter II. Territory Article 2	(a) Japan, recognizing the independence of Korea, renounces all right, title and claim to Korea, including the islands of Quelpart, Port Hamilton and Dagelet.
Second joint Anglo-American draft treaty (June 14, 1951)	Chapter II. Territory Article 2	(a) Japan, recognizing the independence of Korea, renounces all right, title and claim to Korea, including the islands of Quelpart, Port Hamilton and Dagelet.

The document pointed out three major issues with respect to Korea. The first was territorial issues, the second was Korea's participation in the peace conference and its status as an Allied Power, and the third was the need for special provisions on Korea. The second and third issues were inter-related.

First, the territory of Korea was described as follows in Article 2 of Chapter II of the joint Anglo-American draft treaty of May 3.

Japan renounces all rights, titles and claims to Korea (including Quelpart, Port Hamilton and Dagelet), [Formosa and the Pescadores], and also all rights, titles and claims in connection with the mandate system [or based on any past activity of Japanese nationals in the Antarctic area]. Japan accepts the action of the United Nations Security Council of April 2, 1947,

Lot 56D527, Box 6, Folder "Treaty-Draft-Mar. 23, 1951."

in relation to extending the trusteeship system to Pacific Islands formerly under mandate to Japan.

The UK expressed reservation to the content shown inside brackets. The US modified this provision as follows:

(a) Japan, recognizing the independence of Korea, renounces all right, title and claim to Korea, including the islands of Quelpart, Port Hamilton and Dagelet.[141]

A number of countries made comments regarding territorial issues. In a memorandum dated May 1, 1951, the Canadian government requested that Japan be asked to renounce all rights, titles and claims to its former territories and that their disposition be determined outside the peace treaty. Most of the British Commonwealth countries also criticized the US draft treaty for adopting an overly imprecise method of specifying Japanese territory, and recommended that the method employed by the UK be used instead. In other words, they were asking that the islands to be included in and excluded from Japan be specifically listed in the text of the treaty, that Japanese territory be clearly marked using degrees of longitude and latitude, and that these provisions be clearly visualized through the inclusion of a map annexed to the treaty. In doing so, they were emphasizing the need to construct the Japanese territorial clause in a manner consistent with the spirit and principles of the territorial clauses agreed upon by the Allied Powers under the Cairo and Potsdam Declaration.

The views expressed by the New Zealand government were the most noteworthy with regard to territorial issues. Stating that "In view of the need to ensure that none of the islands near Japan is left in disputed sovereignty," New Zealand expressed its preference for delineating the territories owned by Japan using degrees of longitude and latitude as proposed in Article 1

---

141 "Japanese Peace Treaty Working Draft and Commentary," (Jun. 1, 1951), Chapter II, Territory, Article 2, p. 1.

of the British draft treaty. It added that such a method would help clarify that Habomais and Shikotan, which were at that time being occupied by Russia, were henceforth part of Japan.[142] The US DoS made the following comment in this regard.

> Comment: In the discussions at Washington the British agreed to drop this proposal when the US pointed to the psychological disadvantages of seeming to fence Japan in by a continuous line around Japan. The Japanese had objected to the British proposal when it was discussed with them in Tokyo. US willingness to specify in the treaty that Korean territory included Quelpart, Port Hamilton and Dagelet also helped to persuade the British. As regards the Habomais and Shikotan, it has seemed more realistic, with the USSR in occupation of the islands, not specifically to stipulate their return to Japan.[143]

The US proposed to specify Quelpart, Port Hamilton, and Dagelet as part of Korean territory in order to persuade the UK that it was necessary to discard the Japanese territorial clauses of the Potsdam Declaration as well as to eliminate the specific delineation of limits of Japanese territory and those areas to be renounced by Japan. In other words, the specific mention of Quelpart, Port Hamilton, and Dagelet was a US concession of sorts to get the UK to agree to disregard the Japanese territorial clauses under the Potsdam Declaration, i.e. the detailed specification of islands that were to remain part of Japan and those to be excluded.

The rationale for why Quelpart, Port Hamilton, and Dagelet were specifically mentioned as part of Korean territory is found in the US memorandum on the first Anglo-American meeting. The UK government suggested the desirability of disposing of the islands between Korea and Japan by specific mention, and as a solution, the US government proposed to insert "including Quelpart" after "Korea." Consequently, the sentence

---

142 *Ibid.,* p. 4.
143 *Ibid.*

stating "Japan renounces all rights, titles and claims to Korea" was modified into "Japan renounces all rights, titles and claims to Korea including Quelpart."[144] In short, the US sought to satisfy the UK's request for the specific mention of the islands lying between Korea and Japan through the mere mention of the single most symbolic island lying between them. As the Japanese government and some scholars would later argue, the insertion of Quelpart after Korea was not intended by the US and the UK to specify those islands that would be excluded from Japan and included in Korea; rather, it was merely the outcome of a procedural concession to address the UK's request for a detailed delineation of all islands existing between the two countries by mentioning only one single representative island of Korea. No further discussions were made regarding the ownership of the various other islands in the vicinity. And while record is found of the US proposal to include Quelpart in response to the UK's request, nowhere is there any record of how and when it was decided to insert Port Hamilton and Dagelet behind Quelpart. All that is known is that, at some point during the Washington meetings, the UK Foreign Office proposed to insert the names of the islands lying between Korea and Japan, and as a compromise solution the US DoS proposed to insert only Quelpart, and somewhere further down the line, it was decided to make specific mention of three representative islands—Quelpart, Port Hamilton and Dagelet.

The US government must have been aware of the fact that such ambiguously-worded territorial provisions could lead to territorial disputes between Japan and its nearest neighbors in the future. Nonetheless, the specification of the islands to be included in Japanese territory, the use of degrees of longitude and latitude for territorial delineation, the specification of the many islands to be included in Formosa, and the specification of the four islands attached to the Kurils, all of which were

---

144 The original text reads as follows: "Article 2. British suggested omission of US Article 2, questioned necessity of reference to territorial waters. British mentioned desirability of disposing of islands between Japan and Korea by specific mention. This might be done by inserting "(including Quelpart)"after "Korea" in US Article 3. British accepted US 29 for Ryukyus and US provisions on Habomais and Shikotan."

judiciously provided for in previous draft treaties of the US DoS, were now deleted altogether. It might perhaps be safely conjectured that the US just gave up on addressing who has sovereignty rights over which of the many islands in the region. However, as a result of the Anglo-American talks, only Quelpart, Port Hamilton, and Dagelet were specifically mentioned as belonging to Korea. This was the result of the US wanting to close down the discussion at this point, but by no means did it signify that the US had reached a significant agreement or decision with the UK on the sovereignty status of these islands.

The second issue concerning Korea's eligibility to be a party to the treaty and its status as an Allied Power, and the third issue concerning the inclusion of special provisions on Korea were mutually related. Both during its talks with Japan (April 1951) and those with the UK (April–May 1951), the US had intended to have Korea included as a party to the treaty. Faced with strong opposition from both countries, however, the US decided not to invite Korea as a signatory to the treaty, but instead grant it certain rights under the treaty by way of new provisions.

In other words, during its talks with Japan and the UK between April and May of 1951, the US proposal that Korea be a party and a signatory to the treaty came to be opposed by both countries. Leading up to the first Anglo-American talks in Washington, the US continued to argue in favor of Korea's participation in the peace settlement as a signatory country. However, this determination gradually weakened under pressure and eventually a compromise was sought.

Consequently, in the memorandum of May 16, 1951, the US retreated from its position to support Korea's right to be a party and signatory to the treaty. As a compromise, a new provision was to be inserted granting Korea the same "benefits" as the Allied Powers. The position of the US in this regard was reaffirmed in the *Japanese Peace Treaty Working Draft and Commentary* of June 1, 1951. Eventually, in the second Anglo-American draft treaty (June 14, 1951), Korea was deleted from the list of Allied Powers in the preamble to the treaty and instead specified as a country that would receive certain benefits under a special article (Article 21). Thus, the decision was made that Korea would not be invited to attend the peace conference or to sign the treaty.

2) The second Anglo-American draft treaty of June 14, 1951: Exclusion of Korea from Allied Power status and abandonment of the Allied Powers' war-time provisions on Japanese territory

The draft treaty of June 14, 1951 was the second joint Anglo-American draft treaty and a revision of the first one of May 3. The name of the document was *Draft Japanese Peace Treaty*. The preamble, which had been omitted from the March 1951 draft treaty, was added again in this draft. This second joint draft treaty reflected some key decisions regarding Korea. The first was withdrawal of Korea's status as a signatory to the treaty and the creation of a special article regarding Korea. The second was deletion of the article pertaining to the renunciation of claims of Japanese nationals to property in Korea. And, the third was a partial modification of the territorial clause.

First, Korea was stripped of its prior status as a party and signatory to the peace conference. Second, the draft treaty stipulated in Article 21 that Korea would be granted the benefits of the other Allied Powers under Article 2 (Territory), Article 9 (Limitation of Fishing and the Conservation and Development of Fisheries on the High Seas), and Article 12 (Commercial Agreements). Article 25 of the draft specified that the Allied Powers were to be limited to the states at war with Japan and only those states would sign and ratify the treaty. Instead, an exceptional provision was made for Korea and China under Article 21. In other words, Korea was not recognized as a State at war with Japan, thus effectively excluding it from signing and ratifying the treaty, but it would be granted special rights provided for in a limited number of provisions under the treaty. The US tried to have Korea as a party to the treaty but faced a strong opposition of the UK and Japan. The US also tried to consider Korea's interests by adding a few special articles, but such an arrangement for Korea merely ended up excluding it from the peace settlement process. Not much was to be gained from the articles on territory, fisheries, and commercial agreements. Korea's independence was already a *fait accompli*; as such, it was not something that could be changed or compromised. Meanwhile, the fisheries and commercial agreements were to be resolved directly between Korea and Japan.

Second, the renunciation of property claims of Japanese nationals in Korea, which was the second most important issue for Korea aside from being a party to the treaty, was deleted or modified. Instead, the draft provided that disposition of property and claims were to be settled through consultation between Japan and the relevant authorities involved.[145] Specifically for Korea, this meant that the disposition of property of Japanese nationals in Korea and their claims, and the disposition of property of Korean nationals in Japan and their claims would henceforth be subject to special arrangements made between Korea and Japan. Upon receiving the draft treaty of July 3, 1951, which incorporated this provision almost verbatim in paragraph (a) of Article 4, the Korean government was utterly dismayed. According to Yu Jin-o, leaving it up to Korea to negotiate with Japan the disposition of the property of Japanese nationals in Korea, which at the time accounted for more than 80 percent of the Korean economy, was no different than leaving it up to Korea to negotiate its own independence with Japan.

Third, the territorial provisions related to Korea were modified slightly from that of the May 3 draft treaty as follows:

Chapter II. Territory
Article 2
(a) Japan, recognizing the independence of Korea, renounces all right, title and claim to Korea, including the islands of Quelpart, Port Hamilton and Dagelet.[146]

---

145 Kim Tae-gi, 1999, "US Foreign Policy toward Korea in the Beginning of the 1950s: The US Political Position on the Exclusion of Korea from the Japanese Peace Treaty and the First Korea-Japan Negotiations", Korean Political Science Association, *Korean Political Science Review*, Vol. 33, No. 1 (Spring Issue).

146 "Revised United States – United Kingdom Draft of Japanese Peace Treaty," (June 14, 1951), *FRUS*, 1951, vol. VI, p. 1121.

Again, the most significant change in the territorial clauses was the deletion of the precise specification of Japanese territorial boundaries. The detailed listing of islands to be included in Japan also disappeared. No changes were made to the parts relating to Korea, and Dokdo was no longer mentioned at all, either as Korean or Japanese territory. The treaty's territorial policy remained consistent in this respect.

3) The third joint Anglo-American draft treaty of July 3 and July 20, 1951: Sent to all countries involved

Upon his return from London, Dulles appeared before the US Senate Committee on Foreign Relations and then set about revising the draft treaty. After it was confirmed that the UK Foreign Office and the US DoS had both obtained the consent of their respective legislative bodies, he revised the joint draft treaty and decided to send it to the countries involved. According to a US DoS memorandum, the July 3rd draft treaty was based in part on 1) the US draft treaty of March 1951 sent to the countries that had been at war with Japan, 2) the draft treaty of April 1951 independently formulated by the UK government and then circulated to the British Commonwealth countries during that same period of time, and 3) the feedback on the joint Anglo-American draft treaty from the various governments involved.[147] Meanwhile, it was decided that the signing of the Japanese peace treaty would take place on September 3 of the same year.

The July 3rd draft treaty was the first joint Anglo-American draft sent to all involved countries. The most important agreement reached by the US and the UK was the decision to invite neither Nationalist China nor Communist China. Meanwhile, the US and the UK had some different views on issues relating to shipbuilding and navigation. On July 9, the joint draft treaty, together with its multiple annexes, was sent to all the

---

147 "Memorandum," (July 1951), RG 59, Office of Northeast Asia Affairs, Records Relating to the Treaty of Peace with Japan-Subject File, 1945-51, Lot 56D527, Box 6. Folder, "Treaty-Draft-July 20-August 12, 1951".

countries at war with Japan, except China, Italy, and three Associated States—Vietnam, Laos, and Cambodia.[148] Released to the media on July 12, the draft became the first draft of the peace treaty with Japan to be made public.

Entitled *Draft Japanese Peace Treaty*, the July 3rd draft treaty was given the same name as that of the June 14th draft treaty. The territorial provisions of the two draft treaties were also identical. Korea was addressed in paragraph (a), Article 2 of Chapter II, which provided that "Japan, recognizing the independence of Korea, renounces all right, title and claim to Korea, including the islands of Quelpart, Port Hamilton and Dagelet."[149]

The draft was conveyed to Yang You-chan, Korean Ambassador to the US, on July 9. As mentioned before, the Korean government was utterly shocked by paragraph (a) of Article 4,[150] which provided that the disposition of property of Japanese nationals in Korea and their claims, and the disposition of property of Korean nationals in Japan and their claims would henceforth be subject to special arrangements to be made between the governments of the two countries themselves. This provision seemed completely unacceptable to Korea as it implied that the disposition of enemy property that had been taken over by the US military government and subsequently transferred to the Korean government would have to be settled through negotiations with the postwar government of Japan.

4) Final draft treaty of August 13, 1951

Following the last modifications made on August 11, 1951, the final draft treaty for signature was sent to 50 countries on August 14, 1951. Among

---

148 "Summary of Negotiations Leading Up To the Conclusion of the Treaty of Peace With Japan," by Robert A. Fearey (Sept. 18, 1951), p. 13, RG 59, Office of Northeast Asia Affairs, Records Relating to the Treaty of Peace with Japan-Subject File, 1945-51, Lot 56D527, Box 1.

149 "Draft Treaty of Peace with Japan," (Jul. 20, 1951), RG 59, Office of Northeast Asia Affairs, Records Relating to the Treaty of Peace with Japan-Subject File, 1945-51, Lot 56D527, Box 6. Folder, "Treaty-Draft-July 3-20, 1951".

150 Yu Jin-o, "Review of the Draft Treaty of Peace with Japan," seven-installment series, *Dong-A Ilbo* (Jul. 25, 27 to 31, 1951).

those invited to the peace conference were Argentina, Australia, Belgium, Bolivia, Brazil, Burma, Canada, Ceylon, Chile, Colombia, Costa Rica, Cuba, Czechoslovakia, Dominican Republic, Ecuador, Egypt, El Salvador, Ethiopia, France, Greece, Guatemala, Haiti, Honduras, India, Indonesia, Iran, Iraq, Lebanon, Liberia, Luxembourg, Mexico, the Netherlands, New Zealand, Nicaragua, Norway, Pakistan, Panama, Paraguay, Peru, the Philippines, Poland, Saudi Arabia, Syria, Turkey, South Africa, the Soviet Union, the United Kingdom, Uruguay, Venezuela, and Yugoslavia.[151] On August 23, invitations were also sent to three Associated States—Vietnam, Laos, and Cambodia. Three countries—Yugoslavia, Burma, and India—rejected the invitation: Yugoslavia stated its reasons for rejecting as that it had no interests involved with Japan, Burma felt that no acceptable reparations were provided for in the treaty, and India stated that the Soviet Union and China would not be participating, it did not agree to the US stationing of forces on the Ryukyu Islands, and the ownership of Formosa, the Kurils, and Southern Sakhalin was not clearly specified in the treaty. In total, 50 countries accepted the invitation to participate with the US and Japan.

The provisions on Japanese territory and Korea remained the same as in the third joint Anglo-American draft treaty of July 1951. Paragraph (a) of Article 2 in Chapter II stated that "Japan, recognizing the independence of Korea, renounces all right, title and claim to Korea, including the islands of Quelpart, Port Hamilton and Dagelet." This wording remained unchanged leading up to the formal conclusion of the peace treaty at the San Francisco Peace Conference.

On September 4, 1951, the Peace Conference was held in San Francisco. Of the 52 countries in attendance, the Soviet Union, Poland, and Czechoslovakia raised issues with regard to the rules of order as well as the exclusion of Communist China from taking part in the conference,

---

[151] Department of State Memorandum (Aug. 14, 1951), RG 59, Office of Northeast Asia Affairs, Records Relating to the Treaty of Peace with Japan-Subject File, 1945-51, Lot 56D527, Box 6. Folder, "Treaty-Draft-July 20-August 12, 1951".

and refused to sign the treaty. On September 8, 1951, the plenipotentiary representatives of 49 countries signed the treaty.

Chapter 4

British Draft Treaties of Peace with Japan and Anglo-American Consultations (1951)

1

Confirmation of Korea's Sovereignty over Dokdo in the British Draft Treaties (March 1951)

1) The UK's formulation of a draft treaty of peace with Japan

The UK had an interest in signing an early peace treaty with Japan in tandem with the US. Following the initial US groundwork for a Japanese peace treaty in 1947, the UK also began preparations for a treaty with Japan.[1]

The UK, Australia, New Zealand, and other members of the British Commonwealth met three times to discuss the proposed Japanese peace treaty. Conferences of the Prime Ministers of the British Commonwealth countries were held in Canberra (August 1947, Prime Ministers), Colombo (January 1950, Foreign Ministers), and London (January 1951, Prime Ministers). Then in May 1950, the Commonwealth Working Party of Officials on the Japanese Peace Treaty gathered again in London to study all matters pertaining to it.[2]

The general attitude with which the UK and other British Commonwealth countries approached the anticipated peace conference with Japan was little different from the one embarked upon for the peace treaty with Italy after World War II, i.e. a typical call for punitive reparations.

The discussions held by the British Commonwealth Foreign Ministers in Colombo in January 1950 reveal the highly uncompromising approach they took in their dealings with Japan. During the Colombo Conference,

---

1   The main points of this passage are based on the following citation: Jung, "The UK FCO's Draft of the Treaty of Peace with Japan and Its Attached Map (Mar. 1951) and Reconfirmation of Korea's Sovereignty over Dokdo" and *Journal of Korean Independence Movement Studies*, Vol. 24.
2   TNA, FO371/92532, FJ1022/91 "Parliamentary Question" (Feb. 19, 1951).

the ministers agreed that the basic objectives of the peace conference with Japan would be as follows:[3]

1. The complete disarmament and demilitarization of Japan;
2. The enforcement in concert with the other Powers concerned of measures to obviate the possibility of renewed Japanese aggression;
3. The development of a peace-loving Japan which will have no desire to menace other nations.[4]

The above objectives clearly illustrate that the basic purpose of the peace conference was to prevent a resurgence of Japanese militarism in the future. Such a stance was reiterated in the security clauses *per se*, which provided for the prohibition of all military and para-military organisations and all forms of military training; the total prohibition for an indefinite period of the production of all war materials and military equipment, aircraft, alumina and magnesium, synthetic oil and synthetic rubber; limitation of production for an indefinite period of such industries as shipbuilding, iron and steel, aluminum ingots, and industrial explosives.[5]

The UK also took a firm stance on reparations, stating that they should be taken from "industrial plant and equipment in Japan rendered surplus; all monetary gold and bullion and, all stocks of precious metals and jewels found in Japan; merchant vessels declared surplus to Japan's present needs; all Japanese assets located outside Japan with certain minor exceptions."[6]

The British government saw no specific issues with regard to territory, as the four major Allied Powers (the United Kingdom, the United States, the Soviet Union and China) were committed to the view that Japanese sovereignty be limited to the islands of Honshu, Hokkaido, Kyushu, Shikoku, and such minor islands as they would later determine. The

---

3   "United Kingdom Paper on the Japanese Peace Treaty Discussed at Colombo-January 1950," RG 59, Department of State, Decimal File, 694.001/1-950

4   *Ibid.*, p. 6.

5   *Ibid.*, p. 7.

6   *Ibid.*, pp. 10-11.

government did not foresee any difficulties with respect to territorial issues involving Formosa, Southern Sakhalin, the Kuril Islands or Korea, stating that various commitments had already been made in this regard, and thus none of these issues was to be discussed at the peace conference. The government anticipated that the major territorial issue to be discussed at the peace conference would involve those minor islands that would remain under Japanese sovereignty. As such, the disposition of the Ryukyu and Bonin Islands (Ogasawara), Volcano Island (Iwo Jima), and Marcus Island (Minami-Tori-Shima) would be the key issues under discussion.[7] As far as Japan's territorial issues were concerned, the UK government would only concern itself with how the islands to be included under Japanese sovereignty would be specified. This approach was in line with the spirit of the Cairo and Potsdam Declarations. The UK's basic position with regard to its peace treaty with Japan was to follow what was internationally popular at the time, i.e., an approach that would hold Japan accountable for the war and have it return the territories it had acquired during the war and make war reparations.

The Commonwealth Working Party of Officials on the Japanese Peace Treaty met in London from May 1 to 17, 1950 to review all aspects related to the peace treaty. The basic position remained consistent with that expressed at the Colombo meeting in January 1950.[8] The territorial clauses were organized into the following three provisions:

31. It was generally agreed that:

(a) Japanese sovereignty should be confined to the four main islands and to

---

7   *Ibid.*, pp. 13-14.

8   "Commonwealth Working Party on Japanese Peace Treaty, 1st May to 17th May, 1950. Report," (undated), RG 59, Japanese Peace Treaty Files of John Foster Dulles, 1946-52, Lot 54D423, Box 13. The British Embassy communicated this report to the US Department of State on September 20, 1950. British Embassy to the Secretary of State, Subject: Commonwealth Working Party on Japanese Peace Treaty (Sept. 20, 1950), RG 59, Department of State, Decimal File, 694.001/9-2050.

a number of adjacent minor islands whose precise definition would be a matter for the Peace Conference.

(b) The disposition of the territories to be ceded by Japan need not be dealt with in the Peace Treaty itself. In the Peace Treaty Japan might merely renounce all claims to the ceded territories.

32. The question of Japanese interests in the Antarctic area was discussed and representatives of Australia, South Africa and New Zealand all stressed the importance of including in the treaty a clause whereby Japan would renounce all political and territorial claims, whether actual or prospective, in the Antarctic continent and the islands adjacent thereto.[9]

Following the US government's appointment of John Foster Dulles as the special ambassador to negotiate a peace treaty with Japan in May 1950, consultations between the UK and the US as well as activities targeting an early conclusion of a Japanese peace treaty accelerated. From September 1950 onwards, the governments of the British Commonwealth made steady progress toward that end through a series of informal exchanges of opinions at the working level. In his three different visits to Japan in June 1950, January-February 1951, and April 1951, Dulles concluded discussions with his Japanese counterpart, establishing a more specific timeline leading up to the signing of a peace treaty with Japan.[10]

After a meeting with Sir A. Gascoigne of the UK in Tokyo, Dulles flew to Australia on February 15, 1951 where he held a tripartite meeting with his counterparts in Australia and New Zealand. Soon after this meeting, the British government began to create its own draft treaty. In a February 24 telegram to Washington (Telegram No. 753), the British Foreign Office informed the US that the first British draft treaty would be proposed to the US by mid-March. Immediately thereafter, Charles H. Johnston, head

---

9 "Commonwealth Working Party on Japanese Peace Treaty, 1st May to 17th May, 1950. Report" (undated), pp. 8-9.

10 Annex I: Elaboration of Exception to General Waiver of War Claims, RG 59, Department of State, Decimal File, 694.001/2-1051.

of the Japan and Pacific Department of the British Foreign Office, began working with legal advisors of the foreign office to draft a Japanese peace treaty.[11] The Foreign Office subsequently created three drafts.

The first draft was completed on February 28, 1951. In a letter (dated March 1, 1951) to A. E. Percival of the UK Board of Trade, Johnston stated that "this is a very rough preliminary draft".[12] The draft was typed and officially titled *Japanese Peace Treaty*. It was 22 pages long and was comprised of 89 articles.[13] In terms of length and format, it was far longer and more complex than any US drafts created during the period of 1947 to 1951.

The British Foreign Office felt driven to create a draft treaty both because it had promised to propose one to the US, and also because it needed to clarify the British government's position on the issue. The most significant matters considered in the first draft treaty related to commerce and the economy. Consequently, the first draft treaty was distributed mainly to economy-related government departments.[14] Created by the Japan and Pacific Department of the British Foreign Office based on advice from its legal advisers, the draft was still quite literally "a very rough preliminary draft" developed primarily for review by other departments of the foreign office as well as by other related government agencies.

On March 16, a group of 18 representatives from seven government departments—Foreign Office (4), Treasury (2), Commonwealth Relations Office (1), Colonial Office (3), Trade Office (6), Ministry of Transport (1), one other agency (1)—chaired by G. G. Fitzmaurice from the Foreign Office met to discuss the formulation of a peace treaty with Japan. At the meeting, the representatives decided to prepare materials for the proposed Japanese

---

11 TNA, FO 371/92532, FJ 1022/97, Letter from C. H. Johnston to A. E. Percival (Mar. 1, 1951).

12 TNA, FO 371/92532, FJ 1022/97, Letter from C. H. Johnston to A. E. Percival (Mar. 1, 1951).

13 FO 371/92532, FJ 1022/97, "Japanese Peace Treaty," pp. 102-123.

14 The first draft treaty was distributed to the Colonial Office, the Department of Defense, the Chief of the General Staff, the Civil Aviation Agency, the Department of the Army, the Department of War, the Department of the Navy, the Department of Transportation, and the Department of the Interior.

peace treaty based largely on the government's existing peace treaty with Italy.[15] As a result, the second draft treaty came out. Entitled the *2nd Draft of the Japanese Peace Treaty*, the draft was 48 pages in length, including 40 pages in the body proper and 8 pages in the annex.[16] While the second draft was being prepared, the Under Secretary of the British Foreign Office, Robert H. Scott, met with Allison, head of the US delegation on March 21, 1951 in London. The main topic of the talks related to the participation of China, but also discussed was the participation of Korea.[17]

The final, official draft treaty of the British government was completed on April 7, 1951. Officially titled *A provisional draft of a Treaty of Peace with Japan*, the document consisted of nine chapters, 40 articles, and five annexes, for a total of 20 pages.[18] Johnston, who was in charge of the working-level negotiations with the US, stated in his report to the British Deputy Under Secretary of State for Foreign Affairs, Sir Roger Makins, on April 5, 1951, that the draft had undergone a legal review and had received feedback from all related divisions within the Foreign Office, as well as from 13 government departments.[19] As such, the process of formulating a draft treaty began with the first draft initiated by the Japan and Pacific Department of the British Foreign Office (February 28, 1951) and was finalized with the crafting of the third and final draft (April 7, 1951), which was then reviewed and officially approved by all 18 divisions of the Foreign Office as well as 13 other government departments. The procedures by

---

15   FO 371/92535, FJ 1022/167, "Japanese Peace Treaty: Record of Meeting held at the Foreign Office on the 16th March 1951," pp. 53-60.

16   FO 371/92535, FJ 1022/171, "Japanese Peace Treaty: Second revised draft of the Japanese Peace Treaty," (March 1951), pp. 70-117.

17   Lee, *The Starting Point of Dealing with the Past Affairs between Korea and Japan*, pp. 30-31.

18   FO 371/92538, FJ 1022/222, "Provisional Draft of Japanese Peace Treaty (United Kingdom)," (Apr. 7, 1951), pp. 15-50. The British draft treaty was edited alongside the US draft treaty for purposes of comparison. As a result, approximately 14 pages of the March 17, 1951 US draft treaty were incorporated into the British draft. The British draft, which contained a two-page explanatory note, a one-page table of contents in the front, and a two-page line of distribution at the end, totaled 39 pages including the additions from the US draft.

19   FO 371/92538, FJ 1022/222, C. H. Johnston to Sir R. Makins (Permanent Under-Secretary) (Apr. 5, 1951), pp. 4-5.

which the British draft treaty was finalized were much more complicated than those by which the US draft treaty was formulated. If reaching an agreement with the military authorities was the biggest issue on the table for the US Department of State (DoS), the biggest problem of concern for the UK was obtaining the consent of the other departments of the Cabinet. Following its approval in house, the British Government sent the third draft treaty to the US DoS. According to British Foreign Secretary Herbert Stanley Morrison, this preliminary draft was prepared at the working-level and thus was still subject to change. Nevertheless, the British Commonwealth governments of Canada, Australia, New Zealand, South Africa, India, Pakistan, and Ceylon were notified of the draft.[20] The British government concluded that the reason its draft treaty was noticeably longer than the US version was because of the government's prior experience in drafting the Italian peace treaty.

It is of interest to note that in creating the final draft, the UK did not make reference to the US preliminary draft treaty, which was already completed on March 17, 1951.[21]

2) Korea-related provisions in the British draft treaty

First draft treaty (February 28, 1951)

The drafts of the British peace treaty with Japan had one thing in common in that they all clearly laid down the war responsibility of Japan. The preamble of the first draft introduced the Allied and Associated Powers as signatories to the treaty on one side and Japan on the other. As

---

20   Though Morrison stated that this was a preliminary document that was not an expression of a consensus of the British Commonwealth governments, it was the outcome of ongoing coordination and feedback between the British Commonwealth countries. [FO 371/92538, FJ 1022/222, Mr. Morrison to Sir O. Franks (Washington), no. 401 (Apr. 7, 1951)].

21   FO 371/92538, FJ 1022/222, Memorandum by the United States Government (Communicated by the State Department to His Majesty's Embassy in Washington on 23rd March, 1951); FJ 1022/222, Mr. Morrison to Sir O. Franks (Washington) no. 401 (Apr. 7, 1951).

was clarified during a joint Anglo-American meeting in May 1951, "Allied Powers" referred to the major powers like the UK and the US that would participate in the drafting of a peace treaty with Japan, while "Associated Powers" referred to the various other countries that had been at war with Japan.[22]

By specifying in the preamble that the responsibility for the outbreak and continuation of the war lay with Japan, the UK made it clear that the treaty's primary foci would be punitive in nature, i.e., on clarifying who was responsible for causing the war, on outlining the expectations of the Allies with regard to economic reparations, on specifying political and military restrictions to be placed upon postwar Japan, and on territorial reorganization of lands annexed by colonial Japan prior to and during the war. Having such a focus for the treaty was not just a UK decision but a view common to the rest of the British Commonwealth countries as well.

However, because the preliminary draft of the treaty was "very rough," it contained a number of errors and loopholes. The first draft provided the following territorial clauses with regard to Japanese territory.

Territorial Clauses

6. Japanese sovereignty shall continue over all the islands and adjacent islets and rocks lying within an area bounded by a line…. (Omitted)

   The line should include Hokkaido, Honshu, Shikoku, Kyushu, the Suisho, Yuri, Akijiri, Shibotsu, Oki and Taraku islands, the Habomai islands, Kuchinoshima, Utsuryo (Ulling) island, <u>Miancourt rocks (Take island)</u> <u>Quelpart (Shichi or Chejudo) island</u> and Shikotan.

---

22 The UK distinguished the main parties (Allied Powers) that would be involved in the formulation of a draft treaty of peace with Japan from other lesser players that would only be given the opportunity to provide input on the treaty (Associated Powers). The term Associated Powers was in the end deleted during the 7th Anglo-American meetings (May 1, 1951) [FO 371/92547, FJ 1022/376, British Embassy Washington to C. P. Scott, O.B.E., Japan and Pacific Department, Foreign Office, no.1076/357/5IG, "Anglo-American meetings on Japanese Peace Treaty, Summary Record of Seventh meeting," (May 3, 1951)].

The line above described is plotted on the map attached to the present Treaty (Annex 1). In the case of a discrepancy between the map and the textual description of the line, the latter shall prevail.[23] (Underlined by the author)

The first draft treaty had the following more specific provisions regarding territory under Japanese control. First, in addition to the four major islands of Honshu, Hokkaido, Shikoku, and Kyushu, it established the northern boundary of Japan at the Habomai Islands and Shikotan in the northern part of Hokkaido, the southern boundary at Kuchinoshima in the Ryukyu Islands, and the western boundary adjoining Korea at Oki, Dokdo, Dagelet, and Quelpart.

Second, by mentioning the names of the islands that were to remain part of Japan, the territorial clauses naturally excluded all areas not mentioned within the boundaries specified in the treaty. Together with the provisions specifying Japan's war crimes and those holding Japan accountable for the war, the territorial clauses were clearly punitive in nature and designed to execute the return of "territories that Japan had seized by aggression" to their respective sovereign states as per the agreement under the Cairo Declaration. The draft treaty's careful delineation of the islands that would form Japan's postwar borders was also an application of the provisions of the Potsdam Declaration regarding the islands that were to remain under Japanese sovereignty. Under the Cairo Declaration and the Potsdam Declaration, the Allied policy was that those islands that would remain part of Japanese territory were to be clearly specified. The various draft treaties of the US and the UK were reflective of this underlying policy. In other words, Allied policy consisted of: 1) specifying the islands to be included in postwar Japan, 2) delineating Japanese territory by degrees of longitude and latitude in order to clarify those territories included in and those excluded from Japan, and 3) producing a map that would visualize the written provisions.

---

23   FO 371/92532, FJ 1022/97, "Japanese Peace Treaty," p. 103

Third, the first British draft treaty was in many ways a "rough" draft that lacked organization. Above all, it mistakenly described Dokdo as being within the western boundary of Japanese sovereignty. It also included Ulleungdo (described as Utsuryo) and even Jejudo (described as Quelpart, Shichi) as part of Japanese territory. As we shall soon see, this was quickly recognized as a mistake and was thus changed in subsequent drafts. Not only have Dokdo, Ulleungdo, and Jejudo always been part of Korean territory, but they were also clearly and unmistakably confirmed as being a part of Korean territory in memorandum 677 from the General Headquarters of the Supreme Commander for Allied Powers (SCAPIN 677, January 29, 1946). The flaw in the first British draft is an indication that it was made based on partial and incomplete information.

Fourth, some geographical locations were named incorrectly in the first draft of the UK treaty. For example, the name Liancourt, which was the international name for Dokdo, was mistakenly written as Miancourt. Also, Akiyuri was wrongly typed Akijiri.

Finally, the first draft was created without a thorough investigation or accurate understanding of the countries to which various and sundry islands belonged. The islands of Kuchinoshima and Oki, for example, which in SCAPIN 677 were specified as being under Japanese control, were excluded from Japanese sovereignty, while the islands of Dokdo, Ulleungdo, and Jejudo, which were placed under Korean sovereignty in SCAPIN 677, were mistakenly described as being Japanese territory. Such mistakes suggest that, to some extent, the drafters failed to verify all the information. Also, though the draft text referred to a map attached to the treaty (Annex 1), no such map was forthcoming at the time. Such a map was only included along with the second draft.

Additionally, the first draft treaty made the following statement regarding the independence of Korea.

7. Japan hereby renounces any claim to sovereignty over, and all right, title and interest in, Korea, and undertakes to recognize and respect all such arrangements as may be made by or under the auspices of the United Nations regarding the sovereignty and independence of Korea.[24]

What is particularly noteworthy in this statement is an emphasis made on the role of the United Nations with respect to Korea and its sovereignty. This is probably because the Korean War was ongoing at the time and Korea's ultimate status and fate as a nation state remained undetermined. Also, the possibility of an eventual unification of the Korean Peninsula by the United Nations was taken into consideration.

Second draft treaty (March 1951)

The British Foreign Office finalized its second draft treaty following a review by various divisions within the Foreign Office and related government departments. The biggest difference between the first and second drafts was in the territorial clauses.

> (6) Japanese sovereignty shall continue over all the islands and adjacent islets and rocks lying within an area bounded by a line from Latitude 30°N in a North-Easterly direction to approximately Latitude 33°N 128°E. then northward between the islands of Quelpart, Fukue-Shima bearing North-Easterly between Korea and the island of Tsushima, continuing in this direction with the islands of Oki-Retto to the South-East and Take Shima to the North-West curving with the coast of Honshu, then Northerly skirting Rebun Shima passing Easterly through Soya Kaikyo approximately 145°40″N, [...] The line above described is plotted on the map attached to the present Treaty (Annex I). In the case of a discrepancy between the map and the textual description of the line, the latter shall prevail.[25]

Compared to the first draft, the second draft provided a clearer description of the delimitations of Japanese territory. If the first draft

---

24   *Ibid.*

25   FO 371/92535, FJ 1022/171, "Japanese Peace Treaty: Second revised draft of the Japanese Peace Treaty," (March 1951), p. 73

employed a rather ambiguous description of Japanese territory, the second clearly enunciated what was to be considered part of Japanese territory and what was not.

Key characteristics of the second draft were as follows: First, it specified Japanese territory using degrees of latitude and longitude, adopted accurate place names, and provided a drawing of the boundary line of Japan to clearly show its territorial limits. Second, it rectified various flaws evident in the first draft such as, for example, making it clear that Jejudo, Ulleungdo, and Dokdo were not Japanese territory but Korean territory. Third, the territorial limits of Japan as specified in the second draft treaty were carried over into the third and final draft treaty. Fourth, the second draft treaty delineated Japanese territory by use of a visual line of demarcation. The purpose for doing so was to clarify the relevant provisions of the Potsdam Declaration, which specified that Japanese sovereignty shall be limited to the four major islands and such minor islands as the Allies so determine. According to the declaration, the Allies would enumerate each and every one of the numerous islands adjacent to Japan and specify whether or not they belonged to it. However, it would have been practically impossible to specify all of the thousands of islands involved within the space limitations of the treaty. Thus, the drafters of the treaty chose to delineate Japanese territory using degrees of latitude and longitude in order to clarify which islands were or were not a part of Japan. In this sense, the British draft was still in keeping with the provisions of the Potsdam Declaration. Meanwhile, the same method was employed by the US DoS in the various draft treaties that it crafted from 1947 onwards. A strikingly similar method of delineation had been used in memorandum 1033 of the General Headquarters of the Supreme Commander for Allied Powers (SCAPIN 1033, June 22, 1946) titled *Area Authorized for Japanese Fishing and Whaling*, which was more widely known as the MacArthur Line. Thus, such a method had become an established practice that policy-makers on multiple fronts showed no qualms in using. Fifth, an annex map was officially produced along with the second draft treaty, visualizing the intended meaning of the territorial clauses.

Chapter 4

Third draft treaty (April 7, 1951)

The British government's third draft, which was its official and final draft treaty of peace with Japan, was almost identical to the second draft except for a few minor corrections. The parts relating to Korea were as follows:

> (6) Japanese sovereignty shall continue over all the islands and adjacent islets and rocks lying within an area bounded by a line from Latitude 30°N in a North-Westerly direction (a) to approximately Latitude 33°N 128°E. then Northward between the islands of Quelpart, Fukue-Shima bearing North-Easterly between Korea and the island of Tsushima, continuing in this direction with the islands of Oki-Retto to the South-East and Take Shima to the North-West curving with the coast of Honshu, then Northerly skirting Rebun Shima passing Easterly through Soya Kaikyo approximately 142°E (b) [...] The line above described is plotted on the map attached to the present Treaty (Annex I). In the case of a discrepancy between the map and the textual description of the line, the latter shall prevail.[26] (Underlined by the author)

The few minor changes from the second draft were: (a) the change of Northeasterly direction to Northwesterly, and (b) the change of 142°40″N to 142°E. As further shown on the map, the changes were made to rectify the flaws in the second draft.

The territorial clause of the third draft made reference to a map being attached to the treaty in Annex I.[27] The only remaining copy of this map can be found at the National Archives and Records Administration in the US.

---

26   FO 371/92538, FJ 1022/222, "Provisional Draft of Japanese Peace Treaty (United Kingdom)," (Apr. 7, 1951), p. 15.
27   (1) FO 371/92538, FJ 1022/222, "Provisional Draft of Japanese Peace Treaty (United Kingdom)," (Apr. 7, 1951), pp. 15-50, (2) FO 371/92538, FJ 1022/224, "Provisional Draft of the Japanese Peace Treaty and list of contents," (undated), pp. 90-140. (1) is a printed version and (2) a typed version.

3) Characteristics of the British map / Korean sovereignty over Dokdo reaffirmed

The map attached to the third draft treaty is 72.0 centimeters wide and 68.5 centimeters long, and entitled *The Territory under Japanese Sovereignty as Defined in Art. I of the Peace Treaty*. The map was produced by the Research Bureau of the British Foreign Office in March 1951, an indication that the map was produced about the same time the second draft was being made (March 1951). Also, based on the changes in the third draft, it seems likely that the text of the third draft was changed after the line delineating Japanese territory had been added to the map. The following summarizes the main characteristics of the map and contents related to Dokdo.

First, the map delineates the territory to remain under Japanese control around the four major home islands of Japan. This characteristic common to all three of the British draft treaties seems to be a strict application of the Potsdam Declaration, which marked out the territory to remain under Japanese control based on the four major home islands of Japan.

Second, not only were the territorial boundaries of Japan specified in a way that left little room for controversy, they were further visually reinforced through the use of a clear, bold line. While the first draft had used the more tedious method of listing the islands under Japanese control one by one, thus naturally excluding from Japan's postwar territory those islands not listed, the second and third drafts further clarified Japan's boundaries by their use of the more flexible method of a boundary line. However, this method was still not as advantageous for Japan as the method ultimately employed at the San Francisco Conference.

Third, there seem to be three primary reasons behind the UK government's use of a boundary line to define Japan's territory.

First and foremost was the territorial clause of the Potsdam Declaration. Article 8 of the Potsdam Declaration provided for Japan's postwar territory to be as follows: "The terms of the Cairo Declaration shall be carried out and Japanese sovereignty shall be limited to the islands of Honshu, Hokkaido, Kyushu, Shikoku and such minor islands as we determine." The UK subsequently interpreted the words "minor islands as the Allies

[Figure 4-1] Map attached to the British draft treaty (March 1951)

determine" to mean those minor islands in the immediate vicinity of Japan's four major islands.

Second, by drawing a boundary line, the UK may have wanted to forestall any future territorial disputes between Japan and its neighbors. The use of a line to visually depict Japan's postwar territory would help overcome any ambiguities and inaccuracy in wording, thus offering the advantage of removing potential sources of conflict between Japan and its neighbors. In fact, had the final draft of the Treaty of San Francisco included a map defining Japanese territory as clearly as the map had done in the British draft, it would likely have prevented any further territorial disputes that Japan might have engaged in with neighboring countries.

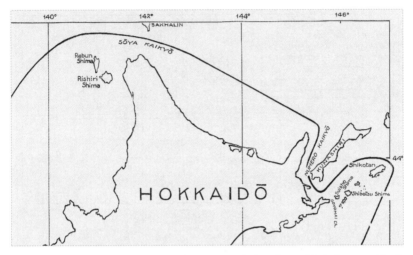

[Figure 4-2] Shikotan and Habomai on the map attached to the British draft treaty (March 1951)

Finally, the delineation method sent a clear message to Japan that it would be held accountable for its acts of aggression during the war. In other words, as a pre-condition to the peace treaty initiated by the US, the UK may have wanted to establish clear territorial limits to postwar Japan that would restore those lands taken by Japan by aggression to their original states. In particular, the draft imposed considerably disadvantageous territorial clauses on Japan by excluding Amami Oshima, the Ryukyu Islands, and even the islands south of Kyushu from Japanese territory.

Fourth and most importantly, the draft made it clear that Dokdo was part of Korea, and not Japan. Furthermore, the map included in Japanese territory Shikotan and Habomai, which are two of the four islands in the North over which Japan is currently involved in territorial disputes with Russia, while excluding Ryukyu, which became a trust territory of the US. At the Yalta Conference held before the end of the war, the US, the UK, and the USSR agreed to transfer Sakhalin and Kuril to the Soviets. However, the Soviet Union occupied Shikotan and Habomai after the war ended. Japan had argued that Shikotan and Habomai were an integral part of Hokkaido, and not the Southern Kurils, and had called for their return. Therefore, the inclusion of Shikotan and Habomai in Japanese territory in the British draft was an indication that Japan's position had been considered.

Meanwhile, the map's significance with respect to Dokdo can be summarized as follows: First, it was the only official map produced by the UK government in preparation for the San Francisco Conference. It was also the only map created by any Allied member to delineate the territorial limits of postwar Japan. Though the US DoS did produce its own version of a map, it never made one to go with the official draft. Likewise, no map was attached to the final draft of the San Francisco Treaty. Thus, the map attached to the British draft became by default the only official map reflecting the views of the Allies with respect to the territorial boundaries of postwar Japan as of April 1951.

Second, by reflecting the views of the UK rather than the US per se, this map perhaps documented the views of the Allies as a whole from a more objective, third-person perspective. Since the UK was somewhat less influenced by Japanese lobbying at the time, its map perhaps adds supportive rationale to the fairness of its territorial provisions with respect to Dokdo.

Third, in addition to the views of the UK, the map also reflected the general views of the other British Commonwealth countries: Canada, Australia, New Zealand, South Africa, India, Pakistan, and Ceylon. In other words, it was produced based on consultation and agreement between at least eight countries of the British Commonwealth between March and April 1951, meaning that they all agreed that Dokdo was part of the territory of Korea, not Japan.

Fourth, the map clearly and decisively showed Dokdo as outside the limits of Japanese sovereignty. It showed both Dokdo and Ulleungdo as part of Korea. This was all the more significant in that it constituted the official and final view of the UK government in the months leading up to the San Francisco Conference where the final draft of the treaty was signed. In other words, the map stood out as the only official map made by the UK government for use as an annex map in its draft treaty. Additionally, it was also the most recent and up-to-date map produced prior to the signing of the 1951 San Francisco Peace Treaty, and for that reason superseded all

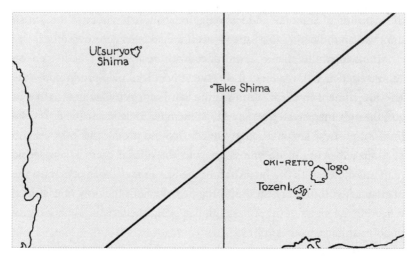

[Figure 4-3] Dokdo on the map attached to the British draft treaty (March 1951)

the older maps of the 18th and 19th centuries, the SCAP administrative maps of the 1945-1950 period, as well as the working maps produced by the US DoS. Since the SCAPIN 677 memorandum of January 1946, this map provided the clearest evidentiary support for Korea's sovereignty over Dokdo.

Fifth, and perhaps even more important to note is the fact that the UK government mistakenly described Dokdo, Ulleungdo, and even Jejudo as belonging to Japan in its initial draft. Then, in the second draft onwards, it had officially corrected these errors, recognizing that these areas were not under Japanese territorial sovereignty. In short, by correcting its initial mistake in the first draft, the UK government reaffirmed Korea's sovereignty over Dokdo, making it clear that the previous determinations in this regard had merely been an oversight. Thus, the argument of some that this was a sheer mistake grounded on SCAPIN 677 fails to be convincing.[28] The UK government had finalized its draft treaty independently of the US without reference to the draft that the US had produced in March 1951.

---

28 Tsukamoto, "The Treaty of Peace with Japan and Takeshima (Review)," p. 46.

Sixth, although this map was not incorporated in the final peace treaty, its existence carries significance in that it reaffirms Korea's sovereignty over Dokdo. Japan has repeatedly argued since that time that the lack of any specific wording in the San Francisco Treaty text excluding Dokdo from its postwar boundaries is proof of its right of dominium over it. However, a careful examination of the process by which the British draft treaty was created and why it underwent the changes that it did over the course of its various drafts reveals such an argument to be groundless. The territorial principles of the Cairo Declaration, reaffirmed through the Potsdam Declaration, became the official guidelines used by the Allies to further develop their policies regarding Japan's postwar territorial boundaries from then onwards. The Allies applied these principles to: 1) specify the islands to be included in and those to be excluded from Japanese sovereignty, 2) delineate Japanese sovereignty using degrees of longitude and latitude, and 3) develop an annex map to practically illustrate the execution of such a policy.

Intended to put into action the policies of the Allies with respect to Japanese territory as provided for in the Cairo and Potsdam Declarations, such a method was consistently employed throughout the various drafts produced by the US DoS and the UK Foreign Office during the period of 1947-1951. The US and the UK drew up their draft treaties separately without consulting one another, but they both adopted the same method. The Japanese territorial clauses of the Cairo and Potsdam Declarations, which defined the international wartime agreements regarding the postwar disposition of territories occupied by Japan during the war, remained significantly influential following the end of the war, their influence extending undoubtedly until as late as 1951. Some records of the Anglo-American meeting held in London in June 1951 indicate that the two countries agreed to specify in the final treaty those areas that would be excluded from Japan. Such a specification of territory, discussed at a meeting where no minutes or records were left, was ultimately not reflected in the draft treaty, however. This is because the US and the UK discarded the Allies' earlier agreements of the Cairo and Potsdam Declarations at the meeting but did not leave any resolution or even documentation of their agreement. Furthermore, no official consent was obtained from the countries involved *ex ante* or *ex post* with regard to such a decision, so even if the decision had been officially documented in the draft treaty, it would have failed to be effective. Such a course of action would have constituted a negation of the international agreements under the Cairo and Potsdam Declarations, undermining the Allies' officially established policies for dealing with Japan in the postwar era.

As a result, the areas to be included in and excluded from Japan were simply eliminated from the final treaty, with the overall tenor of the remaining territorial provisions turning in favor of Japan. While they scrapped the Japanese territorial clause of the Cairo and Potsdam declarations, the UK and the US failed to come up with a new territorial principle.

2

Anglo-American Consultations of 1951 and Discussions on Korea and Territorial Issues

With the communization of mainland China in 1949, the friendly relations of good will and cooperation among the four major Allies during World War II—the US, the USSR, the UK, and China—came to an end. Amidst a Cold War with the Soviets, the UK emerged as the most important negotiating partner of the US given the latter's East Asia strategy including the peace talks with Japan. The UK held considerable influence over many of the British Commonwealth countries, of which Australia and New Zealand were key Allied members with respect to the Peace Treaty with Japan. Thus, obtaining the consent of the UK and of the British Commonwealth countries was an urgent priority for an early conclusion of a treaty of peace with Japan.

In this connection, US Secretary of State, Dean Acheson, met with UK Foreign Secretary, Ernest Bevin, in Washington in September 1949 to lay the foundation for bilateral cooperation. The US Department of State (DoS) hurriedly put together a draft proposal in preparation for the Colombo Conference scheduled to take place in January 1950 (the Commonwealth Conference of Foreign Ministers). Meanwhile, the UK had been preparing a separate draft treaty in consultation with other British Commonwealth countries. In May 1950, the Commonwealth Working Party of Officials on the Japanese Peace Treaty met in London to review all aspects related to the treaty.[29]

During his visit to Tokyo in February 1951, Dulles met twice with the UK Ambassador to Japan. Immediately after his visit to Japan, he also

---

29   TNA, FO 371/92532, FJ 1022/91 "022/9132, of Question 2 (Feb. 19, 1951).

visited the Philippines, Australia, and New Zealand. Based in part on these contacts between the US, the UK, and British Commonwealth countries, the UK and the US completed their separate drafts of a proposed peace treaty with Japan about the same time.

The UK completed its draft between the end of February and early April 1951 and immediately sent it to the British Commonwealth countries for review. In tandem, the US also finalized its draft in March 1951 and sent it to the relevant countries. At this point, the UK and the US began their discussions in full swing.

In 1951, the two countries engaged themselves in three rounds of consultations. The first round involved a visit by Allison (Dulles' right-hand man in the Japanese Treaty negotiations) to London for unofficial consultations with officials of the UK Foreign Office (March 20-21, 1951). The second round consisted of the first official Anglo-American talks held during the visit of Charles H. Johnston, head of Japan and Pacific Department of the British Foreign Office, and his delegation to Washington (April 25-May 4, 1951). Through these talks, the first joint Anglo-American draft treaty was finalized and sent to the British Commonwealth countries for review. The third round of consultations was held during Dulles' visit to London (June 2-14, 1951). The outcome was a revised joint draft (June 14, 1951), which was sent to all the relevant countries for the first time. While the first and second rounds of consultations were held at the working level, the third round of consultations was the final series of meetings between Dulles and the UK Foreign Secretary to coordinate and make decisions at the highest level.

1) Consultations of March 1951

During the period of March-April 1951, the UK's major concerns with respect to the anticipated peace treaty with Japan were: 1) the participation of the Soviet Union and China to the talks, 2) the participation of Japan to the talks, and 3) Japan's renunciation of rights to Formosa.[30] Some key discussions regarding Korea related to 1) the status of Korea as a negotiating party and potential signatory to the Japanese peace treaty, i.e. Korea being a party to the treaty, and 2) sovereignty over Dokdo. At this point in time, the UK and the US held different positions over the role of Korea in the talks, with the US highly supportive of Korean participation and the UK opposed to it. No serious deliberations had yet been undertaken regarding territorial sovereignty over Dokdo, but while the UK recognized Korean sovereignty, the US had not as yet put forward any decided policy on the issue.

On March 12, 1951, the UK Foreign Office communicated to Dulles the British government's position on territorial issues via a diplomatic memorandum,[31] which concurred with the principles under the Potsdam Declaration that Japanese sovereignty was to be limited to the four major islands of Japan and such minor islands as the Allies were to determine. In other words, the British policy was to specify Japanese territory and draw a clear line to delineate those areas to be excluded from postwar Japan. At this point, the UK's second draft was being worked on, thus the articulation of such a policy would only have been natural. With respect to Korea, however, the memorandum only stated that "Japan shall recognize the independence of Korea."

In response, the US made a preliminary report, which stated that it was in general agreement with the proposed territorial provisions of the UK. The US specifically agreed to incorporate the following in the draft:

Territory
The United States Government agrees in general with the territorial clauses of the United Kingdom aide-memoire and in particular agrees that the following should be recorded in the Treaty
(i) Japan should recognise the independence of Korea.

---

30   FO 371/92535, FJ 1022/174, "022/174, on the Japanese angle of the problem of Chinese & Russian non participation & the question of Japanese participation of Japanese Peace Treaty" (Mar. 22, 1951).

31   "AIDE-MEMOIRE" (Mar. 12, 1951), handed to Mr. John Foster Dulles by the British Charge d'Affaires on March 12, 1951, RG 59, Japanese Peace Treaty Files of John Foster Dulles, 1947-1952, Subject File, Lot 54D423, 1946-52, Box 13.

(ii) The Ryukyu and Bonin Islands should be placed under a United States trusteeship.

(iii) Japan should renounce all special rights and interests in China.

(iv) Japan should specifically renounce all her rights and claims in respect of her pre-war mandated territories.[32] (Underlined by the quoter)

The US agreed to the British government's proposals that Japan should recognize the independence of Korea, the Ryukyu and Bonin Islands be placed under US trusteeship, and Japan renounce its rights in China as well as in other territories formerly under its mandate. However, the US had different views regarding the future status of Southern Sakhalin, the Kuril Islands, and the Antarctic Continent.

Subsequently, Allison visited London from March 20 to 21, 1951. He met with officials of the UK Foreign Office, though not in an official setting.[33] During these meetings, the two sides discussed various topics related to the Japanese peace treaty, and both sides agreed that there were no major differences between the UK and US drafts. The US was most interested in the provisions on war responsibility, Japan's shipbuilding capacity, and security. R. H. Scott, the British Assistant Under-Secretary of State, stated that because the British Foreign Office was under the supervision of the Cabinet, it would follow the Cabinet's decision regarding the provision on Japan's war responsibility. He also indicated that Australia had concerns about the security of Japan. The issue of Soviet and Chinese participation in the talks was also discussed, but this was not a big issue. Then, the two sides discussed the participation of Korea as a party to the treaty.

Allison stated that the US government was planning to send its draft to the members of the Far Eastern Commission and certain other governments soon. Assistant Under-Secretary Scott agreed to this point, but requested that the draft be sent to the individual "members" of the Far

---

32   *Ibid.*

33   David K. Marvin, Amembassy, London to the Secretary of State, Subject: Japanese Peace Treaty (Mar. 28, 1951), RG 59, Department of State, Decimal File, 694.001/3-2851.

Eastern Commission, rather than to the commission itself. Since China would not be a signatory to the treaty, the UK felt it would be inappropriate to send the draft treaty to the Far Eastern Commission of which China was a member. Scott was also opposed to sending a copy of the draft to Korea, which was not a member of the Far Eastern Commission. His stated reason was that Korea had a different legal status. What the UK meant by this was that Korea had technically been a colony of Japan until the end of World War II and as such was neither a country that had been at war with Japan nor one that had declared war on Japan.

Allison responded that there was a very good political reason for sending a copy of the draft to Korea. He stressed the political need to do so and to have it participate in the peace conference with Japan and sign the treaty. This was the position of the US DoS ever since John J. Muccio, US Ambassador to Korea, had formally requested that Korea take part in the peace conference. Allison explained that, Korea being at the heart of the free world's cold war confrontation with communism, the US now placed a greater political significance on its participation.

This was the first exchange of opinions between the UK and the US regarding Korea's participation in the peace conference and its signing of the treaty. The UK was still looking at Korea's juridical status at the time Japan surrendered in 1945, while the US was emphasizing Korea's emerging political status and significance at the time.

The future status of the Ryukyu Islands was also dealt with at these meetings. Allison stated that US trusteeship over the islands would merely be a headache since the US had no intention of annexing the islands and would therefore at some time or other have to return them to Japan.

2) The first Anglo-American talks (April 25-May 4, 1951) including discussions on Korea's participation in the peace treaty settlement and territorial issues

On April 25, 1951, a UK delegation comprised of legal and economic experts and headed by Charles H. Johnston, head of the Japan and Pacific Department of the British Foreign Office, arrived in Washington. The

US representative for the Anglo-American talks was John Allison, and attending the meeting along with him were U. Alexis Johnson, Arthur Ringwalt (First Secretary in the UK), Noel Hemmendinger, Robert A. Fearey, and C. Arnold Fraleigh. The meeting of the joint working group was chaired by Allison of the Dulles delegation along with his counterpart, Johnston, from the British Foreign Office. At the meeting, the two sides reviewed both the UK and the US drafts. The meetings were held from April 25 to May 4, 1951.[34]

Some important topics concerning Korea were discussed at the meetings, including its being a party and signatory to the Japanese peace treaty, and the Dokdo sovereignty issue. According to the Foreign Relations of the United States series (FRUS), no detailed minutes of those first Anglo-American talks in Washington are on record in the US DoS files. It appears that no official minutes were taken down of the talks. Those first Anglo-American talks in Washington consisted of nine sessions in all. US DoS files contain records of the meetings held from April 25 to 27, 1951, while UK Foreign Office files contain records of the meetings from May 1 to 4, 1951(6 th -9th meetings).

Korea's participation in the peace treaty settlement

A document reviewing and comparing the respective positions of the US and the UK during the Anglo-American talks from Wednesday, April 25 to Friday, April 27, 1951 was found on file in the US DoS. A careful review of the US draft treaty (March 1951) and the British draft treaty (April 1951), and the discussions that had taken place over the three days, shows the differences between the positions of the two countries.[35]

What follows is a brief summary of the discussions.[36] For the preamble, the two sides seemed to be in disagreement regarding which countries had

---

34   "Editorial Note," *FRUS*, 1951, Vol. VI, p. 1021.
35   "Check List of Position Stated by US and UK at April 25-27 Meetings" (undated), RG 59, Department of State, Decimal File, 694.001/4-2751.
36   *Ibid.*

been at war with Japan and thus would be signatories to the treaty.

The US had included Korea as a "potential signatory to the treaty" and as "an Allied Power" with the intention of having it take part in the peace conference. As mentioned before, the US had taken a positive stance toward the participation of Korea in the conference as a signatory ever since the US Ambassador to Korea, Muccio, had requested in December 1949 that Korea take part in the peace conference with Japan. The outbreak of the Korean War, in particular, led the US to lend Korea its support in this regard. However, between May and June of 1951, the US changed its position towards not having Korea participate at the peace conference. What influenced such a change of position was opposition from the UK and Japan.[37]

The UK's argument against Korea's participation was that Korea did not have Allied Power status during World War II. The UK had even opposed the idea of the US sending its preliminary draft to Korea, but during his visit to London on March 21, 1951, Allison told British Foreign Under-Secretary Scott that it was necessary to do so for political reasons. On April 7, 1951, the UK completed its own draft of a treaty. In a memorandum sent to the US government (April 16, 1951), British Foreign Secretary Morrison stated that "though Korea's participation is not desirable, we would not oppose it if the US considered it important."[38] The UK government's position was that it would not oppose the participation of Korea should the US strongly argue in favor of it. After having reviewed Morrison's memorandum, however, different opinions emerged within the British Cabinet. The British government led by the Labour Party was now strongly opposed to Korea's participation in the peace conference.[39]

37　Kim, "US Foreign Policy toward Korea in the Beginning of the 1950s," pp. 362-363; Lee, *The Starting Point of Dealing with Past Affairs between Korea and Japan*, pp. 27-28.

38　Chihiro Hosoya, 1989, *Leading up to the Peace Treaty of San Francisco*, Chuokoronsha, p. 228 (re-quoted Kim Tae-gi, "US Foreign Policy toward Korea in the Beginning of the 1950s," p. 366).

39　Cheong Sung-hwa, *The Politics of Anti-Japanese Sentiment in Korea: Japanese-South Korean Relations Under American Occupation, 1945-1952*, New York, Greenwood Press, 1991, pp. 91-93 (re-quoted Kim, *US Foreign Policy toward Korea in the Beginning of the 1950s*, p. 366)

During the joint UK-US working group meeting in Washington, the British government insisted that Korea should not be a signatory. The relevant documents show that the two sides discussed Korea's participation in the treaty at least three times during their meetings, with the UK delegation expressing their strong opposition to it at least twice.

The two sides debated this issue for the first time at the seventh meeting on May 1, 1951 when Allison raised the question of which countries should be included as Allied Powers in the preamble and how those not mentioned in the preamble should be addressed. At this point, the two sides were brought face to face with the question of whether or not to include Korea. F. S. Tomlinson of the UK expressed his concerns that if Korea were allowed to be a signatory to the treaty while China was excluded, regardless of whether or not the latter had willingly decided to do so, it may become significantly more difficult to obtain the cooperation of some Asian countries for purposes of making the treaty.[40] Records of the meeting show that Allison noted Tomlinson's point but "it was clear that he wasn't affected by it too much." Afterwards, the two delegations decided to delete the term Associated Powers from the phrase "the Allied and Associated Powers."

On the following day, May 2, during a follow-up meeting between the UK delegation and Dulles and Allison, the issue of Korea's participation in the treaty was brought up again. The two sides had scheduled this meeting to discuss the procedures of the peace conference with Japan. On this day, Dulles emphasized again that Korean participation in the peace conference was necessary. Dulles' statement is recorded as follows in a document sent by Sir O. Franks, UK Ambassador to the US, to the British Foreign Office.

Mr. Dulles said that there would be political advantages in allowing the Republic of Korea to sign the Treaty as principal party in view of the agg-

---

40   FO 371/92547, FJ 1022/376, British Embassy, Washington to C. P. Scott, O.B.E., Japan and Pacific Department, Foreign Office, no.1076/357/5IG, "Anglo-American meetings on Japanese Peace Treaty, Summary Record of Seventh meeting" (May 3, 1951).

ressions committed against it. The Japanese Government had however expressed the hope that the Treaty would not give the advantageous status of many Allied nationals to the Korean minority in Japan whom are communists. There was also some reason to suppose that the Burmese and Indonesian Governments, judging by certain hints made by their representatives here, might be averse to signing a Treaty signed by the Republic of Korea. Any legal difficulties attendant on the problem could probably be solved to conform with the solution which seemed best on political grounds. Possibly the best solution would be to provide for Korea to sign the Treaty some time after the original signing by other Powers.[41] (Underlined by the quoter)

Dulles viewed Korean participation as necessary not so much because of Japan's aggression against Korea and its past history of colonization but because of Korea's present value as a country that had taken a firm stand against communism in North Korea and China. From the view of the present, Dulles judged that having Korea sign the treaty would present a distinct political advantage. His political intention was not so much to include Korea in the peace treaty because the interim government of Korea had fought against Japan as did the other Allied Powers but to fully acknowledge its status as a US ally against communist powers.[42]

Dulles later gave two reasons for changing his mind about Korea being a signatory to the treaty. The first was strong opposition from Japan. It is likely that Dulles conveyed the position of the Japanese government on this issue. What was said at the meeting was consistent with the memorandum *Peace Conference with Korean Participation* (April 23, 1951) that Japanese Prime Minister Shigeru Yoshida had delivered to Dulles during the latter's third visit to Tokyo just prior to the first Anglo-American talks. The

---

41   FO 371/92547, FJ 1022/370, Sir O. Franks, Washington to Foreign Office, "Japanese Peace Treaty: Records of meeting between our representative and Mr. Dulles," no. 393(s) (May 3, 1951).
42   Cheong, The Politics of Anti-Japanese Sentiment in Korea, p. 81; Lee, *The Starting Point of Dealing with the Past Affairs between Korea and Japan*, pp. 29-30 (re-quoted from Kim, *US Foreign Policy toward Korea in the Beginning of the 1950s*, p. 362).

Anglo-American talks were held only a week after Yoshida had delivered his memorandum to Dulles requesting that Korea not be allowed to take part in the peace treaty. His stated reason for making this request was that Koreans in Japan, who were either communist or criminals, should be stopped from ruining Japan's economy. In retrospect, it seems plausible that the strong request of the Japanese government had an influence on Dulles' thinking. The message that "communist Koreans living in Japan" posed a danger to Japan was first conveyed by Japanese Prime Minister Shigeru Yoshida to John Foster Dulles, and then to British Ambassador to the US, Sir O. Franks. Of note is that during the high-level meeting of the UK and the US, such false accusations against Korea and Koreans residing in Japan were quoted as undeniable fact. The second reason for Dulles' change of heart was opposition from Burma and Indonesia. Though the specific reasons were unknown, Dulles anticipated that Burma and Indonesia would oppose a treaty in which Korea was included as a participant. In fact, Burma did not take part in the San Francisco Peace Conference due to its dissatisfaction over compensation issues, while Indonesia took part in the conference and signed the treaty.

The compromise solution that Dulles came up with was to have Korea sign the treaty but only after the initial signatories had signed it. Though his support for Korean participation as a signatory to the treaty was still strong, he seems to have beaten a tactical retreat. After receiving a report on the meetings from the British Ambassador to the US, British Foreign Under-Secretary Scott expressed his views in his commentary of May 9 that should the US continue to argue in favor of Korean participation as a signatory to the Japanese peace treaty, the UK could possibly support it through the addition of a special clause.[43] Thus, both the US and the UK announced that they were willing to make concessions to meet half way on the issue.

The US and the UK discussed both Dulles' proposal that Korea sign the

---

43   FO 371/92547, FJ 1022/370, Sir O. Franks, Washington to Foreign Office, "Japanese Peace Treaty: Records of meeting between our representative and Mr. Dulles," no. 393(s) (May 3, 1951).

treaty after the initial signatories had signed it and Scott's proposal to allow Korean participation by a special clause. Both proposals were, however, a far cry from Korea participating as a signatory to the treaty. Both parties had in fact moved away from invitation and participation of Korea towards non-invitation and exclusion of it.

Finally, at the 9th session of the meetings on May 4, the UK and the US again discussed Korea's participation in the treaty. At the 8th meeting on the previous day, the two sides had completed a joint draft treaty and circulated it.[44] The meeting of May 4 was the last session of the meetings, and there the two sides reviewed the joint draft sentence by sentence. While reviewing the preamble, Fitzmaurice of the UK again expressed his opposition to including Korea as a signatory to the treaty.[45] He argued that Korea had never been at war with Japan and thus most of the provisions in the treaty did not apply to it.[46] Throughout the first Anglo-American talks in Washington, the UK persistently made an issue of Korea's legal status to put pressure on the US. In the end, Allison, head of the US delegation responsible for the working-level talks, agreed to take note of the British position.

In short, the US had argued in favor of Korea's signing the treaty up until the Anglo-American talks of early May 1951. But from that time onwards, it came to hold a more nuanced view of Korean participation. In April 1951, both the UK and Japan persistently insisted that 1) Korea was not an Allied Power and 2) the granting of Allied Power status to Korea would unduly benefit communist Koreans living in Japan and cause trouble for the Japanese government. Consequently, the US became increasingly concerned that 1) if Korea participated in the treaty while

---

44   FO 371/92547, FJ 1022/377, British Embassy, Washington to C. P. Scott, O.B.E., Japan and Pacific Department, Foreign Office, no.1076/365/5IG, "Anglo-American meetings on Japanese Peace Treaty, Summary Record of Eighth meeting held on 3rd May" (May 4, 1951).
45   "Joint United States-United Kingdom Draft Peace Treaty"" (May 3, 1951), FRUS, 1951, Vol. VI, p. 1024.
46   FO 371/92547, FJ 1022/378, British Embassy, Washington to Foreign Office, no.1076 /366/5IG, "Anglo-American meetings on Japanese Peace Treaty, Summary Record of Eighth meeting held on 3rd May" (May 4, 1951).

China was excluded, it may trigger unwanted opposition from Burma, Indonesia, and other Asian countries, and that 2) communist and criminal Korean elements living in Japan could take undue advantage of their newly acquired status as Allied citizens. Thus, Dulles proposed a special clause by which the Allied Powers would sign the treaty first and then Korea would be allowed to sign it afterwards. This, however, was clearly a retreat from the initial position. Also, such a proposal was not one to which the Allies could easily consent considering its priority, political significance, and feasibility. Agreeing to such a half-step concession could easily lead to still further concessions.

Meanwhile, one cannot exclude the possibility that the Korean government's first response to the preliminary US draft of March 1951 (April 27, 1951), received by the US DoS on May 7, 1951, may have had a negative impact on Dulles' thinking as well. Having faced such strong opposition from Japan (April 1951) and the UK (April-May 1951) regarding Korea's participation in the treaty, the US DoS was disappointed by Korea's first response to its draft.[47] The person who reviewed and recorded the US DoS's comments to Korea's reply was Fearey who had been involved in development of the draft since 1947 at the Office of Northeast Asian Affairs, Bureau of Far Eastern Affairs of the US DoS. In his comments, Fearey reacted negatively to all four arguments that Korea gave to legitimate its status as a member of the Allied Powers. To sum up, though the US had initially been in favor of Korea's participation in the treaty, it saw its resolve weaken by the inadequate and unacceptable requests from Korea while it was already faced with rigorous and persistent opposition from the UK, its strongest ally, as well as from Japan.

---

47 "Korea File" (undated), RG 59, Japanese Peace Treaty Files of John Foster Dulles, 1946-52, Lot 54D423, Box 8.

Abrogation of the Japanese territorial clauses under the Cairo
Declaration and the Potsdam Declaration

The US and the UK were also not in agreement concerning the clauses
on Japanese territory. The UK proposed to delete provision "2. The Allied
Powers recognize the full sovereignty of the Japanese people over Japan
and its territorial waters" from Article 2 of Chapter II on Sovereignty in the
US draft treaty. The American and British drafts differed significantly on
Japanese territory. The US draft had no such provisions, while the British
draft contained some that were as detailed and specific as those in the US
drafts prior to 1949. The British draft included a detailed specification of
the islands to be included as part of Japanese territory, the delineation
of Japanese sovereignty using degrees of longitude and latitude, and an
attached map showing the territory to be under Japanese sovereignty.
Such were the chief characteristics of the Japanese territorial clauses of the
Potsdam Declaration.

What the specific discussions regarding Japanese territory were about
is not known, except that the US was strongly opposed to the territorial
provisions and map of the British draft. Due to the lack of meeting minutes,
it is unclear who opposed it and when. But according to the *Japanese Peace
Treaty Working Draft and Commentary* (June 1, 1951), which the US
DoS produced after its talks with the UK, this issue was discussed at the
Washington talks. The US mentioned Japan's "psychological disadvantage"
to persuade the UK to drop the Japanese territorial clauses in its draft.[48]

The US comments were made in the form of a reply to the feedback
of the New Zealand government on the US draft treaty (March 1951).
Noting that the US draft did not clearly specify the various minor islands
to be included under Japanese sovereignty, the New Zealand government
argued that Japanese sovereignty should be accurately delineated by the

---

48 "Japanese Peace Treaty Working Draft and Commentary" (June 1, 1951), Chapter II,
Territory, Article 2, p. 4, RG 59, Office of Northeast Asia Affairs, Records Relating to the Treaty
of Peace with Japan-Subject file, 1945-51, Lot 56D527, Box 6, Folder "Treaty-Draft-Mar. 23 1951".

specification of its boundaries using degrees of latitude and longitude as in Article 1 of the British draft so that territorial disputes over various islands adjacent to Japan can be prevented.[49]

Immediately prior to the talks with the UK (April 23, 1951), the US delegation held discussions with the Japanese government regarding the British draft. During these discussions, Shigeru Yoshida vehemently opposed the delineation of Japanese territory using a fence-like line in the draft. The very fact that the US government was willing to discuss the draft treaty of the UK, which was a third party to the discussions, with the Japanese government is surprising. What is more shocking is that the US so willingly accepted the Japanese views. After feedback was received from William J. Sebald in November 1949 expressing strong objection to the territorial clauses, the US government was already beginning to give up on the Japanese territorial clauses agreed upon by the Allies. By August 1950, it had deleted the provision specifying the islands to be included as a part of Japanese sovereignty. As far as territorial issues were concerned, the Japanese first were able to persuade Sebald, then succeeded in persuading the US DoS through Sebald, and then finally succeeded in persuading the UK government through Dulles.

The Dulles delegation brought the British draft along when they arrived in Tokyo on April 16. At this point, they had neither the time nor the opportunity to discuss with the UK how the two countries would approach the draft treaty, and especially the fact that the US might discuss the British draft treaty with Japan. A review of the relevant files of the US DoS and of the UK Foreign Office revealed no records that the US government consulted with the UK government or obtained its consent regarding its intention to present the British draft to Japan. Time-wise, it wasn't until the end of April that the economic experts within the US DoS were able to present their perspective regarding the economic provisions of the British draft treaty, so it is almost certain that the Dulles delegation did not consult

---

49 "Japanese Peace Treaty Working Draft and Commentary" (June 1, 1951), Chapter II, Territory, Article 2, p. 4.

on this with the UK government.

Furthermore, during the Washington talks, the US failed to inform the UK that it had reviewed the British draft with Japan. The US delegation went as far as using Shigeru Yoshida's statement on "the psychological disadvantage created by the fencing of Japan in by drawing a continuous line around it" as if these were its own views. It is likely that the US delegation did not belabor the fact that the Japanese government was opposed to such territorial provision during its talks with the UK.

About a week later, the intense opposition of the Japanese Prime Minister was conveyed by the US DoS to the UK government, not as the views of Japan but as the views of the US. Eventually, the UK government decided to drop its proposed territorial provisions. This was the moment that the Allies' territorial clauses on Japan under the Cairo and Potsdam declarations were abandoned. In other words, at the Washington talks in April and May 1951, the US and the UK, the two most important countries working on the formulation of the Japanese peace treaty, decided to abrogate the Allies' territorial clauses on Japan in the Cairo Declaration of 1943 and the Potsdam Declaration of 1945. And the backdrop that led to this decision was the review of the British draft by the US and Japanese governments, Japan's strong opposition to it, and the US consent to it. In other words, the US accepted Japan's objection to the territorial provisions and persuaded the UK, which in turn gave up on its proposed territorial provisions.

With regard to Korea, the UK and the US debated the issue of how to describe the islands situated between Japan and Korea. Two records were found in this regard, the first being the minutes of the meetings held on April 25-27, 1951. According to this document, the UK "argued that it would be desirable to place the islands between Japan and Korea via a special mention." The US proposed to add "including Quelpart" after Korea in Article 3 of the US draft reading "3. Japan renounces all right, title and claim to Korea, Formosa and the Pescadores." In other words, the US proposed the addition of Quelpart in that specific provision in exchange for asking the UK to give up on its proposal to specify the islands in between Korea and Japan. Though the British proposed to clearly specify all the islands within and outside of Japanese boundaries for the sake of preventing territorial disputes, the US wanted to scrap the Japanese territorial clauses of the Cairo and Potsdam declarations and thus avoid specifying all of the islands in the draft if possible.

In this respect, the *Japanese Peace Treaty Working Draft and Commentary* (June 1, 1951) read "US willingness to specify in the treaty that Korean territory included Quelpart, Port Hamilton and Dagelet also helped to persuade the British." This shows that in addition to Quelpart, Port Hamilton and Dagelet were also added to the text of this draft. It is apparent that the US "willingly proposed" to include a specific mention of Quelpart, Port Hamilton, and Dagelet as being under the territorial sovereignty of Korea as a concession to the UK for giving up on its proposed Japanese territorial clause. The rationale that the US gave for this request was that it would cause "psychological disadvantage to Japan." Thus with the specific mention of the three islands of "Quelpart, Port Hamilton, and Dagelet," Korea was now treated differently from Formosa or the Pescadores, which in the US draft of March 1951 had been mentioned in the same way as Korea. Thus, it appears that the strange structure of Article 2 of the first joint Anglo-American draft treaty dated May 3, 1951, in the form of "Japan renounces all rights, titles and claims to Korea (including Quelpart, Port Hamilton and Dagelet), [Formosa and the Pescadores]" was the outcome of a compromise agreement between the US and the UK. The US draft treaties prior to September 1950 had listed and specified in detail the islands to be under the territorial sovereignty of Formosa and the Pescadores, but all of this was omitted from the draft treaties made after September 1950. The same was the case with respect to Korea. But at the Anglo-American meetings of April-May 1951 in Washington, the US willingly proposed to include a specific mention of Quelpart, Port Hamilton, and Dagelet as a compromise for the UK government to scrap its Japanese territorial provisions. However, no mention was made of the islands of Formosa and the Pescadores, which were in the same situation as Korea with regard to their territorial sovereignty rights.

Meanwhile, insufficient records of the Washington meetings remain on the British side. In the British Foreign Office files, there are only records of the sixth (May 1, 1951), seventh (May 2, 1951), eighth (May 3, 1951), and ninth sessions of the meetings (May 4, 1951).[50] Of these, the following was found regarding the discussions held on the Korea-related provisions at the seventh session (May 2, 1951).[51]

United States Chapter III

Both Delegations agreed that it would be preferable to specify only the territory over which Japan was renouncing sovereignty. In this connection, United States Article 3 would require the insertion of the three islands: Quelpart, Port Hamilton and Dagelet. It was left undecided whether the sentence in British Article 2 requiring Japan to recognize whatever settlement the United Nations might make in Korea should be maintained or not.[52]

The plan to specify those areas to be excluded from Japanese territory reflected favorably on the Japanese position. Accordingly, the UK decided to accept the US proposal to include Quelpart, Port Hamilton, and Dagelet among the islands over which Japan would relinquish sovereignty. This is how Article 2 of the first joint Anglo-American draft treaty of May 3, 1951, which provides that "Japan renounces all rights, titles and claims to Korea (including Quelpart, Port Hamilton and Dagelet), [Formosa and

---

50   FO 371/92547, 6th meeting: FJ 1022/372, British Embassy, Washington to C. P. Scott, O.B.E., Japan and Pacific Department, Foreign Office, no. 1076/332/5IG, "Summary Record of Sixth Meeting of Anglo- American meetings on Japanese Peace Treaty," (May 2, 1951); 7th meeting: FJ 1022/376, no. 1076/357/5IG, "Anglo-American meetings on Japanese Peace Treaty, Summary Record of Seventh meeting," (May 3, 1951); 8th meeting: FJ 1022/377, no.1076/365/5IG, "Anglo-American meetings on Japanese Peace Treaty, Summary Record of Seventh meeting held on 3rd May," (May 3, 1951); 9th meeting: FJ 1022/378, no.1076/366/5IG, "Anglo-American meetings on Japanese Peace Treaty, Summary Record of ninth and final meeting held on 4th May," (May 4, 1951).
51   FO 371/92547, FJ 1022/376, British Embassy, Washington to C. P. Scott, O.B.E., Japan and Pacific Department, Foreign Office, no.1076/357/5IG, "Anglo-American meetings on Japanese Peace Treaty, Summary Record of Seventh meeting," (May 3, 1951).
52   "Anglo-American meetings on Japanese Peace Treaty, Summary Record of Seventh meeting," (May 3, 1951), p. 66.

the Pescadores]," came with the addition of (including Quelpart, Port Hamilton and Dagelet) in parentheses. The UK and the US still remained undecided about whether or not to include these islands in this sentence. Also undecided was whether to include the provision of the British draft that Japan shall concur in any actions of the United Nations.

The sovereignty over Dokdo (Liancourt Rocks) was not even brought up during the course of these discussions. The US merely proposed to include the specific mention of Quelpart (and possibly Port Hamilton and Dagelet at a later date) in the draft, and this as a concession in exchange for the British agreeing to discard the remainder of its Japanese territorial provisions and attached map. The two sides were already well on their way to a joint draft more in line with the simpler and briefer US version, so compromises and changes were made in such a way to abridge the longer UK version.

During these meetings, the UK and the US discussed the status of Ryukyu, Ogasawara, and the Southern Kurils. Allison expressed his disfavor with the UK proposal that Japan be required to renounce its sovereignty rights over Ryukyu and Ogasawara (Bonin). His rationale was that given the fact that the US would at some point give up its control over these islands, requiring Japan to renounce its sovereignty over them may later trigger an international dispute. Thus, it would be easier to legally restore the islands to Japan at the outset. This exchange clearly showed the pro-Japanese nature of the US territorial policy towards Japan.

At this point, Dulles was already facing difficulties in his efforts to negotiate with the UK, so much so that at a meeting with his staff during his second visit to Tokyo (April 17, 1951) he asked if it was at all possible for the US to exclude the British altogether and sign a separate treaty with Japan. Dulles' reaction to the British draft is recorded as follows:

He said that he believed that a team of people in the UK Foreign Office has been working on the British draft for many years, as had been the case in the State Department, and that this long and detailed draft was the logical result of such prolonged consideration. He said that he had never expected that the final treaty would be as short as our original proposal. If the British wish to include detailed provisions which will be the length of the treaty but to which the Japanese and the US do not have substantive objections it might be desirable to accept the British proposals.[53]

Though the basic policy was to have a simple draft treaty, the US felt that it had little choice but to accept the UK proposals. As an alternative, the US sought to conclude its negotiations with the British by symbolically incorporating part of the British draft, if not all of its details. At the Anglo-American meetings, the US revealed its conciliatory posture towards Japan by announcing its support of Ryukyu being excluded from those islands over which Japan would be required to renounce its sovereignty, given that the US would be returning Ryukyu to Japan at some point after a certain period of US trusteeship. It is currently unknown what exactly was decided regarding Dokdo at these meetings. What is clear is that Dokdo was not addressed as an important issue and, based on the available records, it appears that it was not discussed at all. At their Washington meetings, the UK and the US discarded the Allies' previous agreement on the territorial policy toward Japan without leaving so much as a single note or memo on file of having done so. In this respect, no discussions or agreements were made between the countries that had been at war with Japan or had declared war on it, i.e. the major Allied and Associated Powers of World War II. The signatory countries that took part in the San Francisco Peace Conference knew little or nothing about the discussions, agreements, and decisions of the UK and US regarding Japanese territory, nor did they have any influence to speak of over them.

As indicated by the above discussion, the strict territorial clauses of the Potsdam Declaration were discarded as a result of the Anglo-American meetings in Washington, where it was decided not to specify the islands to be included in and excluded from Japanese sovereignty. The UK and

---

53 "Minutes-Dulles Mission Staff Meeting, Dai Ichi Building, April 17, 9:00 A.M." by R. A. Fearey, RG 59, Office of Northeast Asia Affairs, Records Relating to the Treaty of Peace with Japan-Subject File, 1945- 51, Lot 56D527, Box 6.

the US dropped the method of clearly specifying such, describing the limits of Japanese sovereignty through the use of degrees of longitude and latitude, and delineating the territory on an annexed map as was done in the British draft treaty of April 1951 and the US treaty drafts of 1947-1950. The main rationale that drove the two countries in this direction was Japan's argument that doing so would put it in a position of "psychological disadvantage," but at the heart of it was the intensification of the Cold War and the rising status that Japan held in US policy formation following the outbreak of the Korean War. As a consequence, the more precise territorial provisions of the previous drafts were dropped in favor of an ambiguous and indecisively-worded provision more to the liking of Japan and a provisory clause stating "to specify only the territory over which Japan was renouncing sovereignty was adopted" was recorded. Such modifications left the door open for Japan to later engage in international territorial disputes with its neighbors. With the Allies failing to exercise their rights to determine those islands to which Japanese sovereignty shall be limited, a right that Japan had accepted as a condition for ending the war, they for all practical purposes gave Japan the right to dispute with its neighbors over the sovereignty status of many smaller islands that still remained in abeyance

There may have been several reasons why the US gave up on the territorial clauses of the Cairo and Potsdam declarations. The first and foremost reason was the varying interests on this issue of the US, the USSR, and China in the intensifying Cold War. At the time, no decisions had been made during the war regarding the disposition of or jurisdiction over the territories in the South Pacific that had formerly been under Japanese jurisdiction over which the US was now to have trusteeship, and the Ryukyu and Bonin Islands. While the US was given trusteeship over Japan's former territories following a decision made on April 2, 1947 by the United Nations Security Council, no specific agreement had been reached by the allies regarding the disposition of the islands of Ryukyu, Bonin, and Iwo Jima. The Soviet Union was the most strongly opposed to the US being given jurisdiction over these former Japanese territories, the reason being that there had not been any wartime discussions or agreements reached on their disposition. India was also opposed to the US being given any rights over these islands. Ironically, the Soviets argued strongly in favor of Japanese sovereignty over these islands. While meekly accepting US trusteeship over them, Japan requested that the sovereignty rights over those islands be exercised by Japan, or else be jointly administered by the US and Japan. Eventually, the US changed its position and accepted that though it would have trusteeship over these islands, Japan would retain the right to "potential sovereignty" over them in the future.

The timely disposition of Japan's former mandated territories in the South Pacific, the Ryuku and Bonin islands, the Southern Kurils and Sakhalin, and Formosa was hindered by the allies' wartime agreement, the development of a new Cold War, and the non-participation in the conference and/or strong opposition of the Soviet Union and China, which were two of the four major Allied Powers during the war. In 1951, the US began to feel that the territorial clauses of the Cairo and Potsdam declarations had perhaps outlived their usefulness. Because the Allies had failed to dispose of these territories of the utmost importance within the policy framework established at Potsdam, it seemed insignificant if not irrelevant to continue to hold onto the territorial clauses any longer.

The second reason was the early US decision to pursue a pro-Japanese territorial policy. The execution of the Japanese territorial clauses of the Cairo and Potsdam declarations would have required as a package the specification of which islands were to be included in and those to be excluded from Japanese sovereignty, a clear delineation of Japanese sovereignty using degrees of longitude and latitude, and the use of an annex map. Thus, it was only logical and reasonable that the drafts crafted by the US DoS from 1947 onwards as well as the draft put together by the UK Foreign Office in 1951 had such features. After receiving Sebald's feedback in December of 1949, however, the US DoS practically gave up on including detailed provisions on Japanese territory in the final draft treaty. After the emergence of Dulles as the chief negotiator for the US in 1950, the use of such detailed territorial provisions was axed completely from the final treaty. This was in blatant violation of the Allies' policy on Japanese territory agreed upon at Cairo and Potsdam. In particular, the package settlement of a peace treaty with a security agreement and an administrative agreement that the Dulles Delegation hastily made with the government of Japan in February of 1951 may have had a decisive impact. The unfavorable turn of events in the Korean War, marked by the stunning retreat of United Nations forces on January 4th, 1951 after Chinese communists entered the Korean War on a massive scale, added to the urgency for the US to sign an early peace treaty and security pact with Japan. The Dulles Delegation quickly flew to Tokyo and, in an unprecedented act in the history of postwar peace settlements, initialed a peace treaty with Japan then and there. At this point, the UK had not yet begun drafting its own version of a peace treaty, and as such, no prior consultations had been completed or agreements reached between the US and the UK regarding the peace treaty with Japan. After having initialed a provisional peace treaty with Japan, the US only then held its first meeting with the UK two months later. As such, the US was already constrained by its prior agreements with Japan and so, instead of going back on its agreement with Japan, focused its efforts on persuading the UK to accept the US draft. This was due to the stickiness of policy at the time.

The third reason was the prior agreements the US had committed itself to with Japan while the US had already given up the wartime territorial policy framework of the Allied powers toward Japan. The US went so far as to show Japan the British draft, stressing how friendly the US agreements with Japan were in comparison. In its meetings with the UK, the US for the most part tried to steer the negotiations towards what it had already agreed on with Japan without informing the UK of these agreements. The wartime policy framework was discarded, the Soviet Union and China were excluded from the treaty process, and the US had already reached *de facto* agreements with Japan. The detailed territorial provisions on Japanese territory, i.e. the specification of the islands to be included and those to be excluded from Japanese sovereignty, the delineation of Japanese territory using degrees of longitude and latitude, and the use of an annex map had long lost their usefulness. Bound by its prior commitments with Japan, the US easily discarded what it now considered to be outmoded wartime agreements on Japanese territory.

3) The second series of Anglo-American meetings (June 2-14, 1951) and the decision to exclude Korea altogether from participation in the treaty

Following working-level consultations with the UK and high-level consultations with Japan, the US sent Dulles to London from June 2 to 14, 1951 for a final fine-tuning of the draft treaty. During Allison's earlier visit to London, Under Secretary of the British Foreign Office, Robert H. Scott, had requested that Dulles visit the UK for some key pending decisions, such as the participation of China and the disposition of Formosa.

On June 2, Dulles appeared before the Subcommittee on Far Eastern Affairs of the US Senate Committee on Foreign Relations to inform the members of the purpose of his London visit and then flew directly to London with Allison and Colonel Babcock.

On June 4, Dulles met with British Foreign Secretary Morrison and a number of other British Foreign Office officials. While agreeing to a "quick and liberal peace" rather than a punitive treaty, the British emphasized that Japanese atrocities and wrongdoings should not be forgotten and, as such, should not be completely ignored in the treaty text.[54] The meetings continued over the next two days, where the two sides discussed key issues including the participation of China to the treaty and the disposition of Formosa.

The two sides quickly reached a consensus on Formosa. The US proposed that, instead of stipulating to whom Formosa would belong, a provision be included that Japan would henceforth renounce all rights over it. The UK government accepted this proposal.

The invitation of China to participate in the treaty talks was also discussed. Following a series of meetings on the issue, Dulles and Morrison agreed to invite neither Communist China nor Free China to sign the treaty and not to allow them to sign the treaty later either. The two sides

---

54 The Ambassador in the United Kingdom (Gifford) to the Secretary of State (June 4, 1951), *FRUS*, 1951, Vol. VI, pp. 1105-1106.

decided that China and Japan should address their issues in the form of a bilateral treaty of their own.[55]

On June 6, the UK and the US agreed not to invite either Communist China or Free China to the Japanese peace treaty. It was also agreed to provide that Japan should renounce all rights to Formosa in the treaty without specifying where Formosa would belong.[56]

After meeting with British Prime Minister Clement R. Attlee on June 8, Dulles visited Paris from June 9 to 13. On June 12 in Paris, he learned of the decision by the British Cabinet to accept the key provisions on China as agreed to during his meetings with Morrison. On June 13, Dulles flew back to London to consult with the Foreign Office on some other minor issues.

The UK and the US finalized their second joint Anglo-American draft on June 14, which was a revised edition of the first joint draft of May 3, 1951. The draft treaty of June 14 was made public in London on that date and was featured in a New York Times article the next day. Dulles also left London on June 14, and the next day, he along with Secretary of State Acheson briefed the US President on the meetings in London.[57]

Meanwhile, after Dulles' departure, Allison visited Paris, Karachi, New Delhi, Manila, and Tokyo from June 14 until the first week of August. Upon his arrival to Tokyo on June 24, he met with Matthew B. Ridgway and gave him two British government memoranda detailing the British concerns about Japan's shipbuilding capabilities. Allison advised Ridgway to come up with ways for Japan to set the Pacific Rim countries at ease prior to the start of fisheries negotiations provided for under the Japanese peace treaty. As a result, on July 13, Japanese Prime Minister Yoshida issued a statement in which he assured that Japan's voluntary declaration contained in his letter of February 7, 1951 was intended to embrace fishery conservation

---

55 "Summary of Negotiations Leading Up To the Conclusion of the Treaty of Peace With Japan," by Robert A. Fearey (Sept. 18, 1951), pp. 8-9, RG 59, Office of Northeast Asia Affairs, Records Relating to the Treaty of Peace with Japan-Subject File, 1945-51, Lot 56D527, Box 1.

56 The Ambassador in the United Kingdom (Gifford) to the Secretary of State (June 5 and 6, 1951), *FRUS*, 1951, Vol. VI, pp. 1106-1108.

57 Editorial Note, *FRUS*, 1951, Vol. VI, pp. 1118-1119.

arrangements. Allison also informed Yoshida that consultations had taken place between the US and the UK largely based on the US draft. He explained that the final draft, which incorporated some of the provisions of the British draft, was slightly less favorable to Japan than the initial US draft had been, but that overall it was by no means a harsh peace treaty.[58]

The decision to exclude Korea from participation in the treaty

Some major decisions regarding Korea were made during Dulles' visit to London. Of them, the most important one was not to grant Korea the right to take part in the treaty talks.

Prior to Dulles' visit to London (June 2-14, 1951), Allison submitted to him a shortlist of an agenda to run past the British.[59] Of the twelve agenda items on the list, number three concerned Korea and read "3. US is inclined to accept UK idea that Korea should not be a signatory and is drafting an article which will give Korea certain rights under the Treaty." [60]This meant that Korea would not be invited to the peace conference or be a signatory to the treaty; rather, it would be granted certain rights under the treaty. Establishing such a provision at a multilateral international peace conference to which Korea was not even a party was somewhat unrealistic, especially considering the US preference for a "simple treaty."

Such a new position of the US DoS was explained in the *Japanese Peace Treaty Working Draft and Commentary* (June 1, 1951).[61] On this document, the US proposed the following Article 10:

---

58   Yoshida, *Kaiso Junen*, p. 33.

59   Memorandum by the Deputy to the Consultant (Allison) to the Consultant to the Secretary (Dulles) (May 16, 1951), Subject: Talk with Sir Oliver Franks Regarding Japanese Peace Treaty, *FRUS*, 1951, Vol. VI, pp. 1042-1043.

60   Subject: Talk with Sir Oliver Franks Regarding Japanese Peace Treaty, *FRUS*, 1951, Vol. VI, p. 1043.

61   "Japanese Peace Treaty Working Draft and Commentary" (June 1, 1951), RG 59, Office of Northeast Asia Affairs, Records Relating to the Treaty of Peace with Japan-Subject file, 1945-51, Lot 56D527, Box 6, Folder "Treaty-Draft-Mar. 23 1951"; *FRUS*, 1951, Vol. VI, pp. 1068-1069.

Article 10. The Republic of Korea shall be deemed an "Allied Power" for the purposes of Articles 5, 10 (to be 11), and 13(to be 14) of the present Treaty, effective at the time that the Treaty first comes into forces.[62]

This was followed by the following long explanation:

The reason for this is that the United States now considers, in agreement with the British position, that Korea is not entitled to be a signatory to the treaty. The US and other major powers deliberately refrained from recognizing the "Provisional Government of Korea" as having any status whatsoever during World War II. The facts that that government declared war on Japan, and that Korean elements, mostly long time resident in China, fought with the Chinese forces, do not, therefore, have any bearing on the question.

The Korean Government has cited the fact that Poland was permitted to sign the Versailles Treaty. On examination, however, Korea's case for participation in the Japanese treaty does not gain much support from this example. The Polish National Committee set up in Paris in 1917 under Paderewski was "recognized" and dealt with by all the principal western Allies. Although it has not been possible to determine definitely that it declared war on Germany it was set up for the purpose of fighting Germany and liberating Poland and can, therefore, be assumed to have done so. When Germany surrendered the Committee and the Regency Council, which had been set up by the Central Powers at Warsaw, combined and formed a Provisional Government of Poland which was recognized as such by the Powers before the Versailles Conference was convened. Poland had an army fighting in France even before 1917.

While it is not believed that Korea should be allowed to sign the treaty it is considered that it should derive the benefits of certain of its provisions. The proposed article would ensure Korea the full advantages of Article 5 (treatment of Japanese property in renounced or ceded territories), Article

---

62　"Japanese Peace Treaty Working Draft and Commentary" (June 1, 1951), *FRUS*, 1951, Vol. VI, p. 1068.

10 (fisheries), and Article 13 (commercial relations) from the time that the treaty is first brought into force.[63]

Instead of acknowledging Korea's right to sign the treaty, the US decided to insert a special provision under Article 10 in the draft that the benefits of Articles 5, 10 and 13 would be applied to it. This proposal was discussed at the second Anglo-American talks (June 1951) in London.

During those meetings, the US and the UK officially agreed to exclude Korea. Instead, they decided to stipulate in the draft that Korea would be granted the basic benefits even though it was not an "Allied Power." The US proposal to include a special provision guaranteeing special benefits to Korea was reflected in Article 21 of the second joint Anglo-American draft treaty of June 14, 1951, which read as follows:

Article 21. Notwithstanding the provisions of Article 25 of the present Treaty, China shall be entitled to the benefits of Articles 10 and 14, and Korea to the benefits of Articles 2, 9 and 12 of the present Treaty.

Article 25 related to the Allied Powers. Though Korea was not stipulated as an Allied Power, it was granted along with China certain benefits of an Allied Power under Article 2 (Territory), Article 9 (Limitation of fishing and the conservation and development of fisheries on the high seas, and Article 12 (Commercial agreements) of the draft treaty.[64]

As noted above, it was provided in the draft treaties produced from December 1949 to early May 1951 that Korea would participate in the peace conference. However, US support for Korean participation began to

---

63 "Japanese Peace Treaty Working Draft and Commentary" (June 1, 1951); *FRUS*, 1951, Vol. VI, pp. 1068-1069.

64 Kim, "US Foreign Policy toward Korea in the Beginning of the 1950s," p. 368; "Draft Japanese Peace Treaty" (June 14, 1951), RG 59, Office of Northeast Asia Affairs, Records Relating to the Treaty of Peace with Japan–Subject File, 1945-51, Lot 56D527, Box 6. Folder, "Treaty-Draft-June 14, 1951"; RG 59, Japanese Peace Treaty Files of John Foster Dulles, 1946-52, Lot 54D423, Box 12.

crumble under strong opposition from the UK and Japan, and ultimately the US decided not to push any further to have Korea included as a signatory to the treaty; instead, at the second Anglo-American meetings of June 1951, the US proposed to insert some special Korea-related provisions in the draft treaty. Thus, Korea's hopes of taking part in the peace conference fell apart. On July 9, 1951, Dulles notified Korean Ambassador to the US, Yang You-chan, of the final decision that, since Korea was not a nation at war with Japan during World War II, the Korean government would not be allowed to be a signatory to the treaty.[65]

After receiving notification from Dulles that Korea would not be recognized as a signatory to the peace treaty with Japan, the Korean Embassy in the US copied the Korean government's initial response to the US DoS of April 27, 1951 to the government of the UK on July 20, 1951 in a last ditch effort to try to obtain the latter's support for its participation. However, as the UK government had already made its policy decision clear in its talks with the US and in the joint Anglo-American draft treaty, it was already too late to change its decision and grant Korea its support.

The UK government's analysis of the Korean government's memorandum was almost identical to that of the US DoS. The UK government had already made a firm policy decision in the second joint Anglo-American draft treaty of June 14, 1951. That decision was to deny Korea Allied Power status but balance it with a special article (Article 21) in support of Korea's national interests. Related to this was the UK comment "Article 21 extends the benefits of Articles 2, 9 and 12 to Korea" under Article 7 in the table below. Regarding Article 14 on Claims and Property, the UK also commented that "The settlement of property claims between Japan and Korea has been left for settlement between the two Governments under Article 4. Korea will have the whip hand because Japanese property in Korea will be within their jurisdiction."

---

65 Memorandum of conversation, Subject: Japanese Peace Treaty (July 9, 1951), RG 59, Department of State, Decimal File, 694.001/7-951.

Decisions on the territorial provisions related to Korea

As stated above, Article 2 of Chapter II of the second joint Anglo-American draft treaty of June 14 read that "(a) Japan, recognizing the independence of Korea, renounces all right, title and claim to Korea, including the islands of Quelpart, Port Hamilton and Dagelet."[66]

Although the draft treaty did not specify the names of the Allied and Associated Powers that would take part in the peace conference, it did explicitly exclude Korea. In a joint statement made on June 19, 1951, the UK and the US also announced their decision not to invite China to the peace conference.[67]

A US document made immediately following the Dulles delegation's visit to London contained a summary of agreements that the US had reached with the UK leading up to the completion of their June 14 joint draft treaty. Regarding the political and territorial clauses, the document noted that Korea, while not an "Allied Power," would be granted the same basic benefits.[68]

As noted above, neither the Communist Chinese government nor the Nationalist Chinese government was invited to participate in the peace conference or to sign the peace treaty with Japan. Instead, it was decided that both should seek to resolve their outstanding issues with Japan through bilateral treaties of their own. Meanwhile, the provision on the eventual restoration of Formosa to the "Republic of China," stipulated in the Cairo Declaration, was not included in the draft treaty. The treaty only included a provision that Japan would renounce all territorial claims to Formosa. The treaty also specified that Japan would renounce the Sakhalin Islands

---

66 "Revised United States-United Kingdom Draft of a Japanese Peace Treaty" (June 14, 1951), FRUS, 1951, Vol. VI, p. 1120.

67 "Draft Joint Statement of the United Kingdom and United States Government," Chinese Participation and Formosa (June 19, 1951), FRUS, 1951, Vol. VI, p. 1134.

68 "United Kingdom" (June 15, 1951), RG 59, Japanese Peace Treaty Files of John Foster Dulles, 1947-1952, Subject File, 1946–52, Lot 54D423, Box 13.

[Table 4-1] British Foreign Office Review of Korean Government
Note Dated July 20, 1951

Related provision	Proposed Amendment	Origin	Comment
Preamble	The term "Allied Powers" to be defined specifically to include Korea	Korean Government in Notes dated 20th and 25th July (FJ 1022/799, FJ 1022/847)	This is not acceptable because Korea is not at war with Japan.
Preamble	Any future status of Japan in connection with membership of the United Nations to be limited to an equivalent status for Korea	Korean Government (see Note of 20th July at FJ 1022/799)	Although this request is somewhat obscure it should be rejected if it is intended to mean that Japan should not be admitted to the United Nations unless Korea is also admitted. Decisions concerning admission to the United Nations are the concern only of that organization.
Preamble	Korean nationals resident in Japan to be guaranteed the rights, privileges and protection accorded to the nationals of other Allied Powers	Korean Government (see Note of 20th July at FJ 1022/799)	This is unacceptable because the large minority in Japan are very trouble-some and are used by the Communists to create disturbances.
Article 2	The island of Tsushima to be transferred to Korea	Korean Government (Note of 20th July from Korean Minister)	This is unacceptable because Tsushima has been Japanese since the dawn of Japanese history and the inhabitants are Japanese by speech, race and choice.
Article 5	Consideration to be given to the importance of Korea in the maintenance of peace and security in the Pacific	Korean Government (Note of 20th July from Korean Minister)	The Koreans have made no specific request for an amendment to the Treaty. Presumably they want some guarantee or participation in a defence arrangement with the United States. It seems that no amendment to the Treaty is called for.

Article 7	The rights of Korea which naturally has no pre-war bilateral treaties with Japan to be safeguarded as effectively as are those of Allied Powers which have such treaties	Korean Government (Note of 20th July from Korean Minister)	Because Korea has no such treaties it is impossible to put her in the position as if she had. It is impossible to select any list of bilateral treaties or any particular clauses as being universal or standard. This request is substantially covered by Article 21 which extends to Korea the benefits of Articles 2, 9 and 12.
Article 9	The "MacArthur Line" defining areas available to Japanese and Korean fishermen to be given the same status as pre-war bilateral treaties	Korean Government (see Note of 20th July at FJ 1022/799)	This request is met by the present draft of Article 9. No addition to this Article is called for or is likely to be accepted by the Americans.
Article 14 (Reparations)	Detailed provisions to be added to ensure that Korean property in Japan shall be recognized as Korean and that Korea shall be entitled to seize Japanese property in Korea more freely than is at present provided by Article 14	Korean Government (Note of 20th July from Korean Minister)	This request is based upon the false assumption that Korea is an Allied Power. The settlement of property claims between Japan and Korea has been left for settlement between the two Governments under Article 4. Korea will have the whip hand because Japanese property in Korea will be within their jurisdiction.
Article 22	Korea to be made a party to the International Court of Justice	Korean Government (Note of 20th July from Korean Minister)	It will not be possible to provide in the Treaty for Korea to become a party to the Statute of the International Court.

[Source] "Japanese Peace Treaty: Proposed Amendments with Comments," (undated), RG 59, John Foster Dulles File, Lot 54D423, Box 12, Folder "Treaty Drafts, May 3, 1951".

and the Kurils,[69] but the draft made no mention of whether or not they would be transferred or ceded to the Soviet Union. As for Korea, the draft stated that though Korea was not an "Allied Power," it would be granted the same basic benefits as one. This was an explicit reference to the fact that

---

69   Article 2 of Chapter II of the second Anglo-American draft treaty of June 14, 1951 made the following stipulations: "(c) Japan renounces all right, title and claim to the Kurile Islands, and to that portion of Sakhalin and the islands adjacent to it over which Japan acquired sovereignty as a consequence of the Treaty of Portsmouth of 5 September 1905." *FRUS*, 1951, Vol. VI, p. 1120.

Korea would not be included as either an Allied or Associated Power in the treaty. It was also a reference to the basic benefits—the lapse of all property claims by Japanese residing in Korea and the possibility of concluding a future bilateral fishery agreement and peace treaty with Japan—that Dulles emphasized to the Korean Ambassador to the US during their meeting of July 9, 1951 when it was announced that Korea would not be invited to the conference.

In the formulation of the joint Anglo-American draft treaty of June 14, 1951, three issues were discussed and decided upon in relation to Korea, i.e. its participation in the treaty (as an Allied Power), territorial issues, and reparations. First, Korea's participation in the treaty process was denied. Though a special provision would be inserted to ensure Korea's national interests (under articles related to fisheries and commercial agreements), such provisions were not effective as they were to be addressed through further negotiations and agreements between Korea and Japan. The UK and the US closed their discussions on territorial issues by deciding to include the specific mention of Quelpart, Port Hamilton, and Dagelet. The provisions ensuring Korea's national interests and the specific mention of these territories that would be under Korean sovereignty were maintained up until the final treaty.

Finally, several minor changes were made to the text of the treaty regarding the issues of reparations and territorial claims. Unlike the previous drafts, the June 14 draft stipulated that any further claims by Japanese to property in Korea that had been confiscated by the US military government and transferred to the Korean government would need to be worked out between the Korean and Japanese governments themselves. However, following a strong protest by the Korean government, the US modified this provision in a way that legalized the confiscation and transfer of Japanese property by the US military government in Korea.

The second joint Anglo-American draft treaty of June 14, 1951, as agreed to by the US and the UK, the US's most important ally, became the prototype for the final treaty signed in September 1951.

Chapter 5

US-Japan Negotiations (1951)

1

The First Visit to Japan by Dulles in 1951 and Major US-Japan Treaty-Related Agreements

1) Japan's preparations for the Seven Principles of the Treaty with Japan (November 1950 to January 1951)

The US Seven Principles of the Treaty with Japan were made known to the press on October 6, 1950 and officially announced on November 24. The Japanese Ministry of Foreign Affairs was in charge of preparing for the Principles, and commenced preparations in December 1950 for an upcoming visit by John Foster Dulles, US special envoy to the Treaty of Peace with Japan and later US Secretary of State.[1] Shigeru Yoshida remarked that the Principles were "unexpectedly generous," and exceeded what Japan had expected and therefore encouraged the country.[2] Takeso Shimoda, head of the Foreign Ministry's Treaty Section I and Executive Secretary of the Executive Committee for Research on a Peace Treaty, also noted regarding the Principles that, while they excluded the USSR, they were favorable to the US and generous to Japan. That is, the USSR's plan to exercise a veto at the peace conference was thwarted in advance, and according to the Principles, the US would be able to exercise administrative authority over the Ryukyu and Ogasawara Islands after Japan's independence and have its forces stationed on Japanese territory. For its part, Japan would not suffer any economic restrictions after regaining its independence, its entrance

---

1   Takeso Shimoda, 1984, *Sengo Nihon Gaiko No Shogen (Testimony to Japan's Postwar Diplomacy: How Japan Revived) Vol.1*, edited by Nobutoshi Nagano, Tokyo, Research Institute for Public Administration, p. 59; Kumao Nishimura, 1971, *Japan's Diplomatic History 27: The Treaty of Peace with Japan*, Kajima Research Institute Press, pp. 80-85.
2   Shigeru Yoshida, 1958, *Kaiso Junen*, Vol.3, Tokyo, Shinchosha, pp. 29-30.

into the UN would be supported, and the Allies would, in principle, waive their right to demand compensation. They were, indeed, very generous terms.[3]

After the Principles were announced, Japan took an interest in three main issues, namely security assurances, territories, and rearmament.[4] Regarding territorial issues, Japan argued that, if the US insisted on trusteeship over Okinawa and Ogasawara, it should be for a set period as in the ten-year trusteeship in Somaliland, Italy's old colony, and Japan should be designated as the joint authority.[5] It saw as a favorable result of misfortune the suggestion of putting the ultimate destiny of Southern Sakhalin and the Kurils in the hands of the UN General Assembly. Regarding rearmament, Japan contended that its security should be ensured in ways other than rearmament to overcome the widespread fear of future hostilities among the Japanese public after the Pacific War and worries of neighboring countries over Japan's invasion, and Japan's economic reconstruction. As an alternative, Japan contended that the personnel and equipment of the reserve police force and maritime security force should be immediately reinforced. The Japanese Foreign Ministry reviewed NATO military agreements and gathered former Japanese *gunbatsu* military personnel at the official residence of the Foreign Minister to discuss the size and type of police force needed in Japan. The resulting opinion was that 150,000 police on land, 50,000 managerial-level personnel, coast guard vessels ranging from 1,500-ton corvettes to 80,000-ton ships, and the like were required to maintain domestic public order.[6]

---

3   Shimoda, *Sengo Nihon Gaiko No Shogen*, p. 61.

4   "Preparations for Dulles' Visit to Japan (Project D)" (Dec. 27, 1940), "Revised Project D" (Jan. 5, 1951), and "2nd-Revision Project D" (Jan. 19, 1951), Ministry of Foreign Affairs of Japan, 2007, *Japanese Diplomatic Documents: Negotiations with the US for the San Francisco Peace Treaty*, pp. 112-120, pp. 129-142.

5   "Action in Case the US Insists on the Trusteeship of the Okinawa and Ogasawara Islands" (Jan. 26, 1951), Ministry of Foreign Affairs of Japan, 2007, *Ibid.*, pp. 162-164.

6   "Meeting with Former *Gunbatsu* Military Personnel at the Foreign Minister's Official Residence in Tokyo's Meguro District," (Jan. 19, 1951), Ministry of Foreign Affairs of Japan, 2007, *Ibid.*, pp. 142-148.

As such, Japan had already defined its stance on the Seven Principles before Dulles' arrival in Tokyo in January 1951. Quite different from the 1919 Treaty of Versailles after WWI as well as the peace treaties with Italy and Romania after WWII, Japan was able to figure out the gist of a draft treaty made public by the US and had sufficient time to fully prepare for negotiations with it.

2) Dulles' first visit (January to February 1951) and the *de facto* initialing of principal treaties

Under these circumstances, Dulles arrived at Tokyo's Haneda Airport on January 25, 1951. His delegation included John M. Allison, deputy special envoy to the Treaty of Peace with Japan; Earl D. Johnson, Assistant Secretary of the Army; Major General Carter B. Magruder; Colonel Conrad S. Babcock; John D. Rockefeller III, and Robert A. Fearey. John Allison was a US diplomat most commonly known for being US Ambassador to Japan. Before 1953, he had been a Foreign Service officer in China, Japan and other places, and Deputy Director of the Bureau of Far Eastern Affairs and Director of the Office of Northeast Asian Affairs within the US Department of State (DoS). After his appointment as Ambassador to Japan in 1953, he actively supported Japan's position regarding the Dokdo issue.[7] Carter Magruder was a China specialist who had been with the Office of Strategic Services (OSS) and built his career in China during the Pacific

---

7   John Moore Allison was born in Kansas in 1905, graduated from the University of Nebraska in 1927, and taught English in Japan from 1927 to 1929 before embarking on a foreign service career as a deputy clerk in Shanghai in 1930. He was appointed as Vice Consul in Kobe in 1931 and became a formal diplomat the same year. He was assigned to Tokyo in 1932; became Vice Consul in Tokyo in 1934; Consul in Dalian in 1935 and successively Consul in Tsinan, Qingdao, Nanking, and Shanghai; Consul in Osaka in 1939-41; back at the US Department of State in 1942; Second Secretary-Consul in London in 1942; Deputy Chief of the Division of Japanese Affairs on May 15, 1947; Chief of the Division of Northeast Asian Affairs on October 5, 1947; Deputy Director of the Bureau of Far Eastern Affairs in November 1948; and Director of the Office of Northeast Asian Affairs in October 1949 (*Register of the Department of State, April 1, 1950*, Office of Public Affairs, Department of State, p. 11).

War. He later served as Eighth US Army Commander in Korea at the time of the April 19th Movement of 1960. The two most interesting figures are Babcock and Fearey. They had both attended Groton High School, a private college preparatory boarding school in Massachusetts and served as military attaché and personal assistant to Ambassador Joseph C. Grew at the US Embassy in Tokyo, respectively, when the Pacific War broke out. Grew, a Groton graduate himself, spent his own money to serve as patron to his elite junior alumni, hiring them as personal assistants for two years and introducing them into the diplomatic circles. Fearey's predecessor, Marshall Green, was also from Groton and would later be Deputy Chief of Mission at the US Embassy in Seoul at the time of the 1961 coup d'état that brought Major-General Park Chung-hee to power, and US Ambassador to Indonesia when Suharto led his successful coup in 1965. They were Grew's "men" within the US DoS. The so-called "Grotonians" were influential people and exhibited a pro-Japanese tendency. The selection as part of the delegation of Babcock and Fearey, who were at the US Embassy in Tokyo at the outbreak of the war but remained supporters of Japan as well as Allison who had worked at POLAD—Japan and the US DoS Bureau of Far Eastern Affairs after the war, showed the delegation's political inclinations toward Japan. Allison and Fearey represented a pro-Japanese stance that favored appeasement within the US DoS in Washington and POLAD—Japan and the SCAP Diplomatic Section in Tokyo while Babcock fulfilled a similar role within the Department of Defense (DoD).[8]

As soon as they arrived in Tokyo, the delegation presented a Suggested Agenda to discuss to the Prime Minister, Shigeru Yoshida. The important items among the 13 on the agenda were as follows:

---

8   Robert A. Fearey, "Diplomacy's Final Round," *Foreign Service Journal*, American Foreign Service Association, December 1991; Robert A. Fearey, "Tokyo 1941: Might the Pacific War Have Been Avoided?" *The Journal of American East Asian Relations*, Spring 1992, Chicago; Robert A. Fearey, 2002, "Fumimaro Konoe: A Full Account of Maneuvers Targeting the US Regarding a Peace Treaty," translated by Kouichirou Fukui, *Bungeishunju*, January issue; Robert A. Fearey, class of 1937, "In Memoriam-Marshall Green, Class of 1953," *Groton School Quarterly*, 1999.

1. Territory: How will the surrender term that "Japanese sovereignty shall be limited to the islands of Honshu, Hokkaido, Kyushu, Shikoku and such minor islands as we determine" be implemented?

2. Security assurance: How will Japan's security be guaranteed after the end of the occupation?

3. Rearmament: By which clauses, if they can be established, will Japan's future rearmament be restricted?

10. The right to demand reparations and war indemnities: Which treaty clauses should be in place in this regard? What about Japan's gold?

11. Postwar indemnities: How will Japan handle GARIOA (Government and Relief in Occupied Areas) liabilities?

12. War criminals: Who will have jurisdiction over those found guilty at the military tribunal?[9]

In general, the agenda was not disadvantageous toward Japan. It was also thoroughly expected by the Japanese Foreign Ministry, which had prepared for the talks based on the Seven Principles of the Treaty with Japan since October 1950.

In response, Japan submitted a memorandum titled "Our Observations" on January 30.[10] It specifically set out Japan's stance on the 13 agenda items put forward by the US and generally contained demands that were so out of place that it is difficult to believe they were made by a defeated country to a victorious one in peace negotiations following a war. Some examples:

First, under "1. Territory," Japan demanded the following conditions based on the Seven Principles which placed the Ryukyu and Ogasawara Islands under UN trusteeship with the US as the administering authority: (a) These islands should be returned to Japan when there was no need for further trusteeship; (b) their residents should retain Japanese nationality; (c) Japan should be a joint authority together with the US; (d) the right

---

9   "Suggested Agenda" (Jan. 26, 1951), Ministry of Foreign Affairs of Japan, 2007, *Japanese Diplomatic Documents: Negotiations with the US for the San Francisco Peace Treaty*, pp. 172-174.
10   "Our Observations" (Jan. 30, 1951), Ministry of Foreign Affairs of Japan, 2007, *Ibid.*, pp. 177-188.

of return for some 8,000 residents originally from the Ogasawara Islands and Iwo Jima who had been evacuated to the mainland by the Japanese government during the war should be granted, and more. In a nutshell, the Japanese demands implied that Japan would accept US trusteeship but it should be stipulated that both sovereignty and administrative authority over the islands lay with Japan. Southern Sakhalin and the Kurils were not mentioned.

Under "2. Security Assurance," Japan argued that it should be given responsibility for domestic public order after independence while its external security should be guaranteed by the UN and the US through an appropriate method, and in this regard, there should be a separate US-Japan defense relationship in addition to a peace treaty. Under "3. Rearmament," it declined the prospect of rearmament citing such reasons as the collapse of the Japanese economy due to a lack of resources; the Japanese population's fear of war; and the surrounding nations' fear of Japan's rearmament. In essence, Japan would accept temporary US trusteeship of the Ryukyu and Ogasawara Islands while its territorial, political, and military sovereignty was acknowledged and a US-Japan bilateral security treaty would be concluded, but did not intend to rearm itself.

Japan also clearly demonstrated its stance on economic reparations. Under "10. The Right to Demand Reparations and War Indemnities," it argued that no more compensation with regard to industrial facilities should be made other than facilities already disposed of for such purpose, and reparations from current production or monetary reparations should not be demanded.[11]

According to Shigeru Yoshida, industrial facilities were disposed of for compensation purposes as part of the interim reparations program before the conclusion of a peace treaty, and after its conclusion, no formal reparations were made and only *de facto* reparations in service were made.[12] According to reports by the US reparations mission to Japan

---

11   *Ibid.*, pp. 182-187.
12   Yoshida, *Kaiso Junen*, Vol. 3, p. 151.

led by Edwin W. Pauley in November 1946 and another mission led by engineer Clifford S. Strike and sponsored by the US Department of the Army in January 1947, immediate delivery to war-devastated countries as advance reparations transfers were put into place for no more than 30 percent of the categories listed as Japanese facilities and equipment which had been set aside for reparations-related removal to cripple Japan's war industry capacity from April 1947. China received 15 percent of the available material; the Philippines, 5 percent; the Netherlands, for the Indies, 5 percent; and the United Kingdom, for Burma, Malaya and other far-eastern colonies, 5 percent. The total value amounted to the equivalent of 1939 valuation of 164 million yen. The "no-reparations" peace formula was the backbone of the process of working out a peace treaty. The major participants in the war, such as the US, the Commonwealth, and the Netherlands agreed not to demand heavy reparations that could harm the Japanese economy in the long term and the Kuomintang of China also refrained from demanding reparations. In reality, partial reparations were made but the peace formula was widely known for its lack of reparations as the principle constituting the backbone of the treaty. The Treaty of Peace with Japan adopted a new method of reparations - reparations in service - making available the services of the Japanese people in processing and delivering materials provided by countries with the right to indemnity, salvaging and dismantling ships sunken in their coastal waters, and other work. It was designed to prevent Japan from incurring foreign currency debt and to compensate for war damages. The biggest reason for the adoption of this method was that the larger the amount of compensation for damages Japan had to pay, the heavier the burden on the US as the victorious country providing major assistance. As the US could not just ignore demands for reparations from other Allies participating in the peace treaty, reparations in service were adopted as a compromise.[13] As such, Article 14 of the treaty stated that, "it is recognized that Japan should pay reparations to the Allied Powers for the damage and suffering caused

---

13   Yoshida, *Kaiso Junen*, Vol. 3, pp. 156-161.

by it during the war. Nevertheless it is also recognized that the resources of Japan are not presently sufficient, if it is to maintain a viable economy, to make complete reparation for all such damage and suffering and at the same time meet its other obligations."

Regarding war indemnities, the Japanese Foreign Ministry claimed as follows:

(a) Japan's properties overseas: <u>All Japanese properties in the Allied countries which actually engaged in hostilities with Japan should be returned.</u> It is implored that special consideration should be made for Japanese properties owned by private citizens. When private properties are used to pay war indemnities, compensation for their owners should be left to the discretion of the Japanese government.

(b) <u>Return of plundered assets: While most of them have already been returned, this issue will be concluded with the signing of a peace treaty.</u>

(c) Allied properties in Japan: Action is required to promptly complete the redemption of Allied properties in Japan.

(d) Japan's gold: All the gold currently confiscated should be returned.[14] (underlined by the quoter)

The underlined sentences reveal the basic perspective of the Japanese Foreign Ministry: while the Japanese properties in nations that had been at war with Japan should be returned to it, properties Japan looted from other nations had already been returned and thereby this issue should no longer be discussed after a peace treaty was signed. If this was Japan's attitude toward war-time enemies and occupied territories, its attitude toward former colonies does not need further explanation. According to Japan, no properties had been looted from its colonies and thereby there was nothing to return while Japanese properties in former colonies, including

---

14 "Our Observations" (Jan. 30, 1951), Ministry of Foreign Affairs of Japan, 2007, *Japanese Diplomatic Documents: Negotiations with the US for the San Francisco Peace Treaty*, pp. 182, 187-188.

properties owned by Japanese citizens, should be returned to Japan.

Under "11. War Criminals," Japan demanded that there should be no more indictments; there should be a general amnesty on the occasion of the conclusion of a peace treaty; and the responsibility for the execution of prison sentences should be transferred to the Japanese authorities. The Ministry announced that there were 1,378 incarcerated and two on trial within Japan and 759 incarcerated and 36 on trial overseas as of January 1, 1951.[15]

As stated above, Japan suggested terms that were advantageous to itself in its negotiations with the US in January 1951. They were already aware that the position the US was taking on a peace treaty was changing and intended to gain maximum leverage as a negotiating party. Shigeru Yoshida wrote that, at the US-Japan negotiations from January to February 1951, requests were made to Dulles that reforms made during the US occupation should not be perpetuated through the peace treaty; reparations should be rendered in service not to burden Japan with foreign currency debts; and no more war criminals should be indicted. It was also suggested that ways should be explored to exonerate convicts or reduce their sentences.[16] The above demands by the Ministry were delivered to the US unchanged.

Dulles talked to Shigeru Yoshida on three different occasions: January 29, January 31, and February 7. Yoshida recorded the talks in his own notes, where he wrote that Dulles said in their first talks that the conditions would have been much worse if a treaty had been concluded three years previously and that the US was now prepared to sign the treaty as a friendly nation, not as a victor concluding peace with a loser.[17] Dulles said that, when Japan was independent again and part of the free world, it should make contributions to strengthen the free world and asked what

---

15   "Our Observations" (Jan. 30, 1951), Ministry of Foreign Affairs of Japan, 2007, *Ibid.*, pp. 183, 188.

16   Yoshida, *Kaiso Junen*, Vol. 3, pp. 30-31.

17   "Yoshida and Dulles Talks (1st talks)" (4 pm, Jan. 29, 1951), Ministry of Foreign Affairs of Japan, 2007, *Japanese Diplomatic Documents: Negotiations with the US for the San Francisco Peace Treaty*, pp. 175-177.

contribution Japan would be able to make in the war the US was fighting for freedom around the world. According to a prewritten scenario, Yoshida refused the possibility of rearmament, saying it would render Japan's economic independence impossible, give rise to concern and suspicion in other nations, and might lead to the resurgence of Japanese *gunbatsu*. Dulles expressed his displeasure at this. Allison, the aide to Dulles, wrote that Yoshida was clearly an anticommunist, but in his talks with Dulles, he expressed objection to Japan's remilitarization and rearmament and tried to avoid detailed discussion on the security issue.[18] At the meetings from January to February 1951, Dulles did not hide his displeasure and frustration at Yoshida's half-hearted and evasive attitude because the US had shown a large degree of good will and favor but Yoshida, who should have been grateful, only responded passively. In particular, Dulles harbored ill feeling against Yoshida's decision to decline the possibility of Japan's rearmament for which he had strong hopes. Contrary to American expectations, it was Yoshida who ended up taking a laid-back attitude that displayed a lack of concern during the negotiations.

According to Takeso Shimoda, Yoshida offered a "99-year lease of the Ryukyu and Ogasawara Islands to the US" at the talks, which presumed automatic reinstatement of Japanese sovereignty over the islands 99 years later. The US did not react to the offer in any way on the spot but later declared that Japan had "potential sovereignty" over them. In reality, they were returned to Japan in less than 20 years.[19] At the second Dulles-Yoshida talks on January 31, 1951, the aforementioned "Our Observations" was delivered to the US.[20]

The high-level talks between Dulles and Yoshida were followed by working-level talks, which boiled down to Japan's rearmament and a US-Japan security treaty. Other issues such as fisheries and property did not

---

18   John M. Allison, *Ambassador from the Prairie*, Boston, Houghton Mifflin, 1973, p. 156.

19   Shimoda, *Sengo Nihon Gaiko No Shogen*, p. 62.

20   "Yoshida and Dulles Talks (2nd talks)" (Jan. 31, 1951), Ministry of Foreign Affairs of Japan, 2007, *Japanese Diplomatic Documents: Negotiations with the US for the San Francisco Peace Treaty*, pp. 189-192.

receive much attention. According to the records of the Japanese Foreign Ministry, four "US-Japan Working-Level Talks" were held. At the first talk on February 1, 1951, Japan delivered four memorandums which were mainly about security assurances and a US-Japan security treaty.[21]

At the second talk (February 2, 1951), Japan proposed the establishment of a Ministry of National Security while the US submitted a draft US-Japan security treaty, "US-Japan Cooperation Agreement for Mutual Security."[22] After the talks, Japan submitted its comments on the draft agreement in the evening of the same day.

According to those comments, Japan already regarded a US-Japan mutual security treaty as a certainty and they were merely working out clauses and their details.[23]

Japan delivered its statement on remilitarization on February 3 that included establishing a security force of 50,000 army and navy troops, operating a reserve force and a maritime security force separately, and placing them under the Defense Force Department of a Ministry of National Security.[24]

The third US-Japan Working-Level Talks (February 5, 1951) were attended by Dulles and plundered assets, Allied properties in Japan, and the like were discussed. Dulles provided Japan with the "Provisional Memorandum" that established the key points of the peace treaty.[25]

The fourth US-Japan Working-Level Talks (February 6, 1951) discussed a US-Japan security treaty, fisheries, and similar issues.[26] At the meeting,

---

21 "US-Japan Working-Level Talks (1st talks)" (Feb. 1, 1951), Ministry of Foreign Affairs of Japan, 2007, *Ibid.*, pp. 192-195.

22 "US-Japan Working-Level Talks (2nd talks)" (Feb. 2, 1951), Ministry of Foreign Affairs of Japan, 2007, *Ibid.*, pp. 202-203.

23 "Observations on the Draft US-Japan Cooperation Agreement for Mutual Security" (Feb. 2, 1951), Ministry of Foreign Affairs of Japan, 2007, *Ibid.*, pp. 217-218, 221.

24 "Statement on Remilitarization" (Feb. 2, 1951), Ministry of Foreign Affairs of Japan, 2007, *Ibid.*, pp. 222-224.

25 "US-Japan Working-Level Talks (3rd talks)" (Feb. 5, 1951), Ministry of Foreign Affairs of Japan, 2007, *Ibid.*, pp. 224-226.

26 "US-Japan Working-Level Talks (4th talks)" (Feb. 6, 1951), Ministry of Foreign Affairs of

the US delivered a draft "US-Japan Security Treaty" and a relevant draft administrative agreement to Japan,[27] and Japan provided its comments on the "Provisional Memorandum".[28]

Through the working-level talks, the US and Japan completed three tasks related to the peace treaty. First, they virtually completed reviewing the content of the proposed treaty. Although what was reviewed was a draft, the Provisional Memorandum written by the US was not very different from the actual treaty signed in September 1951 as far as the general structure and main items were concerned. Second, the content of the US-Japan Security Treaty was, in effect, already written. It still needed to be partially amended, approved by both governments, and ratified by the US Congress and Japanese Diet, but the major task was done. Third, the draft of the US-Japan Administrative Agreement (later, US–Japan Status of Forces Agreement (SOFA)) was completed. This was a separate agreement that accompanied the security treaty to govern the use of facilities and areas granted to the US as well as the status of US armed forces in Japan. These three agreements laid the foundation for US-Japan relations that promoted peace and security.

Once the working-level talks were completed, Yoshida met with MacArthur (February 6, 1951) to discuss progress and held the third and final round of talks with Dulles (February 7, 1951). With the US-Japan talks completed, John Allison and Vice Foreign Minister Sadao Iguchi

---

Japan, 2007, *Ibid.*, pp. 237-239.

27 "Draft US-Japan Security Treaty" (Agreement between the United States of America and Japan for Collective Self-defense Made Pursuant to the Treaty of Peace between Japan and the Allied Powers and the provisions of Article 51 of the Charter of the United Nations); "Draft US-Japan Administrative Agreement" (Administrative Agreement between the United States of America and Japan to implement the provisions of the agreement they have entered into for collective defense) Ministry of Foreign Affairs of Japan, 2006, *Japanese Diplomatic Documents: Preparations for the San Francisco Peace Treaty*, pp. 240-242, 242-248.

28 "Observations and Survey on the Provisional Memorandum" (Feb. 6, 1951), Ministry of Foreign Affairs of Japan, 2007, *Japanese Diplomatic Documents: Negotiations with the US for the San Francisco Peace Treaty*, pp. 249-252.

signed five serial-numbered memorandums on February 9.[29] They were signed by neither Dulles nor Yoshida, each party's chief representative, to emphasize the fact that the documents did not constitute an official treaty but were merely temporary and provisional. Nevertheless, the two parties involved effectively agreed on the framework of a peace treaty on that day. Looking back, the key issues for such a peace treaty were then worked out between the US and Japan; all three fundamental agreements for peace, security, and administration were negotiated in full; and they were effectively initialed.

This was when the UK had neither finished devising a draft treaty nor started full-fledged discussions with the US. Having excluded the USSR and China, and not talked with the UK, the US reached a unilateral agreement with Japan in a surprise move.

I . Provisional Memorandum (Feb. 8, 1951) (five pages in the text and three pages in the annex)[30]

II . Draft US-Japan Security Treaty (Agreement between the United States of America and Japan for Collective Self— defense Made Pursuant to the Treaty of Peace between Japan and the Allied Powers and the provisions of Article 51 of the Charter of the United Nations) (two pages)[31]

III. Addendum to the draft US-Japan Security Treaty (Addendum to the Agreement between the United States of America and Japan for Collective Self— defense Made Pursuant to the Treaty of Peace between Japan and the Allied Powers and the provisions of Article 51 of the

---

29   "Memorandum" (Feb. 9, 1951), signed by John M. Allison and S. Iguchi, RG 59, Department of State, Decimal File, 694.001/2-1051.

30   "Provisional Memorandum" (Feb. 8, 1951), Ministry of Foreign Affairs of Japan, 2007, *Japanese Diplomatic Documents: Negotiations with the US for the San Francisco Peace Treaty*, pp. 266-281.

31   "Agreement between the United States of America and Japan for Collective Self-defense Made Pursuant to the Treaty of Peace between Japan and the Allied Powers and the provisions of Article 51 of the Charter of the United Nations," Ministry of Foreign Affairs of Japan, 2007, *Ibid.*, pp. 281-284.

Charter of the United Nations) (one page)[32]

IV. Draft US-Japan Administrative Agreement (Administrative Agreement between the United States of America and Japan to Implement the Agreement They Have Entered into for Collective Defense) (five pages)[33]

V. Addendum to the draft US-Japan Administrative Agreement (Addendum to the Administrative Agreement between the United States of America and Japan to Implement the Agreement They Have Entered into for Collective Defense) (one page)[34]

This brought to an end the first visit to Japan by Dulles from January to February 1951, made when the war situation on the Korean peninsula was extremely critical. The UN troops, which had advanced as far as Baekdusan Mountain at the northern end of the Korean peninsula, had had to pull back rapidly after the intervention of Chinese troops in November 1950, and by early 1951, the situation was so deteriorated that South Korean government officials and other major figures were even considering evacuating to Jeju, an island in the South Sea, or to Japan. Both the US government and its people saw the need to promptly conclude a peace treaty with Japan, encouraging Dulles to seal the deal on the treaties in record time. Though negotiations with other Allies and refinement of the actual text remained, it is no exaggeration to say that a peace treaty with Japan was almost on the eve of completion when Dulles left Tokyo on February 11, 1951.

During his visit, Dulles not only met with Yoshida officially three times

---

32 "Addendum to the Agreement between the United States of America and Japan for Collective Self-defense Made Pursuant to the Treaty of Peace between Japan and the Allied Powers and the provisions of Article 51 of the Charter of the United Nations," Ministry of Foreign Affairs of Japan, 2007, *Ibid.*, pp. 284-286.

33 "Administrative Agreement between the United States of America and Japan to Implement the Agreement They Have Entered into for Collective Defense," Ministry of Foreign Affairs of Japan, 2007, *Ibid.*, pp. 287-298.

34 "Addendum to the Administrative Agreement between the United States of America and Japan to Implement the Agreement They Have Entered into for Collective Defense," Ministry of Foreign Affairs of Japan, 2007, *Ibid.*, pp. 299-300.

but also met the leaders of major political parties such as the Liberal Party, Social Democratic Party, and People's Party including Ichiro Hatoyama (1883–1959) and Tanzan Ishibashi (1884–1973) who had both been barred from politics by SCAP but later became prime ministers, as well as public figures from the Ryukyu Islands.[35]

The biggest issue for Dulles and Japan was Japan's future security assurances. In his speech given at the Japanese Diet on February 2, Dulles promised a positive review of the Japanese government's request to have US forces stationed in Japan without fail if Japan came under a specific treaty system such as a mutual security treaty.

Another interest of the Japanese was territories. They pled to Dulles that Japanese sovereignty would extend beyond the four major islands as indicated in the Potsdam Declaration. The leaders of the four political parties Dulles met with all asked for the return of the Ryukyu, Ogasawara, and Kuril Islands, at the very least. Dulles made it clear that they should not hope for more than what was promised in the Declaration. Dulles told George Clutton, Minister at the UK Liaison Mission to Japan that Yoshida took up the issue with him on two separate occasions.[36] Allison wrote in his memoirs:

> We were deeply impressed by the Japanese plea for the restoration of the Ryukyu and Bonin Islands. While we could not grant their wishes at the time, I believe it was then that Mr. Dulles conceived the idea, which he later announced at the San Francisco Peace Conference, that Japan should retain residual Sovereignty over the islands but that they would be administered by the United States. Japan reacquired the Ogasawara Islands in 1968 and the Ryukyu Islands in 1972.[37]

---

35   FO 371/92532, 213424, FJ 1022/95 Japan (Feb. 17, 1951), Subject: Japanese Peace Treaty: Summaries of Mr. Dulles Interviews with Japanese Officials in Preparation of a Peace Treaty.
36   FO 371/92532, 213424, FJ 1022/95 Japan (Feb. 26, 1951), Mr. George Clutton to Mr. Bevin (no. 66), Subject: Japanese Peace Treaty, Visit of Mr. John Foster Dulles to Japan.
37   Allison, *Ambassador from the Prairie*, p. 156.

The US and Japan further refined the five memorandums between them, but the overall framework did not change. The US completed its first official draft in March 1951 after having worked out the major terms with Japan. It was circulated to the concerned countries in late March, and was the first official draft the US decided to make public.

3) The Japanese government's reply to the US Provisional Draft of March 1951 on April 4, 1951

Japan received the Provisional Draft of a Japanese Peace Treaty (Suggestive Only) from the US political adviser to SCAP William J. Sebald on March 27, 1951. It took only eight days for Japan to deliver a written opinion to the US, which it did on April 4, 1951. They had already become familiar with the draft through negotiations earlier in the year and had even completed refining the details through continuous contact in February and March.

The memorandum delivered by Vice Minister Iguchi to Sebald did not contain anything new or out of the ordinary.[38] The Japanese government thanked its counterpart for having sent the draft and requested a few "small changes." What they requested was as follows:[39]

Their request was to change the name of Ryukyu to Nansei. The memorandum was so brief that it even seems improper to be the Japanese government's official comment on a draft peace treaty. This reveals that the two parties had agreed on all important matters beforehand. Sebald also reported that Nansei appeared to be more historically correct than Ryukyu. Sebald sent a telegram to the US DoS on the same day of the request to the effect that, "…according (to) Jap[anese] usage. "Ryukyu Islands" not coextensive with "Nansei Islands," former term applying only to those

---

[38] "Observations on the Provisional Draft of a Japanese Peace Treaty" (Apr. 4, 1951), Ministry of Foreign Affairs of Japan, 2007, *Japanese Diplomatic Documents: Negotiations with the US for the San Francisco Peace Treaty*, pp. 351-352.

[39] Telegram by Sebald to the Secretary of State, no. 1750 (Apr. 4, 1951), RG 59, Department of State, Decimal File, 694.001/4-451.

islands formerly included within Okinawa prefecture (Okinawa and Sakishima sub-groups, including Daito and Sento Islands)."[40] This reveals the degree of coordination between the Japanese Foreign Ministry and the US political adviser to SCAP in early April 1951 ahead of the signing of the peace treaty. This means that they had concluded discussions on all important matters.

Upon receipt of Sebald's telegram, Fearey, the working-level official at the US DoS, consulted with Samuel W. Boggs, the US DoS geography specialist, on the question. Boggs responded that "Nansei" was the more accurate term and should be used based on his review of *US Hydrographic Survey*.[41]

Fearey pointed out that "Ryukyu" was a much more familiar name and that it was likely that the Japanese government had suggested "Nansei" because it was a pure Japanese word as opposed to the Chinese-sounding Ryukyu (Ryukyu derived from the Chinese word "Loochoo") and they wanted to hint at future ownership. Fearey marked six island groups including five mentioned by Boggs and the Daito Group next to them on the attached map.

As such, by April 1951, preparations for the peace treaty by the Japanese Foreign Ministry were so thoroughly complete as to consider the change of a geographical name included in the treaty text.

---

40   Telegram by Sebald to the Secretary of State, no. 1750 (Apr. 4, 1951), RG 59, Department of State, Decimal File, 694.001/4-451.

41   Memorandum by Fearey to Allison, Subject: Nansei Shoto (Apr. 5, 1951), RG 59, Department of State, Decimal File, 694.001/4-551.

2

Dulles' Second Visit to Japan in 1951 and Japan's Opposition to Korea's Participation

Dulles was back in Tokyo on April 16, 1951, as MacArthur had been removed from command for continued insubordination on April 11, 1951, which came to many as a shock, and Dulles had to assure the Japanese government that MacArthur's sudden departure did not affect US policy on Japan and they would go ahead with the peace treaty as planned.

There was an anecdote right before Dulles left for Tokyo that showed his trust in Japan. The first Anglo-American Meeting on the Japanese Peace Treaty was scheduled to be held in Washington starting on April 25, 1951. UK Foreign and Commonwealth Office (FCO) officials were coming to Washington to compare the US draft with their own and attempt to integrate the two documents. In a telegram sent to Sebald with the signature of Dean Acheson on April 9, Dulles suggested that the Japanese government send a representative of the same rank as Vice Foreign Minister Iguchi who could provide insight and make compromises at the US-UK meeting.[42]

Dulles soon left for Tokyo and the UK delegation arrived in Washington immediately after his return. It seemed that Dulles' suggestion came to nothing. Nonetheless, the idea was unconventional to have a Japanese diplomatic representative serve in a coordinating role in the negotiations with the UK, the US most important ally. It was no accident or coincidence that he provided the Japanese government with the UK draft peace treaty while he was in Tokyo. Dulles trusted them and this was his way of delegating responsibility.

---

42   Telegram from Dulles to Sebald, no. 1441 (Apr. 9, 1951), RG 59, Department of State, Decimal File, 694.001/4-951.

1) Dulles' intentions vs. Japan's intentions

When Dulles' visit was announced on April 13, Japan hastened to make preparations for the visit as they did for his first visit from January to February 1951. The Japanese Foreign Ministry paid special attention to the placement of the Ryukyu and Ogasawara Islands under trusteeship, the right to demand compensation, and property issues.[43]

The Dulles delegation arrived in Tokyo on April 16 and held staff meetings on April 17 and 18 to discuss ways to talk to Japan. In the April 17 meeting, Dulles suggested that it would be desirable to give Iguchi a chance to review the UK draft peace treaty,[44] which was an official draft completed by the UK FCO on April 7, 1951 and delivered to the US Embassy in London on April 9. The UK intended to provide the draft to major Allies like France and the Netherlands only the following week.[45] Nevertheless, Dulles wanted to provide the draft to Japan in Tokyo on April 17. As explained above regarding the UK-US talks, Dulles neither consulted the UK government about providing its draft to the Japanese government nor informed the UK delegation of this fact during the first Anglo-American Meeting on the Japanese Peace Treaty held in Washington after his return.

Dulles' instruction was not to give a copy of the UK draft to Iguchi, but allow him to transcribe the draft and ask him to provide the delegation with the Japanese government's comments on the UK draft before its return. Dulles entrusted Fearey with this task. Dulles decided on this course of action from the standpoint that Japan should be held responsible to some degree with regard to the UK suggestions. Dulles must have wanted to

---

43 "Draft Requests to the US regarding the Peace Treaty Draft" (Apr. 14, 1951), "Materials Prepared for the Prime Minister in Preparation for Yoshida and Dulles Talks" (Apr. 16, 1951), Ministry of Foreign Affairs of Japan, 2007, *Japanese Diplomatic Documents: Negotiations with the US for the San Francisco Peace Treaty*, pp. 363-373.

44 "Minutes-Dulles Mission Staff Meeting, Dai Ichi Building, April 17, 9:00 A.M." by R. A. Fearey, RG 59, Office of Northeast Asia Affairs, Records Relating to the Treaty of Peace with Japan-Subject File, 1945-51, Lot 56D527, Box 6.

45 *FRUS*, 1951, Vol. VI, p. 979, footnote 2; FO 371/92538, 213349, FJ 1022/222, Mr. Morrison to Sir O. Franks (Washington), no. 401(Apr. 7, 1951).

demonstrate to Japan that the "UK draft probably includes all the details the Allies want to put in the treaty."[46]

In the afternoon of April 17, Fearey showed the UK draft to Japanese officials at the SCAP Diplomatic Section. Fearey informed them that if they would review the UK draft side-by-side with the US draft and relay their opinions to the US delegation, the US government would review them together with their UK counterpart.[47] It is believed that Iguchi copied the draft as instructed by Dulles, commenting that the UK draft consisted of ten chapters, 40 articles, and five annexes, and like the Treaty of Peace with Italy, it was a treaty between victorious countries and the defeated.[48]

Dulles' visit in April 1951 did not have any other important items to discuss as the purpose of the trip was to relieve Japan of its concerns over the sudden departure of MacArthur. Other items discussed at the staff meetings on April 17 and 18 include the suggestion of reparations from current production; difficulties associated with talks with the UK; whether to invite Matthew B. Ridgway, the newly appointed Supreme Commander of the Allied Powers, to attend meetings with Yoshida and to a speech to be given at the Diet (April 23); and a venue for signing the treaty.[49] Dulles argued that, based on the Treaty of Peace with Italy, reparations from current production to countries that had requested compensation such as the Philippines, Malaya, and Burma would help restart trade channels. Regarding the venue for signing the treaty, Sebald said he had discussed this with Iguchi and argued the venue should be Tokyo. Dulles borrowed George Clutton's words to argue that, if the event was to be held in Tokyo, such a decision would be detrimental to the future relations between the

---

46　"Minutes-Dulles Mission Staff Meeting, Dai Ichi Building, April 17, 9:00 A.M." by R. A. Fearey, p. 1.

47　"British Draft Peace Treaty for Japan" (Apr. 17, 1951), Ministry of Foreign Affairs of Japan, 2007, *Japanese Diplomatic Documents: Negotiations with the US for the San Francisco Peace Treaty*, pp. 374-375.

48　*Ibid.*, p. 374.

49　"Minutes-Dulles Mission Staff Meeting, April 18, 9:30 A.M." by R. A. Fearey, RG 59, Office of Northeast Asia Affairs, Records Relating to the Treaty of Peace with Japan-Subject File, 1945-51, Lot 56D527, Box 6.

Allies and Japan.

During his second visit, Dulles met up with Yoshida twice: before the first talks on April 18, 1951, in an unofficial capacity together with Ridgway at the SCAP office at 11 am,[50] and during the official talks between Dulles and Yoshida from 3 to 4 pm. They were accompanied by Vice Minister Sadao Iguchi and Kumao Nishimura, Director general of the Treaties Bureau under the Japanese Foreign Ministry, as well as Sebald, Assistant Secretary of the Army Earl D. Johnson, Colonel Babcock, and Fearey. Nothing important was discussed. The most important agenda items would be taken up at the second talks on April 23, 1951 and would include such items as the results of a review of the UK draft and Korea's participation in the negotiations and signing of the treaty.

The minutes of the first talks of April 18 from each side focused on slightly different items.[51] The US minutes recorded that Dulles talked about reparations in kind, revision of the Addendum to the US-Japan Security Treaty, the venue of the signing, the administrative agreement, and other matters. The Japanese minutes recorded that Dulles brought up the UK draft and said that, if Japan would provide its comments on the draft shown to the Japanese the previous day, they would be "helpful in the discussion with the UK delegation" scheduled for the following week in Washington.[52] All that was discussed in the meeting was more or less the deletion of the geographical limitation that restricted the activities of the UN forces to Korea.

50   "Yoshida, Ridgway, and Dulles Talks" (11 am, Apr. 18, 1951), Ministry of Foreign Affairs of Japan, 2007, *Japanese Diplomatic Documents: Negotiations with the US for the San Francisco Peace Treaty*, pp. 382-383.
51   Memorandum of Conversation by R. A. Fearey, Subject: Japanese Peace Treaty (Apr. 18, 1951), RG 59, Office of Northeast Asia Affairs, Records Relating to the Treaty of Peace with Japan-Subject File, 1945-51, Lot 56D527, Box 6; "Yoshida and Dulles Talks (1st talks)," Ministry of Foreign Affairs of Japan, 2007, *Ibid.*, pp. 384-388.
52   "Yoshida and Dulles Talks (1st talks)," Ministry of Foreign Affairs of Japan, 2007, *Ibid.* p. 385.

2) US-Japan discussion on the UK draft treaty and the Dokdo issue

As seen above, Dulles provided the UK draft to the Japanese Foreign Ministry on April 17 and the Ministry, in response, wrote up its comments and Iguchi delivered them to Sebald on April 20.[53] The memorandum titled "Observations on the British Draft Peace Treaty for Japan" clearly manifested Japan's stance at the time.

In general, Japan's main criticism was that the draft was of the same nature of a peace imposed by a victorious country on an enemy country that had surrendered unconditionally and was a repetition of the Treaty of Versailles. It further criticized the draft as certainly promising to greatly disappoint the Japanese public and predicted it would "spoil their desire to work with the Allies and contribute to world peace and security." Japan argued that the content of the treaty copied that of the Treaty of Peace with Italy and the case of Japan was different from that of Italy. Under the Allied occupation of the last six years, all the conditions that had led to the war had been eliminated, the foundation for Japan's demilitarization and democratization had been laid, and the Japanese people were determined to maintain peace on their own volition. It wrote in the memorandum that the US draft was more realistic and desirable in general and the Japanese people also hoped a peace treaty would be concluded based on the US version. Japan, which had expected a non-punitive, generous peace treaty according to the five memorandums signed and exchanged between the US and Japan on February 9, 1951, was shocked by the punitive peace treaty described in the UK draft.

This fervent opposition by Japan to the draft treaty written by the UK, the closest ally to the US, which would determine Japan's fate, reveals how strongly the US supported Japan's position. With the urgency posed by the Korean War, the US had reached an agreement with Japan on the drafts of the fundamental treaties of peace, security, and administration and

---

53 "Observations on the British Draft Peace Treaty for Japan" (Apr. 20, 1951), Ministry of Foreign Affairs of Japan, 2007, *Ibid.*, pp. 388-392.

effectively initialed them with lightning speed in Tokyo in February 1951. The sudden determination by the US in February 1951 encouraged Japan to expect a generous peace. The US did not inform the UK of its *de facto* initial signing of a peace treaty. This is evidence of the relative closeness and magnetism of US-Japan relations in comparison to US-UK relations.

Japan stated in the memorandum that it wanted the US version to take precedence over the UK version in every article in principle. It argued that not a few of the articles in the UK draft were in fact unnecessary and would only stir up Japanese resentment. The examples are Article 9 (Undesirable Political Entities), Article 10 (Protection of Japanese who Cooperated with the Allied Powers), Article 14 (Congo Basin Treaties), Article 23 (Rules on Base Metal and Gemstones), Article 28 (Japanese Property in Neutral and Former Enemy Nations), Article 31 (Prewar Indemnities), Article 34 (Fisheries of Paragraph 2), and Article 40 (Implementation).

On the other hand, Japan commented that some of the articles of the UK draft should be included in the US draft such as the inclusion of Shikotan in Japanese territory, the end of occupation, and the provisions on monetary liabilities.[54] In the overall process leading up to the signing of the peace treaty, this review of the UK draft by the Japanese government got into full swing. It reveals that the Japanese felt neither responsibility nor remorse for the war and paid no attention to the obligations or penalties which a defeated country was usually saddled with. The Japanese Foreign Ministry recorded that it delivered this written memorandum to Sebald on April 20, 1951 but it was not found among the US Department of State's records.

What can be found at the US DoS is an undated document of oral comments by Nishimura, General Affairs Section Head Ando, and technical assistants.[55] According to Japanese Foreign Ministry records, it

---

54 "Observations on the British Draft Peace Treaty for Japan" (Apr. 20, 1951), Ministry of Foreign Affairs of Japan, 2007, *Ibid.*, pp. 388-392.

55 "Japanese Comments on Individual Articles of British Draft Given Orally by Nishis(m)ura, Ando and Technical Assistants," (undated), RG 59, Office of Northeast Asia Affairs, Records Relating to the Treaty of Peace with Japan-Subject File, 1945-51, Lot 56D527, Box 6. Folder "Treaty-Draft-May 3-June 1, 1951".

corresponds to "Comments on the Individual Articles of the British Draft Peace Treaty for Japan" given orally by Nishimura in a meeting with Fearey on April 21, 1951.[56] Four Japanese officials gathered in Fearey's office and verbally explained the Japanese government's understanding of the UK draft. It was meant to supplement the written comments delivered the previous day.[57]

The oral comments given by Nishimura and others were similar to the Iguchi memorandum and very detailed. What was evident was Japan's opposition to the UK draft and preference for the US version: this preference was expressed no fewer than six times throughout the comments. Korea appeared in the comments as follows:

Preamble

Article 1. We wish that not only the 15 nations indicated but as many nations that were at war with Japan as possible would be original signatories. (We approve the omission of Korea from the UK draft).[58]

Articles 2 & 3. We are very dissatisfied with the war crime clauses.

Chapter 1

Territorial clauses

Article 1. The Prime Minister dislikes the figurative fence that surrounds Japan in the surrounding seas. He said it seems to fence Japan in and will clearly remind the Japanese that they have lost their territories. The US draft is greatly preferred.[59] The inclusion of Shikotan in Japanese territory in the

---

56   "Comments on the Individual Articles of the British Draft Peace Treaty for Japan" (Apr. 21, 1951), Ministry of Foreign Affairs of Japan, 2007, *Japanese Diplomatic Documents: Negotiations with the US for the San Francisco Peace Treaty*, pp. 396-406.

57   *Ibid.*, p. 397.

58   The Japanese Foreign Ministry record states that "the preamble mentioned as Allied and Associated Powers the original 11 nations of the Far Eastern Commission as well as Burma, Indonesia, Ceylon, and Pakistan but left out Korea. Our question about the status of Korea will be raised later in connection with Korea's right to participate in the treaty and it is not related to the preamble," *Ibid.*, p. 397.

59   The Japanese Foreign Ministry record states that "the detailed boundaries of Japanese

UK draft is appreciated. It looks like the Habomais are also included and we are certain it should be specified. We are dissatisfied with the loss of Ryukyu between 30° and 29°. The Japanese are very appreciative of the US drawing a line by 29° rather than by 30°.[60] (underlined by the quoter)

Japan was thorough in expressing its interests, generally preferring the US draft for its generosity towards Japan but supported the UK draft where it suited its interests. It "approved" or "appreciated" the exclusion of Korea as a signatory and the indication of Shikotan as Japanese territory from the UK draft. The problem here is that Korea's participation was not discussed with Korea itself but only with Japan. It should also be noted that Prime Minister Shigeru Yoshida was strongly opposed to the method used in the UK draft to clearly demarcate Japanese territory by drawing a line around Japan.

Shigeru Yoshida opposed the "fencing in of Japan" or the "detailed boundaries with latitudes and longitudes" as it would suggest a sense of loss of territory to the Japanese people. He also disliked the use of an attached map due to the significant impact it would have on the national sentiment. However, as seen before, detailed boundaries and the use of an attached map were essential and inevitable to specify islands to be included in and excluded from Japanese territory as stipulated in the Cairo Declaration and Potsdam Declaration. Japan's opposition on the excuse of national sentiment was in fact its complete rejection and disregard of the territorial clauses of the two Declarations it had accepted as the terms of its surrender. Yoshida's rejection and neglect of the territorial clauses of the Declarations and the subsequent US acceptance of this attitude show that the overall nature of the peace treaty with Japan had completely changed.

---

territory with latitudes and longitudes as in Article 1 of Chapter 1 of the UK draft will denote a strong sense of loss of territory to the Japanese people and may lead to future resentment. The Prime Minister also objected to the use of the attached map due to its impact on the national sentiment." *Ibid.* (Apr. 21, 1951), p. 397.

60   "Japanese Comments on Individual Articles of British Draft Given Orally by Nishis(m)ura, Ando and Technical Assistants," (undated), p. 1.

The highlight of the second visit by the Dulles delegation was the second round of talks between Dulles and Yoshida on April 23 where the review of the UK draft and Korea's participation in the treaty negotiations were intensively discussed. Sebald recalled as follows:

> April 23, 1951, the last day of stay by the Dulles delegation, was devoted to a review of a British draft treaty we had just received. Prime Minister Yoshida, Vice Foreign Minister Iguchi Sadao, and Nishimura Kumao, the Director of the Treaties Bureau of the Foreign Ministry and a skilled technician, joined us in my office and the conference lasted several hours. The Japanese officials, who had been given a copy of the British draft, preferred the American version to the technically accurate and comprehensive British version.[61]

The process of reviewing and discussing the UK draft between the US and Japan can chronologically be outlined as follows:

- **April 7, 1951:** The UK FCO completes its draft peace treaty.
- **April 9 1951:** The UK FCO sends the draft to the US Embassy in London.
- **April 16, 1951:** The Dulles delegation arrives in Tokyo.
- **April 17, 1951:** In the morning Dulles instructs Fearey to show the UK draft to Iguchi, which Fearey does in the afternoon.
- **April 18, 1951:** At the talks with Yoshida, Dulles requests the Japanese government's comments on the UK draft.
- **April 20, 1951:** Iguchi delivers the memorandum of comments to Sebald.
- **April 21, 1951:** Nishimura, Ando, Treaties Section Head Takahashi, and Japanese Nationals Overseas Section Head Usiroku meet Fearey and give oral comments on each article of the draft.
- **April 23, 1951:** Yoshida, Iguchi, Nishimura, the Dulles party, and Sebald review the draft. The party leaves Tokyo.
- **April 25, 1951:** The working-level officials of the UK FCO arrive in

---

61   William J. Sebald with Russell Brines, *With MacArthur in Japan: A Personal History of the Occupation*, W.W. Norton & Company, Inc., New York, 1965, p. 266.

Washington, DC for the US-UK talks.

The second visit by the Dulles delegation in April 1951 can be characterized as a joint US-Japan review of the UK draft treaty, or more accurately, Japan's review of the draft and the acceptance by the US of Japan's comments.

One thing certain is that the UK draft clearly excluded Dokdo (Takeshima) from Japanese territory but Japan did not comment on this at all. Judging from Yoshida's objection to an attached map, it is almost certain that the draft Dulles took with him to Japan had an attached map.

With the good offices of the US, Japan was able to review the UK draft and its attached map and clearly learned of the exclusion of the Liancourt Rocks from Japanese territory. However, there was no mention of the Liancourt Rocks (Dokdo) in any of the Japanese records about the review of the UK draft. Under the territorial clauses, the UK (April 7, 1951) draft drew a line that defined Japanese territorial sovereignty between the Oki islands to the southeast and Dokdo to the northwest. This included the Oki Islands (Oki-Retto) in Japanese territory but excluded Dokdo (indicated as "Take Shima") from it.[62]

First, the memorandum, which was written immediately after the Japanese officials received the UK draft from Fearey on April 17, 1951, stated that, "Article 1 of Chapter 1's territorial clauses specifies the area that remains as Japanese territory with latitudes and longitudes from

---

62 FO 371/92538, FJ 1022/222, "Provisional Draft of Japanese Peace Treaty (United Kingdom)," (Apr. 7, 1951), pp. 15-50. The following section is referred to: "Japanese sovereignty shall continue over all the islands and adjacent islets and rocks lying within an area bounded by a line from Latitude 30°N in a North-Westerly direction to approximately Latitude 33°N 128°E, then Northward between the islands of Quelpart, Fukue-Shima bearing North-Easterly between Korea and the island of Tsushima, continuing in this direction with the islands of Oki-Retto to the South-East and Take Shima to the North-West curving with the coast of Honshu, then Northerly skirting Rebun Shima passing Easterly through Soya Kaikyo approximately 142°E... The line described above is plotted on the map attached to the present Treaty (Annex I). In the case of a discrepancy between the map and the textual description of the line, the latter shall prevail."

all directions. What requires caution is that the draft puts the Nansei Islands south of 30° north latitude (it is 29° in the US draft) and Shikotan within Japanese territory to the north. This is a quite detailed and lengthy description."[63] Regarding Korea, it only wrote, "Article 2 waiver of sovereignty over Korea." The Japanese showed absolutely no interest in Dokdo (Takeshima) and failed to state their opinions about it.

Second, no opinion about Dokdo was ever stated in the memorandum Iguchi submitted to Sebald on April 20, "Observations on the British Draft Peace Treaty for Japan", the oral comments given by Nishimura and others to Fearey on April 21, "Comments on the Individual Articles of the British Draft Peace Treaty for Japan", or the review of the UK treaty between the US delegation and representatives of the Japanese government (including Yoshida) on April 23. In summary, based on the records of the Japanese Foreign Ministry and the US DoS, Japanese officials had at least three opportunities to state their views on the UK draft regarding the exclusion of the Liancourt Rocks from Japanese territory and their inclusion in Korean territory, but never once voiced their objections or offered alternate opinions. Therefore, it is perfectly acceptable to interpret such lack of action as Japan's acceptance. Japan reacted very sensitively to and approved the inclusion of Shikotan in Japanese territory while disapproving of the placement of Ryuku south of 30° north latitude. Yet, it remained silent about Dokdo throughout the entire review process.

With not only the UK, the drafter, but also Korea, the party of direct interest, excluded, the Japanese government intensively and exclusively reviewed the draft treaty by the UK FCO and had no less than three opportunities to express its views in April 1951 amid the US one-sided goodwill. They did not object to or protest the exclusion of Dokdo (Takeshima) from Japanese territory or its indication as Korean territory. Even the name used was not the Liancourt Rocks but the Japanese name

---

63 "British Draft Peace Treaty for Japan" (Apr. 17, 1951), Ministry of Foreign Affairs of Japan, 2007, *Japanese Diplomatic Documents: Negotiations with the US for the San Francisco Peace Treaty*, pp. 374-375.

Takeshima. This means that the Japanese Foreign Ministry was fully aware of and acknowledged the exclusion of Dokdo (Takeshima) from Japanese territory.

This was before the Korean government ever had a chance to present its case for territorial sovereignty over Dokdo to the US. Nor was it aware of the publication by the Japanese Foreign Ministry in June 1947 of a pamphlet that falsely described Dokdo as Japanese territory; Sebald's argument specifying Dokdo as Japanese territory based on the pamphlet in December 1949; and a previous draft of the treaty which was completed in December 1949 where Dokdo was indicated as Japanese territory. The Korean government was never given a chance to take a look at the UK draft. In other words, Korea was placed in a completely defenseless position regarding its sovereignty over Dokdo and had not been given a chance to present its side of the story. Despite exclusive opportunities, Japan neither claimed Dokdo (Takeshima) as its territory nor protested where the UK draft placed the island.

The Japanese government's official position on Dokdo shown in the review process of the UK draft in April 1951 is completely different from its claim for sovereignty over Dokdo made in January 1952 in terms of the time they were announced, the cause that led to them, and the background in which they occurred. The US-backed Japanese government exclusively and promptly reviewed the UK draft not once but over several occasions. On the other hand, the UK, the drafter, and Korea, subject to the outcome of the negotiations, were left in the dark, and even in this enviable position, Japan did not raise objections to the exclusion of Dokdo (Takeshima), thereby practically acknowledging it. This fact remains true even though the plan to indicate Japanese territory with longitude and latitude and the use of an attached map were scrapped as the Japanese government insisted due to the potential psychological effect on the Japanese people.

3) Japan's opposition to Korea's participation and false accusations

Another issue in the second Dulles and Yoshida talks on April 23 was whether Korea was qualified to participate in the peace conference. In this regard, there exist two different minutes of the same meeting: one kept by the Japanese Foreign Ministry and the other by the US DoS. These two documents warrant a comparison. The first is part of the record of the Japanese Foreign Ministry: it is quoted unabridged despite its length as follows:

4. Korea's participation as a signatory

What Dulles said: The ROK government has been recognized by the UN General Assembly as the only legitimate government on the Korean peninsula and is formally approved by many UN members. The said government has requested to join the Far Eastern Commission (FEC) but the Commission has not decided whether to accept the request as its members are divided on it by halves and are having difficulty reaching agreement. The US government wants to build up the prestige of the Korean government and believes the Japanese government is of the same mind in this regard. We are well aware that it would put the Japanese government in a difficult situation if the treaty is put in effect and Koreans in Japan acquire and exercise all the compensation and property rights accruing to Allied nationals. As the US government is considering ways to exempt Japan from this mess, we hope that the Japanese government will agree to Korea's participation as a signatory.

The Prime Minister said the Korean minority in Japan is a great nuisance; General MacArthur has been consulted several times about deporting them to their home country but the general has opposed forcible mass repatriation to the south on the grounds that North Koreans would have their heads cut off and thinks now is not the right time from a humanitarian viewpoint; however it is difficult not to send them back. They came to Japan as laborers during the war and worked in mines. After the war they became one of the causes of social unrest; the Japanese communists use them as puppets and most of them have become communists themselves (Ambassador Sebald explained about the ethnic Korean residents being communists in greater detail).[64]

What Dulles said can be summarized in three points. First, at the time, the US wanted to include Korea in the list of treaty signatories as a way to offer it political support. Korea requested to join the FEC but failed due to the split opinions of its member states. The US position was to bolster the status of the Korean government. Second, the US well understood the Japanese government's concerns over ethnic Korean residents in Japan becoming Allied nationals. Third, as the US would work out a way to resolve these concerns, Japan should consent to Korea's participation. His remarks stressed the UN's recognition of the Korean government and the US intention to save it from the political predicament of the time and exhibit political support for it. He acknowledged the Korean minority issue suggested by the Japanese government as the reason for its objection and promised to identify a solution.

The remarks by Yoshida were also very unique: he did not bring up the popular reason for objection used by the UK government or Sebald in November 1949, which was Korea being disqualified for having been a Japanese colony. Instead, he argued Korea should be excluded because the Korean residents in Japan were criminals and communists, treating Korea's participation in the treaty and the issue of the Korean residents in Japan as one and the same. He denied Korea's qualification for participation in the treaty on the basis of a domestic Japanese issue. Yoshida must have raised this issue because he believed not only Sebald and MacArthur but also Dulles were well informed of the danger of those resident Koreans who were both communists and criminals.

The next section is part of the US record which is somewhat different from the Japanese one: it is quoted below despite its length:

Korea's participation: Ambassador Dulles said that he understood that the Japanese government objected to Korea being a signatory of the treaty. Mr. Yoshida replied that this was so and presented a paper containing his government's views. Ambassador Dulles said that he could see the force of

64   "Yoshida and Dulles Talks (2nd talks)," Ministry of Foreign Affairs of Japan, 2007, *Ibid.*, pp. 408-409.

the Japanese argument that Korean nationals in Japan, mostly Communists, should not obtain the property benefits of the treaty. He suggested that this might be taken care of by limiting these benefits to the Allies which were belligerents at the time of surrender. His initial reaction, however, in the light of the world picture and the desire of the US to build up the prestige of the Korean government, was that we would want to continue to deal with Korea on the treaty. If the only practical objection that the Japanese government had to Korea's participation was the one just discussed, this could and should be taken care of. If the Japanese had any other practical objections, the US would be glad to study them.

Prime Minister Yoshida said that his government would like to send almost all the Koreans in Japan back to "their home." The government had long been concerned over their illegal activities. He had raised the matter with General MacArthur, who had opposed their enforced repatriation, partly on the grounds that they were mostly North Koreans and would have their heads cut off by the ROK. Yoshida said that his government had determined that the assassination of the President of the National Railways in the summer of 1949 had been by a Korean but that it had been unable to catch the guilty party, who was believed to have fled to Korea.[65]

The US record shows the context more clearly. Dulles was aware of Japan's objection to Korea's qualification as a treaty signatory. According to a diplomatic document released by the Japanese Foreign Ministry, Japan was already aware in October 1950 of Dulles' plan to include Korea as one of the key countries to participate in the negotiations of the peace treaty with Japan. Hiroto Tanaka, head of Immigration Department I under the Foreign Ministry's General Affairs Bureau, worked side-by-side with the staff of the US DoS Office of Northeast Asian Affairs who were responsible for the practical affairs of the peace treaty from late September to mid-

---

65 Memorandum of Conversation by R. A. Fearey, Subject: Japanese Peace Treaty (Apr. 23, 1951), RG 59, Office of Northeast Asia Affairs, Records Relating to the Treaty of Peace with Japan-Subject File, 1945-51, Lot 56D527, Box 6.

October 1950. Tanaka learned from Fearey that Dulles had planned to talk to the 13 member countries of the FEC and then have additional talks with Korea and Indonesia.[66] It was only on January 26, 1951 in Tokyo when Dulles first talked to Chang Myun, the ROK Ambassador to the US, about Korea's participation in the peace treaty. Fearey was present at the meeting and wrote up the minutes.[67] As such, Japan had already learned that the US was considering including Korea as a key participant three months before Dulles talked to the Korean ambassador in Tokyo. Correspondingly, Fearey had leaked crucial information about how the US regarded Korea to Japan and there is no doubt Japan was fully prepared by the time it had to deal with the issue.

The reason Japan cited for its objection to Korea's participation was far from what Dulles had expected. Dulles must have expected a more accurate and explicit reason, such as that of the UK, which was that Korea had been a Japanese colony and therefore had neither been at war nor declared war against Japan. Then, he came to learn in the comments of the Japanese government submitted by Yoshida that the major reason for Japan's objection was the possibility of ethnic Koreans in Japan, most of whom were allegedly criminals and communists, gaining economic benefit. Dulles suggested as a solution that by defining that only nationals of the Allied Powers which had been at war with Japan at the time of surrender could be compensated, those Koreans would not be qualified to benefit from the treaty. Dulles explained that if the "only practical objection" that the Japanese government had to Korea's participation was this one alone, it could be well addressed by the US.

For his part, Yoshida repeatedly explained how much the Japanese government was obsessed with repatriation of the Korean minority. It is noteworthy that MacArthur was opposed to such an action. Yoshida's

---

66 "Talks with the US Department of State Officials on the Peace Treaty" (Oct. 14, 1950), Ministry of Foreign Affairs of Japan, 2007, *Japanese Diplomatic Documents: Negotiations with the US for the San Francisco Peace Treaty*, p. 57-63.
67 Memorandum of Conversation, by Mr. Robert A. Fearey of the Office of Northeast Asian Affairs (Jan. 26, 1951), *FRUS*, 1951, Vol. VI, p. 817.

objection to Korea's participation due to ethnic Koreans in Japan being criminals and communists was completely lacking in both logic and justification.

More appalling was his accusation that it was a Korean who assassinated the President of Japanese National Railways in the summer of 1949 and assumption that the criminal had fled to Korea, so could not be captured. It is so slanderous an accusation that it is difficult to believe it was uttered by a nation's prime minister. It was incredibly demeaning to ethnic Koreans living in Japan. As the Prime Minister himself made such remarks openly and without reserve in front of the US delegation and at public appearances, it is crystal clear to presume them as the views Japanese government officials and politicians held toward the ethnic Korean minority population. Of course, this accusation could not be found in any of the official diplomatic documents released by the Japanese Foreign Ministry and records by Japanese diplomats. It is clear evidence of how desperate Japan's highest leaders, diplomats, high-ranking officials, and politicians were in attempting to brand the Korean minority as criminals and communists in order to forcibly deport them.

On July 5, 1949, Sadanori Shimoyama, the President of Japanese National Railways (JNR), disappeared on his way to work in an official vehicle. His body was found the next day at a nearby train station. JNR and its labor union had been pitted against each other due to drastic reductions in staff levels since July 1. With conflicting explanations involving suicide and murder, the media aroused suspicions of the Japanese Communist Party being the mastermind behind his disappearance and JNR went ahead with the firing of some 30,000 employees as the first in a series of cutbacks. On July 15, 1949, a train drove into Mitaka Station on the Chuo line in Tokyo, resulting in six deaths and seven injuries. The government blamed this event on the Communist Party and indicted ten people, including nine Communist Party members, on charges of train sabotage, but they were all found not guilty in the first trial in 1950.

On August 17, 1949, a passenger train derailed and overturned near Matsukawa Station in Fukushima Prefecture on the Tohoku main line, taking the lives of three crew members. All arrested, including Communist

Party members, were convicted in the first trial in December 1950, but the verdict was not convincing and lacked compelling evidence. As a result, some 1,000 "organizations to protect Matsukawa" were established across the nation and all were eventually acquitted on appeal at the Supreme Court in September 1963.[68]

All three of these JNR incidents that seems slanderous remain shrouded in mystery to this day and JNR was able to lay off about 90,000 employees in the process. The incidents are regarded as some of the key conspiracies of the occupation period and there was much speculation about the involvement of the Japanese Communist Party. Yoshida's accusation of ethnic Koreans' involvement lacks persuasion.

Now, let us turn our attention to the memorandum Yoshida handed to Dulles at the second talks on April 23, 1951. It was "Korea and the Peace Treaty" and reads as follows:

> The US has suggested its plan to invite Korea to include it in the list of signatories to the coming peace treaty. The Japanese government hopes that the US will reconsider this from the following perspective:
>
> With regards to Japan, Korea is one of the so-called "liberated nations" that will acquire independence with the conclusion of a peace treaty as one of the "special status nations" (June 21, 1948 SCAP memo). Korea has never been at war nor in a state of belligerence with Japan and therefore should not be treated as one of the Allied Powers.
>
> If Korea signed the peace treaty as an Ally, Korean residents in Japan would demand their rights for property, compensation and other privileges. Approximately one million Koreans reside in Japan even today (the number was almost 1.5 million around the end of the war). (If all of them made such

---

68 The following are referred to regarding the Shimoyama incident: Kimio Yada, 1973, *Bosatsu Shimoyama Jiken (Premeditated Murder: Shimoyama Incident)*, Kodansha; Seicho Matsumoto, 1974, *Nihon-No Kuroi Kiri (Black Fog over Japan)*, Vol. 1&2, Bunshun Bunko; Mikio Haruna, 2000, *Himitsu-No File: CIA-No Tainichi Kosaku (Secret File: CIA's Operations in Japan)*, Vol. 1&2, Kyodo News; Yuji Moronaga, 2002, *Homurareta Natsu: Tsuiseki Shimoyama Jiken (Buried Summer: Chasing Shimoyama Incident)*, Asahi Shimbunsha.

demands,) The Japanese government would collapse under the pressure of the various kinds of immense unverifiable demands.[69] The fact that the majority of Koreans are communists should be pointed out.

The Japanese government is convinced that it is best to limit the peace in a way where the Japanese government renounces all rights, titles and claims to Korea (Article 3, Chapter 3 Territory, US Draft) and recognizes its full independence, and to normalize bilateral relations with a treaty that will be concluded when the current situation of Korea is resolved and peace and stability is restored on the peninsula. April 23, 1951[70]

In the above memorandum, there were two main reasons for the Japanese government's objection to Korea's participation. First, with regard to Japan, Korea was a liberated nation that would acquire independence according to a peace treaty and had never been at war or in a state of belligerence with Japan. Second, if Korea were to acquire signatory status, the Korean residents in Japan, who were allegedly communists, would make enormous demands upon the Japanese government regarding property, compensation, and other matters. It would be sufficient for Japan to renounce all rights, titles and claims to Korea and recognize its independence as indicated in the US draft. Bilateral relations should be resolved through a Korea-Japan bilateral treaty. Yoshida's position ① was against giving Korea Allied status; ② hinted at the possibility of the Japanese government going bankrupt if Korean residents were recognized as Allied nationals; ③ attempted to exclude Korea as a treaty signatory; and ④ sought to establish Korea-Japan relations through a direct treaty

---

69   The Japanese document wrote that "if the ethnic Koreans, whose number is close to 1 million even now and amounted to 1.5 million at the end of the war, become able to claim such rights, it would create an unbearable burden on the Japanese government."

70   "Korea and Peace Treaty," (Apr. 23, 1951), RG 59, Japanese Peace Treaty Files of John Foster Dulles, 1946-52, Lot 54D423, Box 1; RG 59, Japanese Peace Treaty Files of John Foster Dulles, 1947-1952, Subject Files, Lot 54D423, Box 7; "Observations on the Korean Government's Participation as a Peace Treaty Signatory" (Apr. 23, 1951), Ministry of Foreign Affairs of Japan, 2007, *Japanese Diplomatic Documents: Negotiations with the US for the San Francisco Peace Treaty*, pp. 413-415.

between the two nations.

Dulles did not accept Japan's demand on that very same day, but recognized the Japanese government's claim had a point in that most of the Korean residents were communists and should therefore not gain economic benefit from the peace treaty, and therefore gave his consent to Japan's objection to Korea's participation. In the afternoon of the day of the meeting, the Japanese government notified Dulles of its intention not to object to Korea being a peace treaty signatory as long as it was undoubtedly guaranteed that ethnic Koreans would not be Allied nationals.[71]

As seen above, the UK and Japan were strongly opposed to Korea's participation in the peace treaty. Both turned around eventually: the UK indicated its intention to accommodate the US position (April 16, 1951) and Japan said it would acquiesce if it did not have to compensate the Korean minority (April 23, 1951). After having talked to the US DoS from March to April 1951, they came to a decision to not object to Korea's participating in and signing the treaty. Now, the ball was in the US court.

The US had already expressed its concerns over Korea's "excessive compensation demands." In a November 1949 correspondence, John J. Muccio, the first US Ambassador to Korea, explained that if compensation was the reason for objection, it could be settled by limiting Korea's rights in that area. The US DoS Division of Research for Far East (DRF) in its report No. 163 commented that Korea's compensation demands were not wise and predicted that the FEC member countries would find them undesirable. The report wrote, "The Republic of Korea would undoubtedly advocate a punitive treaty and seek to obtain special guarantees for Korean residents in Japan" and this is the point Japan used to persuade the US. The logic grounded in the idea that the recognition of the Korean minority in Japan who were criminals and communists as Allied nationals would wreak havoc on the Japanese economy and politics and should therefore

---

71 *FRUS*, 1951, Vol. VI, p. 1011; "Supplementary Statement on Reparations for the Philippines and the Korean Government's Participation as a Peace Treaty Signatory (Supplementary Statement to the Conversation of Friday Morning, April 23, 1951), Ministry of Foreign Affairs of Japan, 2007, *Ibid.*, pp. 421-423.

be prevented proved effective.

In the end, Japan succeeded in persuading the US DoS by associating Korea's treaty participation and its signatory status with the Korean minority issue. It was the Yoshida cabinet that branded the Korean residents criminals and communists but SCAP had already raised similar concerns before the peace treaty negotiations. Also, the Korean government's policy on ethnic Koreans in Japan backfired, furthering the recognition of them as communists.[72]

Sebald, political adviser to SCAP, was certain that many of the approximately 600,000 Korean residents in Japan were communists and extremely opposed to Rhee Syngman.[73] Sebald and the Japanese government spoke the same language regarding the Korean minority. The most aggressive among them were Yoshida and Jiro Shirasu (1902–1985), Councilor of the Central Liaison Office, who was close to Yoshida. He was the go-between for the Japanese government and MacArthur's GHQ after the war. He drove a Porsche, was the one who introduced jeans to Japan, and was known in the country as the "man who reproached MacArthur." (In 2009, NHK produced a drama series based on his life.) Shirasu visited the SCAP Diplomatic Section on July 11, 1949 and expressed Yoshida's inclination to deport most of the Korean residents to the Korean peninsula at the Japanese government's expense. He added it was originally his idea and Yoshida accepted it.[74] Shirasu was Yoshida's private adviser and a friend

---

72 The following are referred to regarding Rhee Syngman's policy on Korean residents in Japan: Kim Tae-gi, 2000, "Cooperation and Conflicts between the Korean Government and the Federation of Korean Residents in Japan," Chonnam National University's Research Institute for Asia Pacific Rim, *Journal of Asia-Pacific Area Studies*, Vol. 3, No. 1; Kim Tae-gi, 1997, *Postwar Japanese Politics and the Issue of Ethnic Korean Residents in Japan*, Tokyo, Keiso Shobo Publishing.

73 Sebald, *With MacArthur in Japan*, p. 71.

74 Memorandum of Conversation by Cabot Coville (Jul. 11, 1949), Subject: Japanese Suggestion for Repatriation of Koreans, RG 84, POLAD for Japan, Classified General Record 1949, Box 48, Folder "350. Political Affairs-Korea"; Kim Tae-gi, 2001, "References 2: Yoshida Correspondences," The Association of Korean-Japanese National Studies, *The Journal of Korean-Japanese National Studies*, Vol. I, No. 1, pp. 267-278.

to many pro-Japanese US DoS officials including W. Walton Butterworth, Assistant Secretary of State for Far Eastern Affairs.[75]

Shirasu joined Minister of Finance Hayato Ikeda in his visit to Washington from April to May 1950[76] and Butterworth invited him to his home to talk. Shirasu set out his opinion that the best way to deal with 600,000 Korean residents was to deport them and it was "very unfair to burden the Japanese government, which intends to eventually pay all its debts to the US that are incurred during the occupation, with an obligation for this parasite group."[77] Shirasu's view of the Korean residents as a parasitic minority population was delivered even to the Secretary of State on May 3, 1950.[78] The view of Shirasu, Yoshida's personal adviser, was reported as the Prime Minister's own view. Shirasu was close enough to Butterworth to pay him a farewell visit on May 9, 1950.[79]

For his part, Yoshida sent a memo to MacArthur around August 1949 to argue for the deportation of the entire one million plus Korean resident

---

75 For instance, Shirasu was friends with Butterworth and his wife for 20 years: Memorandum of Conversation (May 1, 1950), Subject: Japanese Peace Treaty; Koreans in Japan; Japanese Political Forces, etc. by Green, NA. RG 59, Japanese Peace Treaty Files of John Foster Dulles, 1946-52, Lot 54D423, Box 8, Folder "Japanese Peace Treaty." Butterworth was also well acquainted with Count Aisuke Kabayama (1865-1953), Shirasu's father-in-law. Kabayama was the eldest son of Sukenori Kabayama (1837-1922), an admiral in the Imperial Japanese Navy and the first Japanese Governor-General of Taiwan. Aisuke Kabayama served as a member of the House of Peers (upper house of the Imperial Diet) and the President of the Japan-America Society and his second daughter, Masako Kabayama, married Shirasu.

76 Ikeda, as Yoshida's envoy, talked to Joseph Dodge, Ralph Reid, and others about the peace treaty. His visit was aimed at an early conclusion of a peace treaty by allowing US forces to stay in Japan (Michael M. Yoshitsu, *Japan and the San Francisco Peace Settlement*, New York: Columbia University Press, 1982, pp. 33-37).

77 "Memorandum of Conversation" (May 1, 1950), Subject: Japanese Peace Treaty; Koreans in Japan; Japanese Political Forces, etc., RG 59, Japanese Peace Treaty Files of John Foster Dulles, 1946-52, Lot 54D423, Box 3, Box 8.

78 Butterworth to the Secretary of State, Subject: Views of Mr. Jiro Shirasu on a Japanese Treaty (May 3, 1950), RG 59, Japanese Peace Treaty Files of John Foster Dulles, 1946-52, Lot 54D423, Box 3.

79 "Memorandum of Conversation" (May 9, 1950), Subject: Japanese Situation, RG 59, Japanese Peace Treaty Files of John Foster Dulles, 1946-52, Lot 54D423, Box 3

population, saying half of them were illegal immigrants. His reasons were ① that overpopulation could not be allowed due to the food situation in Japan and generous aid from the US could not be used to feed the Korean residents; ② that most of them did not contribute to economic reconstruction at all; and ③ that most of them were criminals. Yoshida contended that Japan "is willing to pay to the last penny its debts arising from US aid but it is unfair to leave debts incurred due to those Koreans to posterity." He emphasized that the Korean criminals were habitual offenders of economic laws and regulations; almost all of them were "communists and their sympathizers and likely to commit political attacks of the worst kind," and at least 7,000 of them were always in jail.[80] The statistics Yoshida submitted about the Koreans who were brought to trial during the years after the war are as [Table 5-1].

Yoshida said the Japanese government intended to deport all the Koreans at its sole expense and allow only "those believed to be able to contribute to Japan's economic reconstruction" to remain. His rejection of the Koreans who had been brought to Japan due to forced mobilization during the Pacific War or the colonial economic structure, and continued focus on labeling them as criminals and communists and deporting them reveals the degree of malice that postwar Japanese society held toward the Korean minority as well as the efforts to slander and maneuver against them in the context of Japan's relations with SCAP.

Sebald also strongly recommended their deportation in a memo to MacArthur (September 9, 1949) and suggested that the Korean Mission in Japan be permitted to enroll Koreans registered in Japan into its nationality.[81] He drafted a correspondence from MacArthur to Yoshida

---

80   Letter from Shigeru Yoshida to Douglas MacArthur (undated), MacArthur Archives (MA), RG 5, SCAP Official Correspondence, Box 3; Rinjirou Sodei, trans. & ed., 2000, *Shigeru Yoshida-Makkasa Ofuku Shokanshu (Correspondences between Shigeru Yoshida and MacArthur) (1945-1951)*, Tokyo, Hosei University Press.

81   Letter (Draft) (undated), enclosure to Memorandum for General MacArthur from W. J. Sebald (Sept. 9, 1949), MA, RG 5, SCAP Official Correspondence, Box 3; Kim, "References 2: Yoshida Correspondences".

[Table 5-1] Statistics Given by Yoshida to MacArthur on Crimes Committed by Korean Residents in Japan

Year	No. of cases	No. of Koreans involved
1945 (after August 15)	5,334	8,355
1946	15,579	22,969
1947	32,178	37,778
1948 (until May 13)	17,968	22,133
Total	71,059	91,235

where he wrote that illegal immigrants were to be deported, but they could be repatriated after the main issues between Korea and Japan were settled and voluntary return was preferred over deportation.[82] Sebald's view of Korean minorities in Japan proved to have an important effect on the 1951 Korea-Japan Talks.

This contemptuous view of the Koreans in Japan to be squashed "as a parasite group", consistently demonstrated by the words of Yoshida, Shirasu, and Sebald, did not at all consider imperial Japan's colonial policies and forced mobilization that had brought Koreans to Japan in the first place. All that was wanted was their complete eradication and banishment. No matter how rational they made it sound, their true purpose remained clear.

---

82   Kim, "References 2: Yoshida Correspondences".

Chapter 6

The Korean Government's Response to the Treaty of Peace with Japan and Korea-US Negotiations (1951)

1

The Korean Government's Preparations for the Peace Treaty from 1948 to 1950

1) Four items on the agenda: Reparations, participation in the treaty, territorial issues, and the MacArthur Line

News of the peace treaty with Japan arrived in 1947 even before official establishment of the Korean government. Korea's preparations for the treaty mainly revolved around four items.

The first was reparations it would receive from Japan. This issue began to gain traction in 1947 when the South Korean Interim Government was in place. The visit to Korea by the US reparations mission led by Edwin W. Pauley in 1946 raised Korean interest and the Interim Government made a wholehearted attempt to launch a research project in this regard in August 1947, which came up with a figure of damages worth 41,092,507,868 yen as of late April 1948. As such, Korea had worked out the details, amount, and logic of its claim for compensation against Japan before establishment of its own government.

Once the ROK government was established, its Ministry of Finance announced "References on the demand for reparations from Japan" (October 9, 1948), the National Assembly adopted a "Petition for a claim against Japan for the payment of unpaid wages to forced laborers" and a "Petition for a claim for compensation against Japan for the deaths of young adults and middle-aged people" (November 27, 1948), and a "Claims Commission against Japan" was established under the Ministry of Planning (February 1949).[1] As a result of these organized efforts and

---

1   Park Jin-hui, 2008, *Korea-Japan Talks: the First Republic's Policy toward Japan and the*

research activities, the Ministry of Planning completed Volume 1 of its "Report on the Demand for Reparations from Japan" on March 15, 1949 and submitted it to SCAP on April 7.[2] The second volume about general reparations was completed in September 1949, which demanded a total of 31,400,975,303 yen or four million Shanghai dollars in claims.[3] In spite of all this research, SCAP rejected Korea's claims against Japan.

The second was about acquiring the status of an Allied Power and therefore a signatory to the peace treaty. This was also taken up by the Interim Government. On August 27, the South Korean Interim Legislative Assembly (SKILA) Chairman, Kim Gyu-sik, requested in Telegram 306 from Seoul to the US Department of State (DoS) that Korea be able to participate in the peace conference. The Working Group on Japan Treaty at the US DoS, which received the telegram, sent a reply in the name of the US DoS indicating that they would do their best.[4] However, at the time, the US did not have a definite plan.

The third was territorial issues. On August 5, 1948, right before establishment of the ROK government, the Patriotic Old Men's Association sent a petition to Sebald to the effect that Dokdo, Ulleungdo, Tsushima, and Parangdo were Korean territory, so should revert to Korea.[5] This petition marks the first case where Korea claimed its territorial sovereignty before the Dokdo issue arose. The biggest issue after establishment of the government was reverting Tsushima to Korea. Dokdo, which became the object of public concern from 1947 to 1948, was not given important consideration then. President Rhee Syngman made an issue around the

---

Process of the Korean-Japan Talks, Sunin Book, pp. 47-59.

2   Yu Jin-o, 1966, "Until the Korea-Japan Talks Were Held: the Complications of 14 Years Ago Told by the Former Chief Delegate of Korea," Vol. 1, *Sasangge*, February Issue, p. 92.

3   Park, *Korea-Japan Talks*, p. 55.

4   Working Group on Japan Treaty (Sept. 3, 1947), RG 59, Office of Northeast Asia Affairs, Records Relating to the Treaty of Peace with Japan-Subject File, 1945-51, Lot 56D527, Box 5.

5   US Political Adviser for Japan no. 612 (Sept. 16, 1948). Subject: Korean Petition Concerning Sovereignty of "Docksum", Ulleungdo, Tsushima, and "Parang" Islands, RG 84, Japan, Office of US Political Adviser for Japan (Tokyo), Classified General Correspondence (1945-49, 1950-), Box 34.

request for reversion of Tsushima and the island was mentioned in Korea's written statement on the draft peace treaty. President Rhee claimed Korea's sovereignty over Tsushima immediately after he took office, a position which generated a fervent response from the press.[6] Japan's Prime Minister Hitoshi Ashida objected to this claim, arguing that it violated the Allied policy presented by the Atlantic Charter and the Potsdam Declaration.[7] Gal Hong-gi, head of the Bureau of Public Information, launched a full-fledged claim on Korea's sovereignty over Tsushima on September 9, 1948,[8] a stance held by the Korean government until 1949.

This position succeeded that of the SKILA and the Patriotic Old Men's Association of 1948, and its nature was basically political and punitive towards Japan. Due to the hard line taken by Korea, the US DoS Office of Intelligence and Research (OIR) did investigate the matter in earnest.[9] The OIR found Korea's claim to Tsushima to be a result of nationalism and anti-Japanese sentiment and a calculated appeal, and regarded it as an attempt to gain even a small concession from the Allied Powers. The US Embassy in Korea concurred with the OIR on this matter: it believed that the Korean government realized it was impossible to prove its sovereignty over Tsushima and would not claim it further.[10] Nevertheless, the Korean government once again demanded the reversion of Tsushima in its comments on a draft peace treaty in 1951. This claim by the Rhee Syngman government was politically motivated: it was foremost a way of reacting to the peace treaty and was also designed to seize the initiative in future talks between Korea and Japan to resolve bilateral issues.[11]

The fourth was the continuation of the MacArthur Line. The stance of the Korean government as well as Korean industry, commerce, and fisheries

---

6   "South Korea Files Claims to Japanese Tsushima Islands," *Stars and Stripes* (Aug. 19, 1948).

7   "Ashida Raps Korean Claim," *Stars and Stripes* (Aug. 19, 1948).

8   *Fisheries Economic Newspaper* (Sept. 10, 1948).

9   OIR Report no. 4900, "Korea's recent claim to the Island of Tsushima" (Mar. 30, 1950), RG 59, Japanese Peace Treaty Files of John Foster Dulles, 1946-52, Lot 543D423, Box 8.

10   *Ibid.*

11   Park Jin-hui, 2005, "Postwar Korea-Japan Relations and the Treaty of Peace with Japan," *Journal of Korean History Studies*, No. 131, p. 28.

was that the MacArthur Line was the minimum defense mechanism for the survival and development of the Korean fisheries industry.

2) The MacArthur Line at issue

On August 20, 1945, SCAP banned navigation of all Japanese water craft, including fishing vessels. At the request of Japan, then suffering from extreme food shortages after its defeat, permission was granted to wooden vessels to operate within 12 miles of the Japanese coast for fishing purposes in a SCAPIN dated September 14, 1945. SCAPIN No. 80 of September 27, 1945 authorized a limited deepwater fishing zone, the first so-called MacArthur Zone of 632,400 square miles. According to the previous studies, the MacArthur Line was extended three times, with the main aim of resolving food shortages.[12]

The first extension came with SCAPIN No. 1033 of June 22, 1946 (subject: Area Authorized for Japanese Fishing and Whaling), which allowed Japanese fishermen to operate in areas covering 864,000 square miles. The fishing area in the East China Sea nearly doubled in size. The MacArthur Line that is generally known in Korea is the one defined in this instruction. Paragraph 3 of the instruction stipulated, "Japanese vessels or personnel thereof will not approach closer than twelve (12) miles to Takeshima nor have any contact with said island."

The MacArthur Line was extended for a second time through SCAPIN No. 2046 of September 19, 1949. The Pacific area was extended 1,000 miles toward Midway and the Hawaiian Islands so that Japanese fishing vessels could travel as far as where they used to catch albacore before the war.[13]

The second extension was accompanied by the expansion of the navigation area of fishery patrol boats, namely, the surveillance area. SCAPIN No. 1033/2 about the Japanese fishery inspection system was

---

12   Bureau of State Affairs, Ministry of Foreign Affairs, 1954, *Theory of the Peace Line*, pp. 48-49; Ji Cheol-geun, 1979, *Peace Line*, Bumwoosa;

13   *Seoul Shinmun* (Sept. 22, 1949).

announced on June 30, 1949. It was about stationing 11 patrol boats along the MacArthur Line at all times to prevent violations of the fishery zone.[14] This was meant to limit operations by Japanese fishing vessels to the SCAP-defined areas. The Japanese Foreign Ministry expected this to be quite effective, but it ended up having no effect from the point of view of the Korean government. On the contrary, the Japanese patrol boats guided and protected Japanese fishermen in their illegal operations outside the boundaries of the line. The Japanese government interpreted the operation of Japanese patrol boats in this area as an easing of the former limit imposed on Japanese vessels as well as a promise that the MacArthur Line would be extended in the future. The navigation area of the patrol boats was almost twice the size of the Japanese fishing vessels' actual fishery zone to the southeast, which indicated to them their potential fishery zone.[15]

What is more surprising is that Korea's Jejudo was part of the surveillance area for these patrol boats.[16] This fact was never known before at the time. The appearance of Japanese fishery patrol boats in the waters around Jejudo was indicative of the constant violations of the island's waters by Japanese fishing boats as well as Korea's territorial waters being monitored by the patrol boats. These waters were not part of the Japanese fishery zone but were seen as part of the navigation area for the Japanese patrol boats.

SCAPIN No. 2046 of September 19, 1949 greatly increased the Japanese fishery zone in the Pacific, which reflected the existing navigation area of the patrol boats.

Korea first took notice of the MacArthur Line under US military rule. The Line was meant to define the boundaries of the fishery zone to prevent reckless advances that aimed to expand the *de facto* fishery zone

---

14   Kim Dae-yeong, 2004, "Reorganization of the Off-Shore Trawl Fishery in Japan," *Maritime Business*, No. 4, pp. 10-11.

15   Special Data Division, State Affairs Bureau, Ministry of Foreign Affairs of Japan, *Monthly Administration Report*, No. 2 (Jul. 1949), "Navigation by Fishery Patrol Boats," compiled and annotated by Takashi Ara, 1991, *Data Collection on the Occupation of Japan & Diplomatic Relations*, Vol. 10, pp. 15-16.

16   Special Data Division, State Affairs Bureau, Foreign Ministry of Japan, *Monthly Administration Report*, No. 2 (Jul. 1949), *Ibid.*, p. 15.

and prevent overfishing by Japanese fishing boats. It was also used as an occupation policy to prevent unnecessary clashes between Japan and its neighbors. Nevertheless, Japanese fishing vessels often violated the MacArthur Line and operated in the waters of Korea's Jejudo and southwest coast, heightening tension with Korean fishermen. This violation was due to SCAP entrusting the observance of the MacArthur Line to the Japanese government.[17] In a press conference during his visit to Korea (February 27, 1950), Harrington, responsible for fisheries at the SCAP Natural Resources Section, said that the responsibility for the supervision and control of the MacArthur Line had been transferred from SCAP to the Japanese government, and SCAP had its naval and air units keep watch and report on vessels violating the MacArthur Line.[18]

At the time, Korea saw the appearance of Japanese fishing vessels in its coastal waters as an intention to reinvade, not just a mere fisheries-related problem. Despite Korea's independence, the Japanese fishermen did not recognize the waters where they had operated with impunity just a few years ago as Korea's territorial waters.[19] Amid such discrepancy in perception, Korea objected to the extension of the MacArthur Line and demanded the seizure of Japanese fishing vessels in its waters while Japan pushed for the line's extension and opposed any attempts to seize Japanese vessels.

The capture of a Japanese fishing vessel named *Koryomaru*, which was fishing off Jejudo, by the Korea Coast Guard on February 4, 1947 was the first seizure by Korea of a Japanese fishing vessel in violation of the MacArthur Line.[20] With coverage by the Korean press of the MacArthur Line in mid-1947, Korea recognized it as a clear indication of Korean

---

17   Ji, *Peace Line*, p. 97 (O Je-yeon, 2005, "Peace Line and the Korea-Japan Treaty," *Critical Studies on Modern Korean History*, No. 14; re-quoted on p. 14).
18   *Kyunghyang Shinmun* (Feb. 28, 1950).
19   Jo Yun-su, 2008, "'The Peace Line' and South Korea-Japan Fishery Negotiation in 1965," *The Korean Journal for Japanese Studies*, No. 28, pp. 205-206; *Yonhap Shinmun* (Jun. 8, 1949).
20   Choi Jong-hwa, 2000, *History of Modern Korean-Japanese Fishery Relations*, Sejong Publishing, p. 16 (O Je-yeon, "Peace Line and the Korea-Japan Treaty," re-quoted on p. 14).

fisheries and a kind of maritime boundary that placed Dokdo within Korean territorial waters.

With the aggravating violations of the MacArthur Line by Japanese fishing boats in 1948, the US Army Military Government in Korea (USAMGIK) issued on April 17, 1948 an instruction (MGJUAS) numbered 546 in the name of USAMGIK Governor William Dean, ordering the capture of Japanese fishing boats violating the MacArthur Line. From December 1947 to August 1948, a total of some 20 Japanese fishing boats were seized for illegal trespassing and turned over to the customs offices in Mokpo, Yeosu, Jeju, Busan, and other ports. However, due to vehement protests by Japan and a SCAP request, another instruction (MGAGR No. 546) was issued three months later on July 28, 1948 to cancel the previous instruction about seizing Japanese fishing boats. It stipulated that the Japanese authorities should capture fishing vessels violating Korea's territorial waters, and when Japanese vessels violating the MacArthur Line were spotted, they should be monitored and reported instead of being captured.[21] The US military government sent back all the Japanese fishing vessels seized before establishment of the ROK government. This was the result of Japanese lobbying efforts to the effect that capturing vessels in international waters violated international law. It practically rendered the MacArthur Line ineffective.

The initial action by the US military government formed the basis for the ROK government's response to the actions taking place in relation to the Line. When it was reported in May to June 1949 that the Japanese government requested SCAP for an extension of the MacArthur Line, the popular movement to reject such an occurrence took on full momentum in Korea.[22] The National Assembly adopted a resolution against the extension

---

21 "Report by the Ministry of National Defense on the Maintenance or Abolition of the MacArthur Line and Korea's National Defense and Fishing Industry" (Jan. 31, 1949), *Monthly Administration Report*, No. 3, pp. 58-59; "MacArthur Line," *Cooperation*, Joseon Financial Cooperative Association, July 1949, Serial No. 23, p. 20; *Kyunghyang Shinmun* (Sept. 23, 1949).
22 "Korean Ambassador to Japan Instructed to Renegotiate Extension of the MacArthur Line," *Gangwon Ilbo* (Jun. 15, 1949); Lee Ji-sin, "The MacArthur Line and Korea's Fisheries",

at the 16th regular session of its third round on June 14, 1949. It argued that the extension and abolition of the MacArthur Line would be politically equivalent to the revival of Japanese aggression and ruin the Korean economy by destroying the Korean fishing industry and encouraging smuggling.[23] The Korean government made requests to SCAP for the restoration of the MacArthur Line to its original status and for the right to seize Japanese fishing boats violating the line through Ambassador Jeong Hwan-beom of the Korean Mission in Japan on May 16 and June 8, 1949.[24] SCAP denied Korea seizure rights and requested that it issue notifications to SCAP about such vessels.

The Korean government continued seizing Japanese fishing vessels until an incident involving SCAP on January 27, 1950. SCAP had prohibited it from seizing those that crossed the MacArthur Line unless they came within 3 miles of the Korean coast, and instead, instructed it only to report the names, tonnage, locations of the boats and other such information. The Korean government's understanding was that when it reported such information as locations, tonnage, the names of captains, and number of crew to SCAP, SCAP would cancel the fishing licenses of those boats.[25] According to Korean press reports on January 1, 1950, the number of seized Japanese fishing vessels was 9 in 1947, 15 in 1948, 4 in 1949, and 5 in 1950, bringing the total number to 33.[26] The confrontation came when the Korean Navy captured five Japanese fishing vessels including one named *Taiyoumaru* (550 tons) to the south of Seogwipo (on Jejudo) on January 12, 1950 for trespassing into Korea's territorial waters. In response, Japan rushed its patrol boats to Jejudo with SCAP permission and SCAP sent a disapproving correspondence to the Korean Mission in Japan on December 14, 1949 and again on January 20, 1950, asking "why fishing boats operating in international waters were seized." These correspondences were not

Saehan Minbo, Jun. 1949, Vol. 3, No. 14, pp. 11-13.

23 *The Third National Assembly Stenographic Records*, No. 16, pp. 349-350.

24 *Kyunghyang Shinmun* (Sept. 23, 1949).

25 *Jayu Shinmun* (Feb. 5, 1950).

26 *Seoul Shinmun* (Jan. 27, 1950).

relayed to the Korean government at home.[27]

On January 27, 1950, SCAP issued an order to send out US destroyers to seize all Korean Navy ships that interfered with the operation of Japanese fishing vessels in international waters. The destroyers were to leave port on the night of January 27 and 28. In the end, at noon on January 27, President Rhee Syngman ordered the Minister of National Defense to suspend the seizure of Japanese fishing vessels by the Navy and let the captured vessels go. The Korean Mission in Japan was instructed to notify SCAP that the Japanese fishing vessels and fishermen would be sent back and to apologize for the late reply.[28] Though it promised to suspend seizure and release detainees, the Korean government was indignant over the armed protest by the US Navy. The Japanese *Asahi Shimbun* reported on the front page on January 28 that President Rhee "made an apology to" SCAP, which incurred the Korean government's anger.[29]

President Rhee pointed out this incident in the memo sent to Ambassador to the US Yang You-chan in August 1951. According to the President, the Japanese fishermen intentionally crossed the MacArthur Line and allowed themselves to be caught to create a test case to resist seizure by the Korean Navy. US naval vessels showed up at the scene and pressured the Korean Navy to release the captured Japanese fishing vessels. They threatened to fire at the Korean Navy if they did not oblige. They promised SCAP would punish those offenders after they were released and almost 100 cases were transferred to SCAP, none of whom were punished in the end. Violations of the MacArthur Line sharply increased and four vessels were captured within 3 miles of the Korean coast.[30]

With the presidential statement on January 27, 1950 and the Korean

---

27 *Seoul Shinmun* (Jan. 28, 1951).

28 Joint Weeka, no. 5 (Feb. 5, 1950), pp. 212-215 (Re-quoted in *Korean History Seen through Data*); *Seoul Shinmun* (Jan. 27, 28, 29, 1950).

29 *Jayu Shinmun* (Feb. 5, 1950).

30 Memorandum by the President to Ambassador Yang (Aug. 3, 1951), compiled by the National Institute of Korean History, 1996, *Collection of Correspondences with Rhee Syngman Vol. 3 (1951): Korean History Data Collection Vol. 30*, pp. 330-337.

government's official memorandum the next day about the suspension of seizures of Japanese fishing vessels crossing the MacArthur Line, release of the seized vessels, and an apology to SCAP, Japanese fishing vessels began constantly violating the MacArthur Line, something which increased rapidly upon outbreak of the Korean War. In 1951 when the conclusion of a peace treaty became likely, the Korean government included the continuance of the MacArthur Line as an important agenda item for the peace treaty and Korea-Japan relations. On February 20, 1951, President Rhee sent instructions to Ambassador to Japan Kim Yong-ju, which included a tall order regarding the MacArthur Line.[31] He saw the preservation of the line as one of the key issues with Japan and instructed the ambassador to "allude" to the Korean government's hard line to the Japanese government and SCAP.

In general, there was not much preparation by the Korean government prior to the peace treaty. Issues they expected to be raised with regard to its relations with Japan included the old treaties between the two countries including the Japan–Korea Annexation Treaty, reparations, disposal of Japanese property in Korea, the MacArthur Line, and ethnic Korean residents in Japan. The Korean government assigned low priority to Korean-Japan relations and the peace treaty. The US and the UK, the leading parties of the peace conference, were in close contact with Japan, but Korea was not in the loop.

The Korean government began serious involvement in the peace treaty process from March 27, 1951 as the US DoS officially provided it with a draft treaty. By then, a general outline of the treaty had already been worked out between the US and Japan and they had agreed on major issues, leaving only partial revisions to be made.

---

31 "Korea-Japan Trade and Other Matters" (President to Ambassador Kim Yong-ju) (Confidential Instruction No. 2, Feb. 20, 1951), National Archives of Korea.

2

Provisional Draft Made Available to Korea (March 1951) and the Korean Government's First Reply (April 27, 1951)

1) Diplomatic efforts in Washington and Tokyo

Since the US decided to conclude the peace treaty early, the Korean government started to respond in earnest to it from January 1951.[32] Korean diplomats began to engage in diplomatic efforts related to the peace treaty in both Washington and Tokyo. They were fully engaged in the diplomatic effort to persuade the US Department of State (DoS) in Washington and SCAP in Tokyo.

Firstly in Washington, Korean Ambassador to the US, Chang Myun, requested that Korea be allowed to participate in the treaty negotiations and sign the treaty in correspondence dated January 14, 1951 to Secretary of State Dean Acheson based on the following two grounds:[33] first, the Provisional Government of Korea had been engaged in anti-Japanese belligerency, and sabotage and guerrilla and intelligence operations were carried out at its behest. Second, Korea had requested military support from the US, but had been rejected, nevertheless fighting with all its might.

Ambassador Chang met Assistant Secretary of State for Far Eastern Affairs Dean Rusk on January 17, 1951 to emphasize the importance of

---

32 Kim Tae-gi, 1999, "US Foreign Policy toward Korea in the Beginning of the 1950s: The US Political Position on the Exclusion of Korea from the Japanese Peace Treaty and the First Korea-Japan Talks", Korean Political Science Association, *Korean Political Science Review*, Vol. 33, No. 1 (Spring Issue), pp. 362-363; Lee Won-deok, 1996, *The Starting Point of Dealing with Past Affairs between Korea and Japan: Japan's Postwar Diplomacy and the Korea-Japan Talks*, Seoul National University Press, pp. 27-28.

33 John M. Chang, Korean Ambassador to Dean Acheson, Secretary of State (Jan. 4, 1951), RG 59, Department of State, Decimal File, 694.001/1-451.

Korea's presence at the treaty conference, and wrote to Secretary of State Acheson on January 20 to request that, if Korea could not be designated a signatory, the treaty signatories should agree on the commencement of separate peace negotiations to resolve Korea-Japan issues and normalize bilateral relations.[34] This was immediately before Chang, who had been appointed prime minister in November 1950, returned to Korea. On his way home, Chang stopped in Tokyo on January 25 and met Dulles the next day to demand that Korea have the right to participate in the treaty.[35] In response, Dulles said that the US planned to include Korea and would talk to its government in this regard in advance. As of January 1951, there was a positive expectation that Korea-US consultations would result in the US granting Korea a seat in the peace conference.

Secondly newspapers in Tokyo reported in January 1951 that the US would renounce the right to demand reparations and war indemnities. This was based on determination that the emergence of Hitler and the outbreak of WWII was because the Treaty of Versailles after WWI imposed huge reparations on Germany. Reading the reports, Ambassador Kim Yong-ju in Japan wrote to SCAP on January 20, 1951.[36]

The Korean Mission in Japan was mainly interested in property, namely, the disposal of Japanese property in Korea as well as the ownership of Korean-flag vessels, property owned by Crown Prince of Korea Yi Un, that of the Mutual Aid Association in Japan, and the like. Already in January 1949, President Rhee Syngman instructed Jeong Han-gyeong of the Mission to contact SCAP and settle the issue of reparations as soon as possible. As such, the Mission's efforts were focused on reparations.[37]

The stance taken by the Korean government of the time was evident in

---

34   John M. Chang, Korean Ambassador to Dean Acheson, Secretary of State (Jan. 20, 1951), RG 59, Department of State, Decimal File, 694.001/1-2051.

35   "Memorandum of Conversation," by Mr. Robert A. Fearey of the Office of Northeast Asian Affairs (Jan. 26, 1951), FRUS, 1951, Vol. VI, p. 817.

36   Kim Yong-sik, 1993, Promise of the Dawn, Gimm-Young Publishers, p. 83.

37   Seoul Shinmun Special Coverage Team, 1984, Secret History of Korean Diplomacy, Seoul Shinmun, p. 49.

the interview President Rhee had with an AP correspondent on January 26, 1951. Rhee declared that while he supported US policy on the peace treaty, he strongly believed that Korea, as Japan's closest neighbor, should be part of it. President Rhee also stated that the old treaties between 1905 and 1910 forced on Korea by Japan should be abolished and new treaties of trade and friendship be concluded. He promised Korea would not demand any "unreasonable reparations" from Japan.[38]

Meanwhile, the Korean government was seeking agreement within itself and at the National Assembly level regarding the peace treaty. An example of these efforts is a document found from the files of the Presidential Secretariat, "The National Assembly and Research on the Peace Treaty with Japan (February 28, 1951)."[39]

Rhee had instructed the Ministry of Foreign Affairs and the National Assembly to discuss the treaty in secret and not make relevant preparations public.

By then, having completed his first visit to Tokyo (January to February 1951), Dulles had got to work on a draft treaty to be distributed to the Allied Powers and the "Provisional Draft of a Japanese Peace Treaty (Suggestive Only)" was finalized in March, 1951.[40] This was different from the previous drafts written to be distributed internally among US officials: it was the first official draft for use in negotiations with external parties.

On April 1, 1951, Prime Minister Chang Myun sent a letter to John Moore Allison, who was responsible for the peace treaty at the US DoS, to request the status of a negotiating party for Korea and to be made aware of the content of the provisional draft.[41] At the same time, Chang requested preservation of the MacArthur Line. Korea's requests that were fixed in

---

38   *Minju Shinbo* (Jan. 28, 1951).

39   "National Assembly and Research on the Peace Treaty with Japan" (President → Minister of Foreign Affairs) (Confidential Instruction No. 3, Feb. 28, 1951), National Archives of Korea.

40   RG 59, Office of Northeast Asia Affairs, Records Relating to the Treaty of Peace with Japan-Subject File, 1945-51, Lot 56D527, Box 1.

41   John Myun Chang, Prime Minister to John M. Allison, State Department Specialist (Apr. 1, 1951), RG 59, Department of State, Decimal File, 694.001/4-151.

stone at this time were its participation in the peace negotiations and the continuation of the SCAP fishery zone. In a reply on April 25, Allison stated that a copy of the Provisional Draft of March 1951 had already been distributed to the Korean side.[42]

At the point when Chang asked for information on the draft treaty, the US DoS had already handed it over to the Korean Embassy in Washington, DC Han Pyo-wook, who then served as First Secretary at the embassy, recalled that the embassy began to fully engage itself in Korea-Japan affairs from around March 1951 and informed the Korean government of the content of the draft on March 27, 1951.[43] The draft had been passed to the embassy after Chang left the US capital.

It was the "Provisional Draft" finalized on March 23, 1951 that the US DoS provided to the Korean government. The US distributed this draft to 14 Allied Powers and Japan on March 27, 1951 and also to Korea, which was very unusual. The non-FEC member countries, which were not involved in the occupation of Japan but still received the Provisional Draft, were precisely three, namely, India, Korea, and Ceylon.[44] This hints that the US then considered inviting Korea to participate in or sign the peace treaty.

2) Seoul's response: Establishment of the Foreign Affairs Committee

How did the Korean government react when it received the "Provisional Draft" on March 27, 1951 via the Korean Embassy in the US? At this critical juncture, once the draft had been reviewed, all the major diplomatic posts of the Korean government in Washington and Busan were either vacant or being reshuffled. Prime Minster Chang, the only person who had ever dealt with the peace treaty in diplomatic terms took up a key role in the

---

42   John M. Allison to John Myun Chang, Prime Minister (Apr, 25, 1951), RG 59, Department of State, Decimal File, 694.001/4-1551.

43   Han Pyo-wook, 1996, *Rhee Syngman and Korean-US Diplomatic Relations*, Joongang Ilbo (1984 revised edition of *The Initial Stages of Korea-US Diplomatic Relations*), p. 260.

44   Department of State (Allison) to POLAD Japan (Sebald) (Mar. 23, 1951), RG 59, Department of State, Decimal File, 694.001/3-2351.

administration and Yu Jin-o, who had dealt with reparations since the Interim Government days, took up a similar role outside government.

Government records that clearly describe the situation at the time have not been found, but based on several testimonies and references, a Foreign Affairs Committee (Committee to Prepare for the Treaty of Peace with Japan) was established under the Ministry of Foreign Affairs on April 16, 1951, with seven to nine people designated as members. The references available commonly mention the names of Minister of Justice Kim Jun-yeon, Korea University President Yu Jin-o, Bae Jeong-hyeon (lawyer), and head of the Bureau of Judicial Affairs of the Ministry of Justice Hong Jin-gi in addition to the Minister of Foreign Affairs and the Prime Minister. They were all engaged in the field of law. A report on the draft to the Korean President was written on March 27 by Kim Sae-sun, a councilor at the Korean Embassy in the US.[45] The President replied to the report, stating that he had already received a draft copy via a personal connection before Washington provided an official one and that he would discuss it with the Prime Minister and cabinet and inform of the results.[46] He mentioned that the draft was being reviewed and that he had instructed the Prime Minister to write a letter to Dulles about the MacArthur Line, not about the Korean government's comments on the draft.[47]

Prime Minister Chang wrote to Dulles on April 10, where he appraised the draft as "very neutral" and pointed out that the Korean government would be affected by the results of a treaty fully debated by the Allied Powers.[48] He also stated that the Korean government got its hands on the draft just a few days ago and was carefully studying it. He cited as the most important concern fishery rights: he argued that as Japanese fishing vessels

---

45   Letter by President to Sae Sun Kim (Apr. 10, 1951), compiled by the National Institute of Korean History, 1996, *Collection of Correspondences with Rhee Syngman Vol. 3 (1951): Korean History Data Collection Vol. 30*, pp. 176-177.

46   *Ibid.*, p. 177.

47   *Ibid.*, pp. 179-180.

48   Letter by John Myun Chang to John Foster Dulles (Apr, 10, 1951), compiled by the National Institute of Korean History, 1996, *Collection of Correspondences with Rhee Syngman Vol.3 (1951): Korean History Data Collection Vol. 30*, p. 183.

were encroaching on Korean fishing grounds, the current MacArthur Line should be included in the text of the treaty. Chang added that he would write to General MacArthur regarding the line. In his April 10 letter to the general, Chang provided statistics on Japanese fishing vessels seized by the Korean government in 1951 and demanded strong action against Japanese violations of the Line.[49] He wrote to MacArthur that Japanese fishing vessels were intentionally crossing the line and stressed the need for the line to be permanently preserved.

The progress up to this point can be summarized as follows: first, the March 27 report about the draft by Kim Sae-sun was sent to Seoul after April 3 along with other correspondence. Second, the Korean government, including the Prime Minister and relevant ministers, started discussing it before April 10 with President Rhee at the helm of the discussion. Third, the Korean government had already obtained a copy through a personal connection before the embassy was able to send an official one. Fourth, the Korean government replied to Dulles on April 10 under the name of Chang Myun to confirm its receipt of the draft.

The next step is to look at the gist of the Provisional Draft reviewed by the Foreign Affairs Committee through the table of contents:

Provisional Draft of a Japanese Peace Treaty (Suggestive Only)

(Preamble)

Chapter 1 Peace: Article 1

Chapter 2 Sovereignty: Article 2

Chapter 3 Territory: Articles 3 to 5

Chapter 4 Security: Articles 6 to 7

Chapter 5 Political and Economic Clauses: Articles 8 to 13

Chapter 6 Claims and Property: Articles 14 to 16

Chapter 7 Settlement of Disputes: Article 17

Chapter 8 Final Clauses: Articles 18 to 22[50]

---

49   *Ibid.*, pp. 186-187.

50   "Provisional Draft of a Japanese Peace Treaty (Suggestive Only)," Allison to Sebald (Mar. 23,

In the Provisional Draft, Korea was explicitly mentioned in Article 3 of Chapter 3 (Territory) that reads, "Japan renounces all rights, titles and claims to Korea, Formosa and the Pescadores."[51] However, it is hardly mentioned throughout the rest of the document. Articles 14 and 15 about claims were of significant importance regarding the disposal of Japanese property in Korea and Korean property in Japan. As such, the Korean government's reply (April 27, 1951) emphasized these matters, which were issues at the core of Korea's interests.

Japanese property in Korea had been transferred to the Korean government through the US military government. Immediately after its defeat, the Japanese argued that private property owned by Japanese citizens could not be confiscated according to Article 46 of the 1907 Hague Convention.[52] This refers to Article 46 of the Laws of War: Laws and Customs of War on Land (Hague IV) (October 18, 1907) adopted at The Hague International Peace Conference. The article reads, "Family honour and rights, the lives of persons, and private property, as well as religious convictions and practice, must be respected. Private property cannot be confiscated."[53] The Japanese who had lived in Korea and returned to Japan tried to get their property back through their government and used the Hague Convention and its laws. This was used as a basis for the return of overseas property as well as Japan's property claims against Korea at the San Francisco Peace Conference and the Korea-Japan talks. The returnees argued that their overseas property was used for the public interest as reparations and thereby the Japanese government should compensate them for it. In 1967, after the normalization of Korea-Japan relations, the Japanese government interpreted Article 46 of the Hague Convention

---

1951), RG 59, Department of State, Decimal File, 694.001/3-2351.

51　The original text reads as follows: 3. Japan renounces all rights, titles and claims to Korea, Formosa and the Pescadores.

52　Hong Jin-gi, 1962, "My Time in Prison," *Sinsajo*, February Issue, pp. 190-191.

53　The original text reads as follows: Art. 46. Family honour and rights, the lives of persons, and private property, as well as religious convictions and practice, must be respected. Private property cannot be confiscated (http://avalon.law.yale.edu/20th_century/hague04.asp: accessed on April 24, 2009).

about the obligation of occupation forces regarding private property and similar matters as referring to the responsibility of aggressor countries under international law that had seized private property, not to that of the home countries of the victims. This was resolved whereby the state was awarded justification and denied legal obligations while the returnees profited personally from the damages.[54]

Regarding the disposal of Japanese property in Korea, both Yu Jin-o and Hong Jin-gi confirmed that President Rhee at first did not understand and objected to this.[55] According to Yu Jin-o, Ambassador Muccio intervened through Choi Du-seon and then Rhee turned around and agreed to it.

After some argument, the Foreign Affairs Committee chose ① Korea's participation in the San Francisco Peace Conference, ② Japanese property in Korea and Korea's claims to Japan, ③ fisheries, ④ trade, and ⑤ Korean residents in Japan as major items to deal with.[56]

3) The Korean Government's first reply (April 27, 1951) and request for the return of Tsushima

What was said in the Korean government's reply to the Provisional Draft? According to *FRUS*, there was no Korean reply to Dulles' first draft, the March 1951 Provisional Draft.[57] Han Pyo-wook, the First Secretary of the Korean Embassy in the US, also testified that no instruction was provided by the home government until July 1951, four months after the draft was sent.[58] However, this is far from the truth.

---

54 Jeong Byeong-uk, 2005, "Activities by the Joseon Government General Officials after Their Return to Japan and Korea-Japan Talks: Centering on the Donghwa Association and Central Japanese-Korean Association in the 1950s and 1960s," *Critical Studies on Modern Korean History*, No. 14, pp. 87-88; Kim Gyeong-nam, 2008, "Return of Japanese Residents from Joseon and Postwar Recognition of Korea," *Journal of Northeast Asian History*, No. 21.

55 Yu, "Until the Korea-Japan Talks Were Held," Vol. 1, p. 96; Hong, "My Time in Prison," p. 191.

56 Hong, "My Time in Prison," p. 191.

57 *FRUS*, 1951, Vol. VI, p. 1183 (Lee Won-deok, *The Starting Point of Dealing with Past Affairs between Korea and Japan*, p. 34, re-quoted in Note 46).

58 Han, *Rhee Syngman and Korean-US Diplomatic Relations*, p. 260.

The Korean government sent a reply immediately to the US DoS, which was found among the US DoS files and Rhee Syngman correspondences. First, it was found in the US DoS Decimal File series 694.001. Kim Sae-sun of the Korean Embassy in the US sent the Korean Government's Official Comments and Suggestions on the Provisional Draft of a Japanese Peace Treaty (April 27, 1951) to Secretary of State Acheson on May 7, 1951.[59]

In addition, *Collection of Correspondences with Rhee Syngman Vol. 3 (1951): Korean History Data Collection Vol. 30* carries two replies.[60] The same book also carries the Korean government's first reply under the title of "Rough Draft - For Comment and Suggestion."[61] The content is the same as what was written by Kim Sae-sun and Korean Ambassador to the UN Im Byeong-jik.

Now, let us look at the reply received by the US DoS. The Korean government's comments and suggestions consist of eight pages written on official embassy letterhead. The date indicated on the reply is April 27, 1951 but it must have been written earlier considering its delivery via diplomatic bag. This reply of April 27, 1951 carries significance in several aspects:

First, the Korean government received the draft treaty in the capacity of a potential negotiating party/signatory to the treaty. It was not clear whether its status was as an Allied Power or a negotiating party/signatory, but it was evident that Korea would be invited to the negotiating table. As such, the Korean government needed to take appropriate and definite response. What Korea emphasized in its reply was its "past value" including the Provisional Government of Korea's declaration of war against Japan and activities by its Independence Army during the war, but the reason why Dulles and the US DoS wanted to include Korea was its "present value" in

---

59   Sae Sun Kim, Charge d'Affaires a.i., to the Secretary of State (Dean Acheson) (May 7, 1951), RG 59, Department of State, Decimal File, 694.001/5-751.

60   Letter by B. C. Limb, Permanent Representative of Korea to the United Nations to John Foster Dulles (Apr, 26, 1951), compiled by the National Institute of Korean History, 1996, *Collection of Correspondences with Rhee Syngman Vol.3 (1951): Korean History Data Collection Vol.30*, pp.233-236.

61   Rough Draft-For Comment and Suggestion, compiled by the National Institute of Korean History, *Ibid.*, pp. 376-381.

the fight against communism to protect the free world.

Second, its comments and suggestions regarding the Provisional Draft formed the basis of Korea's response to the Treaty of Peace with Japan and provided guidance for the US to decide the level of its response to Korea's requests. The reply was the starting point of Korea's response to the treaty and served as the basis of the US response to it. What was required of Korea was the presentation of rational, credible, and consistent arguments and requests in its reply to render them more persuasive and appealing. This would have been possible only by clearly understanding what the US wanted from Korea at this time and why it wanted Korea's presence at the treaty.

Third, although the US provided Korea with a copy of the draft treaty, it did not inform the latter of the process and context in which the draft was discussed, drawn up, and determined; what the UK and other Allied Powers thought of it; and how it was coordinated with Japan. Korea had no idea of what the US was aiming for with the treaty and just received the draft, itself only a fragment of US policy toward Japan. Without an understanding of the context and process that led to the creation of the draft, it was difficult for Korea to properly voice its related opinions. Moreover, its preparations for the peace treaty and conference were inadequate in general, unlike Japan which had spent five full years (since 1945) in such preparations and had sufficiently talked to and negotiated with the US before it even received the draft. Simply put, Korea lagged behind markedly in its preparations. Its comments and suggestions on the draft correspond to the table of contents of the Provisional Draft. Namely, the reply starts with Korea's comments on the Preamble, proceeds with those on Chapter 3 (Territory), Chapter 4 (Security), Chapter 5 (Political and Economic Clauses), Chapter 6 (Claims and Property), Chapter 7 (Settlement of Disputes), and Chapter 8 (Final Clauses), and offers its thoughts and suggestions at the end. The most elaborate and lengthy part is related to Chapter 6. The essence is as follows:

Korean Government's Official Comments and Suggestions on the Provisional Draft of a Japanese Peace Treaty (April 27, 1951)

Preamble

① The Korean Government believes that it is important that the term, "the Allied Powers," as used throughout the draft be defined to include specifically the Republic of Korea.

② The status of the ROK in the Treaty of Peace with Japan is similar to that of Poland in the Treaty of Versailles. The fact that the Provisional Government of Korea declared war on Japan during WWI and organized military units and fought against the Japanese Army in Manchuria and mainland China meets the qualifications of an "Ally" defined in Article 18 of the Provisional Draft of a Japanese Peace Treaty. This is also directly implied in the memo (provided together with the draft by the US) which listed the ROK as one of the nations consulted before the writing of the Provisional Draft. (omitted)

④ …some seven hundred thousand Korean nationals now resident in Japan are entitled to all the rights, privileges and protection accorded to the nationals of the other Allied Powers.

Chapter 3 Territory

⑤ …the Government of the ROK requests that a thorough study be given to the territorial status of the Islands of Tsushima. Historically, the two islands called Tsushima were Korean territory until forcibly and unlawfully taken over by Japan. (omitted) …the ROK requests that Japan specifically renounce all right, title and claim to the Islands of Tsushima and return them to the ROK.[62]

Chapter 6 (Claims and property)

⑧ The Republic of Korea has made no claim for reparations. (omitted)
All property which existed in Korea between December 7, 1941 and September 2, 1945 and was owned by Japan and its nationals should be reverted to Korea according to Article 14 of the Provisional Draft.

---

62 A working-level US Department of State official wrote "ho" here.

The Korean government's first reply (April 27, 1951) was part of closed-door negotiations, so it was not publicly known in Korea. It was made public only after Dulles notified Ambassador Yang You-chan that most of Korea's requests were declined on July 9, two months after the reply was delivered to the US. The content of Korea's reply summarized and provided to the press by Ambassador Yang is as follows:

(1) The term "the Allied Powers" used in the draft should specifically include the Republic of Korea. This opinion of Korea is based on the fact that the Provisional Government of Korea declared war on Japan during WWII and Koreans fought against the Japanese Army in Manchuria and mainland China. This is sufficient for the ROK to be qualified as an Allied Power. The status of Korea in the Treaty of Peace with Japan is similar to that of Poland in the Treaty of Versailles. Poland was part of the treaty.

(2) As Korea currently is only an observer at the UN, any status which may be acquired by Japan in connection with membership in the UN should not exceed that enjoyed by the ROK.

(3) Korean residents in Japan should be able to enjoy a status equal to that held by the nationals of the other Allied Powers, but are in fact denied that.

(4) Japan should renounce rights to Tsushima. It was historically Korean territory but Japan illegally occupied it.

(5) It is desirable that the Allied Powers develop some method or formula to prevent Japan from developing armament that could constitute a threat to Korean security.

(6) The fishing zones of Korea and Japan should be clearly defined in the treaty.

(7) Korean rights regarding its relations with Japan should be equally protected as those of the Allied Powers having prewar bilateral treaties with Japan. Korea was not able to conclude treaties while held under Japanese domination.

(8) Any so-called "treaties" between Japan and Korea should be considered null, void, and of no effect whatsoever.

(9)   The ROK has made no claim for reparations. It is the belief of the Korean government that most questions related to reparations can be settled by a separate bilateral treaty between the two countries.

(10) The Korean government requests that it be made a party to the International Court of Justice to settle issues with other nations.[63]

This reply can be summarized as requesting ① that Korea be granted the status of an Allied Power and a signatory to the treaty and Korean residents in Japan the status of Allied nationals; ② the return of Tsushima; ③ recognition of the confiscation of Japanese property in Korea; and ④ preservation of the MacArthur Line. Among these requests, ① was a political decision to be decided by the US and, as indicated in the DRF recommendation in 1949, the US was considering having Korea at the peace conference and allowing some of its requests to be submitted or inviting it as a "negotiating party," not as an Allied Power or signatory.[64] That is, at this point in time, the US DoS saw the position of Korea as being between an Allied Power/signatory and a negotiating party.

What was directly connected to Korea's political and economic interests was ③ the recognition of the confiscation of Japanese property in Korea. There was not much difference of opinion between Korea and the US in this regard.

On the other hand, ② the return of Tsushima and ④ preservation of the MacArthur Line were the subjects of great controversy. The return of Tsushima was supposed to be a strategic political move for Korea, but in reality, it was impossible to realize. The preservation of the MacArthur Line was given much importance in relation to *realpolitik*, being directly related to the fishing industry. After its receipt of the Provisional Draft from the US DoS, the Korean government took an even harder stance on the MacArthur Line. Prime Minister Chang sent a letter to General

---

63   *Kyunghyang Shinmun* (Jul 13, 1951).

64   DRF Report (Dec. 12, 1949), RG 59, Japanese Peace Treaty Files of John Foster Dulles, 1946-52, Lot 54D423, Box 7.

MacArthur in Tokyo on April 7 and 10 to strongly protest the violation of the MacArthur Line by Japanese fishing vessels.[65]

In general, the Korean government's reply was strongly worded. Its requests for the return of Tsushima, association of Japan's UN membership with that of Korea, and the like were difficult to be received in a positive manner by the international community, leading the rest of the world to doubt the overall integrity, credibility, and genuineness of the reply. It was a mixture of just, excessive, and unreasonable requests and arguments, showing that the Korean government had not yet clearly worked out its strategic priorities in its response to the Treaty of Peace with Japan.

The argument for the return of Tsushima in particular gave the impression that Korea, a "liberated nation after WWII" was making an excessive request in asking Japan to cede territory.

This reply was forwarded by Kim Sae-sun of the Korean Embassy in the US and was received by the US DoS at 8:43 am on May 7, 1951. The US DoS entrusted it to the Office of Northeast Asian Affairs (NA) and the working-level official who reviewed the reply wrote memos on it with a pencil. According to the "Japanese Peace Treaty Files of John Foster Dulles," the official who reviewed the reply was none other than Robert A. Fearey.[66]

The only part Fearey approved of was where all the title to Japanese property in Korea had already been vested in the Korean government according to USAMGIK Ordinance No. 33 (1945) and the Initial Financial and Property Settlement between the US Government and the ROK Government (1948). Here, Fearey wrote, "...probably how to put in a special article to provide for this."

Fearey summarized the Korean comments under 11 numbered items and these were entered into a document titled "Comments on Korean Note Regarding US Treaty Draft" on May 9, 1951.[67] Fearey was assigned to the

---

65   John Myun Chang to MacArthur (Apr. 10, 1951), RG 59, Japanese Peace Treaty Files of John Foster Dulles, 1946-52, Lot 54D423, Box 8.

66   "Korea File," (undated), RG 59, Japanese Peace Treaty Files of John Foster Dulles, 1946-52, Lot 54D423, Box 8. According to this, Fearey wrote the May 9 comments.

67   "Comments on Korean Note Regarding US Treaty Draft," RG 59, Japanese Peace Treaty

Office of the US Political Adviser for Japan in October 1945 and to the US DoS Bureau of Far Eastern Affairs in mid-1946 to work as a Japan specialist and at the Office of Northeast Asian Affairs.

4) The US Department of State's comments (May 9, 1951)

It is now appropriate to look at the review of the Korean government's comments by the US DoS. The "Comments on Korean Note Regarding US Treaty Draft" is a simple two-page document which summarized the Korean requests under 11 items:

1. Korea should be specifically designated an Allied Power.
2. Korea should be permitted to sign the treaty, as Poland was the Versailles Treaty.
3. Japan's admission to the UN should be tied to Korea's.
4. Koreans in Japan should be accorded the status of Allied nationals.
5. Tsushima should be "returned" to Korea.
6. Korea should be included in any Pacific security system.
7. The "MacArthur (fishing) Line" between Korea and Japan should be preserved in the treaty.
8. Korea should be permitted to confiscate all Japanese property in Korea without regard to the exceptions listed in our draft.
9. Korea should have the same right as the Allied Powers to the restoration of Korean property in Japan.
10. "Korea requests that it be made a party to the International Court of Justice."
11. Korea should be specifically included as an Allied Power.[68]

Firstly, about Korea's request to be designated an Allied Power, the

---

Files of John Foster Dulles, 1946-52, Lot 54D423, Box 8.

[68] "Comments on Korean Note Regarding US Treaty Draft," (May 9, 1951), RG 59, Japanese Peace Treaty Files of John Foster Dulles, 1946-52, Lot 54D423, Box 8.

commenter wrote that, "Korea's status as an Allied Power will of course be made clear if it is decided to include Korea in the list of potential signatories in the Preamble of the May 3 draft." By then, the status of Korea as an Allied Power or signatory had not yet been decided.

About the second request, he wrote, "On examination, Korea's case for participation in the treaty does not gain much support from the example of Poland after World War I." His appraisal was that "the fact that government ("Provisional Government of Korea") declared war on Japan, and that Korean elements, mostly long-time residents in Korea, fought with the Chinese forces, would therefore have no significance in our view."

He was also negative about the third request: "The intention in this paragraph is apparently to ensure that Japan is not admitted to the UN if Korea is not. There would seem to be no basis for this position."

On the fourth request for the status of Allied nationals for Koreans in Japan, the commenter quoted the memorandum of April 23, written by Yoshida, where the Japanese government said that it would not persist in its opposition to Korea being a signatory to the treaty "if it is definitely assured that by the said treaty Korean residents in Japan will not acquire the status of Allied Power nationals." He expressed agreement with the Japanese government and rejected the position of the Korean government by writing, "It is believed that the Japanese Government should be allowed after the treaty, and after stability is reestablished in Korea, to require all Korean residents in Japan to opt for Japanese citizenship or to submit to repatriation to Korea."

Fifth, he commented, "Korea's claim to Tsushima is extremely weak."

Sixth, he regarded Korea being party to a Pacific security system as "being ultimately desirable," but further stated that, "nothing can be promised now."

About the seventh request for the MacArthur Line to be preserved in the treaty, he wrote, "The position that Japanese fishermen should be permanently excluded from the fishing grounds on the Korean side of the MacArthur Line even exceeds the requests of our West Coast fishing people, and would in fact be far more serious for the Japanese fishing industry. The Korean demand should be denied for its direct effects..." He added, "Contrary to the impression conveyed by the Korean Government's note, no nation had any bilateral treaties with Japan excluding Japanese fishing vessels from high seas areas adjacent to other nations."

The eighth request to confiscate all Japanese property in Korea was accepted as "justified" without regard to the exceptions listed in the draft. The commenter wrote, "The new Article 5 of the US-UK May 3 draft takes care of it. The Korean Government seems, however, to have misunderstood our exception (iv) in Article 14 of the US March draft. The exception was intended to refer to the following of paper assets into Japan but the Korean Government has interpreted it as exempting from confiscation by Korea physical property removed from Korea to Japan during the war." He further commented that, though the exception had been misunderstood, the Korean government was right in its understanding that Korea would only be permitted to retain properties which were within its territories between December 7, 1941 (the day war was declared) and September 2, 1945 (the day the instrument of surrender was signed).

Regarding the ninth request for the same rights as the Allied Powers in relation to the restoration of Korean property in Japan, the commenter regarded the issue as "simply a misunderstanding." He wrote that "Allied Powers" was intended to include Korea and the plan was to treat Korea as a member when the draft was handed over to Korea in March 1951. He continued on to say, "We have had second thoughts on this question, of course, since the March draft." This means that the US changed its mind and decided to exclude Korea.

Regarding the tenth request for Korea to join the International Court of Justice, he commented, "Article 17 of the US March draft makes special provision so that Allied Powers, not parties to the Court, may be empowered to enjoy the benefits of the treaty disputes provision."

About the eleventh request for Korea to be specifically included as an Allied Power, he took a reserved position as with the first request.

The above comments reflect the overall thought of the US DoS on the Korean comments. From its perspective, the requests by the Korean government can be largely divided into three categories:

First, to Americans, the reasonable requests were item 6 and 8, especially the one about Japanese property in Korea, an issue that had been settled through Korea-US agreements during the US occupation period and at the time of establishment of the Korean government.

Second, the acceptable requests were item 1, 2, 10, and 11. They were all about granting Korea the status of an Allied Power and signatory. The US made it clear that then-US policy on Korea would determine Korea's status. Korea's status was not to be acquired on its own, but to be granted by the US.

Lastly, the excessive and unreasonable requests were item 3, 4, 5, 7, and 9, which the US also saw as punitive against Japan and unreasonable. It is likely that the US saw the requests for the return of Tsushima and the preservation of the MacArthur Line as excessive reparations or even as a form of territory cession. Korea argued that just as Japan was ordered to hand over to the Soviet Union the southern part of Sakhalin as well as the islands adjacent to it and the Kuril Islands, Korea should be given the Islands of Tsushima. This created an impression that Korea, liberated through WWII, was making imprudent demands. The US objected to the indication of the MacArthur Line in the treaty and restrictions on Japanese fishing. It sided with Japan regarding the granting of Allied national status to Korean residents in Japan. It is likely that the Korean note gave a negative impression to the US DoS as its arguments were quite different from what the US had pursued under the principle of a "non-punitive peace treaty that excluded reparations."

As of May 9 when these comments were written, the US and UK had completed the first Anglo-American Meetings on the Japanese Peace Treaty and written the May 3, 1951 draft. At the time, Japan and the UK were critical about Korea's participation in the peace conference but the US maintained a positive attitude. The Korean reply arrived just at this point of time.

3

The US-UK Draft of July 1951 and the Korean Government's Response

1) Denial of Korea's status as a signatory by the US (July 9, 1951)

Korean and American officials met again two months later on July 9, 1951. Ambassador Yang You-chan visited Dulles, who was joined by Fearey and Arthur B. Emmons III, Officer in Charge of Korean Affairs in the Office of Northeast Asian Affairs. There was no other Korean attendee. They met at the request of the US government and it turned into an occasion where the US notified Korea of its decisions regarding Korea's participation in the peace treaty.[69]

Firstly, the US (Ambassador Dulles) handed Korea (Ambassador Yang) the latest draft of the Japanese peace treaty written on July 3, 1951. This was the third joint US-UK draft: it was sent to the concerned nations and was the first draft treaty made public. Dulles also stated that Ambassador Muccio would make a copy of the draft available to the ROK government as soon as possible. This was the second draft treaty received by Korea. Counselor of the US Embassy in Korea, E. Allan Lightner Jr. delivered a copy to Minister of Foreign Affairs Pyun Yung-tai in the afternoon of July 10 in Busan.[70] The reason the US provided Korea with the draft treaty was to encourage a bilateral treaty with Japan instead of permitting Korea to

---

69   Memorandum of Conversation (Jul, 9, 1951), Subject: Japanese Peace Treaty, RG 59, Japanese Peace Treaty Files of John Foster Dulles, 1946-52, Lot 54D423, Box 8; RG 59, Department of State, Decimal File, 694.001/7-951.

70   "Korean Foreign Minister's Comments on the Armistice" (Jul. 10, 1951), *Documents of the Division of Historical Policy Research of the US State Department, Korea Project File Vol. X: Korean War*, Vol. 35, p. 97.

participate in and sign the peace treaty.[71]

Secondly, Dulles pointed out to Yang that the ROK government would not be a signatory to the treaty, since only those nations which had been in a state of war with Japan and were signatories of the UN Declaration of January 1942 or the Atlantic Charter would sign. The exclusion of Korea had already been decided between May and June 1951. He pointed out, however, that Korea would benefit from all of the general provisions of the treaty equally with other nations. Yang expressed his surprise about the revelation that the ROK would not be included as a signatory, and protested that the Provisional ROK Government had in fact declared war against and been in a state of war with Japan. Fearey pointed out that the US government had never recognized the Provisional ROK Government.

Thirdly, Korea's request for the return of Tsushima was denied. Yang asked whether the islands of Tsushima were to be given to Korea under the terms of the treaty. Dulles pointed out that Japan had been in full control of Tsushima for a very long period of time, confirming Tsushima as Japanese territory, one of Japan's minor islands adjacent to Japan.

Fourthly, the MacArthur Line was discussed. Yang asked whether the treaty included provisions which would restrict Japanese fishing in waters in the vicinity of the Korean peninsula, pointing out that this matter, if not resolved, boded ill for future Korea-Japan relations. He stated that some 34 fishing vessels had recently been intercepted and their crews arrested by the ROK Navy while fishing in waters beyond the MacArthur Line. Dulles replied that the treaty did not include provisions which would govern fishing in "specific high seas areas."

In conclusion, the US notified Korea on July 9, 1951 that it rejected the most important requests made in the Korean government's first reply (April 27, 1951), namely, Korea's signatory status, the return of Tsushima, and preservation of the MacArthur Line.

---

71 "Summary of Negotiations Leading up to the Conclusion of the Treaty of Peace with Japan," Robert Fearey (Sept. 18, 1951), p. 13. RG 59, Office of Northeast Asia Affairs, Records Relating to the Treaty of Peace with Japan-Subject File, 1945-51, Lot 56D527, Box 1.

Now the response of the Korean government was bound to be cautious going forward. All the requests concerning Korea's most important interests had been rejected, and moreover, the content of the new draft was very threatening to it.

2) The Korean government's second reply (July 19, 1951)

On the same day, Secretary of State Acheson sent a telegram to the US Embassy in Busan to make known the meeting between Dulles and Yang and instructed a delivery of the July 3 draft to the Korean Ministry of Foreign Affairs.[72] The draft was announced in Washington, DC on July 12 and reported by the Korean press around July 14.[73] The Korean press called it the draft Treaty of Peace with Japan (joint US-UK Treaty).

Even before its announcement, concerns about the draft were raised in Korea. First, US Ambassador to Korea, Muccio, unaware of the progress on the peace treaty, sent Lightner to meet Allison and discuss Korea's position in Tokyo on June 29, 1951. The draft shocked Muccio. He appraised that, "the draft treaty did not give full consideration to Korea's interests or issues considered sensitive in Korea...Korea's position to negotiate is really ruled out."[74]

Muccio criticized the US Department of State (DoS), stating that it "should have a fully-open perspective on the situation" and "Korea is on the receiving end of irrational treatment from the perspective of equality based on exceptional grounds." He suggested to the US DoS that, "Under any circumstances, it is necessary to come up with a multilateral agreement to which the now anxious Korean government will be less likely to object

---

72 Acheson to the Amembassy, Pusan (Jul. 9, 1951), RG 59, Department of State, Decimal File, 694.001/7-951.

73 *Kyunghyang Shinmun* (Jul. 14, 1951).

74 "The US Ambassador to Korea Expressed Concerns about the Omission of Korea's Interests in the Draft Peace Treaty on July 4, 1951," *Documents of the Division of Historical Policy Research of the U.S. State Department, Korea Project File Vol. X: Korean War*, Vol. 35, pp. 179-180 (compiled by the National Institute of Korean History, 2006, re-quoted in Volume 22 of *Korean History Seen through Data*).

to."

The Korean press and political circles reacted extremely sensitively to the content of the treaty. According to press coverage, the July 1951 draft presented two major issues.[75] First, Korea was denied the status of an Allied Power and was regarded as territory given up by Japan. The Korean fight against the Japanese as well as the plunder and repression under Japan's colonial rule were not recognized at all. The second issue was Japan's claim to Japanese property in Korea.

This was when Korea's Foreign Affairs Committee, an advisory body under the Ministry of Foreign Affairs, was working on a reply and strong statements and demonstrations were being prepared to reinforce Korea's position. The Foreign Affairs Committee focused on three items of the draft regarding Korea's interests: Article 2 (a) about territory; Article 4 (a) about the disposition of Japanese property, and Article 9 about the MacArthur Line.

Korea's position was well represented in articles left by Yu Jin-o who participated in the Committee.[76] The issue that received the greatest interest from diplomatic circles, political groups, and the press was the disposition of Japanese property, with the second most important issue being the MacArthur Line. Territory was still of little concern.

Disposition of Japanese property (Article 4 (a) of the July 3, 1951 draft)

Article 4 (a) was like a bolt out of the blue in the opinion of the Korean government. Settling claims to Japanese property which had already been transferred to the Korean government through special arrangements with the Japanese government was equivalent to linking Korea's independence with the fate of Japan.[77]

Minister of Foreign Affairs Pyun Yung-tai pointed out in a press

---

75   *Minju Shinbo* (Jul. 6, 1951).

76   Yu Jin-o, "Review of the Draft Peace Treaty with Japan," seven-installment series, *Dong-A Ilbo* (Jul. 25 and 27-31, 1951); Yu Jin-o, 1963, *Path to Democracy*, Ilchokak, pp. 272-289

77   Yu, "Until the Korea-Japan Talks Were Held," Vol. 1, p. 94.

conference on July 16, 1951 that the draft included a "dangerous and vague provision" that entrusted the disposition of Japanese property to direct bilateral negotiations. Pyun said that the treatment of Japanese property in Korea had been determined by General MacArthur after the end of the war, Japanese property had been transferred to the ROK government through the Initial Financial and Property Settlement (September 11, 1948), and as such, the transfer was already completed and could not be reversed.[78] On the same day, Pyun stated at the National Assembly, "We are naturally entitled to seize property that was a result of exploitation by the Japanese for forty years according to the principles of justice and humanitarianism" and "Korea will never respond to calls for Korea-Japan bilateral negotiations."[79] The *Dong-A Ilbo* pointed out that the disposition of Japanese property, already decided according to USAMGIK Ordinance No. 33 and the Initial Financial and Property Settlement, could not be undone, and argued for the inclusion in the treaty of a line to the effect that, "Japan and its nationals shall renounce their title to any property they owned in Korea before August 9, 1945."[80]

The worst case scenario suggested then in Korea was where Korea was ① found to not have been in a state of war with Japan, ② not accorded the status of an Allied Power, and therefore ③ not entitled to compensation from Japan and having no title to Japanese property in Korea. In such a case, ④ even though Korea was to be compensated by Japan, the amount would be insignificant as compensation was meant to compensate the nationals of belligerents for war indemnities, and an enormous amount of Japanese property minus the small amount assigned to Korea would have to be returned to Japan.[81]

---

78 *Kyunghyang Shinmun* (Jul. 17, 1951).

79 *Dong-A Ilbo* (Jul. 17, 1951).

80 "Editorial: Draft Peace Treaty and Korea's Interests," *Dong-A Ilbo* (Jul. 18, 1951).

81 Yu, *Path to Democracy*, p. 286.

MacArthur Line (Article 9 of the July 3, 1951 draft)

The Korean position on the MacArthur Line was simple: include preservation of the MacArthur Line in Article 9 of the treaty.[82] Yu Jin-o pointed out that although the line was only established with the authority of the occupation force under international law, if it were to be abolished, almost all of the seas of Asia would be monopolized by Japanese fishing fleets, dealing the hardest blow to Korea.[83]

Territory (Article 2 (a) of the July 3, 1951 draft)

This provision specified that, "Japan, recognizing the independence of Korea, renounces all rights, titles and claims to Korea, including the islands of Quelpart, Port Hamilton and Dagelet." This is quite different from Article 3 of Chapter 3 (Territory) in the March 1951 Provisional Draft that read, "Japan renounces all rights, titles and claims to Korea, Formosa and the Pescadores" in that firstly this provision added recognition of Korea's independence by Japan and secondly mentioned Jejudo, Geomundo, and Ulleungdo as Korea's annexed islands.

The Korean interpretation of the first difference was that, if Korea became independent through the Treaty of Peace with Japan, it would contradict the fact that it had already been independent and its independence had been recognized by the UN and many different nations. Korea became independent on August 9, 1945 when Japan accepted the Potsdam Declaration without regard to Japan's independent recognition of this fact.[84]

In addition, Yu took issue with the mentioning of the names of only three individual islands in the treaty while there existed hundreds and even thousands of ancillary islands of Korea. He expressed his concern

---

82 *Kyunghyang Shinmun* (Jul. 17, 1951); *Dong-A Ilbo* (Jul, 18, 1951).
83 Yu, *Path to Democracy*, p. 287.
84 Yu Jin-o pointed out that the initial day in reckoning specified in USAMGIK Ordinance No. 33 (December 6, 1945) was August 9, 1945. (Yu, *Path to Democracy*, pp. 276-277).

over how to mark those other islands and the nation might be left in fear of an "absurd future argument" where only these islands were returned to Korea and the others still remained Japanese territory. On account of this possibility, he stated that the paragraph should be revised so as not to leave any question about the sovereignty of islands belonging to Korea.

Yu contended that Dokdo needed to be specifically mentioned in the treaty to prevent future Korea-Japan disputes and this was due to the influence of Choi Nam-seon. Yu recalled that he first visited Choi to discuss the draft and came to demand Dokdo and Parangdo instead of Tsushima according to the latter's advice.[85] Officially, however, the Korean government did not renounce its claim to Tsushima. The Foreign Affairs Committee meeting held on July 2 discussed the peace treaty, Korea's claim to Tsushima, and other related issues.[86] On August 3, President Rhee instructed Ambassador Yang to appeal strongly to the US DoS about Tsushima being Korean territory.[87] In the process of writing a second reply in July 1951, the issue of Tsushima was not dropped but still considered as part of Korea's territorial claims.

In a political reckoning dating back to 1947, Korea regarded Dokdo, Parangdo, and Tsushima as one distinct set of islands in terms of territorial issues with Japan. However, in the negotiations for the peace treaty in 1951 with Korea's signatory status denied and transfer of vested properties in Korea now in question, other issues including Dokdo and Parangdo were placed on the back burner. The research findings on Dokdo gathered by the Interim Government and the Corean Alpine Club from 1947 to 1948 were neither in the possession of the Korean government nor actively provided to the US government or the Korean Embassy in Washington.

After composing its second reply, the Korean government announced a toughly-worded statement on July 18, the day before its scheduled

---

85   Yu, "Until the Korea-Japan Talks Were Held," Vol. 1, p. 96.

86   *Minju Shinbo* (Jul, 3, 1951).

87   Letter by Syngman Rhee to Yang You Chan (Aug. 3, 1951), compiled by the National Institute of Korean History, 1996, *Collection of Correspondences with Rhee Syngman Vol. 3 (1951): Korean History Data Collection Vol. 30*, pp. 330-337.

dialogue with the US DoS. In the statement, Ambassador Yang requested the Korean government be recognized as a treaty signatory and added that he would demand such status based on the Provisional Government's fight against Japan.[88]

3) Korea-US dialogue (July 19, 1951) and the issue of Dokdo and Parangdo

Ambassador Yang You-chan, accompanied by First Secretary Han Pyo-wook, called upon Dulles at 2 o'clock on July 19, 1951 at the US DoS. In opening the dialogue, Yang presented Dulles with a letter-size, one-page note dated that very day. The review of the draft treaty by Yu Jin-o was long enough to be carried in a seven-installment series by a domestic newspaper in July 1951, but for some reason, Korea's second reply actually submitted to the US government was quite simple. In this note, the Korean government raised three points it wished to have considered for incorporation in the Japanese peace treaty: namely, its claim to Dokdo and Parangdo, legal transfer of vested properties in Korea to the ROK, and preservation of the MacArthur Line.

The most important issue to the Korean government was the disposition of Japanese property, and regarding territory, it replaced Tsushima with Dokdo and Parangdo. The issue of Dokdo was raised after it gave up on Tsushima together with Parangdo.

After reading the note, Mr. Dulles discussed the three points contained therein. With regard to the first point, Dulles was in doubt that the formula confirming Japan's renunciation of certain territorial claims to Korea could be included in the treaty in the form suggested by the ROK. Dulles noted that the first point made no reference to Tsushima and Yang agreed that this had been omitted. The dialogue then immediately moved on to the

---

88 *Kyunghyang Shinmun* (Jul, 21, 1951); Korean Embassy Press Release (Jul, 18, 1951), RG 59, Japanese Peace Treaty Files of John Foster Dulles, 1946-52, Lot 54D423, Box 8.

topics of Dokdo and Parangdo.[89]

> Mr. Dulles then inquired as to the location of the two islands, Dokdo and Parangdo. Mr. Han stated that these were two small islands lying in the Sea of Japan, he believed in the general vicinity of Ullungdo. Mr. Dulles asked whether these islands had been Korean before the Japanese annexation, to which the Ambassador replied in the affirmative. If that were the case, Mr. Dulles saw no particular problem in including these islands in the pertinent part of the treaty which related to the renunciation of Japanese territorial claims to Korean territory.[90] (underlined by the quoter)

This was the first time Dokdo was mentioned in the Korea-US negotiations on the Treaty of Peace with Japan. Han Pyo-wook's remark about Dokdo and Parangdo lying in the vicinity of Ulleungdo revealed that the Korean government did not even know their geographical location, the bare minimum of basic facts about them. They did not have any of the information on Dokdo accumulated through the Dokdo survey that had previously been utilized on such occasions as the bombing of Dokdo and during the writing of the ROK constitution between 1947 and 1948. Nothing more needs to be said about what Korea knew about Parangdo. This was the result of a lack of cooperation between the Korean Ministry of Foreign Affairs and the Embassy in Washington, DC, poor work by the Ministry and the Foreign Affairs Committee, and the immature Korean diplomatic system, all combined.

In regard to the second point, Dulles assured Yang that the US intended to extend protection to Korea regarding Japanese claims to vested properties in Korea and that the US DoS would study this question further.

What stirred the most controversy was the third point on the MacArthur Line. Dulles stated that he could say right off the bat that it

---

89 Memorandum of Conversation, Subject: Japanese Peace Treaty (Jul, 19, 1951), RG 59, Department of State, Decimal File, 694.001/7-1951.
90 The original text reads as follows: Mr. Han stated that these were two small islands lying in the Sea of Japan, he believed in the general vicinity of Ullungdo.

would be impossible to meet the Korean request for the inclusion of the MacArthur Line in the treaty. He pointed out that the US had been under great pressure from the American fishing industry to make the treaty, in effect, a fishing convention for the Pacific. He explained that this did not preclude negotiation of a series of bilateral or multilateral agreements on fisheries with Japan following the conclusion of the treaty.

Dulles and Yang continued to talk about several important issues. Yang talked about the approximately 800,000 Koreans in Japan who were being heavily discriminated against by the Japanese government. Dulles suggested that, "many of these Koreans were undesirables, being in many cases from North Korea and constituting a center for communist agitation in Japan." This is the evidence of the influence of the memorandum, "Korea and the Peace Treaty," provided by Shigeru Yoshida on April 23, 1951. Yoshida's anti-communism propaganda clearly had an impact on Dulles.

Yang expressed the fear that a lenient treaty with Japan would expose Korea to great difficulties in the future unless a stricter treaty were put into effect to which Korea would be a signatory. To illustrate his point, he referred to the fact that Japanese fishing vessels were crossing the MacArthur Line into Korean waters. In concluding the conversation, Yang jocularly suggested that if Korea were accorded the full status of a signatory to the treaty, he thought it could perhaps drop its second and third demands. In spite of these suggested concessions, the conversation ended only with some consolatory diplomatic rhetoric from Dulles.

4

US Department of State's Research on Dokdo and Parangdo and Its Conclusion

The US Department of State (DoS) sent out invitations to the signing ceremony of the Treaty of Peace with Japan (September 8, 1951) to 51 nations on July 20, 1951, the day after the above meeting between Yang and Dulles. The Soviet Union was invited, but not the Republic of China, the People's Republic of China, or Korea. Korea's rights in regard to the treaty were unchanged from those mentioned on July 9, 1951 by Dulles to Ambassador Yang. The final draft was being amended and was scheduled to be announced on August 13. The July 3 US-UK draft was to be amended and submitted around July 20. According to predictions at the time, the draft could be amended if objections were raised between late July and August 10.[91]

1) Review by Samuel Boggs of Dokdo as Korean territory

The US DoS was discussing the Dokdo issue at around the time of the Korea-US meeting on July 19, 1951. The task was given to Samuel W. Boggs, who had been responsible for the peace treaty's territorial issues at the Working Group on Japan Treaty in 1947. Boggs was a geographer who had been with the US DoS since the 1930s and was the best geography specialist on staff. He was then at the US DoS Office of Intelligence and Research (OIR).

Boggs wrote three key documents about Dokdo while the Korea-US negotiations were taking place in July 1951. These were practical and the

---

91   *Dong-A Ilbo* (Jul, 20, 1951); *Kyunghyang Shinmun* (Jul, 22, 1951).

only reports on Dokdo written by the US DoS working group on the peace treaty from July to August 1951. While writing the final draft of the peace treaty, the US DoS needed concrete information on multiple disputed islands, and Boggs was responsible for answering questions in this regard. Two of the reports were written prior to the July 19 Korea-US meeting where Dokdo was referred to as the Liancourt Rocks. The other one was produced after the meeting to try and confirm the existence of Dokdo and Parangdo.

Boggs' first report was written on July 13, 1951. This was produced in the process of providing information on the disputed islands as required by phone by Fearey at the US DoS Office of Northeast Asian Affairs (NA) for the drafting of the peace treaty. Fearey asked for information on two groups of islands, the Spratly Islands & Paracel Islands and the Liancourt Rocks (Dokdo). Fearey was then responsible for reviewing requests from relevant countries to amend the draft treaty.

Boggs wrote a memo on the same day of Fearey's request and its second item covered the issue of Dokdo:

2. Liancourt Rocks

The Liancourt Rocks (Takeshima) were among the islands to which, in a 1949 draft treaty, Japan would have renounced claim to Korea. In a Japanese Foreign Office publication, entitled "Minor Islands Adjacent to Japan Proper", Part IV, June 1947, Liancourt Rocks are included. It may therefore be advisable to name them specifically in the draft treaty, in some such form as the following (Article 2):

(a) Japan, recognizing the independence of Korea, renounces all right, title and claim to Korea, including the islands of Quelpart, Port Hamilton, Dagelet, and Liancourt Rocks (added).[92] (underlined by the quoter)

---

92   Memorandum by Boggs, OIR/GE to Fearey, NA, Subject: Spratly Island and the Paracels, in Draft Japanese Peace Treaty (Jul, 13, 1951), RG 59, Department of State, Decimal File, 694.001/7-1351.

Three facts can be gleaned from Boggs' memo. Firstly, the US DoS geography specialist clearly indicated that the Liancourt Rocks (Dokdo) were Korean territory and should be included as such in the peace treaty. Boggs' memo is important in that he clearly acknowledged the fact that the Japanese Foreign Office publication indicated Dokdo as one of the minor islands adjacent to Japanese territory and yet recommended that Dokdo be specifically named as Korean territory in the treaty.

Secondly, it is readily apparent that the US DoS referred to the Japanese Foreign Office publication produced in June 1947 to specify islands to be included as Japanese territory. As seen above, the pamphlet was used as an important basis for SCAP to ignore the request for the return of Dokdo, Parangdo, and Tsushima by the Patriotic Old Men's Association in 1948; as a justification by which Sebald argued that Dokdo was Japanese territory in 1949, also resulting in the US DoS draft treaty (1949) that indicated Dokdo as Korean territory being revised; and as a reference in 1951 by the US DoS geographer.

Thirdly, the issue of title to Dokdo was so controversial that direct advice by a US DoS geographer was sought after, and even afterwards the US DoS was still unable to make a decision regarding the issue. Also, even Boggs, the highest-level specialist in his field, did not know "Dokdo" was the Korean name of the Liancourt Rocks. He knew that the Japanese name of the Liancourt Rocks was Takeshima, but not the Korean name, Dokdo. This was due to the lack of information and references. From the perspective of Korea, Dokdo, clearly Korean territory dating back to ancient times, was dubbed Japanese territory in the US-led process of writing the treaty due to Japan's false arguments and propaganda and ultimately dropped from the treaty, leading to a completely unnecessary controversy. While Koreans were left clueless, Dokdo emerged as a subject of controversy due to Japanese maneuvering.

Regarding Dokdo, Boggs referred to Volume 1 of *Sailing Directions for Japan*, US Hydrographic Office Publication No. 123A (1st edition, 1945).[93]

---

93   US Hydrographic Office Publication No. 123A, Sailing Directions for Japan, Vol. I (1st ed.,

Boggs' second report was produced three days later on July 16, 1951. This memo quoted Japanese references more specifically and clearly indicated how Dokdo should be dealt with in the draft treaty:

2. Liancourt Rocks

By one 1949 draft treaty with Japan, the Liancourt Rocks (Takeshima) were to have been renounced to Korea; by another draft at about the same time they were to be named as being retained by Japan. A Japanese Foreign Office publication, entitled "Minor Islands Adjacent to Japan Proper," Part IV, June 1947, includes "Liancourt Rocks (Take-shima)" and says:

It should be noted that while there is a Korean name for Dagelet, none exists for the Liancourt Rocks and they are not shown in the maps made in Korea. If it is decided to give them to Korea, it would be necessary only to add "and Liancourt Rocks" at the end of Art. 2, par. (a).[94]

The above is almost the same as the text written on July 13. The difference is that this memo recorded that Dokdo had been marked as Korean territory in one of the 1949 US DoS drafts and then changed to Japanese territory in another draft due to the protest by Sebald based on the Japanese Foreign Office publication. Boggs also quoted the corresponding part of the pamphlet, the cause of all this trouble.

Boggs quoted what was nothing more than a palpable lie and blatantly false information - that there was no Korean name for Dokdo and the island was not shown on any maps made in Korea. This fraudulent information and misleading propaganda was quoted by the US DoS. Even the US DoS geography specialist gave significant consideration to the false information contained in the Japanese pamphlet, the very existence of which was yet to be known to Korea.

In spite of such misleading information provided by Japan, Boggs

---

1945), p. 597.

94   Memorandum by Boggs, OIR/GE to Fearey, NA, Subject: Spratly Island and the Paracels, in Draft Japanese Peace Treaty (Jul. 16, 1951), RG 59, Department of State, Decimal File, FW694.001/7-1351.

judged the Liancourt Rocks to be Korean territory. In the second report, he backtracked and added "if it is decided to give them (Liancourt Rocks) to Korea." This was an unfathomable situation where US DoS officials were trying to determine whether or not to give Dokdo, a historically Korean territory, back to the nation that had always maintained sovereignty over it.

Boggs' third report came out on July 31 due to Ambassador Yang's argument for Korea's sovereignty over Dokdo and Parangdo on July 19. Boggs wrote, "...regarding Dokdo and Parangdo, two islands which Korea desires to have Japan renounce in favor of Korea in the treaty of peace, we have tried all resources in Washington which we have thought of and have not been able to identify either of them."[95] The unfortunate history of Dokdo, which half a century earlier had become the first victim to Japanese imperialism, was repeated again. After Korea's loss of sovereignty, the Korean name Dokdo could not be printed on world maps and thereby the US DoS could not confirm the Liancourt Rocks as Dokdo.

Boggs continued on to say, "I understand that the Korean ambassador has informed the Department that Parangdo is near Ullungdo. The latter is the Korean name corresponding to the name conventionally used in English, Dagelet Island, and to the Japanese name Utsuryo To. That island is found on available maps and charts, by all three names, in approximately 37° 30' N. latitude, 130° 52' E. longitude." Since it was difficult to find the name equivalents in the various languages, he listed the principal islands in which Korea was interested, in three columns giving the names in European, Japanese and Korean forms, as seen below in Table 6-1.

Boggs' explanation about Jejudo, Geomundo, and Ulleungdo was correct but he was wrong in believing there was no Korean name for the Liancourt Rocks. Boggs clearly saw the Liancourt Rocks as Korean territory, but accepted the false argument by the Japanese Foreign Ministry that there was no Korean name. He was further confused by the Korean

---

95   Memorandum by S.W. Boggs, OIR/GE to Robert A. Fearey, NA. Subject: Parangdo and Dokdo (Islands) (Jul. 31, 1951), RG 59, State Department, Records Relating to the Japanese Peace and Security Treaties, 1946-1952, Lot 78D173, Box 2, Folder "Protocol (Notes & Comments)-Japan, July-September 1951".

[Table 6-1] Name comparison of Jejudo, Geomundo, Ulleungdo, Liancourt Rocks, Dokdo, and Parangdo (Boggs)

HO Pub. No. 122B(1947) page	European name	Japanese name	Korean name
606	Quelpart	Saishu To	Cheju Do
584	"Port Hamilton"	Tonai Kai	Tonae Hae
534	Dagelet	Utsuryo To/Matsu-shima(?)	Ullung Do
535	Liancourt Rocks	Take-shima	(none)
	?	?	Dokdo
	?	?	Parangdo

government's argument that Dokdo and Parangdo were near Ulleungdo. The timing was extremely unfortunate and resulted in the worst possible sequence of events from the perspective of Korea.

As seen above, Boggs neither found Dokdo and Parangdo in references nor proved Dokdo to be the Liancourt Rocks. Parangdo was at the time an unidentified, mythical island, so it was no surprise that its location remained unknown. Nevertheless, it was mentioned together with Dokdo and its location near Ulleungdo in the East Sea together with Dokdo was continuously argued, having an impact on the confirmation of Dokdo's true status.

Though he wrote that he was not been able to identify Dokdo and Parangdo in the July 31 memo, Boggs appeared to have determined Dokdo to be the Liancourt Rocks (Takeshima). Fearey submitted a memorandum to Allison on July 30 about the proposed changes for the August 13 draft.[96]

The July 31 memo stated that ① the location of Dokdo and Parangdo

---

96 Memorandum by Fearey to Allison, Subject: Proposed Changes for August 13 Draft (Jul. 30, 1951), RG 59, Records Relating to the Japanese Peace and Security Treaties, 1946-1952, Lot 78D173, Box 2, Folder "Protocol (Notes & Comments)-Japan, July-September 1951".

could not be identified; ② there was no Korean name for the Liancourt Rocks (Takeshima); and ③ the European and Japanese names of Dokdo and Parangdo were not known. According to the July 16 memo, Boggs did not know that the Korean name of the Liancourt Rocks was Dokdo and trusted the false argument by the Japanese Foreign Ministry that the island did not have a Korean name. According to a memo by Fearey from around the same time, Boggs was aware of Dokdo being Takeshima, namely, the Liancourt Rocks, but consented to the deceptive information provided by the Japanese Foreign Ministry that, "Dokdo had been officially claimed by Japan apparently without any protest from Korea in 1905, and it seemed that Korea had never claimed sovereignty over it before either." With no other reference that could be found about Dokdo and Parangdo and the failure by the Korean government and the Korean Embassy in the US to provide accurate information in a timely manner, Boggs came to depend increasingly on the only available reference: the Japanese Foreign Ministry's pamphlet of June 1947.

2) The Korean Government's third reply (August 2, 1951)

In August 1951, the US DoS officials entered the stage where they had to make a final decision on the Dokdo issue. Decisions needed to be made quickly on unsettled issues before finalizing the draft treaty, and with the approaching deadline, the Dokdo issue also needed to be decided. As Boggs failed to identify the locations of Dokdo and Parangdo, Fearey decided to make an inquiry at the Korean Embassy in Washington. According to a memorandum from Fearey to Allison on August 3, after having received a report from Boggs, Fearey asked the US DoS officer in charge of Korean affairs to ask someone at the Korean Embassy to find out where these islands were located.[97] However, the Korean Embassy failed to respond properly or provide accurate data. The officials at the Korean

---

97 Memorandum by Fearey, NA to Allison, Subject: Islands (Aug. 3, 1951), RG 59, Japanese Peace Treaty Files of John Foster Dulles, 1946-52, Lot 54D423, Box 8.

Embassy had no knowledge about Dokdo and Parangdo. Thereby, it can be discerned that no data from the discussions held at the Foreign Affairs Committee in Busan was provided to Washington. The Korean Embassy had no knowledge of the research conducted and discussions held by its home government and the historical, academic, and logical grounds for Korea's claims to the islands. Such was the situation at the Korean Embassy and therefore little could be expected in turn from the US DoS.

The responses by the Korean government at the time were based on its own set of priorities. Its highest priority was the transfer of vested properties in Korea followed closely by the preservation of the MacArthur Line. The Korean Embassy did not have the necessary information and the Korean government that had evacuated to the city of Busan was trying to wage a war and cared more about the political and economic aspects of the peace treaty than about Dokdo.

In the meantime, Japan was making multi-pronged efforts at both the government and private levels to secure its national interests. In particular, they were making strong claims to make the case for islands adjacent to Japan to be considered Japanese territory from July to August 1951. For instance, on August 10, 1951, an organization that represented 230,000 residents on the Amami Islands and 180,000 residents on the mainland originally from Amami presented a petition to Secretary of State Acheson to refrain from placing Amami Oshima under US trusteeship and instead to declare it Japanese territory. According to Article 3 of the peace treaty, the Amami Islands, which belong to the Ryukyu Islands south of 29° north latitude, were to be placed under the UN trusteeship system, with the US as the sole administering authority. The organization enclosed a photo of a mountain-high pile of signed petitions resulting from the petition drive.[98] They sent the same petition to US Ambassador to the UN and UN Security Council Chairman Warren Austin.[99] Pressure was conveyed from New

---

[98] Naotaka Nobori, National Federation of Amami Association to Dean Acheson, Secretary of State, "Petition Regarding Revision on the Draft Japanese Peace Treaty in Respect of Territorial Question," (Aug. 10, 1951), RG 59, Department of State, Decimal File, 694.001/8-1051.

[99] "Protest against the Exclusion of the Ryukyu Islands from Japan's Territory after the Peace

York to Washington. Already in June 1950, public figures from Okinawa presented a letter to Dulles to request the return of Okinawa to Japan.[100] Japanese people who had family members detained in the Soviet Union and China sent letters of appeal detailing their sad stories to the US Secretary of State, Dulles, and other influential officials and these emotional appeals effectively excited American sympathy.[101] Letters including stories such as a mother's appeal for the return of her only son who had yet to come home after 12 years of detainment as a POW in the Soviet Union after the war and a sister's search for her older brother were delivered to Acheson through Niles Bond, a counselor in the Office of the US Political Adviser for Japan.[102] On the other hand, Korea's public and private sectors had almost no diplomatic experience or system and were not acquainted with effective instruments and methods of appeal that were acceptable in the international community to help them achieve their interests.

This was evident in the statement by Korean Minister of Foreign Affairs Pyun Yung-tai on August 1. He raised four points about the peace treaty at a press conference: ① Article 2 of the treaty should provide that Japan confirm that it renounced on August 9, 1945 all right, title, and claim to Korea and the islands which were part of Korea prior to its annexation by Japan, including the islands Quelpart, Port Hamilton, Dagelet, and Dokdo; ② Article 4 should state that Japan renounce its claims to property formerly belonging to Japan and its nationals (including juridical persons) in Korea and against Koreans as of August 9, 1945; ③ Korea will accept Tsushima if it is to become Korean territory, but if not, it should be designated as

---

Treaty," (Aug. 27, 1951), RG 59, Department of State, Decimal File, 694.001/8-2751.

100 "A Petition to State Department Adviser John Foster Dulles Concerning the Problem of Okinawa," (Jun 22, 1950), RG 59, Japanese Peace Treaty Files of John Foster Dulles, 1946-52, Lot 54D423, Box 7.

101 Letter by Zenich Zoshima, Chairman of the National Council of Family, Organization for Speedy Repatriation of the Japanese Abroad to John F. Dulles (Jul 25, 1951), RG 59, Department of State.

102 Despatch no. 171 by Niles W. Bond to the Secretary of State, Subject: Japanese Attitude toward Repatriation Problem (Aug. 2, 1951), RG 59, Department of State, Decimal File, 694.001/8-251.

a demilitarized zone under the UN trusteeship system; and ④ unless SCAP would come up with a new agreement, the present MacArthur Line should be preserved.[103] Pyun's statement shows the high regard the Korean government placed on the transfer of Japanese property and that, though Dokdo was mentioned, Tsushima was still being used for political leverage.

The memorandum from President Rhee to Ambassador Yang on August 3 effectively demonstrates the stance of the Korean government's highest officer on the peace treaty.[104] Rhee stated his views on various issues including Korea's qualifications to be a treaty signatory (anti-Japanese struggle by the Provisional Government and its Independence Army); concerns on Japan's rearmament; the Japanese government's unlawful treatment of 600,000 Korean residents in Japan; reparations by Japan; and the MacArthur Line.

Rhee pointed out three specific issues, the first of which was Tsushima. Rhee wrote that, though the US was not familiar with the Tsushima issue, it was a long-standing issue to Korea. If the US DoS questioned original ownership, Korea would provide historical evidence about its sovereignty over the island. Rhee confessed in the memo that Tsushima could be used as a bargaining chip, and as such, he placed the greatest importance on publicizing the issue (p. 6).[105]

The second was reparations, and Rhee stated that three lists of proposed reparations had been completed. They probably referred to the "Report on the Demand for Reparations from Japan" completed in 1949.

The third was the MacArthur Line. Rhee wrote that, as Japanese fishing vessels frequently violated the MacArthur Line, the Korean government had to instruct its Navy to seize such vessels and confiscate their fishing nets. He requested a separate agreement between Korea and Japan to clearly demarcate the line and Dulles to serve as an intermediary. This did

---

103 *Minju Shinbo* (Aug. 3, 1951).

104 Memorandum by the President to Ambassador Yang (Aug. 3, 1951), compiled by the National Institute of Korean History, 1996, *Collection of Correspondences with Rhee Syngman Vol. 3 (1951): Korean History Data Collection Vol. 30*, pp. 330-337.

105 *Ibid.*, p. 6.

not deviate greatly from the treaty's article that promoted negotiation of a bilateral or multilateral agreement with Japan on fisheries in the high seas. The core of Rhee's argument was Korea's signatory status and reparation demands including the return of Tsushima (p. 6). While Tsushima was still being used as a form of political leverage, Dokdo was not given much importance.

Meanwhile, the Korean Embassy in the US presented the Korean government's third reply (August 2, 1951). It supplemented the second reply (July 19, 1951) with a request for additions to the revised US draft. Yang delivered this third reply listing additional requests, which was slightly different from that covered in the media. It included additional requests about three articles regarding Japanese property in Korea and the MacArthur Line,[106] but did not mention Dokdo or Parangdo.

The emphasis was still on the legal transfer of vested properties in Korea to the Korean government and the MacArthur Line. In the evening of the same day, Ambassador Yang met reporters at the National Press Club and explained Korea's position, which was an aggregation of the second and third replies.[107]

3) The Rusk Letter (August 10, 1951) and conclusion of Korea-US negotiations

As there was a serious lack of information on Dokdo and Parangdo available to the US DoS working-level officials, they cabled American Ambassador to Korea Muccio. Allison, the working-level official responsible for the peace treaty sent the following telegram to Muccio on August 7:

For MUCCIO from DULLES.

---

106 Letter by You Chang Yang to Dean G. Acheson (Aug. 2, 1951), RG 59, Japanese Peace Treaty Files of John Foster Dulles, 1946-52, Lot 54D423, Box 8.
107 *Minju Shinbo* (Aug 6, 1951).

Neither our geographers nor Korean Embassy have been able locate Dokdo and Parangdo Islands. Therefore unless we hear (information on the locations of these islands) immediately cannot consider this Korean proposal to confirm their sovereignty over these islands. Acheson.[108] (information in the parentheses inserted by the quoter)

After having received this short and stern telegram demanding information on Dokdo and Parangdo, the US Embassy in Busan immediately replied to inform the US DoS of the exact coordinates of Dokdo and that the Korean government had withdrawn its demand for Parangdo.[109]

With this reply, the Korean government's official withdrawal of its demand for Parangdo was confirmed and only the Dokdo issue remained. From this point onwards, however, Dokdo was not mentioned again.

By then, most of the issues raised by the Korean government with regard to the peace treaty had been sorted out. First, Korea's requests for Allied Power and signatory status and for preservation of the MacArthur Line were already rejected on July 9, 1951 and the rejection was made known to the Korean Ambassador to the US. The only change the US DoS made to the treaty at the request of Korea was the legal transfer of vested properties of Japanese in Korea to the Korean government. This had already been decided by the USAMGIK ordinance and the Korea-US settlement and the US government thus agreed to settle the affair.

The US DoS made known its final position on the Treaty of Peace with Japan to Korea on August 10, 1951. This notification was drafted by Fearey, who was responsible for Korea at the US DoS NA with regard to the treaty, on August 9. In the official diplomatic correspondence sent under the

---

108 Outgoing Telegram by Secretary of State (Acheson) to Amembassy, Pusan (Muccio) (Aug. 7, 1951); Lee Seok-woo, 2006, *Data Collection on the Treaty of Peace with Japan*, Northeast Asian History Foundation, p. 254; "Treaty Changes" (Aug. 7, 1951), RG 59, Records Relating to the Japanese Peace and Security Treaties, 1946-1952, Lot 78D173, Box 2, Folder 7.

109 Subject: Correspondence regarding Tokto, Island claimed by Korea (Oct. 14, 1952), RG 84, Korea, Seoul Embassy, CGR 1953-1955, Box 12; National Institute of Korean History, comp., 2008, *Dokdo Data Collection Vol. 2 (with regard to the US)*, p. 232.

name of Dean Rusk, the US Assistant Secretary of State for Far Eastern Affairs, to Ambassador Yang, the US DoS summarized the discussion thus far and announced its decisions.

In the letter, Rusk dismissed most of the Korean government's requests made in its July 19 and August 2 replies. First, with respect to the request that Article 2 (a) of the draft be revised to provide that Japan "confirms that it renounced on August 9, 1945, all right, title, and claim to Korea," he wrote that the "United States Government does not feel that the Treaty (referring to Treaty of Peace with Japan) should adopt the theory that Japan's acceptance of the Potsdam Declaration on August 9, 1945 constituted a formal or final renunciation of sovereignty by Japan over the areas (Korea) dealt with in the Declaration" (parentheses added by the quoter). The opinion was that August 9, 1945 did "not seem to be" the day when Japan renounced sovereignty over Korea and when Korea became independent.[110]

Next, Rusk wrote about Dokdo and Parangdo as follows:

As regards the island of Dokdo, otherwise known as Takeshima or Liancourt Rocks, this normally uninhabited rock formation was according to our information never treated as part of Korea and, since about 1905, has been under the jurisdiction of the Oki Islands Branch Office of Shimane Prefecture of Japan. The island does not appear ever before to have been claimed by Korea. It is understood that the Korean Government's request that "Parangdo" be included among the islands named in the treaty as having been renounced by Japan has been withdrawn.[111] (underlined by the quoter)

Dokdo first appeared only in Korea's second reply of July 19 but the US made a decision that it was Japanese territory and notified the Korean government of its decision on August 10, only some 20 days later. The

---

110 Letter by Dean Acheson to You Chan Yang, Ambassador of Korea (Aug. 10, 1951), RG 59, Japanese Peace Treaty Files of John Foster Dulles, 1946-52, Lot 54D423, Box 7; RG 59, Department of State, Decimal File, 694.001/8-1051.

111 *Ibid.*

wording of Rusk's explanation in this memo matches almost exactly the wording of the Japanese Foreign Ministry's pamphlet published in June 1947. The Korean government failed to provide references of its ownership of Dokdo to the US DoS and its Embassy in Washington also failed to answer the US DoS inquiries during these negotiations. Under pressure to complete the draft in a timely fashion, the US DoS decided they could not wait further and made the above decision based on the information that was available to them. There have been no additional documents found that can shed light on the US DoS decision-making process on this matter.

The US DoS also declined Korea's request to preserve the MacArthur Line regarding Article 9. Rusk pointed out that the MacArthur Line would stand until the treaty came into force, and that Korea would have the opportunity of negotiating a fishing agreement with Japan prior to that date. With respect to Article 15(a), he mentioned that Japan has no obligation to return the property of persons in Japan of Korean origin.[112]

The only request the US DoS accepted was the legal transfer of vested properties of Japanese in Korea. In order to meet the view of the Korean government, a new paragraph (b) was added following Article 4 (a) that read, "Japan recognizes the validity of dispositions of property of Japan and Japanese nationals made by or pursuant to directives of United States Military Government in any of the areas referred to in Articles 2 and 3." This confirmed the transfer of property of Japan and of its nationals to the Korean government according to the US military government directive and the very first US-Korean settlement.

The US DoS handed the final draft treaty to the Korean Embassy in Washington on August 15 and to the US Embassy in Busan via diplomatic pouch delivered by air.[113] Foreign Affairs Minister Pyun reported the change of Article 4 of the draft to the Korean National Assembly on August

---

112 This was the request made in Article 3 of Korea's third reply of August 2, 1951 (Korea's interests under Articles 2, 9, 12, and 15(a) in the draft).
113 Outgoing Telegram from U. Alexis Johnson to Amembassy, Pusan (Aug. 15, 1951), RG 59, Department of State, Decimal File, 694.001/8-1551.

17.[114]

The Rusk Letter received by Ambassador Yang was sent to the home government. In his explanation of the US memorandum to the National Assembly on August 17, Pyun reported that Korea's request for the vested property issue was accepted.[115] However, it cannot be known whether the Korean government clearly grasped the decision regarding the ownership of Dokdo in the letter. It is believed that they did not have an accurate understanding of the importance of the Rusk Letter until December 1951. The Korean Ambassador to the US sent relevant correspondences to the Minister of Foreign Affairs on January 13, 1953.[116]

With most of its requests denied and with no practical leverage to use, the Korean government had no choice but to release a strongly-worded statement. On August 20, Pyun criticized the decision to exclude Korea from the peace treaty, when it is Japan's closest neighbor and maintained hostile relations.[117]

In general, the Korean media pointed out the outcomes and limits of the negotiations regarding the peace treaty. According to press coverage, the biggest outcome was the treaty's recognition of the validity of dispositions of Japanese property with limits being the rejections of Korea's signatory status and the preservation of the MacArthur Line.[118]

While the two rejections were strongly criticized, the dismissal of the request for Dokdo and Parangdo was then not publicized at all

---

114 National Assembly Secretariat, *The Eleventh National Assembly Stenographic Records, No. 45* (Aug. 17, 1951).

115 *Minju Shinbo* (Aug. 19, 1951).

116 "Forwarding of Documents on Dokdo" (Korean Embassy in the US, No. 552, Jan. 13, 1953) (Korean Ambassador to the US → Minister of Foreign Affairs), *Dokdo Issue, 1952-53*. The ambassador sent three documents: Ambassador Note of July 19, 1951, Ambassador Note of August 2, 1951, and Assistant Secretary of State Dean Rusk Reply of August 10, 1951. That is, the Korean government's second reply (Jul. 19, 1951), third reply (Aug. 2, 1951), and Rusk Letter (Aug. 10, 1951) were sent.

117 "Treaty of Peace with Japan" (published on Aug. 20, 1951), Pyun Yung-tai, 1956, *My Homeland*, Freedom Publishing, pp. 236-237; *Seoul Shinmun* (Aug. 23, 1951).

118 *Busan Ilbo* (Aug. 24, 1951).

and, therefore there was no reaction in this regard. The intensive hype surrounding Dokdo from 1947 to 1948 was lost in the media in the summer of 1951. The national interest at the time was centered on the ceasefire talks that had just begun.

According to what has since been discovered in documents made public, the Korean government did not officially protest the decision on Dokdo in the Rusk Letter. They raised issues about Korea's signatory status and the MacArthur Line but never mentioned Dokdo.

As explained above, the US DoS rejected the Korean government's request regarding Dokdo and Tsushima on August 10, 1951. The biggest reason for the rejection of the Dokdo request was the Korean government's failure to provide a well-researched and complete history of Korea's ownership. As a result, the US DoS had to rely solely on the Japanese Foreign Ministry pamphlet, almost the only available literature reference, and in the end did not reflect the Korean government's request in the treaty text, which remained the same as the draft. The biggest reason is likely to have been that the information on Dokdo was not accurate in addition to the location and identity of Parangdo remaining unknown. The US DoS made the swift decision that was not meant to confirm Dokdo as Japanese territory, but to finish the amendment of the treaty provisions on Korea by rejecting its request and thereby completing the final draft treaty.

4) Significance and limits of the Rusk Letter

The Rusk Letter did not represent a general opinion or policy agreed upon by relevant US DoS officials or by pertinent countries. It was written by the US DoS Bureau of Far Eastern Affairs for conducting working-level tasks. The correspondence was sent to the Korean Embassy in Washington but not to the US Embassy in Korea, Office of the US Political Adviser for Japan and to the Japanese government, a fact which will be further explained in the last chapter of this study. Even the Secretary of State's office learned of the existence of the Rusk Letter only in November 1952.

The same held true at the US Embassy in Korea, which maintained the position that, although Korea's sovereignty over Dokdo was not stated in

Article 2 of the treaty, contrary to Korea's request, Dokdo was a disputed territory as Korea claimed sovereignty over the island, whose ownership would be determined in Korea-Japan talks in the future.[119] As such, the US Embassy advised the US DoS and Mark W. Clark, Commander of the UN Command, that the US should not be engaged in any territorial dispute arising from Korea's claim to Dokdo. It learned, only after having received a letter dated November 14, 1952 from Kenneth T. Young, Jr., Director of the Office of Northeast Asian Affairs, that the US had already decided sovereignty over Dokdo through the Rusk Letter of August 10, 1951.[120] The American Embassy was shocked at the very existence of such a memorandum and knew only by early December 1952 that it had taken a position different from that of the US DoS.[121]

The situation was the same at the Japanese government. The Rusk Letter was grounded on the Japanese Foreign Ministry publication with no reference from the Korean government to back up the latter's claim to Dokdo and Parangdo. However, this was not based on across-the-board agreement even within the US DoS, let alone agreement with embassies overseas or relevant countries. Consequently, during the Korea-Japan dispute over Dokdo in 1952, the US DoS tried to restrain a hard-line Korean side with the Rusk Letter, and at the same time, was anxious that Japan would become aware of the letter's existence. When a possible collapse became palpable in Korea-US, Korea-Japan, and US-Japan relations resulting from a simple decision made at working-level, the US DoS

---

119 Despatch by E. Allan Lightner, Jr., Charge d'Affaires, ad interim, to Department of State (Nov. 14, 1952), RG 84, Japan, Tokyo Embassy, CGR 1952, Box 1, Folder 320 Japan-Korea Liancourt Rocks 1952.

120 Letter by Kenneth T. Young, Jr., Director, Office of Northeast Asian Affairs to E. Allan Lightner, Esquire, Charge d'affairs, a.i., American Embassy, Pusan, Korea (Nov. 14, 1952), RG 84, Japan, Tokyo Embassy, CGR 1952, Box 1, Folder 320 Japan-Korea Liancourt Rocks 1952.

121 Letter by E. Allan Lightner Jr. to Kenneth T. Young, Jr., Director, Office of Northeast Asian Affairs (Dec. 4, 1952), RG 84, Korea, Seoul Embassy, CGR, 1953-1955, Box 12; E. Allan Lightner, Jr., Counselor of Embassy, Pusan to William T. Turner, Esquire, Counselor of Embassy, American Embassy, Tokyo (Dec. 19, 1952), RG 84, Japan, Tokyo Embassy, CGR 1952, Box 1, Folder 320 Japan- Korea Liancourt Rocks 1952.

realized the large gap between the seemingly simple practical decision and its possible ramifications in international politics. It was perplexed that the quick, practical decision had been, in fact, only documentary verification work, and what was more, that the authenticity and genuineness of the document had not been confirmed. Nevertheless, in hindsight, the issue should have been dealt with by high-level decision makers in view of its ripple effects on international politics.

The Rusk Letter was not reflected in the Treaty of Peace with Japan. With the dispute over Dokdo escalating as the Korean government's declaration of the Peace Line in 1952 and the Japanese government's own claim to sovereignty over Dokdo clashed, the letter caught the attention of US DoS officials from 1952 to 1953. There were quite a few people, including officials at the US DoS Office of Northeast Asian Affairs and the US Embassy in Japan, who wanted to disclose or provide the Rusk Letter to the Japanese government, and thereby reveal the US government's support for Japan's position in the peace conference. This argument, however, was dismissed by Dulles. By the telegram whose draft was written on December 8, 1953 (sent simultaneously to both the US Embassies in Seoul and in Tokyo), Dulles underscored that, even when the US interpretation of the peace conference might have confirmed Japan's claim to Dokdo, the United States was merely one of many signatories of the treaty, and the interpretation only represented the US stance, not the official view agreed upon by the Allied Powers.[122]

Dulles brought up the issue of the Soviet occupation of the northern Habomais, which the US had publicly declared as Japanese territory. He pointed out that, while Japan neither strongly protested to the Soviet Union nor called for a show of force by the US, he did not understand why Japan eagerly wanted heavy-handed US intervention only in regard to Korea. In the end, Dulles instructed that the US should not get involved in the dispute over Dokdo between two countries, and if Korea and Japan failed

---

122 John F. Dulles to the Embassies in Korea and Japan, telegram, no. 1387, RG 59, Department of State, Decimal File, 694.95B/11-2353.

to settle disputes, they should take the issue to the International Court of Justice.

This point in time was a watershed when the US DoS made two important decisions. First, no matter what decision the US might have made regarding Dokdo in the process leading up to the San Francisco Peace Conference, that would have only served as America's viewpoint, not as an official position agreed upon by the Allied Powers which signed the treaty. This confirmed that the Rusk Letter regarding Dokdo did not reflect the official position of the peace treaty. Second, the dispute over Dokdo was a bilateral issue between Korea and Japan in which the US should not be involved. Its resolution should be left to agreement and settlement between the two concerned nations, and if that was not possible, then it should be brought to the International Court of Justice. In a nutshell, the US chose to sit on the fence and decided not to engage in the Korea-Japan dispute over Dokdo. Nevertheless, American hegemony and its decision power in Northeast Asia in 1951 set Korea, a weak nation, on a long, arduous journey to keep Dokdo.

5

Korea's Participation in the San Francisco Peace Treaty in an Informal Capacity

The US Department of State (DoS) informed the Korean government of its decision on Dokdo by referring to the Japanese Foreign Ministry's pamphlet which indicated that since the 1905 incorporation of Dokdo by Japan, there had been no protest by the Korean government. Nevertheless, the veteran officials at the US DoS did not convey this decision to Japan.

Refused the status of an Allied Power and signatory, Korea could not participate in the signing ceremony of the peace treaty even as an observer. Korea was present at the peace conference, not in the capacity of a signatory or observer but in a completely informal capacity.[123]

Ambassador Muccio recommended the participation of Korean officials as observers to the US DoS in Telegram No. 84 from Busan on July 27, but even this request proved difficult to accept. After the notification of the US DoS's final position to Ambassador Yang in the form of the August 10 memorandum under the name of Assistant Secretary of State Rusk, Yang met Rusk on August 17 to request, once again, Korea's participation as signatory. Rusk said the absence of Korean representatives at the conference would not undermine the prestige of Korea and advised not to issue a statement detailing damage to Korea's prestige.[124] Not only did

---

123 Han Pyo-wook wrote that the US permitted participation by observers as a partial acceptance of Korea's requests. The Korean participants numbered three: Korean Ambassador to the UN Im Byeong-jik, Korean Ambassador to the US Yang You-chan, and Han Pyo-wook (Han, *Rhee Syngman and Korean-US Diplomatic Relations*, p. 263).

124 Memorandum of Conversation (Yu Chan Yang, Pyo Wook Han, Dean Rusk, Noel Hemmendinger, H. O. H. Frelinghuysen) (Aug. 17, 1951), RG 59, Japanese Peace Treaty Files of John Foster Dulles, 1946- 52, Lot 54D423, Box 8.

Rusk decline Korea's attendance to the peace conference, but he also tried to forestall an issuance of a statement of protest.

Soon after this meeting, U. Alexis Johnson of the US DoS Office of Northeast Asian Affairs wrote a memo to Dulles on August 20 where he agreed that Korea could not be a treaty signatory but noted that it would be "very useful to have Korea at the conference in a certain capacity."[125] Johnson thought that Korea's presence would promote the conclusion of a Korea-Japan bilateral agreement and lessen the Korean "chip on the shoulder" aggrieved attitude toward Japan.[126] Mentioning the observer capacity for Korea as suggested by Muccio, he wrote that "From an entirely moral point of view, it would be fair for Korea, a nation that suffered for more than 40 years under Japanese oppression, to have their representatives in a certain capacity in San Francisco" and recommended that Korean representatives participate as observers. After reviewing this memorandum, Dulles objected even to observer status for Korea.[127] At that time, the UK, America's key ally, had approved Mao Zedong's People's Republic of China, but was opposing informal observer status for Chiang Kai-shek's Nationalist Chinese government in San Francisco. It must be noted that UK approval was necessary to allow Korea's participation as observer. The US argument for observer participation was to promote bilateral agreements between Korea and Japan, Japan and Italy, and Japan and Portugal,[128] but it was not an easy choice.

On August 22, Dulles met with Yang, who argued for Korea's attendance at the San Francisco Peace Conference once more. He strongly protested

---

125 Office Memorandum by Johnson to Dulles, Subject: Attendance of Korean Observers at Japanese Peace Conference (Aug. 20, 1951), RG 59, Japanese Peace Treaty Files of John Foster Dulles, 1946-52, Lot 54D423, Box 8.

126 The original text reads as follows: lessening the Korean "chip on the shoulder" attitude toward Japan.

127 The original text reads as follows: "While from a strictly Korean point of view I agree with the above, I believe such action would get us into difficulties and open a Pandora's Box which we would regret."

128 Memorandum by Treumann, NA to Johnson, NA, Subject: Korean observers to Japanese Peace Conference (Aug. 13, 1951), RG 59, Department of State, Decimal File, 694.001/8-1351.

Korea's exclusion from the peace conference where communist countries such as the Soviet Union, Poland, and Czechoslovakia would be in attendance. He also mentioned the US mutual defense treaty with the Philippines, the Australia, New Zealand, and US Security Treaty (ANZUS Treaty), and the peace treaty with Japan, their former enemy. In reacting to Yang's protest, Dulles only offered words of consolation. When Yang inquired about whether the US would invite Korea to the peace treaty as a signatory or an observer, Dulles answered neither would be the case since it was decided not to assign observer status to non-signatory nations at the conference. He said Korea would be able to attend only in an informal capacity. Yang asked if Korea could be granted some formal capacity with regard to the conference proceedings but Dulles said no. Yang said he could not foretell how the Korean government would decide on the dispatch of informal representatives to the San Francisco conference. To this, Dulles said that the US would send a message to President Rhee Syngman to request the dispatch of informal representatives and instructed Emmons to write a draft.[129]

However, a decision not to grant observer status to Korea had already been made before this meeting. After the meeting, an aide to Dulles wrote in a memo: "JFD (John Foster Dulles) met Ambassador Yang at 3:30 pm on August 22, 1951 together with Mr. Emmons. We agreed with Mr. Rusk over the phone that we will not offer 'observer' status to them (Korean representatives), but if they wish to participate as 'guests,' we will help them acquire tickets and make reservations."[130] Neither an Allied Power nor a signatory to the treaty, and not even as an observer, Korea was allowed only to sit in the audience as a mere guest, an entirely informal capacity.

On August 27, Yang wrote to Dulles to repeatedly demand Korea's

---

129 Memorandum of Conversation (Yu Chan Yang, Pyo Wook Han, John Foster Dulles, Arthur B. Emmons, 3rd), Subject: Korean Attendance at San Francisco Peace Conference (Aug. 22, 1951), RG 59, Department of State, Decimal File, 694.001/8-2251.

130 Memo by unknown, attached to the Office Memorandum by Johnson to Dulles, Subject: Attendance of Korean Observers at Japanese Peace Conference (Aug. 22, 1951), RG 59, Japanese Peace Treaty Files of John Foster Dulles, 1946-52, Lot 54D423, Box 8.

signatory status. In his reply on the same day, Dulles wrote that, though numerous individual Koreans fought against Japan, Korea was neither a belligerent country nor an Allied Power during the war waged by Japan, and it had lost its independence before the war and regained it only after the end of war. Dulles reiterated that numerous countries which had not been at war with Japan also wanted to be signatories to the treaty but only the actual belligerents could sign the treaty.[131]

The Korean press deplored the poor treatment that Korea received, decrying the decision that Korea could participate in the San Francisco Peace Conference merely as an "observer under the label of 'informal.'"[132] Dulles announced the US DoS stance with regard to Korea on September 6.[133] He cited Japan's official recognition of Korean independence and verification of the return of vested Japanese property in Korea to the Korean government as the rights that Korea could enjoy under the peace treaty.[134] The US basically thought that independence was all Korea, liberated only after WWII, could hope for and its interests were fully represented through its independence, recognition by the UN, and its defense in the Korean War.[135]

However, the decision to not include Korea in the treaty and deprive it of signatory status based only on a legal technicality was not fair to the Koreans. Countries in Indochina which had been under Japanese aggression only for a few years were granted signatory status despite having been colonies of France, the Netherlands, and other European nations. Korea was excluded despite living with Japanese oppression for more than 40 years. As Foreign Affairs Minister Pyun said in his statement, while Korea shed blood as a guardian of the free world against communism,

---

131 Letter by You Chan Yang to John Foster Dulles (Aug. 27, 1951); Letter by John Foster Dulles to You Chang Yang (Aug. 27, 1951), RG 59, Japanese Peace Treaty Files of John Foster Dulles, 1946-52, Lot 54D423, Box 8.
132 *Seoul Shinmun* (Sept. 4, 1951).
133 *Chosun Ilbo* (Sept. 9, 1951); Kim, *Promise of the Dawn*, pp. 87-88.
134 "United Kingdom" (Jun. 15, 1951), RG 59, Japanese Peace Treaty Files of John Foster Dulles, 1946-52, Lot 54D423, Box 12, Folder "Treaty Drafts, May 3, 1951".
135 *Minju Shinbo* (Jul, 21, 1951).

Poland and Czechoslovakia, satellite countries of the Soviet Union who had nothing to do with the Pacific War, were granted signatory status. When the US distributed its Provisional Draft of March 1951, 14 countries received copies, and among them, only India, Korea, and Ceylon were not FEC members.[136] However, when the peace treaty was signed in San Francisco in September 1951, 51 countries were invited to sign the treaty. The exclusion of Korea was truly politically-motivated.

For its part, Japan should have invited Korea and China, its greatest victims during the war, to sign the treaty, in order to truly repent for its past aggression and usher in a new era. Instead, it strongly demanded these victims be excluded for political reasons. By opting for bilateral treaties instead of a multilateral treaty, Japan intended to occupy a dominant position over these major Asian victims. Both Korea and China suffered more than any other nations under Japanese aggression, and therefore Japan had much to compensate and apologize for. It was indeed predictable that bilateral discussions between these nations would hit snags and become protracted. Clearly at work here was the historical perception and political interpretation by Japan that its defeat in the Pacific War was brought on by the US and Soviet Union and that it did not surrender to either China or Korea.[137]

---

136 Department of State (Allison) to POLAD Japan (Sebald) (Mar. 23, 1951), RG 59, Department of State, Decimal File, 694.001/3-2351.
137 Takashi Hatada, 1963, "New Understanding of the Korea-Japan Talks: Japanese' Understanding of Korea," *Sinsajo*, December Issue (*Sekai* December Issue), p. 104.

Chapter 7

Invisible Battle

: Prelude to the Dispute over Dokdo and Actions taken
by Korea, the United States, and Japan

1

Korea

: The Peace Line and Expedition to Parangdo and Dokdo

1) Dokdo inside the Peace Line

Of the petitions made by the Korean government leading up to the San Francisco Peace Conference, only the one concerning the handling of vested properties was accommodated in the text of the treaty.

Denied access to the San Francisco Peace Conference either as a participating nation or as a signatory to the Peace Treaty with Japan, the Korean government began its preparations for a bilateral peace conference with its former oppressor. The fact that Korea, which was only liberated from Japanese colonial rule after World War II, was now expected to "settle its past" with Japan and normalize relations through bilateral talks on equal terms was in itself unfair and a *de facto* judgment in favor of Japan.[1] On July 30, 1951, the Korean government sent Yu Jin-o and Lim Song-bon to Japan for about two months to look for documents that would give Korea the political and economic leverage that it needed. With almost all of its requests ignored or rejected and the US now trying to object even to observer status for Korea, the Korean government needed some kind of leverage to put political pressure on Japan. In the end, Korea came up with the idea of a line to replace the MacArthur Line. This plan would in practice resolve the twin dilemmas of 1) finding a way to maintain enforcement of the MacArthur Line, which Korea had requested but had now been denied, and 2) ensuring the return of Dokdo and Parangdo to

---

1   Lee, *The Starting Point of Dealing with the Past Affairs between Korea and Japan*; Park, *Korea-Japan Talks*.

Korea. It was also a policy initiative that the Korean government had begun working on beginning in April 1951.

In mid-February 1951, the Korean government recognized an anticipated discontinuation of the MacArthur Line, and it established a committee responsible for working out a fisheries agreement with Japan (April 3, 1951). On July 19, 1951, the government learned from the US that it would not be invited to the Peace Conference. On August 10, it received the final notification from the US that most of its requests, except for the one on vested properties, had been denied. Under such circumstances, the government saw the scope of its internal discussions expand from a fisheries protection line to replace the MacArthur Line to a line of sovereignty over adjacent seas, including its sovereignty over Dokdo, the continental shelf issues and national defense. The line of sovereignty over adjacent seas (or the Peace Line), which Korea would enforce as a replacement for the MacArthur Line, became the strongest territorial policy initiative of the Korean government following conclusion of the San Francisco Peace Treaty. The Korean government's fishery initiative, intended to counterbalance the decision of the US and the UK to eliminate the MacArthur Line, evolved in four key stages. The concepts and terminology used in each stage differed, but they were all developed to achieve the same objective of preserving some semblance at least of the MacArthur Line and thus to ensure the preservation of Korean sovereignty rights over Dokdo.

In the first stage, the views of the committee charged with preparing a fishery agreement with Japan was well reflected in its position paper entitled *Comments* of early April. Headed by Minister of Trade and Commerce Kim Hun and including as its other members Vice Minister of Foreign Affairs Jo Jung-hwan, President Jung Mun-ki of the Central Fishery Laboratory, and lawmaker Hwang Seong-su, the committee mirrored the importance placed by the Korean government on the fishery agreement. The committee constituted a policy consultation and policy-making body comprised of the relevant ministers and vice-ministers.[2]

---

2   "Committee in charge of preparing a fishery agreement with Japan," Ministry of Foreign

In a policy brief presented to the Prime Minister on April 11, 1951, the committee recommended a three-stage fisheries strategy with respect to Japan. The document entitled *Comments* was attached to this brief. Thus, by April 1951, the Korean government already had a three-stage strategy in place in view of the imminent revocation of the MacArthur Line.[3] The strategy involved: 1) preservation of the MacArthur Line in the Japanese peace treaty, 2) inclusion of a provision stipulating the need for a bilateral fishing agreement between Korea and Japan, and 3) conclusion of a bilateral fishery agreement with Japan in the form of a fish species conservation agreement.

Although the first priority of the Korean government was ensuring that the Japanese peace treaty provided for both the continuation of the MacArthur Line and conclusion of a bilateral fishing agreement between Korea and Japan, the government realized that such a bilateral fishing agreement could only be reached through the negotiation of a bilateral treaty with Japan. Thus, the bilateral fishing agreement with Japan, which would formally be an agreement on the protection of fish species, became a *de facto* strategy for the Korean government to establish not just its lawful fishing grounds, but also its maritime boundaries.

For the Korean government, continuation of the MacArthur Line was a critical means of protecting its fishing industry. Advanced Japanese fishing vessels had been engaged for some time in sweeping clean the rich fishing grounds off the Korean coast. In 1936, before the war, Japan's maximum annual catch had been 4.33 million tons; by 1952, the country's annual catch had already reached 4.82 million tons, making Japan the number one fishing country in the world. The fishing grounds in the East Sea

---

Affairs, 1952, *Korea's Policy on Protection of Fisheries: Declaration of the Peace Line, 1949-1952* (diplomatic document disclosed in 2005, classification no. 743.4, registration no. 458), p. 1178; "Regarding Fisheries Policy towards Japan" (Apr. 12, 1951) (Kim Hun, Chairman of the Committee → Prime Minister), pp. 1274-1279.

3   This document was attached at the back of the document "Committee in charge of preparing a fishery agreement with Japan" (p. 1178) together with the "Korea-Japan Fisheries Agreement (draft)" (pp. 1179-1181).

and Yellow Sea off the coast of Korea, in particular, provided optimal conditions for dragnet fishing and trawling, threatening the entire Korean fishing industry.[4]

The second stage was set in motion when Korean Ambassador to Japan Kim Yong-ju sent a report to the Korean Ministry of Foreign Affairs on May 10, 1951. Kim's report, entitled *Jurisdiction over Fisheries Resources outside the Territorial Limits of Korea* (May 4, 1951), greatly affected the Korean government's policy stance on fisheries resources jurisdiction. Kim argued that in order to prevent Japanese crossing of the MacArthur Line in violation of Korea's territorial waters, which had caused the fisheries resources to come close to extinction, Korea should demand "jurisdiction" over its territorial waters in the Yellow Sea and in the sea to the southwest of Korea. He believed that a clearly enunciated policy with regard to "jurisdiction over fisheries resources" could effectively replace the MacArthur Line.[5]

Kim's proposal that Korea clearly articulate its jurisdiction over fisheries resources gained an instant and favorable response from the Korean Ministry of Foreign Affairs. On May 16, 1951, the ministry sent an official memo with Kim's report included as a supporting document to the Ministry of Commerce and Industry, requesting that a survey be conducted and maps made of the distance and area to which such a jurisdiction would apply.[6]

On June 16, the Ministry of Commerce and Industry submitted an opinion piece entitled the *Draft on Jurisdictional Waters over Fisheries*, said

---

4   Masaaki Wada, 1965, "A New Beginning of Japan's Fisheries," *The Suisan-Keizai Daily News* 29, pp. 35-37 (Ji, Peace Line, re-quoted from p. 93).

5   "Consultation and request regarding Korea's Policy on Protection of Coastal Fisheries" (Kim Yong-ju, Korean Minister to JapanàMinister of Foreign Affairs), no. 1949 (May 10, 1951), pp. 1354-1369.

6   "Regarding Korea's Policy on Protection of Coastal Fisheries" (Minister of Foreign Affairsà Minister of Commerce & Industry), no. 402 (May 16, 1951), pp. 1371-1372; "Regarding Korea's Policy on Protection of Coastal Fisheries" (Minister of Foreign Affairs → Minister of Commerce & Industry), no. 402 (June 15, 1951), p. 1373.

to be authored by Ji Cheol-geun.[7] Using Kim's report as a reference, the Ministry set a limit on the number of fishing vessels permitted and the areas where trawling was prohibited. More specifically, it established a fisheries conservation jurisdiction beyond Korea's territorial waters in the Yellow Sea, the East and South China Seas, and the waters to the west of Jejudo. This fishing jurisdiction was established in accordance with the *Regulations on the Reproduction and Protection of Fisheries in Joseon* (December 10, 1928) produced by the Joseon Government General during the period of the Japanese colonial rule of Korea. The Ministry also designated certain areas where trawling was to be prohibited in order to prevent the waning of resources due to indiscriminate overfishing by Japanese vessels in Korean coastal waters. The Fisheries Bureau of the Ministry of Commerce and Industry calculated that the establishment of a "fisheries conservation jurisdiction" based on the criteria developed by the Japanese themselves would make it harder for Japan to reject it.[8] According to Ji Cheol-geun, the draft was made mainly with an eye to the interests and concerns of the Korean fishing industry to protect the key fishing grounds of Korea.[9] Dokdo, however, was not mentioned in this document.

In the third stage, following the circulation among and modification of Ambassador Kim's report by the relevant government ministries, the concepts were further clarified and the report was proposed to and passed at a Cabinet meeting (September 1951). During this stage, the concept of fisheries conservation jurisdiction was expanded to encompass conservation management waters and conservation jurisdictional waters. Upon receiving the proposal of the Ministry of Commerce and Industry, the Ministry of Foreign Affairs immediately consulted with the Ministry of Justice and later organized follow-up meetings of the chiefs of the relevant bureaus to garner the views of working-level officials.

The MacArthur Line and fisheries issues were discussed at a meeting of

---

7   "Regarding Korea's Policy on Protection of Coastal Fisheries" (Minister of Commerce & Industry → Minister of Foreign Affairs), no. 368 (June 16, 1951), pp. 1371-1388.

8   Ji, *Peace Line*, pp. 109-118.

9   Ji, *Peace Line*, pp. 115-118.

directors general and directors held at the Gyeongsangnam-do provincial government office on August 25. At the meeting, it was confirmed that the MacArthur Line would be inevitably abolished once the Japanese Peace Treaty went into effect. It was further reported that the Diplomatic Section of MacArthur's Headquarters had notified Korea on April 19, 1951 that the MacArthur Line was neither an international boundary line dividing territorial waters from international waters nor a fisheries boundary establishing respective commercial fishing zones between Korea and Japan.[10] For this reason, the Korean government came to the conclusion that it was now necessary to declare its own fisheries conservation management waters and fisheries conservation jurisdictional waters and then to engage Japan in talks in order to conclude a fishing agreement before the MacArthur Line would become a thing of the past and to protect the fishing grounds in international waters contiguous to the coasts of Korea from overfishing.[11] The meeting concluded that the declaration of such conservation zones was indeed justified based on the Truman Proclamation of September 1945, which established that a country could, for the conservation of its natural resources, extend its territorial waters 200 nautical miles from its coasts, as well as the reported proclamation by Japan of maritime zones of 150 nautical miles following the conclusion of the peace treaty.

At the conclusion of that meeting, a report was produced titled *The Commentary of the Korean Government with Regards to the MacArthur Line*, which argued that, if at all possible, the MacArthur Line should be maintained and that the development of a separate fishing agreement with Japan was needed in order for the line to be sustained internationally. The rationale given for the preservation of the MacArthur Line was that it had been a vested interest of Korea for the past six years, its revocation was a unilateral decision by the Combined Forces Command, and Japan

---

10   "Minutes of Meeting on Fishery Issues with Japan," pp. 1402-1403; "1. MacArthur Line Issue (Government Opinion)," pp. 1405-1408.

11   "(Annexed Paper 2) Summary and Records of Resolutions of the Meeting on Fisheries Agreement with Japan," pp. 1422-1428.

was exploiting fishing resources in the East and South China Seas off the coast of Korea and in the sea southwest of Jejudo.[12] At this stage, the Korean government publicly presented as the bases of its argument the Truman Proclamation of September 1945, the fisheries agreement between the US and Canada (July 26, 1930), the International Convention for the Regulation of Whaling (December 2, 1946), the Northwest Atlantic Fisheries Convention (February 8, 1949), the agreement between the US and Canada on *Ulleulje(seals' penises)*(美加間 膃肭臍協定), and the fishing agreement between the US and Costa Rica.[13]

Though not stated in official documents, it is most likely that Dokdo was included in the fisheries conservation management waters and fisheries conservation jurisdictional waters for the first time during this period. The memoirs of Kim Dong-jo, director general of the Bureau of State Affairs of the Ministry of Foreign Affairs, as well as those of Ji Cheol-geun, director of the Fishery Department of the Ministry of Commerce and Industry, both of whom oversaw progress on this issue at the working level, attest to this fact.[14]

The last stage was from September 1951 to January 1952, when the idea of designating fisheries conservation jurisdictional waters, which had by this time received the approval of the Cabinet council, was expanded to include the concept of sovereignty over adjacent seas. The Minister of Foreign Affairs quickly submitted to the Cabinet council a document titled *Item on the Proclamation of Fisheries Conservation Zones*. The document was subsequently submitted for the President's approval on September 8. According to an attachment to this document, the title of the presidential proclamation was *Proclamation of the President of the Republic of Korea regarding the Conservation of Fisheries in International Waters Contiguous*

---

12   "(Annexed Paper 1) 1. Opinion of the Korean Government regarding the MacArthur Line from The MacArthur Line and the Fisheries Agreement" (Minister of Foreign Affairs → Korean Minister to Japan) (Aug. 29, 1951), pp. 1417-1428.

13   *Ibid.*

14   Kim Dong-jo, 1986, *Memoirs of 30 Years of Korea-Japan Talks*, Joongang Ilbo, pp. 16; Ji, *Peace Line*, pp. 109-129, 167-172.

to the Coasts of Korea.[15]

The document contained a synopsis of the position of the Korean government discussed thus far. The proclamation stated that either the MacArthur Line should be preserved or the Korean government would unilaterally declare fisheries conservation zones beyond Korea's territorial waters in order to protect its waters from overfishing and to delimit its national fishing grounds.[16]

President Rhee Syngman did not give his immediate approval to the document, however.[17] It was only on January 18, 1952 that the Korean government announced the *Presidential Proclamation of Sovereignty over Adjacent Seas* by Proclamation No. 14 of the State Council.[18]

As described above, on the diplomatic front, the Korean government requested the US to keep the MacArthur Line in the Japanese Peace treaty. Internally, the ministries involved worked together on a countermeasure to offset the expiration of this Line. Between August and September of 1951, the government established fisheries conservation zones incorporating sovereignty claims over Dokdo as it prepared for bilateral talks with Japan upon conclusion of the San Francisco Treaty. In other words, Korea's proposed alternative to the MacArthur Line was intended to validate the country's sovereignty claims over Dokdo in addition to protecting its traditional fishing grounds from overfishing. Thus, it was designed to achieve the twofold objectives of sustaining the MacArthur Line in another form and maintaining Korean sovereignty over Dokdo.

---

15 "Regarding the Declaration of Fisheries Conservation Zones" (Minister of Foreign Affairs → President), no. 958 (Sept. 8, 1951), pp. 1485-1493.

16 "Summary of Rationale for Fisheries Measures, Regarding the Declaration of Fisheries Conservation Zones" (Minister of Foreign Affairs → President), no. 958 (Sept. 8, 1951), p. 1478.

17 Kim Dong-jo, 1986, *Memoirs of 30 Years of Korea-Japan Talks*, Joongang Ilbo, pp. 18; Ji, *Peace Line*, pp. 126-129.

18 Ji, *Peace Line*, pp. 109-129, 167-172.

2) 1952 Dokdo expedition by the Corea Alpine Club and the Dokdo bombing incidents

Immediately after Korea's *Proclamation of Sovereignty over Adjacent Seas* was made publicly on January 18, 1952, the Japanese Foreign Office issued a statement (January 20) asserting Japanese sovereignty over Dokdo.[19] The most noteworthy was that, rather than arguing as it does today that Dokdo had been an inherent part of Japan for centuries (the theory of inherent territory) or that Japan had acquired Dokdo as *terra nullius* in 1905 (the *terra nullius* theory), Japan claimed that Dokdo had become Japanese territory under the Japanese peace treaty of 1951.

Following the 1947 expedition to Dokdo, another Dokdo expedition of the Corea Alpine Club was organized in 1952. Though Korea was in a state of war, governmental support was provided to make the expedition. The expedition was organized by the Corea Alpine Club and sponsored by the Ministry of Culture and Education, the Ministry of Foreign Affairs, the Ministry of National Defense, the Ministry of Commerce and Industry, and the Bureau of Public Information, and was given the same name as the earlier expedition in 1947: the Ulleungdo and Dokdo Scientific Expedition. Details of the 1952 expedition can be found in the (*Seventh month of 4285 by the Dangun calendar) Plan for the Ulleungdo and Dokdo Scientific Expedition* and the (*Ninth month of 4285 by the Dangun calendar) Plan for the Ulleungdo and Dokdo Scientific Expedition* owned by Professor Park Byeong-ju, the first Korean to survey Dokdo.[20] The documents present the purpose and missions of the expedition as follows:

(1) To survey the territory of Ulleungdo and Dokdo in every field of the

---

19 *Jayu Shinmun* (Jan. 26, 1952); *Daegu Maeil Shinmun* (Jan. 31, 1952).

20 "(Seventh month of 4285 by the Dangun calendar) Plan for the Ulleungdo and Dokdo Scientific Expedition" and "(Ninth month of 4285 by the Dangun calendar) Plan for the Ulleungdo and Dokdo Scientific Expedition," *Survey of Dokdo 1952-1953: Materials donated by Professor Park Byeong-ju regarding the Ulleungdo and Dokdo Scientific Expedition by the Corea Alpine Club*, kept at the Dokdo Materials Room of the National Library of Korea.

natural sciences (geology, mineral deposits, topography, biology, and meteorology)

(2) To survey the waters around Ulleungdo and Dokdo in every field of the natural sciences (oceanographic research, meteorology, biology, and marine life)

(3) To survey Ulleungdo and Dokdo in every field of the humanities (history, archaeology, language, folklore, geography, social economy, fishing, and agriculture)

(4) To measure Dokdo and its vicinity (measurement painting, photography, film, and media coverage)

(5) To survey the quality of life of Ulleungdo residents and fishermen active in the Dokdo area, conduct medical survey, and offer free medical treatment

(6) To conduct propaganda and produce a survey report[21]

As far as the length of the expedition was concerned, the first plan made in July called for an 11-day trip, while the second plan made in September called for a 10-day trip. The first plan decided the travel sequence as Busan—Pohang—Ulleungdo—Dokdo—Ulleungdo—Pohang—Busan, while the second had Busan—Ulleungdo—Dokdo—Ulleungdo—Busan.

The catalyst behind the expedition was Japan's claim that Dokdo was part of its territory following conclusion of the San Francisco Peace Treaty along with the expectation that Dokdo would emerge as an important diplomatic issue during bilateral talks with Japan. Thus, the plans read, according to the Corea Alpine Club, the objective of the expedition was to shed light on the "fact that, as an island annexed to Ulleungdo, Dokdo is Korean territory."[22]

The expedition headquarters was organized by members of the Corea

---

21 *Materials donated by Professor Park Byeong-ju regarding the Ulleungdo and Dokdo Scientific Expedition by the Corea Alpine Club*, kept at the Dokdo Materials Room of the National Library of Korea, pp. 51, 63.

22 "On the Departure of the Ulleungdo and Dokdo Scientific Expedition," Corea Alpine Club, undated, *Survey of Dokdo 1952-1953*, pp. 122-123.

Alpine Club and, as in the 1947 trip, leading authorities in academia and the cultural sector took part. According to expedition records, the Dokdo expedition was the outcome of close cooperation and thorough preparation between the Korean government and the Corea Alpine Club. Of the two plans made, the July plan called for about 60 people to take part, most of whom were retained in the September plan as well.[23] Meanwhile, based on records of the Corea Alpine Club, 17 women divers were also to take part.[24] In light of their active participation in the 1951 expedition to Parangdo, it appears that divers were to be mobilized again for the 1952 expedition, mainly to conduct a detailed investigation into the geographical features around Dokdo.

The expedition enjoyed broad support from across the administration, as revealed by the mobilized efforts and resources of the Ministry of Culture and Education, the Ministry of Foreign Affairs, the Ministry of National Defense, the Ministry of Commerce and Industry, and the Bureau of Public Information. The budget allocated for the trip totaled 32.58 million won, including 29.58 million won from the government and 3 million won from the club's own funds.

Planning for the trip began in July but actual survey of the island didn't begin until September. The first expeditionary group, comprised of 45 members, departed from the fish market wharf behind the Fifth Army Hospital at 10 am on September 17, 1952.[25] The expedition was to last ten days, with the group returning to Busan on September 26. According to media reports, some of the specialists in the group stayed on Dokdo for two to three days, while the remaining members stayed in Ulleungdo. This shows that the priority of the expedition was on Dokdo.

The *Jinnam-ho*(vessel) arrived in Dodong-hang(port) on Ulleungdo the morning of September 18, 1952. No sooner had it arrived than fear that it may be impossible to go to Dokdo due to the bombing of the island by

---

23   *Ibid.*, pp. 64-66; Park Byeong-ju, 1953, *Survey of Dokdo*, *Yonggwangno* Issue 4 (Commemorating Reconstruction), Busan Technical High School, p. 54.

24   Kim, "Thirty Years' History of the Corea Alpine Club," p. 36.

25   *Chosun Ilbo* and *Dong-A Ilbo* (Sept. 18, 1952).

the US Air Force turned into a reality. On September 20, the head of the Ulleungdo and Dokdo scientific expedition, Hong Jong-in, sent a telegram to the Minister of Commerce and Industry that, on September 15, a plane of unknown origins had dropped four bombs on the west island of Dokdo.[26]

While in Ulleungdo, the expeditionary group contacted the Air Forces authorities and reported news of the bombing to the Minister of Commerce and Industry in order to ensure the safety of its members. In his report to the Minister, Hong Jong-in stated that the Korean Air Force, upon request from residents of Ulleungdo, asked the US Fifth Air Force on April 25, 1952 to stop its bombing runs over Dokdo, and that on May 4, the Fifth Air Force replied that Dokdo was not a bombing range. This fact was conveyed to Gyeongsangbuk-do and Ulleungdo through the Chief of Staff of the Korean Air Force.[27] Thus, on May 4, 1952, it was confirmed in Ulleungdo that Dokdo was not a bombing range for the US Fifth Air Force. Furthermore, in a prepared statement on September 21, the Minister of Commerce and Industry announced that the US Fifth Air Force had confirmed that Dokdo was not a bombing range.[28]

Upon receipt of this report, the Dokdo scientific expedition decided to proceed with its planned trip to Dokdo. At 5:30 am on September 22, the expedition left Dodong-hang Port for Dokdo. Around 11 am, when the expedition was about two kilometers from Dokdo, four US military aircraft began their bombing run over Dokdo.[29]

Following close communication and negotiations by the Korean Navy Headquarters and the Air Force Headquarters with the US Fifth Air Force and the United Nations, the expedition departed for Dokdo again on September 24. At 9:30 am, just about a kilometer off the shores of Dokdo, the expedition encountered yet another bombing run by the US Air Force.[30]

---

26 Bureau of State Affairs of the Ministry of Foreign Affairs, *Introduction to the Dokdo Issue*, pp. 44-47; *Pyeonghwa Shinmun* (Sept. 23, 1952).

27 *Dong-A Ilbo* (Sept. 21, 1952)

28 *Dong-A Ilbo* (Sept. 22, 1952)

29 *Chosun Ilbo* (Sept. 25, 1952)

30 "Fourth Report of the Scientific Expedition," *Dong-A Ilbo* (Sept. 28, 1952).

As can be seen by the above account, around the time that the expeditionary group was dispatched to Dokdo, the US Fifth Air Force was conducting bombing runs over Dokdo. These bombing runs took place on September 15, September 22, and September 24 of 1952. One single-engine plane dropped four bombs on September 15; four twin-engine planes dropped 25 bombs on September 22; and somewhere between two and four fighters bombed Dokdo again on September 24. The Dokdo expedition assumed that Japan must have been behind the US Air Force bombing of Dokdo.

The Corea Alpine Club's original plan was to erect a territorial signpost that read "독도(Dokdo)·獨島·LIANCOURT" on the front and "15th AUG, 1952" on the back. The Korean word for Dokdo was written in the biggest letters on the sign, and Dokdo's international name "Liancourt Rocks" was inscribed on the sign along with it. The date inscribed on the sign was the National Liberation Day of Korea. With the landing on Dokdo becoming impossible to complete, the disappointed expeditionary group left the signpost in the custody of the Ulleung Police Station and returned to Busan on September 26.

The Dokdo bombing incident of September 1952 subsequently became a subject of bitter controversy between Korea, the US and Japan. On February 27, 1953, the Korean military announced that a comprehensive agreement had been reached between the Korean authorities and the United Nations Command in which the Commander in Chief of the United States Forces' Far Eastern Command had guaranteed that there would be no more aerial bombing exercises conducted in the vicinity of Dokdo and that now "the US government also recognized that Dokdo was part of Korean territory."[31]

The Japanese government immediately refuted this statement. It argued that, upon inquiry with the Commander in Chief of the United States Forces' Far Eastern Command, it received reply that "the United Nations Command only informed the Korean government that the bombing exercises would be suspended, but there is nothing more to it."

---

[31] *Dong-A Ilbo* (Feb. 28, 1953).

3) 1953 Dokdo expedition by the Corea Alpine Club and erection of a territorial signpost

From May 1953 onwards, the unlawful intrusion of Japan into the waters off Dokdo and unlawful Japanese landings on Dokdo became very frequent. As will be described later in the following section, Japanese encroachments on Dokdo began after it was officially removed from the list of bombing ranges for US forces on March 19, 1953. Between May and July 1953, patrol boats of the Maritime Safety Agency of Japan and test ships from fisheries experimental stations began to frequent the waters off Dokdo and make illegal landings on the island. The following list delineates some of the most well-known of these incursions:

- **May 28:** The *Shimanemaru* (63 tons), a test ship from the Shimane Prefecture fisheries experimental station, illegally landed on Dokdo, questioned 30 Korean fishermen, and inspected 10 Korean boats.
- **June 23:** The *Noshiromaru* and *Kuzuryumaru* patrol boats of the Maritime Security Agency of the Eighth Precinct illegally intruded into the waters off Dokdo but failed to land on the island due to high seas.
- **June 26-27:** The *Oki* and *Kuzuryumaru* patrol boats of the Maritime Security Agency of the Eighth Precinct illegally intruded into the waters off Dokdo. Thirty Japanese officials illegally landed on Dokdo and interned one Korean fishing boat (a barge) and six fishermen for interrogation. They also erected two Japanese territorial landmarks and two signboards.
- **July 12:** A patrol boat of the Japanese Maritime Security Agency illegally intruded into the waters off Dokdo and encountered three Korean boats that were accompanied by seven policemen. The Japanese officials argued with them for hours that Dokdo was Japanese territory. Then warning shots were fired from the Korean side during the incident.[32]

The Korean authorities immediately reported Japan's illegal landings

---

32   See next section of this chapter entitled "2. Japan: Propaganda and Stratagem."

on Dokdo to the National Assembly. On July 8, the 19th plenary session of the National Assembly recommended that a strong protest be sent "to the Japanese government regarding the unlawful trespassing of Japanese authorities on Dokdo, which is a territory of Korea." The session adopted a resolution to "send to Dokdo a strong local expedition under the oversight of the Corea Alpine Club."[33]

Meanwhile, on July 8, 1953, the Korean Ministry of Foreign Affairs convened a joint meeting of officials from the relevant government entities—the Ministries of Foreign Affairs and National Defense, Legislation, and the Ministry of Home Affairs—to discuss the Dokdo issue. At the meeting, it was decided to 1) build a lighthouse (the Ministry of Foreign Affairs would discuss with the Ministry of Transportation on this), 2) dispatch naval vessels to Dokdo (to verify if Japanese authorities had installed any signposts), 3) request that the Navy Hydrographic Service erect a surveyor's mark, and 4) conduct a historical and geographical survey of the Dokdo area (Ministry of Foreign Affairs).[34] Furthermore, following a request by the Ministry of Foreign Affairs, the Ministry of National Defense dispatched a naval vessel to Dokdo on July 8 to conduct week-long patrol activities there.[35] The Ministry of Transportation was tasked with building a lighthouse, and the Ministry of National Defense with erecting a surveyor's mark.[36]

The series of provocative actions by Japan had a significant impact on the start of the second Korea-Japan talks (April 15-July 13, 1953), which were ongoing at the time. During the fisheries negotiations, Japan proposed that both countries respect the principle of freedom of navigation and not

---

33   Bureau of State Affairs of the Ministry of Foreign Affairs, *Introduction to the Dokdo Issue*, pp. 67-68.

34   "Calling of Meeting of Relevant Ministries to Discuss the Dokdo Issue" (Minister of Foreign Affairs → Ministers of National Defense, Home Affairs, and Legislation), No. 1146 (Jul. 7, 1953), *Dokdo Issue, 1952-1953*.

35   *Pyeonghwa Shinmun* (Jul. 11, 1953); *Dong-A Ilbo* (Jul. 19, 1953).

36   "On the Illegal Invasion of Dokdo by Japanese Authorities" (Jul. 25, 1953) (Minister of Foreign Affairs → Minister of National Defense and the Minister of Transportation), *Dokdo Issue, 1952-1953*.

recognize the jurisdiction of any coastal states over international waters. Japan demanded further that the Peace Line be abolished, but Korea refused.[37] While it was engaged in bilateral talks and fisheries negotiations with Korea, Japan, at the same time, began mobilizing its forces to make further incursions into the Dokdo area and to subject the Koreans working and fishing there to harsh interrogations. In retrospect, it now appears that Japan's strategy was to exercise diplomacy on the one hand, and to engage in power politics on the other.

The Korean government responded by organizing yet another Dokdo expedition by the Corea Alpine Club, and lent it its full support. In a joint meeting of the vice ministers of the relevant ministries (the Ministries of Foreign Affairs, National Defense, Culture and Education, Commerce and Industry, Finance, and Transportation), it was decided to provide various forms of assistance for the expedition, including a fund of 4.5 million won for the trip.[38] The Navy also provided naval vessel No. 905 for the use of the research team during the expedition.

The mission and purpose of the 1953 expedition was more explicit than its 1952 predecessor. Given that Japan was making illegal incursions into Dokdo and openly erecting territorial signposts on the island in 1953, the expeditionary group presented the following as the foremost purposes of the survey of Dokdo and its adjacent waters:

(1) To survey Dokdo and its adjacent waters (geology, meteorology, oceanology, biology, fisheries, history, and geography)
(2) To conduct a land survey and create a map of Dokdo
(3) To conduct an additional survey of Ulleungdo (archaeology, linguistics, social and economic studies, fisheries, and agriculture in addition to the fields mentioned above)

---

37   Park, *Korea-Japan Talks*, pp. 143-144.
38   Kim Jeong-tae, 1977, "The Tenth Campaign to Save our Territory: Ulleungdo (Survey) Scientific Expedition with the Support of the Ministry of Foreign Affairs and the Ministry of National Defense" from "30 Years' History of the Corea Alpine Club," *Korean Mountains* XI (Issue of 1975 and 1976), Corea Alpine Club, pp. 37-38.

(4) To survey the quality of life of the fishermen living on Dokdo and Ulleungdo (medical survey and free medical treatment)

(5) To produce a cultural film titled *Ulleungdo and Dokdo*

(6) To publish a report titled *Ulleungdo and Dokdo*

(7) To submit a press release to the media on the results of the survey (painting, photography, movies, and media coverage)[39]

Headed by Hong Jong-in, the 38-member expedition departed Busan for Ulleungdo on naval patrol boat 905 (commanded by Captain Seo Deok-gyun) on October 11, 1953. They arrived in Ulleungdo at 7 am the following day. The expeditionary group left Ulleungdo at 6 am on October 13 and arrived at Dokdo around noon. However, due to inclement weather, the group was forced to go back to Ulleungdo, arriving at 9 o'clock that night. According to Hong Jong-in, the group encountered a Japanese patrol craft on the way back.[40]

The expeditionary group departed from Ulleungdo at 1 am on October 15 to make the return trip to Dokdo and arrived there at 5:30 am. After the boat was moored to the south of the Island between Dongdo(East Island) and Seodo(West Island), two barges landed the members of the expedition on a pebble strewn beach of Dongdo.[41]

Three different types of survey activities were conducted on the island. First, the territorial signposts erected by the Japanese reading "島根縣 隱地郡 五箇村 竹島," which means "Takeshima, Gokomura, Ochi-gun of Shimane Prefecture" in English, were pulled out.[42] There were two Japanese signposts, one on both Dongdo and Seodo. Upon removal, one signpost was given to the National Assembly and the other to the Navy

---

39 *Survey of Dokdo 1952-1953*, pp. 145-153, 156-159.

40 "The Dokdo expedition (four trips) (1) First landing failed and unmarked Japanese patrol boat appeared in adjacent waters (Hong Jong-in)," *Chosun Ilbo* (Oct. 22, 1953).

41 "The Dokdo expedition (four trips) (2) Encouraged by unexpected "transmission," we begin our expedition in full swing after sunrise (Hong Jong-in)," *Chosun Ilbo* (Oct. 22, 1953); Kim, "The Tenth Campaign to Save our Territory," p. 38.

42 Lee, "Root out the Traces of 'Takeshima' in Dokdo in 1953."

Headquarters.[43]

Second, the signpost that the expedition of 1952 had failed to erect was installed. This signpost was inscribed with the date of August 15, 1952, which was the date on which it was originally supposed to be erected. In addition, the date of October 15, 1953, the date on which the signpost was actually erected, was inscribed on the side. The signpost, which had remained in the custody of the Ulleungdo Police Station for about a year, was erected by Hong Jong-in at a spot a short distance away from the stone erected by Gyeongsangbuk-do in memory of the Dokdo bombing victims.[44] The signpost that the Corea Alpine Club erected was removed by the Japanese government not long after the expedition left Dokdo.

Third and most important, the expedition conducted measurements of the island and completed survey activities. The scientific survey activities, other than the taking of measurements, were concluded fairly quickly,[45] with all scientific activities finished over the four days between October 13 and 16. The survey activities on Dokdo took place for the most part over two days from October 15 to 16.

Meanwhile, all the activities undertaken by the third Dokdo expeditionary group were photographed by Kim Han-yong, a photographer who traveled along with the group.[46] Kim's photos were put on exhibit for the first time in 2004 during an exhibition marking his 80th birthday. Ten of his photos were also published in the *Weekly Dong-A* magazine in 2005.[47] Kim's photos of the Dokdo expedition, which totaled 31, were later featured in the *Kim Han-yong Work Collection, 1947-2003*.[48] In addition,

---

43   Kim, "The Tenth Campaign to Save our Territory," p. 39.
44   "The Dokdo expedition (four trips) (3) Almost became Robinson Crusoe, camped out on the lonely island on the night of the 15th (Hong Jong-in)," *Chosun Ilbo* (Oct. 26, 1953).
45   Park, *Survey of Dokdo*, pp. 53-64.
46   The five pictures of the Dokdo Expedition taken by Park Byeong-ju were featured in *Pictorial Korea 1953-1954*; *Survey of Dokdo 1952-1953*, pp. 173-176).
47   Lee, "Root out the Traces of 'Takeshima' in Dokdo in 1953," pp. 8-11; Lee Jeong-hun, 2005, "Photographer Kim Han-yong makes headlines with his photos of Dokdo from 1953," *Weekly Dong-A*, Serial No. 477 (Mar. 22), pp. 66-67.
48   Kim Han-yong, 2003, *Kim Han-yong Work Collection 1947-2003*, Nunbit, pp. 211-217.

the documentary *Dokdo* of the Ministry of Culture and Communications was filmed by Lee Yong-min who traveled with the expeditionary group.

The debriefing of the 1953 Dokdo Scientific Expedition took place on May 6, 1954 at the Lecture Hall of the Medical School of Seoul National University. At that time, Professor Park Byeong-ju donated to the Dokdo Materials Room of the National Assembly Library his personal materials on the 1952-1953 Dokdo scientific expeditions.[49]

---

[49] Park Byeong-ju donated several records related to the survey to the National Library of Korea. Currently, the 233-page *Survey of Dokdo 1952-1953* is kept at the Library's Dokdo Materials Room.

2

Japan

: Propaganda and Stratagem

1) Propaganda of 1951: Japanese claims of sovereignty over Dokdo

Immediately after its defeat in the war, the Japanese government never once, internally or externally, claimed sovereignty over Dokdo. Nor did it react to the large-scale survey of Dokdo conducted by the Provisional Government of Korea in 1947 or to the Dokdo bombing incident of 1948. As explained in previous chapters, Japan's only claim to sovereignty over Dokdo was made in a publicity paper published by the Japanese Ministry of Foreign Affairs in June 1947 where it claimed that Dokdo and Ulleungdo were part of Japanese territory. Japanese sailing to Dokdo was prohibited under a SCAP mandate, but even so, the unlawful encroachment onto Dokdo by the Japanese was already becoming a troublesome issue of concern to Korea in mid-1947. The following fragmentary records indicate the beginning of a pattern of such encroachments from 1945 to 1951.

According to Kenzo Kawakami, an officer in charge of Dokdo at the Treaties Bureau of the Japanese Ministry of Foreign Affairs, Japanese excursions to Dokdo occurred twice during this period, once in 1949 and the other in 1951. Of course, such ventures were in direct violation of the SCAP mandate. Nevertheless, testimonials exist that, in July 1949, some Japanese from the Wakayama Prefecture sailed to Dokdo on a fishing boat and gathered between 120 and 130 straw bags of sea lion excrement or fowl droppings. They were quoted as saying that their intent was to use the excrement as fertilizer; they also said that while there they found blood stains of Koreans killed by bombs dropped from US aircraft.[50]

Another testimonial of Kawakami stated that, in mid-May 1951, five Japanese sailed to Dokdo on a 5-ton ship and found 50 Koreans and four powerboats there. The Korean people were harvesting seaweed and building a hut for shelter. The Japanese protested to them that "Takeshima is Japanese territory, so leave this island immediately," but the Koreans refused, saying, "We don't know who Takeshima belongs to but we have come here to harvest seaweed every year." The Koreans also informed them that up to 24 motorboats traveled there from Korea at peak times every year.[51] Though these testimonials emerged only after Japan began making ownership claims to Dokdo, they are suggestive of the Korean fishermen's belief that Korea had ownership of Dokdo on account of the fact that they had been coming there every year to harvest seaweed.

However, the booklet *Changes in Fisheries in Takeshima* (August 1953) published by the Second Division of the Asia Affairs Bureau of the Japanese Ministry of Foreign Affairs, which contained Kenzo Kawakami's accounts, is suspected of manipulating the facts of the matter to serve its own purposes. Originally, for example, in the testimonial as it first appeared in Seizaburo Tamura's *A Study of Takeshima, Shimane Prefecture* (March 1954),[52] near the end of April 1951, Japanese fishermen accidentally reached Dokdo after being cast adrift at sea and, while there, they witnessed Korean fishermen "living" and "fishing" there. Upon their return to Japan, they publicized this fact, sparking the conflict over Dokdo. Nowhere in Tamura's accounts was there any mention of the Japanese fishermen protesting or getting into a conflict with the Koreans over the fact that they were living and working there. Thus, it appears highly likely that Kawakami's account of the fishermen's testimonials was somewhat exaggerated and embellished to serve the ends of the Japanese Ministry of Foreign Affairs. Additional evidence of manipulation is found in its version of a July 1953 testimony

---

50   Verbal testimony by Akira Okumura (July 11, 1953, Shimane Prefecture Government's hearing of Yasutaka Hayami), verbal testimony by Shotaro Hamada (Kenzo Kawakami, 1966, *A Study of the History and Geography of Takeshima*, Kokonshoyin, pp. 264, 272).

51   Verbal testimony by Shotaro Hamada, pp. 264, 272, Asia 2, Japanese Ministry of Foreign Affairs, *Changes in Fisheries in Takeshima* (August of the 28th year of Shōwa), pp. 33-34.

52   Seizaburo Tamura, 1954, *A Study of Takeshima, Shimane Prefecture*, Shimane Prefecture, p. 45.

by one of the fishermen in a document published by the Japanese Ministry of Foreign Affairs.[53] In an interview with the Ministry (July 1953), the fisherman testified that he had intentionally sailed to Dokdo and, while there, had an argument with Korean fishermen.[54]

Prior to 1951, the only interest in Dokdo had come from residents of Shimane Prefecture involved in the fishing industry. Interest from the central government or the media was marginal at best. Following the incident described above, however, the Shimane Prefecture began to use the testimony of the fishermen as a launching pad for a large-scale propaganda campaign on Dokdo. According to Tamura, the Shimane Prefecture submitted a petition to the Minister of Foreign Affairs on August 30, 1951, asking it to get Dokdo reaffirmed as Japanese territory in the Japanese peace treaty since the island was a territory of the Prefecture. Prior to departing for the US as a plenipotentiary for the Japanese peace treaty, a Japanese politician named Date, who was serving as a member of the House of Councilors from the Shimane Prefecture, questioned the Ministry of Foreign Affairs about the status of Takeshima. Then, at a press conference on August 31, the Ministry formally announced that Takeshima had been confirmed as Japanese territory in the peace treaty, refuting rumors that the document would separate it from Japan.[55] News of this development became known to Korea in early September 1951 when the *Minju Shinbo* carried an article on the Japanese government's claim to ownership over Dokdo. This is perhaps the first time that Dokdo was ever reported in major Japanese newspapers.[56]

Furthermore, on October 22, a high-ranking official of the Japanese Ministry of Foreign Affairs remarked at the National Diet that Dokdo

---

53 Verbal testimony by Shotaro Hamada (July 9, 1953), Asia 2, Japanese Ministry of Foreign Affairs, *Changes in Fisheries in Takeshima* (August of the 28th year of Shōwa), p. 33.

54 On September 8th, 1951, the *Shimane Prefecture Daily* and the *Mainichi Shimbun* carried an article on Japanese fishermen drifting ashore near Dokdo (Seizaburo Tamura, 1965, *A New Study of Takeshima by Shimane Prefecture*, General Affairs Department of the Shimane Prefecture Government, p. 117).

55 Tamura, *A Study of Takeshima, Shimane Prefecture*, p. 45.

56 "Japan claims sovereignty over Dokdo on September 3, 1951," *Minju Shinbo* (Sept. 5, 1951).

had been confirmed as being Japanese territory in the San Francisco Peace Treaty. During the 6th meeting (October 22, 1951) of the Special Committee on the Peace Conference and Japan-US Security of the House of Representatives, Toshinaga Yamamoto, a committee member from Shimane Prefecture, raised the following question about the status of sovereignty over Takeshima:

- **Toshinaga Yamamoto:** This is a very specific issue particularly relating to Article 3 (of the Peace Treaty). In the Reference Map of Japanese Territory, which we were given as reference material, the line indicating Japanese territory over the Sea of Japan passes just above Takeshima. Ulleungdo may be a part of Joseon, but Takeshima was originally under the jurisdiction of the Shimane Prefecture and it is an important fishing ground. On this map, is Takeshima a part of Japanese territory or has it been transferred to Joseon as an island annexed to Ulleungdo? Of course, the people of Shimane Prefecture interpret this as saying that Takeshima is a part of Japanese territory, but at this point, this certainly needs to be clarified.
- **Ryuen Kusaba, Deputy Minister for Political Affairs of the Ministry of Foreign Affairs:** Takeshima is currently not featured in Japan's administrative division under the Allied occupation, but I was informed that Takeshima would be specified as Japanese territory under the peace treaty, so it seems that Takeshima has been clearly affirmed as being Japanese territory.[57] (Underlined by the quoter)

Toshinaga Yamamoto, a member of the Democratic Party from the Shimane Prefecture, was committed to making an issue of Dokdo in 1951, raising questions about Dokdo several times at the National Diet. His most famous engagement was his question to a Foreign Ministry official at the 10th meeting of the Foreign Affairs Committee of the House of

---

57 "House of Representatives of the Special Committee on the San Francisco Peace Treaty and the US-Japan Safety Guarantee Treaty," 6th Issue (Oct. 22, 1951), No. 349, 12th Edition, *House of Representatives*, http://kokkai.ndl.go.jp (accessed May 1, 2009).

Representatives on February 6, 1951. Referring to Habomai, Shikotan, and Takeshima that were "occupied by the US military government for being located below certain degrees north latitude or other measures," Yamamoto commented that some "special measures" must be considered to regain areas that had been under the jurisdiction of Japan as a circuit (*do*, 道), metropolis (*to*, 都), urban prefecture (*fu*, 府), or prefecture (*ken*, 県) in the past. To this, *Hisanaga Shimazu*, director general of the Bureau of State Affairs at the Ministry of Foreign Affairs, replied that "Sufficient study has been made [...] Again, we have attentively and sufficiently listened to your comments and will further study the matter [...]We ask for your understanding regarding how we deal with this matter."[58] According to Lee Jong-hak, this response was made with reference to Japan's scheme of designating Dokdo as a bombing range.

During one of these sessions, Toshinaga Yamamoto pointed out that the Reference Map of Japanese Territory that the Japanese government had distributed to the members of the National Diet indicated Dokdo was excluded from Japanese territory. Initially, the Japanese Ministry of Foreign Affairs simply denied Yamamoto's remark. Two years later in November of 1953, Japanese Communist Party politician Kanichi Kawakami raised the issue again at the Foreign Affairs Committee of the House of Representatives. Kawakami asked why Takeshima (Dokdo) was excluded from Japan's administrative division under the Allied occupation. Takeso Shimoda, director general of the Treaties Bureau of the Foreign Ministry, replied that though he was not sure about the intent of the SCAP ruling, he believed that SCAP excluded the island for the reason that, in light of the SCAP's occupation policy, it was not desirable to allow the Japanese government or people to frequent an island too far away from the mainland." The following remarks were exchanged between the two at the time:

---

58 "Minutes of the 10th meeting of the Foreign Affairs Committee of the House of Representatives, no. 3" (Feb. 6, 1951), pp. 7-8 [Lee Jong-hak (former Director, Dokdo Museum), "Dokdo Museum Press Release" (Dec. 20, 2001); *Joongang Ilbo* (Dec. 12, 2001)].

- **Kanichi Kawakami, Diet member:** That cannot be. Those islands were excluded for a specific reason. Whether we want to admit it or not, there is a definite reason why they were excluded. So, why was Takeshima excluded? The MacArthur Line was drawn so close to Takeshima, but the island was excluded. Why has the government never questioned why Takeshima was not included on the Japanese side of the MacArthur Line?

- **Takeso Shimoda, Director general of the Treaties Bureau:** I don't know for sure whether we have raised the question before or not, so I will look into the relevant files and get back to you.

- **Kanichi Kawakami:** If the Director of the Treaties Bureau says he doesn't know, then this is proof that the government has never raised the question before. (Omitted) How could this happen? A map was submitted to the National Diet when the peace treaty was ratified. Even on that map, Takeshima is clearly excluded. But there is another line on the map. It's not the MacArthur Line, but a different line. It is the same line as the one separating administrative districts. The government is pretending that it doesn't know, but I think it does. (Omitted)

- **Kanichi Kawakami:** (Omitted) The map that was submitted at the time the peace treaty was ratified, the government hurriedly withdrew it later, but on that map it says Reference Map of Japanese Territory. There, Takeshima is clearly excluded. This map was not submitted to the Committee of the House of Councilors, but only to the House of Representatives. Why was this map not submitted to the House of Councilors? This is indication that the US is not making its position clear. This is why Deputy Prime Minister Ogata replied to a question from the Labor Party that Takeshima is our territory under international law, but he didn't say that Takeshima is our territory under the peace treaty. (Omitted) The government's failure to handle this issue clearly has led the Rhee Syngman government to protest strongly, and the US has gotten the Asians to quarrel on this point. This is also why the Yoshida government is now accused of exploiting this issue to stir up public sentiment in favor of rearmament. Any further mention of this will only exacerbate the dispute, so I will stop here, but let me just say that the US has never said anything clear on the issue. Also, the Japanese government was asked to provide documentation attesting that Takeshima is Japanese territory under the peace treaty but hasn't yet done so. So again, I urge the government to do so.[59] (Underlined by the quoter)

The points made by Kanichi Kawakami were accurate and perceptive. First, the Reference Map (*Map of Japanese Territory*) that the Japanese Ministry of Foreign Affairs submitted to the House of Representatives in October 1951 clearly showed that Dokdo was outside the boundary of Japanese territory. The same issue had been raised two years earlier by Toshinaga Yamamoto. And, as pointed out by Kawakami, this line was different from the MacArthur Line.

Second, after the map became a contentious issue at the House of Representatives, the Japanese Ministry of Foreign Affairs chose not to submit it to the House of Councilors. This was why the map did not become widely known. The actual map appeared under the name *Map of Japanese Territory* at the beginning of the *Japanese Peace Treaty* published by the *Mainichi Shimbun* in 1952.[60] It clearly showed that Ulleungdo and Dokdo in the East Sea, the four islands in the North (Etorofu, Kunashir, Habomai, Shikotan), Kuchinoshima and Amami Islands south of Kyushu, and Nishinoshima to the east of Japan were outside the boundary of Japanese territory. When the map became a contentious issue in October 1951 at the House of Representatives, the Japanese government quickly retrieved it and then intentionally chose not to submit it to the House of Councilors.

Third, Kawakami was demanding an answer from both the US and the Japanese governments about why Dokdo was excluded from Japanese territory. He complained that the US government never made its position clear and that "it has never said anything clear" about where Dokdo belonged. Given that the US had never notified the Japanese government about its position on the issue, Kawakami's point was well taken. Kawakami also pointed out that the US decision to exclude Dokdo from the list of bombing

---

59   "Minutes of the Foreign Affairs Committee of the House of Representatives, no. 5" (Nov. 4, 1953), Northeast Asian History Foundation, 2009, *Collection of Records relating to Dokdo of the National Diet of Japan, I (1948-1976)*, p. 189.

60   Mainichi Shinbunsha, 1952, *Japanese Peace Treaty*, "Map of Japanese Territory."

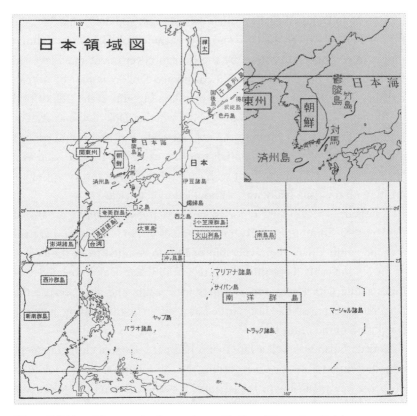

[Figure 7-1] Map of Japanese territory and magnification of the part on Dokdo

ranges was due to the protests on the part of the Korean government. He reviewed the process by which this decision was made, beginning with the initial designation of Dokdo as a training range of the US Air Force, then bombing runs over Dokdo that killed Korean fishermen, the Korean government's subsequent protests about this, and finally the Commander of the US Air Force's decision to exclude Dokdo from its training ranges and its notification of the Korean government of that fact. He believed that this train of events may have led the Korean government to believe that the US recognized Dokdo as Korean territory. He pointed out that if Dokdo had been viewed as Japanese territory from the beginning, then Korea's protests would not have been justified since the Korean fishermen would

471

have come to Dokdo illegally at their own volition and died while illegally fishing there. However, the US decision to exclude Dokdo from its training ranges in response to protests by the Korean government may have led the Koreans to believe that the US considered Dokdo as part of Korean territory. Thus, Kawakami's point was that the ambiguity of the US position on the issue was causing uncertainty about whether Dokdo was Korean or Japanese territory. A Communist Party member, Kawakami argued that the US was, as part of its imperialist policy, using the Dokdo issue as a "stratagem to get Asians to fight with each other," but in this case, the US position on the issue really was, without a doubt, unclear.

Kawakami's views were reported in the *Shimbun Akahata*, a daily of the Japanese Communist Party, on November 9, 1953. Kawakami argued that the conflict over the ownership of Dokdo resulted from the failure of the US to clarify its position with regard to where Dokdo belonged, at times siding with Korea and at others with Japan, and also because the Japanese government had not clarified its position on this leading up to the conclusion of the peace treaty.[61]

Fourth, Japan was well aware that it had not secured a clear statement or endorsement from the US regarding the sovereignty status of Dokdo in the peace treaty. This is why the Japanese government said that Dokdo was Japanese territory according to international law, rather than saying that Dokdo was affirmed as Japanese territory under the peace treaty. Though the government was asked to submit to the National Diet documentation showing that Dokdo was included as Japanese territory under the peace treaty, it had no such documentation to submit as of November 1953. Kawakami's comment that the Yoshida government was exploiting the Dokdo issue as a rationale to stir up public sentiment in favor of rearmament was also in line with the views of the Korean Ministry of Foreign Affairs.

In short, although on the surface the Japanese government was

---

61   Ku Seon-hui, 2007, "Issues in the studies of Dokdo of Korea and Japan with respect to the post-war handling of Dokdo territory by the Allied Powers and future prospects," *Journal for the Studies of Korean History*, No. 28, pp. 363-364.

publicizing Dokdo as being included in Japanese territory at the San Francisco Peace Conference, internally it had serious doubts and concerns that Dokdo may have actually been affirmed as Korean territory. It was also aware that it had no evidential grounds on which to stand that the island was in fact Japanese territory. Thus, it is likely that, following Toshinaga Yamamoto's penetrating questions in October of 1951, the Japanese government moved forward with its scheme to create evidential material in support of its claims over Dokdo.

Following the hearing session in October 1951 at the National Diet, the *Asahi Shimbun* sent a field investigation team to Dokdo. This was a first-of-its kind trip organized by a major Japanese daily newspaper since Japan's defeat in the war. When the *Asahi Shimbun* reporters, six in all, arrived at Dokdo on the morning of November 14, 1951, they found a throng of sea lions and a stone monument erected in memory of bombing victims standing on a rock. The *Asahi Shimbun* provocatively titled its ensuing article *Uninhabited Takeshima returns to Japan*. This was the first time that a major Japanese newspaper ever carried an article about Dokdo after a trip was made there.[62]

This article was reviewed by the *Dong-A Ilbo* in Korea on November 26. In his article, the newspaper's correspondent to Tokyo noted that the *Asahi Shimbun* had called Dokdo, indisputably a territory of Korea, "Takeshima" and that the Japanese newspaper was now under investigation by the authorities because it had sent its correspondents illegally there without following the proper travel procedures established by MacArthur's Headquarters.[63] Thus, soon after the San Francisco Peace Conference was concluded in September 1951, a largely invisible battle over the ownership of Dokdo began to emerge between Korea and Japan.

Having failed to get the US and the UK to settle the Dokdo ownership issue in the Japanese Peace Treaty itself, the Korean government sought

---

[62] "Uninhabited Takeshima returns to Japan," *Asahi Shimbun* (Nov. 24, 1951).

[63] "Japan claims sovereignty over Dokdo, which it calls Takeshima," *Dong-A Ilbo* (Nov. 26, 1951).

instead to resolve it in the form of a fish conservation and fishery demarcation agreement with Japan that would include a "Peace Line." Japan, on the other hand, began to prepare its own basis for claiming sovereignty over Dokdo, based on its understanding that Dokdo was recognized as Japanese territory in the San Francisco Peace Treaty.

Immediately following Korea's *Presidential Proclamation of Sovereignty over Adjacent Seas* in January 1952, Japan refuted it on grounds that Dokdo was its own territory, thus igniting a fiery argument with Korea. This dispute was reminiscent in many respects to the dispute of 1905 when Japan unilaterally annexed Dokdo. In 1905, though it was clearly aware that Dokdo had been a part of Korean territory for centuries, Japan unlawfully declared Dokdo *terra nullius* and used false and fabricated claims to make it part of Japan, announcing this in the Shimane Prefecture gazette. The action was communicated to Korea a year later in 1906 when a Takeshima inspector from the Shimane Prefecture visited Ulleungdo. Korea, which was practically stripped of its sovereignty by Japan at the time, had no energy or time to address this problem as the country was on the verge of ruin. Despite the strong reaction from the Korean media and the general public, Korea had the cards stacked against it. Japan was a well-prepared schemer and determined aggressor.

2) Japan's stratagem in the period 1952-1953: Designation and release of Dokdo as a bombing range

Discussions of "special measures" to secure Japanese sovereignty over Dokdo were held at length in the National Diet between 1952 and 1953. At the heart of these discussions was the designation and release of Dokdo as a bombing range for the US Air Force. Members of the House of Representatives and high-ranking officials of the Foreign Ministry openly discussed this proposal in the Diet.[64]

In February 1952, the US and Japan concluded an administrative

---

64   Lee, "Dokdo Museum Press Release"; *Joongang Ilbo* (Dec. 23, 2001).

agreement on the status of US forces stationed in Japan. And in April, the Japanese peace treaty went into effect. The agreement designating Dokdo as a bombing range was made during this same period. The following dialogue between Toshinaga Yamamoto from the Shimane Prefecture and Kanichiro Ishihara, the Deputy Minister of Foreign Affairs, at a meeting of the 13th Foreign Affairs Committee of the House of Representatives (May 23, 1952) clearly attests to this fact:

- **Yamamoto:** Last time, the Minister of Foreign Affairs said that the Japan-Korea negotiations broke down. <u>Are there any territorial issues that remain unresolved between Japan and Korea?</u>
- **Deputy Minister of Foreign Affairs(Ishihara):** <u>There are no outstanding territorial disputes.</u>
- **Yamamoto:** If so, what is happening with Takeshima, which belongs to the Shimane Prefecture? Reportedly, Korea is claiming sovereignty over it?
- *Ishihara*: Japan considers it to be Japanese territory and the SCAP also approved it as a part of Japan. <u>Only Korea is claiming that it is its territory in its own way.</u>
- **Yamamoto:** That's what I thought. But I hear that <u>the government plans to have Takeshima designated as a bombing range for the US forces in Japan. And I think that plan has the political implication of securing Japanese sovereignty over Takeshima by designating it as a bombing range.</u> Is that right?
- *Ishihara*: <u>We are proceeding along that line.</u>
- **Yamamoto:** As is well known, Takeshima is a fishing ground and a place for hunting sea lions. There are concerns that it will become impossible to hunt sea lions there if the island is designated as a bombing site. I think it should be done in a way that fishing there is not impossible, taking the views of the local people into sufficient consideration. What is the government's view on that?
- *Ishihara*: As you just said, I think the Joint Japan-US Committee will sufficiently consider the interests of the local fishermen when designating Takeshima as a training site.[65] (Underlined by the quoter)

In short, Japan's strategy was to designate Dokdo as a training site for US forces in Japan in order to have the US confirm that Dokdo is Japanese territory. Japan had little rationale otherwise to claim sovereignty over Dokdo in its dispute with Korea.

The US-Japan Administrative Agreement (SOFA) was concluded as a follow-up to the US-Japan Security Treaty of 1951, and the US-Japan Joint Committee was established to oversee its execution. On July 26, 1952, the Joint Committee concluded the *Agreement on Military Facilities and Areas*, which designated Dokdo as a training area for US forces based on an understanding that Dokdo was Japanese territory.

Then, in September 1952, another bombing incident occurred at Dokdo. On September 15, the Korean fishing vessel *Gwangyeongho* was bombed by a US aircraft while fishing there. Then, on September 22 and 24, the Dokdo scientific expedition group witnessed the US bombing of Dokdo from the *Jinnam-ho*. Warnings of the scheduled bombings were only issued to residents of the Shimane Prefecture and the west coast of Honshu. Then, on grounds that the use of Dokdo as a bombing range caused too much trouble for the fishermen of Shimane Prefecture, the Japanese government reversed the decision on March 19, 1953 through a sub-committee of the US-Japan Joint Committee. Just prior to the reversal of this designation, Director general of the Treaties Bureau Shimoda announced at the 15th combined evaluation meeting of the Foreign Affairs Committee and Judicial Affairs Committee of the House of Councilors (March 5, 1953) that "such measures are intended to clearly establish the legal basis of support for the fact that Takeshima is owned by Japan."[66]

Japan's reactions to Korea's claims of sovereignty over Dokdo in 1952 are difficult to understand. When the Korean government first made the *Presidential Proclamation of Sovereignty over Adjacent Seas* in January, Japan argued that Dokdo was its territory. However, no government boats

---

65   "Minutes of the 13th meeting of the Foreign Affairs Committee of the House of Representatives" (May 23, 1952); Tamura, *A New Study of Takeshima by Shimane Prefecture*, pp. 75-76.
66   "Minutes of the 15th joint evaluation meeting of the Foreign Affairs Committee and Judicial Affairs Committee of the House of Councilors" (Mar. 5, 1953).

of the Japanese Maritime Security Agency or Fisheries Agency were as yet observed in the waters off Dokdo. Nor did they try to land on Dokdo. At first, the Japanese government merely engaged in exchanges of charges and countercharges with Korea through diplomatic channels. From May 28, 1953 onwards, however, it began initiating a series of physical aggressions, i.e. violating the waters off Dokdo, making unlawful landings, and installing territorial signposts. Thus, Japan's stratagem of designating and then later releasing Dokdo as a bombing range served as an interim strategy in between its initial engagement with Korea in tit-for-tat diplomatic exchanges in 1952 and its aggressive attempts to physically occupy Dokdo in 1953.

Japan's actions during this period lead to several insightful observations. First, in 1952, Japan lacked any kind of substantial rationale for its claims to Dokdo. Thus, it sought to produce the documentation it lacked indirectly and discretely by exploiting the US to its own advantage. Second, it was obvious why no Japanese patrol boats or fishing vessels appeared in the waters off Dokdo or tried to land there from 1952 t1953: they knew that Dokdo was used as a bombing range for US forces. Third, as soon as Dokdo's designation as a bombing range was revoked on March 19, 1953, Japan immediately began engaging in a series of aggressive actions to establish its ownership. Fourth, after engaging in a twofold offensive in the form of unlawful landings on Dokdo while at the same time sending diplomatic memos to Korea between May and July, Japan began to claim that the designation and release of Dokdo as a bombing range constituted evidence of Japan's sovereignty over it. The events surrounding the island in 1952 and 1953 were not merely accidental; they were interconnected like the spokes of a wheel, being the result of an elaborately planned counteroffensive on the part of Japan.

Each Japanese aggressive action in the form of unlawful attempts at landing on Dokdo and installing Japanese territorial posts there between May and July of 1953 were met with strong reactions on the part of the Korean government. In its counteroffensive, Japan first took a card out of the deck that it had kept in reserve for a long time. The Japanese Ministry of Foreign Affairs presented Korea with a paper titled the *Opinion of the*

Government regarding Takeshima in its memorandum of July 13, 1953.[67] In the paper, the Japanese government claimed that the designation of Dokdo and its subsequent release as a bombing range in the *Agreement on Military Facilities and Zones* of the US-Japan Joint Committee was evidence that Dokdo was indeed under the jurisdiction of Japan. This was the culmination of Japan's postwar scheme to secure sovereignty over Dokdo.

But did the agreements that Japan concluded with the US really support Japan's claims? After the Japanese peace treaty went into effect, the Preliminary Working Group established between the US and Japan automatically transitioned into the US-Japan Joint Committee in accordance with Article 26 of the administrative agreement.[68] Contained in an annex to the US-Japan Security Agreement, the US-Japan administrative agreement established the legal basis for the stationing of US forces and their use of garrisons in Japan.

The US-Japan Joint Committee held its first meeting on May 7, 1952. Its primary function at the outset was to inspect military facilities across Japan. At the meeting, a total of ten subcommittees were organized, of which the seventh was called the Maneuvering Areas Subcommittee.[69] Later, the name of that subcommittee seems to have been changed to the Sea Maneuvering and Training Areas Subcommittee. At the 6th Joint Committee meeting held on June 18, 1952, Japan presented a preliminary

---

67 "Opinion of the Government regarding Takeshima" attached to "Memorandum no. 186 dated July 13 of Asia 2, Ministry of Foreign Affairs," Bureau of State Affairs, Japanese Ministry of Foreign Affairs, *Introduction to the Dokdo Issue*, pp. 107-114; English version "Japanese Government's Expression of its Opinion (1)" (Japanese side, Jul. 13, 1953), Ministry of Foreign Affairs, 1977, *Collection of Documents related to Dokdo (I) Exchanged diplomatic documents (1952-1976)*, pp. 19-20.

68 "Opinion of the Government regarding Takeshima" attached to "Memorandum no. 186 dated July 13 of Asia 2, Ministry of Foreign Affairs," Bureau of State Affairs, Japanese Ministry of Foreign Affairs, *Introduction to the Dokdo Issue*, pp. 107-114; English version "Japanese Government's Expression of its Opinion (1)" (Japanese side, Jul. 13, 1953), Ministry of Foreign Affairs, 1977, *Collection of Documents related to Dokdo (I) Exchanged diplomatic documents (1952-1976)*, pp. 19-20.

69 Memorandum to Ambassador Robert Murphy, Subject: Progress Report of the Joint Committee (no. 2) (May 15, 1952), RG 84, Japan, Tokyo Embassy, CGR 1952. Box 3.

list of approximately 500 facilities. At the 12th Joint Committee meeting held on July 26, 1952, the two sides arrived at an agreement on the military facilities and zones to be used by the US forces in Japan.[70] Since the agreement itself dealt with the Japanese facilities and zones to be provided to US forces, it was implicitly presumed that those facilities and zones were owned by Japan.

The July 26 issue of the *Asahi Shimbun* carried a report on the *US-Japan Military Facilities and Zones Agreement*. The article reported that Japan and the US agreed for the US military to have use of 1,428 general facilities such as barracks and airfields, of which 26 at-sea exercise sites were shown on a separate list, and negotiations were still on-going concerning the possible use of 15 other sites.[71] Meanwhile, the Japanese Ministry of Foreign Affairs officially announced the designation of Takeshima as a bombing range by Notification No. 34 (July 26, 1952),[72] according to which Dokdo was to become a 24-hour, 365-day exercise site for the US military. The same information is also found in US records. This meant that Dokdo was a 24-hour all-time danger zone. Curiously, however, no mentions were made of Dokdo in the July 26 issue of the *Asahi Shimbun* or in the separate list. This silence on the part of the Japanese government is an indication that the Japanese Ministry of Foreign Affairs wanted to keep the designation of Dokdo as a bombing range a secret.

Meanwhile, some records remain of the process by which Dokdo was removed from the list of training sites. The progress report of the 45th Joint Committee meeting of March 19, 1953 read that "4. The request of the sub-committee to exclude the Liancourt Rocks from the list of bombing ranges used by the US forces was approved."[73] The following account was made by

---

70 Memorandum to Ambassador Robert Murphy, Subject: Progress Report of the Joint Committee (no. 10) (Jul. 29, 1952), RG 84, Japan, Tokyo Embassy, CGR 1952.

71 "Four all-time danger zones, at-sea exercise sites," *Asahi Shimbunsha* (Jul. 26, 1952).

72 Kawakami, *A Study of the History and Geography of Takeshima*, pp. 252-253.

73 Despatch by Amembassy, Tokyo (John A. Steeves, First Secretary of Embassy) to the Department of State, Subject: Joint Committee Progress Report (Mar. 23, 1953), RG 84, Japan, Tokyo Embassy, CGR 1953-1955, Box 19.

[Figure 7-2] Map showing US military facilities and zones determined by the US-Japan Joint Committee (*Asahi Shimbun*, July 26, 1952)

a US Embassy officer attending the meeting.

9. Gen. Lewton referred to a recommendation by the Sea Maneuvering and Training Areas subcommittee regarding Liancourt Rocks. The subcommittee recommended that the Liancourt Rocks bombing range be deleted from the list of US facilities as agreed on June 2, 1952 since the Rocks are no longer required by the United States forces. I had not realized that the Joint Committee was going to take any action on this matter but approval of this recommendation is simply recognition of the present situation which had been informally discussed with the Japanese last December, so that I do not think this action by the Joint Committee will have any particular effect on the present controversy over the status of the (Liancourt) Rocks. I have referred this matter to Mr. Lamb who will probably send a telegram about it to Washington and Pusan.[74] (Underlining and parentheses by the quoter)

This account reveals several important facts. The first is that Dokdo had already been designated as an exercise site as early as June 1952. Second, in December 1952, Japan and the US unofficially discussed the possibility of dropping Dokdo from the list of training sites. Third, the Sea Maneuvering and Training Areas Subcommittee recommended on March 19, 1953 that Dokdo should be deleted from the list of US military facilities on the grounds that US forces were no longer using it, and the US-Japan Joint Committee approved the recommendation. Thus, the US Embassy and the US forces in Japan readily shouldered the political risk that the US confirmation of Dokdo as Japanese territory entailed. Once its plot had apparently succeeded, Japan was quick to register its claims with the Korean government that the designation and release of Dokdo as a bombing range was proof that the US recognized it as Japanese territory. The abovementioned account was recorded by Richard B. Finn.

Of the diplomatic documents disclosed to date, Finn's are the strongest in their advocacy of Japanese sovereignty over Dokdo. In a letter dated April 1953, he encouraged his home country to announce Dokdo as Japanese territory, insisting that there were no political ramifications to speak of for the Joint Committee deleting Dokdo from the list of bombing ranges in March 1953. In doing so, he failed to report to Washington and the US Embassy in Korea the issue, which had already become a political hot potato. As a staff member in charge of tracking the Dokdo issue at the Office of the US Political Adviser for Japan, Finn held pro-Japanese views and boldly advocated Japan's interests before the Joint Committee. However, his approach was more in keeping with the basic policy of the American Embassy in Japan than a personal tendency. Seemingly unrelated incidents and circumstances were interconnected like in an unbreakable chain.

Meanwhile, though the Japanese Ministry of Foreign Affairs has only scant records on file about the designation and release of Dokdo as a bombing range, a detailed account of how Dokdo became a bombing

---

74 Memorandum for the Ambassador, Subject: Progress Report of the Joint Committee (45th Meeting) (Mar. 20, 1953), p. 3. RG 84, Japan, Tokyo Embassy, CGR 1953-1955, Box 19.

range for the US Air Force by the Joint Committee is recorded in a book written by Kenzo Kawakami and Seizaburo Tamura (officer of the Shimane Prefecture Government).[75]

The book explains that: 1) Dokdo was first designated as a bombing range by the SCAPIN 2160 directive of July 6, 1951; 2) the US forces wished to continue using Dokdo as a bombing range following conclusion of the San Francisco Peace Treaty; 3) the Joint Committee, which was established to implement the agreements of the US-Japan Security Treaty, on July 26, 1952 designated Dokdo as a sea maneuvering and training area for the US forces in accordance with Article 2 of the Administrative Agreement; and 4) the Japanese Ministry of Foreign Affairs publicly announced such an intent in Notification No. 34 of the same date.[76] In other words, Dokdo had been designated a bombing range as early as July 6, 1950 (by SCAPIN 2160) and, because the US forces wished to continue using it as such after the peace treaty was concluded, the Joint Committee designated it as a bombing range on July 26, 1952, which was officially made public by Notification No. 34 of the Japanese Ministry of Foreign Affairs.

As for the release of Dokdo as a bombing range, the book explains that: 1) on May 20, 1952 the Governor of Shimane Prefecture petitioned the Minister of Foreign Affairs and the Minister of Agriculture and Forestry to dispense with that use[77]; 2) the reason was that the US Air Force had stopped using it from December 1952; 3) as a result, the Joint Committee on March 19, 1953 decided to remove Dokdo from the list of bombing ranges, and 4) the release was made public by Notification No. 28 (May 14, 1953) of the Japanese Ministry of Foreign Affairs.

However, two important pieces of information are missing from the above accounts. The first is that it was Japan that was committed to designating Dokdo as a bombing range, not the US. The designation was

---

75   Kawakami, *A Study of the History and Geography of Takeshima,* pp. 252-262; Tamura, *A Study of Takeshima, Shimane Prefecture;* Tamura, A New Study of Takeshima by Shimane Prefecture, pp. 74-75.

76   Kawakami, *A Study of the History and Geography of Takeshima,* pp. 252-253.

77   Tamura, *A New Study of Takeshima by Shimane Prefecture,* p. 74.

the outcome of the strategizing discussed between lawmaker Toshinaga Yamamoto and Vice Minister of Foreign Affairs Kanichiro Ishihara during a meeting of the Foreign Affairs Committee of the House of Representatives. Furthermore, by this point in time, both the US Embassy and the US forces in Japan were aware that Korea and Japan were embroiled in conflict over Dokdo.

Second, the book makes no reference to the bombing incidents on the 15th, which sank a Korean fishing boat, or those on the 22nd and 24th of September 1952. These incidents were the primary reason why the US Air Force stopped using Dokdo as a bombing range from December 1952 onwards, as these incidents made Dokdo a heated political issue. In reply to strongly worded protests from the Korean government, the US Air Force stopped bombing runs over Dokdo and notified the Korean government accordingly the same month. Then in November 1953, lawmaker Kanichi Kawakami raised the issue at a meeting of the Foreign Affairs Committee of the House of Representatives.

> • **Kawakami:** On July 26 last year, it was announced that Takeshima was added to the list of areas that Japan would provide to the US forces as a bombing range. Reportedly, Korea made an issue of it and, owing to these protests, the US decided to take Takeshima off the list. Furthermore, the US authorities immediately notified Korea of this action. The Japanese government claims that it has asked the US authorities about it and was given the reply that the US authorities had notified Korea. How could Korea have been notified first?[78] (Underlined by the quoter)

Thus, the reason why Dokdo was dropped from the list of bombing ranges for the US forces is because, following a series of bombings that killed Korean fishermen, the Korean government issued strong protests

---

78 "Minutes of the Foreign Affairs Committee of the House of Representatives, no. 5" (Nov. 4, 1953), Northeast Asian History Foundation, 2009, *Collection of Records relating to Dokdo of the National Diet of Japan, I (1948-1976)*, pp. 189-190.

and then the US Air Forces Command decided to halt bombing runs over it and notified the Korean government of this decision. If, according to the Japanese logic, the designation of Dokdo as a bombing range was proof of the US confirmation that Dokdo is under Japanese sovereignty, then by the same logic, the notification of the Korean government by the US of its decision to stop using Dokdo as a bombing range was proof of the US recognition that Dokdo is Korean territory. Furthermore, following the prior Dokdo bombing incidents of 1948, the US reaffirmed that Dokdo was fishing grounds for Korean fishermen and Korean territory. For this reason, the US authorities notified the Korean government of the decision to cease bombing training there, and it was only after the Korean government made this public that the Japanese government became aware of what had transpired and then inquired with the US authorities about the case.

After removing Dokdo from the list of training sites for the US military, the Japanese government strongly protested to the US authorities for failing to consult with Japan first about its decision to do so and also for its decision to notify the Korean government of this and not Japan. During a visit to the US Embassy on March 5, 1953, a representative of the Japanese Ministry of Foreign Affairs asked why the US had made the decision without notifying the Japanese government through the US-Japan Joint Committee first. The representative remarked that "of course no question sovereignty over islands rests with Japan, which Foreign Office understands is view of the United States, and that at some future time Foreign Office might find it necessary to ask that United States clarify its views on subject."[79] Thus, at this point, the Japanese Ministry of Foreign Affairs was not clear about the US position on the sovereignty over Dokdo.

The reason why the US did not notify the Japanese government first of its decision to stop using Dokdo as a bombing range was because of the US

---

[79]　Telegram from Amemb (Murphy), Tokyo to the Secretary of State, no. 187 (Mar. 5, 1953), RG 84, Entry 2846, Korea, Seoul Embassy, CGR, 1953-1955, Box 12; compiled by the National Institute of Korean History, 2008, *Dokdo Collection, Vol. 2 (about the US)*, pp. 278-280.

Embassy's concern that an official notification to the Joint Committee of such a decision could be used by the Japanese government as yet additional support for its claim to sovereignty over Dokdo. US Ambassador to Japan Robert Murphy had forewarned that "Japanese will probably authorize dispatch fishing and other vessels to area. ROK reaction can be anticipated."[80] The US knew that Japan would exploit anything it could to propagandize its sovereignty claim to Dokdo, but it had no other choice but to be dragged into the middle of the controversy by Japan. Also in play was the inertia of the political process. The US Embassy in Japan was also supportive of the Japanese political agenda with regard to Dokdo.

The decision to dispense with the use of Dokdo as a bombing range, which had already been made by the US Far Eastern Air Force in December 1952, was referred as a formal agenda for the Joint Committee to pass on March 19, 1953.[81] This was nothing more than a political ploy on the part of Japan to secure sovereignty over Dokdo by exploiting US forces.

On May 14, 1953, about two months following the decision by the Joint Committee, the Japanese Ministry of Foreign Affairs made its first public announcement regarding the designation and release of Dokdo as a bombing site through Notification No. 28.[82] Having taken all the necessary legal steps to secure Dokdo under its sovereignty, the Japanese government now began to "send fishing boats and other vessels to the area" from May 28, 1953 onwards, just as had been predicted by the US Embassy in Japan.

Japan's public explanation regarding the designation and release of Dokdo as a bombing range reveals how it sought to use the Dokdo bombing incidents of 1952 to its own advantage. As a result of Japan's maneuvering, Dokdo became a bombing range for the US forces and, just like in 1948, Korean fishermen and members of the Dokdo scientific expedition

---

80 Ibid.

81 Kawakami, *A Study of the History and Geography of Takeshima*, p. 254; Tamura, *A New Study of Takeshima by Shimane Prefecture*, p. 77.

82 The Ministry of Foreign Affairs sent an official letter no. 695 to the Governor of Shimane Prefecture on April 4, 1953, informing him that Dokdo was now officially excluded from bombing ranges (Tamura, *A New Study of Takeshima by Shimane Prefecture*, pp. 76-77).

witnessed multiple bombings of Dokdo in September 1952. In response, the Korean government strongly protested to the US Embassy in Korea and to the US Far East Command, and urgent and prolonged discussions took place between Korea and the US in this regard. At the heart of the discussions were the discontinuation of bombing and the release of Dokdo as a bombing range.

Faced with strong protest from the Korean government with regard to Korean casualties in the vicinity of Dokdo, the US Far East Command and the Fifth Air Force felt compelled to revoke the designation of Dokdo as a bombing target, even as Japan sought to solidify its territorial interest in Dokdo through exploitation of that process.

More importantly, after plotting to designate and release Dokdo as a bombing range for the US forces, the Japanese Ministry of Foreign Affairs next made the relevant decisions public through a series of notifications. The situation developed in the same way as in 1905, when the Cabinet of Japan first announced in the Shimane Prefecture Gazette that Dokdo was incorporated to Japan as *terra nullius*, and then sent an inspection team to Dokdo the following year. Similarly, in 1952, Japan first announced the designation and release of Dokdo as a bombing range for the US forces through a public notification of the Japanese Ministry of Foreign Affairs and later notified the Korean government. The events of 1952 and 1953 appear to be a reenactment of what had taken place in 1905. This makes Korea's criticisms of Japan's act as equivalent to "the plundering of a burning house" or "an act no different from international pick pocketing" seem more understandable than otherwise.[83]

To Korea, the strategy used by the Japanese Ministry of Foreign Affairs and the National Diet in 1952 and 1953 was nothing less and nothing more than an unbelievable conspiracy. First, the primary reason why the Japanese government came up with such a plot in the first place was because it had no confidence in the grounds for its sovereignty claims over Dokdo. In

---

83   Bureau of State Affairs, Ministry of Foreign Affairs, *Introduction to the Dokdo Issue*, pp. 23, 123.

other words, even the Japanese government itself must have judged that whatever evidence it had at the time would, upon close investigation, not be sufficient to negate Korea's sovereignty rights over Dokdo. Thus, it was in dire need to "craft" new evidence in order to reinforce its position. The designation of Dokdo as a bombing target thus became a policy alternative for the Japanese government as the Korean government's vocal claims to sovereignty over Dokdo began to surface in coherent form in the international arena. In 1905, having inadequate historical evidence and documentation in support of its unlawful annexation of Dokdo, the Japanese government had, through Yosaburo Nakai, illegally crafted territorial incorporation documents at the national level. Likewise, in 1952, the government worked out a scheme to make up for its lack of supporting documentation.

The Japanese Ministry of Foreign Affairs first devised the scheme, the National Diet discussed it, and finally Japan sought to enlist the support of the US as its counterpart in the plot. Under the Japanese scheme, the US would play the role of guarantor of Japan's sovereignty claims over Dokdo even as Korean fishermen became the bloodied victims of bombings by the US Air Force on the waters where they and their ancestors had made a living. Although no damage to speak of had been inflicted upon them, the fishermen of Shimane Prefecture were depicted as victims and stakeholders that Japan used to confirm its sovereignty claims. Meanwhile, the US allowed itself to be exploited by good will, Korea was threatened with the loss of part of its territory, and Japan secured a fabricated document purportedly proving its territorial rights. When Japan presented this document to Korea in 1952 as evidence that it was now the rightful owner of Dokdo, the act was by itself the true mirror of Japan's basic attitude towards Korea and the Korean people.

Most important to note was how Japan manipulated the facts and technically completed the documentation that it needed in support of its sovereignty claims to Dokdo. Furthermore, despite appearances to the contrary, its scheme was neither fortuitous nor accidental but rather the outcome of deliberate planning, involved discussions, and carefully timed decisions made collaboratively by the Japanese Ministry of Foreign Affairs and the National Diet. As previously stated, this manipulative proffering of Japan's sovereignty claims to Dokdo, orchestrated between the Foreign Affairs Ministry and the Japanese Diet in 1952 and 1953, mirrored in many respects Japan's unlawful annexation of Dokdo in 1905 and 1906. The Japanese Ministry of Foreign Affairs and the National Diet were acting on what they had learned from Japan's past historical experience.

Second, the Japanese government saw the US, and not Korea, as the key stakeholder that it needed to influence on the Dokdo issue. This view rested on Japan's longstanding arrogant attitude towards Korea and its reluctance to recognize its former colony as an equal negotiation partner able to exercise its due rights. More importantly, however, Japan considered the US to be the primary mediator and decision-maker for the new postwar order emerging in the East Asian region. In other words, it viewed the US as the key power broker that needed to be influenced with regard to its territory (the four major islands and the various minor islands to be included in Japanese territory as determined by the Allied Powers) leading up to conclusion of the San Francisco Peace Treaty. Thus, Japan initiated a plan to mobilize the US forces in Japan to designate Dokdo as a bombing range and then subsequently revoking the designation based on a petition from the fishermen of Shimane Prefecture. By doing so, Japan wanted to secure some rudimentary documentation recognizing Dokdo as its territory. At the same time, by having the US military involved in the designation and release of Dokdo as a bombing range, it hoped to acquire confirmation from the US that Dokdo was Japanese territory. That is, the Japanese scheme had as its hidden intent to not only secure documentation confirming Japanese sovereignty over Dokdo but also to get the US involved in the confirmation process. Indeed, statements issued by the Japanese Ministry of Foreign Affairs following the designation and release of Dokdo as a bombing range were mostly aimed at fetching in the US as a third party to confirm this sovereignty.

Third, from the perspective of the Korean people, the designation and release of Dokdo as a bombing range by the Japanese government was barbarous and cruel. Dokdo had already been first designated as a bombing range for the US Air Force in 1947, and bombings of the area in

1948 by the US Air Force caused scores of casualties and other collateral damage to Korea. In 1950, Korea erected a stone monument on Dokdo in memory of the bombing victims. No casualties were incurred by Japanese fishermen in the 1948 bombings by the US Air Force because the Japanese government had informed its fishermen along the western coast of Dokdo's designation and had issued a ban on fishing in that area. In addition, even without the ban, Japanese vessels and fishermen were already prohibited from accessing Dokdo under the military mandate of the MacArthur Line. In short, Dokdo had been, prior to this time, Korean fishing grounds— Korean territory where Korean fishermen went fishing on a regular basis. Thus, access by Japanese fishermen to Dokdo had already been blocked on multiple grounds and only Korean fishermen had the right to fish there. Accordingly, all the casualties of the 1948 bombings were Koreans. Despite the tragic loss of life, the Japanese government again in 1952 designated Dokdo as a bombing range in a conspiracy to secure sovereignty over it. Japan neither notified Korea of the decision in advance nor shared any bombing-related information with Korea. Even though Korean fishermen had a long tradition of working around and on Dokdo and no Japanese fishermen could go out to fish there, the Japanese government again only notified Japanese fishermen residing in the western coast of Japan, including the Shimane Prefecture, of the ban on fishing there. Neither Korean fishermen nor the Korean government knew or could have known that the US Air Force was, based on an agreement reached in confidence with the Japanese government, to engage in renewed bombing exercises over Korean territory. It was a clear infringement of Korea's rights as a sovereign nation, a provocation, and an outright deception of the US on Japan's part.

By logical inference, the Japanese government succeeded in getting the US Air Force to unwittingly execute its scheme, not so much concerned about bombings on Korean fishermen and fishing vessels. As the bombing incidents of 1948 had already demonstrated, it was crystal clear that the designation of Dokdo as a bombing range would result in the death of Korean fishermen and destruction of Korean fishing vessels. At the heart of this plot lay Japan's intent to secure its interests at the expense of the lives and property of the people in neighboring countries.

Moreover, at the time, Korea was desperately fighting against communist aggressors, and thus was preoccupied with dealing with North Korea and China. From the Korean perspective, the Japanese government's scheme was to cause the unexpected bombing of unarmed Korean fishermen on the east coast as a way of acquiring US confirmation of Japan's sovereignty over Dokdo. Such was the basic approach of the postwar Japanese government towards Korea, the Korean government, and the Korean people. The primary reason that the Japanese government resorted to such a plot was probably because it had witnessed how the Dokdo bombing incident of 1948 had been dealt with. To shore up its claims to Dokdo in 1952, Japan plotted to capitalize on the grave tragedy of the bombing incident in 1948 as a maneuver. In September 1952, the Korean fishing vessel *Gwangyeongho* was bombed by a US aircraft while fishing off the coast of Dokdo.

Fourth, by first designating and then releasing Dokdo as a bombing range, Japan was paradoxically undermining the very sovereignty claims that it set out to strengthen. Japan's willingness to allow Dokdo to be bombed was intended to support its claims of sovereignty over it. At the time, the US-Japan Joint Committee discussed a large number of garrisons, shooting ranges, and bombing ranges for the US forces; the designation of Dokdo as a bombing range was only a part of that discussion. However, the strategy of granting the US permission to bomb its own territory, not for military purposes but for the purpose of securing further documentary evidence as well as the confirmation of an ally that Dokdo was indeed its own territory, can hardly be seen as a sensible act of diplomacy by a modern, civilized nation state. If a clear historical precedent and documentary record had been available to Japan in support of its claim to Dokdo, it may not have resorted to such an outlandish scheme.

If, on the contrary, Korea had been the one to designate and then release Dokdo as a bombing range for the US Air Force for the purpose of asserting its own sovereignty claim, it is clear to assume how the Korean people and the Japanese government would have responded. The Korean people would have strongly opposed it while Japan would have vehemently and publicly condemned the Korean government before the entire international community for being so inhumane and uncivilized. Japan's scheme deserves such a harsh condemnation as well.

3) Mid-1953: Japanese encroachment on Dokdo and installation of Japanese signposts

The Dokdo issue began to surface in earnest in the Japanese media from the end of May 1953. Japan sent patrol boats to Dokdo and took a series of bold steps to further assert its sovereignty, such as interrogating and blackmailing Korean fishermen working in the waters off Dokdo, tearing down Korean territorial landmarks and signboards, and installing signposts of their own. Japan's landing on Dokdo and the resulting physical conflict with Koreans there provided great news value and Dokdo soon turned into a major international issue. There were three principal reasons why Japan set about seeking to occupy Dokdo by force in late May 1953.

First, at the US-Japan Joint Committee meeting of March 19, 1953, Dokdo was removed from the list of bombing ranges for the US forces. Then on May 14, the decision was made public by the Japanese Ministry of Foreign Affairs through Notification No. 28. Japan's scheme of designating and releasing Dokdo as a bombing range had come to fruition. After having secured the necessary documentation to legitimize its sovereignty claims over Dokdo, Japan felt confident that its claims had been acknowledged by the US as a fact. Up until May 28, 1953, no Japanese government vessels had been allowed access to Dokdo, and no Japanese officials had landed there. Nor were there any attempts to land.

Second, Japan's provocations were closely intertwined with the second series of Korea-Japan talks (April 15-July 13, 1953) that were ongoing at the time. As one of its top priorities was to get rid of the Peace Line, Japan began "putting into action its evil scheme of completing its sovereignty claims over Dokdo by infringing upon the Peace Line by force and dispatching patrol boats there."[84]

---

84   Bureau of State Affairs, Ministry of Foreign Affairs, *Introduction to the Dokdo Issue*, p. 52.

Third, through engaging in such provocative actions and stimulating a response from Korea, Japan perhaps was seeking to create a rationale for its rearmament. Japan's provocative actions on and around Dokdo between May and August of 1953 prompted a strong response from the Korean Police and Navy, and the Japanese media and Coast Guard used these circumstances to reinforce their argument for rearmament. On September 1, 1953, the Japanese Coast Guard developed a Four-Year Defense Plan, in which it proposed to recruit a land force of 210,000 soldiers, a fleet with a combined tonnage of 145,000, and 1,400 aircraft within the next five years. To this end, in September 1953, the Japanese government dispatched a large fishing fleet to Korean waters near Geomundo, inducing the Korean Navy to seize it. Thus, Japan appeared to have used Dokdo and the Peace Line as a rationale for further reinforcing its defense capacity.[85]

The Korean Ministry of Foreign Affairs recorded that if 1952 was "a year of diplomatic war by correspondence between Korea and Japan," then 1953 was "the year when Japan's unlawful encroachment upon Korean territory began." That comment hit the mark.

Japan's first encroachment on Dokdo: May 28, 1953[86]

Japan's first encroachment on Dokdo occurred on May 28, 1953. According to the records of the Korean Ministry of Foreign Affairs, at 11 am on May 28, 1953, the experiment ship *Shimanemaru* appeared off Dokdo carrying 30 crew members, six of whom made an unlawful landing on Dokdo carrying cameras and binoculars. While they were on shore, they attempted to interrogate Kim Jun-hyeok (32) from Jugam-dong,

---

85   Bureau of State Affairs, Ministry of Foreign Affairs, *Introduction to the Dokdo Issue*, pp. 98-100.

86   Classification of the encroachments from the first to the fifth is based on the criteria of the Bureau of State Affairs of the Japanese Ministry of Foreign Affairs ("Regarding the invasions of Dokdo by Japanese vessels" (no. 1200, Aug. 11, 1953) (Minister of Home Affairs → Minister of Foreign Affairs), *Dokdo Issue, 1952-1953*; Bureau of State Affairs, Ministry of Foreign Affairs, *Introduction to the Dokdo Issue*, pp. 52-83).

Buk-myeon, Ulleungdo who was fishing there at the time, but they failed to communicate due to the language barrier. The Japanese gave Kim a Japanese magazine and three packs of cigarettes and inquired about the fishing conditions on the island, and then returned to their boat at around 1 o'clock in the afternoon.[87]

That encounter, however, was only made public a month later. According to a report in the *Yomiuri Shimbun* on June 22, 1953, the Japanese Ministry of Foreign Affairs was planning to lodge a protest with the Korean government regarding Korean vessels engaging in what it viewed to be illegal fishing activities off Dokdo in late May.

The Japanese Ministry of Foreign Affairs did in fact send a protest to the Korean Diplomatic Mission in Japan on June 23, which read "Takeshima has clearly been Japanese territory since the 38th year of Meiji." The letter went on to point out that Korea violated Japan's fisheries-related law and immigration law on numerous occasions.[88] In an immediate reply dated June 26, Korea responded that Dokdo was Korean territory, pointing out that 1) of Japanese-claimed territory, Dokdo was under direct administration by US forces, not by the Japanese government and 2) the distribution of plants on Dokdo was the same as that on the mainland of Korea.[89]

The encroachment incident had already been reported by Korean media on June 9. According to these news reports, officials from the Fisheries Experiment Station of Japan found a group of about thirty Korean fishermen aboard about ten vessels in the waters off Dokdo and questioned

---

87   Bureau of State Affairs, Ministry of Foreign Affairs, *Introduction to the Dokdo Issue*, pp. 52-53.

88   "Japan submits strongly worded protests to Korea for invasion of its territorial waters of Takeshima,"; "Government registers protests with the Korean government regarding Korean fishing in Takeshima," *Asahi Shimbun* (Jun. 25, 1953); *Busan Ilbo* (Jun. 27, 1953); "Memorandum no. 167 dated June 22 of Asia 2, Ministry of Foreign Affairs," Bureau of State Affairs, Ministry of Foreign Affairs, *Introduction to the Dokdo Issue*, pp. 53-54.

89   *Dong-A Ilbo* (Jun. 29, 1953); "Memorandum of the Korean Mission in Japan dated June 26, 1953," Bureau of State Affairs, Ministry of Foreign Affairs, *Introduction to the Dokdo Issue*, pp. 54-55.

them. The Korean fishermen told them that they had been coming there regularly since April 1953 to gather seaweed and catch fish.[90] There was nothing wrong with Korean fishermen fishing in Korean waters.

The Japanese Fisheries Agency notified the Ministry of Foreign Affairs that Korean vessels were fishing regularly off Dokdo, then the Ministry of Foreign Affairs heard testimony from witnesses and, using the photographs taken during a field survey by Fisheries Agency patrol boats, gathered that Korean nationals were drying abalone and harvested seaweed on Dokdo, and then concluded that this was clearly an "invasion of Japan's territorial waters."[91]

Japan's second encroachment on Dokdo: June 25, 1953

Korean fishermen continued to engage in fishing activities on and around Dokdo, which to them was Korean land. According to the records of the Korean Ministry of Foreign Affairs, six Korean nationals, including Jeong Won-jun (aged 34) from Jeo-dong, Jung-myeon, Ulleungdo, witnessed Japanese officials land on Dokdo three times (on June 25, 27, and 28) during their stay on Dokdo from June 11, 1953 to July 1, 1953.[92] According to their testimony, they had been staying and fishing on Dokdo for about 20 days or so. At 4:30 pm on June 25, 1953, a 100-ton wooden Japanese vessel flying a US flag approached Dokdo, and nine of the crew members went ashore. They questioned the Koreans there about their reason for being there, took photographs of them and of a stone monument erected by the Korean government, and left at 7 pm.[93]

90　*Minju Shinbo* (Jun. 9, 1953).

91　"The Japanese government considering an 'evacuation order' with respect to the Takeshima incident and soon to lodge a protest with the Korean government," *Yomiuri Shimbun* (Jun. 22, 1953).

92　"Regarding the investigation of illegal entries into Dokdo by Japanese" (no. 1141, Jul. 7, 1953) (Director of Public Order, Ministry of Home Affairs → Director of State Affairs, Ministry of Foreign Affairs), *Dokdo Issue, 1952-1953*; Bureau of State Affairs, Ministry of Foreign Affairs, *Introduction to the Dokdo Issue*, pp. 59-63.

93　Bureau of State Affairs, Ministry of Foreign Affairs, *Introduction to the Dokdo Issue*, p. 59.

However, this time no report was put forward by the Japanese media about Japan's June 25 landing. Only the *Yomiuri Shimbun* reported that the Japanese Maritime Security Agency dispatched the *Noshiromaru* and *Kuzuryumaru* patrol vessels to Dokdo before dawn on June 23, 1953, but the waves were high and they did not find any traces of vessels or men.[94]

Japan's third encroachment on Dokdo: June 27, 1953

The third encroachment on Dokdo by Japanese officials was witnessed by Jeong Won-jun and five other fishermen from Ulleungdo. According to their testimonies, a 60-ton Japanese fishing vessel flying a US flag approached Dokdo at about 10 am on June 27, 1953. Eight of the crew members landed. They asked the Korean fishermen why they were there, took down their names and addresses, and left the island at around 3 pm.[95]

According to a Japanese news article on this incident, the Japanese Maritime Security Agency dispatched the patrol vessels *Okimaru* and *Kuzuryumaru* to Dokdo during the night of June 26, 1953 and began investigating the area. On June 27, the patrol boats reported that "at dawn, a Korean barge (about three meters long) was found near the island and on board were six Korean nationals, whom we are now questioning."[96] The incident was also covered in the Korean media, where it was reported that on June 26, around 30 officials from the Police, the Immigration Bureau, and the Secretariat of the Shimane Prefecture aboard two patrol boats made an illegal landing on Dokdo and tried to pressure six Koreans residing there to leave the area.[97] According to another media report, the Japanese

---

94   "Telegram from vessel patrolling around Dokdo verifying the landing of Koreans" *Yomiuri Shimbun* (Jun. 27, 1953).

95   "Regarding the investigation of illegal entries into Dokdo by Japanese" (no. 1141, Jul. 7, 1953) (Director of Public Order, Ministry of Home Affairs → Director of State Affairs, Ministry of Foreign Affairs), *Dokdo Issue, 1952-1953*; Bureau of State Affairs, Ministry of Foreign Affairs, *Introduction to the Dokdo Issue*, pp. 59-60.

96   "Telegram from vessel patrolling around Dokdo verifying the landing of Koreans," *Yomiuri Shimbun* (Jun. 27, 1953).

97   *Pyeonghwa Shinmun* (Jun. 30, 1953); *Dong-A Ilbo* (Jul. 8, 1953).

government in the morning of June 27 "kidnapped six Korean fishermen and one fishing boat from Dokdo and questioned them."[98] The Korean fishermen said that they came to Dokdo with a port of entry permit from the police, that they generally engaged in fishing activities there between April and July of every year, and that they were told by the authorities to be cautious every time they went there.[99] This shows that Dokdo was viewed by Korea not only as part of its territory and an area specially administered by the Korean Police and the Korean government, but also as a place where fishermen from Ulleungdo came on a regular basis to make a living. It also indicates that advance warnings were routinely given to fishermen and vessels traveling to Dokdo to beware of Japanese intruding on the island. The fishermen's statement that they were not sure whether Dokdo was Korean or Japanese territory was in all likelihood made to avoid unnecessary trouble at the moment as they were being subjected to unwanted intimidation by the Japanese.

Japan's fourth encroachment on Dokdo: June 28, 1953

According to Korean fishermen present on Dokdo at the time, at about 8 am on June 28, 1953, two Japanese vessels flying US flags (presumed to be destroyers but their port of origin was unidentified) approached Dokdo. About 30 Japanese nationals on board went ashore carrying revolvers and cameras. On Dongdo (East Island), the Japanese erected two landmarks and two signboards that they had brought with them. The landmarks read "日本 島根縣 隱地郡 五個村 竹島" ("Takeshima, Gokomura, Ochi-gun, Shimane Prefecture, Japan" in English) measured 2 meters 30 centimeters high by 15 centimeters wide. They had written in dark ink on both sides.[100] The two landmarks and the two signboards were erected to the north, south, east, and west of the memorial stone erected in memory

---

98   *Dong-A Ilbo* (Jun. 29, 1953).

99   Kawakami, *A Study of the History and Geography of Takeshima*, p. 265.

100   Bureau of State Affairs, Ministry of Foreign Affairs, *Introduction to the Dokdo Issue*, p. 60-62.

of the Dokdo bombing victims at a distance of about 15 meters from the monument, as if circumscribing it.

The Japanese questioned the Koreans living there and photographed them fishing and taking their meals. They even threatened the Korean fishermen saying in Korean, "This island is Japanese territory, so should you infringe upon it again in the future, you will be taken to the Japanese Police," as one of them who had lived in Korea for 18 years could speak Korean. The Japanese left at around 10 pm.[101] The Japanese officials also removed a landmark that had been erected by the Corean Alpine Club on the island in 1947.[102]

Meanwhile, the Japanese media reported that their landing on Dokdo occurred on June 28, not on the 27th.[103] The Korean media also reported that Japanese officials erected landmarks on Dokdo proclaiming Dokdo as Japanese territory.[104] The landmarks are presumed to be the first territorial landmarks and signboards that Japan placed on Dokdo since the end of the war. In summary, Japanese officials illegally landed on Dokdo for the first time on May 28, 1953 and then again on June 27 or 28 to erect Japanese territorial landmarks and signboards that they had made in Japan and brought with them.

Following media reports on Japan's illegal encroachment onto Dokdo and its setting up of territorial landmarks there, the Korean Diplomatic Mission in Japan lodged formal protests with the Japanese Ministry of Foreign Affairs on June 29 and 30. The Minister of Home Affairs then

---

101 "Regarding the investigation of illegal entries into Dokdo by Japanese" (no. 1141, Jul. 7, 1953) (Director of Public Order, Ministry of Home Affairs → Director of State Affairs, Ministry of Foreign Affairs), *Dokdo Issue, 1952-1953*; Bureau of State Affairs, Ministry of Foreign Affairs, *Introduction to the Dokdo Issue*, p. 61.

102 The petition of the Provincial Assembly of Gyeongsangbuk-do (Jul. 10, 1953) stated that the Japanese had destroyed Korean territorial markers and the memorial stone. During a scientific expedition in October 1953, the Corea Alpine Club verified that the memorial stone was intact. The stone was later lost in a typhoon.

103 *Asahi Shimbun* (Jun. 28, 1953); Bureau of State Affairs, Ministry of Foreign Affairs, *Introduction to the Dokdo Issue*, p. 65-66.

104 *Daegu Maeil Shinmun* (Jun. 29, 1953).

announced on June 3 that the Police Headquarters of Gyeongsangbuk-do had removed two landmarks and signboards that Japan had erected on the island.[105]

In a nutshell, beginning in mid-June 1953, the Japanese Maritime Security Agency, Shimane Prefecture, the Fisheries Agency, and the Ministry of Foreign Affairs encroached on Dokdo repeatedly on a daily basis by dispatching patrol boats and experiment ships like the *Shimanemaru, Noshiromaru, Kuzuryumaru,* and *Okimaru.* The conflict situation continued to exacerbate due to Japan's organized encroachments and sovereignty claims.

Japan's fifth encroachment on Dokdo: July 12, 1953

On July 12, 1953, a shooting incident occurred. A marked discrepancy exists between the Korean and Japanese accounts. First, the following is the historical records of the Korean Ministry of Foreign Affairs:[106]

In response to the growing number of encroachments by Japan on Dokdo, the Ulleungdo Police Station organized a patrol team comprised of Lieutenant Kim Jin-seong, Sergeant Choi Heon-sik, and policeman Choe Yong-deuk to protect the Korean fishermen living and fishing on Dokdo and to monitor Japanese intrusions.[107] Armed with two light machine guns, the team left Ulleungdo at 11 am on July 11, 1953 and arrived off

---

105 *Dong-A Ilbo* (Jul. 9, 1953). According to records of the Ministry of Foreign Affairs, the landmarks and signboards that were removed were transported from Ulleungdo to the Police Headquarters of Gyeongsangbuk-do and kept there, "Regarding the invasions of Dokdo by Japanese vessels" (no. 1200, Aug. 11, 1953) (Minister of Home Affairs → Minister of Foreign Affairs), *Dokdo Issue, 1952-1953*; Bureau of State Affairs, Ministry of Foreign Affairs, *Introduction to the Dokdo Issue*, p. 67).

106 "Regarding the investigation of illegal entries into Dokdo by Japanese" (no. 1141, Jul. 7, 1953) (Director of Public Order, Ministry of Home Affairs → Director of State Affairs, Ministry of Foreign Affairs), *Dokdo Issue, 1952-1953*; Bureau of State Affairs, Ministry of Foreign Affairs, *Introduction to the Dokdo Issue*, pp. 76-79.

107 "Regarding the invasions of Dokdo by Japanese vessels" (no. 1200, Aug. 11, 1953) (Minister of Home Affairs → Minister of Foreign Affairs), *Dokdo Issue, 1952-1953*.

Dokdo at 7 pm the same day. They found about 10 Koreans fishing there. After spending the night on board their vessel, the patrol team noticed a boat approaching Dokdo at around 5 am on July 12, 1953. At 5:40am, when the boat came to within 300 meters northwest of the Korean patrol boat, it hoisted a Japanese flag. As the boat came to a halt, Lieutenant Choi approached it for an official inspection. The captain of the Japanese boat then ordered its crew to turn the vessel around, after which it sped around Dokdo and then fled in the direction of Japan. The Korean Police ordered the boat to stop. The boat failed to heed the order, so the police fired several rounds as a warning. The Japanese boat fled anyway.

According to the *Yomiuri Shimbun*'s account of the encounter, a Japanese Maritime Security Agency patrol boat found three Korean fishing boats intruding in the waters off Dokdo. The Korean boats were fishing in the vicinity, escorted by seven policemen. As the officials of the Japanese patrol boat were getting ready to disembark, an interpreter and two policemen came over and approached them on a lighter craft. The policemen asked, "What brings you to Korean waters?" The officials on the patrol boat replied that they were in Japanese waters. The two sides talked for hours but to no avail. Then while the patrol boat "was patrolling on the east side of the island" on a security check, rounds of ammunition were fired at them from the Korean fishing boats. Without reacting, the patrol boat returned to the Port of Sakai that evening. Only slight damage was done to the patrol boat in the form of two bullet marks on the body of the ship.[108] According to another media report, the patrol boat was the *Hegura*, belonging to the Maritime Security Agency of the Eighth Maritime District of the Tottori Prefecture in Japan. The patrol boat had left Sakai and arrived in Dokdo in the morning of July 12 when they met the Korean fishing boats.[109]

Following this incident, the Japanese Ministry of Foreign Affairs lodged a formal protest with the Korean government by sending a note verbale

---

[108] "Korea fires shots at Japanese patrol boat off the waters of Takeshima," *Asahi Shimbun* (Jul. 13, 1953).
[109] *Dong-A Ilbo* (Jul. 15, 1953).

to the Korean Mission in Japan at 8 pm on July 13, 1953.[110] The Japanese government again sent a patrol boat to Dokdo on July 20 to keep watch on Korean fishing activities there. On July 30, the government lodged another protest about the shooting with the Korean Mission in Japan, claiming that Dokdo was Japanese territory.

In response, the Korean government staged a strong, formal protest on August 4, 1953, to the effect that it was deeply regretful that the Japanese had intruded into the waters of Dokdo, which were Korean territory, not Japanese.[111] On August 8, Japan delivered a memorandum refuting this claim to the Korean Diplomatic Mission.[112] Then, through a memorandum of the Korean Mission dated August 22, the Korean government lodged an even stronger protest regarding the situation. In the memorandum, the government explained that on July 12, 1953, about 30 Japanese nationals intruded into Korean waters near Dokdo and were notified by the Korean authorities there that they had made an illegal intrusion into Korean territorial waters and thus were ordered to report to the Ulleungdo police station. Instead of complying, however, the Japanese boat fled and as a result the Korean police fired several rounds of ammunition as a warning.[113]

Following these incidents, the Japanese National Diet and the media began complaining that Japan's diplomatic response was inadequate so the Coast Guard should instead be allowed to resort to armed force to cope with such incidents. However, herein lay Japan's dilemma. Under Article 9 of the Japanese Constitution of 1947, which provided that "the Japanese

---

110 "Memorandum no. 187 dated July 13 of Asia 2, Ministry of Foreign Affairs," Bureau of State Affairs, Ministry of Foreign Affairs, *Introduction to the Dokdo Issue*, pp. 79-80; "Ministry of Foreign Affairs announces Takeshima is Japanese territory," *Asahi Shimbun* (Jul. 14, 1953).

111 "Counter-protests by Korea regarding the sovereignty of Takeshima," *Yomiuri Shimbun* (Aug. 4, 1953); "Korea protests back on the Takeshima issue," *Asahi Shimbun* (Aug. 5, 1953); "Memorandum of the Korean Mission in Japan dated August 4," Bureau of State Affairs, Ministry of Foreign Affairs, *Introduction to the Dokdo Issue*, pp. 70-72.

112 "Memorandum no. 205 dated August 8 of Asia 2, Ministry of Foreign Affairs," Bureau of State Affairs, Ministry of Foreign Affairs, *Introduction to the Dokdo Issue*, pp. 72-73.

113 "Memorandum dated August 22," Bureau of State Affairs, Ministry of Foreign Affairs, *Introduction to the Dokdo Issue*, pp. 80-82.

people shall forever renounce war as a sovereign right of the nation and the threat or use of force as means of settling international disputes," Japan had renounced the right of belligerency as well as the right to maintain military forces. Accordingly, based on the premise that Dokdo was Japanese territory, Japan could send its police force to patrol the area, but the use of force to settle its international dispute with Korea was banned by the Constitution. At a meeting of the Fisheries Committee of the House of Representatives (July 28, 1953), Takeso Shimoda, director general of the Treaties Bureau of the Ministry of Foreign Affairs, replied that "Enforcement measures may be used to the extent that the police are cracking down on illegal entrants into the country, but because Article 9 of the Constitution prohibits the use of force as a means of settling international disputes, the use of force to resolve the international dispute over Takeshima is prohibited by the Constitution."[114] The best force that Japan could exercise was to mobilize its police force and conduct patrols to prevent "unlawful entries." Thus, an armed conflict with Korea would be the worst-case scenario. First, it would constitute an outright violation of the Japanese Constitution by going against its renouncement of the right of belligerency. Furthermore, Japan's engagement in an armed conflict with no less than a former colony so soon after it had recovered its own sovereignty would have with all likelihood engendered a storm of criticism from the international community.

Against this backdrop, the Minister of the Japanese Maritime Security Agency, in an appearance before the Foreign Affairs Committee of the House of Representatives on August 5, 1953, acknowledged that it could not confront Korean warships.[115] So the only options available to Japan were to influence public opinion by appealing to the international community, to ask for mediation from the US or the UK, or to take the issue to the International Court of Justice.

---

114 "Minutes of the 16th meeting of the Fisheries Committee of the House of Representatives," No. 19 (Jul. 28, 1953); Northeast Asian History Foundation, 2009, *Collection of Records relating to Dokdo of the National Diet of Japan, I (1948-1976)*, p. 105.

115 "Maritime Safety Agency cannot stand up to Korean warships with regards to Takeshima," *Asahi Shimbun* (Aug. 6, 1953).

August-October 1953: Japan's culminating encroachment on Dokdo

Japan again illegally intruded into Korean waters and landed on Dokdo on August 7, September 17, September 23, and October 6, 1953, but Korea was not aware of this at the time. On August 7, Japanese officials re-planted the Japanese landmarks that had been removed, but no further record was made of the events that transpired in relation to it.[116] According to diplomatic documents on file in Korea, at around 9 am on August 23, the steel-hulled Japanese vessel *Oki* was spotted about 500 meters north of Dokdo. The vessel was equipped with two machine guns and there were about 30 persons on board. "Dispatched patrols" accordingly ordered the vessel to stop but to no avail. In consequence, some warning shots were fired in the air and the vessel turned and fled in the easterly direction.[117] After this encounter, the Korean Minister of Defense sent a naval ship to Dokdo and Ulleungdo for an investigation and then reported back to the Minister of Foreign Affairs (August 28, 1953) along with five photographs of the Japanese landmarks, three photos of the Japanese vessel *Hegura*, and three photos of Dokdo with the stone monument.[118]

On September 17, 1953, the *Shimanemaru*, a fisheries scientific experimentation ship of the Shimane Prefecture, illegally landed on Dokdo and then returned to Hamada the next day. The vessel arrived off Dokdo at 9:30 am on September 17. At the time, there were no Korean fishermen or vessels in the area. At 12:30 pm, the people on board the ship landed on Dokdo via a lighter craft and found the landmark reading "島根縣 五箇村領 (Territory of Ochi-gun, Shimane Prefecture)," which the Fisheries Administrative Department of the Shimane Prefecture Government had previously erected. At 5:30 pm, the ship left Dokdo and returned to

---

116 Kawakami, *A Study of the History and Geography of Takeshima*, p. 271.

117 "Current state of invasions by Japanese vessels" (Sergeant Han Dong-sul, Special Information Department, Public Security Bureau), *Dokdo Issue, 1952-1953*.

118 "On the illegal invasion of Dokdo by Japanese Authorities" (no. 19, Aug. 28, 1953) (Minister of National Defense → Minister of Foreign Affairs), *Dokdo Issue, 1952-1953*.

Japan with a catch of 2,000 squid.[119] According to diplomatic records of the Korean Government, the Ulleungdo Police Station inspected Dokdo on September 17 and removed two Japanese landmarks, one erected on Dongdo (East Island) and the other on Seodo (West Island).[120]

On September 23, the *Daisenmaru* (47 tons), a fishery experiment ship from Tottori Prefecture, surveyed Dokdo and found that the two Japanese landmarks previously erected on August 7 had been removed. Consequently, the patrol ship *Hegura* (450 tons) was dispatched from Sakai, on orders from the Maritime Safety Agency Headquarters, to Dokdo on October 6 for the purpose of erecting a third Japanese landmark. At 7 pm on October 5, the *Hegura* left the Port of Sakai with Kashiwa Sakai, head of the Maritime Safety Agency, and one official from the Shimane Prefecture Government. The ship arrived in the waters off Dokdo the next day. It sailed around the island and, after confirming that there were no people or boats in the vicinity, the people on board landed on the island by boat and erected the landmark. They also collected the debris left from the previous landmark and returned to Japan.[121] This new landmark was the third to have been erected by Japan on Dokdo in 1953.[122]

To sum up, on June 27 and 28, 1953, Japanese officials removed two territorial landmarks that the Corean Alpine Club had erected on August 20, 1947 and replaced them with two Japanese territorial landmarks and two signboards. These were promptly removed by the Police Headquarters of Gyeongsangbuk-do on July 3, 1953. On August 7, Japan again illegally landed on Dokdo and erected another Japanese territorial landmark, which the Ulleungdo Police summarily removed on September 17. Japanese officials built a third territorial landmark on October 6, but the

---

119 "No traces of Koreans found in Takeshima and Japanese station pole remains intact, reported by the *Shimanemaru*," *Asahi Shimbun* (Sept. 20, 1953).

120 "On the illegal invasion of Dokdo by Japanese Authorities" (no. 1617, Oct. 7, 1953) (Vice Minister of Foreign Affairs → Korean Minister in Japan), *Dokdo Issue, 1952-1953* (Classification no. 743.11JA, registration no. 4565).

121 "Landmarks planted for the third time," *Asahi Shimbun* (Oct. 7, 1953).

122 "Territorial landmarks removed again, Takeshima representatives to investigate the issue," *Asahi Shimbun* (Oct. 18, 1953).

Corea Alpine Club promptly removed it during their scientific expedition in Dokdo on October 15 and 16, 1953. The territorial landmark erected by the Corea Alpine Club on October 15, 1953 was subsequently removed by Japanese officials on October 21, and then on October 23, Japan erected a fourth Japanese territorial landmark. Thus, from 1953 to 1954, Japan removed Korean territorial landmarks from Dokdo twice and replaced them with Japanese territorial landmarks four times.

During this time of increased tension and anxiety between Korea and Japan, the Corea Alpine Club carried out another expedition to Dokdo from October 13 to 16, 1953. According to Korean records, the members of this expedition encountered some Japanese during their visit there. The expedition's head, Hong Jong-in, recorded that the group encountered the ship *Nagara*, on board which was lawmaker Masanobu Tsuji of the Japanese House of Representatives.

For some reason, the Japanese media failed to report very accurately on this encounter, however. According to the *Asahi Shimbun*, Member of the House of Representatives Masanobu Tsuji, Deputy Director of the Ministry of Foreign Affairs Kawakami Kenzo, and Chief of the Public Safety Division of the Eighth Precinct's Maritime Safety Agency Komori embarked from the Port of Sakai, Tottori Prefecture at midnight on October 17, 1953 (by which time the Korean expeditionary group had already left Dokdo) aboard the 270-ton patrol ship *Nagara* of Sakai's Maritime Safety Agency to further look into the "Takeshima issue."[123] They arrived off Dokdo at noon on October 17 but were unable to go ashore due to inclement weather. They only viewed the island from the boat for about an hour before returning to Sakai at about 5 am in the afternoon of October 18. Upon their return, Tsuji commented to the effect that "the Dokdo issue and the Rhee Syngman Line are a complete defeat for Japan."[124]

Meanwhile, the Tsuji delegation's intrusion into Korean territory in the vicinity of Dokdo on October 17 did not occur by chance. The Japanese

---

123 *Ibid.*
124 *Ibid.*

government at this point had initiated a large-scale investigation into the Peace Line (the Rhee Syngman Line), and its intrusions into Korean territory there were intimately related to the investigation. According to Tsuji's records, he crossed the Peace Line twice to the east of Jejudo from October 7 to 14, 1953, his purpose being to hold maritime talks with a Korean warship there.[125] He stated that his investigation into the Peace Line was approved by the House of Representatives and consented to by the Minister of the Maritime Safety Agency.

Meanwhile, immediately after the Tsuji delegation returned from Dokdo, the Japanese Ministry of Foreign Affairs sent one of its own teams to the south of Jejudo and another to Dokdo to investigate the Peace Line and Dokdo. The Peace Line investigative team, along with 11 reporters, was at first sent along an almost identical route to that taken by Tsuji. From October 14 to 17, 1953, the "Group Appointed for the Investigation of Joseon Waters," which was jointly organized by the Japanese Ministry of Foreign Affairs, the Fisheries Agency, and the Maritime Safety Agency, crossed the channel aboard the 450-ton patrol boat *Iki* of the Maritime Safety Agency to further investigate the Peace Line. The group departed from Port Moji in Fukuoka and explored a total of 750 miles of the Rhee Line before returning to Port Nagasaki.[126] Some members of the group were charged with investigating Dokdo. The crossing of the Peace Line by the Foreign Ministry's investigative group and the intrusion into Korean territory in the vicinity of Dokdo by Masanobu Tsuji had both been planned in advance.

On October 21, the *Shimanemaru*, a fisheries scientific experimentation ship from Shimane Prefecture, landed on Dokdo. The people on board

---

125 Masanobu Tsuji wrote in the December issue of *Bungeishunju* about his experience of encroaching on Korean territorial waters on two occasions. The text of his accounts was also translated into English in the IRR files. Tsuji Masanobu, "Crossing the Stormy Rhee Line, Seeking Korean Warships," *Bungei-Shunju*, December 1953, RG 319, IRR File, Box 458, XA529038: Tsuji Masanobu.

126 Exploring the ocean's 38th parallel latitude, Rhee Line, on board the patrol boat Iki," *Asahi Shimbun* (Oct. 17, 1953).

found a landmark that had been installed on October 15 by the Corea Alpine Club along with a 170 centimeter-long stone memorial erected in memory of the Dokdo bombing victims. They also found four red and white ranging poles on the summit of Dongdo. They also noted that the Japanese territorial landmark had been removed. A photo of the Korean territorial landmark was featured first in Japan's *Asahi Shimbun*.[127]

On the day that the *Shimanemaru* intruded into Korean waters off Dokdo, a second investigative group arrived from Japan as well. The group was sent to restore the Japanese territorial landmarks and to remove the various survey signs left by Korea that the *Tsuji* delegation had discovered during their visit to Dokdo on October 17.[128] In the evening of October 21, Japan sent the patrol boat *Nagara* (from the Maritime Safety Agency in Sakai) along with the 270-ton patrol boat *Noshiro* (from the Maritime Safety Agency in Hamada). The boats docked at Dokdo in the morning of October 22 and removed one Korean territorial landmark and six of seven ranging poles that they found half way up and on the top of the sole peak on the island. They also installed two landmarks, one reading "島根縣 穩地 郡 五箇村 竹島" ("Takeshima, Gokomura, Ochi-gun, Shimane Prefecture" in English) and the other one reading "Fishing by Koreans is illegal."[129] Thus, the landmarks erected by the Corea Alpine Club on October 15 were removed only seven days after they were put up.

The illegal intrusion into Korean waters off Dokdo by Japanese boats and illegal landings on Dokdo itself continued unabated into 1954.[130] On August 23, 1954, the 450-ton patrol boat *Oki* (from the Maritime Safety

---

127 "Korean territorial landmark and measuring poles confirmed in Takeshima by the Shimanemaru," *Asahi Shimbun* (Oct. 23, 1953).

128 "Korean territorial landmarks removed from Takeshima," *Yomiuri Shimbun* (Oct. 26, 1953); *Dong-A Ilbo* (Oct. 27, 1953).

129 "Japanese territorial landmarks erected again for the fourth time," *Asahi Shimbun* (Oct. 25, 1953).

130 Bureau of State Affairs, Ministry of Foreign Affairs, *Introduction to the Dokdo Issue*, pp. 84-96; Kawakami, *A Study of the History and Geography of Takeshima*, p. 266; Jung Byung-joon, 2012, "Korea-Japan conflict on Dokdo in 1953-1954 and Korea's policy to safeguard Dokdo," *Journal of Korean Independence Movement Studies*, Vol. 41.

Agency) was fired on with approximately 400 rounds of ammunition by the Korean authorities that were on Dokdo at the time. One of the rounds passed through the boat's right exhaust pipe and several more rounds hit the boat, but none of the crew was injured. On August 26, the Japanese Ministry of Foreign Affairs lodged a protest with the Korean Diplomatic Mission in Japan concerning the encounter.[131] On August 28, the Korean Ministry of Foreign Affairs rejected Japan's protests, criticizing Japan instead for illegally intruding into Korean territorial waters with the intention of landing on Dokdo.[132] Following this incident, the Cabinet of the Korean government adopted a resolution on August 31, 1943 to station "hundreds of policemen" on Dokdo "to protect it from Japanese encroachment at all cost."[133] The government also drew up a plan to build a lighthouse there as a follow-up measure.[134]

In conclusion, from 1952 to 1954, Korea and Japan exchanged a series of diplomatic memoranda clarifying their respective claims of sovereignty over Dokdo, installed competing territorial landmarks and signboards on Dokdo, and automatic weapons were even discharged. During this period, the two governments produced memoranda clarifying their respective positions on the issue. The position of the Japanese government is well summarized in the *Viewpoints of the Japanese Government on Takeshima of July 13, 1953* and the *Viewpoints of the Japanese Government Refuting the Korean Government's Viewpoint Enclosed in the Note of the Korean Mission in Japan dated September 9, 1953*.[135] The position of the Korean government is clarified in the Korean Government's Refutation of the Japanese Government's Views Concerning Dokdo (Takeshima) dated July 13, 1953 and the Views of the Korean Government (Korean Mission in Japan) Refuting the Viewpoints of the Japanese Government Enclosed in

131 *Yomiuri Shimbun* (Aug. 27, 1954).
132 *Yomiuri Shimbun* (Aug. 29, 1954).
133 *Yomiuri Shimbun* (Sept. 1, 1954).
134 *Yomiuri Shimbun* (Sept. 10, 1954).
135 Bureau of State Affairs, Ministry of Foreign Affairs, *Introduction to the Dokdo Issue*, pp. 107-114, 131-151.

the Note of the Japanese Ministry of Foreign Affairs Dated February 10, 1954 on the Possession of Dokdo (Takeshima), Asia 2, No. 15).[136]

The position of the Korean government in response to Japan's territorial offensive was simple: "Dokdo has been and is being very effectively administered by the Korean government authorities in light of the fact that it was originally found and occupied by Koreans, and has been a part of Korean territory for centuries."[137]

---

136 Bureau of State Affairs, Ministry of Foreign Affairs, *Introduction to the Dokdo Issue*, pp. 114-130, 155-189.
137 Bureau of State Affairs, Ministry of Foreign Affairs, *Introduction to the Dokdo Issue*, pp. 121-122.

3
The United States
: From Active Intervention to a Position of Neutrality

1) Disparate views in Busan, Tokyo, and Washington in 1952

The bombing incident on *Gwangyeongho* and the bombing of Korean fishermen and divers on Dokdo on September 15, 1952 were given wide coverage in the Korean media. The incidents were dealt with as a matter of common concern by the US Embassy in Korea, the US Embassy in Japan, and the US Department of State (DoS). At the heart of their discussions were whether or not such bombings had actually occurred, the designation and release of Dokdo as a bombing range, and the Rusk documents of August 10, 1951.

In 1952, the US Embassies in Busan and Tokyo viewed the Dokdo bombing incidents with the same policy inertia that they had in 1951. During this period, the US Embassy in Busan, the US Embassy in Tokyo, and the US DoS in Washington showed subtle differences in their positions, a reflection of the disparate views existing between the local missions and headquarters on the one hand and between the enforcement agencies and the policy-making organization on the other. The Embassies in Busan and Tokyo wanted completely opposite local ambiances and voices to be reflected in US policy. Washington's fear was that any US decision on the matter would cause unmanageably strong reactions from the countries involved.

The position of the US Embassy in Busan was as follows: First, the text of the San Francisco Peace Treaty did not support Korean sovereignty over Dokdo. Second, there existed a dispute between Korea and Japan over the sovereignty of Dokdo. Third, the dispute over Dokdo was an issue that should be resolved during the Korea-Japan talks. Fourth, the US should not intervene in the Korea-Japan dispute over Dokdo.[138] The Embassy, which did not know of the Rusk documents until November 1952, was shocked to learn about their existence from the Office of Northeast Asian Affairs of the US DoS and at the fact that the US had already made a decision on Dokdo. Thus, from December 1952 onwards, the US Embassy in Busan decided that silence was the best policy.

Meanwhile, the US Embassy in Tokyo took a stronger stance on the issue. First, because Dokdo was not listed as a territory to be ceded by Japan in the text of the San Francisco Peace Treaty, the Embassy contended that Dokdo was therefore Japanese territory. Second, since Dokdo was clearly Japanese territory, Korea's claims to sovereignty over Dokdo were invalid. Third, Dokdo could be used as a potential radar point for United Nations aircraft, a possible dumping area of unexpended bomb loads, or a bombing target for the US Air Force. Fourth, since the US-Japan Joint Committee had designated Dokdo as a bombing range for the US forces, it had therefore recognized it as a facility belonging to the Japanese government. Fifth, so long as Korean fishermen were frequenting Dokdo for fishing purposes, there was naturally going to be a high risk of civilian casualties.[139] The US Embassy in Japan also learned about the existence of the Rusk documents only in November 1952. However, the Embassy had already come to the conclusion that Dokdo was part of Japan, and it was with this conviction that it approached its dealings with the San Francisco Conference and the US-Japan Joint Committee. Though it is understandable that diplomatic missions reflect local public opinion in their reports due to their assimilation to the local circumstances with which they are in need of dealing on a daily basis, the US Embassy in Tokyo took a

---

138 Despatch by E. Allan Lightner, Jr., to Robert Murphy, American Ambassador, Tokyo, Japan (Oct. 16, 1952); Memorandum, Subject: Use of Disputed Territory (Tokto Island) as Live Bombing Area (Oct. 15, 1952), RG 84, Japan, Tokyo Embassy, CGR 1952, Box 1, Folder 320 Japan-Korea Liancourt Rocks 1952.
139 Despatch by Amembassy, Tokyo (John M. Steeves, First Secretary of Embassy) to the Department of State, Subject: Koreans on Liancourt Rocks (Oct. 3, 1952), RG 59, Department of State, Decimal File, 694.9513/10-352; RG 84, Japan, Tokyo Embassy, CGR 1952, Box 1, Folder 320 Japan-Korea Liancourt Rocks 1952.

much stronger position on the Dokdo issue than the US Embassy in Busan. Even after learning about the US policy decision of August 10, 1951, the US Embassy in Tokyo disregarded the neutrality guidelines recommended by the Secretary of State, instead requesting that the US DoS disclose the Rusk documents.

As a result, Washington found itself in a dilemma. It was only in November 1952 that the US DoS's Office of Northeast Asian Affairs found out about the Rusk documents and the policy decision made therein regarding Dokdo. However, that decision had not been made either through involved discussions with Korea and Japan or through close cooperation with the US Embassies in Korea and Japan. Nor had the decision been made by the Allied Powers through any kind of a formal decision-making procedure. It had been made at the working level and had not been officially communicated to the diplomatic offices in Seoul and Tokyo or to the Korean and Japanese governments. As a result, while the US Embassy in Tokyo continued to put pressure on the US DoS to maintain its policy decision, inform the Japanese government of the decision, and officially announce it, the US Embassy in Busan sent a warning to the US DoS that Korea's sovereignty claims to Dokdo had reached a fever pitch. In the end, Washington decided to weaken the Korean position by reminding the Korean government of the US policy position set forth in the Rusk documents, while leaving the Japanese government uninformed of the documents. Such an approach was an expression of the US DoS's desire to maintain coherence in its policies while avoiding involvement in the dispute over Dokdo. In response, Tokyo protested vociferously, Busan kept silent, and Washington hoped that the dispute would somehow just go away.

The Korean media refused to let it go away. Nevertheless, while the Dokdo bombing incidents of September 1952 were being widely reported, it was not until two months later (in November) that the issue was first breached with the US DoS through diplomatic channels. However, by early October, both the US Embassies in Japan and Korea were conceiving plans to deal with the issue.

The US Embassy in Japan was the first to report to the US DoS. First,

Embassy Secretary John M. Steeves addressed the Dokdo sovereignty issue in a report entitled *Koreans on Liancourt Rocks* (October 3, 1952). In his report, Steeves argued in support of Japanese sovereignty over Dokdo. He based his argument on the facts that: 1) Dokdo, which at one time had been part of the Kingdom of Korea, was annexed by Japan and became Japanese territory, 2) in Article 2 of the 1951 Peace Treaty, Dokdo was not specified as an area to be renounced by Japan, whilst Quelpart, Port Hamilton and Dagelet were, and 3) with the explicit consent of the Japanese government, the US-Japan Joint Committee had more recently designated Dokdo as a military maneuvering area.[140] Steeves concluded that Dokdo was clearly owned by Japan, that this fact had been recognized by both Japan and the US, and that it was Korea that was making an issue of it, not Japan.

Steeves stated that standing in the open international waters between Korea and Japan, Dokdo had a certain utility to United Nations aircraft returning from bombing runs in North Korean territory. More specifically, he proposed that Dokdo could serve as a radar point, which would permit the dumping of unexpended bomb loads, as well as an actual live bombing target. This argument was more elaborate than the one made by Sebald in 1949 where it was simply proposed to use Dokdo as a radar station and a bombing range. The Joint Committee mentioned by Steeves was a reference to the 12th US-Japan Joint Committee of July 26, 1952. The US Embassy in Japan had already come to an understanding that the designation of Dokdo as a bombing range was based on US recognition of Japan's sovereignty over the island. Meanwhile, Steeves expressed his opinion that since the Dokdo expedition organized by the Corea Alpine Club was intended to establish Korea's claim to sovereignty over Dokdo, the Far East Command, Far East Naval Forces, and United Nations Naval Command in Busan should refrain from granting any further permits for such expeditionary activities.[141] Nowhere in his report did Steeves request that the bombing

---

140 Despatch by Amembassy, Tokyo (John M. Steeves, First Secretary of Embassy) to the Department of State, Subject: Koreans on Liancourt Rocks (Oct. 3, 1952), RG 59, Department of State, Decimal File, 694.9513/10-352.

141 Steeves attached a letter from Son Won-il, the ROK chief of the General Staff of the Navy,

training runs taking place over Dokdo be discontinued. He only suggested that the scientific expeditions and fishing activities by Koreans should be stopped, expressing his concern about incidents happening on Dokdo sometime in the future owing to the crude implementation of government controls by Korea.

In contrast, the report prepared by the US Embassy in Busan took on a completely different tone. In a letter dated October 16, 1952 to Robert Murphy, the American Ambassador to Japan, E. Allan Lightner, Jr. the *chargé d'affaires* of the US Embassy in Korea, wrote that Koreans were very touchy on the Dokdo issue and that the new complication involving the bombing of the island was being discussed in the press. With regard to sovereignty, the American Embassy in Korea viewed the status of Dokdo (Takeshima or the Liancourt Rocks) as still unresolved. Lightner also stated that, despite the Korean government's request in July 1951 that the Japanese renounce any claims to this island in the Peace Treaty, no action had been taken to insert such a provision in the draft treaty and so Korea continued to claim sovereignty over the island.

Given that the implication of the Joint Committee's decision was that the US had recognized the Japanese as having sovereignty over Dokdo, Lightner stated that the US should not get involved in the controversy between Korea and Japan over it. He stated that the Dokdo expedition by the Corea Alpine Club was a "government-sponsored expedition" and "undoubtedly intended to strengthen Korean claims to ownership of the island." He noted that while the expeditionary group was attempting to land on Dokdo, bombs were dropped on the island two times, causing the local press to complain that such bombings were an infringement upon Korean sovereignty. He went on to express concerns that the continued use of Dokdo as a live bombing area may involve the US in the territorial dispute and cause adverse publicity and/or legal action in the event

---

requesting permission for the Jinnam-ho, on which the Corea Alpine Club boarded for its expedition to Dokdo, to travel, and the article from *Dong-A Ilbo* regarding the Dokdo bombing incident (Sept. 21, 1952).

that fishermen were killed or injured by bombs. Lightner concluded by suggesting that the American Embassy in Tokyo resolve the matter since the decision to use the island as a bombing target had been made in Tokyo. More specifically, he suggested that the Ambassador mention the subject to the Commander of the United Nations Forces, General Mark W. Clark, or the Commander of the Far East Air Force, General Otto P. Weyland, with a view to discontinuing the use of the island for bombing practice, which would otherwise entail potentially explosive political implications.[142]

On October 20, Lightner communicated the relevant records regarding the Korea-Japan dispute over Dokdo and the bombing incidents to General Thomas W. Herren, Commanding General of the Korean Communications Zone.[143] Subsequently, an investigation of the Dokdo bombing incidents was initiated. The Air Attaché of the American Embassy visited the Fifth Air Force Headquarters in Daegu but was unable to locate information there concerning the plane or the pilot that bombed Dokdo. This was because the bombs had been dropped by the US Air Force stationed in Japan, not in Korea.[144] However, General Clark, the Commanding General of the Far East Command, stated in his letter to Lightner that he had initiated an investigation into the bombing incident.[145]

In October 1952, Busan and Tokyo each came up with a report reflective of the ambiance in their respective locales. The conflict was further exacerbated when the Korean Ministry of Foreign Affairs lodged a formal

---

142 Despatch by E. Allan Lightner, Jr., to Robert Murphy, American Ambassador, Tokyo, Japan (Oct. 16, 1952); Memorandum, Subject: Use of Disputed Territory (Tokto Island) as Live Bombing Area (Oct. 16, 1952), RG 84, Japan, Tokyo Embassy, CGR 1952, Box 1, Folder 320 Japan-Korea Liancourt Rocks 1952.

143 Letter by Edwin A. Lightner, Jr. to Thomas W. Herren (Oct. 20, 1952), RG 84, Korea, Seoul Embassy, CGR 1953-55, Box 12.

144 Memorandum by Alben B. Culp, Air Attache, American Embassy to Bushner, Political Section (Oct. 20, 1952), RG 84, Korea, Seoul Embassy, CGR, 1953-1955, Box 12.

145 Letter by Mark W. Clark, CINC, Far East Command to E. Allan Lightner, Jr., (undated), RG 84, Korea, Seoul Embassy, CGR, 1953-55, Box 12 (compiled by the National Institute of Korean History, 2008, *Dokdo Data Collection, Vol. 2: US*, p. 242).

protest two months after the bombing incident on Dokdo.[146] Lightner forwarded the Korean Government's letter to General Clark (November 14, 1952) and requested that the bombing runs be discontinued. He also sent a copy to the Fifth Air Force Command and the US Embassy in Tokyo.[147] Lightner viewed the Korean government's decision to lodge a protest two months after the incident as designed to support its sovereignty claims over Dokdo. He anticipated that if the US chose to ignore Korea's protest, the Korean government would argue strongly that the US effectively acknowledged Korean sovereignty over Dokdo due to the fact that the US had thus far chosen to remain silent on Korea's very vocal claims to sovereignty over Dokdo. On the other hand, Lightner stated that the US may only get itself further embroiled in the Dokdo dispute by making its position clear. He also noted that the US had to a certain degree already involved itself in the Dokdo dispute by agreeing to Japan's proposal to designate Dokdo as a bombing range at the US-Japan Joint Committee. In conclusion, Lightner asked General Clark if the US position on Dokdo should perhaps be stated clearly in Clark's reply to the Korean government. Given that sovereignty had not yet been resolved and was at the heart of the dispute between Korea and Japan, he proposed including the following wording at the end of the letter to be sent to the Korean government:

The Embassy has noted the statement contained in the Ministry's note that 'Dokdo Island (Liancourt Rocks)... is a part of the territory of the Republic of Korea'. The United States Government understands that ownership of this island is in dispute and therefore feels that clarification of the exact status will depend initially on the outcome of negotiations between the Republic of Korea and the Japanese Government.[148] (Underlined by the quoter)

---

146 Bureau of State Affairs, Ministry of Foreign Affairs, *Introduction to the Dokdo Issue*, p. 47.

147 Copy of Letter (E. Allan Lightner, Jr., Charge d'Affairs, ad interim) to General Clark (Nov. 14, 1952), RG 84, Japan, Tokyo Embassy, CGR 1952, Box 1, Folder 320 Japan-Korea Liancourt Rocks 1952.

148 Despatch by E. Allan Lightner, Jr., Charge d'Affaires, ad interim, to Department of State (Nov. 14, 1952), RG 84, Japan, Tokyo Embassy, CGR 1952, Box 1, Folder 320 Japan-Korea

In short, Lightner was asking the US DoS Headquarters about how the Dokdo sovereignty issue should be addressed, including the proposed wording above.

On November 14, 1952, Kenneth T. Young, Jr., director of the Office of Northeast Asian Affairs notified the US Embassy in Busan of the US DoS's stance on the Dokdo issue.[149] The position came as a shock to both the US Embassies in Busan and Tokyo, as they had never been informed of it before. Young pointed out the following: First, Korea's claim to sovereignty over Dokdo had been dismissed at the conclusion of the San Francisco Peace Treaty and thus Dokdo was now considered to be a territory of Japan. Second, the action of the US-Japan Joint Committee in designating these rocks as a facility of Japan was thus justified. Third, the Korean claims to sovereignty over Dokdo, based on SCAPIN 677 (January 1, 1946), did not permanently preclude Japan from exercising its sovereignty over Dokdo in the future. In particular, the details of the Korea-US dialogue held in Washington in July-August, 1951 was first made public at this time.

The US Embassy in Tokyo reacted promptly. On November 25, it forwarded Young's letter to the Commanding General of the Far East Command, underlining the US DoS's position that Dokdo was Japanese territory. This correspondence was drafted by Finn.[150]

The US DoS's overall assessment of the situation was well reflected in the telegram sent by Robert J. G. McClurkin, Deputy Director of the Office of Northeast Asian Affairs of the US DoS, to Busan and Tokyo dated November 26, 1952 (No. 365, received in Busan, November 27, 1952; No. 1360, received in Tokyo, November 28, 1952). The US DoS's position was stated as follows:[151]

Liancourt Rocks 1952.

149 Letter by Kenneth T. Young, Jr., Director, Office of Northeast Asian Affairs to E. Allan Lightner, Esquire, Charge d'affairs, a.i., American Embassy, Pusan, Korea (Nov. 14, 1952), RG 84, Japan, Tokyo Embassy, CGR 1952, Box 1, Folder 320 Japan-Korea Liancourt Rocks 1952.

150 Letter by John M. Steeves, First Secretary of Embassy, to Commander-in-Chief, Far East (Nov. 25, 1952), RG 84, Japan, Tokyo Embassy, CGR 1952, Box 1, Folder 320 Japan-Korea Liancourt Rocks 1952.

151 Telegram from Department of State (Robert J. G. McClurkin, Deputy Director, Office

First, the Department agreed that the US should not become involved in any territorial dispute arising from Korea's claim to Dokdo. In other words, it maintained its position that the dispute over Dokdo arose from Korea's claims to the island and the US would not intervene in the dispute. The department's foremost concern was not to get involved in the Dokdo dispute if at all possible through re-affirming existing policy and excluding the use of clear expressions.

Second, three bases were given regarding Japan's sovereignty over Dokdo: the position already taken by SCAP, by Rusk in the note dated August 10, 1951 to the Korean Ambassador in Washington, and by the designation of Dokdo as a facility of the Japanese government by the US-Japan Joint Committee. Of these, it is unclear what the position taken by SCAP means. The Office of Northeast Asian Affairs concluded that the already established facts and policy decisions were appropriate.

Third, the Office of Northeast Asian Affairs instructed the US Embassy in Korea to modify Lightner's proposed wording as follows:

> The Embassy has noted the statement contained in the Ministry's note that 'Dokdo Island (Liancourt Rocks)… is a part of the territory of the Republic of Korea. <u>The US Government's understanding of territorial status of this island was stated in Assistant Secretary Dean Rusk's Note to Ambassador Yang dated August 10, 1951.</u>[152] (Underlined by the quoter)

In short, Lightner's proposed wording that "clarification of the exact status will depend initially on the outcome of negotiations between the Republic of Korea and the Japanese government" was to be replaced by a reference to the Rusk documents of August 10, 1951, which contained

---

of Northeast Asian Affairs) to Amembassy Pusan (no. 365), repeated Tokyo (no. 1360) (Nov. 26, 1952), RG 84, Japan, Tokyo Embassy, CGR, 1952-1954, Box 1, Folder 320. Japan-Korea, Liancourt Rocks, 1952.

152 Telegram from Department of State (Robert J. G. McClurkin, Deputy Director, Office of Northeast Asian Affairs) to Amembassy Pusan (no. 365), repeated Tokyo (no. 1360), RG 59, Department of State, Decimal File, 694.9513/11-1452.

mention that Dokdo had been under the jurisdiction of Japan. However, the wording did not in itself explicitly state who had sovereignty over Dokdo, leaving anyone not familiar with the Rusk Documents clueless as to its meaning. Being fully aware of the potentially explosive political implications of the Dokdo issue, the Office of Northeast Asian Affairs seemed to have thought a great deal about it. While recognizing the inertia existing in the policy-making arena, the Office wanted to avoid further involvement in the issue if at all possible. Though such wording was understandable to officials at the Office of Northeast Asian Affairs of the US DoS, and to the US Embassies in Busan and Tokyo, it was a politically savvy exercise in ambiguity that left third parties clueless for the most part as to what was actually being said. The intent behind such wording was to avoid Korea's opposition to unjustifiable policy decision articulated in the Rusk documents, the weak rationale behind the US decision, doubts regarding the degree of consultation and nature of the decision-making process, and the fact that administrative convenience had trumped a key policy decision.

Thus, while internally taking the official stance that Dokdo was Japanese territory, the US DoS tried to take the easy way out by simply referring Korea to the Rusk documents of August 10, 1951, rather than spelling out its position. Towards the end of the telegram, it only quoted the relevant part of the Rusk documents, which stated that Dokdo had been under the jurisdiction of Japan.

Fourth, the main objective of the Office of Northeast Asian Affairs in writing this telegram was to "discourage the Korean government, already in a difficult situation as it was, from raising unnecessary issues for inclusion in the Korea-Japan talks." In other words, the US DoS's primary objective was to have the Korean government back off from its claim to sovereignty over Dokdo. Of interest to note is that the Office of Northeast Asian Affairs deleted part of its original draft of the telegram, which was the phrase "it is suggested that any contrary views held by the Republic of Korea be addressed to the government of Japan" The Office of Northeast Asian Affairs was taking a high-handed approach of threatening and suppressing Korea.

Busan and Tokyo reacted in strikingly different ways to this telegram. The first reaction came from Tokyo. After receiving the telegram on November 28, the US Embassy in Tokyo quickly sent a memorandum to the Commanding General of the Far East Command on December 1. The memorandum, signed by First Secretary Steeves, was again drafted by Finn.[153] The gist of the letter was that the Liancourt Rocks had been determined as being Japanese territory and thus any further policy decisions shall be made accordingly.

The US Embassy in Busan, on the other hand, seemed perplexed. Not only had it received letters from the US DoS referring back to and underlining the importance of the Rusk documents two times on November 14 and 26, it was also provided with specific wording to use in crafting its reply to the Korean government. In the meantime, Lieutenant General Doyle O. Hickey of the Headquarters of the Far East Command replied on November 27, 1952 that it was no longer possible to investigate the bombing incident as more than two months had passed since it had occurred, and that there were no records of any air units requesting the use of Dokdo at that time. The Headquarters of the Far East Command also informed the Embassy that they were preparing to dispense with the use of the Liancourt Rocks as a bombing range and they would notify Korea and other relevant authorities as soon as a decision was made on the issue. It also stated that the question of international sovereignty was, of course, outside General Clark's authority.[154] Thus, the US Embassy now had all the relevant information it needed to respond to the protests of the Korean Ministry of Foreign Affairs. Its response would be that it was impossible at this point to investigate the Dokdo bombing incident, work was being done to dispense with the use of Dokdo as a bombing range, and

---

153 Memorandum by John M. Steeves, First Secretary of Embassy, to the Commander-in-Chief, Far East (Dec. 1, 1952), RG 84, Japan, Tokyo Embassy, CGR 1952, Box 1, Folder 320 Japan-Korea Liancourt Rocks 1952.

154 Letter by Doyle O. Hickey, LTG, Chief of Staff, Far East Command to E. Allan Lightner, Jr. American Embassy, Pusan, Korea (Nov. 27, 1952), RG 84, Korea, Seoul Embassy, CGR, 1953-1955, Box 12.

determination of Dokdo's territorial status was understood by the US DoS as being *fait accompli*.

On December 4, 1952, the US Embassy in Korea conveyed this message to the Korean Ministry of Foreign Affairs by means of memorandum No. 187. Although it was written in the form of a reply to the Korean Foreign Ministry's memorandum of November 10, 1952, which inquired about the bombing incident on Dokdo, the December 4th memo was primarily focused on clarifying the territorial status of Dokdo. The memo read that 1) it was virtually impossible to determine the facts in the Dokdo bombing incident as a very long time had elapsed since the incident had taken place, 2) preparations had been expedited to dispense with the use of Dokdo as a bombing range, and 3) with regard to the Ministry's note that Dokdo was a part of the Republic of Korea, the US Government's understanding of the territorial status of this island had been stated in Assistant Secretary of State Dean Rusk's note to the Korean Ambassador in Washington dated August 10, 1951.[155] Korea asked about the Dokdo bombing incident but the US only answered its position on Dokdo's sovereignty.

Yet, it is unclear how the Korean Ministry of Foreign Affairs interpreted the memo from the US Embassy at this point. It is also not known what kind of further relevant exchanges of opinion took place between Korea and the US. What is known is that Korea continued to advocate its position that Dokdo was Korean territory.

After sending the memo to the Korean Ministry of Foreign Affairs on December 4, 1952, Lightner reported to Young of the Office of Northeast Asian Affairs that he had acted in accordance with the US DoS's instructions. In this report, Lightner wrote as follows:

I much appreciate your letter of November 14 in regard to the status of the Dokdo Island (Liancourt Rocks). The information you gave us had never

---

155 No. 187, American Embassy, Pusan (Dec. 4, 1952), enclosure to the Despatch by American Embassy Pusan (E. Allan Lightner, Jr., Counselor of Embassy) to the Department of State, no. 204 (Dec. 4, 1952), RG 84, Korea, Seoul Embassy, CGR, 1953-1955, Box 12.

been previously available to the Embassy. We had never heard of Dean Rusk's letter to the Korean Ambassador in which the Department took a definite stand on this question.[156]

In short, the US Embassy in Korea was not aware of the policy statement of the US DoS regarding the sovereignty status of Dokdo at all until it was notified as such by the Office of Northeast Asian Affairs. Despite the fact that this issue was politically a very sensitive subject for Korea, the US DoS made a policy decision without knowing who made the call in the first place. Furthermore, the decision, made without so much as a single consultation with the local diplomatic offices, was not even communicated to the US Embassy in Busan. Instead, it was left dormant for over 14 months until the Dokdo dispute between Korea and Japan had reached a fever pitch following the bombing incident. This implied that the decision may not have been an important policy decision at the time, but rather a routine administrative measure taken at the working level. This was why neither the diplomatic office in Seoul nor the one in Tokyo were made aware of it. Nor did they have the slightest hint of a clue that such a decision had been made. And this was also why the US Embassy in Busan, in light of local public opinion, had taken such a different position from that of its headquarters in Washington. The fault lay with Washington's hasty decision and the poor manner with which it handled the matter, betraying a complete lack of a system of cooperation. In brief, these circumstances seem to indicate that Rusk's letter of August 10, 1951 was the result of a hasty decision—an administrative contrivance if you will—on the part of the US DoS as it was nearing finalization of the peace treaty with Japan.

The US Embassy in Korea tried to avoid the Dokdo sovereignty issue as much as possible, focusing its attention and energy instead on the need to discontinue the use of Dokdo as a bombing range. According to a

---

156 Letter by E. Allan Lightner, Jr., to Kenneth T. Young, Jr., Director, Office of Northeast Asian Affairs, Department of State (Dec. 4, 1952), RG 84, Korea, Seoul Embassy, CGR, 1953-1955, Box 12.

report from Tokyo dated December 9, the Far East Command organized a team of three officers to find a replacement site for bombing practice but expressed its intention to continue using Dokdo in the meantime. The Far East Command would immediately notify the relevant units to discontinue use as soon as a replacement site was found.[157] In his reply to William T. Turner, the Counselor of the US Embassy in Japan, dated December 19, 1952, Lightner asked that the US Embassy in Korea be immediately informed of any such decision. In the letter, Lightner also underlined that the US Embassy in Korea had never before heard of Rusk's letter of August 10, 1951.[158] However, that was about all the US Embassy could do. A policy decision had already been made and, despite the fact that Washington's handling of the case was now at the heart of a major international dispute, the local diplomatic office could not alter or object to the decision. On the other hand, the primary reason behind the steadfast silence of the US Embassy in Korea was to ensure coherence with the policy of headquarters in Washington.

2) The responses of Korea and Japan to the release of Dokdo as a bombing range in 1953

In a memorandum to the Korean government dated December 4, 1952, the US Embassy in Korea addressed some of the issues that the Korean Ministry of Foreign Affairs had raised on November 10, 1952, stating that an investigation into the Dokdo bombing incident was not possible, that the territorial issue had been clarified by an existing policy decision, and that what remained to be resolved was dispensing with the use of Dokdo as a bombing range. Thus, throughout January 1953, efforts were

---

157 William T. Turner, Counselor of Embassy, Tokyo to E. Allan Lightner, Jr., Esquire, Counselor of Embassy, Pusan (Dec. 9, 1952), RG 84, Japan, Tokyo Embassy, CGR 1952, Box 1, Folder 320 Japan- Korea Liancourt Rocks 1952.

158 E. Allan Lightner, Jr., Counselor of Embassy, Pusan to William T. Turner, Esquire, Counselor of Embassy, American Embassy, Tokyo (Dec. 19, 1952), RG 84, Japan, Tokyo Embassy, CGR 1952, Box 1, Folder 320 Japan-Korea Liancourt Rocks 1952.

made to this end, but getting the US forces to stop was directly linked to Japan's sovereignty claims over Dokdo, which had far-reaching political ramifications.

On January 5, 1953, William T. Turner of the US Embassy in Japan informed Allan Lightner of the US Embassy in Korea that it had been notified by the Far East Command that Dokdo would no longer be used as a bombing range. He also said that the Liancourt Rocks (located 37° 15′ north, 131° 52′ east) would be replaced by the Far East Command, as of December 18, 1952, with an area ten miles in radius from 37° 30′ North, 132° 30′ East. This message was immediately conveyed to the Commanding General of the Korean Communications Zone, General Herren, and Turner asked him to convey it to the Korean government.[159]

After receiving the information from Tokyo, the US Embassy in Korea sent a letter to General Herren on January 16, 1953 asking if the Embassy could inform the Korean government of the Far East Command's decision to stop using Dokdo as a bombing range as of December 18, 1952.[160] It seems that upon receiving this request, General Herren directly notified the Korean government of this fact. According to Korean records, "On January 20, 1953, the Communications Garrison Command of the United Nations Forces in Korea reported that all units under its jurisdiction were instructed to take the necessary measures following the decision to dispense with the use of the Liancourt Rocks as a bombing range."[161] Here, the Communications Garrison Command means the Headquarters of the Korean Communications Zone under the US Eighth Army.

The US Embassy in Korea looked through its files and discovered that,

---

159 Letter by William T. Turner, Counselor of Embassy, Tokyo to E. Allan Lightner, Jr., Counselor of Embassy, Pusan (Jan. 5, 1953), RG 84, Korea, Seoul Embassy, CGR, 1953-1955, Box 12.

160 Letter by E. Allan Lightner, Jr., Counselor of Embassy, Pusan to Major General Thomas W. Herren, Commanding General, Korean Communications Zone (Dec. 18, 1952), RG 84, Korea, Seoul Embassy, CGR 1953-1955, Box 12.

161 Bureau of State Affairs, Ministry of Foreign Affairs, *Introduction to the Dokdo Issue*, p. 47; Annex 7. Thomas W. Herren's Letter dated January 20, 1953. *Introduction to the Dokdo Issue*, p. 10.

from June to July of 1951, some formal discussions had taken place between the US and Korea regarding the designation of Dokdo as a bombing range.[162] On June 20, 1951, the US Eighth Army had made a request to the Korean government to allow it to use the Liancourt Rocks as a 24-hour bombing range. Subsequently on July 1, 1951, the Korean Prime Minister, the Minister of National Defense, and the Minister of Home Affairs had approved that request. Lightner immediately sent a letter to General Herren of the Korean Communications Zone (January 23, 1953), letting him know that copies of old letters were found among the unorganized files of the Embassy and that, before the documents were found, the US Embassy had not been aware that the US military authorities had asked for and obtained permission from the Korean government to use Dokdo as a bombing range.[163] Lightner also cautiously inquired whether it was necessary to inform the Koreans of the location of the new bombing range that would replace Dokdo since Korean civilians were always fishing there as well.

20 June 1951

Dear Mr. Minister

The Air Force requests authority to use the Liancourt Rocks Bombing Range (3715 north latitude – 13152 east) on a 24-hour basis for training.

The Air Force is prepared to give 15 days advance notice and to clear the area of any personnel or boats.

Will you please inform me as soon as practical if the above meets with your approval?

---

162 This fact was first revealed by Park Jin-hui (Park Jin-hui, compiled by the National Institute of Korean History, 2008, "Explanation," *Dokdo Data Collection, Vol. 2: US*). Lovmo also posted the original relevant documents on his webpage [US Military Requested, and Received, Permission from ROK Prime Minister Chang Myun to Use Dokdo as a Bombing Range, (June 20, 1951), http://dokdo-research.com/page8.html].

163 Letter by E. Allan Lightner, Jr., Counselor of Embassy, Pusan to Major General Thomas W. Herren, Commanding General, Korean Communications Zone (Jan. 23, 1953), RG 84, Korea, Seoul Embassy, CGR 1953-1955, Box 12.

Your cooperation is deeply appreciated and you may be assured of my continued best wishes.

Sincerely yours,

/s/ John B. Coulter

Lieutenant General, United States Army

Deputy Army Commander

The Honorable Chang Myun

Prime Minister

Republic of Korea[164]

Thus, on June 20, 1951, the US Eighth Army had requested the permission of the Korean government to use Dokdo as a bombing range. Such a request could only have been made based on the premise that Dokdo was Korean territory. The response of the Korean government was also found in the files of the US Embassy.

Headquarters

Eighth United States Army Korea (EUSAK)

Office of the Deputy Army Commander

APO 301

7 July 1951

Subject: Progress Report

To: Commanding General (EUSAK)

…a. Liancourt Rocks Bombing Range

---

164 Letter by John B. Coulter, LTG, Deputy Army Commander, to Chang Myun, Prime Minister, Republic of Korea (Jan. 20, 1951), attached to the Letter by E. Allan Lightner, Jr., to Thomas W. Herren (Jan. 23, 1953).

Inquiry made at the office of the Prime Minister on 1 July disclosed that the request for its use by the Air Force had been approved by the Minister of Defense and the Prime Minister, and had been referred to the Minister of Home Affairs because the locality in question is under the jurisdiction of his Ministry. It was learned that the latter had not disposed of the paper because he understood that he was to obtain the fifteen day advance notice before approving it. The Prime Minister's office was informed that we could not give a fifteen day notice until action on the request was known. I was informed that the request was approved and the fifteen day notice was requested.

The above information was furnished by Colonel Patterson, G-3 Section, 1 July.[165]

Since November 1952, Japan, the US Embassy in Japan and the US DoS referred to documents on the designation and release of Dokdo as a bombing range exchanged between the Japanese government and the US forces in Japan as a basis for Japan's claim over Dokdo. Contradictory to this, in June 1951, there had already been a meeting of minds between Korea and the US regarding the territorial sovereignty of Dokdo, with the US Eighth Army recognizing it as Korean territory and the Korean government approving the Eighth Army's request to use it for military purposes. Therefore, having already recognized Korea's sovereignty over Dokdo through a bilateral agreement designating Dokdo as a bombing range in June and July of 1951, the US made the mistake of recognizing it as a Japanese facility as the result of a carefully designed Japanese plot in July of 1952. To sum up, Dokdo had already been designated as a bombing range for the US Eighth Army by consent of the Korean government in July, 1951, but the US-Japan Joint Committee, which was not cognizant of this fact, re-designated it as a bombing range for the US Air force in July, 1952.

However, it is not known whether the Korean government, devastated

---

165 Subject: Progress Report, by Deputy Army Commander, EUSAK (Jul. 7, 1951), attached to the Letter by E. Allan Lightner, Jr., to Thomas W. Herren (Jan. 23, 1953).

by the Korean War at the time, was able to keep track of the document that the US Embassy happened upon among its files. The agreement mentioned in the document had been made two years previously, and a number of top government officials had been replaced over this period [the Prime Minister (Chang Myun→Baek Du-jin), the Minister of National Defense (Lee Ki-bung→Sin Tae-yeong), and the Minister of Home Affairs (Lee Sun-yong→Jin Heon-sik)]. There is no indication that the US Embassy in Korea notified or consulted with the Korean government in this regard. The Embassy only informed the Headquarters of the Korean Communications Zone about it.

Although the decision to release Dokdo as a bombing range and designate another site as such had already been made on December 18, 1952, it was only in February 1953 that the Korean government was notified of this. Considering the close communications between the US Embassy in Korea and the Headquarters of the Korean Communications Zone throughout January 1953, this notification was considerably late. No documents have yet been found regarding how and when the US Embassy in Korea or the Headquarters of the Korean Communications Zone notified the Korean government that Dokdo would no longer be used as a bombing range.

The decision to dispense with this use of Dokdo became known to the Korean people through a public announcement by the Korean Ministry of National Defense on February 27, 1953. The announcement stated that a comprehensive agreement had been reached between Korea and the United Nations Forces authorities regarding the discontinuation of the use of Dokdo as a bombing range and that "the US government also recognizes that Dokdo is part of Korean territory and it was guaranteed by the Commander of the Far East Command that no bombing runs would take place around Dokdo in the future."[166] However, no mention was made regarding the designation or location of the alternate site.

The Ministry's announcement was covered in detail by the Korean media, which soon became an additional source of political controversy,

---

166   *Dong-A Ilbo* (Feb. 28, 1953).

not only because of the US decision to stop bombing Dokdo but also because the announcement stated that the US recognized it as Korean territory. In a telegram to the Secretary of State dated March 3, 1953, the US Ambassador to Korea Ellis O. Briggs stated that the Korean media was quoting from a letter by General Weyland, Commander of the Far East Air Forces and that he presumed that someone in the Korean government had misquoted it.[167] The US Embassy in Korea, on the other hand, claimed that it had no first-hand knowledge of Weyland's letter.

According to Korean diplomatic files, the Korean government tried not to associate the US apology for the bombing incident on Dokdo with the Dokdo sovereignty issue. Such an attempt would have appeared to be stooping to the same kind of logic that Japan had used in seeking to get the US to recognize Dokdo as Japanese territory. The Korean Minister of Foreign Affairs made the following statement in a document sent to the Korean Minister in Japan on August 12, 1953.

The US apology over the bombing of Dokdo by US military aircraft should not be seen as US approval of Korea's sovereignty over Dokdo since such an argument would be in the same vein as Japan's claim that Dokdo is Japanese territory based on their agreement with the US that Dokdo could be used as an exercise range of US forces in accordance with the US-Japan Administrative Agreement, and for this reason alone such an argument should not be made without permission.[168]

Being clearly aware of the Japanese intent, the Korean government did not want to make claims to Dokdo on the same basis as Japan had done. At this point, the conflict between Korea and Japan over the Peace Line was already at its height. On February 4, 1953, two Japanese fishing boats crossed the Peace Line and were found fishing one nautical mile off

---

167 Telegram by Briggs, Pusan to the Secretary of State (Mar. 3, 1953), RG 84, Japan, Tokyo Embassy, CGR 1953-1955, Box 23, Folder 322.1 Japan-Korea Liancourt Rocks.

168 "Regarding the sovereignty over Dokdo" (no. 257, Aug. 12, 1953) (Minister of Foreign Affairs → Korean Minister in Japan), *Dokdo Issue, 1952-1953*.

the coast of Jejudo. Despite orders from a Korean patrol boat to stop, the fishing boats fled, leading the patrols to fire warning rounds that accidently killed one of the fishermen. Japan launched strong protests and the Korean government as well as the Korean Mission in Japan responded in turn that the incident occurred in waters under the jurisdiction of Korea.[169]

Though the Japanese Minister of Foreign Affairs claimed that the incident occurred on the high seas, the area in question was not only on the Korean side of the Peace Line (the Rhee Line) but also within the Clark Line, i.e. the Sea Defense Zone set up by the United Nations Forces or defensive waters. For this reason, General Mark Wayne Clark, the Commander of United Nations Forces, advised that the best way to prevent such a situation happening again was to get the Japanese government to ban all war-related Japanese vessels from entering the sea-defense zone of Korean waters, or else to ban all commercial vessels from entering the waters in question until Korea and Japan could negotiate a resolution on this issue.[170]

The Japanese government reiterated its sovereignty claims over Dokdo at a joint meeting of the Foreign Affairs Committee and the Judicial Affairs Committee of the House of Councilors on March 5. During the meeting, Japanese Vice-Minister of Foreign Affairs Nakamura criticized the Korean government for using the memorandum of the Far East Command for propaganda purposes.[171] The Japanese again resorted to the dual rationale that Dokdo was not included on the list of territories to be excluded from Japan in the San Francisco Peace Treaty and that the designation and release of Dokdo as a bombing range constituted evidence of Japanese sovereignty over Dokdo.

The US DoS also conducted an investigation into Weyland's letter. As a result, both the US DoS and the Department of Defense concluded

169 *Pyeonghwa Shinmun* (Feb. 18, 1953); *Minju Shinbo* (Feb. 23, 1953).
170 Telegram by Murphy, Ambassador, Japan to the Secretary of State, no. 2858 (Mar. 4, 1953), RG 84, Japan, Tokyo Embassy, CGR 1953, Box 13.
171 Telegram by Murphy to the Secretary of State, no. 2894 (Mar. 6, 1953), RG 84, Japan, Tokyo Embassy, CGR 1953-1955, Box 23, Folder 322.1 Japan-Korea Liancourt Rocks

that it did not exist. Meanwhile, Dulles emphasized that the telegram of November 26, 1952 sent to the US Embassies in Busan and Tokyo remained the official position of the US DoS. This was a reference to the one sent by the Office of Northeast Asian Affairs to Busan and Tokyo regarding the US DoS's position on Dokdo. With relatively minor events being blown into major political issues, Dulles instructed the US Embassies in Busan and Tokyo to consult with the US DoS first before making any further public statements on the issue.[172]

However, it does not appear that the US DoS publicly denied the existence of Weyland's letter or sent the relevant documents to the Korean government, the reason being that the situation had already been decided in favor of Japan. Nevertheless, over the protests of the Japanese Ministry of Foreign Affairs, the US officially decided to discontinue using Dokdo as a bombing range through the US-Japan Joint Committee on March 19, 1953. Japan announced the decision through a notification of the Ministry of Foreign Affairs on May 14, 1953, and from May 28, 1953 onwards, it began encroaching into waters off Dokdo in earnest. Japan's actions since 1952 were coherently and carefully planned, and the US was being unwittingly dragged in the direction that Japan wanted.

While Korea resorted to the letter of the US Air Forces Command to argue that Dokdo was under Korean sovereignty, Japan put the discontinuation of the use of Dokdo as a bombing range on the formal agenda of the US-Japan Joint Committee. The US discounted the Korean government's claims about the letter as a distortion and exaggeration, and the Japanese government basically got what it wanted. All the while that Korea and Japan were engaged in this war of words over the sovereignty of Dokdo, public opinion within the US DoS and at the US Embassies in Busan and Tokyo was shifting precipitously in favor of Japan.

---

[172] Telegram by Secretary of State Dulles to Pusan and Tokyo Embassy (Mar. 11, 1953), RG 84, Japan, Tokyo Embassy, CGR 1953, Box 13.

3) Request for intervention by the US Embassy in Tokyo and Dulles' declaration of neutrality

The Dokdo sovereignty dispute, which began with Korea's declaration of the Peace Line in January 1952 and Japan's ensuing claims of ownership over Dokdo, remained at the diplomatic level of tit-for-tat charges and countercharges at least until the end of May 1953. Prior to that, the Korean government had sent a scientific expedition to Dokdo to further substantiate its sovereignty claims, but its plan failed due to bombings by the US Air Force. Instead, it sought to stop the bombings on its territory, Dokdo. In that process, however, it came face to face with the cold and resolute attitude of the US DoS and the US Embassy in Japan, and found itself being criticized as trumping up a non-existent sovereignty dispute by claiming that it had sovereignty rights to Dokdo. The Korean government was also unaware that Japan was intent on misusing the process of designating areas for US military use to contrive additional evidence in support of its own sovereignty claims over Dokdo.

Meanwhile, while confronting Korea's Peace Line declaration with verbal claims, the Japanese government concentrated its efforts on securing additional rationale for its claims by scheming to first designate and then release Dokdo from use as a bombing range for the US Air Force. This plan reached fruition with the decision of the 45th US-Japan Joint Committee to release Dokdo as a bombing range on March 19, 1953. Furthermore, a favorable environment was established for Japan to obtain the friendship and support of the US in its bid to secure sovereignty rights over Dokdo as it became known in diplomatic circles in Washington, Tokyo, and Busan that the US DoS had already taken a clear negotiating position on the issue with the Rusk note of August 10, 1951, though the document was not conveyed to the Japanese government at the time.

From March 1953 onwards, there was a growing demand in both Tokyo and Washington that the Rusk documents be disclosed in order to put an end to the Dokdo sovereignty dispute—in other words, that the conflict should be resolved through a public announcement that Dokdo was Japanese territory, or else that the US should proactively mediate the

Korea-Japan dispute over Dokdo.[173]

As early as January 1952, Sebald, the US political adviser in Japan at the time when Korea declared the Peace Line, expressed his opinion that Japanese sovereignty over Dokdo had been preserved in the text of the San Francisco Peace Treaty.[174] In opposition to the US draft treaty of 1949, which placed Dokdo under Korean territory, Sebald argued that Dokdo should be considered Japanese territory, sowing the seeds of the postwar territorial dispute over Dokdo. Leading up to the conclusion of the San Francisco Peace Treaty, Sebald served in Japan as Director of the Diplomatic Section of SCAP as well as political adviser. Even after Dulles expressed his position of neutrality on the issue in 1953, Sebald was still convinced that Dokdo was Japanese territory, but his position was that the territorial dispute should be negotiated directly between Korea and Japan rather than for the Allied Powers or SCAP to intervene. In November 1954, while Sebald was the Deputy Assistant Secretary of State for Far Eastern Affairs, Shigenobu Shima, Minister of Japan to the United States, inquired about taking the Dokdo issue to the UN Security Council and then to the International Court of Justice. Sebald shared his views that a bilateral resolution was more advised than taking the issue to the court.[175] He also recommended that "Japan should keep its claim alive and not permit its rights to be prejudiced by default," suggesting that "a note to the ROK or other periodic formal statements" would serve this purpose. If Sebald had not left Japan to become the US Ambassador to Burma in April of 1952, Korea would have likely faced a much more difficult situation. The problem was that even after his departure, one who had openly harbored pro-Japanese sentiments and a distrust of Korea, the majority of the diplomats

---

173 Jung, "Essay: Korea-Japan Dispute on the Sovereignty over Dokdo and the Role of the US"; Jung, "Viewpoints of Korea, the US, and Japan regarding the Territorial Dispute on Dokdo Island."
174 Sebald to the Secretary of State (Jan. 29, 1952), RG 59, Department of State, Decimal File, 694.95B/1- 2952.
175 Memorandum of Conversation (Nov. 17, 1954), RG 59, Department of State, Decimal File, 694.95B/11-1754.

at the US Embassy in Tokyo were still pro-Japan.

In April 1953, Second Secretary Finn of the US Embassy in Japan argued that since the sovereignty status of Dokdo was clearly weighted in favor of Japan based on the Treaty of San Francisco and that the US judgment in the Rusk note had already been officially conveyed to Korea, the Rusk documents dated August 10, 1951 should be publicly disclosed to effectively refute Korea's claims to Dokdo and resolve the Korea-Japan conflict over the issue once and for all.[176]

Finn was strongly advocating active US intervention in the territorial dispute as the US had already recognized Japan's claim at the San Francisco Conference and thus should intervene in the stormy relations between Korea and Japan and confirm Japan's sovereignty.

Finn is also the official who ignored the petition of the Patriotic Old Men's Association and failed to report it to the US DoS in August of 1948. Having begun his diplomatic career at the Far Eastern Commission, Finn had become particularly active since 1947 while at the Office of the Political Adviser and the Diplomatic Section of SCAP in Japan.[177] When he was starting out as a diplomat in Tokyo, the influence of Sebald and others was strong and thus the Office was overflowing with pro-Japanese sentiment.

Finn helped strengthen Japan's sovereignty claims to Dokdo by aiding in the decision of the 45th US-Japan Joint Committee (March 19, 1953) to remove Dokdo from the list of US military ranges despite knowing the dangerous political implications that such a decision would entail. Some may think that this was in keeping with established policy, but the facts of the case make it clear that strong pro-Japanese sentiments had a deciding impact.

Upon receiving Finn's memorandum, Bill Leonhart, First Secretary of the Tokyo Embassy, scribbled underneath the memo that he agreed with Finn's recommendation and that his boss should send a document to the

---

176　Memorandum by R. B. Finn to Leonhart, RG 84, Japan, Tokyo Embassy, CGR 1952-63, Box 23, Folder 322.1 "Liancourt Rocks."

177　Department of State, *The Biographic Register 1956* (Revised as of May 1, 1956), p. 215.

US Ambassador to Japan or the Japanese government outlining the US position. In the final analysis, things did not work out quite as Finn or Leonhart had proposed. Nevertheless, their views were not the minority opinion.

Between June and October of 1953, the conflict between Korea and Japan over Dokdo mounted, with Japan intruding into waters off Dokdo at least ten times, making landings, removing Korean territorial landmarks, and planting Japanese territorial landmarks and signboards four times or more. As was to be expected, the Japanese government proceeded to argue that the designation and release of Dokdo as a bombing range constituted evidence of Japan's sovereignty over it. The Korean government countered by strongly denying the veracity of such arguments. When the shooting incident on July 12, 1953 occurred during a Korean police inspection of a Japanese fishing boat that had illegally entered Korean waters off Dokdo, the US DoS became extremely nervous. At that time, it was critical for the US to ensure the stability of Korea. After more than three years of war on the peninsula, with the election of Eisenhower as the US President and the death of Stalin in the Soviet Union, an armistice appeared imminent. However, the Korean government was strongly opposed to the signing of an armistice and had just released a large number of anti-communist POWs (June 18, 1953). To the US, Korean President Rhee Syngman seemed to be simply beyond control. To the eyes of the US DoS, Rhee and his government were seen as wild, irrational, and obstinate, while the Japanese government was in contrast viewed as elegant, submissive, and rational. Such perceptions influenced the way the US DoS undertook its dealings with Korea and Japan on the Dokdo issue.

On July 22, 1953, a memorandum on the possible methods of resolving the Dokdo issue was put together by Alice L. Dunning of the Office of Northeast Asian Affairs.[178] According to the memo, four solutions were

---

178 Memorandum by Mrs. Dunning, NA to Mr. McClurkin, NA, Subject: Possible Methods of Resolving Liancourt Rocks Dispute between Japan and the Republic of Korea (Jul. 22, 1953), RG 59, Department of State, Decimal File, 694.9513/7-2253.

being proposed in Japan following the July 12 incident: 1) crafting an peaceful resolution through direct negotiation with Korea, 2) referring the issue to the United Nations or the UK, 3) bringing this issue to the International Court of Justice in the Hague or the United Nations, or 4) dispatching the Japanese Coast Guard to Dokdo.

Dunning pointed out that the two documents outlining the US policy on the sovereignty status of Dokdo, i.e. the Rusk note (August 10, 1951) and the memorandum of the US Embassy (December 4, 1952), had already been communicated to the Korean government and that the Rusk documents had not yet been officially conveyed to the Japanese government. She commented that the US position in the Rusk note might well come to light were this dispute ever submitted to mediation, conciliation, arbitration or judicial settlement. The Rusk note and the US Embassy memorandum that Dunning pointed to would later become the two most important documents that the US DoS would refer to in its efforts to resolve the dispute. No other subsequent documents from the US DoS ever explicitly stated that Japan had sovereignty over Dokdo. Instead, they simply referred to the Rusk note and the memorandum of the US Embassy.

Dunning predicted that Japan would either opt to: 1) ask the US for arbitration, 2) take the issue to the International Court of Justice, or 3) take the issue to the General Assembly or Security Council of the United Nations. She recommended that the US should take no action in as much as Japan had stated that it would try to settle the dispute with the Korean government. She noted further that Korea would likely reject the option of taking the case to the International Court of Justice, and that Japan would likely not want to further magnify the issue by bringing it to the General Assembly of the United Nations where it could be used by the Soviet Union to its own advantage for propaganda purposes, and where it would be difficult to get the consent of the anti-Soviet bloc. For this reason, the Division of Japanese Affairs of the Office of Northeast Asian Affairs (referred to as NA/J) recommended the following:

1. NA/J recommends that the Department of State take no action at this time inasmuch as Foreign Minister Okazaki has stated that the Japanese

Government will try to mediate the dispute with the ROK Government by direct negotiations.

2. However, if the Japanese Government requests the United States Government to act as a mediator in this dispute, NA/J recommends that the US refuse and suggest that the matter might appropriately be referred to the International Court of Justice or the United Nations.

3. If the Japanese Government requests the legal opinion of the United States Government on this question, NA/J recommends that the United States make available to the Japanese Government the United States position on the Liancourt Rocks as stated in the Rusk note of August 10, 1951.[179]

The above recommendations were also submitted for the review and consent of the Office of Korean Affairs of the Northeast Asian Bureau.[180] After reviewing the memorandum, Director McClurkin of the Office of Northeast Asian Affairs signed the first and second recommendations, but hinted at his rejection of the third recommendation by placing a question mark beside it. Thus, at this point, the scope of action available to the US was to recommend that Japan take the case to the International Court of Justice or to the United Nations. The US had already notified the Korean government of its policy decision regarding the sovereignty of Dokdo two times or more, but the Korean government had ignored these communications and continued to claim territorial sovereignty. The last option the US could take was to disclose the Rusk note, but doing so was likely to generate an irrevocable outcome.

While engaged in confrontation over Dokdo, Korea and Japan held their third bilateral talks on October 6, 1953 under US mediation. However, the talks fell apart in only fifteen days on October 21, 1953 owing to a number of reckless statements made by Kanichiro Kubota, head of the Japanese delegation. Kubota stated: 1) that the establishment of an independent

---

179 *Ibid.*

180 Treumann in charge of Korean affairs at the Office of Northeast Asian Affairs signed the recommendations.

Korean state before the Japanese peace treaty was signed was a violation of international law, 2) that the evacuation of all Japanese from Korea soon after the defeat of Japan in 1945 was a violation of international law, 3) that the confiscation of private Japanese property in Korea was a violation of international law, 4) that the wording "enslavement of the people of Korea" in the Cairo Declaration was the product of wartime hysteria, and 5) that Japan's colonial rule of Korea was beneficial to the Korean people.[181] As a condition for resuming the talks, the Korean delegation asked that Kubota take back his statements and apologize, but Japan had no intention of doing so.

In a telegram to the Secretary of State on November 23, 1953, US Ambassador to Japan Allison argued that the US was not free to say it was "legally not involved" in the Dokdo dispute given the Allied commitment in the Potsdam Declaration that Japanese sovereignty was to be limited to the four major islands and such minor islands as the Allied Powers determine, the exclusion of Dokdo from the islands to be renounced by Japan in the peace treaty, the designation of Dokdo as a bombing range in accordance with the Administrative Agreement, and the Rusk document.[182] As such, the US had a responsibility to resolve the dispute. Allison stated that the US had already recognized Japan's right to Dokdo in the Rusk note and, as such, the proposal to settle the issue at the International Court of Justice was an irresponsible act of reneging on an established policy. Having been the second in the line of command in the Dulles delegation for negotiating the peace treaty with Japan and being the Director of the Office of Northeast Asian Affairs at the US DoS, Allison may well have wanted to justify the policy-decision he was involved in making. Having begun and ended his diplomatic career in Japan, Allison also had an in-depth knowledge of the country.

Subsequently on November 30, 1953, William Turner, Counselor of

---

181 Park Jin-hui, *Korea-Japan Talks*, pp. 178-190.
182 Telegram by Allison, Tokyo to the Secretary of State, RG 59, Department of State, Decimal File, 694.95B/11-2353.

the US Embassy in Tokyo, expressed similar views to those of Allison. He argued that the Korean government should be pressured into accepting the Rusk document, i.e. Japan's territorial claim to Dokdo, and if it would not do so, the issue should be taken to the International Court of Justice. Finally, if Korea refused to agree to this alternative, then the Rusk document should be disclosed.[183]

Thus, besides Ambassador Allison, Counselor Turner, and Second Secretary Finn at the US Embassy in Japan, Dunning at the Division of Japanese Affairs of the Office of Northeast Asian Affairs in Washington also strongly advocated that the US clarify its position on Dokdo by disclosing the Rusk note. For the time being, Director McClurkin of the Office of Northeast Asian Affairs placed the Rusk note under lock and key. However, calls from Japan and within Washington itself to disclose it were echoing through the halls of the US DoS.

Meanwhile, nothing was heard from the US Embassy in Korea during this time. All it was able to come up with were some measures related to the Peace Line, such as US disapproval, withdrawal of US observers from the Korea-Japan talks, or suspension of US support for the ROK Navy and government institutions.[184]

If the astute lawyer-turned-diplomat Dulles had not been the US Secretary of State, the Rusk note would likely have been disclosed in 1953 or 1954, dealing a huge blow to Korea-US and Korea-Japan relations. In his telegram to Seoul and Tokyo on November 19, 1953, Dulles detailed the following instructions:

> 2. With regard to Takeshima issues, it is not necessary or desirable for the US to publicly support Japan. The two embassies need to take the matter to the International Court of Justice as soon as possible taking the example of the Court's judgment on the Channle Islands. If necessary, the US can

---

183 Memorandum by William T. Turner, Subject: Memorandum in regard to the Liancourt Rocks (Takeshima Island) Controversy (Nov. 30, 1953).
184 Telegram by Ellis O. Briggs to the Secretary of State, no. 233 (Nov. 18, 1953); no. 436 (Nov. 20, 1953), RG 84, Japan, Tokyo Embassy, CGR 1953, Box 23.

provide mediation until the judgment is rendered at the Court, and this matter should be explained off the record. Japan must stop arguing that the US, which is not legally involved in this matter, clarify its position on Dokdo.[185] (underlined by quoter)

Dulles' position was clear: 1) that the US could not side with Japan with respect to the Dokdo dispute, 2) that if there was a problem, it should be taken to the International Court of Justice, 3) that the US could arbitrate until the issue was taken to court, and 4) that the Japanese government should stop demanding that the US clarify its position further on the issue.

Ambassador Allison's November 23rd telegram carried a strong counterargument to Dulles' opinion that the US was "not legally involved in" the Dokdo dispute. Despite the above guidelines from the Secretary of State, Allison (November 23), Turner (November 30), and other high-ranking diplomats of the US Embassy in Japan continued to strongly advocate that the US take a more proactive role in the dispute over Dokdo.

The subsequent actions taken by the US Embassy in Tokyo were clearly out of line with Dulles' guidelines. The Embassy informed Washington of the visits of Japanese Liberal Party members and representatives of the fishing industry to the Embassy on November 16, 1953 to deny Korea's sovereignty claims to Dokdo and request active US intervention in the case.[186] Allison also argued that the Korean government should be pressured into relinquishing its sovereignty claims. In his telegram to the Secretary of State on November 27, 1953, he argued that if the Korean government continued to enforce the Peace Line, hold Japanese fishing boats, and refuse to resume its talks with Japan, then the US should withdraw its observers from the Korea-Japan talks, announce its decision to dismiss the Peace Line, and withdraw all logistics support from the Korean

---

185 Telegram by Secretary of State, Dulles to Seoul(no.398), Tokyo(no.1198)(1953. 11. 19), RG 84, Japan, Tokyo Embassy, CGR 1953, Box 23.
186 Despatch by Samuel D. Berger, Counselor of Embassy, Tokyo to the Secretary of State, no. 844 (Nov. 25, 1953). Subject: Rhee Line, Takeshima and Japan-Korean Relations (National Institute of Korean History, *Data Collection*, pp. 120-129).

government and the ROK Navy enforcing the Peace Line. He also argued that the Secretary of State should send a personal message to President Rhee encouraging him to resume the bilateral talks with Japan. Allison's telegram was sent after having obtained the approval of the Commander of the United Nations Forces.[187]

With resistance from Tokyo at its peak, Dulles chose to accommodate some of the protests but also made some key decisions of his own. On December 4, 1953, he sent a nine-page letter to Rhee Syngman. In the letter, Dulles emphasized that the US could not recognize the Peace Line even though it could understand Korea's earnest desire to secure its fishery resources from being exploited by the Japanese fishing industry. Instead, he proposed a variety of economic aid programs to Korea, such as assistance with revival of Korea's fishing fleet, cooperation with protection of its fishery resources, US support in its property claim issue in bilateral talks with Japan, an economic cooperation program with the US, and permission for Korea to participate in wartime procurement.[188] Dulles was offering Korea a variety of economic forms of aid in exchange for its return to the talks with Japan, while at the same time refusing to support enforcement of the Peace Line.

Dulles also responded firmly to the strong petition made by the US Embassy in Tokyo that the Rusk document be disclosed and that the US should publicly announce its position on Dokdo. His telegram sent to the US Embassy in Tokyo on December 9, 1953 outlined the final position of the US DoS regarding the territorial dispute between Korea and Japan over Dokdo between 1951 and 1953.[189] In the telegram (No. 1387 to Tokyo and No. 497 to Seoul), Dulles pointed out that the Peace

187 Telegram by Allison, Tokyo to the Secretary of State and Amembassy, Seoul (Nov. 27, 1953) (compiled by the National Institute of Korean History, *Data Collection*, pp. 134-137).

188 Telegram by Secretary of State to Amembassy, Seoul, no. 1333 (Dec. 4, 1953) (compiled by the National Institute of Korean History, *Data Collection*, pp. 161-169).

189 Telegram by Secretary of State to Amembassies in Tokyo, no. 1387 and Seoul, no. 497 (Dec. 9, 1953), RG 84, Entry 2846, Korea, Seoul Embassy, Classified General Records, 1953-55, Box. 12 (compiled by the National Institute of Korean History, *Data Collection*, pp. 184-186).

Treaty with Japan and the corresponding US administrative decisions had led Japan to expect that the US would act in its favor in the dispute over Dokdo. By his mention of the Peace Treaty, Dulles was referring to the fact that Dokdo was not specified as an island to be excluded from Japan under the territorial clauses, and by his mention of the US administrative decisions, he was referring to the US recognition of Dokdo as a Japanese government facility through its designation and release as a bombing range by the US-Japan Joint Committee in 1952 and 1953. He went on to clarify that the Rusk note of August 10, 1951, in which the US position on the issue was officially conveyed to Korea, had never been communicated to the Japanese government. In other words, while the US policy decision had been forwarded to Korea, it had not been communicated to Japan. He concluded by making it clear that even though it may become necessary or desirable to inform the Japanese government of the US position, in light of the already difficult ROK-Japan negotiations, the US should no longer be expected to intervene in the dispute. Dulles gave the following reasons as to why the US should not intervene:

First, despite US views that the peace treaty was a determination under the terms of the Potsdam Declaration and that the treaty left Takeshima to Japan, and despite the US participation in Potsdam and Treaty and action under Administrative Agreement, it did not necessarily follow that the US was automatically responsible for settling or intervening in Japan's international disputes, territorial or otherwise, arising from the Peace Treaty.

Second, the US view regarding Takeshima was simply that of one of many signatories to the Treaty.

Third, the new element mentioned of the Japanese feeling that the US should protect Japan from ROK pretensions to Takeshima could not be considered as a legitimate claim for US action under the Security Treaty.

Fourth, a far more serious threat to both the US and Japan in the Soviet occupation of the Habomais did not impel the US to take military action against the USSR nor did Japanese seriously contend such was the US obligation despite the public declaration by the US that Habomais are Japanese territory.

Fifth, the US should not become involved in territorial disputes arising from "Korean claim to Takeshima."

Finally, perhaps no action on the US part was required, but in case the issue was revived, the general line of the US should be that this issue, if it could not be settled by Japanese and Koreans themselves, was a kind of issue appropriate for presentation to the International Court of Justice.[190]

His points were premised on an understanding that the Rusk note (August 10, 1951) and the designation and release of Dokdo as a bombing range by the US-Japan Joint Committee (1952-1953) reflected the official US policy decision regarding sovereignty over Dokdo. He also viewed the sovereignty and territorial dispute over Dokdo as originating from "Korea's claim to Takeshima." Such views and assessment of the situation were utterly unacceptable for Korea.

Dulles also made it clear that the US position on Dokdo at the time of the peace conference was merely that of one of the many signatories to the treaty, and not an agreed consensus or decision of all signing countries. This was a very important remark, because as previously explained, the Rusk note had been crafted as an administrative contrivance by a US DoS staff member at a time when the wording of the San Francisco Peace Treaty was in urgent need of being finalized, and was never subjected to the usual process of consultation or deliberation, or high-level negotiation with the relevant countries involved.

Dulles also had a clear understanding of the Japanese agenda. He pointed out that Japan was taking strong actions and putting pressure on the US with respect to Korea, which was weak and in the midst of a crisis fighting against communist aggression at the time. However, Japan was not proactively contesting Russia's claims to sovereignty over the Habomais, which the US had publicly announced as being Japanese territory as well.

Thus, Dulles' policy decision contained some conclusions and

---

190 Telegram by Secretary of State to Amembassies in Tokyo, no. 1387 and Seoul, no. 497 (Dec. 9, 1953), RG 84, Entry 2846, Korea, Seoul Embassy, Classified General Records, 1953-55, Box. 12 (compiled by the National Institute of Korean History, *Data Collection*, pp. 184-186).

assessments that were difficult for Koreans to accept, but, paradoxical as it may sound, his assessment of the situation was also more supportive of Korea's position than those of others in Washington and elsewhere at the time.

The right to decide how Japanese territory would be specified in the San Francisco Peace Treaty lay with the US, and the US Administration had not been aware of the far-reaching implications that its decision on Dokdo would have on Korea-Japan relations. As a result, the US decision, which was largely based on administrative contrivance, resulted in the small nation of Korea becoming embroiled in a harsh and prolonged fight with Japan over Dokdo. The US DoS had notified the Korean government of its official position on Dokdo, but for some reason it had chosen not to notify the Japanese government. On the surface, it appears that the Korea-Japan conflict over Dokdo exploded when Japan strongly protested Korea's declaration of a Peace Line in 1952 and proceeded to publicly declare that Dokdo was Japanese territory. Meanwhile, with two of its most important allies in the Far East now on the verge of a battle to the death over Dokdo in the midst of the Korean War, the US suddenly found itself needing to play the role of an arbitrator. While Korea and Japan were fiercely disputing sovereignty over the island, the US DoS sought to put pressure on Korea by threatening to disclose the Rusk note if Korea refused to relinquish its claims, while at the same time recommending to the Japanese government that it take the issue to the International Court of Justice. Meanwhile, the US was equally concerned that the Japanese government would learn about the US confirmation that Dokdo was under Japanese jurisdiction in the Rusk document.

With the Dokdo dispute between Korea and Japan heating up in 1952 and 1953, officials at the US DoS and the US Embassy in Japan continued to voice their views that the US should disclose the Rusk note as a way to end the dispute and bring about reconciliation between the two countries. Pro-Japanese officials pressured the US DoS to disclose the Rusk note for the sake of policy coherence and consistency. However, nothing is known about how the Korean government responded to the US in this regard.

Had it not been for the prudent and decisive assessment of the situation on the part of US Secretary of State Dulles, the Rusk note would likely have been disclosed between 1953 and 1954, plunging both Korea-Japan and Korea-US relations into turmoil. Dulles emphasized that even though the US interpretation of the San Francisco Conference was in favor of Japanese sovereignty over Dokdo, the US was only one of the many signatories to the treaty and the US interpretation of the situation was not the consensus of the Allied Powers as a whole. He also questioned why Japan was asking the US to play a strong interventionist role with regard to Korea while it was neither protesting the Soviet Union's occupation of the Habomai Islands, nor asking the US for a show of force regarding its claims to these islands, which Japan was disputing over with the Soviets and which the US had made clear were, from their perspective, part of Japan as well. In the final analysis, Dulles' conclusion was that the US should not intervene in the Dokdo dispute and that if Korea and Japan failed to arrive at a solution between themselves, they should take the issue to the International Court of Justice. Thanks to Dulles' assessment and his efforts to contain the political fallout over the issue, the US was able to maintain its relations with both its allies despite the critical conflict situation over Dokdo.

Once it became palpable that the Dokdo issue could not only affect the relations between Korea and Japan but also have explosive implications for US relations with both countries, the US DoS began to adjust its position from that of a decision-maker to that of a neutral party. Despite the emphasis made by Dulles on the need for the US to take a position of neutrality, voices critical of Korea and supportive of Japan were still able to make themselves heard within the US Administration. Such was the daunting situation faced by Korea until the 1960s.

Bibliography

• **Publications in Korean Language**

康晋和編, 1956,『大韓民國建國十年誌』, 建國記念事業會.

고려대학교 아세아문제연구소 육당전집편찬위원회 편, 1973,『六堂崔南善全集2』, 현암사.

공군중앙교육위원회 항공용어제정분과위원회, 1962,『항공용어집(항공작전편)』, 공군본부.

국립민속박물관, 1996,『국립민속박물관 50년사』.

國立民俗博物館, 2007,『처음으로 민속을 찍다: 송석하 소장 민속학 선구자들의 사진자료집』.

국방부 국방군사연구소, 1998,『美國 國務部 政策硏究課 文書(Documents of the Division of Historical Policy Research of the U. S. State Department, Korea Project File, Vol. Ⅹ): 한국전쟁 자료총서』35집.

國史編纂委員會, 1994~1995,『大韓民國史資料集』18~26,「駐韓美軍政治顧問文書」.

_____, 1996,『南北韓關係史料集』16,「大韓民國內政에관한美國務部文書」.

_____, 1996~1997,『大韓民國史資料集』28~37,「李承晚關係書翰資料集」.

_____, 1998~2008,『資料大韓民國史』8~29.

_____, 2008,『독도자료: 미국편』Ⅰ~Ⅲ.

국회도서관 입법조사국, 1967,『헌법제정회의록(제헌의회)』1.

국회사무처,『대한민국국회 속기록』. (National Assembly Secretariat, *Constitutional Assembly Stenographic Records*)

김교식, 2005,『아, 독도 수비대』, 제이제이북스.

金東祚, 1986,『회상30년 한일회담』, 중앙일보사. (Kim Dong-jo, 1986, *Memoirs of 30 Years of Korea-Japan Talks*, Joongang Ilbo)

金龍周, 1984,『風雪時代八十年』, 新紀元社.

김병렬, 1997,『독도: 독도자료총람』, 다다미디어. (Kim Byeong-ryeol, 1997, *Dokdo: Comprehensive Survey of Dokdo Materials*, Dada Media.)

_____, 1997,『이어도를 아십니까』, 홍일문화.

金溶植, 1993,『새벽의 약속』, 김영사. (Kim Yong-sik, 1993, *Promise of the Dawn*, Gimm-Young Publishers)

김원용, 1963,『(국립박물관고적조사보고 제4책) 울릉도(附영암군내동리옹관묘)』.

金俊淵, 1966,「對日講和條約草案의 修正」,『나의 길』, 동아출판사.

김진송, 1996,『이쾌대』, 열화당.

김혁동, 1970, 『미군정하의 과도입법의원』, 평범사. (Kim Hyeok-dong, 1970, *Interim Legislative Assembly under the US Army Military Government*, Pyeongbeom Publishing.)

나이토우 세이쭈우(內藤正中) 지음·권오엽·권정 옮김, 2005, 『獨島와 竹島』, 제이앤씨.

南朝鮮過渡立法議院, 『南朝鮮過渡立法議院速記錄』 1∼5(여강출판사, 1984 영인).

다카사키 소우지(高崎宗司) 지음·김영진 옮김, 1988, 『검증 한일회담』, 청수서원. 〔Soji Takasaki, 1988, *Kensho Nikkan Kaidan (Japan-Korean Talks)*, translated by Kim Yeong-jin, Cheongsuseowon.〕

大韓公論社, 1965, 『獨島』.

大韓民國國防部政訓局戰史編纂委員會, 1953, 『韓國戰亂二年誌』.

도봉섭·심학진, 1948, 『朝鮮植物圖說(有毒植物編)』, 금룡도서주식회사.

도요시타 나라히코(豊下楢彦) 지음·권혁태 옮김, 2009, 『히로히토와 맥아더』, 개마고원. 〔Narahiko Toyoshita, translated by Gwon Hyeok-tae, 2009, *Hirohito and MacArthur (Showa Tenno, Makkasa Kaiken)*, Gaemagowon.〕

도정애, 2003, 『都逢涉 탄생백주년기념자료집』, 자연문화사 백원길.

독도학회 편, 1996, 『독도의 영유와 독도정책』.

_____, 1997, 『독도영유의 역사와 국제관계』.

_____, 1998, 『독도영유권 문제와 해양주권의 재검토』.

_____, 2002, 『독도영유권 연구논집』, 독도연구보전협회.

_____, 2003, 『한국의 독도영유권 연구사』, 독도연구보전협회. (*Research History of Korea's Sovereignty over Dokdo*, Association for the Study and Preservation of Dokdo)

동북아역사재단, 2009, 『일본 국회 독도 관련 기록모음집』I∼II. (Northeast Asian History Foundation, 2009, *Collection of Records relating to Dokdo of the National Diet of Japan*, I-II.)

동북아의평화를위한바른역사정립기획단 편, 2005, 『독도자료집 I』, 다다미디어.

_____, 2005, 『독도논문번역선I』, 다다미디어.

東亞日報社, 1981, 『東亞日報索引(8): 1945∼1955』, 東亞日報社.

東亞日報社編, 1975, 『秘話第一共和國』 5권, 弘字出版社.

민족문화사, 1986, 『재조선미국육군사령부군정청법령집(국문판)』.

박경래, 1965, 『獨島의 史·法的인 硏究』, 日曜新聞社.

박관숙, 1949, 『國際法要論』, 宣文社.

_____, 1954, 『國際法』, 이화여자대학교출판부.

_____, 1959, 『世界外交史』, 博英社.

朴觀淑·裵載湜共著, 1961, 『國際法』, 博英社.

박병섭·나이토 세이추 지음, 호사카 유지 옮김, 2008, 『독도=다케시마 논쟁』, 보고사.

박진희, 2008, 『한일회담: 제1공화국의 대일정책과 한일회담 전개과정』, 선인. (Park Jin-hui,

Bibliography

2008, *Korea-Japan Talks: the First Republic's Policy toward Japan and the Process of the Korean-Japan Talks*, Sunin Book.)

박평종, 2007, 『한국사진의 선구자들』, 눈빛.

방선주, 2002, 『미국소재 한국사 자료 조사보고 3: NARA 소장 RG 242 「선별노획문서」 외』, 국사편찬위원회.

方鍾鉉, 1963, 『一簑國語學論集』, 民衆書館.

卞榮泰, 1956, 『나의 祖國』, 自由出版社. (Pyun Yung-tai, 1956, *My Homeland*, Freedom Publishing.)

山邊健太郎·梶村秀樹·堀和生 지음·林英正 옮김, 2003, 『獨島 영유권의 日本側 주장을 반박한 일본인 논문집』, 경인문화사.

서울대학교 부속도서관, 1974, 『서울대학교법률도서관 소장 雪松文庫도서목록』.

서울신문 특별취재팀, 1984, 『한국외교비사』, 서울신문사.

손경석, 1995, 『등산반세기: 한국산악운동 50년 野話』, 산악문화.

송병기, 1999, 『울릉도와 독도』, 단국대학교출판부. (Song Byeong-gi, 1999, *Ulleungdo and Dokdo*, Dankook University Press.)

_____, 2004, 『독도영유권자료선』, 한림대학교출판부.

_____, 2010, 『울릉도와 독도, 그 역사적 검증』, 역사공간.

스기하라 세이시로우(杉原誠四郎) 지음·홍현길 옮김, 1998, 『무능과 범죄의 사이』, 학문사.

스털링, 페기 시그레이브 지음·김현구 옮김, 2003, 『야마시타골드』, 옹기장이.

신동욱, 1965, 『獨島에 關한 硏究』, 출판사 미상.

신용하, 1996, 『독도, 보배로운 한국영토: 일본의 독도영유권 주장에 대한 총비판』, 지식산업사.

_____, 1996, 『독도의 민족영토사 연구』, 지식산업사.

_____, 1998~2001, 『독도영유권 자료의 탐구』 1~4, 독도연구보전협회. (Sin Yong-ha, 1998~2001, *Study of Materials on Sovereignty over Dokdo*, Vol. 1-4, Dokdo Research and Preservation Association)

_____, 2001, 『독도영유권에 대한 일본주장 비판』, 서울대학교출판부. (Sin Yong-ha, 2001, *Criticism on Japanese Claims of Sovereignty over Dokdo*, Seoul National University Press)

_____, 2003, 『한국과 일본의 독도영유권 논쟁』, 한양대학교출판부.

_____, 2005, 『신용하 교수의 독도 이야기』, 살림출판사.

_____, 2006, 『한국의 독도영유권 연구』, 경인문화사.

양태진, 1998, 『독도연구문헌집』, 경인문화사.

與論社, 1945, 『朝鮮의 將來를 決定하는 各政黨·各團體解說』, 與論社出版部.

영남대학교 민족문화연구소, 1998, 『울릉도 독도의 종합적 연구: 부록 독도관계문헌목록』.

오오타 오사무 지음, 송병권·박상현·오미정 옮김, 2008, 『한일교섭: 청구권문제 연구』, 선인.

(Osamu Ota, 2008, *Korea-Japan Talks: Study on the Right of Claim*, translated by Song

Byeong-gwon, Park Sang-hyeon, and O Mi-jeong, Sunin Book)

외교통상부 외교안보연구원, 1999, 『외교관의 회고: 진필식대사회고록』.

外務部, 1977, 『獨島關係資料集I: 往復外交文書, 1952~76』. (Ministry of Foreign Affairs, 1977, *Collection of Documents related to Dokdo (I) Exchanged diplomatic documents (1952-1976).*)

_____, 1977, 『獨島關係資料集II: 學術論文』.

外務部政務局, 1954, 『평화선의 이론』.

_____, 1955, 『獨島問題槪論』. (Ministry of Foreign Affairs, 1955, *Introduction to the Dokdo Issue.*)

_____, 1959, 『外務行政의 十年』.

유경선 외 엮음, 1995, 『사진용어사전』, 미진사.

유민홍진기전기간행위원회, 1993, 『유민홍진기전기』, 중앙일보사.

유진오, 1963, 「對日講和條約 草案의 檢討」, 『民主政治에의 길』, 一潮閣. (Yu Jin-o, 1963, *Path to Democracy*, Ilchokak.)

이석우, 2003, 『일본의 영토분쟁과 샌프란시스코 평화조약』, 인하대학교출판부.

이석우, 2004, 『독도분쟁의 국제법적 이해』, 학영사.

_____, 2004, 『영토분쟁과 국제법: 최근 주요 판례의 분석』, 학영사.

_____, 2006, 『대일강화조약 자료집』, 동북아역사재단. (Lee Seok-woo, 2006, *Data Collection on the Treaty of Peace with Japan*, Northeast Asian History Foundation.)

_____, 2007, 『동아시아의 영토분쟁과 국제법』, 집문당.

이오키베 마코토(五百旗頭眞)외 지음·조양욱 옮김, 2002, 『일본 외교 어제와 오늘』, 다락원. (Makoto Iokibe et al., 2002, *The Diplomatic History of Postwar Japan*, translated by Jo Yanguk, Darakwon.)

이원덕, 1996, 『한일과거사 처리의 원점: 일본의 전후 처리 외교와 한일회담』, 서울대학교출판부. (Lee Won-deok, 1996, *The Starting Point of Dealing with the Past Affairs between Korea and Japan: Japan's Postwar Diplomacy and the Korea-Japan Talks*, Seoul National University Press.)

이종학, 2006, 『日本의 獨島海洋政策資料集』 1~4, 독도박물관.

이창위, 2008, 『일본 제국 흥망사』, 궁리. (Lee Chang-wi, 2008, *The Rise and Fall of the Empire of Japan*, Kungree.)

이한기, 1969, 『韓國의 領土: 領土取得에 관한 國際法的 硏究』, 서울대학교출판부.

임인식 작·임정의 엮음, 2008, 『우리가 본 한국전쟁: 국방부 정훈국 사진대 대장의 종군 사진 일기 1950~1953(임인식 사진집)』, 눈빛.

정용욱, 1994, 『해방직후 정치사회사 자료집』 2, 다락방.

정인섭, 1995, 『재일교포의 법적 지위』, 서울대학교출판부. (Jeong In-seop, 1995, *Legal*

Bibliography

Status of Ethnic Korean Residents in Japan, Seoul National University Press.)

조영복, 2002, 『월북 예술가 오래 잊혀진 그들』, 돌베개.

中央選擧管理委員會, 1963, 『歷代國會議員選擧狀況』, 보진재.

지철근, 1979, 『평화선』, 범우사. (Ji Cheol-geun, 1979, *Peace Line*, Bumwoosa.)

_____, 1989, 『한일어업분쟁사』, 한국수산신문사.

_____, 1992, 『수산부국의 야망』, 수산신보사.

_____, 2000, 『현대한일어업관계사』, 세종출판사.

崔永禧 外, 1985, 『獨島硏究』, 韓國近代史資料硏究協議會.

최종화, 2000, 『현대한일어업관계사』, 세종출판사. (Choi Jong-hwa, 2000, *History of Modern Korean-Japanese Fishery Relations*, Sejong Publishing.)

한국민속박물관, 1975, 『民俗寫眞特別展圖錄-石南民俗遺稿-』.

韓國法制硏究會, 1971, 『美軍政法令總覽』(국문판).

韓國史學會, 1978, 『鬱陵島·獨島 學術調査硏究』.

한국산악회50년사편찬위원회, 1996, 『한국산악회50년사』, 한국산악회.

한국외국어대학교, 1995, 『독도문제연구회 자료집: 독도의 어제와 오늘』. (Hankuk University of Foreign Studies, 1995, *Dokdo Research Society's Source Book: Dokdo's Yesterday and Today (Aug. 24 to 30, 1995).*)

한국일보사, 1981, 『財界回顧2: 元老企業人篇』, 한국일보사(「金龍周」).

한국해양수산개발원, 2006, 『독도관련논저목록』.

한표욱, 1996, 『이승만과 한미외교』, 중앙일보사(1984, 『한미외교요람기』의 개정판). 〔Han Pyo-wook, 1996, *Rhee Syngman and Korean-US Diplomatic Relations*, Joongang Ilbo (1984 revised edition of *The Initial Stages of Korea-US Diplomatic Relations*).〕

해양수산부, 1990, 『竹島의 歷史地理學的硏究』.

_____, 2000, 『독도자료집』 1~9.

_____, 2004, 『독도자료실 자료해제집』.

黃相基, 1965, 『獨島領有權解說: 부록 평화선문제』(초판·재판은 1954년), 勤勞學生社.

후지와라 아키라·아라카와 쇼지·하야시 히로후미 지음, 노길호 옮김, 1993, 『일본현대사, 1945~1992』, 구월.

• **Publications in English**

Allison, John M., *Ambassador from the Prairie*, Boston, Houghton Mifflin, 1973.

Borton, Hugh, *Spanning Japan's Modern Century: The Memoirs of Hugh Borton*, Lexington Books, 2002.

Cheong, Sung-Hwa, *The Politics of Anti-Japanese Sentiment in Korea: Japanese-South Korean Relations Under American Occupation, 1945~1952*, New York, Greenwood Press, 1991.

Emmerson, John K., *The Japanese Thread: A Life in the U.S. Foreign Service*, Holt, Rinehart and Winston, 1978.

Fearey, Robert A., *The Occupation of Japan, Second Phase: 1948-50*, The MacMillan Company, 1950.

Federal Register Division, National Archives and Records Service, *United States Government Organization Manual, 1945*(Revisions through September 20, 1946); *Revised to May 1, 1947*(Revised to December 1, 1946); *1947*(Revised through June 1, 1947); 1948(Revised through June 30, 1948); *1949*(Revised as of July 1, 1949); *1950-51*(Revised as of July 1, 1950); *1952-53*(Revised as of July 1, 1952).

Finn, Richard B., *Winners in Peace: MacArthur, Yoshida, and Postwar Japan*, University of California Press, Berkeley and Los Angeles, California, 1992.

Headquarters, KMAG, *G-2 Periodic Report, G-2 Weekly Summary*.

_____, USAFIK, *G-2 Weekly Summary*.

Johnson (U. Alexis) with McAllister (Jef Olivarius), *The Right Hand of Power*, Prentice-Hall, 1984.

Sebald (William J.) with Brines (Russell), *With MacArthur in Japan: A Personal History of the Occupation*, W. W. Norton & Company, Inc., New York, 1965.

United States Armed Forces in Korea, *History of the United States Armed Forces in Korea*, Manuscript in Office of the Chief of the Military History, Washington, D. C..

_____, *Summation of U.S. Military Government Activities in Korea*.

United States, Department of State, *Foreign Relations of the United States*, 1947-1952, United States Government Printing Office; 1947, Vol. VI; 1950, Vol. VI, Vol. VII; 1951, Vol. VI, Part 1.

US Military Attache to Amembassy at Seoul, *Joint Weeka*.

Yoshitsu, Michael M., *Japan and the San Francisco Peace Settlement*, New York: Columbia University Press, 1982.

• **Publications in Japanese Language**

高山信武, 1999, 『二人の参謀-服部卓四郎と辻政信』, 芙蓉書房出版.

吉田茂, 1959, 『回想十年』1~4, 新潮社. (Shigeru Yoshida, 1958, *Kaiso Junen*, Vol. 1~4, Tokyo, Shinchosha.)

金太基, 1997, 『前後日本政治と在日朝鮮人問題』, 東京, 勁草書房. (Kim Tae-gi, 1997, *Postwar Japanese Politics and the Issue of Ethnic Korean Residents in Japan*, Tokyo, Keiso Shobo Publishing)

內藤正中, 2000, 『竹島(鬱陵島)をめぐる日朝關係史』, 多賀書店.

內藤正中·朴炳涉, 2007, 『竹島＝獨島論爭』, 新幹社.

동북아역사재단 편, 2009, 『일본 국회 독도 관련 기록모음집』 I부(1948~1976년), II부 (1977~2007년). 〔Northeast Asian History Foundation, 2009, *Collection of Records relating to Dokdo of the National Diet of Japan, I (1948-1976) II (1977-2007)*〕.

李鍾元, 1996, 『東アジア冷戰と韓米日關係』, 東京大學出版會. (Lee Jong-won, 1996, *East Asia Cold War and Korea-US-Japan Relations*, University of Tokyo Press.)

李鍾學 (ed), 2006, 『日本의 獨島海洋政策資料集』1~4, 독도박물관.

每日新聞社編, 1952, 『對日本平和條約』. (Mainichi Shinbunsha, 1952, *Japanese Peace Treaty*.)

山下康雄, 1949, 『領土割讓の主要問題』, 有斐閣.

杉原荒太, 1965, 『外交の考え方』, 鹿島研究所出版會.

森田芳夫, 1939, 『國史と朝鮮』, 綠旗聯盟.

生出壽, 1993, 『惡魔的作戰參謀辻政信稀代の風雲兒の罪と罰』, 光人社文庫.

西村熊雄, 1971, 『日本外交史27: サンフランシスコ平和條約』, 鹿島研究所出版會. (Kumao Nishimura, 1971, *Japan's Diplomatic History 27: The Treaty of Peace with Japan*, Kajima Research Institute Press.)

細谷千博, 1989, 『サンフランシスコ講和條約への道』, 中央公論社. (Chihiro Hosoya, 1989, *Leading up to the Peace Treaty of San Francisco*, Chuokoronsha.)

松本淸張, 1974, 『日本の黒い霧』上·下, 文春文庫. (Seicho Matsumoto, 1974, *Nihon-No Kuroi Kiri (Black Fog over Japan)*, Vol. 1&2, Bunshun Bunko.)

袖井林二郎編譯, 2000, 『吉田茂-マッカーサ往復書簡集 1945-1951』, 法政大學出版局. (Rinjirou Sodei, trans. & ed., 2000, *Shigeru Yoshida-Makkasa Ofuku Shokanshu (Correspondences between Shigeru Yoshida and MacArthur) (1945-1951)*, Tokyo, Hosei University Press.)

矢田喜美雄, 1973, 『謀殺下山事件』, 講談社. 〔Kimio Yada, 1973, *Bosatsu Shimoyama Jiken (Premeditated Murder: Shimoyama Incident)*, Kodansha.〕

奧原碧雲(奧原福市), 1907, 『竹島及鬱陵島』, 報光社. 〔Fukuichi Okuhara, 1907, *Takeshima Oyobi Utsuryoto, (Dokdo and Ulleungdo)*.〕

外務省條約局, 1953, 『竹島の領有』. 〔Ministry of Foreign Affairs of Japan, 1953,

Takeshima No Ryoyu (Sovereignty over Takeshima).〕

日本外務省, 2002, 『日本外交文書: 平和條約の締結に關する調書. 第1冊: I〜III』.

_____, 2002, 『日本外交文書: 平和條約の締結に關する調書. 第2冊: IV〜V』.

_____, 2002, 『日本外交文書: 平和條約の締結に關する調書. 第3冊: VI』.

_____, 2002, 『日本外交文書: 平和條約の締結に關する調書. 第4冊: VII』.

_____, 2002, 『日本外交文書: 平和條約の締結に關する調書. 第5冊: VIII』.

_____, 2006, 『日本外交文書: サンフランシツコ平和條約準備對策』. (Ministry of Foreign Affairs of Japan, 2006, *Japanese Diplomatic Documents: Preparations for the San Francisco Peace Treaty*.

_____, 2007, 『日本外交文書: サンフランシツコ平和條約對米交渉』(Ministry of Foreign Affairs of Japan, 2007, *Japanese Diplomatic Documents: Negotiations with the US for the San Francisco Peace Treaty*.)

日本外務省アジア局第二課, 1953, 『竹島漁業の變遷』(昭和二十八年八月).

田宮英太郎, 1986, 『参謀・辻政信・傳奇』, 芙蓉書房出版.

田村清三郎, 1954, 『島根縣竹島の研究』, 島根縣. 〔Seizaburo Tamura, 1954, *Shimaneken Takeshima No Kenkyu (A Study of Takeshima, Shimane Prefecture)*, Shimane Prefecture.〕

_____, 1965, 『島根縣竹島の新研究』, 島根縣總務部總務課. 〔Seizaburo Tamura, 1965, *Shimaneken Takeshima No Shin Kenkyu (A New Study of Takeshima, Shimane Prefecture)*, General Affairs Department, General Affairs Section, Shimane Prefecture.〕

諸永裕司, 2002, 『葬られた夏追跡下山事件』, 朝日新聞社. 〔Yuji Moronaga, 2002, *Homurareta Natsu: Tsuiseki Shimoyama Jiken (Buried Summer: Chasing Shimoyama Incident)*, Asahi Shimbunsha.〕

朝海浩一郎, 1950, 『外交の黎明』, 讀賣新聞社. (Koichiro Asakai, 1950, *Gaiko No Reimei (Dawn of Diplomacy)*, Yomiuri Shimbun.)

中澤孝之・日暮高則・下條正男, 2005, 『(圖解)島國ニッポンの領土問題: 激怒する隣國, 無關心な日本』, 東洋経済新報社.

川上健三, 1966, 『竹島の歴史地理學的研究』, 古今書院. (Kenzo Kawakami, 1966, *A Study of the History and Geography of Takeshima*, Kokonshoyin.)

春名幹男, 2000, 『秘密のファイルCIAの對日工作』上・下, 共同通信社. 〔Mikio Haruna, 2000, *Himitsu-No File: CIA-No Tainichi Kosaku (Secret File: CIA's Operations in Japan)*, Vol. 1&2, Kyodo News.〕

下田武三著・永野信利編, 1984, 『戰後日本外交の證言: 日本はこうして再生した』上・下, 行政問題研究所. (Takeso Shimoda, 1984, *Sengo Nihon Gaiko No Shogen (Testimony to Japan's Postwar Diplomacy: How Japan Revived)* Vol. 1-2, edited by Nobutoshi

Nagano, Tokyo.)

下條正男, 1999, 『日韓·歷史克服への道』, 展轉社.

_____, 2004, 『竹島は日韓どちらのものか』, 文藝春秋.

_____, 2006, 『(發信)竹島: 眞の日韓親善に向けて: 下條正男-拓殖大學敎授に聞く』, 山陰中央新報社.

下條正男〔外〕, 2002, 『知っていますか, 日本の島』, 自由國民社.

和田正明, 1965, 『日本漁業の新發足』, 水產經濟新聞社. (Masaaki Wada, 1965, *A New Beginning of Japan's Fisheries*, The Suisan-Keizai Daily News.)

荒敬 編輯·解題, 1991, 『日本占領·外交關係資料集』第10卷.

_____, 1994, 『日本占領·外交關係資料集』第2期 第10卷(終戰連絡地方事務局·連絡調整地方事務局資料).

• Theses & Research Papers

고지훈, 2000, 「駐韓美軍政의 占領行政과 法律審議局의 活動」, 『韓國史論』 44, 서울대학교 국사학과.

구선희, 2007, 「해방 후 연합국의 독도 영토처리에 관한 한·일 독도연구 쟁점과 향후 전망」, 『한국사학보』 28호. (Ku Seon-hui, 2007, "Issues in the studies of Dokdo of Korea and Japan with respect to the post-war handling of Dokdo territory by the Allied Powers and future prospects," *Journal for the Studies of Korean History*, No. 28.)

김경남, 2008, 「재조선 일본인들의 귀환과 전후의 한국인식」, 『東北亞歷史論叢』 21호.

김대영, 2004, 「일본 以西저인망어업의 축소재편에 관한 一考」, 『해양비즈니스』 4호. (Kim Dae-yeong, 2004, "Reorganization of the Off-Shore Trawl Fishery in Japan," *Maritime Business*, No. 4.)

김병렬, 1996, 「일본 古地圖에도 독도는 한국땅이라 명시」, 『한국논단』 6월호.

_____, 1996, 「증거를 외면하지 마라」, 『한국논단』 11월호.

_____, 1998, 「대일강화조약에서 독도가 누락된 전말」, 『독도영유권과 영해와 해양주권』, 독도연구보전협회.

_____, 1998, 「日학자에의해 '억지주장' 입증되었다」, 『한국논단』 9월호.

김성보, 1995, 「소련의 대한정책과 북한에서의 분단질서 형성, 1945~1946」, 역사문제연구소편, 『분단 50년과 통일시대의 과제』, 역사비평사. (Kim Seong-bo, 1995, "The USSR's Policy toward Korea and the Process of National Division Shaped in North Korea, 1945-1946," compiled by the Institute of Korean Historical Studies, *Fifty Years of National Division and Tasks for Unification*, Critical Review of History.)

김성원, 2008, 「식민지시기 조선인 박물학자 성장의 맥락: 곤충학자 조복성의 사례」, 『한국과
학사학회지』 30권 2호.

김용섭, 1966, 「日本, 韓國에 있어서의 韓國史敍述」, 『歷史學報』 31.

김정태, 1971, 「1946년 적설기 한라산학술등반기」, 『한국산악』 VII(26년호).

_____, 1977, 「韓國山岳會30年史」, 『한국산악』 XI(1975·1976년호). 〔Kim Jeong-tae, 1977,
    "30 Years' History of the Corea Alpine Club," *Korean Mountains* XI (Issue of 1975
    and 1976), Corea Alpine Club.〕

김태기, 1996, 「일본정부의 재일한국인정책: 일본점령기를 중심으로」, 한국정치학회 연례학
    술회의. (Kim Tae-gi, 1996, "The Japanese Government's Policy regarding Korean
    Residents: Focusing on the Period of the Japanese Occupation over Korea," an
    annual academic conference of the Korean Political Science Association.)

_____, 1999, 「1950년대초 미국의 대한 외교정책: 대일강화조약에서의 한국의 배제 및 제1
    차 한일회담에 대한 미국의 정치적 입장을 중심으로」, 『한국정치학회보』 33집 1호(봄호).
    〔Kim Tae-gi, 1999, "US Foreign Policy toward Korea in the Beginning of the 1950s:
    The US Political Position on the Exclusion of Korea from the Japanese Peace Treaty
    and the First Korea-Japan Negotiations", Korean Political Science Association,
    Korean Political Science Review, Vol. 33, No. 1 (Spring Issue).〕

_____, 1999, 「GHQ/SCAP의 對재일한국인정책」, 『國際政治論叢』 38집3호. (Kim Tae-
    gi, 1999, "The GHQ/SCAP Policy toward Korean Residents in Japan," *The Korean
    Journal of International Relations*, Vol. 38, No. 3.)

_____, 2000, 「한국 정부와 민단의 협력과 갈등관계」, 『아시아태평양지역연구』 3권. (Kim
    Tae-gi, 2000, "Cooperation and Conflicts between the Korean Government and the
    Federation of Korean Residents in Japan," Chonnam National University's Research
    Institute for Asia Pacific Rim, *Journal of Asia-Pacific Area Studies*, Vol. 3, No. 1.)

_____, 2001, 「자료소개2: 요시다서간」, 『한일민족문제연구』 Vol. I, no.1. (Kim Tae-gi,
    2001, "References 2: Yoshida Correspondences," The Association of Korean-Japanese
    National Studies, *The Journal of Korean-Japanese National Studies*, Vol. I, No. 1.)

김태우, 2008, 「한국전쟁기 미공군의 공군폭격에 관한 연구」, 서울대학교 국사학과 박사학위
    논문.

김호동, 2008, 「『竹島問題에 관한 調査研究 最終報告書』에 인용된 일본 에도(江戶)시대 독도
    문헌 연구」, 『인문연구』 55호.

나가사와 유코(長澤裕子), 2007, 「日本의 '朝鮮主權保有論과 美國의 對韓政策: 韓半島分
    斷에 미친 影響을 中心으로, 1942~1951年)」, 고려대학교 대학원 정치외교학과 박사
    학위논문. 〔Yuko Nagasawa, 2007, "Japan's Argument for Sovereignty over Joseon
    and US Policy on Korea with a Focus on Their Effect on the Division of the Korean

Peninsula (1942-1951)," doctoral dissertation, Department of Political Science and International Relations, Korea University Graduate School.]

노관택, 2008,「김홍기(金弘基)」, 서울대학교 한국의학인물사 편찬위원회 편,『한국의학인물사』, 태학사.

도봉섭·심학진, 1948,「국산 '미치광이'의 생약학적 연구」,『약학회지』1권1호.

朴觀淑, 1956,「독도의 법적 지위: 국제법상의 견해」,『국제법학논총』.

_____, 1977,「獨島의 法的地位에 關한 硏究」, 外務部,『獨島關係資料集II: 學術論文』.

朴杰淳, 1992,「日帝下 日人의 朝鮮史硏究學會와 歷史: 高麗史 歪曲」,『독립운동사연구』6집.

박배근, 2001,「『竹島の歷史地理的硏究』에 대한 비판적 검토」,『法學硏究』42권 1호. [Park Bae-geun, 2001, "Critical Review on Takeshima No Rekishi Chirigakuteki Kenkyu," Institute of Law Studies, Pusan University, *Journal of Law Studies*, Vol. 42, No. 1.]

_____, 2005,「독도에 대한 일본의 영역권원주장에 관한 一考」,『국제법학회논총』50권 3호.

박병섭, 2007,「明治時代の資料からみた獨島の歸屬問題」,『독도연구』3호, 영남대학교 독도연구소.

_____, 2008,「시모조 마사오의 논설을 분석한다」,『독도연구』4호, 영남대학교독도연구소.

박봉규, 1985,「제I장 총설 제2절 울릉도·독도의 자연」,『獨島硏究』, 한국근대사자료연구협의회. (Park Bong-gyu, 1985, "Section 2 Nature of Ulleungdo and Dokdo of Chapter I Outline," *Dokdo Research*, Korea Modern Historical Research Society.)

박상윤, 1982,「動物學近代化의 開拓者」,『과학과 기술』2월호.

박성수, 1996,「한일관계사와 독도문제」,『獨島硏究』, 한국정신문화연구원.

박주석, 1988,「현일영(玄一榮)연구」, 중앙대학교 대학원 석사학위논문.

박진희, 2005,「戰後 韓日관계와 샌프란시스코 平和條約」,『한국사연구』131호. (Park Jin-hui, 2005, "Postwar Korea-Japan Relations and the Treaty of Peace with Japan," *Journal of Korean History Studies*, No. 131.)

_____, 2008,「독도영유권과 한국·일본·미국」,『독도자료』1~3(미국편), 국사편찬위원회. (Park Jin-hui, 2008, "Sovereignty over Dokdo and Korea, Japan, and the US," *Dokdo Data Collection*, Vol. 1 to 3 (with regard to the US), National Institute of Korean History.)

방선주, 1987,「美國 第24軍 G2 軍史室 資料 解題」,『아시아문화』3호.

_____, 1998,「美國 國立公文書館 國務部文書槪要」,『국사관논총』79호.

방종현, 1940,「古語 硏究와 方言」,『한글』(1940. 7. 1).

백충현·송병기·신용하, 1981,「(학술좌담) 독도문제 재조명」,『한국학보』24호. [Baek Chung-hyeon, Song Byeong-gi, Sin Yong-ha, 1981, "Shedding New Light on the Dokdo Issue (academic discussion)," *Hankuk Hakbo (Journal of Korean Studies)*, No.

24.]

석주일, 1949, 「朝鮮의 梅毒. 第1報, 梅毒의 統計的 觀察」, 『中央防疫研究所所報』 1권 1호 (1949년 8월).

송병기, 1990, 「日本의 '랑고島(獨島)' 領土編入과 鬱島郡守 沈興澤 報告書」, 『윤병석교수 화갑기념 한국근대사논총』, 한국근대사논총간행위원회.

_____, 1991, 「韓末利權侵奪에 관한 研究: 獨島問題의 一考察: 鬱陵島의 地方官制編入과 石島」, 『국사관논총』 23집.

_____, 1996, 「資料를 통해 본 韓國의 獨島領有權」, 『한국독립운동사연구』 10집.

_____, 1998, 「조선후기의 울릉도경영-搜討制度의확립-」, 『진단학보』 86호.

_____, 1999, 「울릉도의 지방관계 편입과 석도」, 『울릉도와 독도』, 단국대학교출판부. (Song Byeong-gi, 1999, "Ulleungdo's Incorporation in the Government System and Seokdo," *Ulleungdo and Dokdo*, Dankook University Press.)

_____, 1999, 「자료를 통해 본 한국의 독도영유권」, 『울릉도와 독도』, 단국대학교출판부.

_____, 2006, 「안용복의 활동과 울릉도爭界」, 『역사학보』 192호.

_____, 2007, 「獨島(竹島)問題의 再檢討」, 『東北亞歷史論叢』 18호.

_____, 2008, 「安龍福의 活動과 竹島(鬱陵島) 渡海禁止令」, 『동양학』 43집.

시모조 마사오(下條正男), 1996, 「'竹島'가 韓國領이라는 근거는 왜곡돼 있다」, 『한국논단』 5월호.

_____, 1996, 「증거를 들어 실증하라」, 『한국논단』 8월호.

_____, 1998, 「'竹島' 문제의 문제점」, 『한국논단』 8월호.

신용옥, 2008, 「대한민국 헌법 경제조항 개정안의 정치·경제적 환경과 그 성격」, 『한국근현대사연구』 봄호 44집.

_____, 2009, 「제헌헌법의 사회·경제질서 구성 이념」, 『한국사연구』 144집.

신용하, 1989, 「朝鮮王朝의 獨島領有와 日本帝國主義의 獨島侵略: 獨島領有에 대한 實證的 研究」, 『한국독립운동사연구』 3집.

_____, 1992, 「일제하의 독도와 해방 직후 독도의 한국에 반환과정 연구」, 『한국사회사연구회논문집』 34집.

_____, 1993, 「獨島問題와 獨島領有權 歸屬」, 『일본평론』 7집.

_____, 1996, 「韓國의 獨島領有와 日帝의 獨島侵略」, 『한국독립운동사연구』 10집.

_____, 1996, 「역사적 측면에서 본 독도문제」, 『獨島研究』, 한국정신문화연구원.

_____, 1997, 「한국의 獨島領有에 관한 역사적 증거 자료의 발굴과 실증적 연구」, 『省谷論叢』 28집 4권.

_____, 1997, 「일제의 1904~5년 獨島 침탈시도와 그 批判」, 『한국독립운동사연구』 11집.

_____, 1998, 「17세기 조선왕조의 독도영유와 일본의 '竹島고유영토론' 주장에 대한 비판」, 『독도학회국제학술심포지움』.

_____, 1998, 「獨島·鬱陵島의 名稱變化연구-명칭 변화를 통해본 獨島의 韓國固有領土 증명-」, 『韓國學報』第91·92합집.

_____, 1999, 「독도·울릉도의 명칭변화 연구」, 『독도영유권 자료의 탐구』 2권, 독도연구보전협회.

_____, 2000, 「제7부 연합국최고사령부의 독도영유 관계자료와 해설」, 『독도영유권 자료의 탐구』 3권, 독도연구보전협회.

_____, 2001, 「일본측의 '1951년 샌프란시스코 강화조약에서 독도를 한국영토에서 제외시킴으로써 독도가 일본영토임을 인정받았다'는 주장에 대한 비판」, 『독도영유권에 대한 일본주장 비판』, 서울대학교출판부. 〔Sin Yong-ha, 2001, "Criticism of Japan's Claim that the Exclusion of Dokdo from the Korean Territory in the 1951 Treaty of Peace with Japan Acknowledged Dokdo as Japanese Territory," *Criticism on Japanese Claims of Sovereignty over Dokdo*, Seoul National University Press.〕

양태진, 1996, 「문헌적 측면에서 본 독도관계 자료분석」, 『獨島研究』, 한국정신문화연구원.

영남대학교 민족문화연구소, 1998, 「독도관계 문헌목록」, 『울릉도 독도의 종합적 연구』.

오제연, 2005, 「평화선과 한일협정」, 『역사문제연구』 14호. (O Je-yeon, 2005, "Peace Line and the Korea-Japan Treaty," *Critical Studies on Modern Korean History*, No. 14.)

요시자와 후미토시, 2008, 「일본의 한일회담 관련 외교문서의 공개상황에 대하여」; 「(특별부록) 일본 외무성 외교문서 공개 리스트」, 『일본공간』 Vol. IV, 국민대학교 일본학연구소.

柳敎聖, 1952, 「對日外交의 史的考察: 독도 및 울릉도문제를 중심으로」, 『新生公論』 6월호.

윤덕영, 1995, 「해방직후 신문자료 현황」, 『역사와현실』 16집.

윤범모, 2008, 「이쾌대의 경우 혹은 민족의식과 진보적 리얼리즘」, 『미술사학』 8월호.

이병도, 1963, 「독도의 명칭에 대한 사적 고찰」, 『불교사논총』.

이석우, 2002, 「독도분쟁과 샌프란시스코 평화조약의 해석에 관한 소고」, 『서울국제법연구』 9권 1호.

_____, 2002, 「미국립문서보관소 소장 독도 관련 자료」, 『서울국제법연구』 9권 1호. 〔Lee Seok-woo, 2002, "Dokdo-related materials held by the US National Archives and Records Administration," *Seoul International Law Journal*, Vol. 9, No. 1.)

_____, 2002, 「샌프란시스코평화조약에서의 쿠릴, 센카쿠섬의 지위와 독도분쟁과의 상관관계에 대한 소고」, 『서울국제법연구』 9권 2호. 〔Lee Seok-woo, 2002, "Some Observations on the Territorial Disputes over Dokdo (Liancourt Rocks) and Interpretation of the Territorial Clauses of the San Francisco Peace Treaty," *Seoul International Law Journal*, Vol. 9, No. 2.〕

이선근, 1963, 「울릉도 및 독도탐험 소고: 근세사를 중심으로」, 『대동문화연구』 1집.

이숭녕, 1963, 「故一簑의 追憶」, 『一簑國語學論集』, 民衆書館.

이만열, 1981, 「日帝官學者들의植民主義史觀」, 『韓國近代歷史學의理解』, 문학과지성사.

이미령, 2002, 「이쾌대 군상연구: 1948년작을 중심으로」, 이화여자대학교 미술사학과 석사학위논문.

이이화, 1992, 「나의 학문 나의 인생: 4·25교수데모에 앞장선 한학·금석문의 대가―임창순」, 『역사비평』가을호(통권 20호).

이재영, 2008, 「조중삼(趙重參)」, 서울대학교 한국의학인물사 편찬위원회 편, 『한국의학인물사』, 태학사.

이종원, 1995, 「한일회담의 국제정치적 배경」, 『한일협정을 다시 본다』, 아세아문화사. (Lee Jong-won, 1995, "International Political Background of the Korea-Japan Talks," *Reinterpretation of the Korea-Japan Talks*, Asea Culture Publishing.)

이한기, 1977, 「韓國의 領土: 領土取得에 관한 國際法的 研究」, 外務部, 『獨島關係資料集II: 學術論文』.

李弘稙, 1962, 「鬱陵島搜討官關係碑二」, 『考古美術』 3의7(李弘稙, 1972, 『史家의 流薰』, 통문관).

이희성, 2008, 「이근배」, 서울대학교 한국의학인물사 편찬위원회 편, 『한국의학인물사』, 태학사.

임영정, 1996, 「일본의 독도영유권 주장의 근거: 자료를 中心으로」, 『獨島研究』, 한국정신문화연구원.

조명철, 2007, 「독도의 영유권에 대한 전략적 고찰: 일본의 대독도 방침을 중심으로」, 『한국사학보』 28호.

정갑용, 2009, 「쓰카모토 다카시의 "샌프란시스코 평화조약에서 나타난 다케시마에 대한 취급"에 대한 비판적 연구」, 영남대학교 독도연구소, 『독도영유권 확립을 위한 연구』, 경인문화사.

정병준, 1999, 「이승만의 정치고문들」, 『역사비평』가을호.

_____, 2002, 「미 국립문서기록관리청 소장 RG 59(국무부 일반문서) 내 한국 관련 문서」, 『미국소재 한국사 자료 조사보고 1: NARA 소장 RG 59, RG 84 외』, 국사편찬위원회.

_____, 2005, 「영국 외무성의 對日평화조약 草案·부속지도의 성립(1951. 3)과 한국독도영유권의재확인」, 『한국독립운동사연구』 24집. (Jung Byung-joon, 2005, "The UK FCO's Draft of the Treaty of Peace with Japan and Its Attached Map (Mar. 1951) and Reconfirmation of Korea's Sovereignty over Dokdo," *Journal of Korean Independence Movement Studies*, Vol. 24.)

_____, 2005, 「윌리암 시볼드(William J. Sebald)와 '독도분쟁'의 시발」, 『역사비평』 71집. (Jung Byung-joon, 2005, "William J. Sebald and the Dokdo Territorial Dispute," *Historical Criticism*, Vol. 71.)

_____, 2006, 「시론: 한일 독도영유권 논쟁과 미국의 역할」, 『역사와현실』 60집. (Jung Byung-joon, 2006, "Essay: Korea-Japan Dispute on Sovereignty over Dokdo and the Role of the US," *Quarterly Review of Korean History*, No. 60.)

_____, 2006, 「독도영유권 분쟁을 보는 한·미·일 3국의 시각」, 『사림』 26호. (Jung Byung-joon, 2006, "Viewpoints of Korea, the US, and Japan regarding the Territorial Dispute over Dokdo Island," *Sarim*, No. 26.)

_____, 2008, 「패전 후 조선총독부의 戰後 공작과 金桂祚 사건」, 『이화사학연구』 36집.

정병욱, 2005, 「조선총독부 관료의 일본 귀환 후 활동과 한일교섭: 1950, 60년대 同和協會·中央日韓協會를 중심으로」, 『역사문제연구』 14호. (Jeong Byeong-uk, 2005, "Activities by the Joseon Government General Officials after Their Return to Japan and Korea-Japan Talks: Centering on the Donghwa Association and Central Japanese-Korean Association in the 1950s and 1960s," *Critical Studies on Modern Korean History*, No. 14.)

정용욱, 2003, 「미군정 자료 주요 문서철 자료 목록1. 군사실 문서철」, 『미군정자료연구』, 선인.

정인섭, 1996, 「국제법 측면에서 본 독도영유권 문제」, 『獨島研究』, 한국정신문화연구원.

_____, 2006, 「1952년 평화선 선언과 해양법의 발전」, 『서울국제법연구』 13권 2호.

조동걸, 1990, 「植民史學의 成立過程과 近代史 敍述」, 『歷史敎育論集』 13·14.

조성훈, 2008, 「제2차 세계대전 후 미국의 대일전략과 독도 귀속문제」, 『국제·지역연구』 17권 2호.

조윤수, 2008, 「'평화선'과 한일어업협상: 이승만정권기의 해양질서를 둘러싼 한일 간의 마찰」, 『일본연구논총』 28호. (Jo Yun-su, 2008, "'The Peace Line' and South Korea-Japan Fishery Negotiation in 1965," *The Korean Journal for Japanese Studies*, No. 28.)

진실·화해를위한과거사정리위원회, 2008, 「월미도 미군폭격 사건」, 『2008년 상반기 조사보고서』 2권. (Truth and Reconciliation Commission, 2008, "Bombing of Wolmido by the US Forces," *Investigation Report for the First Half of 2008*, Vol. 2.)

塚本孝, 1996, 「샌프란시스코 평화조약시 독도 누락과정 전말」, 한국군사문제연구원, 『한국군사』 3. 〔Takashi Tsukamoto, 1996, "A Full Account of the Omission of Takeshima in the Treaty of Peace with Japan," Korea Institute of Military Affairs, *Korean Military Affairs Journal* 3 (Aug. 1996).〕

최규장, 1965, 「獨島守備隊秘史」, 『週刊韓國』.

최영호, 1998, 「현대 일본인의 한국과 한국인에 대한 인식」, 한일관계사학회, 『한일양국의 상호인식』, 국학자료원. (Choi Yeong-ho, 1998, "Recognition of Korea and Koreans by Contemporary Japanese," The Korea-Japan Historical Society, *Mutual Recognition of Korea and Japan*, Kookhak.)

_____, 2008, 「한반도 거주 일본인의 귀환과정에서 나타난 식민지 지배에 관한 인식」, 『동북아역사논총』 21호. (Choi Yeong-ho, 2008, "Recognition of Colonial Rule as Seen in the Process of Japanese Residents Returning Home from the Korean Peninsula," *Journal of Northeast Asian History*, No. 21.)

최장근, 2008, 「'죽도문제연구회'의 일본적 논리 계발」, 『독도의 영토학』, 대구대학교출판부.

_____, 2009, 「'竹島經營者中井養三郎氏立志傳'의 해석오류에 대한 고찰」, 『영산대학법률논총』 5권 2호.

_____, 2009, 「'竹島經營者中井養三郎氏立志傳'의 해석오류에 대한 고찰」, 영남대학교 독도연구소, 『독도영유권 확립을 위한 연구』, 경인문화사.

최진옥, 1996, 「독도에 관한 연구사적 검토」, 『獨島研究』, 한국정신문화연구원.

_____, 1996, 「독도관계 논저목록」, 『獨島研究』, 한국정신문화연구원.

한철호, 2007, 「독도에 관한 역사학계의 시기별 연구동향」, 『한국근현대사연구』 40집.

_____, 2007, 「明治時期 일본의 독도정책과 인식에 대한 연구쟁점과 과제」, 『한국사학보』 28호.

허영란, 2002, 「독도영유권 문제의 성격과 주요 쟁점」, 『한국사론』 34, 국사편찬위원회.

_____, 2008, 「독도영유권 문제의 주요 논점과 '고유영토론'의 딜레마」, 『이화사학연구』 36집. [Heo Yeong-ran, 2008, "Main Discussion Points of the Dokdo Sovereignty Issue and Dilemma of Inherent Territory Theory," *Ewha Sahak Yeongu (Bulletin of the Ewha Historical Research Center)*, Vol. 36.]

홍성근, 2003, 「독도폭격사건의 국제법적 쟁점 분석」, 『한국의 독도영유권 연구사』, 독도연구보전협회. (Hong Seong-geun, 2003, "Analysis of the Bombing Incident from an International Law Perspective," *Research History of Korea's Sovereignty over Dokdo*, Association for the Study and Preservation of Dokdo.)

홍종인, 1977, 「독도」, 『한국산악』 XI(1975·1976년호), 한국산악회.

Em, Henry H. "Civil Affairs Training and the U.S. Military Government in Korea," Bruce Cumings ed, *Chicago Occasional Papers on Korea*, select paper Vol. VI, The Center for East Asian Studies, 1991, The University of Chicago, Chicago, Illinois.

Frankel, Ernst, 1994, "Structure of United States Army Military Government in Korea," 정용욱 편, 『해방직후 정치사회사 자료집』 2권, 다락방.

Jung Byung-joon, "Korea's Post-Liberation View on Dokdo and Dokdo Policies, 1945~1951," *Journal of Northeast Asian History*, Vol. V-2(Winter 2008).

Lovmo, Mark S., "The June 1948 Bombing of Dokdo"[로브모, 「1948년 6월 8일 독도폭격사건에 대한 심층적 연구」(2003. 5)], http://www.geocities.com/mlovmo.

_____, "Liancourt Rocks Bombing Range 1947~1953".

堀和生, 1987, 「一九○五年日本の竹島領土編入」, 『朝鮮史研究會論文集』 第24號.

金炳烈, 1999, 「本誌98年7·8月號 下條論文「竹島論爭の問題點」に反論する」, 『現代コリア』 4月號.

Bibliography

吉岡吉典, 1962, 「'竹島問題'とはなにか」, 『朝鮮研究月報』11號, 日本朝鮮研究所.

內藤正中, 2005, 「竹島は日本固有領土か」, 『世界』6月號.

梶村秀樹, 1978, 「竹島＝独島問題と日本国家」, 『朝鮮研究』182号 9月.

白忠鉉·宋炳基·愼鏞廈, 1984, 「獨島問題を再照明する」, 『アジア公論』4月號.

山名酒喜男, 1979, 「終戦前後に於ける朝鮮事情概要」, 森田芳夫·長田なか子篇, 『朝鮮終戦 の記録 資料篇 第一卷日本統治の終焉』, 嚴南堂書店.

山邊健太郎, 1965, 「竹島問題の歷史的考察」, 『コリア評論』第7卷·第2號.

_____, 1978, 「竹島＝獨島問題と日本國家」, 『朝鮮研究』182.

森田芳夫, 1961, 「竹島領有をめぐる日韓兩國の歷史上の見解」, 『外務省調査月報』II-5.

_____, 1979, 「竹島領有に關する日韓兩國の見解」, 『外務省調査月報』II-2.

速水保孝, 1954, 「竹島(I)」, 『地方自治』74.

宋炳基著·內藤浩之譯, 1999, 「朝鮮後期の鬱陵島經營」, 『北東アジア文化研究』10號, 鳥取女 子短大學北東アジア文化總合研究所.

辻政信, 1953, 「波荒き李ラインを往く: 韓國軍艦をもとめこ」, 『文藝春秋』12月號. (Tsuji Masanobu, "Crossing the Stormy Rhee Line, Seeking Korean Warships," *Bungei-Shunju*, December 1953.)

李鍾元, 1994, 「韓日會談とアメリカ: '不介入政策'の成立を中心に」, 日本政治學會 編, 『國 際政治』105號.

_____, 1994·1995, 「米韓關係における介入の原型-'エウァ-レデイ計劃'再考-(1)·(2)」, 『法 學』58·59.

田川孝三, 1953. 10, 「竹島問題研究資料: 文獻に明記された韓國領土の東極」.

_____, 1953. 11, 「竹島問題研究資料: 朝鮮政府の鬱陵島管轄について」.

_____, 1953. 12, 「竹島問題研究資料: '于山島'について」.

_____, 1954. 12, 「竹島問題研究資料(歷一): 三峯島について」, 外務省アジア局 第五課.

_____, 1954. 12, 「竹島問題研究資料(歷二): 于山島と鬱陵島名について」, 外務省アジア 局 第五課.

_____, 1954, 「竹島の歷史的背景の素描」, 『親和』7號, 日韓親和會.

_____, 1989, 「竹島領有に關する歷史的考察」, 『東洋文庫書報』20, 東洋文庫.

池內敏, 1999, 「竹島圖解と鳥取藩-元祿竹島一件考-序說」, 『鳥取地域史研究』第一號.

_____, 2001, 「17～19世紀鬱陵島海域の生業と交流」, 『歷史學研究』no. 756.

_____, 2001, 「前近代竹島の歷史學的研究序說」, 『青丘學研究論集』25.

_____, 2001, 「竹島一件の再檢討-元祿六～九年の日朝交涉」, 『名古屋大學文學部研究論 集』, 史學47.

川上健三, 1965, 「今の竹島·昔の竹島」, 『文藝春秋』12月號.

秋岡武次郎, 1933, 「安鼎福筆地球儀用世界地圖」, 『歷史地理』61-2.

_____, 1950, 「日本海西南の松島と竹島」, 『社會地理』第27號(8月).

_____, 1955, 「松島と竹島との混淆」, 『日本地圖史』, 河出書房.

樋畑雪湖, 1930, 「日本海に於ける竹島の日鮮關係に就いて」, 『歷史地理』55-6, 日本歷史地理學會.

塚本孝, 1977, 「海洋法に關連する四つの表(資料)」, 國立國會圖書館 調査立法考査局, 『レファレンス(The Reference)』 no. 315(Apr 1977).

_____, 1983, 「サンラフランシスコ條約と竹島-米外交文書集より-」, 『レファレンス』 no. 389(1983. 6). 〔Takashi Tsukamoto, 1983, "The Treaty of Peace with Japan and Takeshima - FRUS," Research and Legislative Reference Department, National Diet Library, *The Reference*, No. 389 (Jun. 1983).〕

_____, 1985, 「竹島關係舊鳥取藩文書および繪圖(上)」, 『レファレンス』 no. 411(Apr 1985).

_____, 1985, 「竹島關係舊鳥取藩文書および繪圖(下)」, 『レファレンス』 no. 412(May 1985).

_____, 1991, 「米國務省の對日平和條約草案と北方領土問題」, 『レファレンス』 no. 482(1991. 3). 〔Takashi Tsukamoto, 1991, "Draft Treaty of Peace with Japan of the US Department of State and Northern Territorial Issue," *The Reference* no. 482 (Mar. 1991)〕

_____, 1992, 「韓國の對日平和條約署名問題-日朝交渉, 戰後補償問題に關連して-」, 『レファレンス』 no. 494(Mar 1992).

_____, 1993, 「日本と領土問題(上)-北方領土問題の國際司法裁判所ての付託(上)」, 『レファレンス』 no. 504(Jan 1993). 〔Takashi Tsukamoto, 1993, "Japan and Territorial Issues," Vol. 1, The Reference no. 504 (Jan. 1993)〕

_____, 1993, 「日本と領土問題(下)-北方領土問題の國際司法裁判所ての付託(下)」, 『レファレンス』 no. 505(Feb 1993). 〔Takashi Tsukamoto, 1993, "Japan and Territorial Issues," Vol. 2, The Reference no. 505 (Feb. 1993)〕

_____, 1993, 「北方領土問題の經緯(第3版)」, 國立國會圖書館 調査及び立法考査局, 『ISSUE BRIEF(調査と情報)』 no. 227(Sep 28, 1993).

_____, 1993, 「戰後補償問題-總論1」, 『ISSUE BRIEF(調査と情報)』 no. 228(Oct 15, 1993).

_____, 1993, 「戰後補償問題-總論2」, 『ISSUE BRIEF(調査と情報)』 no. 229(Nov 2, 1993).

_____, 1993, 「戰後補償問題-總論3」, 『ISSUE BRIEF(調査と情報)』 no. 230(Nov 16, 1993).

_____, 1994, 「平和條約と竹島(再論)」, 『レファレンス』 no. 518(1994. 3). 〔Takashi Tsukamoto, 1994, "The Treaty of Peace with Japan and Takeshima (Review)," Research and Legislative Reference Department, National Diet Library, *The Reference*, No. 518 (Mar. 1994).〕

_____, 1994, 「竹島領有權問題の經緯」, 『ISSUE BRIEF(調査と情報)』 no. 244(Apr 12, 1994).

Bibliography

_____, 1996,「竹島領有權問題の經緯(第2版)」,『ISSUE BRIEF(調査と情報)』no. 289(Nov 22, 1996).

_____, 2000,「日本の領域確定における近代國際法の適用事例–先占法理と竹島の領土編入を中心に」,『東アジア近代史』3, ゆまに書房.

_____, 2002,「竹島領有權をめぐる日韓兩國政府の見解(資料)」,『レファレンス』no. 617(June 2002).

_____, 2004,「(特輯: 日本の領土・日本の防衛)「竹島領有權紛爭」が問う日本の姿勢」,『中央公論』10月號.

_____, 2007,「奧原碧雲 竹島關聯資料(奧原水夫所藏)をめぐる」,『竹島問題に關する調査研究最終報告書』(Mar 2007), 竹島問題研究會.

_____, 2007,「サンラフランシスコ條約における竹島の取り扱い」,『竹島問題に關する調査研究最終報告書』(Mar 2007), 竹島問題研究會.

下條正男, 1996,「竹島問題考」,『現代コリア』5月號, 日本朝鮮研究所.

_____, 1997,「續・竹島問題考(上)」,『現代コリア』5月號.

_____, 1997,「續・竹島問題考(下)」,『現代コリア』6月號.

_____, 1998,「竹島論爭の問題點」,『現代コリア』7・8月號.

• Korean Newspapers

『江原日報』(*Gangwon Ilbo*)

『京城大學豫科新聞』(*Gyeongseong University Premed Newspaper*)

『京鄕新聞』(*Kyunghyang Shinmun*)

『工業新聞』(*Gongeop Shinmun*)

『南鮮經濟新聞』

『大邱每日新聞』(*Daegu Maeil Shinmun*)

『大邱時報』(*Daegu Shibo*)

『獨立新報』(*Dokrip Shinbo*)

『東光新聞』

『東亞日報』(*Dong-A Ilbo*)

『聯合新聞』(*Yonhap Shinmun*)

『民主新報』(*Minju Shinbo*)

『釜山日報』(*Busan Ilbo*)

『婦人新報』

『새한민보』(*Saehan Minbo*)

563

『서울신문』(*Seoul Shinmun*)

『水産經濟新聞』(*Fisheries Economic Newspaper*)

『自由新聞』(*Jayu Shinmun*)

『朝鮮日報』(*Chosun Ilbo*)

『中央新聞』

『平和新聞』(*Pyeonghwa Shinmun*)

『한겨레신문』(*Hankyoreh*)

『漢城日報』(*Hanseong Ilbo*)

• Korean Magazines

『建國公論』(*Geongukgongron*)

『國際報道』(*Pictorial Korea*)

『文藝』

『民聲』

『思想界』(*Sasangge*)

『史海』(*Sahae*)

『世界』

『施政月報』

『新東亞』

『新思潮』(*Sinsajo*)

『新天地』(*Shincheonji*)

『용광로』(*Yonggwangno*)

『주간동아』(*Weekly Dong-A*)

『주간한국』

『最高會議報』

『漢陽』

『協同』

『希望』

• Japanese Newspapers and Magazines

『讀賣新聞』(*Yomiuri Shimbun*)

Bibliography

『文藝春秋』(*Bungei-shunju*)

『時事』

『朝日新聞』(*Asahi Shimbun*)

• Articles Written in Korean Language

具東鍊, 1947,「鬱陵島紀行」1~4,『수산경제신문』(Sep 20-24, 1947).

권상규, 1947,「동해의 孤島 울릉도행1」,「鬱陵島紀行2」,『大邱時報』(Aug 27 & 29, 1947).

旗田巍, 1963,「한일회담의 재인식: 일본인의 조선관」,『新思潮』12월호. 〔Takashi Hatada, 1963, "New Understanding of the Korea-Japan Talks: Japanese' Understanding of Korea," *Sinsajo*, December Issue (*Sekai* December Issue)〕

김영주, 1949,「상반기의 화단」,『문예』9월호.

김원용, 1947,「울릉도의 여인」,『서울신문』(Sep 6, 1947).

도봉섭, 1937,「鬱陵島植物相; 孤島植物踏查記 特히 天然記念物을 찾아서」1~6,『동아일보』(Sep 3-11, 1937).

李智新, 1949,「맥아더線과 韓國의 水産」,『새한민보』3권 14호(6월호). (Lee Ji-sin, "The MacArthur Line and Korea's Fisheries", *Saehan Minbo*, Jun. 1949, Vol. 3, No. 14.)

박경래, 1962,「독도영유권의 史·法的인 연구」,『최고회의보』.

박대련, 1964,「독도는 한국영토」,『漢陽』(Sep, 1964).

박병주, 1953,「獨島의 測量」,『용광로』4호(재건기념), 부산공업고등학교. (Park Byeong-ju, 1953, Survey of Dokdo, *Yonggwangno* Issue 4.)

방종현, 1947,「獨島의 하루」,『경성대학예과신문』13호. (Bang Jong-hyeon, 1947, "A Day at Dokdo," *Gyeongseong University Premed Newspaper*.)

석주명, 1947,「울릉도의 연혁」,『서울신문』(Sep 2, 1947).

_____, 1947,「울릉도의 자연」,『서울신문』(1947. 9. 9). 〔"Nature of Ulleungdo" by Seok Ju-myeong, *Seoul Shinmun* (Sept. 9, 1947)〕

_____, 1948,「鬱陵島의 人文」,『신천지』1948년 2월호(3권2호).

_____, 1950,「特別附錄·德積群島 學術調査報告」,『신천지』1950년 6월(통권47호).

손연순, 1999,「독도에서 쓰치 마시노부 물리치다」, 홍종인선생추모문집편찬위원회,『대기자 홍박』, LG상남언론재단.

손진태, 1949,「宋錫夏先生을 追慕함」,『民聲』1월호(5권1호).

송석하, 1948,「古色蒼然한 歷史的 遺跡 鬱陵島를 찾어서!」,『국제보도』(Pictorial Korea) 10권(올림픽특집) 3권 1호(신년호), 國際報道聯盟. (Song Seok-ha, 1948, "A Visit to Ulleungdo, Historical Remains!" (Dec 1, 1947), *Pictorial Korea*, International

Publicity League.〕

신석호, 1948, 「獨島 所屬에 對하여」, 『史海』 창간호. 〔Sin Seok-ho, 1948, "Who Dokdo Belongs To", *Sahae*, December Issue (Vol. 1, No. 1)〕

_____, 1960, 「獨島의 來歷」, 『思想界』 8월호. (Sin Seok-ho, 1960, "Origin of Dokdo," *Sasangge*, August Issue.)

양유찬, 1974, 「남기고 싶은 이야기들: 駐美大使 시절 ①∼⑤」, 『중앙일보』(Dec 17-21, 1974).

유진오, 1951, 「對日講和條約案의 檢討」 全7回, 『東亞日報』(1951. 7. 25, 7. 27∼31). 〔Yu Jin-o, "Review of the Draft Treaty of Peace with Japan," seven-installment series, *Dong-A Ilbo* (Jul. 25, 27 to 31, 1951).〕

_____, 1961, 「韓日會談을 回顧하면서」, 『時事』 11월호, 내외문제연구소.

_____, 1966, 「韓日會談이 열리기까지: 前韓國首席代表가 밝히는 十四年前의 곡절」 上, 『思想界』 2월호. (Yu Jin-o, 1966, "Until the Korea-Japan Talks Were Held: the Complications of 14 Years Ago Told by the Former Chief Delegate of Korea," Vol. 1, *Sasangge*, February Issue.)

_____, 1983, 「남기고 싶은 이야기들: 韓日會談(7) 政府意見書 작성」, 『중앙일보』(Sep 5, 1983).

_____, 1983, 「남기고 싶은 이야기들: 韓日會談(9) 歸屬財産 처리」, 『중앙일보』(Sep 7, 1983).

유홍렬, 1962, 「독도는 울릉도의 속도: 영유권을 중심으로」, 『최고회의보』.

이숭녕, 1953, 「내가 본 독도: 현지답사기」, 『希望』.

이정훈, 2005, 「1953년 독도 사진으로 화제 김한용 사진작가」, 『주간동아』 477호. 〔Lee Jeong-hun, 2005, "Photographer Kim Han-yong makes headlines with his photos of Dokdo from 1953," *Weekly Dong-A*, Serial No. 477 (Mar. 22)〕

_____, 2005, 「1953년 독도에서 '다케시마'를 뿌리뽑다」, 『주간동아』 476호. (Lee Jeong-hun, 2005, "Root out the Trace of 'Takeshima' in Dokdo in 1953," *Weekly Dong-A*, Mar. 15, Serial No. 476.)

_____, 2009, 「1953년 독도를 최초로 측량한 박병주 선생」, 『신동아』 1월호.

蔣周孝, 1976, 「慶北登山運動의 變遷過程」, 『한국산악』 XI(창립30주년특간호).

정병준, 2005, 「일본 100년 동안의 조작」, 『한겨레신문』(2005. 3. 16). 〔Jung Byung-joon, "Japan's Fabrication for 100 Years," *Hankyoreh* (Mar. 16, 2005)〕

조중삼, 1950, 「特別附錄·德積群島 學術調査報告」(德積群島의 保健狀況), 『신천지』 1950년 6월(통권 47호, 5권 6호).

주효민, 1960, 「지정학적으로 본 독도위치: 독도는 한국의 最東端」, 『사상계』 8월호.

최규장, 1965, 「독도수비대 비사」, 『주간한국』.

최남선, 1953, 「鬱陵島와 獨島: 韓日 交涉史의 一側面」, 『서울신문』(Aug 10- Sep 7, 1953).

Bibliography

특파원, 1947, 「절해의 울릉도: 학술조사대 답사①」, 『조선일보』(Sep 4, 1947).

한국산악회, 1971, 「韓國山岳會慶北支部略史(1945년~1970년)」, 『한국산악』 VII(제26년호).

韓奎浩, 1948, 「慘劇의 獨島(現地레포-트)」, 『新天地』 7월호(통권27호). 〔Han Gyu-ho, 1948, "Tragic Dokdo (on-site report)," *Shincheonji*, July Issue (Serial No. 27)〕

한찬석, 1962, 「독도비사: 安龍福小傳」, 『동아일보』(Feb, 1962).

홍구표, 1947, 「無人獨島 踏査를 마치고(紀行)」, 『建國公論』 1947년 11월호(3권 5호). 〔Hong Gu-pyo, 1947, "Wrapping up the Expedition of the Unmanned Island Dokdo (travel essay)," *Geongukgongron*, November Issue (Vol. 3, No. 5)〕

홍이섭, 1954, 「鬱陵島와 獨島」, 『新天地』 8월호.

홍종인, 1947, 「鬱陵島 學術調查隊 報告記」 1~4, 『한성일보』(1947. 9. 21, 9. 24, 9. 25, 9. 26). 〔"Ulleungdo Scientific Expedition Report (1-4) by Hong Jong-in," *Hanseong Ilbo* (Sept. 21, 24-25, 1947).〕

_____, 1978, 「다시 獨島문제를 생각한다」, 『신동아』 11월호.

洪璉基, 1962, 「나의 獄中記」, 『新思潮』 2월호. (Hong Jin-gi, 1962, "My Time in Prison," *Sinsajo*, February Issue.)

황상기, 1957, 「독도문제연구」, 『독도영유권해설』, 『동아일보』(Feb-Mar, 1957).

• Articles Written in English

Fearey, Robert A., "Diplomacy's Final Round," *Foreign Service Journal*, American Foreign Service Association, December 1991.

Fearey, Robert A., "Tokyo 1941: Might the Pacific War Have Been Avoided?," *The Journal of American East Asian Relations*, Spring 1992, Chicago: http://www.connectedcommunities.net/robertfearey/pacific_war.htm. ロバート・フィアリー, 福井宏一郎譯, 2002, 「近衛文麿 對米和平工作의全容」, 『文藝春秋』 1月號.

McKinzie, Richard D., "Oral History Interview with Niles W. Bond," December 28, 1973, Harry S. Truman Library.

• References from Korean Institutions

National Institute of Korean History (국사편찬위원회)
『島根縣독도관련사료』 1~7.

National Assembly Library, Dokdo Materials Room (국회도서관 독도자료실)

『1952년~1953년 독도 측량: 한국산악회 울릉도 독도 학술단 관련 박병주 교수 기증자료』.
(*Survey of Dokdo 1952-1953: Materials donated by Professor Park Byeong-ju regarding the Ulleungdo and Dokdo Scientific Expedition by the Corea Alpine Club.*)

· 「(檀紀四二八五年七月) 鬱陵島獨島學術調査團派遣計劃書」. 〔*(Seventh month of 4285 by the Dangun calendar) Plan for the Ulleungdo and Dokdo Scientific Expedition.*〕

· 「(檀紀四二八五年九月) 鬱陵島獨島學術調査團派遣計劃書」. 〔*(Ninth month of 4285 by the Dangun calendar) Plan for the Ulleungdo and Dokdo Scientific Expedition.*〕

· 「(檀紀四二八六年七月) 鬱陵島獨島學術調査團再派遣計劃書」.

· 「9월 최종계획서」.

Dokdo Museum (독도박물관)

「옥승식이력서」.

玉昇植, 「鬱陵島獨島調査報文」.

「鬱陵島及獨島地質調査槪報」(地質鑛物班 玉昇植) 〔"Brief Report on the Geological Survey of Ulleungdo and Dokdo" (geology and mineralogy team, Ok Seung-sik)〕.

Seoul National University (서울대학교)

『光緒九年七月日江原道鬱陵島新入民戶人口姓名年歲及田土起墾數爻成冊』奎17117 (규장각 한국학연구원).

外務部政務局飜譯, 1951, 『對日講和條約第二草案』(서울대학교 도서관 雪松文庫).

Ministry of Foreign Affairs, Diplomatic Archives (외교부 외교사료관)

『독도문제, 1952~53』, 분류번호 743.11JA, 등록번호 4565. 〔*Dokdo Issue, 1952-1953* (Classification no. 743.11JA, registration no. 4565)〕

『독도문제, 1954』, 분류번호 743.11JA, 등록번호 4566.

『독도문제, 1955~59』, 분류번호 743.11JA, 등록번호 4567.

『독도문제, 1960~64』, 분류번호 743.11JA, 등록번호 4568.

『독도문제, 1965~71』, 분류번호 743.11JA, 등록번호 4569.

『독도문제, 1972』, 분류번호 743.11JA, 등록번호 5419.

『한국의 어업보호정책: 평화선 선포, 1949~52』, 분류번호 743.4, 등록번호 458. 〔*Korea's Policy on Protection of Fisheries: Declaration of the Peace Line, 1949-1952* (diplomatic document disclosed in 2005, classification no. 743.4, registration no. 458)〕

『한일회담 예비회담(Oct 20~Dec 4, 1951) 자료집: 대일강화조약에 대한 기본 태도와 그 법적 근거』, 분류번호 723.1JA 자1950, 등록번호 76.

Bibliography

『한일회담예비회담(Oct 20–Dec 4, 1951) 본회의 회의록, 제1~10차, 1951』, 분류번호 723.1JA, 등록번호 77.

• **References from Foreign Institutions**

The U.S. National Archives and Records Administration (NARA)

RG 59, Department of State, Decimal File
· 740.0011PW (Peace) Series.
· 694.95B.
· 694.001.

RG 59, State Department, Special File
· Japanese Peace Treaty Files of John Foster Dulles, 1946–52, Boxes. 1–14, Lot 54D423.
· Office of Northeast Asia Affairs, Records Relating to the Treaty of Peace with Japan–Subject File, 1945–51 (John Moore Allison file), Boxes. 1–7, Lot 56D527.
· Records Relating to the Japanese Peace and Security Treaties, 1946–52, Lot 78D173.
· Records of the Division of Research for Far East, Lot 58D245.

RG 84, Records of the Foreign Service Posts of the Department of State.
· Korea, Seoul Embassy: Classified General Records, 1953–55 Entry 2846.
· Japan, Tokyo Embassy: Classified General Records, 1953–55.
· Japan, Foreign Service Posts of the Department of State, Office of the U.S. Political Advisor for Japan–Tokyo, Classified General Correspondence, 1945–49, 1950– Entry 2828.

RG 319, Records of the Army Staff, Records of the Office of the Assistant Chief of Staff, G–2, Intelligence, Entry IRR Personal, Records of the Investigative Records Repository, Security Classified Intelligence and Investigative Dossiers, 1939–76.
· XA519894: Chu KanRi(李中煥), Boxes. 307–308.
· XA529038: Tsuji Masanobu(辻政信), Boxes. 457–458.
· 辻政信,「國民革命外史(一): 第一成敗の概觀」,『月刊亞東』No. 2 (Aug 15, 1951).
· 辻政信,「國民革命外史(二): 第二破壞の適任者」,『月刊亞東』No. 3 (Sept 15, 1951).
· 辻政信,「國民革命外史(三): 第三勝利の悲哀」,『月刊亞東』No. 4 (Oct 15, 1951).
· 辻政信,「告發された問題の元大本營參謀辻政信氏の演説」(Aug 4, 1951).

· "Ryuten(流轉)," by Tsuji Masanobu.
· 辻政信, 「國民革命外史(五): 第五 蔣獨裁の基盤と支柱」, 『月刊亞東』 No. 6 (Dec 15, 1951).
· "Crossing the Stormy Rhee Line, Seeking Korean Warships," Bungei-Shunju (『文藝春秋』) by Tsuji Masanobu.

RG 554, Records of General HQ, Far East Command, Supreme Commander Allied Powers, and United Nations Command.
· United States Army Forces in Korea XXIV Corps, G-2 Historical Section, Historical Files, 1945-48, Box 41. Box 77.
· USAFIK, Entry A1 1378, United States Army Forces in Korea(USAFIK), Adjutant General, General Correspondence(Decimal Files) 1945-49, Box 108, Box 141.
· Entry A1 1404, USAFIK, US Army Office of Military Government, Box 311.

Air Force Historical Research Agency, Maxwell Air Force Base, Alabama

· History of The 93rd Bombardment Group(VH), Kadena Air Force Base, Okinawa, For the Month of June 1948.
· History, 330th Bombardment Squadron, 93d Bombardment Group, Kadena Air Force Base, Okinawa, For the month of June 1948.
· History of 328th Bombardment Squadron(VH) for June 1948, Narrative History.

MacArthur Memorial Archives (MA)

· RG 5, SCAP Official Correspondence Box 3.

The National Archives (TNA): UK

· FO 371/92532, 213424, FJ 1022/95 Japan, (Feb 17, 1951), Subject: Japanese Peace Treaty: Summaries of Mr. Dulles interviews with Japanese Officials in preparation of a Peace Treaty.
· FO 371/92532, FJ 1022/91, "Parliamentary Question,"(Feb 19, 1951).
· FO 371/92532, FJ 1022/97, Letter from C. H. Johnston to A. E. Percival (Mar 1, 1951).
· FO 371/92535, FJ 1022/167, "Japanese Peace Treaty: Record of Meeting held at the Foreign Office on the 16th March 1951".
· FO 371/92535, FJ 1022/171, "Japanese Peace Treaty: Second revised draft of the

Japanese Peace Treaty,"(Mar 1951).

· FO 371/92535, FJ 1022/174, "Comments on the Japanese angle of the problem of Chinese & Russian non participation & the question of Japanese participation of Japanese Peace Treaty,"(Mar 22, 1951).

· FO 371/92538, FJ 1022/222, "Provisional Draft of Japanese Peace Treaty(United Kingdom),"(Apr 7, 1951).

· FO 371/92547, 213351, FJ 1022/368, Sir O. Franks, Washington to Foreign Office, no. 1382(May 4, 1951), Subject: Japanese Peace Treaty: given text of line taken by State Department in answer to any press enquiries.

· FO 371/92547, FJ 1022/377, no. 1076/365/5IG, "Anglo-American meetings on Japanese Peace Treaty, Summary Record of Seventh meeting held on 3rd May,"(May 3, 1951).

· FO 371/92547, 213351, FJ 1022/383, Mr. Clutton to Mr. Morrison, no. 148, 119/244/51, (May 1, 1951), Subject: Record of Meeting with the Japanese Prime Minister on the 30th April at which the main theme of conversation with the Japanese Peace Treaty.

· FO 371/92547, FJ 1022/370, Sir O. Franks, Washington to Foreign Office, "Japanese Peace Treaty: Records of meeting between our representative and Mr. Dulles," no. 393(s)(May 3, 1951).

· FO 371/92547, FJ 1022/376, British Embassy Washington to C. P. Scott, O.B.E., Japan and Pacific Department, Foreign Office, no. 1076/357/5IG, "Anglo-American meetings on Japanese Peace Treaty, Summary Record of Seventh meeting,"(May 3, 1951).

· FO 371/92547, FJ 1022/377, British Embassy, Washington to C. P. Scott, O.B.E., Japan and Pacific Department, Foreign Office, no. 1076/365/5IG, "Anglo-American meetings on Japanese Peace Treaty, Summary Record of Eighth meeting held on 3rd May,"(May 4, 1951).

· FO 371/92547FJ 1022/372, British Embassy, Washington to C. P. Scott, O.B.E., Japan and Pacific Department, Foreign Office, no. 1076/332/5IG, "Summary Record of Sixth Meeting of Anglo-American meetings on Japanese Peace Treaty,"(May 2, 1951).

Ministry of Foreign Affairs of Japan, Diplomatic Archives

日本外務省外交史料館,『對日平和條約關係準備研究關係』1～7 (Classification no. B'. 4. 0. 0. 1, http://gaikokiroku.mofa.go.jp/mon/mon_b.html). (*Research on a Peace*

Treaty, written by the Executive Committee for Research on a Peace Treaty, had a total of seven volumes.)

The National Diet of Japan

日本国会会議録検索システム (http://kokkai.ndl.go.jp/).

• **Testimonies & Interviews**

· 「권재상 전화 인터뷰」(Mar 18, 2010); 「김한용 인터뷰」(Feb 4, 2009); 「손경석 인터뷰」(Jan 7, 2010); 「이근택 인터뷰」(June 9, 2010); 「이한우 전화 인터뷰」(Jan 6, 2009).
· KBS 현대사발굴특집반, 「도널드 맥도널드(Donald McDonald) 인터뷰」(Nov 12, 1992), 『한국현대사 관련 취재 인터뷰(미국인)』.

Index

A

A Study of the History and Geography of Takeshima 162, 163, 465, 479, 482, 485, 496, 502, 506

Agreement on Military Facilities and Areas 476, 478

American Council on Japan 213

Anglo-American Draft
- First Draft (May 3, 1951) 184, 264-265, 266, 268-270, 318-319, 407
- Second Draft (June 14, 1951) 270, 274, 275, 326, 329-330, 331, 333-334
- Third Draft (July 3, 1951) 277, 279, 409, 419

Anglo-American Meetings
- First joint Anglo-American talks (March 1951) 184
- First Meeting (April-May, 1951) 184, 274, 290, 304, 307-308, 310, 311-319, 321, 354-355, 408
- Second Meeting (June 2-14, 1951) 274, 301, 304, 325-326, 329-330, 331, 333-334

Appendix A 181, 205

Asahi Shimbun 389, 473, 479, 480, 493, 497, 499, 500, 501, 503, 504, 505, 506

Ashida Initiative 116-118, 137

Atlantic Charter 109, 111-112, 116, 132, 135, 138, 383, 410

B

bombing range 27, 30, 32, 71-74, 75, 78, 84-86, 87, 88-89, 94, 167, 246-247, 456, 458, 468, 470-471, 474-486, 488-491, 509-510, 512, 515, 519-521, 522-527, 529-531, 534, 537, 541-542

British Commonwealth Foreign Ministers Conference 181, 214, 245, 283, 284, 285, 303

British Commonwealth Prime Ministers Conference 123, 283

C

Cairo Conference 233

Cairo Declaration (1943) 24, 109-113, 132-135, 148-149, 193, 198, 201, 212, 228, 242, 259, 271, 285, 291, 296, 301-302, 314, 317-318, 322-323, 331, 361, 537

Canberra Conference → British Commonwealth Prime Ministers Conference

ceasefire talks 434

Central Liaison Office (Japan) 84, 105, 108, 114, 145, 374

Chosen Engan Suiroshi (Korean Sea Directory) 61

Chugoku Liaison Office (Japan) 88

Clark Line 529

Coast Guard 48, 49, 53, 70, 338, 386, 492, 500, 535

Colombo Conference → British Commonwealth Foreign Ministers Conference

Committee in charge of preparing a fishery agreement with Japan 446, 447

Commonwealth Working Party of Officials on the Japanese Peace Treaty 283, 285, 286, 303

Congo Basin Treaties 359

Constitution of the Republic of Korea 96, 417

Corean (Corea) Alpine Club 8, 31, 43-58, 63, 69, 90, 95, 415, 453-455, 457, 459-460, 462, 497, 503-504, 506, 512-513

Crowd IV 94

D

Daegu Shibo 37, 39, 45, 49, 57, 76

Daejeonhwan (vessel) 48-49

de facto peace 124-125 131 137

Defense Force Department 347

Disarmament and Demilitarization Treaty (D and D Treaty) 192

Division of Research for Far East (DRF) 189, 238, 241, 373, 403

Dokdo bombing incident (1948) 69, 71, 72, 73-74, 75, 76, 77, 79, 81, 88, 90-96, 464, 484, 490

Dokdo bombing incident (1952) 452, 457, 462, 486, 509, 511, 513, 514, 519-520, 522

Dokdo Research Society 78

Dokdo Scientific Expedition 31, 38, 463, 463, 476, 485, 504, 531

Dokdo sovereignty 56, 301, 308, 484, 512, 516, 520-521, 528, 531

DRF → Division of Research for Far East

Dulles delegation 129, 256, 308, 316, 324, 331, 339, 355, 362-363, 537

Dulles' first draft 398

E

Executive Committee for Coordination 103, 108

Executive Committee for Coordination between Ministries for a Peace Treaty 103, 108

Executive Committee for Research on a Peace Treaty 103-104, 105, 106-107, 132-134, 136, 140, 141, 228-229, 337

F

Far Eastern Commission (FEC) 44, 123-124, 176, 189, 205, 241-242, 245, 262, 306-307, 360, 366-367, 369, 373, 394, 442, 533

FEAF → US Far East Air Force

FEC → Far Eastern Commission

Foreign Affairs Committee (Korean) 72, 394-396, 398, 412, 415, 417, 426

Foreign Relations of the United States (FRUS) 22, 169, 182, 200, 251, 252, 256, 264, 267, 276, 308, 313, 325, 326, 327, 328, 330, 331, 355, 369, 373, 392, 398

FRUS → Foreign Relations of the United States

G

Gimpo Air Base 70

Guksagwan (the present National Institute of Korean History) 44, 46, 56, 58

Gwangyeongho (vessel) 476, 490, 509

H

H. O. 1500 87

Hague Convention 397

Hornet (vessel) 160

I

inherent territory theory 56, 453
Initial Financial and Property Settlement
between the US Government and the
ROK Government (September 11, 1948)
404, 413
Institute of Korean Historical Studies 67
International Court of Justice 256, 333,
403, 405, 407, 436-437, 501, 532, 535-
539, 542-544
Introduction to the Dokdo Issue 44, 62,
164, 456, 459, 478, 486, 491, 492, 493,
494, 495, 496, 497, 498, 500, 506, 507,
508, 515, 523
Italian peace treaty 7, 124, 129-130, 175,
183, 185-186, 216, 248-249, 265, 283,
288-289, 339, 356, 358
Italy's peace treaty 124 129

J

Japanese Coast Guard developed a Four-
Year Defense Plan 492
Japanese Communist Party 370-371, 468,
472
Japanese Emperor 107, 119, 122-123
Japanese landmarks 502-504
Japanese Peace Treaty Files of John Foster
Dulles 171, 259, 285, 305, 314, 329,
331, 333, 372, 375, 403, 404, 405, 409,
416, 425, 427, 429, 431, 438, 439, 440,
441
Japanese property in Korea 330, 333, 390,
392, 397-398, 403-405, 407-408, 412-
413, 429, 441, 537
Jinnam-ho (vessel) 455, 476, 513
John Foster Dulles Files → Japanese Peace
Treaty Files of John Foster Dulles

Joint Soviet-American Commission 168
jurisdictional waters 448, 449-451

K

Korea Modern Historical Research Society
56
Korea-Japan Fisheries Agreement 333,
432, 446, 447, 450, 451
Korea-Japan talks 20, 29, 122, 377, 382,
391, 397, 398, 412, 415, 435, 509, 518,
538-539
– the second Korea-Japan talks (April
15-July 13, 1953) 459, 491
– the third Korea-Japan talks (October
6, 1953) 536
Korean Communications Zone 514, 523-
524, 527
Korean Government's Official Comments
and Suggestions on the Provisional
Draft of a Japanese Peace Treaty (April
27, 1951) 399, 400-401
Korean government's reply (response) 409
– First reply (April 27, 1951) 314, 330,
391, 397, 398-402, 404, 410
– Second reply (July 19, 1951) 170,
411, 415, 416, 429, 431, 433
– Third reply (August 2, 1951) 425,
429, 432, 433
Korean Mission in Japan 376, 388-389,
392, 500, 507-508, 529
Korean territorial landmarks 491, 503-
504, 506, 534
Koreans in Japan 142, 312, 366, 368-369,
374, 377, 405-406, 418
Koryomaru (vessel) 386

L

Laws of War: Laws and Customs of War on Land (Hague IV) 397
Liancourt (vessel) 160
London Conference (1951) 283
long-range, maximum-effort mission 79

M

MacArthur Line 39-41, 45, 61, 65, 294, 333, 381, 383-390, 393, 395-396, 403-404, 406, 408, 410, 412, 413-414, 416-418, 426, 428-430, 432-434, 445-452, 469-470, 489
majority peace 126-129
mandated territory (of Japan) 115, 134, 148-149, 178, 181, 187, 306, 323
Map of Japanese Territory 467-470, 471
Ministry of National Security 347
Minor Islands Adjacent to Japan Proper 148, 151, 158
 – Part I: The Kurile Islands, the Habomais, and Shikotan 149-150, 152, 229
 – Part II: Ryukyu and Other Nansei Islands 149-150
 – Part III: The Bonin Island Group, the Volcano Island Group 149-150
 – Part IV: Minor Islands in the Pacific, Minor Islands in the Japan Sea 149-150, 154, 155, 157, 158, 160, 161, 165, 169, 229, 234, 246, 247, 420, 422
Mongolian People's Republic 216

N

National Institute of Korean History 26, 44, 389, 395, 399, 411, 415, 428, 430, 484, 514, 524, 539, 540, 542
Northeast Asian History Foundation 26,
430, 470, 483, 501
Notification of the Japanese Ministry of Foreign Affairs 486
 – Notification No. 28 (May 14, 1953) 482, 485, 491, 530
 – Notification No. 34 (July 26, 1952) 479, 482

O

Office of Intelligence and Research (OIR) 170, 383, 419, 420, 422, 423
Office of Northeast Asia Affairs, Records Relating to the Treaty of Peace with Japan-Subject File, 1945-51 66, 178, 184, 190, 191, 192, 194, 196, 197-198, 200, 204, 209, 211, 213, 216, 217, 240, 241, 245, 260, 265, 266, 269-270, 277, 278, 279, 315, 321, 325, 327, 329, 355, 356, 357, 359, 368, 382, 393, 410
OIR → Office of Intelligence and Research
Oki Island Magistrate 63, 164
Outline of a Hypothesis on a Peace Treaty with Japan 129, 130, 138
overall peace 18, 127-128, 177

P

Pallada (vessel) 160
partial peace 125
Patriotic Old Men's Association 31, 96, 98, 99, 100, 168-169, 197, 382-383, 421, 533
Peace Constitution 122, 179, 500-501
 – Article 9 126, 177, 501
Peace Line 30, 32, 58, 436, 445-446, 460, 474, 491-492, 504-505, 528-529, 531-532, 538-540, 543
Policy Planning Staff (PPS) 32, 180, 203-205, 207, 220

Policy Review Committee 113, 126

Polish National Committee 325

Potsdam Declaration (1945) 24, 98, 105, 109-112, 116, 132-136, 140, 148-149, 151, 166, 175, 198, 201, 212, 228, 242, 250, 252-253, 258-259, 262-263, 265, 271-272, 285, 291, 294, 296, 301-302, 305, 315, 317-318, 321-323, 351, 361, 383, 414, 431, 537, 541

PPS → Policy Planning Staff

PPS/10, Results of Planning Staff Study of Questions Involved in the Japanese Peace Settlement 180, 203-210

Presidential Proclamation of Sovereignty over Adjacent Seas (January 18, 1952) 28, 452-453, 474, 476

Provisional Government of the Republic of Korea (Provisional Government of Korea) 97, 168, 216, 238, 328, 391, 399, 401, 402, 406, 416, 428, 464

Provisional Memorandum 257-258, 261-262, 266, 347-349

R

radar stations 169, 229, 233-235, 246, 512

Regulations on the Reproduction and Protection of Fisheries in Joseon 449

reverse course 117, 120, 124, 131, 146, 176

Rusk letter (August 10, 1951) 23, 429-437, 509-511, 517-522, 531, 533, 535-538, 540-544

S

San Francisco (Peace) Treaty 5-8, 17, 20, 25, 30, 111, 154, 207, 297, 299, 301, 438, 446, 452, 454, 467, 474, 482, 488, 509-510, 516, 529, 532-533, 542-543

San Francisco Peace Conference 6, 17, 19-20, 22-25, 27-28, 45, 68, 111, 121, 168, 179, 180, 185, 216, 232, 237, 248, 279, 296, 299, 312, 321, 351, 397-398, 437, 439-442, 445, 473, 510, 533, 544

SCAP → Supreme Commander of the Allied Powers

SCAP Instruction → SCAPIN

SCAPIN (SCAP Instruction)
 – SCAPIN No. 80 (September 27, 1945) 384
 – SCAPIN No. 677 (January 29, 1946) 38, 165, 292, 300, 516
 – SCAPIN No. 1033 (June 22, 1946) 38, 294, 384
 – SCAPIN No. 1033/2 (June 30, 1946) 384
 – SCAPIN No. 1778 (September 16, 1947) 84-86
 – SCAPIN No. 2046 (September 19, 1949) 384-385
 – SCAPIN No. 2160 (July 6, 1951) 482

Sea Maneuvering and Training Areas Subcommittee 479-481

separate peace 18, 103, 123, 126-129, 131, 177, 189, 213, 228, 253-254, 392

Seven Principles of the Treaty with Japan 146, 183-184, 251, 254-257, 260, 337, 339, 341

Shimbun Akahata 472

signpost 51, 52-53, 457-462, 477, 491

Sino-Japanese War (1894) 148, 193

SKILA → South Korean Interim Legislative Assembly

SOFA → US-Japan Administrative Agreement

South Korea-Japan Fishery Negotiation 334

South Korean Interim Government 31, 39-41, 43-45, 47, 49-50, 52-53, 55-58, 69, 76, 92, 95-96, 168, 311, 381-382,

395, 415

South Korean Interim Legislative Assembly (SKILA)   65, 66, 67, 168, 217, 382-383

Soviet-Japanese Joint Declaration (1956)   153

State-War-Navy Coordinating Committee (SWNCC)   189-190

Strike mission   343

Supreme Commander of the Allied Powers (SCAP)   19, 25, 32, 70, 76, 78, 84-86, 94, 98, 99, 110, 114-122, 125-126, 137, 139-141, 143-146, 152-153, 166, 168-169, 194, 197, 221, 246, 292, 294, 300, 340, 351-353, 356-357, 371, 374, 376, 382, 384-390, 391-392, 394, 421, 428, 464, 468, 475, 517, 532-533

SWNCC → State-War-Navy Coordinating Committee

Syngman Rhee Line (Peace Line) → Peace Line

T

Taiyoumaru (vessel)   388

Takeshima No Rekishi Chirigakuteki Kenkyu (A Historical and Geographical Study of Takeshima) → *A Study of the History and Geography of Takeshima*

Takeshima No Ryoyu (Sovereignty over Takeshima)   162

Takeshima Oyobi Utsuryoto (Dokdo and Ulleungdo)   164-165

territorial signposts → signpost

Treaty of Commerce and Navigation between Japan and Russia (Treaty of Shimoda)   153

Treaty of Portsmouth   331

Treaty of Saint Petersburg (1875)   153

Treaty of San Francisco → San Francisco Treaty

Treaty of Versailles   104, 106, 183, 185-186, 249, 258, 328, 339, 358, 392, 401, 402, 405

– Versailles Conference   328

Truman Doctrine   113, 117, 176

Truman Proclamation (1945)   450-451

trusteeship   97, 115, 134, 135, 148, 154, 178, 181, 187, 214, 219, 224, 228, 229, 233, 239, 244, 250, 253, 255, 258, 259, 261, 267, 269, 271, 306, 307, 321-323, 338, 341-342, 355, 426-427

U

UK Foreign and Commonwealth Office (FCO)   23-25, 232, 267, 273, 277, 283, 301, 304-306, 308, 316, 320, 323, 354-355, 362, 364

Ulleungdo & Dokdo Scientific Expedition   52, 453, 454, 456

Ulleungdo and Dokdo   159

Ulleungdo police   69-70, 457, 462, 498, 500, 503

Ulleungdo Scientific Expedition   47-48, 49, 54-57, 456, 460

United Nations   112, 182, 215, 233, 251, 254, 255, 258, 268, 270, 292, 319-320, 332, 399, 456, 535-536

– United Nations trusteeship   233, 255, 258

US Far East Air Force (USFEAF) Headquarters   70-72, 79, 84, 86

US political adviser   25, 66, 115, 120-121, 182, 220, 226-227, 235, 352-353, 532

– Office of US political adviser   405, 427, 434, 481

US-Japan Administrative Agreement   324, 348, 350, 474-476, 478, 528

US-Japan Joint Committee   476, 478, 481, 484, 490-491, 510, 512, 515-517, 526,

530, 541-542
- the 12th (July 26, 1952) 476, 479, 512, 541-542
- the 45th (March 19, 1953) 476, 479, 491, 530, 531, 533, 541-542
US-Japan Security agreement 177, 179, 250, 257, 478
US-Japan Security Treaty 19, 347-349, 357, 476, 482
US-Japan Working-Level Talks
- First talk (February 1, 1951) 347
- Second talk (February 2, 1951) 347
- Third talk (February 5, 1951) 347
- Fourth talk (February 6, 1951) 347-348
US-UK Draft→ Anglo-American Draft

W

Weyland's letter 528-530
Working Group on the Treaty with Japan 66, 177, 180, 188, 190-192, 194-196, 204, 212, 221, 382, 419-420

Y

Yalta Agreement 134, 135, 187, 196
- Yalta Conference 135, 153, 298

#

22nd Bombardment Group 79, 89
2nd Draft of the Japanese Peace Treaty 288
93d Bombardment Group (BG) 79-82

Index of Names

A

Acheson, Dean   171, 181, 188-189, 214, 248, 303, 326, 354, 391-392, 399, 411, 426-427, 429-431

Allison, John Moore   21, 170, 183, 214-215, 218, 221, 240, 241, 248, 249, 251, 257, 264, 288, 304, 306-310, 313, 320, 325-327, 339-340, 346, 348, 349, 351, 353, 393-394, 396, 411, 424-425, 429, 442, 537-540

An Jae-hong (안재홍)   31, 44, 46, 60, 63

Anderson, Colin E.   99, 169

Asakai, Koichiro (朝海浩一郎)   113-115, 119, 145

Atcheson, George, Jr.   110, 114-121, 123, 136, 194-197

B

Bacon, Ruth   190-192, 194, 209, 215-216

Baek Chung-hyeon (백충현)   60

Ball, W. McMahon   114, 117

Bang Jong-hyeon (방종현)   58-59

Bevin, Ernest   181, 214, 303, 351

Boggs, Samuel W.   170, 197-203, 206-207, 209-210, 244, 353, 419-425

Bond, Niles   427

Borton, Hugh   120, 180, 188-190, 194-196, 198, 200, 204, 207, 214, 221

Bradley, Omar   178

Briggs, Ellis O.   528, 538

Butterworth, W. Walton   169, 205, 215, 221, 223, 235, 375

Byrnes, James F.   134

C

Chang Myun (장면)   72, 369, 391, 393, 394, 395, 396, 403, 404, 524, 525, 527

Chiang, Kai-shek (蔣介石)   66, 229, 439

Choi Du-seon (최두선)   398

Choi Heon-sik (최헌식)   498

Choi Nam-seon (최남선)   415

Chu In-bong (추인봉)   44

Clark, Mark W.   435, 514-515, 519, 529

Clutton, George   186, 351, 356

D

Do Bong-seop (도봉섭)   46, 49, 63

Dulles, John Foster   21, 23-24, 103, 129, 146, 171, 177-179, 183-186, 194, 238, 245, 248-254, 256-260, 266-267, 277, 285-286, 303-305, 308, 310-312, 314, 316, 320-321, 323-327, 329-331, 333, 337-339, 345-347, 349-351, 354-358, 362-363, 366-369, 371-373, 375, 383, 392-393, 395-396, 398-399, 402-405, 409-411, 416-419, 425, 427-429, 431, 436, 438-441, 530-532, 537-544

E

Eisenhower, Dwight D.   534

Emmerson, John. K.   190

Emmons, Arthur B.   409, 440

581

F

Fearey, Robert A.   170, 178, 180, 192, 194, 198, 199, 207, 215, 218, 221, 240, 241, 243-244, 247, 265, 269, 278, 308, 314, 321, 325, 339-340, 353, 355-357, 360, 362-364, 368-369, 392, 404, 409-410, 420, 422, 423, 424-425, 430

Finn, Richard B.   99, 144, 146, 169, 194, 204, 481, 516, 519, 533-534, 538

Fitzmaurice, G. G.   287, 313

G

Gaminish, Yutaro (神西由太郎)   164

Green, Marshall   213-214, 340

H

Hagiwara, Toru (萩原徹)   108, 109, 110-111, 113, 118

Han Gi-jun (한기준)   44, 56

Han Pyo-wook (한표욱)   394, 398, 416-417, 438

Helmick, G. C.   65

Heo Pil (허필)   88

Hickey, Doyle O.   519

Hildring John H.   189, 190, 191

Hong Gu-pyo (홍구표)   49, 57

Hong Jae-hyeon (홍재현)   61-63

Hong Jin-gi (홍진기)   395, 397, 398

Hong Jong-in (홍종인)   47, 49, 51, 52, 54, 55-56, 57, 63, 90, 91, 456, 461-462, 504

Hunsberger, Warren S.   189, 190

Hwang Seong-su (황성수)   446

I

Iguchi, Sadao (井口貞夫)   257, 348, 349, 352, 354-358, 362, 364

Im Byeong-jik (임병직)   399, 438

Iokibe, Makoto (五百旗頭眞)   104, 105, 106, 113, 120, 122, 195

Ishihara, Kanichiro (石原幹市郎)   475, 483

J

Jang Hak-sang (장학상)   90

Jeong Won-jun (정원준)   494-495

Jeong Yeong-ho (정영호)   56

Ji Cheol-geun (지철근)   384, 449, 451

Jo Jae-cheon (조재천)   95

Jung Mun-ki (정문기)   446

K

Kabayama, Aisuke (樺山愛輔)   375

Kase, Toshikazu (加瀬俊一)   110-111

Kawakami, Kanichi (川上貫一)   468-470, 472, 483

Kawakami, Kenzo (川上健三)   20, 162, 464-465, 482, 504

Kennan, George F.   176, 180, 205

Kim Dong-jo (김동조)   451-452

Kim Gyu-sik (김규식)   66, 217, 382

Kim Hong-rae (김홍래)   57

Kim Jang-ryeol (김장렬)   91

Kim Jeong-tae (김정태)   55, 460

Kim Jin-seong (김진성)   498

Kim Jun-hyeok (김준혁)   492

Kim Jun-seon (김준선)   69

Kim Jun-yeon (김준연)   395

Kim Sae Sun (김세선)   395-396, 399, 404

Kim Yong-ju (김용주)   390, 392, 448-449

L

Lamb, Richard   480

Lee Bong-su (이봉수)   44

Lee Jong-hak (이종학) 140, 468
Lee Ki-bung (이기붕) 527
Lee Kwae-dae (이쾌대) 94
Lee Yeong-ro (이영로) 56
Lee Yong-min (이용민) 463
Leonhart, Bill 533-534
Lewton, William S. 480
Lightner, E. Allan Jr. 409, 411, 435, 510, 513-517, 519-526
Lim Song-bon (임송본) 445

M

MacArthur, Douglas 19, 31-32, 40-41, 43-44, 64, 73-74, 86, 91, 96-98, 108, 110, 113, 118-123, 133, 144-145, 149, 175-176, 181-182, 188-189, 194-196, 204-205, 221, 224, 226-227, 230, 235, 250, 348, 354, 356, 362, 366-369, 374-377, 396, 404, 413, 450, 473
Marshall, George C. 66, 114, 196
Martin, Edwin M. 190
Masanobu, Tsuji (辻政信) 504-505
Matsunaga, Bukichi (Matsunaga, Takekichi, 松永武吉) 164
McClure, Thomas 77
McClurkin, Robert J. G. 516-517, 536, 538
McDonald, Donald 93
Morrison, Herbert Stanley 289, 309, 325-326
Muccio, John J. 182 236-238 241 307 309 373 398 409 411 429 438-439
Murphy, Robert 485, 513

N

Nakai, Yozaburo (中井 養三郎) 27, 161, 487
Nishimura, Kumao (西村熊雄) 143-144, 337, 357, 359-360, 362, 364

P

Park Byeong-ju (박병주) 453-455 462-463
Pauley, Edwin E. 343, 381
Penfield, James K. 190-191, 205
Percival, A. E. 287
Pyun Yung-tai (변영태) 409, 412-413, 427-428, 432-433, 441

R

Reischauer Edwin O. 189, 219-220
Rhee Syngman (이승만) 95, 122, 216, 374, 382-383, 389-390, 392-393, 394, 395, 396, 398-399, 415, 428-429, 438, 440, 452, 469, 504-505, 534, 540
Ridgway, Matthew B. 326, 356-357
Rusk, Dean 23, 170, 188, 391, 429-440, 509-511, 517-522, 531, 533, 535-538, 540-544

S

Sebald, William J. 25, 27-28, 32, 115, 120-123, 141, 143-146, 169-170, 182, 194, 197, 221, 225, 226-240, 242-244, 247, 316, 323, 352-353, 354, 356-359, 362, 364-367, 374, 376-377, 382, 394, 396, 421-422, 442, 512, 532-533
Seo Deok-gyun (서덕균) 461
Seok Ju-myeong (석주명) 52, 63
Shirasu, Jiro (白洲次郎) 374-375, 377
Sim Heung-taek (심흥택) 38, 42, 62-63, 162
Sin Seok-ho (신석호) 44-46, 49, 56, 60-62
Sin Yong-ha (신용하) 20, 25, 60
Son Won-il (손원일) 512
Song Byeong-gi (송병기) 60, 159
Steeves, John M. 510, 512, 516, 519

T

Tomlinson, F. S.   310

Truman, Harry S.   66,

Tsukamoto, Takashi (塚本孝)   21-22, 203,
211, 300

Turner, William T.   435, 522-523, 537-539

W

Whitney, Courtney   116-117

Y

Yamamoto, Toshinaga (山本利壽)   467-
468, 470, 473, 475, 483

Yamana, Mikio (山名酒喜男)   166, 167

Yang Je-bak (양제박)   65

Yang You-chan (양유찬)   170, 278, 330,
389, 402, 409, 416, 438

Yoshida, Shigeru (吉田茂)   104, 106, 118,
128, 137, 140-141, 143, 144, 146, 154,
186, 188, 194, 204, 248, 257, 311-312,
316-317, 326-327, 337, 340, 342, 343,
345-346, 348-351, 355, 356-357, 361-
365, 367-369, 371-372, 374-377, 406,
418

Young, Kenneth T., Jr.   435, 516, 520, 521

Yu Hong-ryeol (유홍렬)   46

Yu Jin-o (유진오)   276, 278, 382, 395, 398,
412, 414, 416, 445

Yun Chi-yeong (윤치영)   91

Index of Place Names

A

Akiyuri (秋勇留島) 292
 – Akijiri 290, 292
Amami Islands 426, 470
 – Amami Oshima 135-136, 154, 298, 426
Amami Oshima → Amami Islands
Antarctica 267, 270, 286, 306

B

Bonin Islands (Ogasawara) 133, 138, 140,
 142, 150, 151, 154, 214, 255, 258, 265,
 269, 285, 306, 320, 322-323, 351

C

Ceylon 216, 241, 262, 279, 289, 299, 360,
 394, 442
Chejudo → Jejudo

D

Dagelet Island → Ulleungdo
Daito Islands (大東島) 150, 154, 196, 353
Dokdo (독도)
 – Dokseom 58-60
 – Dolseom 59-60
 – Liancourt Rocks 6, 32, 73-75, 80,
  84-86, 87, 159-163, 165, 169-170, 181,
  184, 192-194, 197, 199-200, 203, 204,
  207, 208, 211, 217-219, 220, 223, 226,
  229, 230, 233-234, 238-240, 244, 246,
  292, 363-364, 420-425, 431, 457, 479-
  480, 512, 519, 520, 523-525, 534, 536,
  538
 – Matsu-shima 156, 160-161
 – Miancourt rocks (Take island) 290, 292
 – Sambongdo 58-60, 90
 – Seokdo 59-60
 – Takeshima (竹島) 39, 60, 164, 169-
  170, 197, 246, 364, 384, 421, 425, 431,
  461, 465-470, 473-476, 478, 479, 483,
  493, 496, 501, 504, 506, 538, 541-542
 – Tokdo 25
 – Udo (우도) 38
Dokseom (독섬) → Dokdo
Dolseom (돌섬) → Dokdo

E

Etorofu (択捉島) 152-153, 199, 202, 218,
 223, 233, 243, 470

F

Fukue-Shima (福江島) 293, 295

G

Geocheomdo Island (거첨도) 86
Goto Archipelago (五島列島) 193, 218

H

Habomai (歯舞) 152, 199, 202, 215, 223,
 272, 298-299, 361, 436, 468, 470, 541-

544

– Habomai Islands 138-139, 142, 150-153, 218 233, 242-243, 290-291

Hokkaido (北海島) 87, 88, 132-133, 140, 148, 151, 153, 193, 196, 218, 284, 290-291, 296, 298, 341

Honshu (本州) 84-86, 87, 132-133, 148, 151, 193, 218, 284, 290-291, 293, 295-296, 341, 363, 476

I

Indonesia 125, 241, 262, 279, 311-312, 314, 340, 360, 369

Inland Sea 193, 218

Iwo Jima (硫黄島) → Volcano Island

Izu Island (伊豆) 202

– Izu Islands 218

– Izu Oshima 135-136

J

Jejudo, Quelpart (or Chejudo) island (제주도) 40, 169, 292, 294, 300, 350, 385-388, 414, 423, 424, 449, 451, 505, 529

– Chejudo 290, 424

– Quelpart 185, 193, 196, 199, 203, 214, 239, 267-268, 270-274, 276, 278-279, 290-293, 295, 317-320, 331, 334, 363, 414, 420, 424, 427, 512

– Shichi 290, 292

K

Kaiba (海馬島, Kaiba To) 196

Kazan (火山) → Volcano Islands

Komun Do (거문도) → Nan How group

Kuchinoshima (口之島) 290-292, 470

Kunashiri Shima (国後島) 150, 152-153,

199, 202, 218, 223, 233, 243, 470

Kurils 130, 135-136, 151-153, 211-212, 215, 228, 243, 252, 255, 262-263, 273, 279, 298, 333, 338, 342

– Chishima 132

– Kuril Islands 132, 134-135, 138-140, 142, 150-152, 193, 196, 224, 261, 285, 306, 331, 351, 408

– Southern Kuril 142, 153, 215, 243, 298, 320, 323

Kyushu (九州) 80, 87, 132-133, 148, 151, 193, 218, 284, 290-291, 296, 298, 341, 470

L

La Perouse Strait

– Soya Kaikyo (宗谷海峽) 293, 295, 363

Liancourt Rocks → Dokdo

M

Marcus Island (Minami-Tori-shima) 150, 154, 204, 258, 285

Marianas 134

N

Nan How group (San To, or Komun Do) 199, 203, 239

Nanpo Islands (南方諸島) 204

Nansei (南西) 352-353

– Nansei Islands 138, 142, 150, 151, 154, 204, 352, 364

– Nansei Shoto (南西諸島) 154, 353

– Ryukyu Retto → Ryukyu Islands

Nemuro Peninsula (根室半島) 153

Nemuro Province (根室国) 153

Nishinoshima (西之島) 470

O

Ogasawara (小笠原) → Bonin Islands
Oki (隠岐島) 63, 193, 291-292, 458
  – Inshu (Oki Island) 160
  – Oki Islands 38, 84, 86, 160, 163-164, 170, 234, 246-247, 290, 293, 295, 363, 431
  – Oki Retto 85, 218, 363
Okinawa (沖縄) 8, 72, 79-80, 82, 89, 98, 122-123, 132, 135-136, 140, 151, 177-178, 187, 196, 338, 353, 427
  – Okinawa Island 135
Okujiri (奥尻島) 193

P

Paracel 99, 420
Paracel Islands 99, 420
Parangdo (파랑도) 31, 63-65, 67-68, 96-99, 169-170, 382, 415-417, 420-421, 423-425, 429-431, 433-435, 445, 455
  – Parangseo 64
Parece Vela 150, 154, 258
  – Okinotorishima 150, 154
  – Parcoe Vela 258
Pescadores 110, 130, 132-134, 138, 148, 193, 228, 243-244, 252, 255, 258, 262-263, 267, 270, 317-318, 320, 397, 414
Port Hamilton (Tonaikai) 185, 193, 196, 199, 203, 239, 267-268, 270-274, 276, 278-279, 318-320, 331, 334, 414, 420, 424, 427, 512

Q

Quelpart Island → Jejudo

R

Rasa 196
Rebun 193 242
  – Rebun Shima (礼文島) 293, 295, 363,
Riishiri (利尻島) 193
Rosario Island 258
Ryukyu Islands 132-136, 142, 150-151, 154, 181, 193, 195-196, 199-200, 205, 208-209, 210, 211-212, 214-215, 218-219, 250, 253, 255, 258-259, 262, 265, 269, 279, 285, 291, 298, 306-307, 321-322, 337, 341-342, 346, 351-353, 355, 426
Ryukyu Retto (琉球諸島) → Ryukyu Islands

S

Sado (佐渡島) 193, 218
Sakai Minato (境港) Port 38
Sakhalin 130, 142, 151-153, 196 211, 298, 323, 331, 408
  – Southern Sakhalin (Minami-Karafuto) 132, 134-136, 138, 153, 228, 243, 252, 255, 261, 263, 279, 285, 306, 338, 342
Sakishima (先島) 353
Sambongdo (삼봉도) → Dokdo
San To (산도) → Nan How group
Sento Islands 353
Seokdo (석도) → Dokdo
Shibotsu (志発島) 290
Shikoku (四國) 132-133, 149, 151, 193, 218, 284, 290-291, 296, 341
Shikoku (四国) 132-133, 149, 151, 193, 218, 284, 290-291, 296, 341
Spratly Islands 170, 420, 422

T

Taiwan 18, 375

Takeshima → Dokdo

Taraku Islands (多楽島) 290

Tsushima (對馬島)   31, 67-68, 96-99, 133, 137, 142, 149, 154, 156, 159, 169, 193, 218, 242, 293, 295, 332, 363, 382-383, 401-406, 408, 410, 415-416, 421, 427-429, 434

U

Udo (우도) → Dokdo

Ulleungdo (울릉도) 6, 24, 27, 31, 37-38, 39, 40-42, 43, 45, 47-50, 52-53, 54-63, 69-70, 76-78, 80-81, 88, 89, 91, 93-94, 95, 97-99, 150, 151-152, 154-155, 158-159, 161-165, 169, 197, 207, 224-225, 292, 294, 299-300, 382, 414, 417, 423-424, 453-456, 460-462, 464, 467, 470, 474, 493-496, 498, 500, 502-503

– Dagelet Island   150, 154-156, 160, 162-163, 170, 185, 193, 196, 199, 203, 207-208, 234, 239, 246-247, 267-268, 270-274, 276, 278-279, 291, 318-320, 331, 334, 414, 420, 422-424, 427, 512

– Matsu Shima   154, 155, 199, 203, 239, 424

– Utsuryo   154, 155, 193, 196, 290, 292

– Utsuryoto   199, 224, 225, 239, 423, 424

Ullung do → Ulleungdo

Urup   153

V

Volcano Island

– Iwo Jima (硫黄島)   135-136, 138, 151, 154, 195, 285, 342

Volcano Islands 133, 142, 150-151, 154, 258

– Kazan Retto (火山列島)   133, 154

Y

Yokosuka (横須賀)

– Yokosuka Port   181 204

Yuri (勇留) 290

List of Figures & Tables

051   **[Figure 1-1]**   Territorial signposts installed at Dokdo by the Corean Alpine Club (Aug. 20, 1947) © Hong Jong-in/Corea Alpine Club

087   **[Figure 1-2]**   Locations of bombing ranges used by the US occupation forces

157   **[Figure 2-1]**   Attached map, Minor Islands Adjacent to Japan Proper, Part IV (June, 1947)

161   **[Figure 2-2]**   Dokdo section, Minor Islands Adjacent to Japan Proper, Part IV (June, 1947)

206   **[Figure 3-1]**   Map attached to PPS/10 (October 14, 1947)

208   **[Figure 3-2]**   Dokdo in the map attached to PPS/10 (October 14, 1947)

210   **[Figure 3-3]**   Territorial boundaries in the US Department of State's draft treaties of 1947

222   **[Figure 3-4]**   Map attached to the US draft peace treaty with Japan (November 2, 1949)

223   **[Figure 3-5]**   Four islands in the North in the draft treaty of November 2, 1949

224   **[Figure 3-6]**   Ulleungdo and Dokdo in the draft treaty of November 2, 1949

297   **[Figure 4-1]**   Map attached to the British draft treaty (March 1951)

298   **[Figure 4-2]**   Shikotan and Habomai on the map attached to the British draft treaty (March 1951)

300   **[Figure 4-3]**   Dokdo on the map attached to the British draft treaty (March 1951)

471   **[Figure 7-1]**   Map of Japanese territory and magnification of the part on Dokdo

480   **[Figure 7-2]**   Map showing US military facilities and zones determined by the US-Japan Joint Committee (*Asahi Shimbun*, July 26, 1952)

076   **[Table 1-1]**   Claims by Koreans during US Military Rule

142   **[Table 2-1]**   36 Volumes of References in English Forwarded to the US Department of State by the Japanese Ministry of Foreign Affairs

150   **[Table 2-2]**   Minor Islands Adjacent to Japan Proper

266   [Table 3-1]   Organization of Draft Treaties of Peace with Japan (Drafts of February, March, & May 1951)

270   [Table 3-2]   Changes in Korea-related Provisions in Draft Treaties of Peace with Japan (May-June 1951)

332   [Table 4-1]   British Foreign Office Review of Korean Government Note Dated July 20, 1951

377   [Table 5-1]   Statistics Given by Yoshida to MacArthur on Crimes Committed by Korean Residents in Japan

424   [Table 6-1]   Name comparison of Jejudo, Geomundo, Ulleungdo, Liancourt Rocks, Dokdo, and Parangdo (Boggs)